AA

GUEST HOUSES, FARM HOUSES AND INNS IN BRITAIN

Editor: Penny Hicks
Designers: Liz Rosinska and Andrew Turnbull

Gazetteer: Compiled by the Publications Research Unit of the Automobile Association
Maps: Prepared by the Cartographic Services Unit of the Automobile Association
Cover Picture: New Inn, Clovelly (International Photobank).

Head of Advertisement Sales: Christopher Heard Tel 0256 20123 (ext 2020)
Advertisement Production: Karen Weeks Tel 0256 20123 (ext 3525)
Advertisement Sales Representatives:
London, East Anglia, East Midlands, Central Southern and South East England: Edward May
Tel 0256 20123 (ext 3524) or 0256 67568
South West, West, West Midlands: Bryan Thompson Tel 0272 393296
Wales, North of England, Scotland: Arthur Williams Tel 0222 20267

Filmset by: Tradespools Ltd, Frome, Somerset
Printed and bound in Great Britain by William Clowes Ltd., Beccles and London

Every effort is made to ensure accuracy, but the publishers do not hold themselves responsible for any consequences that may arise from errors or omissions. Whilst the contents are believed correct at the time of going to press, changes may have occurred since that time or will occur during the currency of this book. The up to date position may be checked through AA regional offices.

ISBN 0 86145 248 8

Published by the Automobile Association, Fanum House, Basingstoke, Hampshire RG21 2EA

Contents

About this book

In this book we list over 3000 of Britain's guesthouses, farmhouses and inns, the hallmarks of which are a warm welcome and good, homely accommodation. Most are less expensive than hotels, but all have been selected by our inspectors as being good value for money and of a high enough standard to qualify for an AA recommendation. To help you get even better value for money we are including four **money-off vouchers** each of which will enable you to claim a £1 reduction on a bill for accommodation. Full details of the conditions of use can be found on the reverse of the vouchers, printed opposite.

Our colour feature highlights two of the categories of accommodation to be found in the book. The **Inn of the Year** had a large number of contenders and through a lengthy process of elimination we have selected what we consider to be the best all round for accommodation, food and drink and that elusive quality – atmosphere. We also feature the regional winners which all ran a very close race. A holiday **Down on the Farm** may evoke ideas of feeding the animals and riding home atop a laden haycart, but just how involved can visitors get in the serious business of agriculture? We explore the possibilities on page 27.

REQUIREMENTS

Three types of establishment are listed in this guide.

Guesthouses and Private Hotels

These are different from, but not necessarily inferior to AA ap ointed hotels, and they offer an alternative for those who prefer inexpensive and not too elaborate accommodation. Small and private hotels are also included in this category and they all provide clean, comfortable accommodation in homely surroundings. Each establishment must usually offer at least six bedrooms, and there should be a general bathroom and a general toilet for every six bedrooms without private facilities. Fully licensed premises are not usually included, although it is acceptable for an establishment to have a residential or restaurant licence. It should be noted that in several establishments which offer only 'bed and breakfast', it may be difficult to come and go readily throughout the day.

Parking facilities should be reasonably close. All the establishments listed in the London section of the book are small hotels and so their entries are not accompanied by the GH symbol that accompanies all the other guesthouses and private hotels in the book.

Farmhouses

A recent survey undertaken by the AA has found a very high level of satisfaction with both the food and the accommodation offered by farmhouses in Britain. All those listed in this book are, generally, working farms, though it must be emphasized that the modern farm is a highly mechanized and potentially dangerous place. Children, in particular, should be carefully supervised. To qualify for inclusion the farmhouse must have a minimum of two letting bedrooms, which should be light, clean and airy, and preferably fitted with washbasins. A bathroom with hot and cold running water must be provided and there must also be an inside lavatory. A residential or restaurant licence is permissible.

Inns

All the inns listed in this book provide simple overnight accommodation, breakfast and, at least, light meals during licensing hours. By law, the proprietor of an inn is under an obligation to provide food, drink (not necessarily alcoholic) and accommodation for any bona fide traveller, and this definition may encompass small hotels as well as pubs. To be included in this book, the inn must provide a minimum of three and a maximum of 15 bedrooms, each having washbasins with hot and cold running water; most bedrooms should be served by a bathroom and lavatory on the same floor.

A suitable breakfast room must be available, although a lounge is not essential.

Whatever the type of establishment, however, there are certain requirements common to them all, and these include:

i A well-maintained exterior
ii Clean and hygenic kitchens
iii A good standard of furnishing
iv Friendly and courteous service
v Access at reasonable times
vi The use of a telephone
vii Full English breakfast
viii An adequately lighted and heated sitting room when half board is provided (but see Inns)
ix Bedrooms should have comfortable beds, a wardrobe, a carpet beside the bed, a bedside cabinet, a washbasin with soap, towel, mirror and a shaver socket (but see Farmhouses)
x There should be no extra charge for baths or lavatories, and heating should be unmetered.

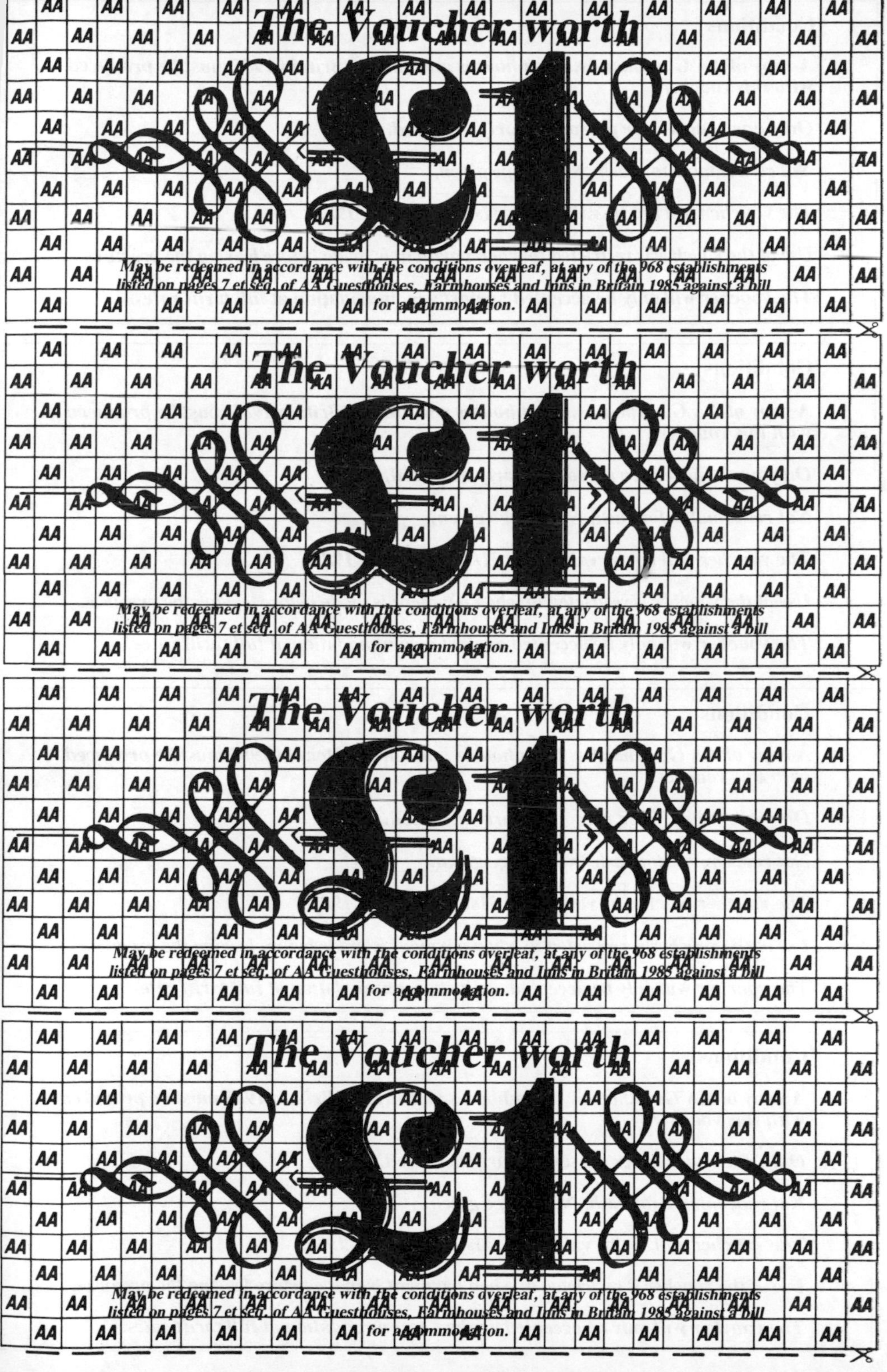
The Voucher worth
£1
May be redeemed in accordance with the conditions overleaf, at any of the 968 establishments listed on pages 7 et seq. of AA Guesthouses, Farmhouses and Inns in Britain 1985 against a bill for accommodation.
The Voucher worth
£1
May be redeemed in accordance with the conditions overleaf, at any of the 968 establishments listed on pages 7 et seq. of AA Guesthouses, Farmhouses and Inns in Britain 1985 against a bill for accommodation.
The Voucher worth
£1
May be redeemed in accordance with the conditions overleaf, at any of the 968 establishments listed on pages 7 et seq. of AA Guesthouses, Farmhouses and Inns in Britain 1985 against a bill for accommodation.
The Voucher worth
£1
May be redeemed in accordance with the conditions overleaf, at any of the 968 establishments listed on pages 7 et seq. of AA Guesthouses, Farmhouses and Inns in Britain 1985 against a bill for accommodation.

Conditions

A copy of AA Guesthouses, Farmhouses and Inns in Britain 1985 must be produced with this voucher.

Only one voucher per person or party accepted.

Not redeemable for cash. No change given.

The voucher will not be valid after 31st December, 1985.

Use of the voucher is restricted to when payment is made before leaving the premises.

The voucher will only be accepted against accommodation at full tariff rates.

Conditions

A copy of AA Guesthouses, Farmhouses and Inns in Britain 1985 must be produced with this voucher.

Only one voucher per person or party accepted.

Not redeemable for cash. No change given.

The voucher will not be valid after 31st December, 1985.

Use of the voucher is restricted to when payment is made before leaving the premises.

The voucher will only be accepted against accommodation at full tariff rates.

Conditions

A copy of AA Guesthouses, Farmhouses and Inns in Britain 1985 must be produced with this voucher.

Only one voucher per person or party accepted.

Not redeemable for cash. No change given.

The voucher will not be valid after 31st December, 1985.

Use of the voucher is restricted to when payment is made before leaving the premises.

The voucher will only be accepted against accommodation at full tariff rates.

Conditions

A copy of AA Guesthouses, Farmhouses and Inns in Britain 1985 must be produced with this voucher.

Only one voucher per person or party accepted.

Not redeemable for cash. No change given.

The voucher will not be valid after 31st December, 1985.

Use of the voucher is restricted to when payment is made before leaving the premises.

The voucher will only be accepted against accommodation at full tariff rates.

AA Money-off voucher scheme

Listed below are those establishments who have agreed to participate in this scheme.

Abbots Bromley
Marsh Farm
Aberdare
Cae-Coed Private Hotel
Aberdovey
Brynmorwydd Private Hotel
Aberfeldy
Nessbank Private Hotel
Abergavenny
Park Guest House
Llanwenarth House
Abersoch
Llysfor Guest House
Aberystwyth
Railway Hotel
Abington
Netherton Farm
Craighead Farm
Acaster Malbis
Ship Inn
Acharacle
Dalilea House
Aldershot
Glencoe Hotel
Aldwark
Lydgate Farm
Alfriston
Pleasant Rise Farm
Alnmouth
Marine House Private Hotel
Alnwick
Aln House
Alston
Middle Bayles Farm
Alverdiscott
Garnacott Farm
Ambleside
Borrans Park Hotel
Gale Crescent Guest House
Oaklands Country House Hotel
The Horseshoe Guest House
Appleby
Gale House
Arbroath
Kingsley Guest House
Ardersier
Milton-of-Gollanfield
Ardgay
Croit Mairi Guest House
Ardrossan
Ellwood House
Arnside
Grosvenor Private Hotel
Arreton
Stickleworth Hall
Ascot
Highclere House
Ashford (Kent)
Downsview
Ashurst
Barn Guest House
Aveton Gifford
Court Barton Farmhouse.
Avonwick
Sopers Horsebrook Farm
Ayr
The Park House Hotel
Babell
Bryn Glas

Bala
Fronddérw Guest House
Baldock
Butterfield House
Ballater
Morvada Guest House
Balmaha
Arrochoile Guest House
Bampton (Devon)
Bridge House Hotel
Bampton (Oxon)
Bampton House
Banbury
Lismore Private Hotel
Banff
Carmelite House Hotel
Barkestone-le-Vale
The Paddocks
Barnstaple
Cresta Guest House
Fair Oak Farm House
Home Farm
Barton-on-Sea
Gainsborough Hotel
The Old Coastguard Hotel
Bassenthwaite
Bassenthwaite Hall Farm (East)
Ravenstone Hotel
Link House Hotel
Bath
Highways House
Carfax Hotel
Edgar Hotel
Wentworth House Hotel
Beaumaris
Sea View Guest House
Bedford
Hurst House
Clarendon House Hotel
Beer
Bay View Guest House
Beeston
Brackley House Hotel
Bell Busk
Tudor Guest House
Betws-y-Coed
Bryn Llewelyn
Henllys (Old Court) Hotel
Mount Garmon Hotel
Bexhill-on-Sea
Dunselma Private Hotel
Bickleigh
Bickleigh Cottage Guest House
Bideford
Kumba Guest House
Birmingham
Heath Lodge Hotel
Lyndhurst Hotel
Tri-Star Hotel
Wentsbury Hotel
Bishopston
Winston Hotel
Black Cross
Homestake Farm
Blackpool
Motel Mimosa
Derwent Private Hotel
Sunnycliff Guest House
Sunray Private Hotel
Ashcroft Private Hotel
Burlees Hotel

Blackwood
Plas Inn
Blaenau Ffestiniog
Don Restaurant & Guest House
Blairgowrie
Rosebank House Guest House
Glenshieling Guest House
Bleadney
Threeway Country House
Hotel & Restaurant
Bletchingley
Whyte Harte Inn
Blore
Coldwall Farm
Bodedern
Crown Hotel
Bognor Regis
Landsdowne Hotel
Boot
Brook House Guest House
Boreland
Gall Farm
Borrowdale
Langstrath Hotel
Boscastle
St Christophers Country House Hotel
Bournemouth
Chawson House Hotel
Penmone Hotel
Dean Court Hotel
Sandelheath Hotel
Cransley Private Hotel
Bursledon Hotel
Eglan Court Hotel
Heather Mount Hotel
East Cliff Cottage Private Hotel
Hotel Bristol
Mae-Mar Private Hotel
Mount Stewart Hotel
Hotel Restormel
Arlington Hotel
Cliff House Hotel
Holmcroft Hotel
Bay Tree Hotel
Hotel Sorrento
Northover Private Hotel
Pine Beech Hotel
Cintra
Myrtle House Hotel
Woodside Private Hotel
Tree Tops Hotel
Grassmere Guest House
The Mariner's Hotel
Sea Shells
Brun-Lea Hotel
Woodford Court Hotel
Bow
East Hillerton House Farm
Bradford
Maple Hill Guest House
Braunton
Brookdale Hotel
Brechin
Wood of Auldbar
Blibberhill Farm
Brenchley
Rose & Crown Inn
Brent Eleigh
Street Farm
Bridestowe
Town Farm
Little Bidlake
Bridgnorth
Severn Arms Hotel
Bridlington
Shirley Private Hotel
Southdowne Hotel

Bridport
Roundham House Hotel
Britmead House

Brighton
Melford Hall Hotel
Marina House Hotel
Rowland House Guest House
Downlands Hotel
Whitehaven Hotel

Brigsteer
Barrowfield

Bristol
Glenroy Hotel
Cavendish House Hotel
Alandale Hotel

Brixham
Cottage Hotel
Raddicombe Lodge

Broad Marston
Broad Marston Manor

Broadstairs
Bay Tree Hotel
Keston Court Hotel
St Augustines Hotel

Broadway
Olive Branch Guest House

Broadwindsor
Hursey Farm

Brompton Regis
Lower Holworthy Farm

Bromsgrove
The Forest Inn

Bryngwyn
Newhouse Farm

Bucknell
Bucknell House

Bude
Pencarrol Guest House
Wayfarer Guest House
Links View Guest House

Budleigh Salterton
Hayes Barton

Burnsall
Manor House

Burntisland
Forthaven Guest House

Burwash
Admiral Vernon Inn

Butleigh
Dower House

Buxton
High House
Griff Guest House
Thorn Heyes Private Hotel

Cabus
Clay Lane Head

Caldbeck
High Greenrigg House
Friar Hall

Callander
Rock Villa Guest House
Kinnell Guest House
Annfield Guest House
Edina Guest House
Arden House
Riverview House Private Hotel

Calstock
Boot Inn

Calvine
Clachan of Struan

Camborne
Pendarves Lodge Guest House
Regal Hotel

Cambridge
Suffolk House Private Hotel

Camelford
Sunnyside Hotel

Canterbury
Castle Court Guest House
Abba Hotel
Pointers Hotel
Red House Hotel

Caputh
Stralochy Farm

Cardiff
Dorville Hotel

Carey
The Cottage of Content Inn

Carlisle
Georgian House

Carlops
Carlophill Farm

Carradale
Drumfearne Guest House
Dunvalanree Guest House

Carrbridge
Mountain Thyme Country Guest House

Carrutherstown
Domaru

Castle Carrock
Gelt Hall Farm

Castle Cary
Greenhills Guest House

Castle Donington
Delven Hotel

Catlowdy
Bessietown Farm

Cerne Abbas
Giants Head Farm

Chagford
Bly House

Chapmanslade
The Spinney Farm House

Chelmsford
Boswell House Hotel

Cheltenham
Hollington House Hotel
Cleevelands House
Beaumont House
Askham Court Hotel
Lawn Hotel

Cheriton Fitzpaine
Brindiwell Farm House

Chester
Malvern Guest House
Redland Private Hotel
Cavendish Hotel

Chideock
Betchworth Guest House

Chiselborough
Manor Farm

Christchurch
Laurels Guest House
St Albans Hotel
Pines Private Hotel
Belvedere Hotel

Church Stoke
The Drewin Farm

Church Stretton
Dudgeley Mill

Cirencester
Raydon House Hotel

Clacton-on-Sea
Chudleigh Hotel

Clawddnewydd
Maestyddyn Isa

Clearwell
Wyndham Arms

Cleobury Mortimer
Talbot Hotel

Clunton
Hurst Mill Farm

Clyro
Crossway Farm

Clyst St Mary
Ivington Farm

Coll (Island of)
Tigh-na-Mara Guest House

Colwyn Bay
Southlea Guest House
Cabin Hill Private Hotel

Combe Martin
Firs Guest House

Compton
Swan Hotel

Comrie
West Ballindalloch Farm

Coniston
Crown Inn

Constantine
Trengilly Wartha Inn

Conwy
Llys Gwilym Guest House
Sunnybank Guest House

Cookley
Green Farm

Coombe
Treway Farm

Coventry
Trinity House Hotel
Croft Hotel

Cowdenbeath
Struan Bank Private Hotel

Crail
Caiplie Guest House

Crediton
Woolsgrove Farm

Crianlarich
Glenardran Guest House

Criccieth
Neptune Private Hotel
Moorings Guest House
Mor Heli Private Hotel
Min-y-Gaer Private Hotel

Crieff
Comely Bank Guest House

Croesgoch
Trearched Farm

Cromer
Chellow Dene Guest House

Cromhall
Varley Farm

Crook
Greenbank Farm

Croxdale
Croxdale Inn

Croyde
The Thatched Barn Inn
Moorsands House Hotel

Croydon
Markington Hall
Friends Guest House

Crymych
Felin Tygwyn Farm

Cullompton
Five Bridges Farm

Dawlish
Lynbridge Private Hotel
Radfords Hotel

Debden Green
Wychbars Farm

Dedham
Dedham Hall

Dersingham
Westdene House Hotel

Devils Bridge
Erwbarfe Farmhouse

Diddlebury
Glebe Farm

Dirleton
Castle Inn

Dolgellau
Clifton Private Hotel

Douglas
Gladwyn Private Hotel
Ainsdale Guest House
Rosslyn Private Hotel
Beachcomber

Dover
Number One Guesthouse
Dover Stop

Downham Market
Crosskeys Riverside Hotel

Droxford
Little Uplands

Dumfries
Fulwood Private Hotel

Dunbar
St Beys Guest House
Springfield Guest House

AA Money-off voucher scheme

Dunoon
Cedars Hotel
Dunster
Foresters Arms
Dunsyre
Dunsyre Mains Farm
Dunvegan
Roskhill Guest House
Dursley
Park Farm
Eastbourne
Eastbourne Health Hotel
Beachy Rise
Southcroft Guest House
St Clare Guest House
Rosforde Private Hotel
Fairlands Hotel
Somerville Private Hotel
Flamingo Private Hotel
Courtlands Hotel
East Budleigh
Hayes Barton
East Calder
Whitecroft Farm
East Cowton
Beeswing Inn
Eastleigh
Pines Farmhouse Hotel
East Mey
Glenearn Farm
East Wittering
Wittering Lodge Hotel
Ebberston
Foxholm Hotel
Edinburgh
Galloway Guest House
Bonnington Guest House
Thrums Private Hotel
Kariba Guest House
Grosvenor Guest House
Buchan Hotel
Glenisla Hotel
Kildonan Lodge Hotel
Salisbury Hotel
Dorstan Private Hotel
Sharon Guest House
Hillview Guest House
Sherwood Guest House
Elie
The Elms Guest House
Elsdon
Dunns Farm
Ely
Castle Lodge Farm
The Nyton Guest House
Erlestoke
Longwater Park Farm
Erwood
Ty-Isaf Farm
Ettington
Whitfield Farm
Ewhurst Green
White Dog Inn
Exeter
Trenance House Hotel
Park View Hotel
Shene Guest House
Trees Mini Hotel
Exmouth
Aliston House Hotel
Falmouth
Tregenna House
Evendale Private Hotel
Hotel Dracaena
Langton Leigh Guest House
Penty Bryn Hotel
Bedruthan Guest House
Collingbourne Hotel
Wickham Guest House
Farnham
The Eldon Hotel
Fazeley
Buxton House Hotel
Felmingham
Felmingham Hall Farm

Feniton
Colestocks House Guest House
Ffestiniog
Newborough House Hotel
Fishguard
Glanmoy Country House
Flushing
Nankersey Hotel
Folkestone
Wearbay Hotel
Fonthill Bishop
The Kings Arms
Forden
Coed-y-Brenin Farmhouse
Fordingbridge
Oakfield Lodge
Fordoun
Ringwood Farm
Forton
Oakfield Guest House
Fort William
Benview Guest House
Stronchreggan View
Rhu Mhor Guest House
Fowey
Carnethic House Guest House
Fownhope
Bowens Farm House
Frinton-on-Sea
Forde Guest House
Galston
Auchencloigh Farm
Gargrave
Kirk Syke Guest House
Gatehead
Old Rome Farm
Gatwick Airport
Trumbles Hotel & Restaurants
Gayhurst
Mill Farmhouse
Gedney Hill
Sycamore Farm
Giggleswick
Close House
Glan-yr-Afon
Llawr-Betws Farm
Glasgow
Dalmeny Hotel
Glastonbury
Cradlebridge Farm
Hawthorn House Hotel
Glossop
Hurst Lee Hotel
Gloucester
Claremont
Golspie
Park House Hotel
Gomshall
The Black Horse Inn
Grampound Road Village
Midway Inn
Grandes Rocques
Hotel Le Saumarez
Grange Over Sands
Elton Private Hotel
Grantown on Spey
Kinross House
Umaria Guest House
Greenhead
Holmhead Farmhouse
Gretna Green
Greenlaw
Gwystre
Bryn Nicholas Farm
Halfway House
The Willows Farm
Halifax
Stump Cross Inn
Haltwhistle
White Craig Farm
Hanmer
Buck Farmhouse

Harberton
Preston Farm
Harlech
Tyddyn Gwynt Farm
Rum Hole Hotel
Harrogate
Abbey Lodge Guest House
The Kingsway
The Cavendish Hotel
Gillmore Hotel
Roan Guest House
The Woodhouse Guest House
Youngs Private Hotel
Shelbourne Guest House
Aygarth Guest House
Harrop Fold
Harrop Fold Farm
Harwich
Hotel Continental
Hastings
Bryn-y-Mor Guest House
Gresford House
Hatherleigh
Bridge Inn
Haugh of Urr
Markfast Farm
Haverfordwest
Cuckoo Grove Farm
Hawkeshead
Ivy House
Highfield House Guest House
Haworth
Ferncliffe Guest House
Heasley Mill
Heasley House
Henstridge
Toomer Farm
Manor Farm
Hereford
Munstone House
Herne Bay
Northdown Hotel
Herstmonceux
Cleaver's Lyng Country Hotel
Holmfirth
White Horse Inn
Holne
Wellpritton Farm
Church House Inn
Holsworthy
Leworthy Farm
Holywell
Green Hill Farm
Honiton
Hill House Country Hotel
Roebuck Farm
Horrabridge
Overcombe Hotel
Horsham St Faith
Elm Farm Chalet Hotel
Howey
Brynhir Farm
Corven Hall Country Guest House
Three Wells
Hugh Town
Brantwood
Hunstanton
Claremont Guest House
Deepdene Hotel
Tolcarne Private Hotel
Sutton House Hotel
Hursley
Kings Head Hotel
Icklesham
Snailham House
Ilfracombe
Headlands Hotel
Briercliffe Hotel
Westwell Hall Hotel
New Cavendish Hotel
Combe Lodge Hotel
Norbury
Elmfield Hotel
Lantern House Hotel

AA Money-off voucher scheme

Wentworth House Private Hotel
Dedes Hotel
Queen's Court Hotel
Ilkley
Moorview House Hotel
Ingleton
Springfield Private Hotel
Invergarry
Faichem Lodge
Lundie View Guest House
Inverness
Whinpark Guest House
Lyndale
Ipstones
Glenwood House Farm
Ipswich
Gables Hotel
Isleworth
Kingswood Hotel
Isle Ornsay
Old Post Office House
Jacobstowe
Higher Cadham Farm
Jedburgh
Ferniehirst Mill Lodge
Kenmore Bank Guest House
Keith
Tarnash House Farm
The Haughs Farm
Kenilworth
Enderley
Keswick
Kings Arms Hotel
Derwent Lodge Guest House
Clarence House
Woodlands Guest House
Priorholm Hotel
Kilmartin
Kilmartin Hotel
Kilve
Hood Arms
Kingham
Conygree Gate
Kingsbridge
Hotel Kildare
Ashleigh Guest House
Kingsey
Foxhill Farm
Kingussie
Sonnhalde Guest House
Kirkconnel
Niviston Farm
Kirkhill
Wester Moniack Farm
Kirk Ireton
Sitch Farm
Kirkoswald
Prospect Hill Hotel
Kirtling
The Queens Head Inn
Kirton
Old Rectory Guest House
Knutsford
Longview Private Hotel
Lancaster
Belle-Vue Guest House
Langho
Mytton Fold Farm Guest House
Langland
Brynteg Hotel
Lanlivery
Treganoon Farm
Largs
Sunbury Guest House
Latheron
Upper Latheron Farm
Laxton
Moorgate Farm
Leamington Spa
Hill Farm
Leeds
Trafford House Hotel
Budapest Private Hotel

Leek
Peak Weavers Hotel
Leicester
Daval Hotel
The Old Tudor Rectory
Leslie
Rescobie Hotel
Lewdown
Venn Mill Farm
Lincoln
Brierley House Hotel
Lindridge
Middle Woodston
Linlithgow
Woodcockdale Farm
Belsyde House
Little Dewchurch
Cwm Craig Farm
Little Mill
Pentwyn Farm
Little Torrington
Lower Hollam
Liverpool
Aachen Hotel
New Manx Hotel
Lizard
Parc Brawse House
Llanarthney
Brynheulog
Llanberis
Lake View Hotel
Llanboidy
Maencochyrwyn Farm
Llanddeiniolwen
Ty'n-Rhos Farm
Llandinam
Trewythen Farm
Llandudno
Brigstock Private Hotel
Capri Hotel
Bryn-y-Mor Private Hotel
Cumberland Hotel
Puffin Lodge Hotel
Warwick Hotel
Heath House Hotel
Braemar Hotel
Lynwood Private Hotel
Brannock Private Hotel
Orotava Private Hotel
Plas Madoc Private Hotel
Llanfair Dyffryn Clwyd
Llanbenwch Farm
Llanfihangel y Pennant
Tynybryn Farm
Llanfihangel-yng-ngwynfa
Cyfie Farm
Llanvair-Discoed
Cribau Mill
Llanwarne
Llanwarne Court
Llanwddyn
Tynymaes Farm
Loddon
Stubbs House Farm
London
E18 Grove Hill Hotel
NW3 Frognal Lodge Hotel
NW6 Dawson House Hotel
NW11 Central Hotel
Croft Court Hotel
SE3 Bardon Lodge
SE19 Crystal Palace Tower Hotel
SE25 Toscana
SW1 Franterre Hotel
Hanover Hotel
SW3 Eden House Hotel
SW19 Wimbledon Hotel
W1 Milford House
Hart House Hotel
Georgian House Hotel
W2 Camelot Hotel
Nayland Hotel
Slavia Hotel
W4 Chiswick Hotel
W8 Atlas Hotel

Longframlington
Granby Inn
Longleat
Stalls Farmhouse
Looe
Kantara
Panorama Hotel
Lostwithiel
Pelyn Barn Farm
Loughborough
Sunnyside Hotel
Lowestoft
Amity Guest House
Ludlow
Cecil Private Hotel
Lulworth (West)
Gatton House Hotel
Shirley Hotel
Luton
Arlington Hotel
Stoneygate Hotel
Lyme Regis
White House Guest House
Kersbrook Hotel
Lynton
Longmead House
Horwood House Guest House
Mayfair Hotel
Valley House Hotel
The Croft Guest House
Woodlands
Alford House
Gable Lodge Hotel
North Cliff Private Hotel
Pine Lodge Guesthouse
Hazeldene Guest House
Lytham St Annes
Beaumont Private Hotel
Harcourt Hotel
Endsleigh Private Hotel
Westbourne Hotel
Maidstone
Rock House Hotel
Gt Malvern
Fromefield Hotel
Manchester
Imperial Hotel
Horizon Hotel
Kempton House Hotel
Margate
Tyrella Private Hotel
Charnwood Guest House
Westbrook Bay House
Masham
Bank Villa Guest House
Mathon
Moorend Court
Matlock
Packhorse Farm
Mawgan Porth
Pandora Guest House
Melksham
Regency Hotel
York Guest House
Melton Mowbray
Sysonby Knoll Hotel
Menheniot
Tregondale Farm
Middlesbrough
The Chadwick Private Hotel
Milborne Port
Venn Farm
Millpool
Chyraise Lodge Hotel
Minehead
The Gascony Hotel
Dorchester Hotel
Minster Lovell
Hill Grove Farm
Monksilver
Rowdon Farm
Montrose
Muirshade of Gallery

AA Money-off voucher scheme

Morecambe
Glendene Guest House
Hotel Warwick
New Hazlemere Hotel

Moretonhampstead
Elmfield
Cookshayes Guest House

Moy
Invermoy House

Moylgrove
Penrallt Ceibwr Farm

Mullion
Belle Vue Guest House

Mumbles
Southend Hotel & Restaurant
Harbour Winds Private Hotel

Mylor Bridge
Penmere Guest House

Nailsworth
Gables Private Hotel

Nantgaredig
Cwmtwrch Farm

Narberth
Jacob's Park Farm

Needham Market
Pips Ford Farm

Newbold on Stour
Berryfield Farm

Newby Bridge
Furness Fells Guest House

Newcastle Upon Tyne
Morrach Hotel
Chirton House Hotel

Newport (Dyfed)
Golden Lion

Newport (Gwent)
Caerleon House Hotel

Newport (I.O.W.)
Shute Inn

Newquay
Fairlands Guest House
Priory Lodge Hotel

Newtonmore
Alvey House Hotel
Coig Na Shee

Newton Stewart
Duncree House Hotel

Normanby
Heather View Farm

North Berwick
Cragside Guest House

North Walsham
Beechwood Private Hotel

Norwich
Grange Hotel

Oakford
Newhouse Farm

Oban
Ardblair Guest House
Heatherfield Private Hotel
Roseneath Guest House

Okeover
Little Park Farm

Onich
Cuilcheanna House Farm
Glenmorven House Guest House

Oswestry
Ashfield Country House

Ottery St Mary
Pitt Farm

Ovington
Highlander Inn

Oxenhope
Lily Hall Farm

Oxford
Tilbury Lodge Guest House
Westgate Hotel
Ascot Guest House
Earlmont Guest House

Paignton
Orange Tubs Hotel
Channel View Hotel
Torbay Sands Hotel
Preston Sands Hotel
St. Weonard Private Hotel
Sunnybank Private Hotel
Commodore Hotel
Clennon Valley Hotel
Chorra Hotel
The Sealawn Hotel

Parkmill
Parc-le-Breos House

Parracombe
Lower Dean Farm

Peebles
Lindores Guest House

Penmachno
Tyddyn Gethin Farm

Pennan
Pennan Inn

Pennant
Bikerehyd Farm

Penzance
Kilindini Private Hotel
Pentrea Hotel
Penmorvah Hotel
Camilla Hotel
Mount Royal Hotel
Dunedin

Perth
The Gables Guest House
Pitcullen Guest House

Pilton
The Long House

Pitlochry
Adderley Private Hotel
Balrobin Private Hotel
Duntrune Guest House

Pluckley
Elvey Farm

Plymouth
Trillium Guest House
St James Hotel
Imperial Hotel
Carnegie Hotel

Polmassick
Kilbol House

Polperro
Penryn House Hotel

Ponthirwaun
Penwernfach

Poole
Sheldon Lodge
Dene Hotel
Ormonde House Hotel

Porlock
Lorna Doone Hotel

Portesham
Millmead Country Guest House

Porthcawl
Minerva Private Hotel

Porthmadog
Owen's Hotel

Port Isaac
Archer Farm Hotel

Portree
Craiglockhart Guest House
Upper Ollach Farm

Portsmouth & Southsea
Chequers Hotel
Beaufort Hotel
St Andrews Lodge
Astor House Guest House
Somerset Private Hotel

Prestayn
The Hawarden House Guest House

Preston
Tulketh House

Pwllheli
Bryn Crin Farm
Gwynfryn Farm

Raglan
Grange Guest House

Ramsgate
St Hilary Private Hotel
Jalna Hotel

Ravenscar
The Smugglers Rock

Ravenstonedale
The Fat Lamb

Redditch
The Old Rectory

Redmile
Peacock Farm

Reigate
Cranleigh Hotel
Priors Mead Guest House

Rhes-y-Cae
Miners Arms Inn

Rhyl
Pier Hotel
Hafod-y-Mor

Rock
Roskarnon House Hotel

Rodbourne
Angrove Farm

Romsey
Adelaide House

Ross-on-Wye
Sunnymount Hotel
Ryefield House
The Arches Country House

Roston
Roston Hall Farm

Rothbury
Orchard Guest House

Rottingdean
Braemar House

Rudyard
Fairboroughs Farm

Rugby
Grosvenor House Hotel

Ruskie
Lower Tarr Farm

Ryde
Teneriffe Guest House
Aldermoor Farm

Rye
Cliff Farm
Mariner's Hotel
The Monastery Hotel & Restaurant

St Albans
Glenmore House Guest House

St Andrews
Number Ten
Arran House

St Aubin
Panorama Private Hotel

St Blazey
Moorshill House Hotel

St Davids
Pen-y-Daith Guest House
Allandale Guest House
Belmont House
The Ramsey Guest House

St Dogmaels
Granant Isaf Farm

St Erme
Trevispian Vean Farm

St Heller
Almorah Hotel

St Ives
Cy-an-Creet Private Hotel
Bay View Guest House
Monowai Private Hotel
Lyonesse Hotel
Sherwell Guest House
Sunrise Guest House
Kandahar & Cortina Guest house
Pondarosa Guest House
Verbena Guest House

St Keyne
Badham Farm

St Margaret South Elmham
Elms House Farm

AA Money-off voucher scheme

St Owens Cross
Aberhall Farm
St Saviour
La Girouette Country House Hotel
Salcombe
Charborough House Hotel
Bay View Private Hotel
Lyndhurst Hotel
Stoneycroft Hotel
Saltdean
Linbrook Lodge
Sandwich
Fleur de Lis Inn
Sarisbury Green
The Dormy Guest House
Saundersfoot
Rhodewood House
Claremont Hotel
Harbour Light Private Hotel
The Sandy Hill Guest House
Scarborough
Avoncroft Hotel
Sefton Hotel
Park Hotel
Scotch Corner
Vintage Hotel
Seaton
Thornfield Guest House
Mariners Homestead
St Margarets
Sebergham
Bustabeck Farm
Semley
Bennett Arms
Shanklin
Bay House Hotel
Overstrand Private Hotel
Curraghmore Hotel
Edgecliffe Hotel
Shawbury
Sowbath Farm
Longley Farm
Shearsby
Knaptoft House Farm
Shepton Mallet
Kings Arms
Sheriff Hutton
Rangers House
Sheringham
Melrose Hotel
Beacon Hotel
Shottle
Shottle Hall Farm Guest House
Skegness
Crawford Hotel
Skipton
Red Lion Hotel
Highfield Hotel
Slaidburn
Parrock Head Farm Guest House
Smeaton, Gt
Smeaton East Farm
Somerton
Church Farm Guest House
Southampton
Banister House Hotel
South Brewham
Holland Farm
Southend-on-Sea
Tower Hotel
West Park Private Hotel
Pavilion Guest House
Mayfair Guest House
The Regency Hotel
Terrace Hotel
South Petherton
Rydon Farm
Southport
Newholme Guest House
The White Lodge Private Hotel
Whitworth Falls Hotel
Orleans Christian Hotel
Sunningdale Hotel

Southwold
Mount Guest House
South Zeal
Poltimore Guest House
Stafford
Abbey Hotel
Steeple Aston
Westfield Farm Motel
Stevenage
Northfield Private Hotel
Steyning
Down House
Stinchcombe
Drakestone House Farm
Stiperstones
Tankerville Guest House
Stockbridge
Old Three Cups Private Hotel
Stockton on Tees
Claireville Hotel
Stoke Holy Cross
Salamanca Farm
Stow on the Wold
Parkdene Hotel
Stratford-upon-Avon
Coach House Guest House
Hunters Moon
Brook Lodge
Ambleside Guest House
Hylands Hotel
Hardwick House
Avon House
Strete
Tallis Rock Private Hotel
Sturminster Newton
Holbrook Farm
Sturton by Stow
Village Farm
Sudbury
Black Boy Hotel
Summercourt
Trenithon Farmhouse
Surbiton
Holmdene Guest House
Sutton
Eaton Court Hotel
The Dene Hotel
Sutton Coldfield
Cloverley Hotel
Swanage
Boyne Hotel
St Michael Hotel
Burlington Hotel
Golden Sands Private Hotel
Firswood Guest House
Havenhurst Hotel
Swansea
Alexander Hotel
Westlands Guest House
Tregare Hotel
Symonds Yat East
Saracens Head
Symonds Yat West
Woodlea Guest House
Tadcaster
Shann House
Tarporley
Perth Hotel
Taunton
Ruishton Lodge Guest House
Rumwell Hall Guest House
Teignmouth
Glen Devon
Bay Cottage Hotel
Tenby
Richmond Hotel
Hildebrand Hotel
Red House Hotel
Ripley St Mary's Hotel
Sea Breezes Hotel
Thornhill
Waterside Mains Farm
Thorpe
Hillcrest House

Thrapston
Court House Hotel
Throwleigh
East Ash Manor
Thurning
Rookery Farm
Tintagel
Trevervan Hotel
Belvoir Guest House
Willapark Manor Hotel
Tintern
Fountain Inn
Parva Farmhouse
Tiverton
Bridge Guest House
Todmorden
Todmorden Edge South
Torquay
Glenorleigh Hotel
Hatherleigh Hotel
Castle Mount Hotel
Stephen House Hotel
Castleton Private Hotel
Ventnor Guest House
Burley Court Hotel
Marlow Hotel
Cranborne Hotel
Westowe Hotel
Torcroft Hotel
Jesmond Dene Private Hotel
Beechmoor Hotel
Carn Brea
Tregantle Hotel
The Blue Waters Hotel
Casey's Court Motel
Trafalgar House Hotel
Skerries Private Hotel
Totland Bay
The Nodes Country Hotel
Lismore Private Hotel
Totnes
Four Seasons Guest House
Trearddur Bay
Moranedd Guest House
Tregaron
Neuaddlas Farm
Tregony
Tregony House Guest House
Trenear
Longstone Farm
Troutbeck
Lane Head Farm
Tunbridge Wells
Firwood Guest House
Uffculme
Houndaller Farm
Ullingswick
The Steppes
Upton Pyne
Pierce's Farm
Usk
Ty Gwyn Farm
Uttoxeter
Popinjay Farm
Venn Ottery
Venn Ottery Barton
Ventnor
Under Rock Hotel
Lake Hotel
Richmond Private Hotel
Wallasey
Sandpiper Private Hotel
Warren Street
The Harrow Inn
Warwick
Guys Cross Hotel
Waterperry
Manor Farm
Waterrow
Hurstone Farmhouse Hotel
Wells
Bekynton House
Welshpool
Tynllwyn Farm

West Chilington
New House Farm
Weston-super-Mare
Scottsdale Hotel
Lydia Private Hotel
Westward Ho!
The Buckleigh Lodge Guest House
Weymouth
Sunningdale Private Hotel
Tamarisk Hotel
Kings Acre Hotel
Wheddon Cross
The Higherley Guest House
Whiddon Down
South Nethercott Farm
Whitby
Old Hall Hotel
Europa Private Hotel
Whitestone
Rowhorne House
Wigmore
Compasses Hotel
Willand
Doctors Farm
Wimpstone
Whitchurch Farm
Wincle
Four Ways Diner Motel

Windermere
Elim Bank Hotel
Rosemount Guest House
Oakfield Guest House
Kenilworth Guest House
Greenriggs Guest House
Cranleigh Hotel
Fairfield Country House Hotel
Brooklands
Windsor
Clarence Hotel
Winterbourne Abbas
Church View Guest House
Wix
New Farmhouse
Wolseley Bridge
Taft Farm
Womenswold
Woodpeckers Country Hotel
Woolacombe
The Castle Guest House
Combe Ridge Hotel
Woolhope
Butchers Arms
Woolley
East Woolley Farm
Wormbridge
Duffryn Farm

Worthing
Camelot House
Windsor House Hotel
Wolsey Hotel
Blair House
Wye
New Flying Horse Inn
Gt Yarmouth
Georgian House Private Hotel
Frandor Guest House
Yatton
Prince of Orange Inn
York
Avenue Guest House
Priory Hotel
Croft Hotel
Albert Hotel
Dairy Guest House
Mayfield Hotel
Clifton Bridge Hotel
Cavalier Private Hotel
Greenside
Beech Guest House
Abingdon Guest House
Inglewood Guest House
Youlgrave
The Bulls Head

The Voucher Scheme

All of the establishments listed above have agreed to participate in our scheme, which will enable you to claim £1 off your bill for accommodation with each of the vouchers. In effect, you can save the cost of this book by using the vouchers.

The following conditions apply to their use:

- A copy of AA Guesthouses, Farmhouses and Inns in Britain 1985 must be produced with the voucher.
- Only one voucher per person or party accepted.
- Not redeemable for cash. No change given.
- The voucher will not be valid after 31st December 1985.
- Use of the voucher is restricted to when payment is made before leaving the premises.
- The voucher will only be accepted against accommodation at full tariff rates.

Scottish Inns – do they exist?

In the pages that follow we announce the results of our nationwide quest for the AA's Inn of the Year. We asked our regional inspectors to nominate the best inns in their area, but it has not been possible to find a top-rate inn in Scotland.

It is not that Scotland does not have any inns, but their character tends to differ so greatly from the accepted idea that it was felt that the ones we looked at would not fit into the context of our feature.

Many of Scotland's inns are of a standard high enough to have been listed, the better ones classified as star-rated hotels or restaurants which would not appear in this guide. Those that we do list here may have more in common with English guesthouses than with their inns.

It would appear that the variance between the two countries is historical, going back to the days when Scottish licensing laws were stricter than the English. Then, in order to serve alcohol seven days a week, it was necessary to have been granted a hotel licence. To get this, there had to be four letting bedrooms (two in the case of smaller communities) and so a large number of 'inns' came into being. When the licensing laws relaxed, these establishments either up-rated themselves to become proper hotels or reverted to being basic drinking places.

The problem, therefore, is really one of definition – when is an inn not an inn, but a hotel, and vice versa? The answer is probably that if you are looking for a good inn in Scotland, you might be best advised to look among the one- and two-star hotels which call themselves inns. Here you might well find the combination of character and quality which the traditional idea of an inn evokes.

INN OF THE YEAR

This year we set ourselves the task of looking for an inn which encompasses the very best of everything that a traditional British inn should have. We looked for a warm welcome, a friendly atmosphere, good food and drink and comfortable accommodation. To find all of these qualities in a single establishment is not always easy, but they can be guaranteed in all of the inns that we feature in the following pages, starting with the overall winner . . .

WINNER

INN OF THE YEAR

THE MILL HOUSE INN Trebarwith

Our nationwide search for the Inn of the Year brought us finally to the Mill House Inn, nestling in a secluded valley away from Cornwall's many beaten tracks.

The West Country is one of our most popular holiday

areas and visitors aiming to sample its delights could do no better than to stay at the Mill House. It is in an ideal situation for holidaymakers, just a short distance inland from the north Cornish coast at Trebarwith Strand. Tintagel, with its ruined cliff top castle and its stories of King Arthur and Merlin, is just a few miles north and all along the rocky coastline are secluded coves and pretty fishing villages.

The inn, as its name suggests, was a corn mill which only ceased production in 1941 after nearly 300 years in operation. It stands in its own 7 acres, most of which form the steep sides of the valley through which the mill stream still runs. Although the mill wheel no longer turns, it can still be seen behind the inn where a narrow path winds up the wooded slopes.

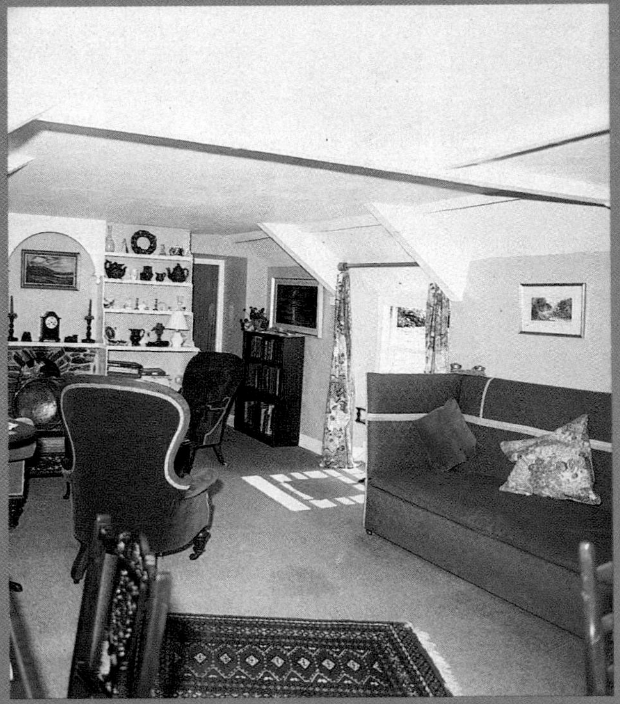

Naturally, extensive work was needed to convert the building for use as an inn, but many of the original features are still in evidence, including grain shafts, in which cupboards have been built, and the ancient flagstone floors in the bar. The building has certainly lost nothing in character and it has been enhanced by the thoughtful approach to its decor and furnishings. A cosy, cottagey atmosphere has been created in the bedrooms with pretty floral wallpaper and matching or toning fabrics. There is some lovely old stripped pine furniture and the little windows reveal just how thick those stone walls are. Each bedroom has its own bathroom, sometimes en suite, and lots of little extras are provided for guests' comfort, such as disposable shower caps and a handy sewing kit. Not only are there facilities for making tea and coffee, but a selection of biscuits is there too. To complete the 'home from home', each room has a colour television and a radio.

On the first floor is a large, comfortable residents' lounge with deep armchairs grouped around a large open fireplace. The sizeable round table contains a bowl of fresh fruit and lots of reading matter. Books of all kinds, from novels to fine art, are everywhere and newcomers to Cornwall will find lots of volumes of local interest to enliven their sightseeing plans.

Visitors who arrive at the Mill House with a healthy appetite will not be disappointed, whether they choose from the delicious home-made bar meals or a more substantial feast in the dining room. A large stone fireplace dominates one end of this room, where some of the old stone walling is exposed and the polished pine tables are divided by low wooden panels. The à la carte menu is changed regularly, but always includes some interesting dishes which are well-cooked and nicely presented by the friendly staff.

There are two bars at the Mill House Inn, although the small, cosy Lounge Bar may not be in use outside the main holiday season. The bar at the back of the building is always busy though, with visitors and locals alike. The age of the building is even more apparent here with the old stone floor and timbers – some of the locals may be of advanced years too and will be able to tell stories of the old mill as it was before.

The first sight a visitor will get of the Mill House from across the car park is of the lovely terracing which provides outdoor seating, with Cornish slate paving and pretty rockery flowers tumbling over the retaining walls.

We certainly feel confident in saying that the Mill House Inn has everything one would expect of a traditional British inn – and a good deal more.

WINNER

SOUTH EAST REGION

THE HARROW INN Warren Street

When the Harrow came up for sale a few years ago, builder Mark Watson snapped it up to convert it into a luxury home. However, after totting up the cost of a conversion he decided that he might just as well direct his efforts towards re-opening the inn as a free house. So it was that in December 1982 a much improved and extended Harrow Inn once again threw open its doors and the ex-builder became the licensee.

The work that has gone into the new-look Harrow certainly reflects the professional touch. The old part of the building, with its original beams and large open fireplaces, has been sympathetically restored; the new has been constructed to be completely in keeping. The theme of dark wood beams, doors and furniture is continued throughout and the doors and windows have lovely brass fittings. The bedrooms, though plain in decor are no less attractive, for the dark-stained wardrobe units and doors set off the cream walls and the lovely plain, deep pink carpets. This is also one of the few inns we looked at which served early morning tea on a tray, rather than providing facilities for guests to make their own.

The residents' lounge on the ground floor is a delightful room with deep chairs and settees and a huge fireplace, complete with wood-burning stove. A lovely old clock, pictures, plants and magazines create a very homely room. Incidentally, this lounge was featured on local television during the last general election – as one of the more unusual polling stations.

Food at the inn is excellent, with some interesting dishes. Starters include a stilton and walnut vol-au-vent or a delicious lentil and bacon soup which may be followed by baked fresh salmon with Pernod and fennel sauce, or

pork fillet in an apricot and cream sauce. Guests with a taste for plainer food will also have plenty of choice. The dining room is very pleasant with some exposed brickwork against the cream walls, pretty china and lots of fresh flowers.

The focal point of any inn is, of course, its bar and the one at the Harrow is a happy place, full of lively chatter every evening. It is a large room, again with beams, ample fireplace and woodburner. In the heart of England's hop county you would naturally expect to find some good ale, and the selection at the Harrow includes Shepherd Neame mild (OG 1031) and bitter (OG 1036), Young's bitter (OG 1036) and Young's Special bitter (OG 1046). Kent is, of course, just as famous for its apples as for its hops and a good local cider is also on sale here.

Mr Watson runs the inn with a manageress, a chef and a large number of part-time staff, one of whom tends the pretty garden at the back of the building. Here, among the trees, shrubs, lawns and flowers, rustic furniture is arranged for fine-weather drinking.

The inn is situated in a tiny village up on the North Downs and is yet only a couple of miles off the main road from Maidstone to Ashford. The Channel ports of Folkestone and Dover are within an hour's drive and so this particular inn would be ideal both for travellers heading for the continent or for holidaymakers exploring the Garden of England and Canterbury.

WINNER

MIDLAND REGION

WHITE BEAR HOTEL
Shipston-on-Stour

The Heart of England, with its Shakespeare country, Cotswold Hills and lovely Vale of Evesham, is certainly a likely place to discover a traditional English inn. Travellers in these parts need look no farther than the White Bear Hotel in the old Warwickshire town of Shipston-on-Stour. This is a particularly accessible inn, too, for a main holiday route, the A34, passes right behind the car park.

The front of the inn looks out onto the Town Square, where many of the old buildings retain their historic character. The oak-beamed bars are hung with interesting old prints, cartoons and lots of photographs of old Shipston. Here visitors can sample the cask-condition beers (Bass and M & B) amidst lively company, and perhaps partake of one of the mouthwatering range of home-made bar meals which are chalked on the blackboard over the bar. Lunchtimes and evenings, it is possible to enjoy a good three-course meal here at a very reasonable price.

The cuisine at the inn enjoys a very high reputation locally and the more formal dining room at the rear is always well patronised. Here the menu is much more elaborate, offering such starters as Duck and Green Lentil Soup which may be followed by Casseroled

Pigeon Breast with juniper berries or Elizabethan Pork, with apples, walnuts and sweet herbs. There is a good range of wines to accompany the meal, including a selection of six house wines.

There are eight letting bedrooms – three on the first floor, all with private facilities, and five on the second floor sharing a bathroom. They are prettily decorated in cottage style and are well-furnished with modern, comfortable beds, nice carpets and lots of little comforts to make for a pleasant stay. Each has its kettle and tray of tea-and coffee-making supplies. Mrs Roberts' interesting collection of paintings adorn the rooms and the landings, adding a particularly individual touch.

The first floor also includes the residents' lounge, a very pleasant room in which the deep, comfortable seating – all with matching loose covers – is arranged in groups around coffee tables. The deep pink walls, hung with old hunting prints and a set of china plates, are set off by an oatmeal-coloured carpet, creating a very restful atmosphere.

There is a colour television for those who wish to view and a large bay window looks out over the square below.

Suzanne and Hugh Roberts have worked extremely hard to achieve the high standard which the White Bear enjoys and their friendliness, and that of their staff, make this a worthy regional winner and well worth a visit.

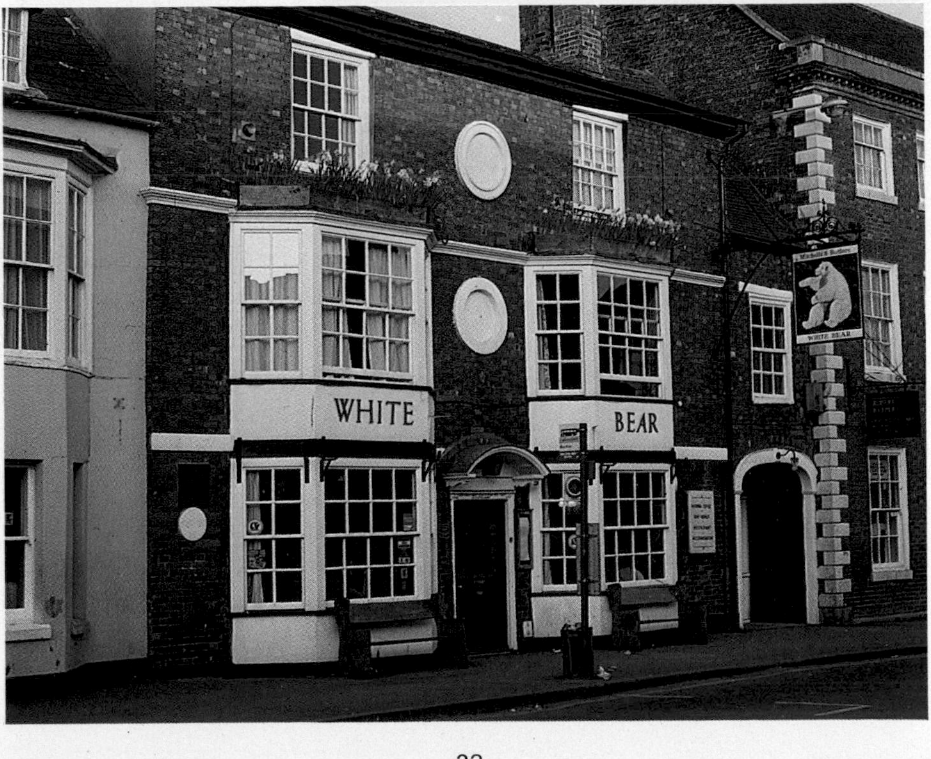

WINNER

WALES

THE SLOOP INN Llandogo

We have explained on page 16 that Scotland is not really in the running for traditional inns, but, contrary to popular belief, England does not have a monopoly, for the Sloop Inn is firmly planted on Welsh soil. Llandogo is a village on the Welsh side of the lovely River Wye, along which the border here runs for a few miles. The river is still tidal and the inn takes its name from the shallow-bottomed barges which sailed from Bristol to Llandogo on the tide, bringing general supplies in return for the broom handles and turned chair legs which were manufactured in the village.

The building has a new appearance, but its facelift, in the form of extensions and alterations, conceals what was once an old mill, powered by the stream that still flows past the inn on its way to join the Wye nearby. The latest addition to the inn was the construction of the four letting bedrooms which were built over an existing single-storey extension just over a

year ago. A thoughtful approach to their design has created rooms of character with dormer windows, dark wood beams and specially constructed cupboard/ wardrobe units. One of the larger rooms is particularly grand with a four-poster bed and french windows leading onto a balcony from where there are beautiful views across the valley. All of the rooms have en-suite bathrooms and are fitted out with colour televisions and tea- and coffee-making facilities. Matching fabrics and good quality carpets add a final touch of comfort.

The inn has two bars. The front bar, on the road side, is large enough to contain a pool table in one corner without its activities encroaching on the non-playing customers. Its ceiling is supported by two massive round timbers – not part of the original mill as one might imagine, but purchased from a veneer factory! Whatever the origin, the effect is still impressive. Among the full range of beers and spirits here are Wadworth's 6X (OG 1041) and Smiles Best Bitter (OG 1040).

At the back of the inn is the lounge bar which doubles as the dining room. It, too, is a large room, at present arranged with tables and chairs in an open-plan fashion, but proprietors George Morgan and Grace Evans have plans to install partitions and create a more intimate atmosphere. If you are lucky enough to find a vacant table by a window you can enjoy the lovely view down the valley, with a bend of the river in sight. The river, as we have said before is still tidal here and sometimes observers will witness the strange sight of driftwood floating upstream. Apparently, one local resident watches for wood going upstream so that he can collect it for firewood on its way back down again! A simple bar menu is offered here including steaks, grills and cold snacks which are excellent value for money.

That the inn is situated in a famous area of outstanding beauty is certainly an advantage, but the main attribute of the Sloop Inn is the cheerfulness and enthusiasm of its proprietors who work extremely hard with a minimum of staff to ensure that their guests have a pleasant stay.

WINNER

NORTH REGION

THREE SHIRES INN Little Langdale

In the days before the English counties were re-organised this inn stood at the point where Cumberland, Westmorland and Lancashire meet, hence its name. It is set in a beautifully peaceful corner of Lakeland, not far from Ambleside or Coniston, on the road which leads over the steep Wrynose Pass to the equally formidable Hard Knott Pass and eventually to the coast. The village of Little Langdale is nothing more than a scattered collection of houses and a small chapel, yet in the 19th century it was a busy quarrying and mining community with six quarries in the area. In those days the inn was a convenient place for the workmen to get a drink or two. It was built in 1872 and as well as catering for the quarrymen, it also offered a resting place for the traveller.

Today, life is quieter and more civilised, especially since the Stephenson's took over at the beginning of 1983. They have completely decorated the inn from top to bottom and they have created a charming downstairs lounge, with an attractive fireplace of Westmorland green slate. As well as smartening up the inside they have also re-designed the garden to create an attractive area for a quiet drink in the summer.

Shelagh and Neil Stephenson, together with their children provide a very friendly, hospitable atmosphere. There is plenty of information about places to visit, as well as comfortable places to relax, including the small television lounge. All members of the family are interested in cooking, and dinner every evening is a filling four-course dinner with several choices, and some sumptuous puddings set out on the sideboard. There is a small, traditional Walkers bar with a slate floor, and a wide range of bar snacks is available.

Views from all the bedrooms are spectacular, with those at the front looking towards the Tilberthwaite Fells. It is a perfect area for walking or for touring around the lakes, although many would be happy to just stay put at this attractive, friendly inn.

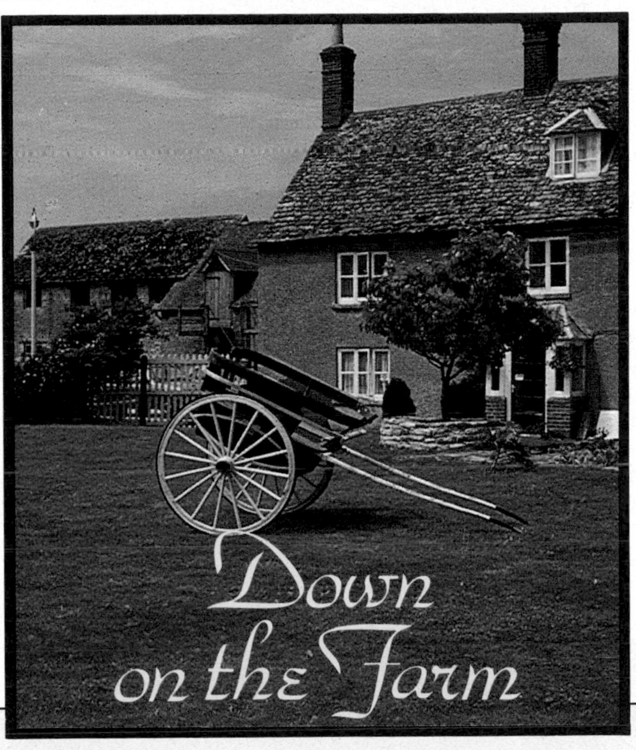

Anyone who takes an interest in the farming programmes on the radio and television will realise that producing the nation's food is just as much an intensive industry as making cars or running computers – more so in most cases. So how do holidaymakers fit into the scheme of things? Will they be made welcome even beyond the confines of the farmhouse, or will they feel more as if they have wandered onto some factory floor?

In the pages that follow we look into some of the problems and give details of some farms we know that will offer their visitors a real taste of country life.

Nearly all of the farms we list in this guide are working farms, but it has to be said that many will run the accommodation side of the business more along the lines of a country guesthouse. Of course, the farmhouse atmosphere will be there, but guests may not be encouraged to venture beyond the house and garden.

The fact is that a farmyard is potentially a very dangerous place and, without exception, every farmer and farmer's wife that we spoke to during our research stressed that this was so. Machinery is a particular hazard and there are often chemicals around. It may be hard to imagine anyone willingly going near a slurry pit, but these, too, have caused many a sticky end in the past. The farms that do allow visitors to wander around will always point out these dangers and ask that children are supervised when in the farmyard – not only for their own safety, but also to avoid upsetting the livestock. The same goes for visitors' pets which are sometimes able to accompany their owners on holiday, but very careful consideration is needed before taking a dog with you to a farm. It is essential that your pet should get along with other animals – farms always have dogs and cats of their own – and that it won't object if it is expected to sleep in the car at night.

Having got all these problems sorted out, there is no doubt that a holiday on a farm can be a very rewarding experience, particularly for town and city dwellers. One of our inspectors, by his own admission 'no longer a wide-eyed child from the city', told us what a thrill it was for him to witness every cow, calf, pig, sheep, lamb, goose, duck and chicken go absolutely wild with noise and activity at the sight of one farmer's wife stepping from the door at feed time and quietly saying 'Come on then'. Imagine how a child would feel to be allowed to help with the feeding!

Sheep graze the orchard at Duffryn Farm.

The farm in question was Middle Woodston Farm at Lindridge, near Tenbury Wells in Worcestershire, a small ten-acre farm in a predominantly fruit-growing area. This just goes to show that it doesn't need to be a large concern with great herds of animals to illustrate what farm life is about. Mrs May's readiness to let visiting children help with the smaller animals makes this an ideal place if there are young ones in the family.

Sick swans recuperate on Duffryn Farm's pond.

Down in the twin county of Hereford, Duffryn Farm at Wormbridge is a quite outstanding example, offering a relaxed holiday with complete freedom to wander around. It is mainly a dairy farm so there are plenty of nice pastures, not all being grazed at the same time. Mr Davies, the farmer, actively preserves his hedgerows and wild flowers which encourage the butterflies, so nature lovers will find plenty to interest them. A small stream runs through the farm and gradually work is being done to widen it in places to encourage the fish. The focal point of the farmyard is a lovely pond, hung over with weeping willows. The Davies' collection of ducks, geese, ornamental pheasants and peacocks reside here, joined occasionally by injured birds which have been brought to the farm to recuperate. The Davies' have four children of their own, who are happy to share their play equipment and the exciting tree-house by the pond. Visitors are also welcome to watch the milking by means of a specially installed observation window in the milking parlour which ensures that the cows are not disturbed by the presence of strangers in their midst.

The Caldon Canal crosses Bank End's farmland

If your family are keen on water, Bank End Farm at Longsdon in Staffordshire would suit them admirably. Although there are few animals here, other than the family cats and dogs, there is a heated swimming pool, a deep brook ideal for fishing and the Caldon Canal which runs through the farm. Visitors have the use of a dinghy to explore this delightful waterway. The Robinsons, who run the farm, have skilfully converted a former milking parlour to provide four double rooms with en-suite bathrooms, a dining room with a small bar and a cosy lounge, complete with television and video. Two other rooms are available within the farmhouse.

Also in Staffordshire, but much more remote, is Glenwood Farm at Ipstones, run by Mr and Mrs Brindley. It is a large farm

Comfortable accommodation at Bank End Farm.

with a great many mixed animals and much to interest the visitor. The accommodation is very comfortable and homely and Mrs Brindley is a mine of information on the area, being a leading light in the local tourism association.

Down in the West Country, nestling in one of Dartmoor's quiet valleys, is Welpritton Farm – an ideal choice for a holiday in this beautiful National Park area. It is a pig farm, with piglets usually to be seen, and Mr Townsend is happy for visitors to watch the animals being fed. From time to time there are also sheep and lambs in the fields and the farm pets are a great attraction – a nanny goat and kid, rabbits, five cats, a Springer spaniel and two donkeys, Noddy and Big Ears, who came from the Donkey Sanctuary at Sidmouth. Children are encouraged to help feed the animals here too and, although the Townsends advertise that they should be over six years old, younger children may be accepted out of the main season.

A sheltered spot in Devon – Welpritton Farm.

Just two of the pets at Welpritton Farm.

For a farmhouse holiday in real style there is Manor Farm at Crackington Haven, close to Cornwall's lovely north coast. Recorded in the Domesday Book as belonging to the Earl of Mortain, half brother of William the Conqueror, the Manor is now presided over by Mr and Mrs Knight. Restored and adapted to accommodate guests, the farmhouse is tastefully furnished with many antiques. Visitors here can watch the computerised milking and see the hens.

Another more compact farm – more a smallholding really – is Penwernfach Farm at Pont Hirwaun in the south west of Wales. The 200-year-old stone farmhouse, with lovely views of the Teifi Valley and Preseli Hills, is surrounded by six acres supporting a variety of animals – chicken, geese, ducks, calves, Shetland and Welsh Mountain ponies and a donkey. Mr and Mrs Moine are very friendly and enthusiastic about their work and will be pleased to show visitors around. Children are encouraged to help out at feeding times and, when they are not occupied thus, there is an adventure playground and a sandpit.

Also in the county of Dyfed is the Preseli Farm Stud, near Whitland amidst the beautiful scenery of the Pembrokeshire National Park. The well-appointed farmhouse is run by Mrs Vaughan who also opens her dining room to the public as a restaurant. Naturally, children would not be allowed to ride the resident horses, but a pony is acquired from a local farm for the summer months and this can be ridden under supervision.

In contrast to the remote, ultra-quiet type of farm, University Farm at Lew in Oxfordshire is popular with plane-spotters, for just across the next field is Brize Norton airfield, a major R.A.F. station where, Mrs Rouse tells us, they sometimes train Concorde pilots in evasive action! No need for alarm though – the aircraft noise is not really a problem. It doesn't even worry the cows who are sensitive creatures at the best of times. The 420-acre farm is mainly milk-producing and so there are some pleasant walks across the pastures (when the weather is dry).

In the far north-east of England is West Ditchburn Farm at Eglingham where, although guests are not really encouraged to wander around at will, conducted tours are arranged in the evenings and guests are sometimes invited to watch Mr Easton work his Border Collies, both with sheep and with

Mellow stone at University Farm, Lew.

geese. Mr Easton is the Vice President of the International Sheep Dog Association and has between ten and twenty dogs of his own at any one time. The farm is also famous for its Charolais cattle and there might be up to forty bulls around. Mr and Mrs Easton are only too pleased to answer any questions about their work.

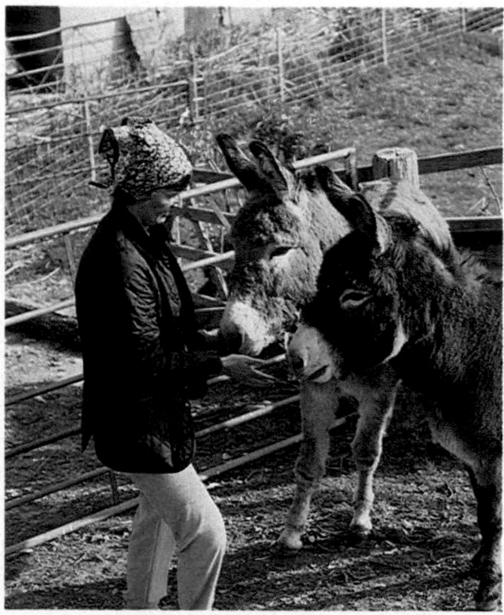

'Noddy' and 'Big Ears' at Welpritton Farm.

Just a few miles away over the hills is Lumbylaw Farm at Edlingham which specialises in the breeding of Limousin Cattle. Other beef cattle and sheep are also kept and the sheep dip is close enough to the house for all to see. On Sundays visitors are treated to an organised tour of the farm, when not only are the farm and stock viewed, but historical features of the neighbourhood are also explained by the farmer, Mr Oates.

Across the country to the west is Bessiestown Farm, which featured in the previous edition of the guide as the North of England's best place for a family holiday. In the context of this article, it certainly deserves another mention. The farm, which is one of very few that can boast an indoor swimming pool, breeds sheep and calves, and visiting children are only too pleased to be invited to help with the feeding. Those who are interested in riding can usually arrange this with Mrs Sissons, her daughter Maria, and her ponies.

Across the border in Scotland, Rockhill Farm is a 200-acre stud and sheep farm on the shore of Loch Awe in Argyll. Guests may wander at will around the farm to see the many thoroughbred mares and foals, sheep and cattle. There is also a private road to the loch edge where guests can fish without a permit, swim, windsurf or sail (if they bring their own craft). There is also a small private lochan on the farm. This is a good area for walking and birdwatching. Nevertheless, because of all the deep water around, Mrs Hodge is reluctant to accommodate children under the age of seven.

Wester Moniack Farm at Kirkhill has the advantage of being situated next door to Scotland's only wine-producing operation at Moniack Castle. It is one of three separate units which make up the farm and, although this particular unit does not include any farm animals, guests can be taken to one of the other units, either to watch the milking or to see any of the other farming operations.

The owners, or in some cases, tenants, of all these farms have demonstrated to us just how well farming and the holiday industry can go together. Both aspects are very hard work and it takes a special kind of family to make it work well by creating just the right atmosphere. Much depends on the attitude of the guests too. One of the more relaxed of the farms we visited had found only one little boy who couldn't be trusted around the farm; another had found only one who could! They, naturally, were rather more wary of offering guests the freedom of their land. Whatever you make of staying on a farm, it certainly cannot be counted as just another type of accommodation – it has a special quality which will not be found in any other kind of holiday.

How to use the gazetteer

Arrangement of gazetteer

The gazetteer includes Great Britain, Channel Islands and the Isle of Man, placenames being arranged in alphabetical order. With the exception of the Isles of Scilly, establishments on off-shore islands are listed under individual placenames and not under the island name. Where applicable the establishments are listed in the following order under their appropriate placenames, Guesthouses (**GH**), Farmhouses (**FH**) and Inns (**INN**). These are listed alphabetically within each category. The establishments are generally more modest in the way of facilities than the AA hotels classified by stars (listed in *AA Members' Handbook* and the AA guide *Hotels and Restaurants in Britain*).

At the back of the book is a 16-page atlas showing the location of the towns and villages mentioned in the gazetteer.

To find a guesthouse, farmhouse or inn

Look at the area you wish to visit in the atlas. *Towns with guesthouses or inns* are marked with a solid dot ●.

Towns with guesthouse/s and/or inn/s plus farmhouse/s are marked with a dot in an open circle ⊙.

Towns with farmhouses only are marked with an open circle ○.

Farmhouses are listed under the nearest identifiable town or village and may in fact be a few miles away.

Reading a map reference

In the gazetteer section of this guide, the main placename is given a two-figure map reference to key with the atlas. In addition, farmhouses have been given six-figure references which can be used in conjunction with a larger scale Ordnance Survey map to pinpoint the exact position.

Example: Two-Figure Reference

*Map **3** ST76:* This is the map reference for Bath in the county of Avon. Turn to Map 3 in the atlas, refer to the large square, ST. Find sub-division 7 from *left* to *right* and sub-division 6 from *bottom* to *top*. While every effort has been made to ensure the correct gazetteering of establishments, in some cases the information received by us has been insufficient. In these instances the establishments have been marked at the nearest town.

Town Plans

A number of town plans have been included in the text to show the positions of establishments in some of the larger towns or cities. As the gazetteer information is continually being updated, some of the establishments shown on the town plans may have been deleted from the text; conversely some more recent gazetteer entries do not appear on the relevant town plans. The mileages at road exits on district plans are calculated from the border of the plan. A list of town plan symbols appears on page 36.

Gazetteer notes

A key to abbreviations and symbols in gazetteer entries appears on the inside covers.

Accommodation for £8 or under

Not all guesthouses, farmhouses or inns shown in this publication provide bed and breakfast for £8 or under per person per night. Those which expect to do so during 1985 carry the appropriate symbol (⊢⊣)

Annexes

The number of bedrooms in an annexe (provided they are of an acceptable standard) is shown in the gazetteer entry, eg (A6). It should be noted that annexes (often used only during the season) may lack some of the facilities available in the main building. It is advisable to check the nature of the accommodation and the charges should be checked before reservations are confirmed.

Bathrooms

The gazetteer entry indicates the number of rooms with private bath or shower and lavatories where applicable.

Central Heating

The heating symbol (▥) in an establishment's entry does not mean that this facility is available all year round. Some places only operate their central heating in the winter months, and then at their own discretion.

Children

Guesthouses and farmhouses usually accommodate children of all ages unless a minimum age is given (*eg* nc8yrs – no children under eight), but it does not necessarily follow that they are able to provide special facilities. If you have very young children find out, before you reserve accommodation, what special amenities (such as cots, high-chairs and, particularly, laundry facilities) are available and whether reductions are made for children. In the gazetteer, establishments which do have special facilities for children are indicated by the symbol ♣. All the following amenities will be found at these establishments: baby-sitting service or baby intercom system, playroom or playground, laundry facilities, drying and ironing facilities, cots and high-chairs, and special meals.

Complaints

If you have any complaints you should inform the proprietor immediately so that the trouble can be dealt with promptly. If a personal approach fails, members should inform the AA.

Credit cards

The numbered boxes below indicate the credit cards which establishments accept.

1 Access/Euro
2 American Express
3 Barclays Visa
4 Carte Blanche
5 Diners

It is advisable to check when booking to ensure that the cards are still accepted.

Deposits

Some establishments, particularly in large towns and holiday centres, require a deposit – especially from chance callers staying for only one night. If you are paying a deposit at the time of advance booking it is advisable to effect insurance cover against possible cancellation, eg *AA Travelsure*. It should be noted that whether or not a deposit is paid, if the booking is subsequently cancelled, compensation may be required.

Disabled Persons

If the wheelchair symbol ♿ is shown in an establishment's entry it means that the disabled can be accommodated. This information has been supplied to the AA by the proprietor but it is advisable to check before making reservations. Details more relevant to disabled persons may be obtained from *The AA Guide for the Disabled Traveller* (1984/5 edition), available from AA offices, free to members, £1.50 to non-members. Members with any form of disability should notify proprietors so that appropriate arrangements can be made to minimise difficulties, particularly in the event of an emergency.

Dogs

Establishments which do not accept dogs are indicated by the symbol ★ but other establishments may impose restrictions on the size of dog allowed. Guide dogs for the blind may also be an exception to the normal rules. The conditions under which pets are accepted should be confirmed with the management when making reservations. Generally dogs are not allowed in the dining room.

Family bedrooms

The gazetteer indicates whether family bedrooms are available by the abbreviation 'fb' together with the relevant number of rooms, eg (2fb).

Farms

Within each gazetteer entry is the six-figure reference to be used in conjunction with Ordnance Survey maps. This number follows the establishment name and is in *italics*.

The acreage of each farm is shown in the body of each entry (*eg* 55acres) followed by the type of farming that predominates (*eg* dairy, arable etc).

Although the AA lists working farms, some may have become 'non-working' if, for instance, the farmer has sub-let or sold land. Potential guests should ascertain the true nature of the farm's activity before booking to ensure their requirements are met.

Fire Precautions

So far as can be ascertained at the time of going to press, every unit of accommodation listed in this publication, provided it is subject to the requirements of the Act, has applied for and not been refused a fire certificate. The Fire Precautions Act 1971 does not apply to the Channel Islands or the Isle of Man, both of which exercise their own rules with regard to fire precautions for accommodation units.

Gazetteer Entry

Establishment names shown in *italics* indicate that particulars have not been confirmed by the management in time for this 1985 edition.

Licences

An indication is given in each entry where a guesthouse is licensed to serve alcoholic drinks. Most places in the guesthouse category do not hold a full licence but all inns do. Licensed premises are not obliged to remain open throughout the permitted hours and may do so only when they expect reasonable trade. Note that at establishments which have registered clubs, club membership does not come into effect – nor can a drink be bought – until 48 hours after joining. For further information refer to leaflet HH20 'The Law about Licensing Hours and

Children/Young Persons on Licensed Premises' available from AA offices.

London

It is common knowledge that in London prices tend to be higher than in the provinces. For hotels, we have tried to select establishments where the accommodation is inexpensive and where bed and breakfast is normally provided. We have also included a few which provide a full meal service and whose charges are consequently higher.

Meals

In some parts of the country such as the north east of Scotland, high tea is generally served in guesthouses although dinner is often also available on request. The latest time that the evening meal can be **ordered** is indicated in the text. In some cases this may be at breakfast time or even at dinner the evening before. On Sundays, many establishments serve their main meal at midday and will charge accordingly. However it is possible that a cold supper will be available in the evening.

Opening dates

Unless otherwise stated, establishments are open all year. Where dates are shown these are inclusive: eg Apr–Oct indicates that the establishment is open from the beginning of April to the end of October.

Prices

Prices are liable to fluctuation and it is advisable to check when you book. Also, make sure you know exactly what facilities are being offered when you are verifying charges, because there are variations in what an establishment may provide within inclusive terms. Weekly terms, for instance, vary from full board to bed and breakfast only. This is shown in the text by the symbol Ⱡ (no lunches) and M̸ (no main meals). At the height of the season some establishments offer accommodation on a weekly basis only. When applicable this is shown in the gazetteer. Some establishments provide packed lunches, snacks or salads at extra cost. All prices quoted normally include VAT and service, where applicable.

*1984 Prices

When proprietors have been unable to furnish us with their proposed 1985 prices, those for 1984 are quoted, prefixed by an asterisk (*).

Requests for Information

If you are writing to an establishment requesting information it is important to enclose a stamped, addressed envelope. Please quote this publication in any enquiry.

Reservations

Please book as early as you possibly can or you may be disappointed. If you are delayed or have to change your plans, let the proprietor know at once. You may be held legally responsible if the room you booked cannot be re-let. Some establishments, especially those in short-season holiday centres, do not accept bookings for bed and breakfast only. Additionally, some guesthouses – particularly in seaside resorts – do not take bookings from midweek to midweek, and a number will not accept period bookings other than at full board rate, *ie* not at nightly bed and breakfast rate plus individual meals.

It is regretted that the AA cannot at the present time undertake to make any reservations.

The hotel industry's Voluntary Code of Booking Practice was introduced in June 1977. Its prime object is to ensure that the customer is clear about the precise services and facilities he or she is buying, and what price he will have to pay, before he commits himself to a contractually binding agreement. The guest should be handed a card at the time of registration, detailing the total obligatory charge, and tariff details may also be displayed prominently at the reception office.

The Tourism (Sleeping Accommodation Price Display) Order 1977 was introduced in February 1978. It compels hotels, motels, guesthouses, inns and self-catering accommodation with four or more letting bedrooms to display in entrance halls the maximum and minimum prices charged for each category of room. This order complements the Voluntary Code of Booking Practice.

Every effort is being made by the AA to encourage the use of the Voluntary Code in appropriate establishments.

Restricted Service

Some establishments operate a restricted service during the less busy months. This is indicated by the prefix rs. For example, rs Nov–Mar indicates that a restricted service is operated from November to March. This may be a reduction in meals served and/or accommodation available. It is advisable to telephone in advance to find out the nature of the restriction.

Tea and Coffee in bedrooms

The symbol ® means that tea and coffee making facilities are available in bedrooms, although they may only be available on request; so please check when booking. The nature of these facilities will vary from one establishment to another.

Telephone Numbers

Unless otherwise stated the telephone exchange name given in the gazetteer is that of the town under which the establishment is listed. Where the exchange for a particular establishment is not that of the town under which it appears, the name of the exchange is given after the telephone symbol ☎ and before the number.

In some areas telephone numbers are likely to be changed by the telephone authorities during the currency of this publication. In case of difficulty check with the operator.

Television

If the gazetteer entry shows 'CTV' or 'TV' this indicates that either colour or monochrome television is available in a lounge. The entry may also show the number of guests' bedrooms with 'CTV' or 'TV' available. This can be in for form of televisions permanently fixed or available on reques from the hotel management. In all cases these points should be checked when making a reservation.

VAT and Service Charge

In the United Kingdom and the Isle of Man, Value Added Tax is payable on both basic prices and any service. The symbol S% in the gazetteer indicates that the inclusive prices shown do not reflect any separate accounting for service made by the establishment. VAT does not apply in the Channel Islands. With this exception, prices quoted in the gazetteer are inclusive of VAT.

Explanation of a gazetteer entry

The example is ***fictitious***

TOWN NAME
Appears in alphabetical order.

MAP REFERENCES
First figure is map page no. Then follows grid reference; read 1st figure across (east), 2nd figure vertically (north).

ORDNANCE SURVEY MAP REFERENCE
Appears only after **farmhouse** name

COUNTY NAME
The administrative region/county names are used throughout. This may not be the complete postal address.

LOOE
Cornwall
Map **2** SX25
GH Ram Hotel *(ST075149)* ☎(07652) 768 Plan **9**
Etr–Oct
12hc (2→4⩍) (1fb) CTV in 6 bedrooms
✱ Ⓡ B&b£9–£11 Bdi£15–£18 W£85–£105 Ⓚ LDO5pm
Lic ▥ CTV 9P nc7yrs
Credit cards 1 3

TELEPHONE NUMBER
The exchange is that of the gazetteer heading town name unless otherwise stated (see above)

CLASSIFICATION
Guesthouse

SPECIFIC DETAILS
Opening times, facilities, prices and terms. See 'Symbols and Abbreviations' on inside covers.

TOWN PLAN
Establishment number on town plan (where applicable).

Symbols used in town plans

- Recommended route
- Other routes
- Restricted roads
- ✝ Church
- *i* Tourist information centre
- *AA* AA service centre
- **P** Car park
- ❻ Guesthouses, inns, etc
- 4 ½m Distances to guesthouse etc from edge of plan
- **KESWICK 12m** Mileages to towns from edge of plan (district plan)

Gazetteer

The gazetteer gives locations and details of AA-listed guesthouses, inns and farmhouses in England, Wales and Scotland. Details of guesthouses in the Channel Islands, Isle of Man and Isles of Scilly are also included, but there are no AA-listed farmhouses within these islands. *NB. There is no map for Isles of Scilly*. The gazetteer is listed in alphabetical order of placenames. Details for islands are shown under individual placenames, the text also gives appropriate cross-references. A useful first point of reference is to consult the location maps which show where AA-listed accommodation is located.

GUESTACCOM & MINOTEL
The above consortia are highlighted in the gazetteer. The Central Reservation Office telephone numbers are; Guestaccom: Brighton (0273) 722833, Minotel: Brighton (0273) 731908

ABBERLEY
Hereford & Worcester
Map **7** SO76

FH Mrs S Neath **Church** *(SO754678)* ☏Great Witley (029921) 316
Apr–Oct
An early Victorian farmhouse in the peaceful village of Abberley. Off A443 on B4202, in ¼m turn right into village.
2hc (1fb) ✱ ✻B&bfr£8 W£56 M
TV 4P 300 acres arable beef

ABBOTS BICKINGTON
Devon
Map **2** SS31

FH Mrs E Bellew ***Court Barton*** *(SS385133)* ☏Milton Damerel (040926) 214
May–Oct
Stone-built farmhouse in an area of great natural beauty. Panoramic views from most windows. Rough shooting, fishing and riding available.
4rm 3hc (2fb) ✱ LDO5.30pm
TV 10P nc4yrs 600acres arable beef sheep

ABBOTS BROMLEY
Staffordshire
Map **7** SK02

⊢⊣**FH** Mr & Mrs W R Aitkenhead **Fishers Pit** *(SK098244)* ☏Burton-on-Trent (0283) 840204
Early Victorian two-storey brick-built farmhouse, ½m from village on B5234.
5hc (2fb) ✱ Ⓡ B&b£7–£8 Bdi£12–£13 W£84 Ⱡ LDO6pm
CTV 6P 84acres dairy sheep

⊢⊣**FH** Mrs M K Hollins **Marsh** *(SK069261)* ☏Burton-on-Trent (0283) 840323
Closed Xmas
Large two-storey, cement rendered farmhouse set in open countryside 1m from village.
2rm (1fb) B&b£7–£7.50 Bdi£10–£10.50 W£49 M LDO6.30pm
Ⅲ CTV 6P 87acres mixed
Ⓥ

ABERDARE
Mid Glamorgan
Map **3** SO00

GH *Cae-Coed Private Hotel* Craig St, off Monk St ☏(0685) 871190
A neat but modestly appointed guesthouse.
7hc (1fb) LDO4pm
Lic Ⅲ CTV nc2½yrs
Ⓥ

ABERDEEN
Grampian *Aberdeenshire*
Map **15** NJ90

GH Broomfield Private Hotel 15 Balmoral Pl ☏(0244) 588758
9hc (1fb) Ⓡ ✻B&b£11.50 Bdi£16 LDO5pm
Ⅲ CTV 16P

GH Kilbreck 410 Great Western Rd ☏(0224) 36115
Closed Xmas & New Year
Well appointed small hotel with some ground floor bedrooms.
6hc (1fb) ✱ B&b£9–£9.50 Bdi£13–£15 LDO3pm
Ⅲ CTV 3P

GH Mannofield Hotel 447 Great Western Rd ☏(0224) 35888
10rm 7hc (3fb) B&b£17.25–£19.55 Bdi£23.85–£25.15 W£116.95–£183.05 Ⱡ LDO6pm
Lic Ⅲ CTV 14P nc10yrs

⊢⊣**GH Strathboyne** 26 Abergeldie Ter ☏(0224) 593400
7hc (2fb) ✱ B&b£8–£9 Bdi£12–£13 W£82–£90 M LDO4pm
Ⅲ CTV

GH *Tower Hotel* 36 Fonthill Rd ☏(0224) 24050
Small, traditionally furnished and decorated hotel with business clientele.
7hc (3fb) LDO6.45pm
Lic Ⅲ CTV 8P

GH Western 193 Great Western Rd ☏(0224) 596919
Closed Xmas & New Year
Well maintained granite house with gardens; on road on outskirts of city centre.
6hc (2fb) ✱ Ⓡ B&b£9–£10 W£60–£65 M
Ⅲ CTV 6P nc5yrs

ABERDOVEY
Gwynedd
Map **6** SN69

GH *Brynmorwydd Private Hotel* ☏(065472) 606
6hc 3⇌ (3fb) ✱
Lic CTV 10P sea
Ⓥ

ABEREDW
Powys
Map **3** SO04

⊢⊣**FH** Mrs M M Evans **Danycoed** *(SO079476)* ☏Erwood (09823) 298
Etr–Oct
Stone-built, two-storey farmhouse. Pleasant situation on edge of River Wye.
3rm 2hc ✱ B&b£7–£7.50 Bdi£10.50–£11 W£70–£75.50 Ⱡ LDO5.30pm
P 230acres sheep mixed

ABERFELDY
Tayside *Perthshire*
Map **14** NN84

GH Balnearn Private Hotel Crieff Rd ☏(0887) 20431
Large house with modern bedroom wing and some antiques.
13hc (2fb) Ⓡ B&bfr£10.35 Bdifr£16.10 Wfr£112.70 Ⱡ LDO7pm
CTV 15P ♿

GH Guinach House Urlar Road ☏(0887) 20251
Mar–Oct
Attractive house standing in its own well tended gardens in a quiet spot close to the town centre.
7hc (1fb) TV in 1 bedroom Ⓡ B&b£11–£12.50 Bdi£17.50–£20 W£110–£126 Ⱡ LDO8pm
Lic Ⅲ CTV 12P 2🚗

GH Nessbank Private Hotel Crieff Rd ☏(0887) 20214
rs Nov–Mar
A very comfortable little hotel with high standards throughout.
7hc Ⓡ B&b£11.50 Bdi£18 W£110 Ⱡ LDO7pm
Lic CTV 7P
Ⓥ

⊢⊣**FH** Mr A Kennedy **Tom of Cluny** *(NN875515)* ☏(0887) 20477
Small hillside farmhouse reached by long steep tarmac/rough drive. Magnificent views southwards across the River Tay and Aberfeldy.
2rm B&b£7.50 Bdi£10 LDO4pm
CTV 2P 220acres arable beef sheep mixed

ABERGAVENNY
Gwent
Map **3** SO21

GH Belchamps 1 Holywell Rd (Guestaccom) ☎(0873) 3204
5hc (2fb) ✱ ✻B&b£7.50–£9 Bdi£12.50–£14 W£49.88–£59.85 LDO5pm
▥ CTV 5P

GH Llanwenarth House Govilon ☎Gilwern (0873) 830289
5rm 4⇌ 1⋒ (1fb) CTV in 4 bedrooms ® B&b£17.50–£19.50 Bdi£27.50–£29.50 LDO8.30pm
Lic ▥ CTV 10P 2🚗
Credit cards ② ⑤ Ⓥ

GH Park 36 Hereford Rd ☎(0873) 3715
Proprietor run small guesthouse offering a warm welcome.
7hc (1fb) B&b£8.50–£9 Bdi£12.75–£13.50 W£55–£65 M LDO6pm
Lic ▥ CTV 8P
Ⓥ

FH Mrs D V M Nicholls **Newcourt** *(SO317165)* Mardy ☎(0873) 3734
16th-century, stone built farmhouse with views of Sugar Loaf Mountain.
3hc (1fb) CTV in 1 bedroom ✱ B&bfr£10
▥ TV P 🚗 nc6yrs 85acres dairy

ABERHOSAN
Powys
Map **6** SN89

⊢⊣ **FH** Mrs A Lewis **Bacheiddon** *(SN825980)* ☎Machynlleth (0654) 2229
Apr–Oct
From the windows there are lovely views of the surrounding mountains and countryside. Off unclassified road linking Machynlleth and Dyliffe/Staylittle (B4518).
3⋒ (1fb) ✱ B&bfr£8 Bdifr£13 W£90 L
CTV P 850acres sheep mixed

ABERPORTH
Dyfed
Map **2** SN25

GH *Ffynonwen Country* ☎(0239) 810312
Proprietor run, rural guesthouse with a residents' bar.
12hc 1⇌ (2fb)
Lic ▥ 30P

ABERSOCH
Gwynedd
Map **6** SH32

GH Llysfor ☎(075881) 2248
Etr–Oct
Detached Victorian house near beach and shops.
8rm 7hc 1⇌ (2fb) ® B&b£9–£10 Bdi£13.50–£14.50 W£63–£70 L LDOam
Lic CTV 12P
Credit card ③ Ⓥ

ABERYSTWYTH
Dyfed
Map **6** SN58
See plan

GH *Glan-Aber Hotel* 7–8 Union St ☎(0970) 617610 Plan **1** *B2*
Victorian house in side street opposite the railway terminus.
12hc (1fb) ® LDO6pm
Lic ▥ CTV

GH Glyn-Garth South Rd ☎(0970) 615050 Plan **2** *A2*
Closed 2 wks Xmas rs Oct–Etr
Victorian, mid-terrace property adjacent to beach and harbour, ¼m from the shops.
10rm 4hc 4⇌ 2⋒ (3fb) CTV in all bedrooms ® ✻B&b£8–£15 Bdi£14.50–£21.50 W£55–£100 L LDO4pm
Lic ▥ CTV nc7yrs

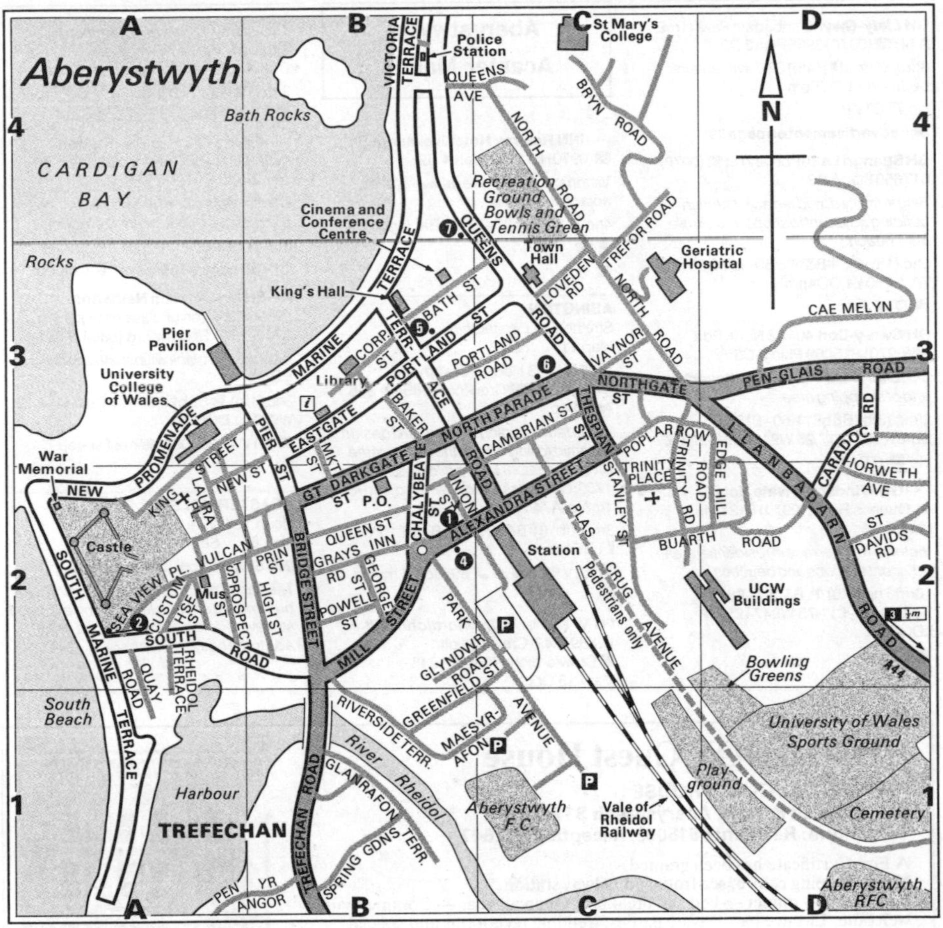

Aberystwyth

Aberystwyth

1 Glan-Aber Hotel
2 Glyn-Garth
3 Llety-Gwyn
4 Railway Hotel (*Inn*)
5 Shangri-La
6 Swn-y-Don
7 Windsor Private Hotel

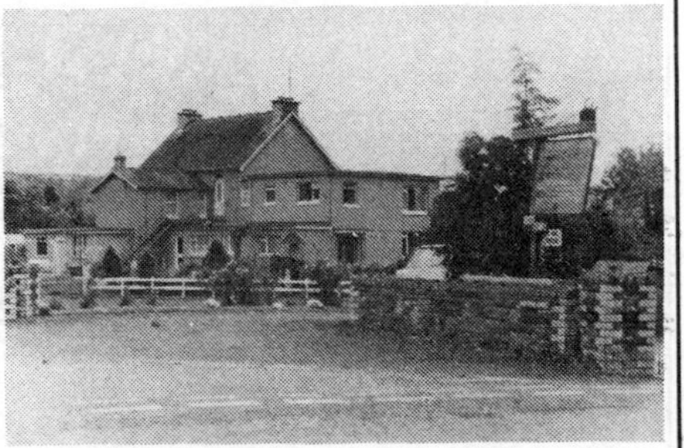

GH *Llety-Gwyn* Llanbadarn Fawr (1m E A44) ☎(0970) 3965 Plan **3** *D2*

8hc (A 5hc 3fl) (4fb) CTV available in bedrooms LDO6pm

Lic ₩ CTV P

See advertisement on page 39

GH Shangri La 36 Portland St ☎(0970) 617659 Plan **5** *B3*

Single fronted, mid terrace Victorian building adjacent to shops and ¼ mile from beach.

6hc (1fb) ® *B&b£6.50 Bdi£9.50 W£45.50 Ł LDO4pm

₩ CTV ₽

GH Swn-y-Don 40–42 North Pde ☎(0970) 615059 Plan **6** *C3*

Double fronted Victorian mid terrace at end of shopping area.

25hc (3fb) B&b£11.50–£12.50 Bdi£16.10–£17.25 W£109–£112.70 Ł

Lic ₩ CTV 7P

GH Windsor Private Hotel 41 Queens Rd ☎(0970) 612134 Plan **7** *B4*

Victorian mid terrace in residential area adjacent to shops and beaches.

10rm 7hc (2fb) B&b£7–£8 Bdi£10.75–£11.75 W£47–£53 M LDO5pm

₩ CTV ₽

INN Railway Hotel Alexandra Rd ☎(0970) 611258 Plan **4** *B2*

Victorian inn opposite railway station, adjacent to shops.

4hc ® B&b£7–£7.50 Bar lunch £2

₽

Ⓥ

ABINGTON
Strathclyde *Lanarkshire*
Map **11** NS92

FH Mr G Hodge **Craighead** *(NS914236)* ☎Crawford (08642) 356 Apr–Sep

Large farm building in courtyard design. Set amid rolling hills on the banks of the River Duneaton. Main buildings date from 1780. Off unclassified Crawfordjohn rd. 1m N of A74/A73 junc.

3rm (1fb) ® B&bfr£6.50 Bdifr£10 W£65 Ł LDO4pm

₩ CTV 6P 2 800acres mixed

Ⓥ

FH Mr D Wilson ***Crawfordjohn Mill*** *(NS897242)* Crawfordjohn ☎Crawfordjohn (08644) 248 May–15 Oct

Two-storey, brown brick farmhouse. Situated off the A74 1m SE of Crawfordjohn on an unclassified road.

3rm (1fb) LDO6.30pm

₩ TV 4P 180acres arable dairy

FH Mrs M E Hamilton **Kirkton** *(NS933210)* ☎Crawford (08642) 376 Jun–Sep

Comfortable stone farmhouse in picturesque tree-screened gardens.

3rm B&b£7

CTV 3P nc4yrs 750acres beef sheep

FH Mrs J Hyslop **Netherton** *(NS908254)* (on unclass road joining A74 & A73) ☎Crawford (08642) 321

A converted black whinstone shooting lodge.

3hc (1fb) B&b£7.50–£8 Bdi£11–£12 W£50 Ł LDO6pm

₩ CTV 4P 3000acres beef sheep

Ⓥ

ACASTER MALBIS
North Yorkshire
Map **8** SE54

INN Ship ☎York (0904) 705609

The period features of this 18th-century building are still visible including exposed stonework and beamed ceilings which add to the cosy atmosphere.

5hc ★ Ⓡ B&b£9–£11 W£57–£70 M Bar lunch £1.25–£3.50 D9.30pm £4.50–£7.50
CTV 40P
Credit cards 1 3 Ⓥ
See advertisement on page 282

ACHARACLE
Highland *Argyllshire*
Map **13** NM66
FH Mrs M Macaulay **Dalilea House** *(NM735693)* ☎Salen (096785) 253
Etr–Oct
A splendid turreted house with surrounding grounds giving excellent views over farmland hills and Loch Shiel. A blend of the ancient and modern.
6hc (1fb) Ⓡ B&bfr£9.77 Bdifr£15.50 Wfr£96.60 L LDO7pm
P 18000acres beef sheep hill
Ⓥ

AINSTABLE
Cumbria
Map **12** NY54
FH Miss K Pollock **Basco Dyke Head** *(NY529450)* Basco Dyke ☎Croglin (076886) 254
Mar–Oct
1½m S off unclass rd.
2hc (1fb) B&b£6 Bdi£10 W£40 M LDO8.30pm
CTV 4P 2 245acres arable dairy mixed

ALDERSHOT
Hampshire
Map **4** SU85
GH Cedar Court Hotel Eggars Hill ☎(0252) 20931
Closed 24 Dec–1 Jan
Large private house with comfortable annexe accommodation.
8rm 5hc 3 (A 4rm 1 3) (2fb) CTV in 8 bedrooms ★ Ⓡ B&b£12 Bdi£18 LDOnoon
Lic lift CTV 13P
GH Glencoe Hotel 4 Eggars Hill ☎(0252) 20801
Friendly, nicely appointed private house with spacious bedrooms.

Acaster Malbis — Alnwick

12hc 3 (2fb) ★ Ⓡ B&b£12 W£84 M
CTV 12P
Credit card 1 Ⓥ

ALDWARK
Derbyshire
Map **8** SK25
FH J N Lomas **Lydgate** *(SK228577)* ☎Carsington (062985) 250
Stone-built traditional farmhouse, about 300 years old, in quiet rural setting.
3rm (1fb) ★ B&b£8.50 Bdi£12 W£59.50 M LDO4pm
CTV 3P 2 300acres beef dairy sheep
Ⓥ

ALFRISTON
East Sussex
Map **5** TQ50
FH Mrs D Y Savage **Pleasant Rise** *(TQ516027)* ☎(0323) 870545
Very attractive farm with large bright and clean accommodation, delightfully appointed. Badminton, cricket nets and extensive tennis facilities. Adjacent to B2108 Seaford road.
4hc 1 (1fb) CTV in 1 bedroom Ⓡ B&bfr£8.50
CTV P hard 100acres beef
Ⓥ

ALKMONTON
Derbyshire
Map **7** SK13
FH Mr A Harris ***Dairy House*** *(SK198367)* ☎Great Cubley (033523) 359
16th-century brick farmhouse, comfortably modernised yet retaining character. Nature Reserve.
4rm 3hc (1fb) ★ Ⓡ LDO7pm
Lic CTV 6P 82acres dairy

ALLENSMORE
Hereford & Worcester
Map **3** SO43
FH Mrs O I Griffiths **Mawfield** *(SO453366)* ☎Hereford (0432) 277266
May–Oct
Large farmhouse set in a narrow lane off the beaten track, but close enough for Hereford's amenities.
4rm 2hc (1fb) ★ B&b£7–£8.50 Bdi£10–£12.50 W£45–£55 M LDO4pm
CTV P nc8yrs 176acres arable beef sheep

ALNMOUTH
Northumberland
Map **12** NU21
GH Marine House Private Hotel
1 Marine Dr ☎Alnwick (0665) 830349
8rm 4hc 2 (4fb) B&b£11–£13 Bdi£17.50–£19.50 W£116–£130 L LDO4pm
Lic CTV 8P
Ⓥ

ALNWICK
Northumberland
Map **12** NU11
GH Aln House South Rd ☎(0665) 602265
rs Xmas
Large comfortable house with young friendly proprietors.
8rm 6hc 2 (2fb) TV in 1 bedroom ★ B&b£8–£8.50 Bdi£12.50–£13 W£50–£54 M LDO5.30pm
Lic CTV 8P
Ⓥ

GH Aydon House South Rd ☎(0665) 602218
10hc (4fb) ★ B&b£7.50–£9.50 Bdi£12–£15 W£50–£65 M LDO5pm
Lic CTV 12P
Credit cards 1 2 3 4 5
GH Bondgate House Bondgate Without ☎(0665) 602025
Closed Xmas rs Oct–Apr →

8rm 7hc 1⋔ (3fb) Ⓡ B&b£8–£9.50 Bdi£13–£14.50 W£55–£66.50 ⱡ LDO4pm

Lic ▥ CTV 8P

GH *Georgian* 3–5 Hotspur St ☎(0665) 603165

5hc (1fb) TV in all bedrooms ★ Ⓡ

▥ ⊉

⊢⊣ **GH Hope Rise** The Dunterns ☎(0665) 602930

In quiet residential area, house offers comfortable accommodation and a friendly atmosphere.

7hc (2fb) ★ Ⓡ B&b£8–£8.50 W£55–£57 M LDO6pm

▥ CTV 12P nc5yrs

Credit cards 2 3

⊢⊣ **FH** Mrs A Davison **Aldyke** *(NU208124)* ☎(0665) 602193 May–Oct

1m E on A1068.

3rm 2hc (1fb) ★ Ⓡ B&b£9 Bdi£13 W£56 M LDOnoon

CTV 8P nc5yrs 320acres mixed

ALSTON
Cumbria
Map **12** NY74

⊢⊣ **FH** Mrs P M Dent **Middle Bayles** *(NY706451)* ☎(0498) 81383 Closed Xmas & New Year rs Nov–Mar

Alnwick — Ambleside

Charming old world hill farm overlooking South Tyne Valley. Attractive accommodation.

2hc (1fb) ★ B&b£6.30–£7 Bdi£9.50–£10.50 W£66 ⱡ LDO6pm

▥ TV 2P 300acres beef sheep hill

Ⓥ

ALTRINCHAM
Gt Manchester
Map **7** SJ78

GH Bollin Hotel 58 Manchester Rd ☎061-928 2390

10hc (3fb) B&b£12.65

CTV 12P

ALVERDISCOTT
Devon
Map **2** SS52

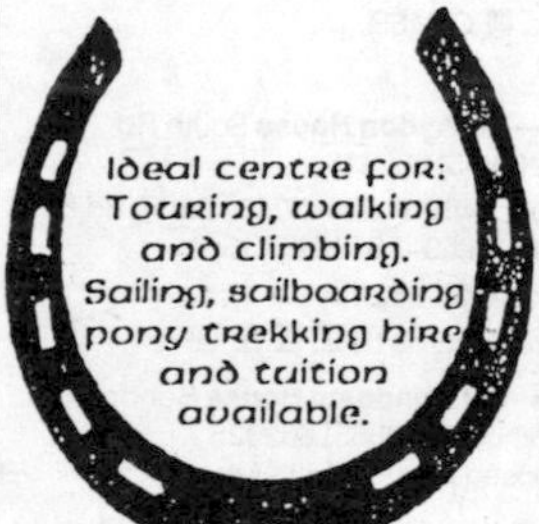

⊢⊣ **FH** Mrs C M Tremeer **Garnacott** *(SS516240)* ☎Newton Tracey (027185) 282
Mar–Nov

Farmhouse standing in small garden surrounded by open fields. Traditional farmhouse furnishings. Facilities nearby include fishing, golf and bathing.

3rm 2hc (2fb) ★ B&b£6.50–£7 Bdi£8.75–£9.25 W£58–£63 ⱡ LDO1pm

CTV 4P 85acres arable beef sheep mixed

Ⓥ

AMBLESIDE
Cumbria
Map **7** NY30

GH Borrans Park Hotel Borrans Rd ☎(0966) 33454
Feb–Nov

Georgian house in secluded position between lake & village. Completely refurbished and modernised.

9rm 2hc 2⇌ 5⋔ (1fb) CTV in 7 bedrooms TV in 2 bedrooms ★ Ⓡ B&b£13.50–£16 Bdi£27–£32 W£138–£158 ⱡ LDO5pm

Lic ▥ 20P ♿

Credit cards 1 3 Ⓥ

GH Chapel House Hotel Kirkstone Rd ☎(0966) 33143
Closed Jan

Former 16th-century cottages, carefully converted to retain their old world charm and atmosphere.

9hc (2fb) ★ Bdi£15.20–£16.50 W£98–£105 ⱡ LDO7pm

Lic ▥ ⊉

↦ **GH Compston House Hotel** Compston Rd ☎(0966) 32305
10hc (2fb) ✱ B&b£7.95–£8.95 Bdi£12.95–£13.95 W£95 Ⅼ LDO5pm
Lic ▥ CTV ⚑

GH Gables Private Hotel Church Walk, Compston Rd ☎(0966) 33272
Mar–Oct
15rm 12hc 1⇌ 2⋒ (6fb) B&b£9–£10 Bdi£13.50–£14 Wfr£94.50 Ⅼ LDO5.30pm
Lic ▥ CTV 8P

GH Gale Cresent Lower Gale ☎(0966) 32284
Apr–Oct
8rm 6hc 2⋒ (1fb) Ⓡ *B&b£9 W£63 M
CTV 8P
Ⓥ

GH *Hilldale* Church St ☎(0966) 33174
8hc 1⋒ (3fb) ✱ LDO6.30pm
▥ CTV ⚑

GH Horseshoe Rothay Rd ☎(0966) 32000
Mar–3 Jan
Town centre guesthouse overlooking park. Dinner available at local restaurant at reduced rate.
12rm 7hc 5⋒ (6fb) B&b£8.95–£11.50 Bdi£14.25–£16.80 W£60–£75 M
▥ CTV 11P
Ⓥ

Ambleside

GH Oaklands Country House Hotel Millans Park ☎(0966) 32525
Closed Xmas
8rm 3hc 2⇌ 3⋒ (3fb) CTV in all bedrooms ✱ Ⓡ B&b£8.50–£14 Bdi£15.50–£21 W£97–£105 Ⅼ LDO4pm
Lic ▥ 8P
Ⓥ

GH Park House Compston Rd ☎(0966) 33542
Closed Dec & Jan
A small friendly house overlooking the park in the town centre.
6hc (2fb) TV in all bedrooms Ⓡ *B&b£7.50–£8.50 W£70–£80 Ⅼ LDOnoon
CTV ⚑ nc5yrs

GH *Romney Hotel* Waterhead ☎(0966) 32219
Etr–Oct
A tranquil country house atmosphere prevails and the resident proprietors give service in keeping.
19hc (4fb) LDO6.45pm
Lic CTV 20P 3🚗 lake

GH Rothay Garth Hotel Rothay Rd ☎(0966) 32217
Hotel offers very relaxing atmosphere and comfortable accommodation.
15rm 5hc 4⇌ 6⋒ (3fb) CTV in 6 bedrooms TV in 2 bedrooms Ⓡ B&b£16–£20.50 Bdi£21–£26 W£137–£168 Ⅼ LDO7.30pm
Lic ▥ CTV 12P 1🚗
Credit cards 1 3 5

GH Rydal Lodge Hotel (2m NW A590) ☎(0966) 33208
Closed Jan
Part Georgian house with attractive gardens, it offers charming bedrooms, comfortable lounges and home cooking.
8hc (1fb) B&b£13 Bdi£20 W£88 M
LDO6pm
Lic CTV 12P
Credit cards 1 3
See advertisement on page 44

GH Rysdale Hotel Kelsick Rd ☎(0966) 32140
Closed Xmas
9hc (4fb) TV in all bedrooms ✱ B&b£8.50–£9.50 Bdi£13.50–£14.50 W£90–£95 Ⅼ S% LDO5pm
Lic ▥ ⚑ nc 3yrs

↦ **GH Smallwood Hotel** Compston Rd ☎(0966) 32330
Mar–Oct
→

13rm 11hc 1⋒ (5fb) B&b£8–£9.50 Bdi£14–£15.50 W£95–£105 M LDO5pm
CTV 10P nc2yrs

ANNAN
Dumfries & Galloway *Dumfriesshire*
Map **11** NY16

GH *Ravenswood* St Johns Rd
☎(04612) 2158
Mar–Jan
Sandstone Villa dating from 1880 standing in residential street close to town centre.

9hc (2fb) LDO5pm
Lic CTV

APPLEBY-IN-WESTMORELAND
Cumbria
Map **12** NY62

GH Bongate House ☎(0930) 51245
7rm 3hc 1→ 3⋒ (3fb) B&b£8.50–£9.50 Bdi£13–£14 W£51–£57 L LDO6pm
Lic CTV 6P 2

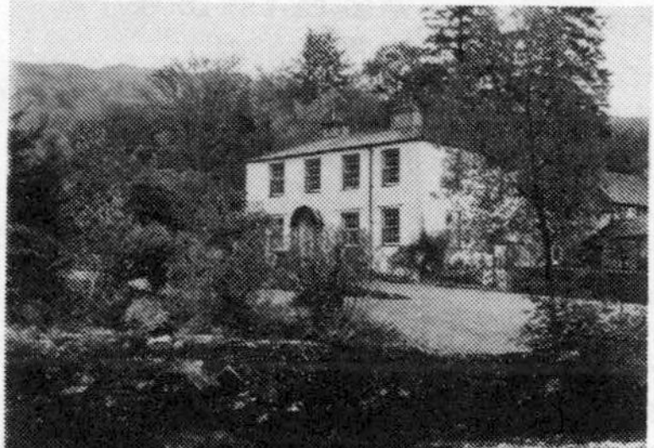

GH Howgill House ☎(0930) 51574
Etr–Oct
6hc (3fb) ® B&bfr£7 Bdifr£11 LDO6pm
TV 6P
Credit cards 1 2 3 4

FH Mrs M Wood **Gale House** *(NY695206)* ☎(0930) 51380
Apr–Sep
Farmhouse standing in small garden surrounded by open fields. Traditional farmhouse furnishings. Facilities nearby include fishing, golf and bathing.

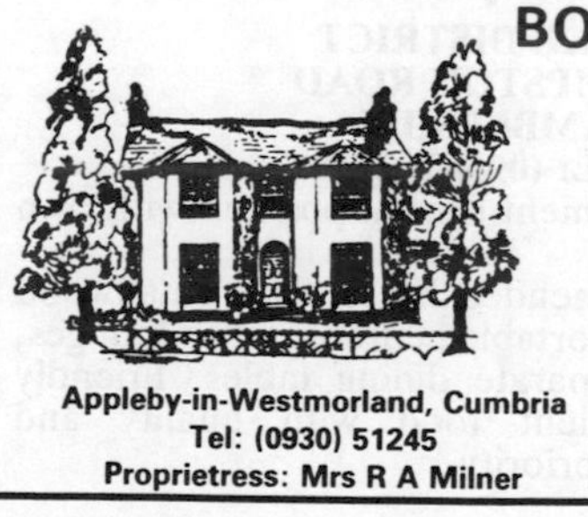

2rm (1fb) ✖ B&b£7 W£49 M
3P nc5yrs 165 acres dairy
Ⓥ

APPLEDORE
Kent
Map **5** TQ92
INN Red Lion 15 The Street ☎(023383) 206
Simple, comfortable accommodation complimented by freshly cooked food and specialising in locally caught fish.
4hc CTV in 1 bedroom B&b£9–£10 W£63 M L£3.50alc D10pm£3.50alc
CTV 6P
Credit card 3

ARBROATH
Tayside *Angus*
Map **12** NO64
GH Kingsley 29 Market Gate ☎(0241) 73933
15hc (5fb) *B&b£7.50–£8 Bdi£9.80–£10.50 W£45–£50 M
Lic CTV
Ⓥ

ARDBRECKNISH
Strathclyde *Argyllshire*
Map **10** NN02
FH Mrs H F Hodge **Rockhill** *(NN072219)* ☎Kilchrenan (08663) 218
Apr–Oct

Loch shore farm. Trout and perch fishing (free), and at the farm's private loch by arrangement.
6hc (4fb) B&b£8.50–£9.50 Bdi£13.50–£15.50 W£80–£100 L LDO7pm
Lic CTV 6P nc6yrs 200acres sheep horses

ARDEN
Strathclyde *Dunbartonshire*
Map **10** NS38
FH Mrs R Keith **Mid Ross** *(NS359859)* ☎(038985) 655
Apr–Sep
Farmhouse pleasantly located close to Loch Lomond 3m N of Balloch off A82.
3hc (1fb) ✖ B&b£5–£8 W£45 M
CTV P 40acres arable beef sheep mixed

ARDERSIER
Highland *Inverness-shire*
Map **14** NH85
FH Mrs L E MacBean **Milton-of-Gollanfield** *(NH809534)* ☎(0667) 62207
Apr–Oct

Stone farmhouse set on north side of A96 5m W of Nairn.
3rm 2hc (1fb) ✖ B&b£7.50–£10 W£54 M
CTV P 360acres arable beef sheep mixed
Ⓥ

ARDFERN
Strathclyde *Argyllshire*
Map **10** NM80
FH Mrs M C Peterson **Traighmhor** *(NM800039)* ☎Barbreck (08525) 228
Apr–Oct
Modern bungalow at loch side with three small croft farms nearby.
3rm (1fb) B&b£8.50 Bdi£15 W£52.50 L (W only Jul & Aug) LDO 3pm
CTV 6P 72acres mixed

ARDGAY
Highland *Sutherland*
Map **14** NH58
GH Croit Mairi Kincardine Hill ☎(08632) 504
Closed 2 wks Nov
Comfortable modern style house in secluded loction with pleasant views.
6rm 5hc (1fb) B&b£7.50 Bdi£12 W£52.50 M
Lic CTV 10P nc4yrs
Credit cards 1 2 3 5 Ⓥ

Ardrossan — Ascot

ARDROSSAN
Strathclyde *Ayrshire*
Map **10** NS24
⊢⊣ **GH Ellwood House** 6 Arran Pl
☎Kilmarnock (0294) 61130
Victorian stone house of good appearance situated on sea front.
9hc (2fb) B&b£7 W£49 M
CTV P
Ⓥ

ARINAGOUR
Coll, Island of Strathclyde *Argyllshire*
Map **13** NM25

Details are listed under COLL (Island of)

ARNSIDE
Cumbria
Map **7** SD47
GH Grosvenor Private Hotel The Promenade ☎(0524) 761666
Mar–Oct
Large stone built house overlooking the Kent estuary and lakeland hills beyond.
15rm 10hc (6fb) Ⓡ B&b£9.50 Bdi£14.50 W£98 L LDO5pm
Lic ⓜ CTV 10P
Ⓥ

See advertisement on page 45

ARRAN, ISLE OF
Strathclyde *Buteshire*
Map **10**
See **Blackwaterfoot, Corrie, Lamlash, Lochranza, Sannox**

ARRETON
Isle of Wight
Map **4** SZ58
GH *Stickworth Hall* ☎(098377) 233
May–Sep
Lovely 18th-century home in extensive grounds with lake for fishing.
25hc 2🚿 14⋒ (6fb) ★ Ⓡ LDO7pm
Lic ⓜ CTV 50P nc5yrs
Ⓥ

ARUNDEL
West Sussex
Map **4** TQ00
⊢⊣ **GH Arden** 4 Queens Ln ☎(0903) 882544
Small house with friendly, homely atmosphere.
8hc (1fb) ★ B&b£8–£10 Bdi£12–£14 W£50–£62 M LDO5pm
ⓜ CTV 6P

GH *Bridge House* 18 Queen St
☎(0903) 882142
Closed Xmas Wk
Well maintained with good homely atmosphere in attractive situation overlooking river and facing the castle.
11hc 2⋒ (5fb) CTV in 2 bedrooms Ⓡ
ⓜ CTV 6P 2🚗 river

INN Swan Hotel High St ☎(0903) 882314
Georgian style inn, overlooking the River Arun.
11rm 8🚿 3⋒ CTV in all bedrooms ★ Ⓡ B&b£12.50–£20 Bdi£17.50–£25 W£75–£120 M L£5&alc D9.30pm£5&alc
ⓜ P 🚗
Credit cards 1 2 3

ASCOT
Berkshire
Map **4** SU96
GH Highclere House Kings Rd, Sunninghill ☎(0990) 25220
Well appointed and decorated property run by friendly young proprietor.
12hc 5⋒ (3fb) CTV in all bedrooms Ⓡ B&b£12–£15 Bdi£17–£22 LDO9pm
Lic ⓜ CTV 14P 2🚗 🏠 🐴

ASCOTT-UNDER-WYCHWOOD
Oxfordshire
Map **4** SP31

INN *Wychwood Arms Hotel* ☎Shipton-under-Wychwood (0993) 830271
Closed Xmas & New Year
Attractive, Costwold stone, village inn offering antique furnished bedrooms.
5⇌ CTV in all bedrooms
40P nc

ASHBURTON
Devon
Map **3** SX77

GH Gages Mill Buckfastleigh Rd ☎(0364) 52391
Closed Xmas
Attractive old mill in quiet situation with large, well kept garden.
7rm 2⋒ (1fb) ® B&b£9–£10.50 Bdi£14.50–£16.50 W£89–£94
Lic CTV 7P nc5yrs

FH Mrs H Young ***Bremridge*** *(SX785701)* ☎(0364) 52426
Clean and brightly decorated farmhouse, parts of which date back to early 16th century.
6rm 5hc 1⇌ (4fb)
CTV 6P 8acres beef

ASHFORD
Kent
Map **5** TR04

GH Croft Hotel Canterbury Rd, Kennington ☎(0233) 22140
Closed Xmas
Comfortable simple accommodation with more modern annexe.
15hc 1⇌ 7⋒ (A 12hc 8⇌ 7⋒) (9fb) CTV in all bedrooms ® B&b£12–£22 LDO8.30pm
Lic CTV 36P
Credit card 3

GH Downsview Willesborough Rd, Kennington ☎(0233) 21953
16rm 10hc 3⋒ (2fb) CTV in 6 bedrooms TV in 9 bedrooms B&b£12.30 Bdi£18.60 W£61.50 LDO8.30pm

Lic CTV 20P
Credit cards 1 3 ⓥ

INN *George* High St ☎(0233) 25512
Small, olde worlde inn with cosy well decorated bedrooms.
14hc 1⇌
CTV 8P 6

ASHURST
Hampshire
Map **4** SU31

GH Barn 112 Lyndhurst Rd ☎(042129) 2531
Apr–Sep
Attractive detached house offering comfortable bedrooms.
6hc B&b£8–£8.50
CTV 8P
ⓥ

See advertisement on page 318

ASHWELL
Hertfordshire
Map **4** TL23

INN Three Tuns Hotel 6 High St ☎(046274) 2387
Country inn with pleasant individually furnished bedrooms.
7rm 4hc 2⋒ (A 5rm 1hc 2⇌ 4⋒) CTV in all bedrooms ® B&b£16–£26 L£1.25–£10 D10pm (10.30pm wknds) £3–£10
18P billiards
Credit cards 1 2 5

ATHERSTONE
Warwickshire
Map **4** SP39

INN Three Tuns Hotel 95 Long St ☎(08277) 3161
14rm 4hc 5⇌ 5⋒ TV in all bedrooms ® B&bfr£12.50 Bdifr£15.50 LDO10.30pm
CTV 20P
Credit cards 1 2 3 5

ATTLEBOROUGH
Norfolk
Map **5** TM09

INN Griffin Hotel Church St ☎(0953) 452149
A friendly inn recently renovated to a high standard offering good fare.
7hc TV in all bedrooms B&b£13 Bar lunch 75p–£2 D8.45pm £4.50&alc
20P

AUCHENCAIRN
Dumfries & Galloway *Kirkcudbrightshire*
Map **11** NX75

FH Mrs D Cannon **Bluehill** *(NX786515)* ☎(055664) 228
Etr–Sep
A comfortable house with nice bedrooms and panoramic views towards Solway Firth.
3hc (1fb) ® B&b£8.50–£9
CTV 6P nc12yrs 120acres dairy

AUSTWICK
North Yorkshire
Map **7** SD76

FH Mrs M Hird **Rawlinshaw** *(SD781673)* ☎Settle (07292) 3214
Etr–Sep
200-year-old farmhouse with attractive views to the front of the house.
2hc (2fb) ® B&b£6.50–£7 W£45–£49
CTV P U 206acres dairy sheep pony trekking

AVETON GIFFORD
Devon
Map **3** SX64

FH Mrs G M Balkwill **Court Barton** *(SX695477)* ☎Loddiswell (054855) 312
Closed Dec
6hc (2fb) *B&b£6–£8 W£42–£56
CTV 10P 350acres arable beef
ⓥ

AVIEMORE
Highland *Inverness-shire*
Map **14** NH81

GH Aviemore Chalets Motel Aviemore Centre ☎(0479) 810618
Chalet style accommodation in blocks of four units.
80⋒ (32fb) CTV in 48 bedrooms ® B&b£10.10–£17.30 Bdi£16–£25 Wfr£108 ⱡ LDO9pm
⋓ CTV 800P ⌧(heated) ♩ squash U billiards sauna bath

GH Corrour House Inverdruie ☎(0479) 810220
Closed Nov
Stone-built house standing in tree-studded grounds ½m E of Aviemore on B970.
11rm 9hc (5fb) ® B&b£12 Bdi£19.50 Wfr£133 ⱡ LDO6.30pm
Lic ⋓ CTV 12P ⌂
Credit card 3

⊢⊣ **GH Craiglea** Grampian Rd ☎(0479) 810210
Detached stone house with garden and childrens play area.
11rm 10hc 1⋒ (4fb) B&b£8–£8.75 W£55–£60 M S%
CTV 12P sauna bath

GH Ravenscraig ☎(0479) 810278
Detached house on main road at north end of Aviemore, with annexe to the side.
5rm 4hc 1⋒ (A 5rm 2⋒) (2fb) B&b£8.50–£9.50 Bdi£13–£14 LDO5pm
⋓ CTV 10P ⌂

AVONWICK
Devon
Map **3** SX75

FH Mrs C Scott **Sopers Horsebrook** *(SX711587)* ☎South Brent (03647) 3235
May–Oct rs Mar & Apr
Old farmhouse situated in quiet valley overlooking brook.
2hc (1fb) ✱ ® ✻B&b£6.50–£8 Bdi£10.50–£12 W£68–£73 ⱡ LDO4pm
CTV 2P ⌒ ♩ 100acres beef sheep mixed
Ⓥ

AXBRIDGE
Somerset
Map **3** ST45

⊢⊣ **FH** Mr L F Dimmock **Manor** *(ST420549)* Cross ☎(0934) 732577
Closed Xmas
1m W of A39
8rm 2hc (3fb) B&bfr£7.75 Bdifr£12.65 W£52.33 M LDO5pm
CTV 10P U 250acres mixed

AXMINSTER
Devon
Map **3** SY39

⊢⊣ **FH** Mrs S Clist **Annings** *(SY299966)* Wyke ☎(0297) 33294
Etr–Sep
Large secluded farmhouse with modern furnishings. Situated in elevated position with fine views. Coast nearby. S of town on unclassified road between A35 and A358.
4rm 3hc (2fb) ✱ B&b£7–£7.50 Bdi£10.50–£11 W£73 ⱡ LDO4.30pm
CTV 4P ♩ 54acres dairy

AYR
Strathclyde *Ayrshire*
Map **10** NS32

GH Clifton Hotel 19 Miller Rd ☎(0292) 264521
Detached sandstone house with rear gardens situated in residential area.
11rm 6hc 5⋒ (2fb) CTV in 5 bedrooms ✱ B&b£10–£12.50 Bdi£16–£19 W£70–£87.50 ⱡ LDO6pm
Lic CTV 16P
Credit cards 2 3

GH Lochinver Hotel 32 Park Circus
☎(0292) 265086
Two-storey Victorian terraced house standing in residential crescent.
8hc (3fb) B&b£8.50–£9 Bdi£11.50–£12 W£59.50–£63 M (W only Jul & Aug) LDOam
Lic CTV 4P

GH *Parkhouse Hotel* 1A Ballantine Dr
☎(0292) 264151
Apr–Sep
Situated in a quiet residential area to the south of the town centre.
8hc (3fb) TV in all bedrooms LDO5pm
Lic CTV
Ⓥ

GH *Windsor Hotel* 6 Alloway Pl
☎(0292) 264689
Victorian stone house on main road near to sea front.
13hc (4fb) LDO4.30pm
CTV

FH Mr & Mrs A Stevenson **Trees** *(NS386186)* ☎Joppa (0292) 570270
Closed Xmas & New Year
White farmhouse offering good quality accommodation at modest prices.
3hc (1fb) B&b£7–£8 Bdi£12–£13 W£80 LDO6pm
CTV 4P 75acres grazing

AYTON GREAT
North Yorkshire
Map **8** NZ51

INN *Royal Oak Hotel* High Green
☎(0642) 722361
5hc 1 LDO9pm
CTV 10P

BABELL
Clwyd
Map **7** SJ17

FH Mrs M L Willams **Bryn Glas** *(SJ155737)* ☎Caerwys (0352) 720493
Comfortable modern farmhouse situated in a quiet, rural area near Mold.
2hc (2fb) TV in bedrooms B&b£7.50 W£50 M
CTV 3P 40acres sheep mixed
Ⓥ

BACUP
Lancashire
Map **7** SD82

GH Burwood House Hotel Todmorden Rd ☎Rochdale (0706) 873466
11rm 6 (2fb) B&b£10.50–£14 Bdi£14–£18 LDO9pm
Lic CTV 12P

BAKEWELL
Derbyshire
Map **8** SK26

GH Merlin House Country Hotel Ashford Ln, Monsal Head ☎Great Longstone (062987) 475
early Mar–early Nov
7rm 5hc 2 (1fb) Ⓡ B&b£9–£15 Bdi£17–£23 W£119–£147 LDO6.30pm
Lic CTV 8P nc5yrs

BALA
Gwynedd
Map **6** SH93

GH Frondderw ☎(0678) 520301
Closed Xmas
Detached Georgian country house set high over Bala ½m from village.
7rm 6hc 1 (3fb) Ⓡ B&b£9.50–£12 Bdi£15–£17.50 W£59.85–£72.50 M LDO6pm
Lic CTV 10P (grass)
Credit cards 2 5 Ⓥ

GH Plas Teg Tegid St ☎(0678) 520268
Semi-detached Victorian house in lane off High Street.
8hc (4fb) Ⓡ B&b£8.25 Bdi£14.20 Wfr£85 LDO6pm
Lic CTV 12P

FH Mrs E Jones **Eirianfa** *(SH967394)* Sarnau (4m N on A494) ☎Llandderfel (06783) 389
Mar–Nov
This modernised farmhouse rests on the edge of the Berwyn Mountains. Free trout fishing is available in the farms private lake.
3hc (1fb) ✱B&b£7 Bdi£10.50 W£65 L LDO8pm
TV 5P 150acres mixed

FH Mr D Davies ***Tytandderwen*** *(SH944345)* ☎(0678) 520273
Apr–Oct
Two-storey manor house-style farmhouse in open country. Stone-built and modernised in parts. Borders on the River Dee.
3rm 2hc (3fb)
40acres mixed

BALDOCK
Hertfordshire
Map **4** TL23

GH Butterfield House Hitchin St ☎(0462) 892701
Once a rectory built in 1874, this guesthouse has been internally reconstructed, offering modernised rooms with all facilities and services.
13 (1fb) CTV in all bedrooms Ⓡ B&b£16.10–£24.15 Bdi£22.60–£30.65 S% LDO8.30pm
Lic 12P
Credit cards 1 2 3 Ⓥ

BALLACHULISH
Highland *Argyllshire*
Map **14** NN05

GH *Lyn-Leven* White St ☎(08552) 392
Closed Xmas
Comfortable and well appointed modern bungalow, situated close to the A82 overlooking Loch Leven.
8hc 2 (3fb) LDO8pm
CTV 12P Loch

BALLATER
Grampian *Aberdeenshire*
Map **15** NO39

GH Glenbardie Braemar Rd ☎(0338) 55537
Apr–Oct
5hc 2 (2fb) B&b£8–£9 W£53–£60 M
CTV 5P
Credit card 2

GH Moorside Braemar Rd (Guestaccom) ☎(0338) 55492
May–Oct
Small tourist hotel offering modern décor and furnishing throughout.
8hc 1 3 (2fb) Ⓡ B&bfr£9 Bdifr£14 Wfr£60 M LDO7pm
Lic CTV 10P

GH Morvada ☎(0338) 55501
Apr–Oct

Granite house built in 1880 standing in own ground, near village centre.
6rm 4hc 2 Ⓡ B&b£9–£10 Bdi£13–£14 LDO6pm
Lic CTV 6P
Ⓥ

GH Netherley 2 Netherley Palace ☎(0338) 55792
Feb–Oct
10hc 1 (1fb) B&bfr£8 Bdi£12.50 W£80 L LDO6pm
CTV nc5yrs

BALMACLELLAN
Dumfries & Galloway *Kirkcudbrightshire*
Map **11** NX67

FH Mrs P Porritt **Craig** *(NX682757)* ☎New Galloway (06442) 228
Isolated but spacious farm mansion. 3m SE of village.
4rm (1fb) B&b£7 Bdi£11 W£49 M
CTV 6P 400acres beef sheep

FH Mrs J Shaw **High Park** *(NX644765)* ☎New Galloway (06442) 298
Apr–Oct
Neat roadside farmhouse with pleasant bedrooms. 2m S on A713.
3hc (1fb) B&b£6–£6.50 Bdi£9–£9.50 W£60 L LDO6.30pm
CTV 3P 124acres dairy

BALMAHA
Central *Stirlingshire*
Map **10** NS49

GH Arrochoile ☎(036087) 231
Apr–Oct
Attractive white painted house, set back from the main road and looking west across Loch Lomond.
6hc (2fb) B&b£7 W£49 M
CTV 12P
Ⓥ

BAMPTON
Devon
Map **3** SS92

GH Bridge House Hotel Luke St ☎(0398) 31298
Character hotel, approximately 250 years old with good local hunting, fishing and walking.
6rm 3hc 2 1 (2fb) B&b£9.20–£10.35 Bdi£13.50–£14.65 W£60–£70 M LDO9pm
Lic CTV
Credit cards 1 3 Ⓥ

GH *Courtyard Hotel* ☎(0398) 31536
6rm 3hc 1 (1fb) Ⓡ LDO9.30pm
Lic CTV 25P

FH Mrs R Cole **Hukeley** *(SS972237)* ☎(0398) 31267
Etr–Oct
16th-century farmhouse, on edge of Exmoor with fine old beams. Rooms are comfortable and well decorated.
2hc (2fb) B&b£7.50 Bdi£10.50 W£70 L LDO4pm
CTV 4P 198acres arable beef sheep mixed

BAMPTON
Oxfordshire
Map **4** SP30

GH Bampton House Bushey Row ☎Bampton Castle (0993) 850135
Closed Xmas
Georgian house with large garden situated in a pleasant Cotswold village.
6rm 1hc 1 3 (1fb) ✱B&b£9.50–£12.50 Bdi£17–£20 W£107–£119 L LDO5pm
Lic CTV 14P
Ⓥ

FH Mrs J Rouse **Morar** *(SP312026)* Weald St (½m SW off A4095) ☎Bampton Castle (0993) 850162
Closed 21–27 Dec
A recently built farmhouse of Cotswold stone with a pleasant garden.
3rm 2hc Ⓡ B&b£9.80 W£64.60 M
CTV 4P nc6yrs 440acres arable beef dairy mixed

BANAVIE
Highland *Inverness-shire*
Map **14** NN17

FH Mrs A C MacDonald **Burnside** *(NN138805)* Muirshearlich ☎Corpach (03977) 275
Apr–Oct
Small, stone-built farmhouse with open views over Caledonian Canal, Loch and north face of Ben Nevis. 3m NE off B8004.
3hc B&b£5.50–£6.50 Bdi£8.50–£9.50 W£63 L LDO4.30pm
CTV 3P 60acres mixed

BANBURY
Oxfordshire
Map **4** SP44

GH Lismore Hotel & Restaurant 61 Oxford Rd (Guestaccom) ☎(0295) 62105
Homely hotel offering comfortable bedrooms and more than most in the way of well priced food.
14rm 6hc 7 1 (3fb) CTV in all bedrooms Ⓡ ✱B&b£12–£23 Bdi£15.50–£30.25 W£100–£161 M LDO9pm
Lic CTV 6P 1
Credit cards 1 3 Ⓥ

GH Tredis 15 Broughton Rd ☎(0295) 4632
Small family hotel with friendly informal atmosphere.

6hc (1fb) CTV in all bedrooms Ⓡ B&b£8–£11 Bdi£11.50–£14.50 LDOnoon
𝍖 CTV

BANFF
Grampian *Banffshire*
Map **15** NJ66
GH Carmelite House Hotel Low St ☎(02612) 2152
Town house set back from shopping street in lower part of town.
8hc (2fb) B&b£8.95–£10.50 Bdi£12.90–£15.25 W£56–£66 M LDO8.15pm
Lic CTV 8P
Ⓥ

GH Ellerslie 45 Low St ☎(02612) 5888
A terraced building in the lower shopping street, with accommodation of first floor and above.
6hc (1fb) ★ Ⓡ B&b£9 Bdi£12 W£63 M LDO5pm
Lic CTV
Credit card 2

BANTHAM
Devon
Map **3** SX64
INN Sloop ☎Kingsbridge (0548) 560489
5rm 1hc 4 TV in 3 bedrooms Ⓡ

Banbury — Barnstaple

B&b£10.50–£12 Bdi£15–£17 W£108–£120 L £4.50–£6&alc D10pm £4.50–£6&alc
𝍖 30P

BARHAM
Kent
Map **5** TR25
INN Old Coach House A2 Trunk Rd ☎Canterbury (0227) 831218
9hc CTV in all bedrooms B&b£12.50–£14 Bdi£16.50 Wfr£75 M Lfr£4.50&alc D10pm fr£5
𝍖 60P
Credit cards 1 2 3 4 5

BARKESTONE-LE-VALE
Leicestershire
Map **8** SK73
FH Mrs S H Smart **The Paddocks** *(SK781351)* ☎Bottesford (0949) 42208
Closed Xmas
North of village off 'The Green'.
2hc (A 2hc) (2fb) TV in all bedrooms ★ B&b£8.50 Bdi£13.50 W£55 M LDO4pm
𝍖 CTV 8P (heated) U 150acres arable sheep
Ⓥ

BARMOUTH
Gwynedd
Map **6** SH61
GH *Cranbourne* 9 Marine Pde ☎(0341) 280202
Feb–Nov
10hc 5 (5fb) CTV in all bedrooms ★ Ⓡ LDO4.30pm
Lic 𝍖 CTV 4P sea

GH Lawrenny Lodge ☎(0341) 280466
Apr–Oct
Detached Edwardian house on outskirts of town ¼m from shops and beach.
10hc (3fb) B&b£9.20 Bdi£13.22 W£92 L LDO5.30pm
Lic CTV 15P

GH *Morwendon* Llanaber ☎(0341) 280566
Apr–Sep
Detached Victorian house overlooking Cardigan Bay, located 1m N A496.
6hc (3fb) ★ LDO5.30pm
Lic CTV 10P nc5yrs sea

BARNSTAPLE
Devon
Map **2** SS53
GH Cresta 26 Sticklepath Hill ☎(0271) 74022
Closed Xmas
Semi-detached house on main Barnstaple to Bideford road. →

5rm 4hc 1⋔ (A 1⋔) (1fb) CTV in all bedrooms ★ ® B&b£9–£11 W£49–£63 M̸

Ⅲ CTV 6P

Ⓥ

GH *Northcliffe* Hele Manor 8 Rhododendron Av (off A39) ☎(0271) 42524
Closed Xmas
Chalet style house build during the 1940's in quiet backwater of Barnstaple.
8hc (1fb)
Lic Ⅲ CTV 12P

GH Yeo Dale Hotel Pilton Bridge ☎(0271) 42954
Blue and white fronted terraced house in Pilton overlooking the river.
12hc (4fb) ★ B&b£9–£9.50 Bdi£12–£14 W£90–£98 Ⱡ LDO5pm
Lic Ⅲ CTV 3P

⊢⊣ **FH** Mrs G Hannington **Fair Oak** *(SS530348)* Ashford ☎(0271) 73698
Apr–Oct
Modern farmhouse arranged as mini-farm specially catering for children, with pets corner and aviaries with mixed birds. Overlooks Taw Estuary.
4hc (3fb) ★ B&b£6–£7.50 Bdi£10–£12 W£60–£72 Ⱡ LDO3pm
Ⅲ CTV 6P 89acres beef sheep mixed

⊢⊣ **FH** Mrs M Lethaby **Home** *(SS555360)* Lower Blakewell, Muddiford ☎(0271) 42955
Mar–Oct
Farmhouse situated in peaceful North Devon countryside. Pony, many pets and Wendy House available for children.
4hc (3fb) ® B&b£7–£9 Bdi£9–£11 W49 M̸ LDO6pm
CTV 4P 70acres beef dairy sheep mixed
Ⓥ

BARRASFORD
Northumberland
Map **12** NY97

INN *Barrasford Arms* ☎Humshaugh (043481) 237
Closed Xmas
5hc ® D8.30pm
Ⅲ CTV 45P 2🚗

BARROW-IN-FURNESS
Cumbria
Map **7** SD16

GH Barrie House Hotel 179 Abbey Rd ☎(0229) 25507
A well-furnished, semi-detached house privately owned. Located on A590.
10hc 3⋔ (1fb) ★ ® ✱B&b£17.50 Bdi£25 W£115 Ⱡ LDO9pm
Temperance Ⅲ CTV P̸

GH Lisdoonie Private Hotel Abbey Rd ☎(0229) 27312
rs Sun & Bank Hols
Large family run house with very well furnished bedrooms.
12rm 7→ 5⋔ (1fb) CTV in 5 bedrooms TV in 7 bedrooms ® ✱B&b£22.50 Bdi£30 LDO7.30pm
Lic Ⅲ CTV 33P

BARRY
South Glamorgan
Map **3** ST16

GH Aberthaw House Hotel Porthkerry Rd ☎(0446) 737314
Closed 24 Dec–3 Jan
9rm (2fb) CTV in all bedrooms ® B&b£15.50–£16.50 Bdi£20–£22.50 W£100–£110 M̸ LDO9.30pm
Lic Ⅲ

GH Maytree 9 The Parade ☎(0446) 734075
Closed Xmas
Victorian seafront house with lounge for residents at the front.
15rm 13hc 2⋔ (2fb) B&b£10.35–£11.50 Bdi£13.85–£15 W£46.50–£50 M̸ (W Jul & Aug) LDO7pm
Lic Ⅲ CTV 4P

GH *Sheridan* 11 The Parade ☎(0446) 738488
An attractive guesthouse overlooking the seafront with comfortable bedrooms and warm welcome.
5hc (5fb) TV in 1 bedroom ★ ®
Ⅲ CTV sea

BARTON-ON-SEA
Hampshire
Map **4** SZ29

GH Cliff House Hotel Marine Drive West ☎New Milton (0425) 619333
10 Feb–3 Nov
Clifftop hotel with panoramic views, offering nicely appointed bedrooms, spacious sunlounge and family run restaurant.
10hc (1fb) B&b£13–£14 Bdi£18.50–£20 W£112–£120 Ⱡ LDO7pm
Lic Ⅲ CTV 20P
Credit cards 1 2 3 5

GH Dome Hotel Barton Court Av ☎New Milton (0425) 616164
15hc 7→ 4⋔ (2fb) ® B&bfr£14.95 Bdifr£19.55 Wfr£120 Ⱡ
Lic lift Ⅲ CTV 18P

GH Gainsborough Hotel 39 Marine Drive East ☎New Milton (0425) 610541
9rm 6hc 3→ (1fb) CTV in 3 bedrooms ® ✱B&b£12.50–£14 Bdi£17.60–£19.10 W£85 M̸ LDO6.30pm
Lic Ⅲ CTV 12P 2🚗 nc8yrs
Ⓥ

GH Old Coastguard Hotel 53 Marine Drive East ☎New Milton (0425) 612987
8rm 7hc 1⋔ ✱B&b£11.50–£12.50 Bdi£16.50–£17.50 W£105–£110 Ⱡ LDO5pm
Lic Ⅲ CTV 10P nc12yrs
Ⓥ

BASINGSTOKE
Hampshire
see **Sherfield-on-Loddon**

BASSENTHWAITE
Cumbria
Map **11** NY23

GH *Link House Hotel* ☎Bassenthwaite Lake (059681) 291
Etr–Oct

Home Farm

**Lower Blakewell, Muddiford,
Nr. Barnstaple, N. Devon.
Tel: Barnstaple (0271) 42955**

Mixed farm. Ideal for children, Wendy House, swings, pony, pets. Tea trays and wash basin in all rooms. Colour TV. High chair, cot and baby-sitting included. Farm situated approx 2 miles from Barnstaple and 7 miles from Ilfracombe. Also available cottage and caravan with or without meals provided.
SAE for brochure.
Proprietor Mrs M Lethaby.

A Victorian house comfortably converted to offer well appointed bedrooms and cosy lounges.

7hc 6⋒ (1fb) TV in 6 bedrooms ✱ Ⓡ LDO7.30pm

Lic ▥ 7P lake

Ⓥ

GH *Ravenstone Hotel*
☏Bassenthwaite Lake (059681) 240
Apr–Oct

Country house style with very comfortable lounges and attractive dining room.

12hc (9fb) Ⓡ LDO6.30pm

Lic ▥ CTV 14P lake

Ⓥ

Bassenthwaite — Bath

⊢⊣ **FH** Mrs P Trafford **Bassenthwaite Hall (East)** *(NY231322)*
☏Bassenthwaite Lake (059681) 393
Closed Xmas

Fully modernised 17th-century farmhouse in picturesque village close to quiet stream.

2hc (2fb) B&b£6–£8

▥ CTV 3P ⌂ 200acres mixed

Ⓥ

FH Mrs D Mattinson ***Bassenthwaite Hall (West)*** *(NY228323)* ☏Bassenthwaite Lake (059681) 279
Apr–Nov

On west side of village not to be confused with the Bassenthwaite Hall Farm on east side.

3hc (1fb) ✱ LDO4pm

CTV 4P 135acres mixed

BATH
Avon
Map **3** ST76
See plan on page 56

GH Arden Hotel 73 Great Pulteney St ☏(0225) 66601 Plan **2** *E4* →

Jan–15Dec
12rm 8hc 1⇌ 3ᐱ (3fb) ★ ® B&b£15–£17
Lic ||| CTV

GH Ashley Villa Hotel 26 Newbridge Rd
☎(0225) 21683 Plan **3** *A3*
Closed 2wks Xmas
15rm 6hc 3⇌ 6ᐱ (2fb) CTV in all bedrooms B&bfr£13 Bdifr£18 Wfr£91 M
LDO9pm
Lic ||| CTV 10P ♿ ≈ (heated)
Credit cards 1 3

GH Carfax Hotel Great Pulteney St
☎(0225) 62089 Plan **5** *D4*
rs Xmas

Bath

35rm 14hc 13⇌ 8ᐱ (4fb) CTV in all bedrooms ★ ® B&b£12.10–£21.65
Bdi£17.35–£27.15 W£114.45–£178.50 L
LDO8pm
Temperance lift ||| CTV 13P 4🚗
Credit cards 1 2 3 V

⊢⊣ **GH Dorset Villa** 14 Newbridge Rd
☎(0225) 25975 Plan **7** *A3*
Etr–Oct
6hc ★ B&b£7.50
||| CTV 6P nc12yrs
Credit card 3

GH Edgar Hotel 64 Great Pulteney St
☎(0225) 20619 Plan **8** *E4*
11rm 7hc 4ᐱ (2fb) ★ B&b£12–£17
W£84–£139 M
Lic ||| CTV 🚫
V

See advertisement on page 53

GH Gainsborough Hotel Weston Ln
☎(0225) 311380 Plan **9** *A3*
Closed Xmas & 1st 2wks Jan

15rm 12→ 3⋒ (2fb) CTV in all bedrooms ✱ Ⓡ B&b£18–£20

Lic 🍽 18P

Credit cards 1 2 3

GH Glenbeigh Hotel 1 Upper Oldfield Park ☎(0225) 26336 Plan **10** *B1*
Closed Jan

12hc 3⋒ (4fb) CTV in 3 bedrooms Ⓡ B&b£9.50–£12 W£60–£76 M

Lic 🍽 CTV 7P 3🚗

GH Grove Lodge 11 Lambridge, London Road ☎(0225) 310860
Plan **11** *C4*
Closed Oct

8hc (2fb) CTV in 7 bedrooms TV in 1 bedroom B&b£9 W£58 M

Lic 🚫

GH Highways House 143 Wells Rd ☎(0225) 21238 Plan **12** *B1*
Closed Dec

5hc 2⋒ Ⓡ B&bfr£10

🍽 CTV 6P

Ⓥ

GH Kennard Hotel 11 Henrietta St ☎(0225) 310472 Plan **13** *D4*
Closed Xmas

12rm 5hc 6⋒ (3fb) CTV in all bedrooms Ⓡ B&b£12–£15

🍽 TV nc2yrs

Bath

GH Leighton House 139 Wells Rd ☎(0225) 314769 Plan **14** *B1*
Closed Dec

A comfortable, enthusiastically run hotel with good degree of hospitality.

7rm 1hc 2→ 2⋒ (2fb) CTV in 4 bedrooms TV in 3 bedrooms Ⓡ B&b£9.50–£13 W£65–£85 M

🍽 CTV 7P 2🚗 nc5yrs

GH Lynwood 6 Pulteney Gdns ☎(0225) 26410 Plan **15** *E2*
Mar–Dec

14rm (3fb) CTV in 12 bedrooms TV in 2 bedrooms Ⓡ B&b£13–£14

🍽 CTV 2P nc3yrs

Credit cards 1 2 3 5

GH Millers Hotel 69 Great Pulteney St ☎(0225) 65798 Plan **16** *E4*
Closed Xmas

12hc 2→ (3fb) ✱ B&b£13–£14 LDO5pm

Lic 🍽 CTV 3P

GH Oldfields 102 Wells Rd ☎(0225) 317984 Plan **17** *A1*
mid Jan–mid Dec

14rm 6hc 1→ 7⋒ (2fb) TV in all bedrooms ✱ Ⓡ B&b£9–£15

🍽 P sauna bath

Credit cards 1 3

GH *Oxford Private Hotel* 5 Oxford Row, Lansdown Rd ☎(0225) 314039
Plan **18** *C4*

8hc 1⋒ (2fb) ✱

CTV 🚫

GH Paradise House Hotel Holloway (Guestaccom) ☎(0225) 317723
Plan **19** *B1*
mid Jan–mid Dec

An elegant, comfortably appointed hotel in cul-de-sac overlooking the city. Splendid walled garden.

9rm 5hc 2→ 2⋒ (1fb) CTV in all bedrooms ✱ Ⓡ B&b£12–£16 W£76–£100 M

🍽 2P 3🚗

Credit cards 1 3

GH Hotel St Clair 1 Crescent Gdns, Upper Bristol Rd ☎(0225) 25543
Plan **20** *A4*

10rm 8hc 2⋒ (1fb) CTV in 1 bedroom TV in 9 bedrooms Ⓡ B&b£12–£20 Bdi£17–£25 LDO7.30pm

Lic 🍽 🚫 nc2yrs

↦ **GH Tacoma** 159 Newbridge Hill ☎(0225) 310197 Plan **22** *A3*

8hc (3fb) 🚭 Ⓡ B&b£8–£9

▥ CTV 5P

See advertisement on page 55

GH Villa Magdala Private Hotel Henrietta Rd ☎(0225) 66329
Plan **23** *D4*
Closed Jan

17rm 9🛁 8🚿 (3fb) CTV in all bedrooms 🚭 Ⓡ B&b£15–£17

▥ 15P nc5yrs

GH Waltons 17 Crescent Gdns ☎(0225) 26528 Plan **24** *B3*

17rm 16hc 1🚿 (4fb) B&b£18–£20 Bdi£23–£25 W£120–£135 M LDOnoon

Lic ▥ CTV

GH Wentworth House Hotel
106 Bloomfield Rd ☎(0225) 310460
Plan **25** *B1*

20rm 10hc 10🛁 (3fb) TV in all bedrooms Ⓡ B&b£13–£15 Bdi£19.50–£21.50 W£103.95–£135.45 M LDO5pm

Lic ▥ CTV 16P ≋

Credit cards 1 3 5 Ⓥ

See advertisement on page 58

INN *County Hotel* 18–19 Pulteney Rd ☎(0225) 66493 Plan **6** *E4*

24hc 1🛁 6🚿 (2fb) CTV in 5 bedrooms

▥ CTV 60P

BATLEY

West Yorkshire
Map **8** SE22

GH Alder House Hotel Towngate Rd, Healey Ln ☎(0924) 475540

Handsome Georgian country house standing in 2½ acres of attractive gardens and grounds.

13rm 4🛁 7🚿 CTV in all bedrooms 🚭 B&b£18–£24 Bdi£26–£32 W£120–£170 M

Lic ▥ CTV 23P 5🚗

Credit cards 1 3

See advertisement on page 58

BATTLE

East Sussex
Map **5** TQ71

FH Miss A Benton **Little Hemingford** *(TQ774149)* Telham (2½m SE on N side of A210) ☎(04246) 2910

Picturesque, part 17th-century farmhouse in 26 acres with lovely sheltered garden. Has peaceful, well equipped bedrooms.

5🛁 (A 5🛁) (1fb) CTV in all bedrooms Ⓡ Bdi£20–£24 W£130–£153 L

Lic ▥ CTV 20P nc12yrs 🎾(grass) 🐟

26acres dairy sheep mixed

See advertisment on page 58

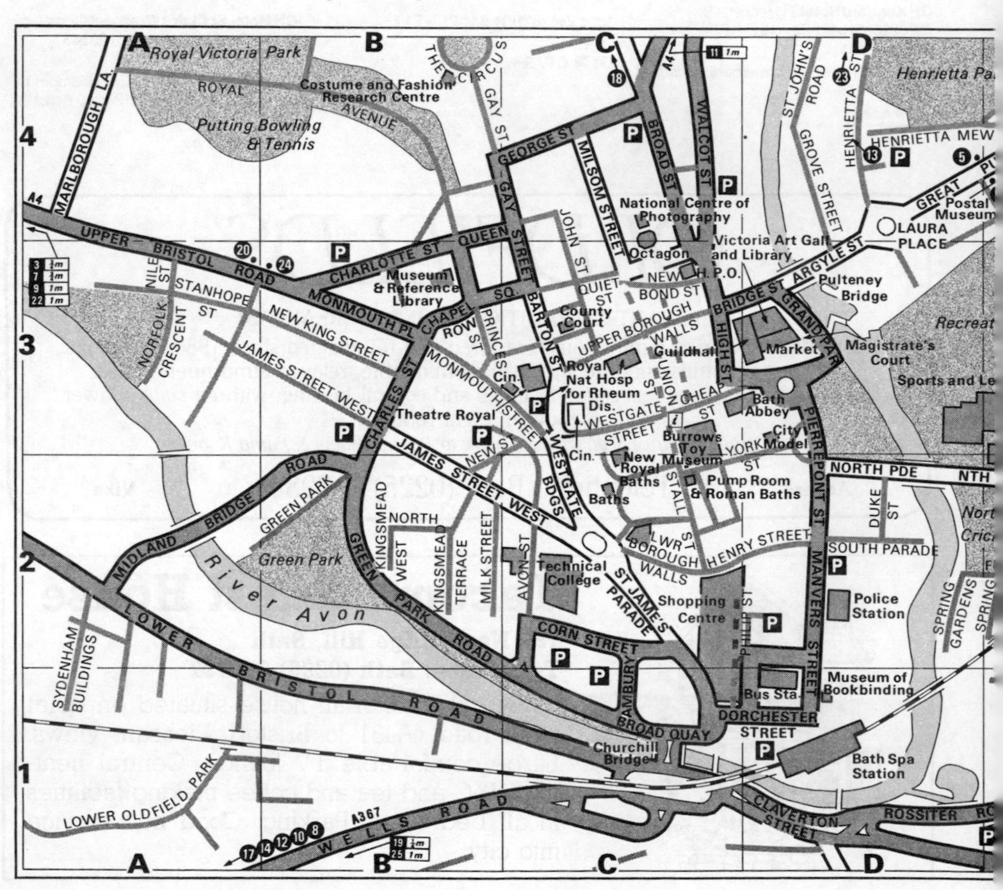

BEAMINSTER
Dorset
Map **3** ST40

GH Hams Plot Bridport Rd ☎(0308) 862979
Apr–Sep & Xmas

6rm 3hc 3⇌ ✱ Ⓡ B&b£11–£14 Bdi£19–£22 W£69.30–£88.20 M̸

Lic 𝍖 CTV 6P nc7yrs ⛆ 𝒫(hard)

BEAULY
Highland *Inverness-shire*
Map **14** NH54

⊢⊣ **GH Chrialdon** Station Rd ☎(0463) 782336
Apr–Oct

Detached house in own grounds on main road.

11hc (4fb) B&b£8–£9 Bdi£13–£14 W£90–£98 M̸ LDO7.45pm

Lic 𝍖 CTV 14P

⊢⊣ **GH Heathmount** Station Rd ☎(0463) 782411
Closed Xmas & New Year

Comfortable well appointed accommodation situated on a main road, close to shops.

5hc (2fb) B&b£7.50 Bdi£12.50 W£84 L̸ (W only Jun–Sep) LDO7pm

Lic 𝍖 CTV 5P

BEAUMARIS
Gwynedd
Map **6** SH67

⊢⊣ **GH Sea View** 10 West End ☎(0248) 810384
Closed Xmas

Single fronted Victorian house at water's edge adjacent to the shops.

6hc ✱ B&b£8 Bdi£13

TV 5P nc10yrs

Ⓥ

BECCLES
Suffolk
Map **5** TM49

⊢⊣ **GH Riverview House** Ballygate ☎(0502) 713519

11hc (4fb) CTV in 8 bedrooms TV in 1 bedroom ✱ Ⓡ B&b£7.80–£11.50 Bdi£11.80–£15.50 W£54.60–£62 LDO4pm

𝍖 CTV ⌂

BECKERMET
Cumbria
Map **11** NY00

INN Royal Oak Hotel ☎(094684) 551

8⇌ CTV in all bedrooms Ⓡ B&b£17–£19 L£1–£4&alc D10pm £6&alc

𝍖 26P

BEDDGELERT
Gwynedd
Map **6** SH54

GH Sygyn Fawr Country House Hotel ☎(076686) 258 →

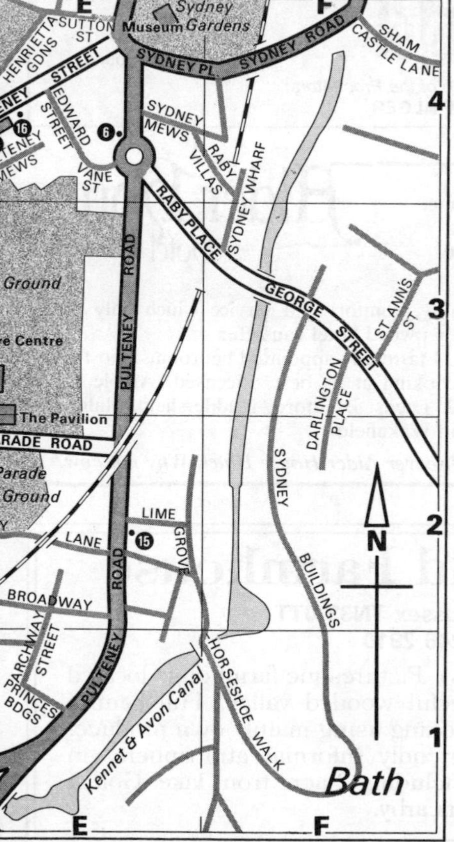

Bath

2 Arden Hotel
3 Ashley Villa Hotel
5 Carfax Hotel
6 County Hotel (*Inn*)
7 Dorset Villa
8 Edgar Hotel
9 Gainsborough Hotel
10 Glenbeigh Hotel
11 Grove Lodge
12 Highways House
13 Kennard
14 Leighton House
15 Lynwood
16 Millers Hotel
17 Oldfields
18 Oxford Private Hotel
19 Paradise House Hotel
20 Hotel St Clair
22 Tacoma
23 Villa Magdala Private Hotel
24 Waltons
25 Wentworth House

18th-century stone country house in own grounds 1m from village.

7rm 2⇌ 4⋒ (1fb) ® B&b£12.50–£14.50 Bdi£19–£21 W£120–£135 𝑘 LDO7.30pm

Lic CTV 30P

BEDFORD
Bedfordshire
Map **4** TL04

GH Clarendon House Hotel 25/27 Ampthill Rd ☏(0234) 66054

Comfortable Edwardian house run by young professional couple.

12rm 4hc CTV in all bedrooms ✱ ® B&b£13–£19.50 Bdi£18.75–£25.25 LDO8pm

Lic ▥ CTV 16P

Credit cards [1] [2] [3] Ⓥ

GH Hurst House Hotel 178 Hurst Gv ☏(0234) 40791

6hc (2fb) CTV in all bedrooms ® B&b£12 Bdi£15.50 W£75.60 M LDO7.30pm

Lic ▥ CTV 5P

Credit cards [1] [2] [3] [5] Ⓥ

GH Kimbolton Hotel 78 Clapham Rd ☏(0234) 54854
Closed wk after Xmas

Three storey Victorian house run by four friendly partners.

16rm 4hc 12⋒ CTV in 15 bedrooms ✱ ® ✻B&b£15–£20 Bdi£22–£27 W£98–£133 M LDO7.15pm

Lic ▥ CTV 18P

BEER
Devon
Map **3** SY28

⊢⊣ **GH Bay View** Fore St ☏Seaton (0297) 20489
Etr–Oct

Property at end of village overlooking the beach and sea.

6hc (2fb) B&b£7.50–£9.50 W52–£56 M

CTV nc5yrs

Ⓥ

BEESTON
Nottinghamshire
Map **8** SK53

GH Brackley House Hotel 31 Elm Av ☏Nottingham (0602) 251787

13hc 2 1 (1fb) CTV in 1 bedroom TV in 12 bedrooms B&bfr£17.50 Bdifr£25.45 W£100–£120 M LDO9.15pm

Lic CTV 20P billiards

Credit cards 1 2 3 Ⓥ

BELFORD
Northumberland
Map **12** NU13

INN Black Swan Market Sq ☏(06683) 266

Simple village inn with informal atmosphere. Situated in village centre on A1.

7hc 1 Ⓡ B&b£10.50 Bdi£16 Bar lunch 50p–£2.50 D8.30pm £5.50

CTV 20P 2

BELL BUSK
North Yorkshire
Map **7** SD95

⊢⊣ **GH Tudor** ☏Airton (07293) 301

This friendly hospitable little guesthouse by the Settle–Carlisle line was once Bell Busk station.

5hc (2fb) Ⓡ B&b£7.50–£8.50 Bdi£12 W£52.50 M LDO4pm

Lic CTV 8P nc5yrs billiards

Ⓥ

BELSTONE
Devon
Map **2** SX69

INN Tors ☏Sticklepath (083784) 689

3hc CTV in 2 bedrooms Ⓡ *B&b£9–£10 Bdi£13–£15 W£75–£85 Bar lunch £1.25–£2.50 D£4–£4.75&alc

CTV P

BEPTON (Near Midhurst)
West Sussex
Map **4** SU81

GH Park House Hotel ☏Midhurst (073081) 2880

Part 17th-century house with homely welcome and accommodation. Set in attractive lawns for croquet, putting and tennis.

11rm 7 2 (A 2rm) CTV in all bedrooms Ⓡ B&b£20.27–£25.50 Bdi£31.62–£34.50 W£241.50 LDO8.30pm

Lic CTV 15P 2 (heated) (grass)

BERRYNARBOR
Devon
Map **2** SS54

GH *Lodge Country House* ☏Combe Martin (027188) 3246
Closed Xmas

6hc (A 1hc) (3fb) LDO6pm

Lic CTV 7P nc4yrs

See advertisement on page 119

BETHESDA
Gwynedd
Map **6** SH66

⊢⊣ **FH** Mrs D Williams **Maes Caradog** *(SH635626)* Nant Ffrancon ☏(0248) 600266

2hc (1fb) B&b£6–£7 Bdi£10–£11 Wfr£45 LDO6pm

CTV 10P 670acres sheep

BETWS GARMON
Gwynedd
Map **6** SH55

⊢×⊣ **GH Bryn Gloch Farm** ☎ Waunfawr (028685) 216
Converted farmhouse with glorious views, on edge of Snowdonia National Park.
3hc (1fb) B&b£7.50–£8 Bdi£12.50–£13 W£52.50–£56 M̸ LDO7pm
Lic CTV 8P 🎣

BETWS-Y-COED
Gwynedd
Map **6** SH75

⊢×⊣ **GH Bryn Llewelyn** Holyhead Rd ☎(06902) 601
Three-storey building near the village centre.
5hc (2fb) ✱ B&b£6.50–£7.50
▥ CTV 6P nc7yrs
Ⓥ

GH Glenwood ☎(06902) 508
Feb–Nov
Pre-war detached house set back from the A5 on edge of village.
6hc ✱ B&b£10–£11
▥ CTV 12P nc6yrs

GH Hafan ☎(06902) 233
Detached Victorian house in rural surroundings, near centre of village.
7rm 1🛁 4🚿 (4fb) CTV in 4 bedrooms TV in 3 bedrooms Ⓡ B&b£8.50–£11.50
Lic ▥ CTV 10P nc3yrs

GH *Henllys (Old Court) Hotel*
☎(06902) 534
Converted police station and cells, adjacent to village centre.
11hc 2🛁 6🚿 (2fb) CTV in 8 bedrooms TV in 2 bedrooms LDO9pm
Lic 12P river
Ⓥ

GH Mount Garmon Hotel ☎(06902) 335
Closed Dec
Victorian semi detached house alongside the A5 in the centre of village.
5rm 2hc 3🚿 ✱ B&b£9–£12.50 Bdi£15–£18.50 W£100–£125 L̸ LDO6pm

Lic ▥ CTV 5P nc5yrs
Ⓥ

BEXHILL-ON-SEA
East Sussex
Map **5** TQ70

GH Dunselma Private Hotel 23 Marina ☎(0424) 212988
Etr–12 Oct
A warm friendly atmosphere in a well appointed guesthouse.
11hc 2🛁 (2fb) TV in 2 bedrooms B&b£10.93–£13.80 Bdi£16.10–£18.40 W£87.40–£103.50 L̸ LDO7.30pm
Lic ▥ CTV nc5yrs
Ⓥ

GH *Moorings Hotel* Hastings Rd ☎(0424) 213668
Charming Edwardian style house within its own grounds offering comfortable rooms and a peaceful atmosphere.
7hc (3fb) CTV in 1 bedroom Ⓡ LDO6.30pm
Lic ▥ CTV 6P

BICKINGTON (*Near Ashburton*)
Devon
Map **3** SX77

GH Privet Cottage ☎(062682) 319
May–Sep
Attractive, white stone, cottage style house in central position for touring south Devon.
5hc
CTV 4P

BICKLEIGH (*Near Tiverton*)
Devon
Map **3** SS90

GH Bickleigh Cottage ☎(08845) 230
May–Sep rs Apr & Oct
10rm 8hc 2🛁 (2fb) ✱ B&b£10.50–£12.50 Bdi£16–£18 W£73.50–£87.50 M̸ LDO5pm
CTV 10P nc5yrs 🎣
Ⓥ

BIDEFORD
Devon
Map **2** SS42

⊢×⊣ **GH Edelweiss** 2 Buttgarden St ☎(02372) 2676
Jan–Nov & 4 days Xmas
Proprietor-run guesthouse with à la carte restaurant.
8rm 6hc (2fb) B&b£7–£9.50 Bdi£13–£15.50 W£42–£59.50 M̸ LDO9pm
Lic ▥ CTV ⚑ nc5yrs
Credit cards 1 2 3 5

⊢×⊣ **GH Kumba** Chudleigh Rd, East-the-Water ☎(02372) 2133
7hc (4fb) B&b£7–£8 Bdi£11–£12 W£70–£79 L̸ LDO4pm
Lic CTV 10P
Ⓥ

GH *Mount Private Hotel* Northdown Rd ☎(02372) 3748
Detached Georgian house standing in attractive walled garden with terrace at front.
6hc 2🚿 (2fb) TV in 2 bedrooms
Lic ▥ CTV 4P 1⌂

GH *Sonnenheim Private Hotel*
Heywood Rd, Northam ☎(02372) 4989
Large detached Victorian house, 1m from Bideford.
10hc 1🚿 (3fb) LDO7pm
Lic ▥ CTV 10P

GH *Tadworthy House Hotel* Tadworthy Rd, Northam (2m N off A386) ☎(02372) 4721
6hc 1🚿 (2fb) CTV in 4 bedrooms TV in 2 bedrooms Ⓡ LDO8.30pm
Lic CTV 10P ⌂ sea

BIGBURY-ON-SEA
Devon
Map **3** SX64

GH *Easton House Private Hotel*
☎(054881) 296

17hc 9→ 2⋒ (11fb) TV available in bedrooms
Lic 🔥 CTV 20P ⌂

BINGLEY
West Yorkshire
Map **7** SE13

GH Hall Bank Private Hotel Beck Ln
☎Bradford (0274) 565296
Closed Xmas

Large, well-furnished house overlooking Aire Valley. Family run

8rm 6hc 2→ 1⋒ (A 2rm) (1fb) ★
B&b£10.06–£12.65 Bdi£15.52–£17.82
LDO10am

🔥 CTV 20P nc2yrs

BIRMINGHAM
West Midlands
Map **7** SP08
See plan on pages 62–63

GH Alexander 44 Bunbury Rd
☎021-475 4341 Plan **1**
rs Xmas

12hc (2fb) ® B&b£11.50 Bdi£17.50
Wfr£70 ⱡ LDO6.30pm

Lic 🔥 CTV 12P

GH *Bridge House Hotel* 49 Sherbourne Rd, Acocks Gn ☎021-706 5900 Plan **2**

18rm 12hc 6→ 6⋒ (1fb) CTV in 2 bedrooms TV in 6 bedrooms ®
LDO9.30pm

Lic 🔥 CTV P

GH *Cape Race Hotel* 929 Chester Rd, Erdington ☎021-373 3085 Plan **3**

Spacious converted private house with large rear garden containing lawns and hard tennis court.

6hc 2⋒ (1fb) CTV in all bedrooms ★ ®
LDO8.30pm

Lic 🔥 CTV 16P

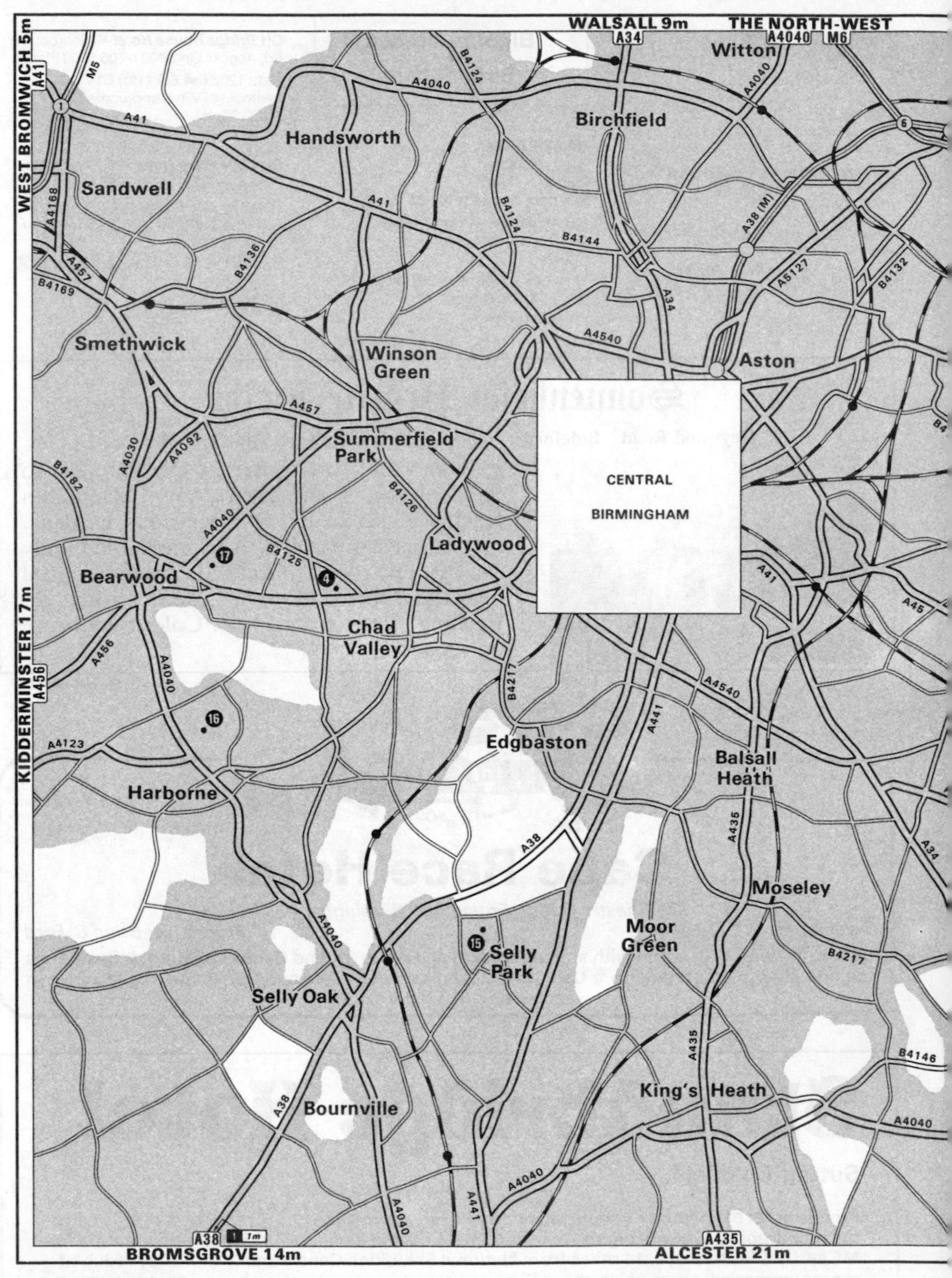

Birmingham & District

1	Alexander	4	Hagley Court Hotel	7	Kerry House Hotel
2	Bridge House Hotel	5	Heath Lodge Hotel	8	Linden Lodge Hotel
3	Cape Race Hotel	6	Hurstwood Hotel	10	Lyndhurst Hotel

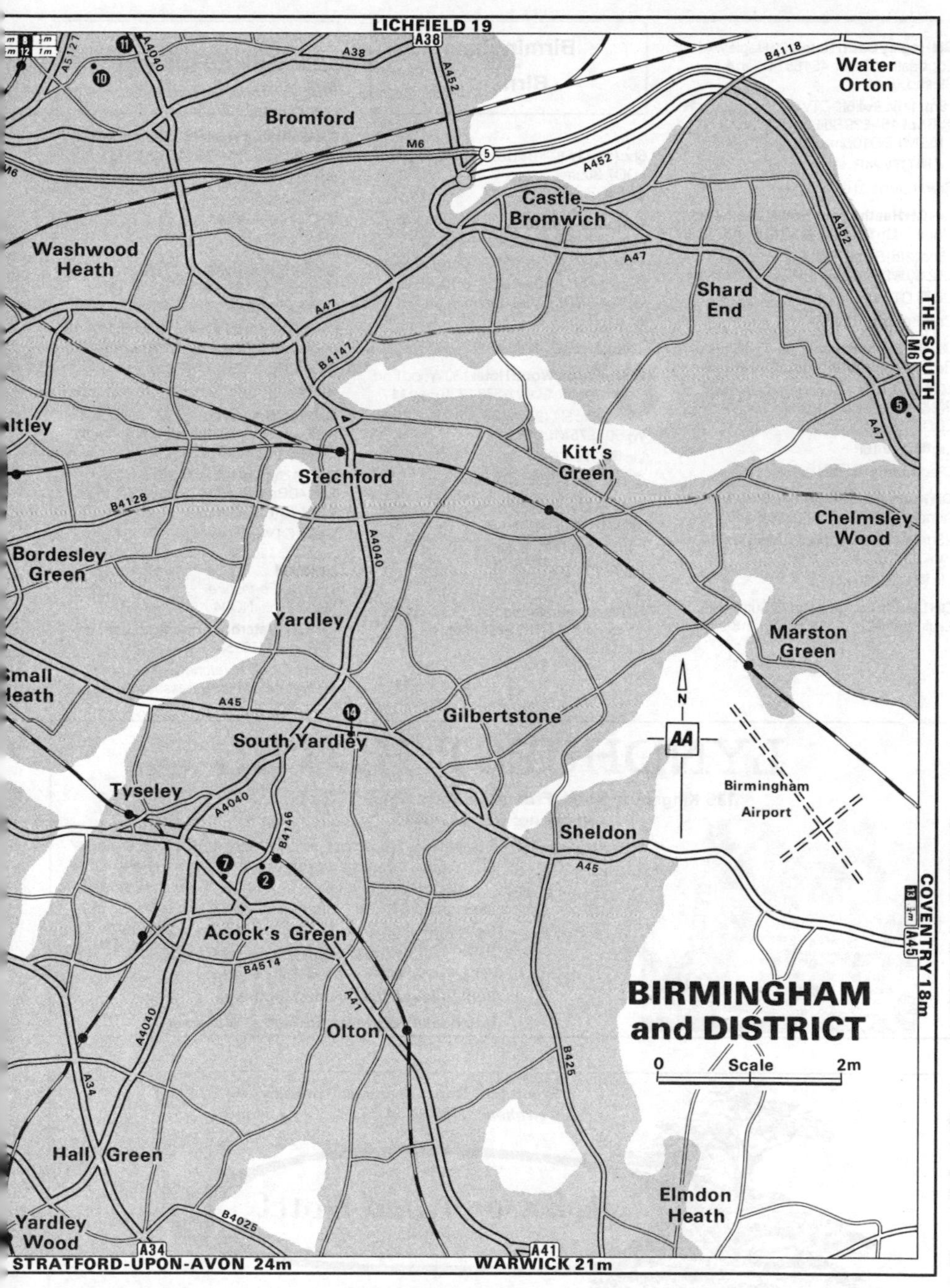

11 Rollason Wood Hotel
12 Standbridge Hotel (*Listed under Sutton Coldfield*)
13 Tri-Star Hotel
14 Welcome House
15 Wentsbury Hotel
16 Wentworth Hotel
17 Westbourne Lodge

GH Hagley Court Hotel 229 Hagley Rd, Edgbaston ☎021-454 6514 Plan **4**
Closed Xmas
25rm 11hc 8→ 6⋒ CTV in all bedrooms ✱ ®B&b£15–£29 Bdi£21–£35 W£117–£185 M LDO10pm
Lic ▥ CTV 24P
Credit cards 1 3

⊢⊣ **GH Heath Lodge Hotel** Coleshill Rd, Marston Gn ☎021-779 2218 Plan **5**
15hc (2fb) B&b£7.50–£10 Bdi£10–£12.50 W£52.50–£70 M S% LDO9.30pm
Lic ▥ CTV 15P
Credit cards 1 3 Ⓥ

GH Hurstwood Hotel 775–777 Chester Rd, Erdington ☎021-382 8212 Plan **6**
10⋒ (2fb) CTV in all bedrooms ✱ ® *B&b£18.98 Bdi£26.50 W£100 M LDO9pm
Lic ▥ CTV 16P
Credit cards 1 2 3 5

GH Kerry House Hotel 946 Warwick Rd, Acocks Gn ☎021-707 0316 Plan **7**
23rm 3⋒ CTV in 10 bedrooms B&b£16 Bdi£23 W£96 M LDO7pm
Lic ▥ CTV 23P nc3yrs

GH Linden Lodge Hotel 79 Sutton Rd, Erdington ☎021-382 5992 Plan **8**

Birmingham — Birnam

6hc (1fb) ✱ ® *B&b£8.50 Bdi£10.50 LDO7.30pm
▥ CTV 8P

GH Lyndhurst Hotel 135 Kingsbury Rd, Erdington ☎021-373 5695 Plan **10**
15rm 14hc 1⋒ (2fb) CTV in 6 bedrooms ✱ B&b£11.50–£13.80 Bdi£16.10–£19 W£70–£75 M LDO8.30pm
▥ CTV 15P
Credit cards 1 2 3 5 Ⓥ

GH Rollason Wood Hotel 130 Wood End Rd, Erdington ☎021-373 1230 Plan **11**
33rm 28hc 5⋒ (2fb) *B&b£6.75–£13.75 W£50–£75 M LDO9pm
Lic ▥ CTV 40P
Credit cards 1 2 3 4 5

GH *Tri-Star Hotel* Coventry Rd, Elmdon ☎021-779 2233 Plan **13**
14hc (1fb) LDO7.30pm
Lic ▥ CTV 20P
Ⓥ

GH Welcome House 1641 Coventry Rd, Yardley ☎021-707 3232 Plan **14**
Closed 24 Dec
7hc 1⋒ (1fb) CTV in 1 bedroom TV in 6 bedrooms ✱ *B&b£10 W£70 M
▥ 8P nc5yrs
Credit cards 1 3

GH Wentsbury Hotel 21 Serpentine Rd, Selly Park ☎021-472 1258 Plan **15**
8hc (2fb) ® B&b£12.50 Bdi£18 W£115 M S% LDO4pm
▥ CTV 10P 1🚗
Ⓥ

GH Wentworth Hotel 103 Wentworth Rd, Harborne ☎021-427 2839 Plan **16**
Closed Xmas wk
21hc 7⋒ (3fb) CTV in 4 bedrooms TV in 17 bedrooms ® B&b£10–£14 Bdi£15–£19 LDO9pm
Lic ▥ CTV 14P

GH Westbourne Lodge 27–29 Fountain Rd, Edgbaston ☎021-429 1003 Plan **17**
Closed Xmas wk
20rm 12hc 6→ 2⋒ (1fb) B&b£11.50–£18.40 Bdi£18.40–£25.30 W£72.45–£120.75 M LDO7pm
Lic ▥ CTV 14P

BIRNAM
Tayside *Perthshire*
Map **11** NO04

⊢⊣ **GH Waterbury House** Murthly Ter ☎Dunkeld (03502) 324
Forming part of a stone-built terrace on the main street of this by-passed village.

6hc (2fb) TV in 1 bedroom B&b£7–£8 Bdi£11–£12 W£45–£52 ⱡ LDO5pm

Temperance 𝍖 CTV 6P

Credit cards 1 2 3

BISHOP'S CLEEVE
Gloucestershire
Map **3** SO92

GH Old Manor House 43 Station Rd ☎(024267) 4127

Proprietor run guesthouse in the village.

6hc (3fb) B&bfr£8.50 Bdifr£14.50 Wfr£59.50 M LDO9.30am

CTV P

BISHOPSTON
West Glamorgan
Map **2** SS58
See also Langland Bay and Mumbles

GH Winston Hotel 11 Church Ln, Bishopston Valley ☎(044128) 2074
Closed 24–29 Dec

Well equipped small hotel with good indoor heated pool, sauna and solarium.

14rm 3hc 3⋔ (A 5rm 4➡ 1⋔) (2fb) CTV in 5 bedrooms Ⓡ B&bfr£10 Bdifr£16

Lic 𝍖 CTV 20P ▭(heated) billiards sauna bath

Ⓥ

See advertisement on page 337

BISHOP WILTON
Humberside
Map **8** SE75

INN Fleece ☎(07596) 251

4hc ✶ B&b£9.50 Bdi£16 L£5alc D9pm £6.50&alc

𝍖 CTV 20P nc10yrs

BLACK CROSS
Cornwall
Map **2** SW96

FH Mr & Mrs J P Edwards **Homestake** *(SW910606)* ☎St Austell (0726) 860423
Apr–Oct

Pleasant house with garden on main village road. In central position for touring Cornwall.

8hc (4fb) *B&b£6.50–£7 Bdi£8.50–£9 W£56–£59.50 ⱡ (W only Jun–mid Sep) LDO4pm

CTV 12P (hard) 82acres sheep mixed

Ⓥ

See advertisement on page 255

BLACKPOOL
Lancashire
Map **7** SD33
See plan

GH *Arandora Star Private Hotel* 559 New South Prom ☎(0253) 41528 Plan **1** *A1* Jan–Oct & Xmas

18hc (3fb) LDO4pm

Lic 𝍖 CTV 12P 4 sea

GH Arosa Hotel 18–20 Empress Dr ☎(0253) 52555 Plan **2** *B5*
Etr–Oct & Xmas

21rm 12hc 2➡ 7⋔ (6fb) Ⓡ B&b£10–£12 Bdi£10.50–£14 W£63–£80 ⱡ LDO4pm

Lic 𝍖 CTV 6P

GH Ashcroft Private Hotel 42 King Edward Av ☎(0253) 51538 Plan **2A** *A5*
Apr–Oct

11hc (3fb) B&b£7.25–£9.50 Bdi£8.95–£11.95 W£59–£79 ⱡ LDO5pm

Lic 𝍖 CTV 4P

Ⓥ

GH Berwick Private Hotel 23 King Edward Av ☎(0253) 51496 Plan **3** *A5*

8rm 1⋔ (4fb) ✶ Ⓡ B&b£7.50–£9.50 Bdi£9–£12 W£49–£63 M LDO3.30pm

Lic 𝍖 CTV nc3yrs

Credit card 1

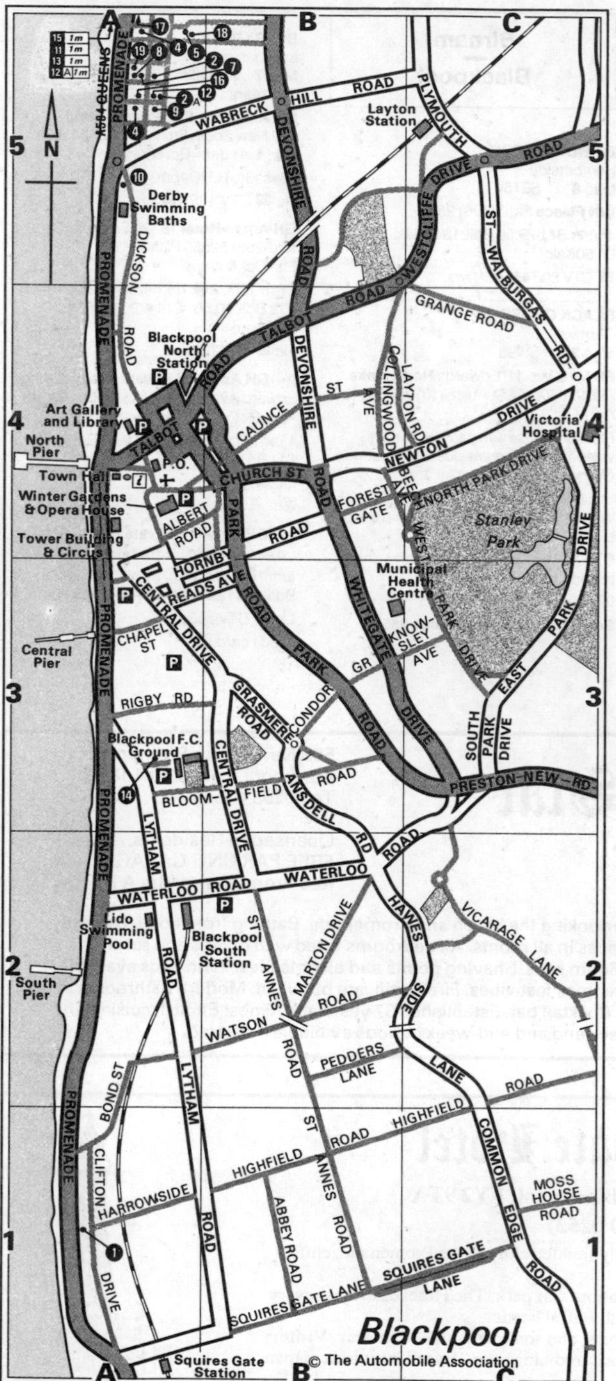

GH Brabyns Hotel 1–3 Shaftesbury Av ☎(0253) 52163 Plan **4** *A5*

Detached modernised hotel in side road just off the Promenade.

22rm 19⇌ 3⋒ (A 3rm 1⇌ 2⋒) (9fb) CTV in all bedrooms Ⓡ B&b£15–£18 Bdi£18.50–£21.50 W£85–£106 M LDO6pm

Lic ▥ CTV 14P

Credit cards 1 3

GH Burlees Hotel 40 Knowle Av ☎(0253) 54535 Plan **5** *A5*

Apr–Nov rs Mar

10hc (2fb) Ⓡ B&b£8.50–£9.50 Bdi£11.50–£12.50 W£57–£60 Ꝃ LDO5.15pm

CTV 5P 1⌂

Ⓥ

GH Cliftonville Hotel 14 Empress Dr, Northshore ☎(0253) 51052 Plan **7** *B5*

Apr–Nov

20rm 18⋒ ✶ Ⓡ B&b£8.50–£11 Bdi£10.50–£17 W£60–£91 Ꝃ LDO5pm

Lic ▥ CTV 4P

Blackpool

- **1** Arandora Star Private Hotel
- **2** Arosa Hotel
- **2A** Ashcroft Privatre Hotel
- **3** Berwick Private Hotel
- **4** Brabyns Hotel
- **5** Burlees Hotel
- **7** Cliftonville Hotel
- **8** Croydon Private Hotel
- **9** Denely Private Hotel
- **10** Derwent Private Hotel
- **11** Garville
- **12** Lynstead Private Hotel
- **12A** Manxonia Hotel
- **13** Mavern Private Hotel
- **14** Motel Mimosa
- **15** New Heathcot Hotel
- **16** North Mount Private Hotel
- **17** Sunnycliff
- **18** Sunray Private Hotel
- **19** Surrey House Hotel

GH *Croydon Private Hotel* 12 Empress Dr ☎ (0253) 52497 Plan **8** *A5*
Etr–Nov
11hc (6fb) ★
CTV 8P

⊢→ **GH Denely Private Hotel** 15 King Edward Av ☎ (0253) 52757 Plan **9** *A5*
9hc 1⋔ (2fb) ★ B&b£8–£9 Bdi£9.50–£10.50 W£56–£63 M LDO4.30pm
▥ CTV 5P

See advertisement on page 65

⊢→ **GH Derwent Private Hotel** 8 Gynn Av ☎ (0253) 55194 Plan **10** *A5*

Blackpool

12rm 8hc 4⋔ (2fb) B&b£7.50–£9.50 Bdi£10.50–£12.50 W£66–£79 V LDO4pm
Lic ▥ CTV 5P 1⌂ nc3yrs
Ⓥ

⊢→ **GH Garville** 3 Beaufort Av, Bispham (2m N) ☎ (0253) 51004 Plan **11** *A5*
Closed Dec
7rm 5hc 2⇨ (4fb) B&b£5.75 Bdi£8.25 W£40.25 M LDO5.30pm

Lic ▥ CTV 5P

GH Lynstead Private Hotel 40 King Edward Av ☎ (0253) 51050 Plan **12** *A5*
Closed 1st wk Jan
10rm 5hc 5⋔ (4fb) ★Ⓡ B&b£8.50–£9.50 Bdi£10.35–£11.50 W£72–£80 V LDO3pm
Lic lift ▥ CTV

⊢→ **GH Manxonia Hotel** 248 Queens Prom, Bispham (1m N A584) ☎ (0253) 51118 Plan **12A** *A5*
24hc (3fb) CTV in all bedrooms B&b£8 Bdi£10 W£69 V LDO5.30pm
Lic ▥ CTV 8P

GH Mavern Private Hotel 238 Queens Prom, Bispham (1m N A584) ☎(0253) 51409 Plan **13** *A5*
25rm 22hc 3⋒ (6fb) ✱ B&b£9.50–£10 Bdi£11–£12 W£66.50–£70 LDO4pm
Lic lift 🍽 CTV 15P

GH Motel Mimosa 24A Lonsdale Rd ☎(0253) 41906 Plan **14** *A3*
Closed 23 Dec–3 Jan
15rm 9⇌ 6⋒ CTV in all bedrooms ® B&b£10.80–£12 W£72.45–£78.50 M
🍽 12P 1⌂ nc7yrs
Credit card 3 V
See advertisement on page 67

Blackpool

GH New Heathcot Private Hotel 270 Queens Prom ☎(0253) 52083 Plan **15** *A5*
Closed Jan
9hc (4fb) Bdi£7.50–£8 Bdi£9–£9.50 W£63–£66.50 LDO5.30pm
Lic 🍽 CTV 6P

GH North Mount Private Hotel 22 King Edward Av ☎(0253) 55937 Plan **16** *B5*
8hc (3fb) ® ✱ B&b£7–£8.50 Bdi£9–£10.75 LDO3pm
Lic 🍽 CTV 1P

GH Sunnycliff 98 Queens Prom, Northshore ☎(0253) 51155 Plan **17** *A5*
Etr–Nov & Xmas
12hc (4fb) ® B&b£8–£9.25 Bdi£10–£11 W£70–£72 LDO5pm
Lic CTV 8P
V

GH Sunray Private Hotel 42 Knowle Av, Queens Prom ☎(0253) 51937 Plan **18** *B5*
Closed Xmas & New Year

Comfortable small hotel in quiet residential area, close to Queens Promenade and Blackpool's many attractions.

9⋔ (2fb) TV in all bedrooms Ⓡ B&b£8.75–£10.75 Bdi£13.75–£15.75 W£87–£99 LDO4pm

Ⅲ CTV 6P

Ⓥ

⊢⊣ **GH Surrey House Hotel**
9 Northumberland Av ☎(0253) 51743
Plan **19** *A5*
Apr–Oct rs Mar & early Nov

12rm 3hc 2➡ 7⋔ (2fb) Ⓡ B&b£6.75–£8.75 Bdi£8.95–£11.95 W£47.25–£61.25 M LDO4.45pm

Ⅲ CTV 6P 1🚗

BLACKWATERFOOT
Isle of Arran Strathclyde *Buteshire*
Map **10** NR92

INN Greannan Hotel ☎Shiskine (077086) 200

Attractive white hotel in lovely country with modern style dining room.

12hc Ⓡ B&b£10.50–£11.50 Bdi£13.50–£15 W£73.50–£80.50 M L£1.50–£2.50 D9.30pm £3.50–£6.45

Ⅲ CTV 50P 🚗

BLACKWOOD
Gwent
Map **3** ST19

INN Plas Gordon Rd ☎(0495) 224674

Comfortable and popular family run inn enjoying elevated location.

6rm 4⋔ CTV in all bedrooms Ⓡ B&b£13–£18 L£4.65–£8&alc D9.45pm £6.50alc

Ⅲ 80P

Credit cards 1 3 Ⓥ

BLAENAU FFESTINIOG
Gwynedd
Map **6** SH74

⊢⊣ **GH Don** 147 High St ☎(0766) 830403

Three storey stone Victorian house near centre of village.

6hc (3fb) ★ B&b£7–£7.50 Bdi£10.50–£11 W£49–£52.50 M LDO7pm

Lic Ⅲ CTV 2P 2🚗

Ⓥ

BLAIRGOWRIE
Tayside *Perthshire*
Map **11** NO14

⊢⊣ **GH Glenshieling** Hatton Rd, Rattray ☎(0250) 4605
Closed Dec

Comfortable accommodation in house standing in its own gardens.

6hc (2fb) ★ Ⓡ B&b£8–£9 Bdi£13–£14 W£88–£92 ⅃ LDO5pm

Lic Ⅲ CTV 18P

Ⓥ

GH Rosebank House Balmoral Rd ☎(0250) 2912
28Dec–Oct

Privately owned and run white painted house standing in its own attractive garden.

7rm 6hc (3fb) B&b£9–£10.50 Bdi£12–£16.95 W£95–£105 ⅃ LDO7pm

Lic Ⅲ TV 16P nc10yrs

BLEADNEY
Somerset
Map **3** ST44

GH *Threeway Country House Hotel & Restaurant* ☎Wells (0749) 78870
Closed Xmas

10hc 3➡ 1⋔ (1fb) CTV in 4 bedrooms ★ LDO9pm

Lic Ⅲ CTV 60P 3🚗

Ⓥ

BLETCHINGLEY
Surrey
Map **4** TQ35

INN Whyte Harte ☎Godstone (0883) 843231

Popular roadside inn, dating from 1388, with compact modern or character bedrooms and a good restaurant.

9rm 5hc 4➡ ★ B&bfr£16.43 Lfr£6.50&alc D9.45pm fr£10.50&alc S%

CTV 50P 🚗

Credit cards 1 2 3 5 Ⓥ

BLITHBURY
Staffordshire
Map **7** SK02

FH Mrs H Hodgkinson ***Blithbury Bank*** *(SK083206)* Uttoxeter Rd ☎Hamstall Ridware (088922) 284

Large 18th-century farmhouse in elevated position with good views, situated on B5014 S of Abbots Bromley.

3rm 2hc (1fb) ★ LDO5pm

Ⅲ CTV 3P nc7yrs 59acres dairy

BLORE
Staffordshire
Map **7** SK14

⊢⊣ **FH** M A Griffin **Coldwall** *(SK144494)* Okeover ☎Thorpe Cloud (033529) 249
Etr–Oct

Stone built farmhouse approximately 200 years old. Good views of the surrounding hills. 4 miles NW of Ashbourne.

2hc (2fb) ★ B&b£6.50 Bdi£10 LDO6pm

TV 6P 250acres mixed

Ⓥ

BLUE ANCHOR
Somerset
Map **3** ST04

⊢⊣ **GH Camelot** ☎Dunster (064382) 348
Mar–Oct

5hc ★ B&b£7–£7.50 Bdi£10.50–£11 W£45–£48 M LDO5.30pm

Ⅲ CTV 6P nc14yrs

BODEDERN
Gwynedd
Map **6** SH38

INN Crown Hotel ☎Valley (0407) 740734

Old country coaching inn with pleasant homely atmosphere, situated a few miles from holiday beaches and the Irish car ferry terminal.

5hc CTV in 1 bedroom ✱B&b£7

Ⅲ 80P

Ⓥ

BODIAM
East Sussex
Map **5** TQ72

GH Justins Hotel Sandhurst Rd ☎Staplecross (058083) 372
Closed Dec

Attractive and well run country house, in peaceful surroundings.

9rm 2hc 2➡ 5⋔ (4fb) Ⓡ B&b£17.10 Bdi£23.43 W£138.25 ⅃ LDO8pm

Lic Ⅲ CTV 12P nc3yrs

Credit cards 1 3

BODMIN
Cornwall
Map **2** SX06

GH *Washaway Your Troubles* Washaway (Guestaccom) ☎(0208) 4951
Closed Xmas

7hc (1fb) ★ LDO8pm

Lic Ⅲ CTV 15P nc10yrs

BOGHEAD
Strathclyde *Lanarkshire*
Map **11** NS74

⊢⊣ **FH** I McInally **Dykehead** *(NS772417)* ☎Lesmahagow (0555) 892226

Rough cast, two-storey farmhouse just fifty yards from Strathaven/Lesmahagow Road.

2rm (1fb) B&b£6.50–£7 W£42 M

Ⅲ CTV 3P 1🚗 200acres dairy sheep

BOGNOR REGIS
West Sussex
Map **4** SZ99

GH *Landsdowne Hotel* 55–57 West St ☎(0243) 865552

Modernised property incorporating cottage style restaurant, set in a quiet residential area away from sea front.

8hc (4fb) LDO9.30pm

Lic Ⅲ CTV 5P sea

Ⓥ

See advertisement on page 70

Lansdowne Hotel & Farthings Restaurant

Bognor Regis, West Sussex
Telephone: Bognor Regis (0243) 865552

This family run hotel and restaurant is centrally situated to Esplanade, Floral Gardens, Bowling Greens, Tennis Courts, Grazy Golf, Bognor Pier and amusements, Sailing Club, Children's Zoo and Hotham Park, Boating Pool, Angling Festivals, Punch and Judy.
The Town Centre, Bus and Rail Stations all are within a 5 minute walk. Fontwell Races 5 miles, Goodwood Races 9 miles

Member of S.E. England Tourist Board

The Halfway House Hotel

BONTDDU, DOLGELLAU, NORTH WALES
Tel: Bontddu 635. (STD 034 149)

Picturesque village. Coaching Inn set in spectacular mountain scenery.
Completely modernised bedroom accommodation.
Intimate, candle-lit dining room specialising in Welsh lamb, local salmon and seafood.

Resident proprietors: Maggie and Bill Hutchinson

The Grange

Grange-in-Borrowdale,
Near Keswick, Cumbria CA12 5UQ
Telephone: 059 684 251

Owned and managed by Mr & Mrs G Jenkinson

The Grange is a small, friendly hotel in the village of Grange in one of the loveliest valleys, Borrowdale in the Lake District. This is an excellent centre for walking, rock-climbing, boating and touring, and for less energetic occupations. There are 6 bedrooms, 3 bathrooms (one private) all rooms have central heating and lovely views. Food is good and guests are sure of personal attention. Ample parking space. Dogs are accommodated at the management's discretion.

Langstrath Hotel

ENGLISH LAKELAND **Stonethwaite, Borrowdale, Keswick, Cumbria, CA12 5XG**

Tranquillity, friendliness and old-world charm – a cosy, family-run hotel in a delightful setting. With no passing traffic, the paths along the valley and onto the fells begin at our door. Rivers, lakes, mountains and forests vie for your attention. Central heating, open fires and a well-stocked residential bar will ensure your total comfort at the end of the day. Home cooking to suit the most discerning palate and satisfy the heartiest appetite. Step into another world where nothing is too much trouble to make your holiday truly memorable.

For more information ask for our colour brochure by ringing
Borrowdale (059 684) 239

BOLLINGTON
Cheshire
Map **7** SJ97

INN *Turners Arms Hotel* 1 Ingersley Rd ☎(0625) 73864
Part modernised stone built public house occupying a corner site.
5rm 4hc TV in 4 bedrooms
▥ 5P

BOLNEY
West Sussex
Map **4** TQ22

GH *Bolney Grange House Hotel* ☎Burgess Hill (04446) 45164
Country house, set in rural surroundings with swimming pool, fishing lakes and horse riding available.
15hc (1fb) ✱
Lic ▥ CTV 30P

BONDLEIGH (Near North Tawton)
Devon
Map **3** SS60

FH Mrs M C H Partridge **Cadditon** *(SS644050)* ☎North Tawton (083782) 450
Etr–Oct
1¼m W unclass rd.
3hc (1fb) ✱ Ⓡ *B&b£5.50–£6 Bdi£9–£10 W£63–£70 Ⱡ
CTV P 147acres beef dairy mixed

BO'NESS
Central *West Lothian*
Map **11** NS98

FH Mrs A Kirk **Kinglass** *(NT006803)* Borrowstoun Rd ☎(0506) 822861
Charming sandstone farmhouse overlooking Firth of Forth. Bedrooms are very well decorated and the welcome is warm and friendly.
7rm 6hc (1fb) TV in 6 bedrooms ✱ Ⓡ B&b£8.50–£9.50 Bdi£13.50–£14.50 W£91.50 Ⱡ LDO8pm
Lic ▥ CTV 20P 120acres arable

BONTDDU
Gwynedd
Map **6** SH61

INN Halfway House Hotel ☎(034149) 635
Half timbered inn in centre of small village.
4rm 3hc 1→ Ⓡ B&b£10–£11.50 Bdi£18.50–£20 W£70–£73.50 Ⱡ Bar lunch £2.50alc D9pm £8.75
CTV 12P 3🚗 ⛳

BOOT
Cumbria
Map **7** NY10

GH Brook House ☎Eskdale (09403) 288
Closed Dec
6rm 4hc 2⋔ (2fb) TV in all bedrooms Ⓡ B&b£9–£11.50 Bdi£14.50–£17 W£95–£112.50 Ⱡ LDO8.30pm
Lic ▥ 10P
Ⓥ

Bollington — Bournemouth

BORELAND
Dumfries & Galloway *Dumfriesshire*
Map **11** NY19

⊢⊣ **FH** Mrs I Maxwell **Gall** *(NY172901)* ☎(05766) 229
Apr–Oct
Well appointed modern farmhouse with delightful views across rolling countryside and distant hills.
3hc (2fb) ✱ Ⓡ B&b£7–£8 Bdi£11 £12 W75 Ⱡ LDO4pm
CTV 3P 🏠 1066acres beef sheep
Ⓥ

BORROWDALE
Cumbria
Map **11** NY21

GH Greenbank Country ☎(059684) 215
10rm 3hc 3→ 4⋔ (2fb) B&b£9–£11.30 Bdi£14.25–£16.80 W£56–£69 M LDO5pm
Lic ▥ CTV 12P

GH Langstrath Hotel ☎(059684) 239
mid Mar–Oct
13rm 11hc 2⋔ (3fb) B&b£13.50 Bdi£18.50 W£120 Ⱡ LDO2pm
Lic ▥ 20P
Ⓥ

BOSCASTLE
Cornwall
Map **2** SX09

GH St Christophers Country House Hotel High St (Guestaccom) ☎(08405) 412
Mar–Oct
6rm 5hc 1⋔ B&b£9–£10 Bdi£15–£16 W£103–£118.50 Ⱡ LDO7pm
Lic ▥ CTV 7P
Ⓥ

BOSWINGER
Cornwall
Map **2** SW94

GH Van Ruan House ☎Mevagissey (0726) 842425
May–Sep rs Oct–Dec
5hc ✱ Ⓡ B&bfr£9 Bdifr£15 LDOnoon
Lic ▥ CTV 6P nc11yrs

BOTALLACK
Cornwall
Map **2** SW33

FH Mrs J Cargeeg **Manor** *(SW368331)* ☎Penzance (0736) 788525
Previously known as 'Nanparra'; home of Ross Poldark from the television series filmed here. Area steeped in history.
6hc (1fb) ✱ Ⓡ B&b£8 W£56 M
▥ CTV 6P 180acres arable beef mixed

BOUGHTON MONCHELSEA
Kent
Map **5** TQ75

GH Taynard Wierton Hill ☎Maidstone (0622) 44705
Set in 1 acre, this 14th-century building has comfortable character bedrooms.
5rm 4→ 1⋔ (1fb) B&b£18.40–£27.60 Bdi£30.47–£39.67 W£213.29–£277.69 Ⱡ LDO8pm
Lic ▥ CTV 10P nc5yrs
Credit cards 1 2 3 5
See advertisement on page 239

BOURNEMOUTH AND BOSCOMBE
Dorset
Map **4** SZ09

See Central Plan (page 76), Boscombe and Southbourne Plan (pages 78–79) and Westbourne & Branksome Plan (page 82)
For additional guesthouses see **Poole** and **Christchurch**

GH *Alcombe Private Hotel* 37 Sea Rd, Boscombe ☎(0202) 36206 Boscombe & Southbourne plan **27** *C2*
Closed Xmas
Near shops, and within walking distance from sea front and pier.
12hc (4fb) LDO4.30pm
CTV 6P

GH Alum Bay Hotel 19 Burnaby Rd, Alum Chine ☎(0202) 761034 Westbourne & Branksome plan **80** *B2*
Within short walking distance of sea front.
12hc 1⋔ (4fb) *B&b£8.05–£9.20 Bdi£11.50–£13.80 W£51.75–£59.80 M LDO6pm
Lic ▥ CTV 10P

GH Alumcliff Hotel 121 Alumhurst Rd, Alum Chine ☎(0202) 764777 Westbourne & Branksome plan **81** *B1/2*
Well appointed guesthouse located at the sea end of Alum Chine.
17hc 2→ 8⋔ (4fb) CTV in all bedrooms Ⓡ *B&b£16.50–£17.25 Bdi£20.50–£25.60 LDO6.30pm
Lic ▥ CTV 12P nc7yrs
Credit cards 1 2 3

GH *Alum Grange Hotel* 1 Burnaby Rd, Alum Chine ☎(0202) 761195 Westbourne & Branksome plan **82** *B2*
Closed Nov
Within two minutes walking distance of the sea.
14hc 4→ 4⋔ (5fb) CTV in 10 bedrooms ✱ Ⓡ LDO6pm
Lic ▥ CTV 8P nc3yrs
See advertisement on page 72

GH Anfield Private Hotel 12 Bradbourne Rd ☎(0202) 290749 Central plan **1** *B3*
Centrally located in quiet position backing onto central gardens. →

16hc (3fb) ✯ B&b£9.20–£11.50 Bdi£12.59–£15 W£69.75–£89.99 Ⱡ LDO3pm

Lic CTV 12P nc5yrs

Credit cards 1 2

GH Arlington Hotel Exeter Park Rd ☎(0202) 22879 Central plan **1A** *D2*
Mar–Nov & Xmas

Neat and well furnished, in fine position with good views.

30hc 2⇌ 6ⓜ (6fb) B&b£9–£15 Bdi£12–£18 W£63–£105 (W only Jul & Aug) LDO7pm

Lic ▥ CTV 21P

Ⓥ

Bournemouth

⊢×⊣ **GH Bay Tree Hotel** 17 Burnaby Rd, Alum Chine ☎(0202) 763807 Westbourne & Branksome plan **84** *B2*

Adjacent to Alum Chine, a few minutes from beach.

12rm 7hc 2ⓜ (5fb) ✯ Ⓡ B&b£7–£11 Bdi£11–£15.50 W£47–£75 Ⓜ LDO6pm

Lic CTV 7P nc3yrs

Ⓥ

⊢×⊣ **GH Blinkbonnie Heights Hotel** 26 Clifton Rd, Southbourne ☎(0202) 426512 Boscombe & Southbourne plan **30** *F1/2*
Mar–Oct

12hc 1⇌ (4fb) ✯ Ⓡ B&b£8–£11 Bdi£10.50–£13.50 W£69–£90 Ⱡ LDO6.15pm

Lic ▥ CTV 12P ♿

GH Blue Cedars Hotel Portchester Pl ☎(0202) 26893 Boscombe & Southbourne plan **30A** *A3*

12hc (3fb) ✯ *B&b£7–£8.50 Bdi£10.50–£12 W£45–£59 Ⓜ LDO3pm

Lic ▥ CTV 8P

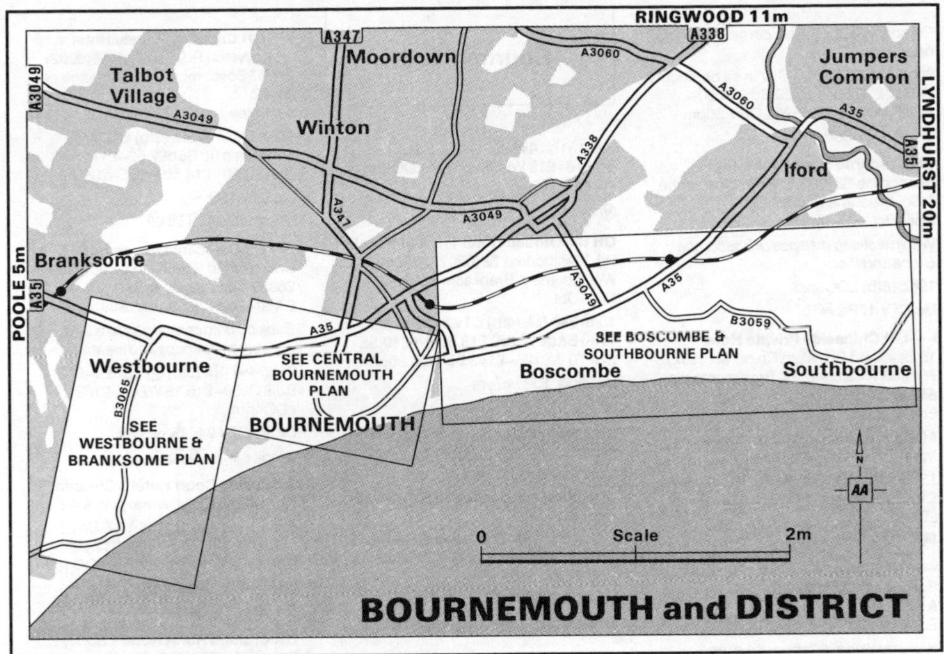

GH *Borodale Hotel* 10 St Johns Rd, Boscombe ☎(0202) 35285 Boscombe & Southbourne plan **31** *B2*

Short distance from Boscombe pier with nearby shopping complex.

17hc 4🚿 Ⓡ

Lic ♨ CTV 18P

GH Bracken Lodge Private Hotel 5 Bracken Rd, Southbourne ☎(0202) 428777 Boscombe & Southbourne plan **32** *E2*

Mar–Nov

In quiet residential Southbourne area near to shops and sea front.

12rm 10hc 1🛁 1🚿 (2fb) CTV in 2 bedrooms ★ Ⓡ *B&b£8.05–£13.80 Bdi£13.80–£17.25 W£56.35–£80.50 M LDO2.30pm

Lic ♨ CTV 14P nc3yrs

⊢⊣ **GH Braemar Private Hotel** 30 Glen Rd, Boscombe ☎(0202) 36054 Boscombe & Southbourne plan **33** *C2*

Apr–Oct & Xmas

Family run hotel near shops and sea front.

11rm 9hc 1🛁 1🚿 (4fb) Ⓡ B&b£8–£11 Bdi£10–£15 W£60–£85 L (W only Jun–Aug) LDO6pm

Lic ♨ CTV 6P

⊢⊣ **GH Hotel Bristol** Terrace Rd ☎(0202) 27007 Central plan **2** *B2*

Central popular hotel convenient to theatres.

28hc 6🛁 2🚿 (6fb) ★ B&b£7.50–£11 Bdi£10–£15 W£60–£97 M LDO7.30pm

lift ♨ CTV 2P Ⓥ

GH *Britannia Hotel* 40 Christchurch Rd ☎(0202) 26700 Boscombe & Southbourne plan **34** *A2*

Closed Xmas

On main Christchurch road into Bournemouth.

28hc ★

♨ CTV 30P nc3yrs

⊢⊣ **GH Brun-Lea Hotel** 94 Southbourne Rd ☎(0202) 425956 Boscombe & Southbourne plan **35** *E2*

Situated in Southbourne area, near shops and seafront.

15hc 4🚿 (3fb) ★ B&b£7.50–£9 Bdi£12–£15 W£50–£60 L LDO6.45pm

Lic ♨ CTV 11P nc8yrs

Ⓥ

GH Bursledon Hotel 34 Gervis Rd ☎(0202) 24622 Central plan **3** *E3*

Central position on East Cliff within short walking distance of shops and theatres.

23hc 2🛁 7🚿 (4fb) B&b£10.35–£15 Bdi£13.80–£21.85 W£96.60–£140.30 M LDO6.30pm

♨ CTV 14P 5🚗 nc3yrs

Credit card 3 Ⓥ

GH Carisbrooke Hotel 42 Tregonwell Rd ☎(0202) 290432 Central plan **4** *C1*

Mar–Nov

Modern family run hotel near the Winter Gardens.

24hc 1🛁 6🚿 (3fb) Ⓡ B&b£9–£13.50 Bdi£13–£17.50 W£54–£76 M LDO5pm

Lic CTV 19P

⊢⊣ **GH Carysfort Lodge Private Hotel** 19 Carysfort Rd, Boscombe ☎(0202) 36751 Boscombe & Southbourne plan **36** *B3*

rs Dec–Mar

In residential area near shops.

9hc (3fb) ★ B&b£6.50–£8 Bdi£9.50–£11.50 W£42–£55 M

Lic CTV 7P nc6yrs

⊢⊣ **GH Charles Taylor Hotel** Knyveton Gdns, 40–44 Frances Rd ☎(0202) 22695 Boscombe & Southbourne plan **37** *A2*

Mar–Nov

Named after owner who personally supervises. Pleasant location overlooking bowling greens.

28hc 11🛁 (9fb) ★ Ⓡ B&b£8–£12 Bdi£11.34–£15.34 W£54–£72 L LDO6.30pm

Lic ♨ CTV 12P nc3yrs

⊢⊣ **GH Chawson House Hotel** 72 Lansdowne Road North ☎(0202) 22317 Central plan **5** *F4*

In select residential area with secluded rear garden.

14hc (1fb) ★ B&b£7.50–£8.50 W£49–£56 M

♨ CTV 15P 1🚗 nc4yrs

Credit card 3 Ⓥ

GH Chequers Hotel 17 West Cliff Rd ☎(0202) 23900 Central plan **6** *A1*

Mar–Nov

→

Personally supervised, corner sited hotel near Durley Chine.

28hc 8⇌ 10⋒ (6fb) CTV in all bedrooms ✈ B&b£10.50–£15.50 Bdi£14.50–£22.50 W£65–£105 M LDO7.30pm

Lic ⅏ CTV 35P

GH *Chilterns Hotel* 44 Westby Rd, Boscombe ☎(0202) 36539 Boscombe & Southbourne plan **38** *C2*
Apr–Oct

Within walking distance of Boscombe Chine and Pier.

19hc (8fb) LDO5pm

Lic CTV 17P 2⛍

⊢⊣ **GH Chineside Private Hotel** 15 Studland Rd, Alum Chine ☎(0202) 761206 Westbourne & Branksome plan **85** *B2*
Etr–4 Oct

Modern, well appointed hotel near sea front.

13rm 10hc 3⋒ (3fb) ✈ Ⓡ B&b£7.50–£10 Bdi£10.50–£15 W£50–£67 Ł LDO6.15pm

⅏ CTV 13P nc4yrs

⊢⊣ **GH Cintra** 10–12 Florence Rd, Boscombe ☎(0202) 36103 Boscombe & Southbourne plan **39** *C2*
Etr–Oct

Within walking distance of pier and shopping centre.

Bournemouth

39rm 31hc 4⇌ 4⋒ (20fb) B&b£7–£10 Bdi£10–£13 W£49–£70 M LDO6pm

Lic ⅏ CTV 10P ⌂

Ⓥ

GH Cliff House Hotel 113 Alumhurst Rd, Westbourne ☎(0202) 763003 Westbourne & Branksome plan **86** *B2*
Mar–Oct

10rm 2⇌ 6⋒ (4fb) CTV in all bedrooms ✈ Ⓡ B&b£12.65–£13.50 Bdi£19.55–£20.70 W£126–£143 Ł LDO6.30pm

Lic lift ⅏ 10P nc7yrs

Ⓥ

GH Clifton Court Hotel 30 Clifton Rd ☎(0202) 427753 Boscombe & Southbourne plan **40** *F1*

Well furnished guesthouse with modern extension.

12rm 10hc 2⇌ (2fb) *B&b£8.50–£12 Bdi£11.50–£16.50 W£50–£70 M LDO9am

Lic ⅏ CTV 10P 1⛍

See advertisement on page 72

⊢⊣ **GH Cransley Private Hotel** 11 Knyveton Rd, East Cliff ☎(0202) 20067 Boscombe & Southbourne plan **41** *A2*
Apr–Nov

12rm 5hc 4⇌ 3⋒ (2fb) CTV in 4 bedrooms Ⓡ B&b£7.50–£11 Bdi£10.50–£14.50 W£55–£85 Ł

Lic CTV 10P

Credit cards 1 3 Ⓥ

⊢⊣ **GH Crescent Grange Hotel** 6–8 Crescent Rd, The Triangle ☎(0202) 26959 Central plan **8** *B3*
6 Mar–2Nov rs 5 Jan–5 Mar

Backing onto central gardens and convenient to shops and theatres.

21hc 4⇌ 4⋒ (3fb) Ⓡ B&b£8–£12 Bdi£11.50–£15.15 W£75–£102 Ł LDO4pm

Lic ⅏ CTV 24P ♿ nc3yrs

Credit cards 1 3

GH Cresta Court Hotel 3 Crescent Rd ☎(0202) 25217 Central plan **9** *A3*

20rm 17hc 2⇌ 1⋒ (4fb) CTV in all bedrooms Ⓡ B&b£9.50–£12.50 Bdi£14–£17 W£95–£115 Ł LDO4pm

Lic ⅏ CTV 17P nc4yrs

Credit cards 1 3

GH Croham Hurst Hotel 9 Durley Rd, Boscombe ☎(0202) 22353 Central plan **10** *B1*
Etr–mid Nov

24rm 10hc 9➡ 5ƒ (6fb) CTV in all bedrooms ✱ ® B&b£8.50–£12 Bdi£11.50–£16 W£56–£77 M LDO6.30pm

Lic CTV P

GH Crossroads Hotel 88 Belle Vue Rd, Southbourne ☎(0202) 426307 Boscombe & Southbourne plan **42** *G2*

Near to shops and a few minutes walking distance from beach.

10rm 6hc 4ƒ (6fb) ✱ *B&bfr£6.50 Bdifr£11 Wfr£45 L (W only July & Aug)

Lic ⅢⅢ CTV 12P nc5yrs

GH Dean Court Hotel 4 Frances Rd ☎(0202) 28165 Boscombe & Southbourne plan **43** *A2*
Closed Nov

Near to shops and clubs of Lansdowne.

11hc (4fb) B&b£7–£10 Bdi£10.50–£13.50 W£60–£85 L

Lic ⅢⅢ CTV 5P nc3yrs

Credit cards 1 2 3 V

GH Derwent House 36 Hamilton Rd, Boscombe ☎(0202) 309102 Boscombe & Southbourne plan **44** *B2*

Short distance from Boscombe shops and pier.

10hc (5fb) *B&b£7–£8.50 Bdi£9.50–£11.25 W£57–£70 L

Lic ⅢⅢ CTV 12P

Bournemouth

GH Dorset Westbury Hotel
62 Lansdowne Road North ☎(0202) 21811 Central plan **11** *F4*
Closed Dec

Unusual 'ranch house' dining room and attractive, intimate bar.

17rm 11hc 3➡ 3ƒ (5fb) B&b£8.05–£12.07 Bdi£12.65–£16.67 W£82.80–£110.97 L LDO2pm

Lic ⅢⅢ CTV 20P

GH Earlham Lodge 91 Alumhurst Rd, Alum Chine ☎(0202) 761943 Westbourne & Branksome plan **88** *B2*
Feb–Nov & Xmas

Few minutes walk from sea front.

14rm 8hc 6ƒ (4fb) ✱ ® B&b£8.50–£11 Bdi£12.50–£15 W£85–£99 L LDO6pm

Lic ⅢⅢ CTV 9P

Credit cards 1 2 3

GH *East Cliff Cottage Private Hotel*
57 Grove Rd, East Cliff ☎(0202) 22788 Central plan **12** *F3*
Etr–Oct

Cottage in quiet area near East Cliff.

10hc 3➡ 1ƒ (1fb) ® LDO4.30pm

ⅢⅢ CTV 8P nc5yrs

V

GH Egerton House Private Hotel
385 Holdenhurst Rd, Queens Park ☎(0202) 34024 Boscombe & Southbourne plan **44A** *B3*

8hc (3fb) ✱ B&b£7.50–£8.50 Bdi£11.50–£12.50 W£46.50–£55 M LDO6pm

ⅢⅢ CTV 8P

GH Eglan Court Hotel 7 Knyveton Rd ☎(0202) 290093 Boscombe & Southbourne plan **45** *A2*
Mar–Dec

Located in pine clad avenue near to sea.

15rm 11hc 4ƒ (4fb) CTV in 12 bedrooms ® B&b£7.50–£8.50 Bdi£10.50–£11.50 W£50–£57.50 M LDO10am

Lic ⅢⅢ CTV 10P nc5yrs

Credit card 3 V

GH Farlow Private Hotel
13 Walpole Rd, Boscombe ☎(0202) 35865 Boscombe & Southbourne plan **46** *B3*

Well maintained guesthouse with sound furnishings and personal service.

12hc (2fb) CTV in 2 bedrooms ✱ B&b£7–£8 Bdi£10.50–£11.50 W£47–£54 L LDO4pm

CTV 12P nc3yrs

Credit card 1

GH Florida Hotel 35 Boscombe Spa Rd ☎(0202) 34537 Boscombe & Southbourne plan **46A** *B1* →

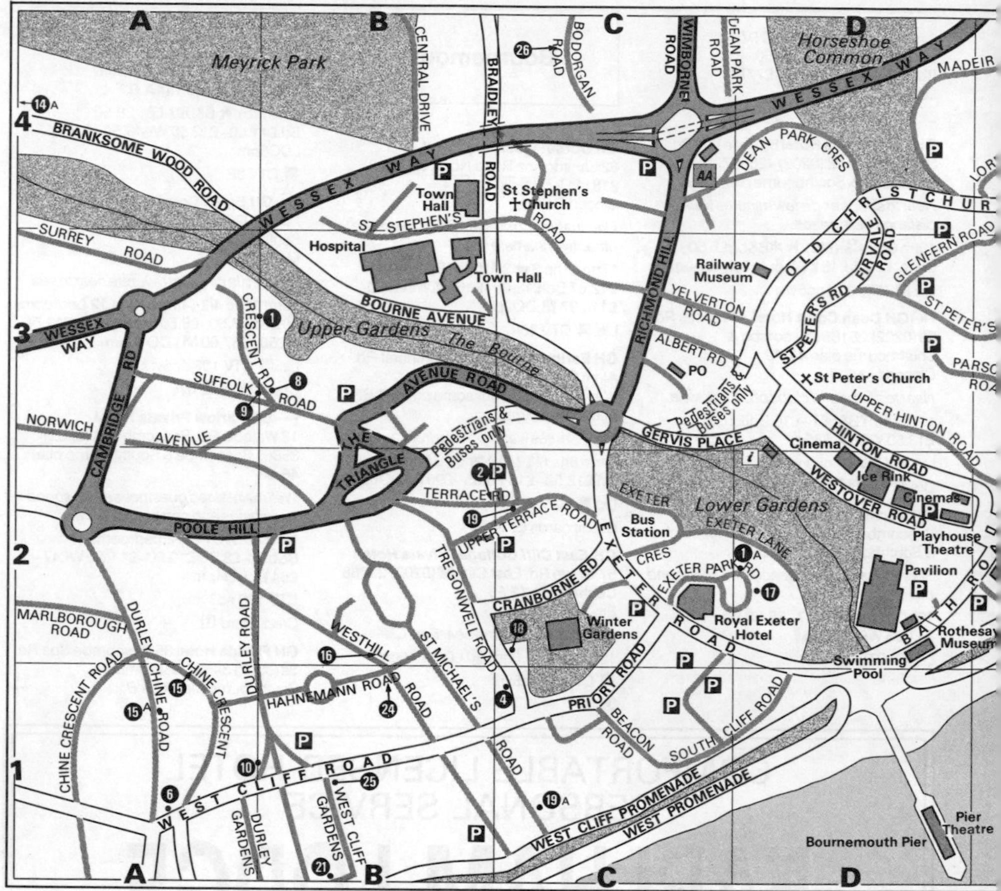

Detached two-storey, red brick building close to Boscombe shopping centre. Sea views.

25rm 19hc 6⇌ (3fb) *B&b£6.95–£10 Bdi£7.95–£12 W£42–£69 M LDO1pm

Lic CTV 20P 2

GH Freshfields Hotel 55 Christchurch Rd ☎(0202) 34023 Boscombe & Southbourne plan **47** *B1*

Situated on main A35 Christchurch road.

11rm 6hc 3⇌ 2ᗑ (5fb) Ⓡ B&b£7.50–£13 Bdi£12–£17.50 W£52–£80 M LDO3pm

Lic CTV 9P

GH Gervis Court Hotel 38 Gervis Rd ☎(0202) 26871 Central plan **13** *E3* Etr–Oct

Amidst pines on East Cliff.

18rm 12hc 3⇌ 3ᗑ (2fb) Ⓡ B&b£11.25–£13.25 Bdi£14.25–£16 W£69–£105 L LDO7.15pm

Llc CTV 15P 2

GH Golden Sands Hotel 83 Alumhurst Rd ☎(0202) 763832 Westbourne & Branksome plan **88A** *B2* Apr–Sep

Pleasant guesthouse with well maintained accommodation.

13hc 2ᗑ (1fb) CTV in 9 bedrooms Ⓡ B&bfr£10 Bdifr£14.25 Wfr£88 L LDO5.30pm

Lic CTV 9P

GH Gordons Hotel 84 West Cliff Rd, Alum Chine ☎(0202) 765844 Westbourne & Branksome plan **89** *B2*

Within walking distance of beach.

17rm 13hc 4ᗑ (3fb) Ⓡ B&b£9–£10.50 Bdi£12.50–£14 W£68–£98 L LDO3pm

Lic CTV 14P

GH Grassmere 5 Pine Av, Southbourne ☎(0202) 428660 Boscombe & Southbourne plan **48** *E2* Etr–mid Oct

In quiet residential Southbourne area.

10hc (3fb) B&b£7–£8 Bdi£10.50–£11.50 W£70–£75 L LDO4.30pm

Lic CTV 10P nc3yrs

Ⓥ

GH Hamilton Hall Private Hotel 1 Carysfort Rd ☎(0202) 35758 Boscombe & Southbourne plan **49** *B2*

Short walk from Boscombe shops and gardens.

10rm 4hc 2⇌ 2ᗑ (3fb) B&b£5.75–£8.60 Bdi£8.90–£11.60 W£35–£56 M (W only Jul & Aug) LDOnoon

Lic CTV 10P nc5yrs

GH Hawaiian Hotel 4 Glen Rd ☎(0202) 33234 Boscombe & Southbourne plan **50** *C2* Apr–Oct

Nice, bright property near Boscombe Pier and shops.

13rm 8hc 4⇌ 1ᗑ (3fb) Ⓡ B&b£7.48–£9.20 Bdi£8.63–£10.35 W£64.40–£78.20 L (W only Jul & Aug) LDO6pm

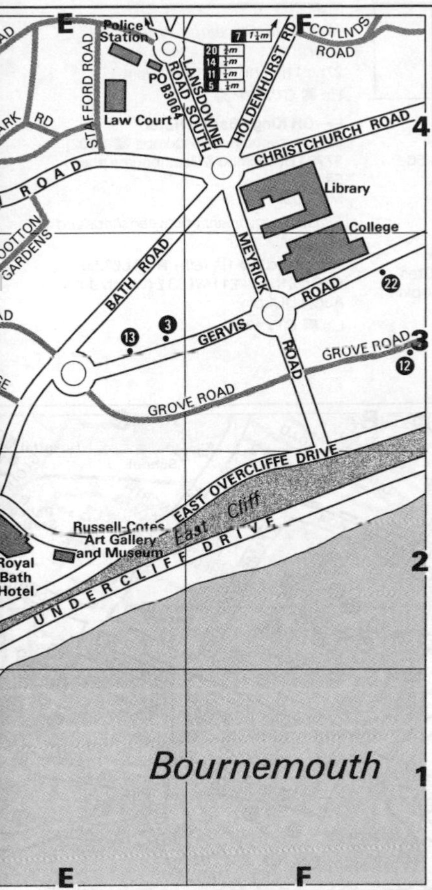

Central Bournemouth Plan

1 Anfield Private Hotel
1A Arlington Hotel
2 Hotel Bristol
3 Bursledon Hotel
4 Carisbrooke Hotel
5 Chawson House Hotel
6 Chequers Hotel
8 Crescent Grange Hotel
9 Cresta Court Hotel
10 Croham Hurst Hotel
11 Dorset Westbury Hotel
12 East Cliff Cottage Private Hotel
13 Gervis Court Hotel
14 Heather Mount Hotel
14A High Trees Hotel
15 Kensington Hotel
15A Langton Hall Hotel
16 Mae-Mar Private Hotel
17 Monreith Hotel
18 Mount Stuart Hotel
19 Hotel Restormel
19A Safari Hotel
20 Silver Trees Hotel
21 Tower House Hotel
22 Tudor Grange Hotel
24 West Leigh Hotel
25 Whitley Court Hotel
26 Windsor Court Hotel

CTV 9P nc4yrs
Credit card 3

GH Heathcote Hotel 2 Heathcote Rd, Boscombe ☎(0202) 36185 Boscombe & Southbourne plan **51** *C2*

Short distance from shops and pier.

16rm 12hc 2→ 2⋒ (7fb) ★ B&b£7.50–£9.50 Bdi£11–£13.50 W£69–£86.50 ⱡ
Lic CTV 14P

GH Heather Mount Hotel
70 Lansdowne Rd ☎(0202) 24557
Central plan **14** *F4*

Within walking distance of shops and sea front.

20rm 12hc 4→ 2⋒ (5fb) B&b£8–£10 Bdi£11.50–£13.50 W£56–£70 M LDO2pm

Lic CTV 16P nc7yrs
Credit cards 1 2 V

GH Highlin Private Hotel 14 Knole Rd ☎(0202) 33758 Boscombe & Southbourne plan **52** *B2*

In a quiet area near Boscombe Chine. →

12rm 11hc 1 (8fb) ® B&b£7–£8 Bdi£11–£12 W£49–£59 LDO4pm

Lic CTV 8P 1

GH High Trees Hotel 3 Glenferness Av (0202) 761380 Central plan **14A** *A4*

9hc 6 (3fb) B&b£9.50–£12.50 Bdi£11.50–£14.50 W£69–£92 (W only mid Jul–mid Aug) LDO6.30pm

Lic CTV 10P nc3yrs

See advertisement on page 77

GH Holmcroft Hotel 5 Earle Rd, Alum Chine (0202) 761289 Westbourne & Branksome plan **90** *B2*

Apr–Oct

Adjacent to the beautiful wooded slopes of Alum Chine.

Bournemouth

21rm 13hc 1 7 (5fb) CTV in all bedrooms ® B&b£10.50–£14.50 Bdi£13.50–£17.50 W£65–£85 LDO5pm

Lic CTV 17P nc3yrs

Credit cards 1 2 3 5 V

GH *Kensington Hotel* 18 Chine Cres, West Cliff (0202) 27434 Central plan **15** *A1*

Mar–Dec

Near Durley Chine in quiet residential area.

27hc 11 (7fb) ® LDO7.30pm

Lic CTV 23P

GH Kings Barton Hotel 22 Hawkwood Rd, Boscombe (0202) 37794 Boscombe & Southbourne plan **54** *C2*

Mar–Oct

Situated conveniently between shops and sea front.

13rm 10hc 2 1 (6fb) B&b£7.50–£8 Bdi£10.50–£11 W£83 (W only Jul & Aug) LDO3pm

Lic CTV 17P

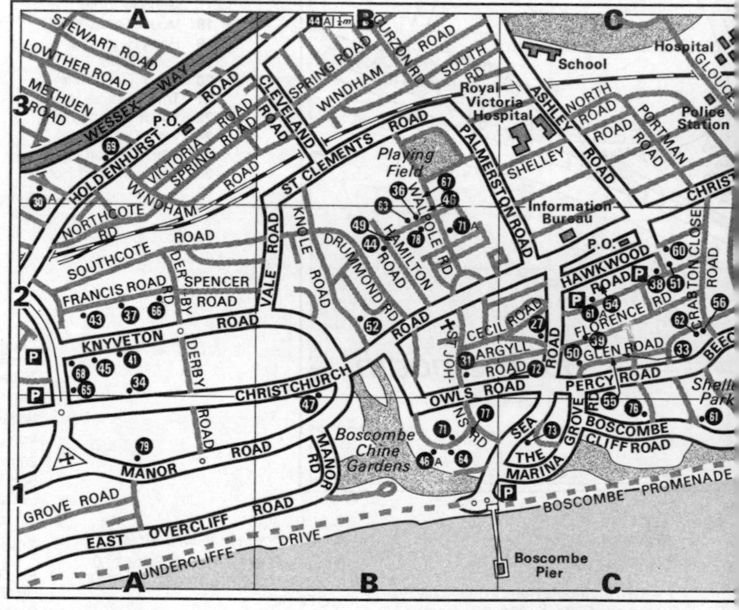

Bournemouth

GH Kingsley Hotel 29 Glen Rd, Boscombe ☎(0202) 38683 Boscombe & Southbourne plan **55** *C2*

Few minutes walk from Boscombe Pier and shops.

12rm 9hc 1→ 2⋔ (3fb) ✻ Ⓡ *B&b£8–£12.50 Bdi£11–£15.50 W£66.70–£95 Ł LDO4.30pm

Lic 🎹 CTV 6P

Credit cards 1 3

GH Langton Hall Hotel 8 Durley Chine Rd, West Cliff ☎(0202) 25025 Central plan **15A** *A1*

22rm 13hc 8→ 1⋔ (5fb) CTV in 5 bedrooms Ⓡ B&b£8–£14 Bdi£11–£17 W£65–£105 Ł LDO6.30pm

Lic 🎹 CTV 22P

Credit cards 1 2 3

GH Linwood House Hotel 11 Wilfred Rd ☎(0202) 37818 Boscombe & Southbourne **56** *C2*

2 Mar–2 Nov

Near Boscombe shops and pleasant walking distance from pier.

10rm 5hc 3⋔ (4fb) CTV in 1 bedroom TV in 3 bedrooms Ⓡ B&b£7–£10.50 Bdi£10.50–£14 W£46–£66 Ł (W only 22 Jun–7 Sep) LDO6pm

Lic 🎹 CTV 9P nc4yrs

GH Mae-Mar Private Hotel 91–93 West Hill Rd, West Cliff ☎(0202) 23167 Central plan **16** *B2*

In the heart of West Cliff hotel area.

28hc (7fb) B&b£8.63–£10.35 Bdi£10.35–£13.80 W£60–£92 Ł LDO6.30pm

Lic lift 🎹 CTV

Ⓥ

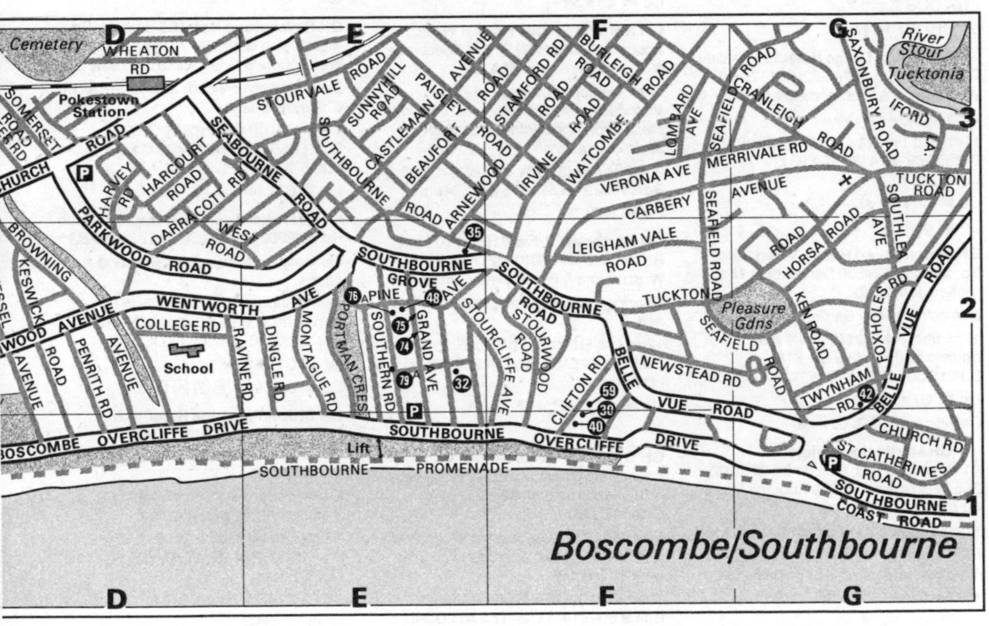

Boscombe & Southbourne Plan

27 Alcombe Private Hotel
30 Blinkbonnie Heights Hotel
30A Blue Cedars
31 Borodale Hotel
32 Bracken Lodge Private Hotel
33 Braemar Private Hotel
34 Britannia Hotel
35 Brun-Lea Hotel
36 Carysfort Lodge Private Hotel
37 Charles Taylor Hotel
38 Chilterns Hotel
39 Cintra Hotel
40 Clifton Court Hotel
41 Cransley Private Hotel
42 Crossroads Hotel
43 Dean Court Hotel
44 Derwent House
44A Egerton House Private Hotel
45 Eglan Court Hotel
46 Farlow Private Hotel
46A Florida Hotel
47 Freshfields Hotel
48 Grassmere
49 Hamilton Hall Private Hotel
50 Hawaiian Hotel
51 Heathcote Hotel
52 Highlin Private Hotel
54 Kings Barton Hotel
55 Kingsley Hotel
56 Linwood House Hotel
59 Mariner's Hotel
60 Myrtle House Hotel
61 Naseby-Nye Hotel
61A Norland Private Hotel
62 Oak Hall Private Hotel
63 Penmone Hotel
64 Pine Beach Hotel
65 St Johns Lodge Hotel
66 St Ronans Hotel
67 St Wilfreds Private Hotel
68 Sandelheath Hotel
69 Sea Shells
71 Sea View Court Hotel
71A Sherbourne Hotel
72 Hotel Sorrento
74 Stratford Hotel
75 Tree Tops Hotel
76 Valberg Hotel
76A Vine Hotel
77 Waldale Hotel
78 Wenmaur House Hotel
79 Wood Lodge Hotel
79A Woodside Private Hotel

Bournemouth

⊢⊣ **GH Mariners Hotel** 22 Clifton Rd, Southbourne ☎(0202) 420851 Boscombe & Southbourne plan **59** *F2* Mar–Oct

Close to cliff top and Southbourne zig-zag path to beach.

15hc (2fb) B&b£7.50–£10 Bdi£10.50–£13 W£50–£62 Ⱡ LDO6.15pm

♨ CTV 20P ⌂

Ⓥ

GH Monreith Hotel Lower Gdns, Exeter Park Rd, ☎(0202) 290344 Central plan **17** *D2* Apr–Oct rs Xmas

In own grounds overlooking bandstand, and central gardens.

30hc (6fb) ✶ Ⓡ B&b£10–£14 Bdi£14–£18 LDO6.30pm

Lic CTV 24P nc4yrs

⊢⊣ **GH Mount Lodge Hotel** 19 Beaulieu Rd, Westbourne ☎(0202) 761173 Westbourne & Branksome plan **91** *B2*

Adjacent to Alum Chine.

11rm 9hc 1⇥ 1⋔ (1fb) ✶ Ⓡ B&b£7.50–£11 Bdi£9–£14 W£56–£98 Ⱡ LDO6.30pm

Lic ♨ CTV 6P ⌂

Credit card ①

GH Mount Stuart Hotel 31 Tregonwell Rd, ☎(0202) 24639 Central plan **18** *C2* Closed Jan & Feb

Behind the Winter Gardens on West Cliff.

17rm 8hc 1⇥ 8⋔ (7fb) CTV in 9 bedrooms Ⓡ B&b£9.50–£16 Bdi£13.50–£20 W£75–£125 Ⱡ LDO7pm

Lic ♨ CTV 15P

Credit cards ① ② ③ ⑤ Ⓥ

⊢⊣ **GH Myrtle House Hotel** 41 Hawkwood Rd, Boscombe ☎(0202) 36579 Boscombe & Southbourne Plan **60** *C2*

Short distance from Boscombe shops and pier.

10hc (6fb) B&b£6.50–£11 Bdi£8–£14 W£55–£92 Ⱡ LDO4pm

Lic ♨ CTV 8P ⌂

Credit card ① Ⓥ

GH *Naseby-Nye Hotel* Byron Rd, Boscombe ☎(0202) 34079 Boscombe & Southbourne plan **61** *C1*

13hc 3⇥ (4fb)

Lic ♨ CTV 10P nc5yrs sea

GH *Newfield Private Hotel* 29 Burnaby Rd, Alum Chine ☎(0202) 762724 Westbourne & Branksome plan **92** *B2*

Short distance from beach in Alum Chine area.

12hc 1⇥ 3⋔ (3fb) ✶

Lic ♨ CTV 5P

GH Norland Private Hotel 6 Westby Rd, Boscombe ☎(0202) 36729 Boscombe & Southbourne plan **61A** *C2*

Semi-detached gabled red-brick Victorian property adjacent to Boscombe Pier & shopping centre. Neat, well-appointed rooms.

9rm 8hc 1⇥ (5fb) ✶ ✻B&b£6–£8.50 Bdi£9–£12 W£57–£75 Ⱡ LDO4pm

Lic ♨ CTV 7P

GH Northover Private Hotel 10 Earle Rd, Alum Chine ☎(0202) 767349 Westbourne & Branksome plan **93** *B2*

Overlooking Alum Chine, 400 yds from sea.

12rm 7hc 5⋔ (4fb) Ⓡ B&b£8.95–£10.95 Bdi£12.95–£15.95 W£54.95–£65.95 Ⱡ LDO5pm

Lic ♨ CTV 10P

Ⓥ

GH Oak Hall Private Hotel 9 Wilfred Rd, Boscombe ☎(0202) 35062 Boscombe & Southbourne plan **62** *C2* Closed 8 Dec–14 Jan

Situated within easy reach of shops and Boscombe Pier and less than 5 minutes walk to Overcliff.

10hc (3fb) Ⓡ B&b£8.50–£9.50 Bdi£9.50–£14 W£58–£65 M LDO4pm

Lic ♨ CTV 6P nc6yrs

⊢⊣ **GH Penmone Hotel** 17 Carysfort Rd, Boscombe ☎(0202) 35903 Boscombe & Southbourne plan **63** *B2*

In residential area, close to shops.

9hc (5fb) B&b£6–£7.50 Bdi£8–£10.50 W£42–£52 Ⱡ

Lic CTV 12P ⌂

Credit cards ② ③ Ⓥ

GH *Pine Beach Hotel* 31 Boscombe Spa Rd, Boscombe ☎(0202) 35902 Boscombe & Southbourne plan **64** *B1* Closed Nov–Apr

Situated in a quiet, elevated position overlooking Boscombe Pier and the sea.

21hc (4fb) LDO6pm

Lic CTV 17P nc4yrs sea

Ⓥ

GH Ravenstone Hotel 36 Burnaby Rd, Alum Chine ☎(0202) 761047 Westbourne & Branksome plan **94A** *B2*

Detached villa property adjacent to Alum Chine and beach.

11hc (5fb) Ⓡ ✻B&b£8–£11.50 Bdi£11.50–£15 W£75–£102 Ⱡ LDO6.30pm

Lic ♨ CTV 9P

⊢⊣ **GH Hotel Restormel** Upper Terrace Rd ☎(0202) 25070 Central plan **19** *B2*

Centrally located for the theatre and shops.

18rm 16hc 1⇥ 1⋔ (2fb) CTV in 8 bedrooms B&b£7.50–£12.50 Bdi£12–£17 W£52.50–£87.50 Ⱡ LDO7pm

Lic ♨ CTV 8P ♿

Credit cards ① ② ③ ④ ⑤ Ⓥ

GH St John's Lodge Hotel 10 St Swithun's Rd ☎(0202) 290677 Boscombe & Southbourne plan **65** *A2* Closed Xmas

Close to shops and within walking distance of the Chine and pier.

18hc (3fb) Ⓡ B&b£9.20–£12.65 Bdi£11.50–£14.95 W£76–£96.60 Ⱡ LDO6.30pm

Lic CTV 14P solarium

Credit card ②

Bournemouth

⊢⊣ **GH St Ronans Hotel** 64–66 Frances Rd ☎(0202) 23535 Boscombe & Southbourne plan **66** *A2*
Closed Oct
Located in quiet area overlooking Knyveton Gardens.
14hc (7fb) Ⓡ B&b£7.28–£11.66 Bdi£10.20–£14.58 W£50.96–£81.62 M (W only Jun–Aug) LDO5pm
Lic ▥ CTV 8P

GH *St Wilfreds Private Hotel* 15 Walpole Rd, Boscombe ☎(0202) 36189 Boscombe & Southbourne plan **67** *B3*
Near the shops and within walking distance of the Chine and sea.
7hc (4fb) ★ LDO6pm
CTV 6P ⌂

GH Safari Hotel 91 St Michaels Rd, West Cliff ☎(0202) 290782 Central plan **19A** *C1*
end Mar–Oct
Welcoming guesthouse with attractive, very comfortable accommodation and well appointed public rooms.
16rm 1hc 6➡ 9⋒ (7fb) ★ B&b£12–£16
Lic ▥ CTV 16P nc6yrs

GH *Sandelheath Hotel* 1 Knyveton Rd, East Cliff ☎(0202) 25428 Boscombe & Southbourne Plan **68** *A2*
Situated in a pine clad avenue in a quiet area of Lansdowne.
15hc (5fb) ★ Ⓡ LDO7pm
Lic ▥ CTV 12P
Ⓥ

GH Sea-Dene 10 Burnaby Rd, Alum Chine ☎(0202) 761372 Westbourne Branksome plan **96** *B2*
Mar–Nov
7rm 3hc 4⋒ (3fb) Ⓡ B&b£9.50–£12.50 Bdi£13–£17 W£70–£98 M LDO7.30pm
Lic ▥ CTV 4P nc5yrs

GH Sea Shells 201–205 Holdenhurst Rd ☎(0202) 292542 Boscombe & Southbourne plan **69** *A3*
Closed 24 Dec–Jan
Located near to shops on main road.
12hc (5fb) CTV in 1 bedroom TV in 4 bedrooms Ⓡ ✱B&b£8.65–£9.80 W£55–£9.80 M
CTV 25P
Credit cards 1 3 Ⓥ

GH Sea View Court Hotel 14 Boscombe Spa Rd ☎(0202) 37197 Boscombe & Southbourne plan **71** *B1*
Mar–Oct
Close to Boscombe Pier and Chine and in a quiet position.
20hc 3➡ 6⋒ (8fb) Ⓡ ✱B&b£6–£9.50 Bdi£9–£12.50 W£40–£58 M LDO6pm
Lic ▥ CTV 25P

GH Sherbourne Hotel 6 Walpole Rd, Boscombe ☎(0202) 36222 Boscombe & Southbourne plan **71A** *B2*
Detached red brick corner property adjacent to shopping area.
10hc (5fb) ★ ✱B&b£5.50–£8.50 Bdi£8.50–£11.50 W£37–£59 M LDO5.30pm
Lic CTV 10P
Credit cards 1 3

GH Silver Trees Hotel 57 Wimborne Rd ☎(0202) 26040 Central plan **20** *F4*
A modernised, late Victorian house standing in its own grounds and offering comfortable accommodation.
9rm 5hc 4⋒ (2fb) CTV in 5 bedrooms TV in 4 bedrooms B&b£11–£12.50 Bdi£16–£17.50 W£80–£110 L LDO5pm
▥ 12P nc5yrs
Credit cards 1 2 3 5

GH Hotel Sorrento 16 Owls Rd, **Boscombe** ☎(0202) 34019 Boscombe & Southbourne plan **72** *C2*
30 Mar–Oct
A comfortable and friendly hotel situated in the Alum Chine area.
19rm 15hc 4⋒ (4fb) Ⓡ B&b£8.62–£13 Bdi£11.50–£17 W£51.75–£78 M LDO6pm
Lic CTV 16P

GH Hotel Sorrento 8 Studland Rd, **Alum Chine** Westbourne ☎(0202) 762116 Westbourne & Branksome plan **98** *B2*
Closed Nov
The resident proprietors offer a friendly atmosphere and good cuisine.
19rm 12➡ 7⋒ (3fb) Ⓡ B&b£10–£12 Bdi£15–£17 W£103–£115 L LDO5.30pm
Lic ▥ CTV 12P nc5yrs
Ⓥ

GH Stratford Hotel 20 Grand Av, Southbourne ☎(0202) 424726 Boscombe & Southbourne plan **74** *E2*
13hc (7fb) ✱B&b£6.50–£9.50 Bdi£8.50–£13 W£38.50–£64 M S%
LDO6pm
Lic ▥ CTV 8P

GH Tower House Hotel West Cliff Gdns ☎(0202) 290742 Central plan **21** *B1*
Apr–Oct & Xmas
A quiet, friendly hotel near to West Cliff Lawns.
34rm 15hc 19➡ (15fb) Ⓡ B&b£11–£13 Bdi£11.50–£17 W£72.50–£114 L LDO6.30pm
Lic lift ▥ CTV 36P nc5yrs

⊢⊣ **GH Tree Tops Hotel** 16 Grand Av, West Southbourne ☎(0202) 426933 Boscombe & Southbourne plan **75** *E2*
Etr–Oct
Situated close to the shops and cliff top.
14hc (4fb) CTV in 7 bedrooms TV in 7 bedrooms Ⓡ B&b£8–£10.50 Bdi£10.68–£14 W£74.75–£98 L (W only Jul & Aug) LDO5pm
Lic ▥ CTV 12P
Credit cards 1 3 Ⓥ

GH Trent Private Hotel 16 Studland Rd ☎(0202) 761088 Wesbourne & Branksome plan **99** *B2*
Etr–Oct
12rm 6hc 6⋒ (3fb) ★ Ⓡ B&b£9.50–£12 Bdi£14.50–£17 W£60–£75 L LDO6.15pm
Lic CTV 10P nc4yrs

GH Tudor Grange Hotel 31 Gervis Rd ☎(0202) 291472 Central plan **22** *F3*

Centrally located mock Tudor house with neat grounds.

12rm 11hc 1➡ (5fb) B&b£10–£13.50 Bdi£14–£18 W£86–£115 Ⱡ LDO7pm

Lic ⅢⅢ CTV 8P

Bournemouth

⊢⊣ **GH Valberg Hotel** 1A Wollstonecraft Rd, Boscombe ☎(0202) 34644 Boscombe & Southbourne plan **76** *C1*
Closd Xmas

A comfortable, modern hotel in a quiet location near the gardens.

10⋒ (2fb) ✻ Ⓡ B&b£6.50–£9 W£39–£57 M (W only mid Jun–mid Sep)

ⅢⅢ CTV 8P nc5yrs

⊢⊣ **GH Vine** 22 Southern Rd, Southbourne ☎(0202) 428309
Boscombe & Southbourne plan **76A** *E2*
Closed New Year

8rm 2hc 6⋒ (1fb) B&b£8–£12 Bdi£12–£15 W£70–£86 Ⱡ

Lic ⅢⅢ CTV 8P

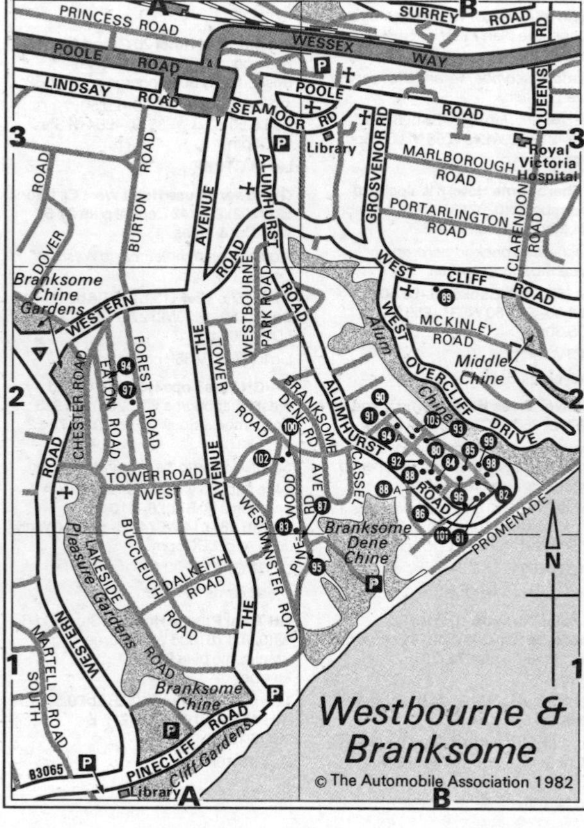

Westbourne & Branksome Plan

80 Alum Bay Hotel
81 Alumcliff Hotel
82 Alum Grange Hotel
83 Avalon Private Hotel (*Listed under Poole*)
84 Bay Tree Hotel
85 Chineside Private Hotel
86 Cliff House Hotel
87 Dene Hotel (*Listed under Poole*)
88 Earlham Lodge
88A Golden Sands Hotel
89 Gordons Hotel
90 Holmcroft Hotel
91 Mount Lodge Hotel
92 Newfield Private Hotel
93 Northover Private Hotel
94 Ormonde House Hotel (*Listed under Poole*)
94A Ravenstone Hotel
95 Redcroft Private Hotel (*Listed under Poole*)
96 Sea Dene
97 Sheldon Lodge (*Listed under Poole*)
98 Hotel Sorrento
99 Trent Private Hotel
100 Twin Cedars Hotel (*Listed under Poole*)
101 West Dene Private Hotel
102 Westminster Cottage Hotel (*Listed under Poole*)
103 Woodford Court Hotel

GH Waldale 37–39 Boscombe Spa Rd ☎(0202) 37744 Boscombe & Southbourne plan **77** *B1*
Mar–Oct
20rm 12hc 8⇌ (4fb) Ⓡ B&b£10–£15.50 Bdi£13–£19.63 W£60–£90 M (W only Jun–Aug) LDO7pm
Lic 🍽 CTV 17P 4🚗 nc7yrs

⊢⊣ **GH Wenmaur House Hotel** 14 Carysfort Rd, Boscombe ☎(0202) 35081 Boscombe & Southbourne plan **78** *B2*
Closed New Year
Enjoying quiet location near to Boscombe shops.
12hc (7fb) ✱ B&b£7–£8.50 Bdi£10.50–£12 W£65–£80 Ł (W only 14 Jul–30 Aug) LDOnoon
Lic 🍽 CTV 10P 🏠

GH *West Dene Private Hotel* 117 Alumhurst Rd, Westbourne ☎(0202) 764843
Etr–Oct
Not on plan
Overlooking sea at foot of Alum Chine.
17hc 5⇌ 2⋒ (4fb) ✱
CTV 20P sea

⊢⊣ **GH West Leigh Hotel** 26 West Hill Rd ☎(0202) 292195 Central plan **24** *B1*
31rm 20⇌ 8⋒ (8fb) CTV in 3 bedrooms B&b£7–£14 Bdi£11–£18 W£45–£95 Ł (W only Jul–Oct) LDO7.15pm
Lic lift CTV 30P 🏠 ≋ (heated)
Credit cards 1 2 3 5

GH Witley Court Hotel West Cliff Gdns ☎(0202) 21302 Central plan **25** *B1*
Closed 10 Nov–15 Dec
Situated in the West Cliff area enjoying ideal location for shops and sea.
15rm 2⋒ (6fb) B&b£9–£11.50 Bdi£13–£15.50 W£65–£95 Ł LDO4pm
Lic 🍽 CTV 12P

GH Windsor Court Hotel 32 Bodorgan Rd ☎(0202) 24637 Central plan **26** *C4*
Occupying quiet location, ideal for shops and sea.
40rm 20hc 20⇌ (15fb) CTV in 30 bedrooms B&b£9–£14 Bdi£11–£16.50 W£60–£110 Ł LDO7pm
Lic 🍽 CTV 24P ≋ (heated)

⊢⊣ **GH Woodford Court Hotel** 19–21 Studland Rd, Alum Chine ☎(0202) 764907 Westbourne & Branksome plan **103** *B2*
Apr–Nov
Overlooking Alum Chine enjoying a quiet location near beach.
23rm 12hc 3⇌ 12⋒ (7fb) Ⓡ B&b£8–£12 Bdi£10.50–£15 W£56–£84 M LDO6pm
Lic 🍽 CTV 14P nc2yrs
Credit card 1 Ⓥ

GH *Wood Lodge Hotel* 10 Manor Rd, East Cliff ☎(0202) 290891 Boscombe & Southbourne plan **79** *A1*

Bournemouth — Braunton

Etr–Oct
16hc 2⇌ 6⋒ (3fb)
Lic 🍽 CTV 12P

⊢⊣ **GH Woodside Private Hotel** 29 Southern Rd, Southbourne ☎(0202) 427213 Boscombe & Southbourne plan **79A** *E2*
Apr–Oct
11hc ✱ B&b£7–£8.50 Bdi£10.50–£12.50 W£70–£85 Ł
Lic 🍽 CTV 5P nc12yrs
Credit cards 3 Ⓥ

BOURTON-ON-THE-WATER
Gloucestershire
Map **4** SP12

GH Southlands Hotel Rissington Rd ☎(0451) 20724
Closed 18 Dec–14 Jan rs 15 Jan–Apr
7hc 5⇌ 1⋒ (1fb) CTV in all bedrooms ✱ Ⓡ ✻B&b£8.50–£12.50 Bdi£14–£18 LDO7pm
Lic 🍽 CTV 7P nc6yrs

INN Mousetrap ☎(0451) 20579
Small inn on the outskirts of this attractive village.
3hc TV in all bedrooms Ⓡ B&b£12–£13.25 Bdi£21–£22.50 W£140 Ł Bar lunch £2.50alc D9pm £7alc
🍽 11P nc14yrs

BOVEY TRACEY
Devon
Map **3** SX87

FH Mrs H Roberts **Willmead** *(SX795812)* ☎Lustleigh (06477) 214
Closed Xmas & New Year
Farmhouse dating from 1327 and situated on the edge of Dartmoor National Park in a delightful valley.
3hc B&b£12 W£84 M
🍽 CTV 10P nc10yrs 32acres beef

BOW
Devon
Map **3** SS70

FH Mrs V Hill **East Hillerton House** *(SX725981)* Spreyton ☎(03633) 393
Closed Xmas
The farm is located 2m NE of Spreyton village.
3hc ✱ ✻B&b£6–£7 Bdifr£11 LDO8pm
🍽 CTV P 🎾 180acres arable beef sheep mixed
Ⓥ

BOWNESS-ON-WINDERMERE
Cumbria
Map **7** SD49

Guesthouses are listed under Windermere

BRADFORD
West Yorkshire
Map **7** SE13

GH Belvedere Hotel 19 North Park Rd, Manningham ☎(0274) 492559
13rm 10hc (1fb) CTV in 6 bedrooms Ⓡ B&b£15 Bdi£22 LDO7.15pm
Lic 🍽 CTV 10P nc5yrs
Credit card 1

GH Maple Hill 3 Park Dr, Heaton ☎(0274) 44061
Large, comfortable Victorian house with many original features.
10hc (1fb) CTV in all bedrooms ✱ B&b£10.50–£11.50 Bdi£15–£16 W£100–£107 M LDO9pm
🍽 CTV 12P 4🚗 nc5yrs
Ⓥ

BRADNINCH
Devon
Map **3** SS90

FH Mrs E J Yendell ***Poundapitt*** *(ST001024)* Hele (adjacent to B3181) ☎Exeter (0392) 881282
3hc (1fb) Ⓡ LDO5pm
🍽 CTV 5P 🏠 172acres dairy

BRAEMAR
Grampian *Aberdeenshire*
Map **15** NO19

GH *Braemar Lodge Hotel* ☎(03383) 617
Jun–Sep
8hc (2fb) LDO6pm
Lic 🍽 CTV 8P

GH Callater Lodge Hotel ☎(03383) 275
26 Dec–mid Oct
Small friendly hotel set in own grounds with hill views.
9hc (1fb) B&b£11.10 Bdi£18.60 W£124.50 Ł LDO8pm
Lic 🍽 CTV 20P

BRANSCOMBE
Devon
Map **3** SY18

GH The Bulstone ☎(029780) 446
6hc (4fb) ✻B&b£8–£9.50 Bdi£14.50–£16 W£89–£99 Ł LDO6pm
Lic 🍽 CTV 12P 🏠

BRAUNTON
Devon
Map **2** SS43

GH *Brookdale Hotel* 62 South St ☎(0271) 812075
Victorian double fronted house in narrow street 50yds from village.
9hc (3fb) ✱ LDO5pm
Lic 🍽 CTV 14P 1🚗 🏠
Ⓥ

⊢⊣ **FH** Mr & Mrs Barnes **Denham Farm Holidays** *(SS480404)* North Buckland ☎Croyde (0271) 890297
Closed Dec →

Large farmhouse, parts of which date from the 18th century, set in lovely countryside, 2 miles from Croyde and within easy reach of Barnstaple and Ilfracombe.

8hc (5fb) ✱ B&b£7–£8 B&di£12–£14 W£80–£85 ⱡ (W only last 2wks Jul–1st wk Sep) LDO4pm

Lic CTV 7 🚘 160acres beef

BRECHIN
Tayside
Map **15** NO56

FH Mrs M Stewart **Blibberhill** *(NO553568)* (5m WSW off B9134)
☎Aberlemno (030783) 225

Spacious, well-appointed farmhouse in peaceful surroundings.

3rm 2hc 1➡ ✱ *B&bfr£6.50 Bdifr£10.50

▥ CTV 3P 300acres arable beef mixed
Ⓥ

⊢⊣ **FH** Mrs J Stewart **Wood of Auldbar** *(NO554556)* Aberlemno ☎Aberlemno (030783) 218

Fairly large farmhouse well back from road amidst wooded land, 5m SW on unclassified road, between B9134 and A932.

3rm (1fb) ✱ B&bfr£6.50 Bdifr£9.50

▥ TV 4P 187acres arable mixed
Ⓥ

BREDE
East Sussex
Map **5** TQ81

GH ***Roselands Private Hotel***
☎(0424) 882338
15 Jan–15 Dec

Peaceful and secluded house in 7 acres of land with scenic views.

16hc (2fb) Ⓡ LDO6pm

▥ CTV 10P

BREDWARDINE
Hereford & Worcester
Map **3** SO34

GH Bredwardine Hall
☎Moccas (09817) 596
Apr–Nov

An early 19th-century manor-house set in mature gardens offering elegant accommodation in a quiet and tranquil village setting.

5rm 3➡ (2fb) ✱ Ⓡ *B&b£9–£10 Bdi£14–£15 W£88–£95 ⱡ LDO6.30pm

▥ CTV 6P nc10yrs

BRENCHLEY
Kent
Map **5** TQ64

INN Rose & Crown High St
☎(089272) 2107
Closed Xmas

A historic 16th-century road-side inn, complemented by a well managed restaurant, good standards of cooking, and friendly and efficient service.

3➡ CTV in 2 bedrooms TV in 1 bedroom B&b£15 Bdi£23 L£6.95–£12&alc D9pm £8.95–£13&alc

▥ 13P 🚗

Credit cards 1 3 5 Ⓥ

BRENDON
Devon
Map **3** SS74

FH Mrs C A South ***Farley Water*** *(SS744464)* ☎(05987) 272
May–Oct

Comfortable farmhouse adjoining the moors. Good home cooking and freedom for children.

5rm 4hc (2fb)

CTV P 223acres beef sheep

BRENT ELEIGH
Suffolk
Map **5** TL94

FH Mrs J P Gage **Street** *(TL945476)*
☎Lavenham (0787) 247271
Apr–Oct

A most beautiful period house, tastefully furnished to a high standard.

2hc ✱ B&bfr£9.50

▥ CTV P nc14yrs 142acres arable
Ⓥ

BRIDESTOWE
Devon
Map **2** SX58

FH Mrs M A Down **Little Bidlake** *(SX494887)* ☎(083786) 233
May–Sep

Neat, clean and efficient farmhouse adjacent to A30 between Bridestowe and Launceston.

2hc ✱ LDOnoon

▥ CTV P 🚘 ♪ 150acres beef dairy
Ⓥ

FH Mrs M A Ponsford **Stone** *(SX503890)*
☎(083786) 253
mid May–mid Sep

Large Victorian farmhouse with gardens and fishing lake at rear.

6hc (2fb) ✱ *B&b£8 Bdi£11 W£70 ⱡ LDO5pm

▥ CTV 6P ♪ billiards 260acres beef sheep mixed

⊢⊣ **FH** Mrs J Northcott **Town** *(SX504905)* ☎(083786) 226
May–Oct

Tile-hung farmhouse, with a pleasant homely atmosphere.

3hc Ⓡ B&b£6.50–£8 Bdi£10–£12 W£70 ⱡ LDO6pm

▥ CTV 3P 150acres dairy
Ⓥ

FH Mrs M Hockridge ***Week*** *(SX519913)*
☎(083786) 221

Attractive red brick farmhouse in pleasant countryside.

6hc (4fb) LDO4pm

CTV ▥ 10P 163acres dairy mixed sheep

See advertisement on page 261

BRIDGERULE
Devon
Map **2** SS20

⊢⊣ **FH** Mrs S A Gardener **Buttsbeer Cross** *(SS266043)* ☎(028881) 210
May–Sep →

Modernised farmhouse dating from 15th century. Within easy reach of Bude and North Cornish coast.
3rm 2hc ★ B&b£6.50–£6.75 Bdi£9–£9.25 W£65 ⱡ LDO3pm
CTV 3P nc6yrs 230acres mixed

BRIDGNORTH
Shropshire
Map **7** SO79

GH Croft Hotel St Mary's Street
☎(07462) 2416
Lovely 18th-century house, tastefully preserved and modernised.
7rm 4hc 1⟶ 2⋒ (2fb) B&b£11–£14 Bdi£14.95–£17.95 W£86–£101.50 ⱡ LDO7.30pm
Lic ▥ CTV
Credit cards 1 3

GH Severn Arms Hotel Underhill St
☎(07462) 4616
Closed Xmas wk
11rm (5fb) B&b£10–£12 Bdi£15–£16 W£66–£80 Ⓜ LDO7pm
Lic ▥ CTV
Ⓥ

INN *Ball Hotel* East Castle St ☎(07462) 2478
6hc CTV in 2 bedrooms TV in 1 bedroom ★ D9.30pm
▥ 11P ⇎

INN King's Head Hotel Whitburn St
☎(07462) 2141
An authentic 17th-century coaching inn close to town centre.
5hc CTV in 2 bedrooms ★ Ⓡ B&b£10–£11 L£2–£5 D10pm £2–£5
8P ⇎
Credit card 3

BRIDLINGTON
Humberside
Map **8** TA16

GH Langdon Hotel Pembroke Ter
☎(0262) 73065
Jan–Oct & Xmas rs Nov & Dec
Comfortable hotel with smart, cosy lounge and sea views.
21rm 12hc 9⋒ (6fb) TV in 6 bedrooms ★ B&b£9.50–£11.50 Bdi£13.50–£17 W£60–£70 ⱡ LDO7pm
Lic ▥ CTV

GH *Shirley Private Hotel* 47–48 South Marine Dr ☎(0262) 72539
Apr–Oct
Comfortable, well furnished guesthouse with spacious lounge and attractive dining room.
39hc 1⟶ 6⋒ (10fb) CTV available in bedrooms LDO10.45pm
Lic lift CTV 5P sea
Ⓥ

GH Southdowne Hotel South Marine Dr
☎(0262) 73270
10hc (3fb) ★ Ⓡ B&b£10.35–£10.93 Bdi£12.65–£13.23 W£72.45–£76.51 ⱡ LDO6pm
Lic ▥ CTV 10P
Credit card 3 Ⓥ

BRIDPORT
Dorset
Map **3** SY49

GH Britmead House 154 West Bay Rd (Guestaccom) ☎(0308) 22941
Between Bridport and West Bay harbour.
8rm 5hc 3⟶ (2fb) TV in all bedrooms Ⓡ B&b£10.50 Bdi£16 W£101.50 ⱡ LDO6pm
Lic ▥ CTV 8P nc5yrs
Credit cards 1 3 Ⓥ

GH Roundham House Hotel West Bay Rd ☎(0308) 22753
Country type residence in elevated position off Bridport to West Bay road.
9rm 4hc 2⟶ 3⋒ (3fb) CTV in 3 bedrooms TV in 1 bedroom B&b£11.50–£13.50 Bdi£17.35–£19.35 W£99–£112 ⱡ LDO9pm →

Lic 🏨 CTV 14P
Credit card 1 Ⓥ

INN King Charles Tavern 114 St Andrews Rd ☎(0308) 22911

Situated a short distance from the town centre alongside the Beaminster to Yeovil road.

4hc TV in 2 bedrooms ✱ Ⓡ
*B&b£8.50–£10 Bdi£12–£14.50 W£50–£70 M L£1.50–£5 D9pm £2–£6
CTV 6P 2🚗

Bridport — Brighton & Hove

BRIGHTON & HOVE
East Sussex
Map **4** TQ30
See plan.
See also Rottingdean and Saltdean

GH Adelaide Hotel 51 Regency Sq ☎(0273) 24987 Plan **1** *B1*
Closed 1st 2 wks Dec & last 2 wks Jan

11rm 1→ 10⋒ (1fb) CTV in all bedrooms ✱ Ⓡ B&di£17.50–£19.50 W £110–£122.90 M
Lic 🏨 ⊁
Credit cards 1 2 3 5

GH Ascott House 21 New Steine, Marine Pde ☎(0273) 688085
Plan **1A** *E2*
Closed Xmas

Small Victorian guesthouse run by friendly proprietors, only a short walk from shops and sea front.

10hc (3fb) B&b£8.50–£10.50 W£56–£63 M
🏨 CTV ⊁ nc10yrs

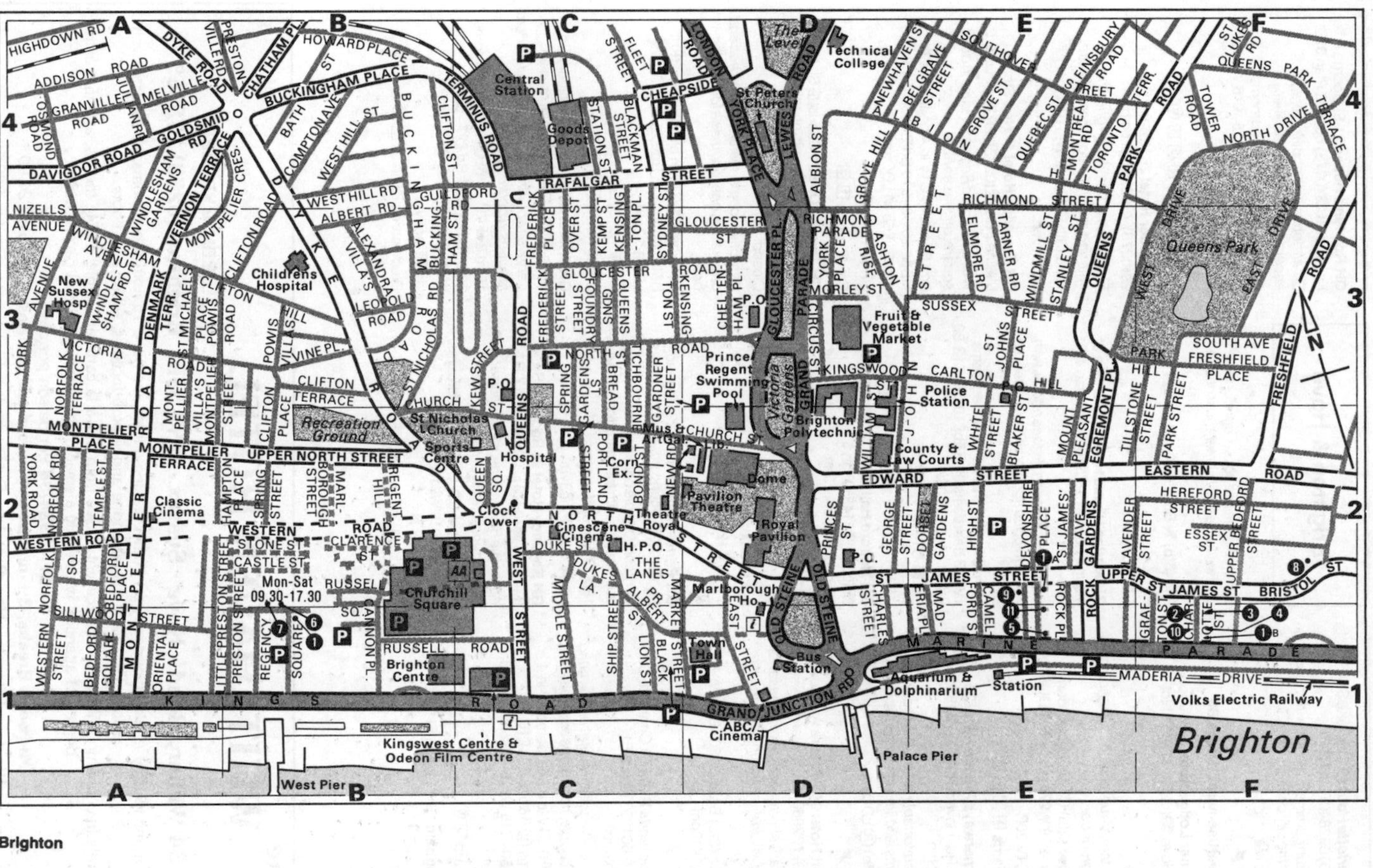

Brighton

1 Adelaide Hotel
1A Ascott House
1B Charlotte House
2 Downlands Hotel
3 Langham
4 Marina House Hotel
5 Melford Hall Hotel
6 Prince Regent Hotel
7 Regency Hotel
8 Rowland House
9 Trouville
10 Twenty-One

Brighton & Hove

GH *Charlotte House* 9 Charlotte St ☎(0273) 692849 Plan **1B** *F1*

Family-run commercial hotel within easy reach of the city centre.

8rm 4hc 4fl (1fb)

CTV

See advertisement on page 86

GH Corner Lodge Hotel 33 Wilbury Gdns, Hove ☎(0273) 775931 Not on plan
rs Xmas

A small, family-run residence, standing in its own grounds.

15hc 10→ (2fb) CTV in all bedrooms B&b£14–£18 W£74–£119 M LDO6pm

Lic CTV 20P

Credit cards 1 2 3 5

GH *Cornerways Private Hotel* 20 Caburn Rd, Hove ☎(0273) 731882 Not on plan

Small comfortable house with modern bedrooms and limited lounge facilities.

10hc (2fb) Ⓡ LDO4pm

Lic CTV

GH Croft Hotel 24 Palmeira Av, Hove ☎(0273) 732860 Not on plan

Well established guesthouse, pleasantly situated within easy walking distance to the beach.

11rm 9hc (3fb) B&b£10.50–£12 W£70–£80 M LDO8pm

Lic CTV

GH Downlands Hotel 19 Charlotte St ☎(0273) 601203 Plan **2** *F1*
Closed Xmas

A five storey Victorian house run by young friendly couple, near shops and sea front.

10hc (2fb) CTV in 6 bedrooms TV in 4 bedrooms Ⓡ B&b£8.50–£10 Bdi£13.50–£15 W£56–£62 M LDO10am

CTV

Credit card 3 Ⓥ

GH Langham 16 Charlotte St ☎(0273) 682843 Plan **3** *F1*
Closed Dec

Victorian terraced house, comfortable and well run establishment, just off sea front.

9hc (3fb) B&b£8.50–£9 Bdi£14 W£60 M

CTV nc7yrs

GH Marina House Hotel 8 Charlotte St, Marine Pde ☎(0273) 605349 Plan **4** *F1*
Feb–Nov

Five storey terraced Victorian hotel, with well equipped accommodation, near sea front.

10rm 3hc 4fl (3fb) CTV in 7 bedrooms TV in 3 bedrooms Ⓡ B&b£10.35–£13.80 W£69.45–£93.60 M

Lic CTV

Ⓥ

GH Melford Hall Hotel 41 Marine Pde ☎(0273) 681435 Plan **5** *E1*
Closed 24 Dec–2 Jan

Situated on sea front with well appointed accommodation.

12rm 6hc (5fb) CTV in 11 bedrooms TV in 1 bedroom B&b£13–£14

Lic CTV 12P

Ⓥ

GH *Prince Regent Hotel* 29 Regency Sq ☎(0273) 29962 Plan **6** *B1*

Very comfortable commercial guesthouse, with friendly attentive family.

18fl CTV in all bedrooms

Lic CTV nc3yrs

GH Regency Hotel 28 Regency Sq (Minotel) ☎(0273) 202690 Plan **7** *B1*

Attractive Regency house offering charm, comfort and attentive management.

14rm 4hc 1→ 9fl CTV in all bedrooms Ⓡ B&b£18 W£108 M

Lic CTV

Credit cards 1 2 3 5

GH Rowland House 21 St George's Ter, Kemptown ☎(0273) 603639 Plan **8** *F2*

Small house with above average accommodation and facilities.

10hc (1fb) CTV in all bedrooms Ⓡ B&b£10–£11 Bdi£15.75–£16.75 W£70–£77 M LDO5pm

Lic CTV 1P nc9yrs

Credit cards 1 2 3 5 Ⓥ

GH Tatler Hotel 26 Holland Rd, ☎(0273) 736698 Not on plan

Five storeyed family-run guesthouse catering mainly for commercial trade.

12hc (3fb) B&b£12 W£70 M

Lic CTV

GH Trouville Hotel 11 New Steine, Marine Pde ☎(0273) 697384 Plan **9** *E2*

Well appointed Regency house in quiet square, off the sea front.

9rm 5hc (2fb) CTV in 4 bedrooms *B&b£8.50–£10 Bdi£13.50–£15 W£55–£65 M LDOam

Lic CTV

Credit cards 1 3

GH Twenty One 21 Charlotte St, Marine Pde (Guestaccom) ☎(0273) 686450 Plan **10** *F1*
Closed Jan

Attractive rooms, tastefully furnished and decorated, one room has a fourposter bed.

6rm 2hc 4fl CTV in all bedrooms Ⓡ B&b£11.50–£15 Bdi£23–£26.50 S% LDO8.30pm

Lic nc12yrs

Credit cards 1 2 3 5

GH Whitehaven Hotel 34 Wilbury Rd, Hove ☎(0273) 778355 Not on plan

Very well appointed house with all modern facilities in bedrooms.

15rm 8→ 7fl (1fb) CTV in all bedrooms Ⓡ B&b£20–£21 Bdi£27–£28 W£112–£126 L LDO8.30pm

Lic nc8yrs

Credit cards 1 2 3 5 Ⓥ

BRIGSTEER *(Near Kendal)*
Cumbria
Map **7** SD48

⊢⊣ **FH** Mrs E A Gardner **Barrowfield** *(SD484908)* ☎Crosthwaite (04488) 336
Apr–Oct
Comfortable Elizabethan farmhouse surrounded by beautiful walks and lake and sea views. 1½m N unclass road.
3rm 2hc (1fb) ✱ B&b£7 W£49 M
▥ CTV 3P 180acres dairy sheep
Ⓥ

BRISTOL
Avon
Map **3** ST57
See Plan on pages 90–91

GH Alandale Hotel Tyndall's Park Rd, Clifton ☎(0272) 735407 Plan **1** *C4*
Closed Xmas
Comfortable hotel within easy reach of the city centre.
15rm 10hc 5⇌ (1fb) CTV in all bedrooms Ⓡ B&b£10–£14 W£70–£98 M
Lic ▥ 10P
Ⓥ

GH Alcove 508–510 Fishponds Rd, Fishponds ☎(0272) 653886 Plan **2** *F4*
10hc (3fb) CTV in all bedrooms ✱ Ⓡ *B&b£9 Bdi£12 W£56 M LDO6.30pm
Lic ▥ 8P 1⌂

Brigsteer — Bristol

GH Birkdale Hotel 11 Ashgrove Rd, Redland ☎(0272) 733635 Plan **4** *C5*
Closed Xmas
Commercial hotel off Whiteladies Road.
18rm 3⇌ 5⋔ (2fb) CTV in all bedrooms Ⓡ B&b£17.20 Bdi£21.95 LDO8pm
Lic ▥ 15P billiards
Credit card ③

GH Cavendish House Hotel
18 Cavendish Rd, Henleaze ☎(0272) 621017 Plan **6** *C5*
Pleasant small proprietor run hotel.
8hc (3fb) B&b£12
▥ CTV 5P
Credit card ③ Ⓥ

GH Chesterfield Hotel 3 Westbourne Pl, Clifton ☎(0272) 734606 Plan **5** *B5*
Closed wknds & Xmas
Pleasant small commercial hotel convenient to Clifton and local restaurants.
13hc B&bfr£10
▥ CTV ⊁

GH Glenroy Hotel 30 Victoria Sq, Clifton ☎(0272) 739058 Plan **8** *B3*
Closed Xmas wk
Pleasing private hotel in Clifton near to restaurants.
31rm 28hc 3⇌ (A 16⋔) (13fb) CTV in all bedrooms Ⓡ B&b£13.50 W£94.50 M
Lic ▥ 15P
Ⓥ

GH Oakdene Hotel 45 Oakfield Rd, Clifton ☎(0272) 735900 Plan **9** *B/C4*
Small, proprietor run hotel.
14hc (1fb) CTV in all bedrooms ✱ Ⓡ *B&b£12.65
▥ ⊁

GH Oakfield Hotel 52–54 Oakfield Rd, Clifton ☎(0272) 735556 Plan **10** *C4*
Closed 24–31 Dec
Proprietor run private hotel.
27hc (4fb) B&b£12–£12.50 Bdi£16–£17 Wfr£75 M LDO6.45pm
▥ CTV 10P 2⌂
See advertisement on page 92

GH Pembroke Hotel 13 Arlington Villas, Clifton ☎(0272) 735550 Plan **11** *B4*
Closed Sat, Sun & Xmas
Pleasant small commercial hotel.
13hc (2fb) B&bfr£10
▥ CTV 10P
Credit cards ① ③

GH Rodney Hotel 4 Rodney Pl, Clifton Down Rd ☎(0272) 735422 Plan **12** *A3*
Closed Xmas & New Year

In Clifton village near to restaurants.

25hc (4fb) ✱ B&b£13.50

CTV

GH Seeleys Hotel 19–27 St Pauls Rd, Clifton (Minotel) ☎(0272) 738544
Plan **13** *C4*
Closed Xmas wk

Bristol

Lively hotel conveniently situated for city centre.

40rm 9→ 17ffi (A 20rm 6→ 3ffi) (22fb)
CTV in all bedrooms ✱ Ⓡ B&b£11.50–£13.50 Bdi£16.75–£18.75

LDO10.30pm

Lic 12P 18

Credit cards 1 2 3

GH Washington Hotel 11–15 St Pauls Rd, Clifton ☎(0272) 733980 Plan **14** *C4*

Pleasant small hotel.

32rm 28hc 4ffi (3fb)

CTV 13P

Credit cards 1 3

GH Westbury Park Hotel 37 Westbury Rd, Westbury-on-Trym ☎(0272) 620465 Plan **15** *C5*

Small comfortable hotel adjoining downland, with relaxed atmosphere and offering interesting home-made dishes.

9rm 6hc 2⇨ 1⋒ CTV in all bedrooms B&b£12.50–£20 Bdi£18.50–£26 LDO 8.45pm

Lic ⊞ 6P

BRIXHAM
Devon
Map **3** SX95
See Plan on page 92

GH *Cottage Hotel* Mount Pleasant Rd ☎(08045) 2123 Plan **1** *B2*

8hc (3fb) ✶

Lic ⊞ CTV 5P nc2yrs sea

Ⓥ

GH *Harbour View Hotel* King St ☎(08045) 3052 Plan **2** *C2*
Closed Xmas

10hc 1⋒ (2fb) CTV in 4 bedrooms TV in 6 bedrooms

CTV sea

⊢⊣ **GH *Pola*** 63–65 Berry Head Rd ☎(08045) 2019 Plan **3** *C2*

12hc (5fb) LDOnoon

CTV sea

GH Raddicombe Lodge
105 Kingswear Rd ☎(08045) 2125
Plan **4** *A1*

9hc (3fb) B&b£8.55–£10.50 Bdi£12.80–£15.85 W£89.60–£99.75 ⱡ LDO4.30pm

Lic CTV 10P

Credit cards 1 3 Ⓥ

See advertisement on page 93

GH Ranscambe House Hotel
Ranscambe Rd ☎(08045) 2337
Plan **5** *C2*

10hc 7⇨ 3⋒ (4fb) Ⓡ B&bfr£10 Bdifr£15 Wfr£96 ⱡ LDOnoon

Lic ⊞ CTV 14P

⊢⊣ **GH Sampford House** 57–59 King St ☎(08045) 7761 Plan **6** *C2*
Apr–Oct

6hc (4fb) ✶ B&b£7–£8 W£49–£56 M

CTV ✗

BROAD CHALKE
Wiltshire
Map **4** SU02

INN Queens Head ☎(072278) 344

4⇨ CTV in all bedrooms ✶ Ⓡ B&b£16.50–£37 L£7–£11.50&alc D9.30pm £7–£11.50&alc

⊞ CTV 40P ⚐ nc14yrs

Credit card 3

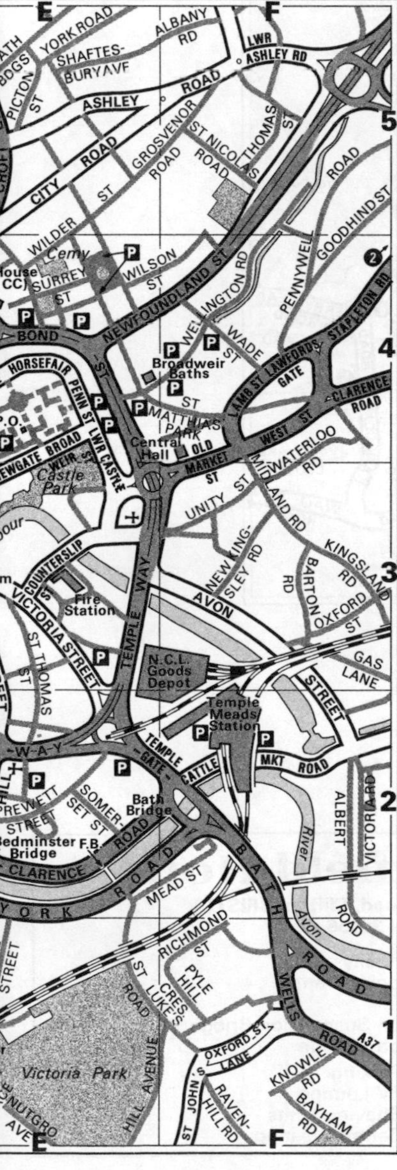

Bristol

1 Alandale Hotel
2 Alcove
4 Birkdale Hotel
5 Chesterfield Hotel
6 Cavendish House Hotel
8 Glenroy Hotel
9 Oakdene Hotel
10 Oakfield Hotel
11 Pembroke Hotel
12 Rodney Hotel
13 Seeleys Hotel
14 Washington Hotel
15 Westbury Park Hotel

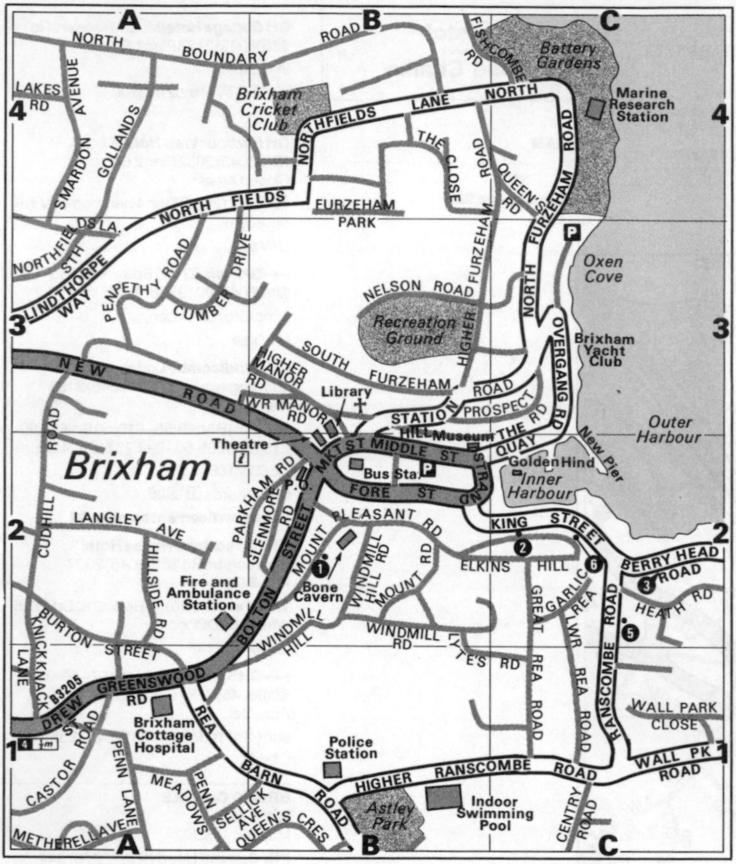

Brixham

1 Cottage Hotel
2 Harbour View Hotel
3 Pola
4 Raddicombe Lodge
5 Ranscambe House Hotel
6 Sampford House

BROADFORD
Isle of Skye, Highland *Inverness-shire*
Map **13** NG62

GH Hilton ☎(04712) 322
Apr–Oct
Two-storey bungalow with sea views.
8hc (2fb) B&b£7–£8.50 Bdi£12.75–£14.50 LDO6pm
Lic CTV 16P

BROAD HAVEN *(Near Haverfordwest)*
Dyfed
Map **2** SM81

GH Broad Haven Hotel ☎(043783) 366
Feb–Oct
Large, lively family hotel facing beach.
38rm 3hc 33 2 (12fb) CTV in all bedrooms Ⓡ B&b£9–£14 Bdi£15–£20 W£60–£90 S% LDO8.30pm
Lic CTV 100P (heated)
Credit cards 1 3

BROAD MARSTON
Hereford & Worcester
Map **4** SP14

GH *Broad Marston Manor* ☎Stratford-upon-Avon (0789) 750252
Closed Xmas
7hc 1
CTV 30P nc12yrs
Ⓥ

See advertisement on page 328

BROADSTAIRS
Kent
Map **5** TR36

GH Bay Tree Hotel 12 Eastern Esp ☎Thanet (0843) 62502
May–Sep rs Mar–Apr & Oct
Well run, comfortable hotel with spacious bedrooms and sea views.
9hc 1 (2fb) Ⓡ B&b£8.50–£10 Bdi£12.50–£14 W£55–£65 LDO4pm
Lic CTV 9P nc3yrs
Ⓥ

GH Dutch House Hotel 30 North Foreland Rd ☎Thanet (0843) 62824
Homely type house with simple accommodation. Overlooking the sea.
10hc B&b£8.50–£9.50 Bdi£14.50–£15.50 W£51–£58 LDO6.30pm
Lic CTV 6P

GH East Horndon Private Hotel
4 Eastern Esp ☎Thanet (0843) 68306
Well managed hotel with well equipped bedrooms most facing the sea, complemented by a good choice of home cooking, and friendly hospitable service.
10hc 2 2 (3fb) CTV in 2 bedrooms TV in 8 bedrooms Ⓡ B&b£12 Bdi£17 W£84 LDO7pm
Lic CTV
Credit cards 1 3 5

GH Keston Court Hotel
14 Ramsgate Rd ☎Thanet (0843) 62401
Simple and comfortable homely type accommodation, run by friendly Hungarian landlady.
9hc (3fb) Ⓡ B&b£8–£11 Bdi£12.50–£14.50 W£54–£66 LDO6pm
Lic CTV 5P nc2yrs
Ⓥ

GH Rothsay Private Hotel
110 Pierremont Av ☎Thanet (0843) 62646
Detached double fronted house with nicely appointed rooms and run by the proprietor and his wife.
14rm 9hc 5 (4fb) Ⓡ B&b£10–£12 Bdi£14.75–£16.75 W£88.50–£100.50
Lic CTV

GH St Augustines Hotel 19 Granville Rd ☎Thanet (0843) 65017
Cheerful and bright modern bedrooms complemented by small lounge with bar. Near the sea. →

15rm 11hc 4⋒ (5fb) TV in 13 bedrooms Ⓡ B&b£10 Bdi£16 W£78–£86 Ⱡ LDO7pm
Lic 🔥 1P
Credit cards 1 3 Ⓥ

⊢⊣ **GH Seapoint Private Hotel**
76 Westcliff Rd ☎Thanet (0843) 62269
May–Sep
Hotel offering well decorated and comfortable accommodation, run by friendly, helpful resident proprietors.
9hc (4fb) TV in 6 bedrooms B&b£7.50–£9 Bdi£11–£13 W£48–£52 Ⱡ LDO4pm
Lic CTV 10P

BROADWAY
Hereford & Worcester
Map **4** SP03
GH *Olive Branch* 78–80 High St
☎(0386) 853440
Closed Xmas
8hc (2fb) ★
CTV 8P
Ⓥ

BROADWINDSOR
Dorset
Map **3** ST40
⊢⊣ **FH** Mrs C Poulton **Hursey**
(ST433028) ☎(0308) 68323
Closed Xmas & New Year

Comfortable and well-designed farmhouse accommodation enjoying quiet location in rolling Dorset countryside.
2hc ★ Ⓡ B&bfr£8 Bdifr£12 W£75 Ⱡ LDOnoon
🔥 3P nc5yrs 2½acres non-working
Ⓥ

BROMLEY
Gt London
London plan **4** *F2*
(pages 222–223)
GH Bromley Continental Hotel
56 Plaistow Ln ☎01-464 2415
Plainly furnished detached Victorian house with own garden.
20hc 1➡ (6fb) ✱B&b£11.20–£16.50 Bdi£16.70–£22 LDOnoon
Lic 🔥 CTV 14P
Credit cards 1 3

BROMPTON REGIS
Somerset
Map **3** SS93
⊢⊣ **FH** Mrs G Payne **Lower Holworthy**
(SS978308) ☎(03987) 244
Closed Xmas
Small 18th-century hill farm overlooking and bordering Wimbleball Lake in Exmoor National Park.
3hc ★ Ⓡ B&b£8 Bdi£13.50
🔥 CTV 6P 🏠 200acres beef sheep
Ⓥ

BROMSGROVE
Hereford & Worcester
Map **4** SO97
INN Forest 290 Birmingham Rd
☎(0527) 72063
6hc TV in all bedrooms Ⓡ ✱B&b£13.25 L£2.75alc D9.30pm £5alc 🔥 70P
Credit card 1 Ⓥ

BROUGH
Cumbria
Map **12** NY71
⊢⊣ **FH** Mrs J M Atkinson **Augill House**
(NY814148) ☎(09304) 305
Closed Xmas & New Year
Stone built Victorian farmhouse 1m from village. Quiet, clean and comfortable.
4hc (1fb) Ⓡ B&b£7.50 Bdi£13.50 W£45.50 M LDO4pm
🔥 CTV 6P nc12yrs 40acres dairy

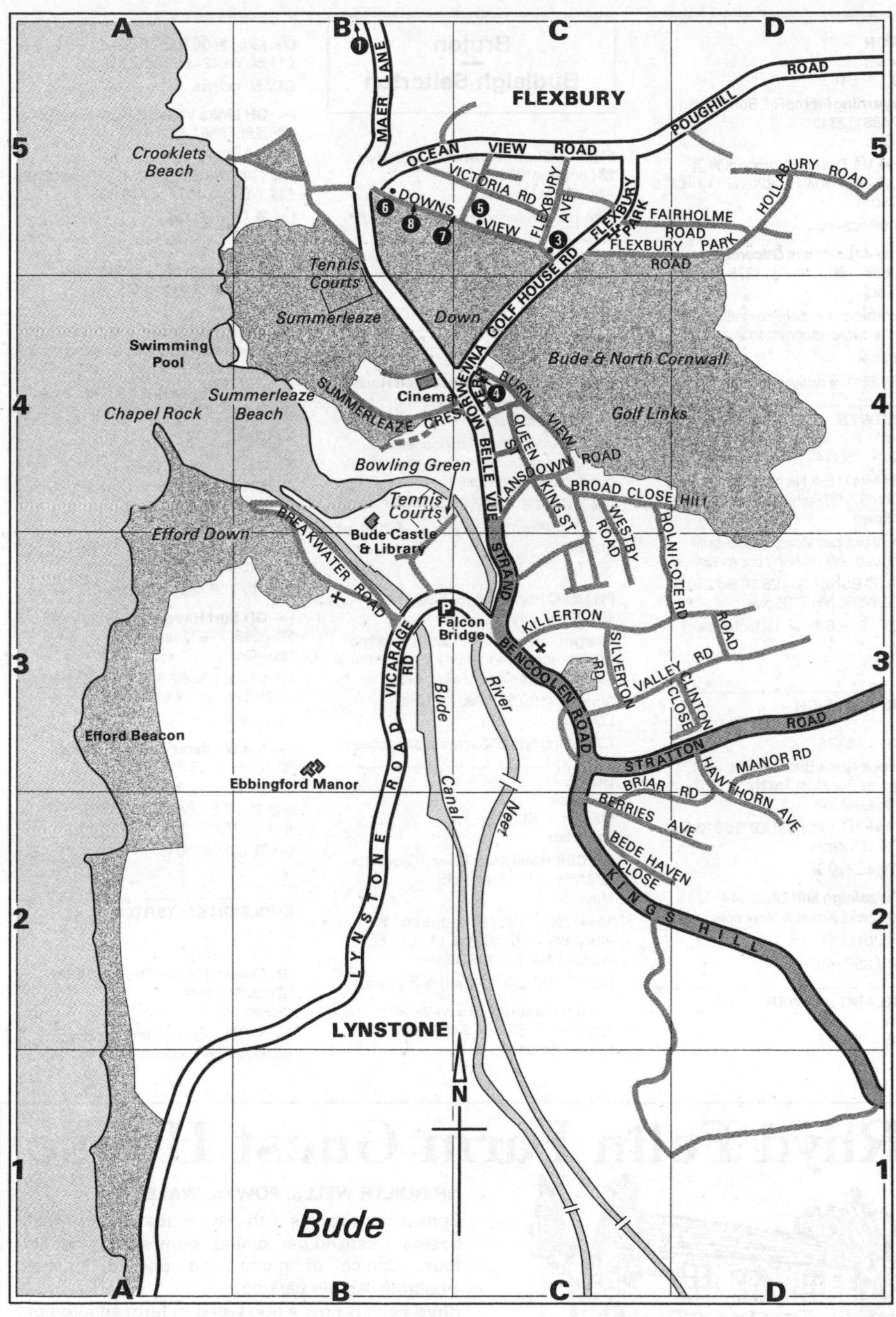

Bude

1 Cliff
3 Kisauni
4 Links View
5 Pencarrol
6 Sandiways
7 Wayfarer
8 Surf Haven

BRUTON
Somerset
Map **3** ST63

GH Fryerning Frome Rd, Burrowfield
☎(074981) 2343
Mar–Dec
4rm 3🛁 1🚿 TV in all bedrooms 🐕 ®
B&b£13–£14 Bdi£17–£20 W£119–£126
🍴LDO3pm
Lic 🔥 8P nc8yrs

FH Mrs A M Eastment ***Gilcombe*** *(ST696364)* ☎(074981) 3378
Apr–Sep
Hospitable owners offer a limited amount of comfortable accommodation.
3rm 2hc 🐕
🔥 CTV 6P 1🚗 nc5yrs 400acres dairy

BRYNGWYN
Powys
Map **3** SO14

⊢⊣**FH** Mrs H E A Nicholls **Newhouse** *(SO191497)* ☎Painscastle (04975) 671 (after 5pm)
200 year old, two storey, stone-built farmhouse set in rolling countryside.
2hc 🐕 ® B&b£7.50–£8.50 Bdi£10.50–£12.50 W£50 M LDO6pm
🔥 CTV 2P nc8yrs 🎣 150acres beef sheep
ⓥ

BUCKFASTLEIGH
Devon
Map **3** SX76

GH Black Rock Buckfast Rd, Dart Bridge (at Buckfast 1m N)
☎(0364) 42343
11hc 1🛁 1🚿 (3fb) B&b£9 Bdi£13.50 W£85 🍴LDO9pm
🔥 CTV 45P 🏠 🎣

GH *Furzeleigh Mill* ☎(03644) 2245
Closed 2wks Xmas & New Year
18hc (3fb) LDO7pm
Lic CTV 25P river

BUCKLAND BREWER
Devon
Map **2** SS42

FH Mrs M Brown ***Holwell*** *(SS424159)*
☎Langtree (08055) 288
Apr–Oct rs Nov–Mar
16th-century farmhouse with a friendly and homely atmosphere.
5hc (3fb)
CTV P 300acres mixed

BUCKNELL
Shropshire
Map **7** SO37

FH Mrs B E M Davies **Bucknell House** *(SO355735)* ☎(05474) 248
mid Jan–mid Dec
Mellow, listed Georgian house in secluded grounds on fringe of village, overlooking Teme Valley.
2🛁 ✱B&b£8–£10 W£56–£70 M
🔥 CTV 3P nc13yrs 🎾(hard) 🎣 70acres grazing
ⓥ

FH Mrs C Price **Hall** *(SO356737)*
☎(05474) 249
A large Georgian farmhouse providing homely accommodation in peaceful rural surroundings close to village centre.
3rm 2hc (1fb) 🐕 ✱B&b£7 Bdi£11 LDOam
CTV 6P nc7yrs 250acres arable sheep

BUDE
Cornwall
Map **2** SS20
See Plan

GH Cliff Hotel Maer Down, Crooklets
☎(0288) 3110 Plan **1** *B5*
May–Oct
15🛁 (9fb) CTV in all bedrooms 🐕 ✱B&b£10–£12.50 Bdi£14–£16.50 W£83–£100 🍴LDO6.30pm
Lic CTV 16P 🏊(heated) ⛳ 🎾(hard)

⊢⊣**GH Kisauni** 4 Downs View
☎(0288) 2653 Plan **3** *C5*
Closed Xmas
6hc (3fb) 🐕 ® B&b£6.50–£8 Bdi£10–£11.50 W£42–£51 M LDO5pm
CTV 5P nc2yrs

⊢⊣**GH Links View** 13 Morwenna Ter
☎(0288) 2561 Plan **4** *C4*
Closed Dec
6hc (3fb) 🐕 B&b£6.50–£7.50 Bdi£9.50–£11 W£40–£48 M LDO6.30
Lic 🔥 CTV 2P 1🚗
ⓥ

⊢⊣**GH Pencarrol** 21 Downs View
☎(0288) 2478 Plan **5** *C5*
Closed Dec
Double fronted, end of terrace Victorian house overlooking the downs and close to beaches.
9hc (2fb) ® B&b£6–£7.50 Bdi£9.50–£11 W£42–£52.50 🍴LDO5pm
CTV 1🚗
ⓥ

⊢⊣**GH Sandiways** 35 Downs View
☎(0288) 2073 Plan **6** *B5*
Mar–Oct
11hc (5fb) 🐕 B&b£7–£7.50 Bdi£10.50–£11 W£45–£48 M LDO5pm
Lic CTV 10P nc3yrs billiards

⊢⊣**GH Surf Haven** 31 Downs View
☎(0288) 2998 Plan **8** *B5*
Mar–Oct
10hc (5fb) B&b£7.50–£9 Bdi£11.50–£13 W£68–£80 🍴LDO5pm
Lic CTV 6P

⊢⊣**GH Wayfarer** 23 Downs View
☎(0288) 2253 Plan **7** *B5*
Mar–Oct
9rm 7hc (5fb) B&b£7–£7.50 Bdi£10.75–£11.75 W£49–£52.50 M LDO4pm
Lic 🔥 CTV 4P 🏠 U
ⓥ

BUDLEIGH SALTERTON
Devon
Map **3** SY08

GH Tidwell House Country Hotel
☎(03954) 2444
Closed 25 Dec–1 Jan
Large Georgian building standing in considerable grounds.

9rm 6hc 1→ (5fb) Ⓡ *B&b£13.50–£15 Bdi£17–£18.85 W£84–£90 L LDO9pm

CTV 16P 3

GH Willowmead 12 Little Knowle ☎(03954) 3115

6hc (1fb) B&b£9.50–£9.75 Bdi£14.50–£15.50 W£75–£80 L LDO7pm

CTV 7P

Credit card 3

BUILTH WELLS
Powys
Map **3** SO05

FH Mrs Z E Hope **Cae Pandy** *(SO023511)* Garth Rd (1m W A483) ☎(0982) 553793

3hc (1fb) *B&b£6.50–£7 W£44.50 M

TV 6P 50acres mixed

BULKWORTHY
Devon
Map **2** SS31

FH Mrs K P Hockridge **Blakes** *(SS395143)* ☎Milton Damerel (040926) 249
Apr–Oct

Pleasant, comfortable and well decorated house in peaceful setting close to the River Torridge.

2hc (1fb) B&bfr£8.50 Wfr£60 M

CTV 4P nc13yrs 150acres arable beef dairy sheep

BURFORD
Oxfordshire
Map **4** SP21

GH Corner House Hotel High St ☎(099382) 3151
Mar–Nov

Charming Cotswold stone building in picturesque High Street. Comfortable antique furnished bedrooms.

9rm 5→ 4 (2fb) B&b£15 Bdifr£18.85 LDO9pm

Lic CTV

BURGH ST PETER
Norfolk
Map **5** TM49

FH Mrs R M Clarke **Shrublands** *(TM473926)* ☎Aldeby (050277) 241

1m SSW unclass rd.

3hc (1fb) B&b£7.50–£8.50

CTV 6P (hard) 350acres arable beef mixed

BURNSALL
North Yorkshire
Map **7** SE06

GH *Manor House* ☎(075672) 231
Mar–Oct

Small private hotel whose gardens run down to River Wharfe.

7hc (2fb) LDO5pm

Lic CTV 7P river

Ⓥ

Budleigh Salterton — Buxton

BURNTISLAND
Fife
Map **11** NT28

GH Forthaven 4 South View, Lammerlaws ☎(0592) 872600

Homely guesthouse looking out across the Firth of Forth.

4hc (2fb) TV in all bedrooms B&b£6–£7 W£35–£40 M

4P

Credit card 2 Ⓥ

BURROW BRIDGE
Somerset
Map **3** ST33

GH *Old Bakery* ☎(082369) 234

6hc 1→

Lic CTV 12P 1

BURTON UPON TRENT
Staffordshire
Map **8** SK22

GH Delter Hotel 5 Derby Rd ☎(0283) 35115

5hc (1fb) CTV in 4 bedrooms TV in 1 bedroom B&b£10–£12 Bdi£15–£18 W£70–£84 M LDO6pm

Lic CTV 8P

BURWASH
East Sussex
Map **5** TQ62

INN Admiral Vernon Etchingham Rd ☎(0435) 882230

Small 16th-century inn with beautiful gardens, overlooking Rother Valley.

5hc CTV in 2 bedrooms B&b£14 Bdi£27 W£75 M L£4 D9pm £6

CTV 30P 2 nc10yrs

Ⓥ

INN *Bell* High St ☎(0435) 882304

15th-century inn with character. Well appointed dining room with country style cooking.

5hc Ⓡ D9pm sn

15P

INN Burwash Motel High St ☎(0435) 882540

17th-century inn, skilfully extended to provide spacious, well-equipped bedrooms. Imaginative home cooking.

8→ CTV in all bedrooms Ⓡ B&b£17 Lfr£5.50 D9.30pm fr£7

CTV 25P 8

Credit cards 1 3

BURY ST EDMUNDS
Suffolk
Map **5** TL86

GH Swan 11 Northgate St ☎(0284) 2678
Closed Xmas

9hc (3fb) B&b£9.50–£10.50 W£63–£66 M

CTV

BUTE, ISLE OF
Strathclyde *Buteshire*
Map **10**
See Rothesay

BUTLEIGH
Somerset
Map **3** ST53

FH Mrs J M Gillam **Dower House** *(ST517333)* ☎Baltonsborough (0458) 50354
Feb–Nov

Pleasant 18th-century farmhouse with large garden. Guests share a large table at mealtimes.

4rm 3hc 1→ (A 2hc) (1fb) Ⓡ B&b£8 Bdi£11.50 W£60 M (W only Jun–Sep LDO4pm

CTV 6P 8acres beef, calves small holding

Ⓥ

BUTTERLEIGH
Devon
Map **3** SS90

FH Mrs B J Hill ***Sunnyside*** *(ST975088)* ☎Bickleigh (08845) 322
Closed Xmas

The farmhouse, built about 1700, is situated in the heart of the Devonshire countryside, 3m W of Cullompton.

5hc (3fb)

CTV 6P 140acres mixed

BUXTON
Derbyshire
Map **7** SK07

GH Fairhaven 1 Dale Ter ☎(0298) 4481

7hc (3fb) TV in all bedrooms Ⓡ B&b£7–£8 Bdi£10–£11 W£45–£54 M LDO4.30pm

CTV

GH Griff 2 Compton Rd ☎(0298) 3628
Closed Dec

6hc (3fb) B&b£7–£7.50 W£45–£47.50 M

CTV 5P

Ⓥ

GH Hawthorn Farm Fairfield Rd ☎(0298) 3230
Mar–Oct

6hc (A 7hc) (2fb) B&b£8–£8.50 Bdi£14 W£78.20 L S% LDOnoon

CTV 12P

GH Kingscroft 10 Green Ln ☎(0298) 2757

9hc (2fb) CTV in 4 bedrooms Ⓡ B&b£7.25–£7.50 Bdi£10 W£45–£50 L LDO5pm

Lic CTV 9P 2

GH Nithen Corner 45 Manchester Rd ☎(0298) 2008
6hc (3fb) ® B&b£7–£8.50 Bdi£11–£12.50 W£46–£49 ⱡ LDO6.30pm
CTV 6P

GH Old Manse 6 Clifton Rd, Silverlands ☎(0298) 5638
Closed Dec & Jan
8hc (4fb) *B&b£7.50–£8 Bdi£11–£12 W£49–£51 M LDO4.30pm
Lic CTV 4P

GH Roseleigh Private Hotel 19 Broad Walk ☎(0298) 4904
Closed Xmas & New Year rs Dec–1 Mar
13hc 2fl (1fb) B&b£9.78 Bdi£14.95 W£63.46 ⱡ LDO5pm
Lic CTV 12P 1 nc7yrs

GH *Templeton* 13 Compton Rd ☎(0298) 5275
Mar–Oct
6hc LDO3pm
CTV 10P

GH Thorn Heyes Private Hotel 137 London Rd (Guestaccom) ☎(0298) 3539
Closed Jan
Local stone built house dating from 1860, once a gentlemans residence, it still retains a Victorian theme throughout. Set in gardens.
7rm 3hc 4fl (2fb) CTV in 4 bedrooms ® B&b£9.50–£10 Bdi£14–£14.50 Wfr£80 ⱡ LDO5pm
Lic CTV 11P
Ⓥ

GH Westminster Hotel 21 Broadwalk ☎(0298) 3929
Feb–Oct & Xmas
13rm 9hc 2 2fl (4fb) ® B&bfr£9.50 Bdifr£14.50 Wfr£60 M LDOnoon
Lic CTV 12P
Credit card 1

FH Mrs C Heathcote ***High House*** *(SK065714)* Foxlow Farm, Harpur Hill ☎(0298) 4219
Mar–Oct
3rm (1fb) LDO9pm
CTV 6P 230acres dairy
Ⓥ

Buxton — Caernarfon

FH Mrs M A Mackenzie **Staden Grange** *(SK075717)* Staden Ln (1½m SE off A515) ☎(0298) 4965
Private shooting available on farm.
4rm 3hc 1 (1fb) ® B&b£9 Bdi£14 W£90 ⱡ LDO4.30pm
Lic CTV 20P U 250acres beef dairy

CABUS
Lancashire
Map **7** SD44

FH Mrs J Higginson **Clay Lane Head** *(SD490474)* ☎Garstang (09952) 3132
2 Jan–23 Dec
A comfortable farmhouse of some character, with fine furniture and log fires. 1½ miles north of Garstang on the A6.
3hc (1fb) B&b£7.50–£8.50 Bdi£11.50–£12.50 W£80 ⱡ LDO5.30pm
CTV 4P 1 U 30acres beef
Ⓥ

CADNAM
Hampshire
Map **4** SU21

FH Mrs A M Dawe **Budds** *(SU310139)* Winsor Rd, Winsor ☎Southampton (0703) 812381
Apr–Oct
Picturesque dairy farm adjacent to the New Forest with thatched roof and attractive gardens.
2hc (1fb) B&b£8–£8.50 W£56 M
TV 3P 200acres beef dairy

FH Mr & Mrs R D L Dawe **Kents** Winsor Rd, Winsor ☎Southampton (0703) 813497
Etr–Sep
Picturesque thatched farmhouse, recently renovated. Accommodation of a high standard. 2m NE unclass rd.
2rm 1 1fl (1fb) B&b£8 W£54 M
CTV 6P nc2yrs 200acres beef dairy

CAERNARFON
Gwynedd
Map **6** SH46

GH Caer Menai 15 Church St ☎(0286) 2612
Feb–Dec
Mid terrace Victorian building situated a short walk from the castle.
7hc (3fb) B&b£7–£8 W£49–£56 M
CTV

GH Menai View Hotel North Rd ☎(0286) 4602
Mar–Oct rs Nov–Feb
Single fronted mid terrace Victorian building overlooking the Menai Straits.
6hc (1fb) TV in all bedrooms B&b£8.25 Bdi£14.75 W£57.75 M S% LDO8pm
TV
Credit cards 1 3

GH Plas Treflan Caeathro ☎(0286) 2542
Mar–Oct
3hc (A 7fl) (2fb) CTV in all bedrooms ® *B&b£9.50–£10.50 Bdi£12.50–£13.50 W£52.50–£60 M LDO10pm
Lic 15P
Credit cards 2 3

INN Black Boy Northgate St ☎(0286) 3604
Closed Xmas
14th-century inn in the centre of town.
15hc 6fl *B&b£10–£12 Bdi £15–£17.75 L£3.50&alc D9pm £5.75–£7.75&alc
CTV 8P

CALDBECK
Cumbria
Map **11** NY33

GH High Greenrigg House
☎(10036) 430
Closed Xmas
8hc ✶ *B&b£10 Bdi£16 W£96 ⱡ
Lic ₩ CTV 8P
Ⓥ

⊢⊣ **FH** Mrs D H Coulthard **Friar Hall Farm** *(NY324399)* ☎(06998) 633
Apr–Oct
Modernised two-storey stone-built farmhouse, well decorated and containing good quality furniture. Overlooks river and village church.
3hc (1fb) B&b£7.50–£8.50 Bdi £12.50–£13 W£80–£85 ⱡ LDO10am
CTV 3P 140acres dairy sheep
Ⓥ

CALLANDER
Central *Perthshire*
Map **11** NN60

GH Abbotsford Lodge Stirling Rd ☎(0877) 30066
Large stone house on main street in its own garden, at S entrance to the town.
19hc (7fb) Ⓡ *B&b£8.25 Bdi£14.50 W£94 ⱡ LDO7pm
Lic ₩ CTV 20P

⊢⊣ **GH Annfield** 18 North Church St ☎(0877) 30204
Mar–Oct
Attractive stone-built house on quiet street in the town centre.
8hc (2fb) B&b£6.50 W£45.50 M
CTV 10P
Ⓥ

⊢⊣ **GH Arden House** Bracklinn Rd ☎(0877) 30235
Attractive stone house standing on hillside close to golf course, formerly used in the making of 'Dr Finlay's Casebook'.
10rm 9hc 1⋒ (3fb) Ⓡ B&b£7.50–£8.50 Bdi£12.50–£14.50 W£80–£92 ⱡ LDO7pm
₩ CTV 12P
Ⓥ

GH *Ashlea House Hotel* Bracklinn Rd ☎(0877) 30325
Apr–Oct
Imposing stone-built house with modern extension, close to the golf course.
20hc 2⋒ (4fb) ✶ LDO6pm
₩ CTV 18P

⊢⊣ **GH Edina** 111 Main St ☎(0877) 30004
Stone house forming part of a long terrace on main street.
9hc 1➡ (A 2hc 1➡ 1⋒) (1fb) Ⓡ B&b£7.20–£7.77 Bdi£11.22–£11.79 W£73.60–£77.07 ⱡ LDO7.30pm
CTV 8P
Ⓥ

⊢⊣ **GH Greenbank** 143 Main St ☎(0877) 30296
Pleasant house standing in the main street.
6hc (2fb) B&b£6.50–£7 Bdi£11.50–£12 W£75–£80 ⱡ LDO7pm
Lic ₩ CTV 6P

GH Highland House Hotel South Church St ☎(0877) 30269
Apr–Oct
Hotel stands on a quiet street in the town centre offering a high standard of accommodation.
10rm 5hc 4⋒ (1fb) B&b£9–£11.50 Bdi£16.50–£19 W£110–£125 ⱡ LDO7.30pm
Lic ₩ CTV

⊢⊣ **GH Kinnell** 24 Main St ☎(0877) 30181
Friendly house in main street, also functions as a tea room. →

8hc (3fb) B&b£7–£8 Bdi£11–£12 W£72–£79 L LDO6pm

CTV 7P

Ⓥ

GH **Riverview House Private Hotel** Leny Rd ☎(0877) 30635
Mar–Oct

6rm 4hc 2⋒ (1fb) Ⓡ B&b£8 Bdi£13 W£56 L LDO7.15pm

Lic CTV 8P

Ⓥ

GH **Rock Villa** 1 Bracklinn Rd ☎(0877) 30331
Etr–Sep

Detached house in corner site set back from the main road.

7hc (1fb) B&b£7–£7.50 W£46–£50 M

7P

Ⓥ

CALSTOCK
Cornwall
Map **2** SX46

INN Boot Fore St ☎Tavistock (0822) 832331

2rm Ⓡ B&b£11.50 Bdi£17.50 W£69 M L£4.95alc D10pm £10alc

2P

Credit cards 1 2 3 5 Ⓥ

CALVINE
Tayside *Perthshire*
Map **14** NN86

FH Mrs W Stewart **Clachan of Struan** *(NN802654)* ☎(079683) 207

½m S on B847

2rm (1fb) B&b£7 W£49 M

CTV 5P 10,000acres sheep Ⓥ

CAMBORNE
Cornwall
Map **2** SW64

GH Pendarves Lodge ☎(0209) 712691
May–Sep

Late Georgian stone-built house pleasantly situated in own grounds adjacent to B3303.

8hc (2fb) B&b£9 Bdi£13.50 W£90 L LDO7.30pm

Lic CTV P

Ⓥ

GH Regal Hotel Church Ln ☎(0209) 713131
rs Sun

Small hotel in the heart of town, adjacent to church.

13hc 2 (2fb) B&b£10 Bdi£15 W£64 M LDO9.15pm

Lic CTV 9P

Ⓥ

CAMBRIDGE
Cambridgeshire
Map **5** TL45

GH All Seasons 219 Chesterton Rd ☎(0223) 353386

10hc (3fb) CTV in all bedrooms B&b£7.50–£8.50 Bdi£11–£12.50 W£52–£59 M LDO2pm

4P

GH Ayeone Cleave 95 Gilbert Rd ☎(0223) 63387

6rm 4hc 2⋒ (1fb) TV in 6 bedrooms Ⓡ B&b£10.50

CTV 6P

GH Belle Vue 33 Chesterton Rd ☎(0223) 351859
Closed Xmas

7hc (2fb) B&b£8–£10

CTV 6P 2

GH *Cambridge Lodge Hotel* 139 Huntingdon Rd ☎(0223) 352833

11hc 2 6⋒ CTV in all bedrooms LDO10pm

Lic 20P

GH Fairways 143 Cherryhinton Rd ☎(0223) 246063
Jan–20 Dec

12hc (2fb) CTV in all bedrooms Ⓡ B&b£9.50–£10 W£66.50–£70 M

CTV 20P

GH Hamilton 88 Chesterton Rd ☎(0223) 314866

7hc (2fb) CTV in all bedrooms Ⓡ B&b£8.50–£11.50 W£59.50–£80.50 M

CTV 6P nc4yrs

GH Helen's Hotel 167–169 Hills Rd ☎(0223) 246465
Closed 11 Dec–9 Jan

25rm 6hc 1 12⋒ (A 6rm 3hc 3⋒) (3fb) CTV in all bedrooms B&b£14–£20 Bdi£21–£28 LDO7pm

Lic CTV 20P

Credit cards 1 3 5

GH Lensfield Hotel 53 Lensfield Rd ☎(0223) 355017
Closed 2 wks Xmas

36rm 4hc 14⋒ (6fb) CTV in 33 bedrooms TV in 3 bedrooms B&b£12–£20 B&di£18–£26

Lic CTV 10P

Credit cards 1 2 3 5

GH Suffolk House Private Hotel 69 Milton Rd ☎(0223) 352016

8rm 7hc 1 (2fb) CTV in 3 bedrooms TV in 5 bedrooms *B&b£9.75–£12.50 LDO10am

CTV 7P

Ⓥ

CAMELFORD
Cornwall
Map **2** SX18

GH Sunnyside Hotel Victoria Rd ☎(0840) 212250
Closed Nov

Large detached house with sun lounge, ¼ mile from village.

10hc (6fb) B&b£10–£12 Bdi£15–£18 W£76–£90 L LDO8pm

Lic CTV 16P

Ⓥ

Camelford — Canterbury

⊢⊣ **GH Warmington House** 32 Market Pl ☎(0840) 213380

Creeper hung, large double fronted house set in the middle of Camelford.

7rm (3fb) Ⓡ B&b£7–£8 Bdi£11–£12 W£70–£75 Ⱡ LDO5pm

Lic ▥ CTV 3 ⌂

Credit card 3

FH Mrs H MacLeod ***Melorne*** *(SX099856)* Camelford Station ☎(0840) 213200

Etr–Oct

Situated approximately 1m N of village near site of old railway station. Fishing and rough shooting available to guests.

7rm 6hc (2fb)

CTV 12P 100acres dairy

⊢⊣ **FH** Mrs R Y Lyes **Pencarrow** *(SX108825)* Advent ☎(0840) 213282

Apr–Nov

Large stone farmhouse in pretty hamlet, 1½ miles from Camelford.

2hc ✱ B&b£6–£7 W£38–£45 M

TV 2 ⌂ 40acres dairy

CANONBIE

Dumfries & Galloway *Dumfriesshire*

Map **11** NY37

INN Riverside ☎(05415) 295

Closed 2 wks Jan & Sun lunch

Charming 17th-century converted family home in a delightful setting overlooking the River Esk.

6 ⇌ CTV in all bedrooms Ⓡ B&b£18 Bdi£29 Bar lunch £2.75alc D8.30pm £11alc

▥ 25P 2 ⌂

Credit card 3

CANTERBURY

Kent

Map **5** TR15

GH Abba Hotel Station Road West ☎(0227) 64771

Comfortable modern well maintained accommodation with basement dining room.

19rm 16hc 3⋔ (3fb) ✱B&b£9–£10 Bdi£15–£16 W£63–£70 M LDO9.30pm

Lic ▥ CTV 7P

Ⓥ

GH Castle Court 8 Castle St ☎(0227) 63441 (due to change to 463441)

Georgian style building in city centre with delightful coffee lounge and walled patio garden. Peaceful position yet close to Cathedral, shops and gardens.

12hc B&b£8–£10 W£49–£63 M S% LDO9.30pm

CTV nc2yrs

Credit cards 1 3 Ⓥ

GH Ebury Hotel New Dover Rd ☎(0227) 68433

Closed 25 Dec–13 Jan

Large Victorian gabled building in three acres of grounds. Cheerfully decorated spacious well equipped accommodation.

15rm 13⇌ 2⋔ (4fb) CTV in all bedrooms B&b£14–£25 Bdi£17.75–£32.50 W£110–£130 Ⱡ LDO8.30pm

Lic ▥ CTV 20P 1 ⌂

Credit cards 1 2 3

GH Ersham Lodge 12 New Dover Rd ☎(0227) 63174 (due to change to 463174)

Closed Dec & Jan

Comfortable modern accommodation with well equipped bedrooms and some very compact annexe rooms.

14rm 1hc 2⇌ 7⋔ (A 11rm 3hc 1⇌) (4fb) CTV in 14 bedrooms TV in 11 bedrooms ✱ B&b£11–£21 Bdi£20–£30 LDOnoon

Lic ▥ CTV 17P 2 ⌂

See advertisement on page 104

The ideal hotel for visiting south east Kent

- ★ Charming Victorian hotel
- ★ 6 miles Canterbury, 9 miles coast
- ★ 2½ acres including lawns, flowers beds and vegetable garden
- ★ Children's play area including sandpit & swing
- ★ Happy atmosphere and good service
- ★ Horse riding, fishing, golf & tennis nearby
- ★ A wealth of historical places to visit just a short car ride away
- ★ **Farm Holiday Guide diploma winner for accommodation & food 3 years running 1979, 80 and 81 (consecutively)**

The Woodpeckers Country Hotel Ltd.

Womenswold, Nr Canterbury, Kent
Barham 319 (STD 022782)

- ★ Heated swimming pool, water slide & diving board
- ★ Television lounge and quiet lounge
- ★ 16 comfortable rooms all with H/C water & tea & coffee-making facilities
- ★ **Four-poster, Georgian, brass bedstead, bridal bedrooms all en suite**
- ★ Warm air central heating
- ★ Highly recommended for traditional country home baking as reported in 'The Daily Express', 'The Guardian', the 'Dover Express', 'The Telegraph' and 'Kentish Gazette'
- ★ Packed lunches
- ★ Licensed

'A Taste of England' *Personal attention from resident proprietors*

Canterbury

GH Highfield Hotel Summer Hill, Harbledown ☎(0227) 62772 (due to change to 462772)
Closed Xmas & New Year

Georgian style country house, family run and providing value for money.

10rm 8hc 2⋔ (3fb) ✶ ✱B&b£8.50–£11
Lic Ⅲ CTV 12P nc3yrs
Credit cards [1] [3]

GH *Kingsbridge Villa Hotel* 15 Best Ln ☎(0227) 66415

Small city centre hotel, friendly and comfortably furnished.

12hc 3⋔ CTV in 1 bedroom TV in 2 bedrooms LDO8pm
Lic Ⅲ CTV 7P

⊢⊣ **GH Magnolia House** 36 St Dunstans Ter ☎(0227) 65121
Feb–Nov

Small, homely house offering simple but comfortable accommodation.

6hc (3fb) ✶ B&b£7.50–£8
Ⅲ CTV 3P

GH *Pilgrims* The Friars ☎(0227) 64531
14hc 2⋔ (2fb)
Ⅲ CTV 4P 4⌂

GH Pointers Hotel 1 London Rd ☎(0227) 56846 (due to change to 456846)
Closed Xmas–New Year

Tastefully furnished and well equipped Regency style hotel.

14rm 11hc 2⇒ 1⋔ (2fb) CTV in all bedrooms Ⓡ B&b£12–£14 Bdi£18.50–£20.50 W£105–£112 Ⱡ LDO8.30pm
Lic Ⅲ 9P
Credit cards [1] [2] [3] [5] Ⓥ

GH Red House Hotel London Rd, Harbledown (1m W A2) ☎(0227) 63578

An attractive manor house set in one acre of mature grounds offering simple overnight accommodation mostly in separate external annexes.

4⇌ (A 11rm 8hc 1⇌ 2ⁿ) (5fb) CTV in 4 bedrooms ✱ B&b£11.50–£25.30 Bdi£20–£32 W£126–£216 ʟ LDO7.30pm

Lic ▥ CTV 16P

Credit cards 1 3 Ⓥ

GH St Stephen's 100 St Stephen's Rd ☎(0227) 62167 (due to change to 462167)

Tudor style building with modern extension to rear.

9rm 8hc B&b£8.62–£9.77

Lic ▥ CTV 8P 2🚗

Credit card 2

GH Victoria Hotel 59 London Rd ☎(0227) 59333 (due to change to 459333)

Comfortable, friendly hotel with modern extension.

24rm 5hc 15⇌ 4ⁿ (4fb) CTV in 21 bedrooms Ⓡ B&b£15–£17 LDO9pm

Lic ▥ 24P ⌂

Credit cards 1 2 3 5

Canterbury — Cardiff

CAPUTH
Tayside *Perthshire*
Map **11** NO04

⊢⊣ **FH** Mrs R Smith **Stralochy** *(NO086413)* ☎(073871) 250 May–Oct

Situated in lovely spot looking down a valley with trees merging in Sidlaw hills.

3rm (1fb) ✱ B&b£6.50 Bdi£9.50 W£45.50 M LDO4.30pm

TV 3P ⌂ 239acres arable beef sheep mixed

Ⓥ

CARDIFF
South Glamorgan
Map **3** ST17

GH Ambassador Hotel 4 Oakfield St, Roath ☎(0222) 491988 Closed Xmas

A friendly but modestly appointed hotel bar for residents.

16hc (3fb) ✱ *B&b£10.50 Bdi£16 LDOnoon

Lic ▥ CTV 12P

GH Balkan Hotel 144 Newport Rd ☎(0222) 463673

Modest commercial hotel convenient to city.

14rm 1⇌ (3fb) CTV in 10 bedrooms ✱ Ⓡ *B&b£9–£12 Bdi£13–£17 Wfr£85 ʟ LDO6pm

▥ CTV 16P

GH *Clayton Hotel* 65 Stacey Rd, Roath ☎(0222) 492345 Closed Xmas & New Year

Commercial guest house just off the main Newport road.

10hc (1fb) LDOnoon

Lic ▥ CTV 6P nc3yrs

GH *Domus* 201 Newport Rd ☎(0222) 495785

A proprietor run guest house with small bar.

10hc 2ⁿ (2fb) ✱ LDOnoon

Lic ▥ CTV 10P

GH Dorville Hotel 3 Ryder St ☎(0222) 30951

Proprietor run establishment within walking distance of the city centre.

13hc (3fb) ✱ B&b£10–£11 W£70 M

▥ CTV

Ⓥ

GH Ferrier's (Alva Hotel) 130/132 Cathedral Rd ☎(0222) 23413 (due to change to 383413)
Closed Xmas wk rs Fri, Sat & Sun
Well-equipped and comfortable family run hotel offering a good standard of service.
27rm 19hc 1➡ (3fb) CTV in 16 bedrooms TV in 1 bedroom B&b£12–£15 LDO7.45pm
Lic 🎹 CTV 8P
Credit cards 1 2 3 5

GH Princes 10 Princes St, Roath ☎(0222) 491732
Proprietor run guest house.
6hc (2fb) ✱ B&b£9–£9.50 Bdi £13.50–£14 LDOnoon
🎹 CTV 3P

GH Tane's Hotel 148 Newport Rd ☎(0222) 491755
Within easy distance of the city centre, a proprietor run establishment.
9hc (1fb) ✱ B&b£9.20–£10.35 Bdi£13.80–£14.95 W£96.60–£104.65 M LDO7pm
🎹 CTV P

CAREY
Hereford & Worcester
Map **3** SO53

INN Cottage of Content ☎(043270) 242

Closed Xmas Day
3hc Ⓡ B&b£10–£12 Bdi£15–£20 W£98–£112 L L£12alc D9.30pm £12alc
🎹 CTV 30P
Credit card 1 Ⓥ

CARLISLE
Cumbria
Map **12** NY45

⊢⊣ **GH Angus Hotel** 14 Scotland Rd ☎(0228) 23546
Closed Xmas & New Year
8hc (2fb) B&b£7.50–£8 LDO4pm
Lic 🎹 CTV 🐕

⊢⊣ **GH East View** 110 Warwick Rd ☎(0228) 22112
Closed 22 Dec–7 Jan
9hc (3fb) ✱ B&b£7–£7.50 Bdi £9.75–£10.25 W£65–£70 L LDO5pm
🎹 CTV 🐕

GH Georgian House 40–44 London Rd ☎(0228) 23805
Closed Xmas Day
14rm 13➡ 1⋔ (4fb) ✱ *B&b£12.65 Bdi£15.65 LDO9pm
Lic 🎹 CTV 9P 2🚗
Ⓥ

⊢⊣ **GH Kenilworth Hotel** 34 Lazonby Ter ☎(0228) 26179
Small, friendly, guesthouse, family run
6hc (2fb) B&b£6.50–£10
🎹 CTV 5P

CARLOPS
Borders *Peeblesshire*
Map **11** NT15

⊢⊣ **FH** Mrs J Aitken **Carlophill** *(NT155556)* (½m SW unclass) ☎West Linton (0968) 60340
May–mid Oct
3rm ✱ B&b£7.50–£8 W£50
🎹 CTV 6P 2000acres beef sheep mixed
Ⓥ

CARNO
Powys
Map **6** SN99

⊢⊣ **FH** P M Lewis **Y Grofftydd** *(SN981965)* ☎(05514) 274
Farmhouse is situated off A470 overlooking typical mid-Wales scenery. Ideal centre for walking. Sporting clay-pigeon shooting on premises.
4hc (2fb) B&b£8 Bdi£12 W£56 L LDO7pm
🎹 CTV P 180acres sheep

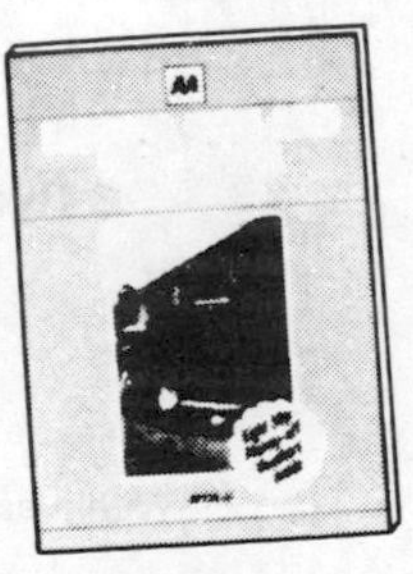

CARNOUSTIE
Tayside *Angus*
Map **12** NO53

GH Dalhousie Hotel 47 High St
☎(0241) 52907
Closed Jan
Small family run hotel with friendly atmosphere, situated in town centre.
6rm 5hc 1⋒ (2fb) *B&b£7.50–£8.50 Bdi£12.50–£13.50 W£92 ⅄ LDO9.30pm
Lic ▥ CTV 7P
Credit card ③

CARRADALE
Strathclyde *Argyllshire*
Map **10** NR83

GH Ashbank Hotel ☎(05833) 650
Adjacent to golf course offering comfortable but compact accommodation.
5hc 1⋒ (1fb) ® B&b£8 Bdi£13.50 W£80 ⅄ LDO7pm
Lic CTV 6P

GH *Drumfearne* ☎(05833) 232
May–Sep
Detached stone house in own grounds on a hill behind the harbour.
6rm 5hc (2fb) ★ LDO6pm
TV P sea Ⓥ

GH *Duncrannag* ☎(05833) 224
Apr–Sep
Two storey painted house with adjoining tearoom/dining room in elevated position overlooking harbour & sound.
11hc
Temperance 8P

GH Dunvalanree Portrigh
☎(05833) 226
Etr–Oct
Large house with attractive rockery garden beside small sandy bay to the south of Carradale Harbour.
12hc (2fb) B&b£7–£7.50 Bdi£10.50–£11 W£49–£50 Ⓜ (W only Jul & Aug) LDO4pm
Lic ▥ CTV 9P
Ⓥ

CARRBRIDGE
Highland *Inverness-shire*
Map **14** NH92

GH Ard-na-Coille Station Rd
☎(047984) 239
6hc (1fb) B&b£7.50–£8.50 Bdi£11.50–£12.50 W£52.50–£59.50 Ⓜ LDO4.30pm
▥ TV P

GH Mountain Thyme Country Station Rd ☎(047984) 696
A comfortable and nicely appointed country guesthouse. Situated ½m W of Carrbridge station.
6hc (2fb) ★ ® B&b£7–£8.50 Bdi£11–£12.50 LDO7pm
▥ CTV 8P
Ⓥ

GH Old Manse Private Hotel Duthil
☎(047984) 278
Closed Nov
Situated 2m from Carrbridge, just off A939 in 8 acres of grounds.
8hc (2fb) ® B&b£8 B&di£13 W£84 Ⓜ LDO1pm
Lic ▥ CTV 7P ⌂

CARRONBRIDGE
Central *Stirlingshire*
Map **11** NS78

FH Mrs J Morton **Lochend** *(NS759856)* ☎Denny (0324) 822778
Modernised, 18th-century hill farm, set in quiet, isolated position. Pleasant farmyard with rose garden in centre. 1½m off unclass road towards Bannockburn.
3rm 1hc ★ B&b£6.50–£7 Bdi£11–£11.50 W£43.50 Ⓜ LDO3pm
▥ CTV P nc3yrs 650acres beef sheep

CARRUTHERSTOWN
Dumfries & Galloway *Dumfriesshire*
Map **11** NY17

FH Mrs J Brown **Domaru** *(NY093716)* ☎(038784) 260
Mar–Oct
Modern, detached, two-storey farmhouse built at side of farm road. About 300 yards from farm buildings. Carrutherstown ½ mile.
3rm 2hc TV in all bedrooms B&b£6.50–£7 Bdi£10–£11 W£45.50 Ⓜ LDO7.30pm
▥ 3P 150acres dairy
Ⓥ

CASTLE CARROCK
Cumbria
Map **12** NY55

FH B W Robinson **Gelt Hall** *(NY542554)* ☎Hayton(022870) 260
An olde-worlde farmhouse built around a courtyard directly off the main street of this tiny village.
3rm 1➡ (1fb) ★ B&b£8 Bdi£12 W£52 Ⓜ
CTV 6P 120acres mixed
Ⓥ

CASTLE CARY
Somerset
Map **3** ST63

GH Greenhills Ansford Hill
☎(0963) 50464
Closed Xmas
6rm 2hc 3➡ ★ ® *B&b£9.50–£12.50 Bdi£17–£20 W£96–£116 ⅄ LDO7pm
Lic ▥ CTV 12P nc10yrs
Ⓥ

CASTLE DONINGTON
Leicestershire
Map **8** SK42

GH Delven Hotel 12 Delven Ln
☎Derby(0332) 810153
7hc (1fb) ★ B&b£14.38 Bdi£17.88 LDO11pm
Lic ▥ CTV 5P 2🚗 nc
Credit cards ① ③ Ⓥ

GH Four Poster 73 Clapgun St
☎Derby(0332) 810335
Tastefully restored end terrace house close to town centre and Donington Park Racing Circuit. Comfortable, tourist and commercial, accommodation.
7hc (1fb) ★ B&b£11.50
▥ CTV 10P 4🚗

CATÊL (CASTEL)
Guernsey, Channel Islands
Map **16**

GH La Galaad Hotel Rue Des Francais ☎Guernsey(0481) 57233
Mar–Oct
11rm 4hc 1➡ 6⋒ (2fb) CTV in all bedrooms ★ B&b£8–£12 Bdi£14–£18 LDO6.30pm
Lic ▥ CTV 15P ♿ nc4yrs

CATLOWDY
Cumbria
Map **12** NY47

FH Mr & Mrs J Sisson **Bessiestown** *(NY457768)* ☎Nicholforest(022877) 219
Neat farmhouse, comfortable and tastefully furnished. Visitors are welcome to stroll around the farm buildings.
10hc 5➡ 3⋒ (2fb) ★ B&b£9.50–£11 Bdi£14.50–£16.50 W£100 ⅄ LDO5pm
Lic ▥ CTV 12P ⊡(heated) U 55acres beef sheep mixed
Ⓥ

See advertisement on page 108

CATON
Lancashire
Map **7** SD56

INN Ship Hotel Lancaster Rd ☎(0524) 770265
4hc TV in all bedrooms ★ B&b£11–£11.50 Bar lunch £3alc
▥ TV 20P 3🚗 nc

CAWOOD
North Yorkshire
Map **8** SE53

GH Compton Court Hotel
☎Selby(075786) 315
rs Sat & Sun
8rm 3hc 1➡ (A 2hc) (1fb) TV in all bedrooms ® B&b£16.50 Bdi£21.50 W£91 Ⓜ LDO9pm
Lic ▥ CTV 8P
Credit cards ① ③

CEMMAES
Powys
Map **6** SH80

⊢⊣ **FH** Mrs D Evans-Breese **Rydygwiel** *(SH826056)* ☎ Cemmaes Road (06502) 541
Remote, detached, stone-built farmhouse on north side of the Dovey Valley with attractive gardens to rear of the house.
3rm (1fb) B&b£6.50–£7.50
P 200 acres mixed

CERNE ABBAS
Dorset
Map **3** ST60

⊢⊣ **FH** R & M Paul **Giants Head** *(ST675029)* Old Sherborne Rd ☎ (03003) 242
Etr–Sep
A modernised, detached farmhouse in elevated position at the head of the famous Cerne Giant. Open rural views.
5rm 3hc ✱ B&b£7.50–£8.50 W£50–£56 M
Lic CTV 10P nc7yrs 4acres sheep
Ⓥ

CHAGFORD
Devon
Map **3** SX78

GH Bly House Nattadon Hill ☎ (06473) 2404
Feb–Oct
8rm 3hc 5⇌ Ⓡ B&b£10.25–£13 Bdi£15–£17.75 W£98–£117 ⱪ LDO7pm
▥ CTV 10P nc10yrs
Ⓥ

GH Glendarah ☎ (06473) 3270
7hc (A 1rm 1⇌) (2fb) CTV in 1 bedroom Ⓡ B&b£8.50–£9.50 Bdi£14–£16 W£94.50–£105 ⱪ LDO6.30pm
Lic ▥ CTV 9P ⌂

CHALE
Isle of Wight
Map **4** SZ47

INN Clarendon Hotel & Wight Mouse (Guestaccom) ☎ Niton (0983) 730431
Delightful antique furnished rooms.
13rm 7hc 3⇌ 3⋒ Ⓡ B&bfr£11.50 Bdifr£18.40 W£109.25 ⱪ Bar lunch fr£2.50 D5pm fr£5.50
▥ CTV 100P

CHALFONT ST PETER
Buckinghamshire
Map **4** TQ09

INN Greyhound High St ☎ Gerrards Cross (0753) 883404
Modernised and comfortable 14th-century inn where Judge Jeffries held court. Reputed to have a ghost.
11hc CTV in all bedrooms ✱ Ⓡ
*B&b£17.50 L£2.25–£7.85 D10pm £2.90–£8.05
▥ 40P
Credit cards 2 3 5

CHANNEL ISLANDS
Map **16**
Places with AA listed accommodation are indicated on location map 16. Full details will be found under individual placenames within the gazetteer

CHAPELHALL
Strathclyde *Lanarkshire*
Map **11** NS76

GH Laurel House Hotel 101 Main St ☎ Airdrie (02364) 63230
A comfortable house with good standards, run by friendly proprietors.
6rm 5hc (1fb) B&b£10 Bdi£13.50 S% LDO6pm
Lic ▥ CTV 6P

Chapelton — Cheltenham

CHAPELTON
Strathclyde *Lanarkshire*
Map **11** NS64

⊢⊣ **FH** Mr R Hamilton **East Drumloch** *(NS678521)* ☎(03573) 236
Large stone-built farmhouse with a modern, well-furnished interior.
4rm 2hc (2fb) B&b£6–£6.50
CTV 10P 260acres beef sheep mixed

FH Mrs E Taylor **Millwell** *(NS653496)* ☎East Kilbride (03552) 43248
Small, 18th-century farmhouse set in tree-studded land.
3rm *B&b£5.50 Bdi£7.50
CTV P 94acres

CHAPMANSLADE
Wiltshire
Map **3** ST84

FH Mrs M Hoskins **Spinney** *(ST839480)* ☎(037388) 412
Two-storey stone-built farmhouse surrounded by fields and woodland.
3hc (1fb) Ⓡ B&b£8.50 Bdi£14.50 W£48 M LDO4pm
CTV 6P 1 4 acres sheep goats
Ⓥ

CHARD
Somerset
Map **3** ST30

⊢⊣ **GH Watermead** 83 High St ☎(04606) 2834
9hc (2fb) B&b£8–£8.50 Bdi£11.75–£12.25 W£50–£55 M LDO1pm
Lic CTV 9P 2

CHARLTON
West Sussex
Map **4** SU81

GH Woodstock House Hotel ☎Singleton (024363) 666
mid Feb–early Nov
Country house dating back to the 12th century with antique furnishings throughout and beautiful well kept gardens.
11rm 5hc 2 4 B&b£14–£17.50 Bdi£19.50–£25 W£125–£150 L LDO7.30pm
Lic CTV 11P nc9yrs

CHARLTON MUSGROVE
Somerset
Map **3** ST72

FH Mrs A Teague **Lower Church** *(ST721302)* ☎Wincanton (0963) 32307
Apr–Oct
18th-century brick built farmhouse with inglenook fireplace and beams.
2hc (1fb) Ⓡ *B&b£8 Bdi£12 W£50 M LDO2pm
CTV 4P 60acres dairy sheep

CHARLWOOD
Surrey
Map **4** TQ74
For accommodation details see under Gatwick Airport

CHARMOUTH
Dorset
Map **3** SY39

GH Newlands House Stonebarrow Ln ☎(0297) 60212
Mar–Oct
Standing in own grounds on edge of village, minutes walk from beach.
12rm 7 5 (2fb) CTV in all bedrooms Ⓡ B&b£9.50–£12 Bdi£14.75–£17.25 W£100–£116 L LDOnoon
Lic CTV 12P

GH White House 2 Hillside ☎(0297) 60411
Attractive Georgian house offering high standard of accommodation and pretty bedrooms.
7hc 6 1 (3fb) CTV in all bedrooms Ⓡ B&b£14.50–£16.50 Bdi£23–£25 W£140 £150 L LDO9.30pm
Lic 15P
Credit cards 1 3

CHEDINGTON
Dorset
Map **3** ST40

FH Lt Col & Mrs E I Stanford **Lower Farm** *(ST485054)* ☎Corscombe (093589) 371
Closed Xmas & New Year
17th-century thatched farmhouse with extensive views over unspoilt Dorset and Somerset countryside. Jacob sheep, Suffolk Punch horses and ornamental waterfowl are to be seen. Boating available on farm lakes.
3hc *B&b£10 W£60 M
CTV 4P nc4yrs 128acres pig sheep heavy horses

CHELMSFORD
Essex
Map **5** TL70

GH Beechcroft Private Hotel 211 New London Rd ☎(0245) 352462
Closed Xmas & New Year
An older style hotel with two lounges, and offering friendly service.
26hc (2fb) B&bfr£14.40 Wfr£70.80 M
CTV 15P

GH Boswell House Hotel 118–120 Springfield Rd ☎(0245) 87587
Closed 10 days Xmas
Recently renovated to provide a good modern standard yet retaining traditional charm.
13rm 9 4 (2fb) CTV in 7 bedrooms Ⓡ B&b£17.25–£24.50 Bdi£22.75–£30 LDO7pm
Lic CTV 15P
Credit cards 1 2 3 5 Ⓥ

GH Newholme Hotel 440 Baddow Rd, Great Baddow ☎(0245) 76691
Closed Xmas wk
Well equipped comfortable private hotel with modern accommodation.
8hc 2 (2fb) CTV in 2 bedrooms Ⓡ B&b£16 Bdi£21.95 W£112 M LDO8pm
Lic CTV 8P
Credit cards 1 3 4

GH Tanunda Hotel 219 New London Rd ☎(0245) 354295
Closed Xmas wk
Fairly large modern hotel with good restaurant facilities and effective management.
20rm 11hc 2 7 CTV in 9 bedrooms B&b£14.50–£21 Bdifr£20.50 LDO7.30pm
Lic CTV 20P

CHELTENHAM
Gloucestershire
Map **3** SO92
See also Bishop's Cleeve

GH Askham Court Hotel Pittville Circus Rd ☎(0242) 525547
Cotswold stone Regency house within walking distance of the town centre.
19rm 13hc 3 2 (1fb) CTV in 5 bedrooms Ⓡ B&b£12–£13 Bdi£18.50–£19.50 W£76–£80 M LDO4.30pm
Lic CTV 20P
Ⓥ

GH Beaumont House 56 Shurdington Rd ☎(0242) 45986
Substantial Regency house with garden, and spacious attractive bedrooms.
8hc (2fb) B&b£10–£12 Bdi£15.50–£17.50 W£50–£70 M LDO5.30pm
Lic CTV 12P
Credit cards 1 3 Ⓥ

GH Bowler Hat Hotel 130 London Rd ☎(0242) 523614
Proprietor run guesthouse.
6rm 5hc 1 (4fb) CTV in all bedrooms B&b£9–£11 Bdi£13–£15.50 W£55–£70 M LDOam
Lic 8P

GH Carrs Hotel 42 Clarence St ☎(0242) 524003
Closed Xmas
15rm 13hc 2 (3fb) *B&b£10–£11.50 Bdi£15–£16.50 W£63–£72.50 M S% LDO6pm
Lic CTV
Credit cards 1 2 3 5

GH Central Hotel 7/9 Portland St ☎(0242) 524789
Proprietor run hotel situated in town centre, at present undergoing major refurbishment.
12hc (2fb) *B&b£12 Bdi£18 W£80 M LDO6pm
Lic CTV 6P

GH Cleevelands House 38 Evesham Rd ☎(0242) 518898
Closed Xmas wk
13rm 12hc 1⋒ (4fb) CTV in all bedrooms Ⓡ B&b£9–£10 W£59.50–£66.50 M̸
▥ CTV 12P ♿
Ⓥ

GH Cotswold Grange Hotel Pittville Circus Rd ☎(0242) 515119
Closed Xmas
Cotswold stone house attractively appointed.
20rm 11hc 9⇥ (3fb) Ⓡ ✻B&b£14–£17.50 LDO7.15pm
Lic ▥ CTV 20P billiards

GH Hollington House Hotel 115 Hales Rd ☎(0242) 570280
Closed Xmas
Attractive Cotswold stone detached house in small pleasant gardens.
6rm 2⋒ (2fb) CTV in 2 bedrooms Ⓡ B&b£11.20–£12.20 Bdi£17.20–£18.20 W£70–£80 M̸ LDO10am
Lic ▥ CTV 8P
Ⓥ

⊢⊣ **GH Ivy Dene** 145 Hewlett Rd ☎(0242) 521726
Proprietor run guesthouse, modestly appointed.

Cheltenham — Chepstow

9hc (2fb) Ⓡ B&b£7–£7.50 W£49–£52.50 M̸
▥ CTV 9P

GH Lawn Hotel 5 Pittville Lawn ☎(0242) 526638
9hc (2fb) B&b£8.50–£9 Bdi£12.50–£13 W£56–£60 M̸ LDOnoon
▥ CTV
Ⓥ

GH North Hall Hotel Pittville Circus Rd ☎(0242) 520589
rs Xmas
Semi-detached house of local stone, with large bedrooms.
21hc (3fb) CTV in 4 bedrooms TV in 1 bedroom Ⓡ B&bfr£11.21 Bdifr£15.25 Wfr£91.44 L̸ LDO6.30pm
Lic ▥ CTV 20P

GH Regency 50 Clarence Sq ☎(0242) 582718
Closed Xmas & New Year
8rm 7hc 1⇥ (3fb) CTV in all bedrooms Ⓡ B&b£8.50–£9 Bdi£13–£14 W£56–£60 M̸ LDOnoon
Lic ▥ 2🚗 ⌂

GH Wellington House Hotel Wellington Sq ☎(0242) 521627
Semi-detached house of local stone, with large bedrooms.
10rm 8hc (3fb) ★ Ⓡ B&b£10.50–£11.50 Bdi£16–£17 W£70–£77 M̸ LDO5pm
Lic ▥ CTV 6P

GH Willoughby 1 Suffolk Sq ☎(0242) 522798
Closed 2wks Xmas
Proprietor run Regency house.
10rm 7hc (2fb) CTV in 9 bedrooms Ⓡ B&b£10.50 Bdi£15 W£70 M̸ LDO4pm
CTV 10P

CHEPSTOW
Gwent
Map **3** ST59

GH First Hurdle Hotel 9 Upper Church St ☎(02912) 2189
Pleasing hotel with pretty bedrooms equipped with Edwardian furniture.
10rm 9hc 1⋒ (1fb) B&b£12–£14 Bdi£18–£20 LDO9pm
Lic ▥ CTV ⚑
Credit cards 1 2 3

CHERITON FITZPAINE
Devon
Map **3** SS80

FH Mrs D M Tricks **Brindiwell** *(SS896079)*
☎(03636) 357
Period farmhouse with oak beams and panelling; on the side of a valley with views of the Exe Valley and Dartmoor.
4rm 2hc (2fb) ✱ ® B&b£8.05–£9.20 Bdi£12.65–£13.80 Wfr£56.35 M̸ LDO6pm
CTV 4P ⌂ 120acres sheep
ⓥ

CHESTER
Cheshire
Map **7** SJ46

GH Brookside Private Hotel 12 Brook Ln ☎(0244) 381943
Closed Xmas wk
24rm 10🛁 4🚿 (5fb) CTV in all bedrooms ® B&b£12.07–£16.10 Wfr£84.49 M̸ LDO8.30pm
Lic ▥ CTV 14P
Credit card 3

GH Cavendish Hotel 44 Hough Green
☎(0244) 675100
Comfortable, elegantly furnished Victorian house in own grounds.
11rm 10hc 1🛁 (4fb) CTV in all bedrooms B&b£12.50–£15 Bdi£19–£21.50 W£120 Ł LDO7pm

Cheriton Fitzpaine — Chester

Lic ▥ CTV 12P
Credit cards 1 2 3 5 ⓥ

GH Chester Court Hotel 48 Hoole Rd
☎(0244) 20779
rs Xmas wk
8rm 4hc 3🚿 (A 12rm 6🛁 6🚿) (8fb) CTV in all bedrooms B&b£12–£15 Bdi£19.50–£22.50 LDO8.30pm
Lic ▥ 30P
Credit cards 1 2 3 5

GH *Devonia* 33–35 Hoole Rd ☎(0244) 22236
A small establishment catering for tourists and business people. On A56 1½m from city centre.
10hc (6fb) CTV in 3 bedrooms TV in 7 bedrooms ® LDO4pm
▥ CTV 14P

GH Eversley Private Hotel 9 Eversley Park (Guestaccom) ☎(0244) 373744
Small, privately owned hotel with relaxing atmosphere.
8hc 4🛁 (4fb) CTV in all bedrooms ✱ ® B&b£13.50 Bdi£18.50 W£84.50 M̸ LDO8pm
Lic ▥ CTV 10P nc3yrs
Credit card 3

⊢⊣ **GH Gables** 5 Vicarage Rd, Hoole
☎(0244) 23969
7hc (2fb) B&b£7.50–£9 W£63 M̸
▥ CTV 7P

GH Green Bough Hotel 60 Hoole Rd
☎(0244) 26241
Closed 2wks Xmas
11rm 3hc 2🛁 6🚿 (2fb) CTV in all bedrooms ® B&b£10–£20 Bdi£16–£26 W£107–£165 Ł LDO7pm
Lic ▥ CTV 11P nc4yrs
Credit cards 1 3

GH Hamilton Court 5–7 Hamilton St
☎(0244) 45387
12hc (6fb) CTV in all bedrooms ✱ ® B&b£10–£11 Bdi£14–£15 W£98–£105 Ł LDO7.30pm
Lic ▥ CTV 10⌂
Credit card 3

⊢⊣ **GH Malvern** 21 Victoria Rd
☎(0244) 380865
8hc (2fb) ✱ ® B&b£7–£8.50 Bdi£10–£11.50 W£42–£51 M̸ LDO6pm
▥ CTV nc2yrs
ⓥ

GH Redland Private Hotel 64 Hough Green ☎(0244) 671024
Feb–Nov
10rm 8hc 2⋔ (2fb) ★ B&b£11–£17.50
Lic ▥ CTV 12P 2🚗 billiards
Ⓥ

GH Riverside Private Hotel 22 City Walls off Lower Bridge St ☎(0244) 26580
Closed Xmas rs Nov–Feb
14hc 11➡ (4fb) CTV in 11 bedrooms TV in 3 bedrooms Ⓡ B&b£13.50–£17 Bdi£19.50–£23 LDO8.15pm
Lic ▥ CTV 20P

CHICKERELL
Dorset
Map **3** SY68

INN Turks Head 6–8 East St ☎Weymouth (0305) 783093
Closed 23–28 Dec
4rm 4➡ CTV in all bedrooms Ⓡ B&b£12–£15 Bdi£18.50–£21.50 W£115–£135 Ⱡ L£2.85–£4.50 D9.30pm £8alc
▥ 12P 🚫
Credit cards 1 3

CHICKLADE
Wiltshire
Map **3** ST93

GH Old Rectory ☎Hindon (074789) 226
Closed 1st 2wks May, 1st 2wks Oct, & 1wk Xmas
8hc (2fb) B&b£9–£10 Bdi£13–£14.50 W£80–£87 Ⱡ LDO2pm
▥ CTV 8P 1🚗
Credit cards 1 3

CHIDDINGFOLD
Surrey
Map **4** SU93

INN Crown Petworth Rd ☎Wormley (042879) 2255
One of the oldest inns in English history dating from 12th century, now providing comfortable, modern facilities and a high standard of cuisine.
8rm 4➡ 4⋔ CTV in all bedrooms Ⓡ B&b£30 L£5.75–£12&alc D10pm £12
▥ 12P
Credit cards 1 2 3 4 5

CHIDEOCK
Dorset
Map **3** SY49

GH Betchworth ☎(029789) 478
6rm 4hc 2⋔ (1fb) B&b£9–£10.50 Bdi£13.50–£15.50 W£63–£73.50 M LDO6pm
Lic ▥ CTV 15P nc7yrs
Credit cards 1 2 3 5 Ⓥ

CHILLINGTON
Devon
Map **3** SX74

GH White House Hotel ☎Kingsbridge (0548) 580580
Apr–Oct
9hc 1➡ (1fb) ★ Ⓡ *B&b£11.50 Bdi£16.50 W£98 Ⱡ LDO5pm
Lic ▥ CTV 8P
Credit card 2

CHIPPING SODBURY
Avon
Map **3** ST78

GH *Moda Hotel* 1 High St ☎(0454) 312135
7hc (A 3hc) (1fb) ★ LDO8.30pm
Lic ▥ CTV 10P

CHIRNSIDE
Borders *Berwickshire*
Map **12** NT85

INN *Mitchell's Hotel* West End ☎(089081) 507
Small, friendly family run inn. Modern conversion of six stone houses.
4hc (1fb) TV in all bedrooms (1fb) ✱ CTV 15P

CHISELBOROUGH
Somerset
Map **3** ST41

FH Mrs E Holloway **Manor** *(ST468151)* ☎(093588) 203
Mar–Oct
Comfortable 19th-century house built of ham stone with well appointed rooms.
4hc (1fb) ✱ B&b£9 Bdi£14 W£92 Ł S% LDO5pm
CTV 6P 🐄 500acres arable dairy sheep mixed
ⓥ

CHRISTCHURCH
Dorset
Map **4** SZ19
For details of additional guesthouses see **Bournemouth**

⊢⊣ **GH Belvedere Hotel** 59 Barrack Rd ☎(0202) 485978
Large Victorian hotel on main Christchurch to Bournemouth road.
10hc 1⋒ (3fb) TV in all bedrooms B&b£8–£8.50 Bdi£14–£15 W£55–£58 M̸ S%
Lic 🍴 CTV 12P 1🚗
ⓥ

GH Broomway Hotel 46 Barrack Rd ☎(0202) 483405
Closed Xmas
On main road near to town centre and convenient to Bournemouth.
9hc (3fb) B&b£10–£11.50 W£72–£85 Ł
Lic CTV 12P nc2yrs

GH Ferndale 41 Stour Rd ☎(0202) 482616
Closed Xmas
Corner sited on main road near the town and Tucktonia.
6hc (1fb) ✱B&b£6.50–£8
🍴 CTV 6P

⊢⊣ **GH Laurels** 195 Barrack Rd ☎(0202) 485530
On main road out of town.
15rm 12hc B&b£8–£10 Bdi£11.50–£14 W£70–£85 Ł LDO5.30pm
Lic 🍴 CTV 14P
ⓥ

GH Park House Hotel 48 Barrack Rd ☎(0202) 482124
Closed Xmas & New Year
Attractive, well appointed house on main road out of town.
9hc 2⋒ (4fb) CTV in 4 bedrooms ✱ ® B&bfr£11 Wfr£66 M̸
Lic 🍴 CTV 12P nc3yrs
Credit cards [1] [3]

GH Pines Private Hotel 39 Mudeford Rd ☎(0202) 475121
Quiet location close to Mudeford Quay and beaches.
13rm 7hc 6⋒ (2fb) CTV in 6 bedrooms ® B&b£11–£15.50 Bdi£15.25–£16.50 W£93–£99 Ł LDO5.30pm
Lic 🍴 CTV 14P 🏠
ⓥ

⊢⊣ **GH St Albans Hotel** 8 Avenue Rd ☎(0202) 471096
Detached villa in quiet road.
9rm 7hc 2⋒ (4fb) B&b£8–£8.50 Bdi£11.50–£12.50 W£55–£58 M̸ LDO4pm
Lic CTV 12P
ⓥ

GH Sea Witch Hotel 153/5 Barrack Rd ☎(0202) 482846
On main A35, a short distance from the town centre.
9hc (2fb) B&b£9.50–£10.50 Bdi£14.25–£15.25 W£62–£68 M̸ LDO6.30pm
Lic 🍴 CTV 15P

GH *Shortwood House Hotel* 1 Magdalen Ln ☎(0202) 485223
Standing in own grounds enjoying a quiet location adjacent to the park.
7hc 1⋒ (4fb) ✱ ® LDO5.3;pm
Lic 🍴 CTV 12P

CHURCHILL
Avon
Map **3** ST45

FH Mrs S Sacof ***Churchill Green*** *(ST429602)* ☎(0934) 852438
Modernised 16th-century farmhouse still retaining its character, the large garden faces south overlooking the foothills of the Mendips.
7hc (4fb) ✱
Lic 🍴 TV 50P 🏠 25acres arable beef

CHURCHINFORD
Somerset
Map **3** ST21

⊢⊣ **FH** M Palmer **Hunter Lodge** *(ST212144)* ☎Churchstanton (082360) 253
Detached, two-storey farmhouse with slate roof and large garden. Set in the Blackdown Hills.
4rm 3hc (2fb) B&b£6–£7 Bdi£9–£10 W£63–£70 Ł LDOnoon
CTV 6P 🏊 (heated) 30acres mixed

CHURCH STOKE
Powys
Map **7** SO29

⊢⊣ **FH** Mrs C Richards **Drewin** *(SO261905)* ☎(05885) 325
Mar–Oct
A border farmhouse with beams and inglenook fireplace. Fine views of surrounding countryside. Offa's Dyke footpath runs through the farm.
2rm 1hc (1fb) TV in 1 bedroom ✱ ® B&b£6.50 Bdi£10 W£70 Ł LDO8pm
CTV 4P 🏠 1000 acres mixed
ⓥ

CHURCH STRETTON
Shropshire
Map **7** SO49

GH Dudgeley Mill All Stretton (2m N B4370) (Guestaccom) ☎(0694) 723461
Tastefully modernised old mill in peaceful, picturesque setting. Stables available for guests to bring their own horses.
7hc (1fb) ♞ Ⓡ B&b£9.50–£10 Bdi£15–£15.50 W£100 Ⱡ LDO7.30pm
Lic 10P ♤ ♪
Ⓥ

GH Mynd House Private Hotel Ludlow Rd, Little Stretton (2m S B4370)
☎(0694) 722212
Feb–mid Dec
13rm 7hc 3➡ (3fb) Ⓡ B&b£9–£14 Bdi£14.25–£19.25 W£90–£115 Ⱡ LDO8pm
Lic ▥ CTV 16P
Credit cards 1 3

⊢⊣ **FH** Mrs J C Inglis **The Hall** (*SO478925*) Hope Bowdler (1m E B4371) ☎(0694) 722041
Mar–Oct rs Nov & Feb
17th-century farmhouse which has recently been modernised to a high standard. Set on the edge of the tiny village of Hope Bowdler and surrounded by hills.
3hc (1fb) ♞ B&b£7.50–£8
▥ 6P nc10yrs ⚲(hard) 22acres sheep

CINDERFORD
Gloucestershire
Map **3** SO61

⊢⊣ **GH Overdean** 31 St White's Rd
☎Dean (0594) 22136
A small, pleasant guesthouse.
6hc (2fb) CTV in 1 bedroom B&b£8–£9 Bdi£13–£14 W£85–£95 Ⱡ
▥ CTV 6P 2🚘 ♤

INN *White Hart Hotel* St White's Rd, Ruspidge (B4227) ☎Dean (0594) 23139
rs Xmas
Satisfactory inn with good value restaurant.
6hc 1➡ 1⋒ CTV in 2 bedrooms TV in 4 bedrooms Ⓡ D9.45pm
50P 1🚘

CIRENCESTER
Gloucestershire
Map **4** SP00

GH Raydon House Hotel 3 The Avenue (Guestaccom) ☎(0285) 3485
Pleasant, small guesthouse, run by proprietors.
16rm 9hc 6➡ 1⋒ (4fb) ♞ Ⓡ B&b£12–£15 Bdi£18.50–£19.50 W£80 M LDO8.30pm
Lic ▥ CTV 12P
Credit cards 1 3 Ⓥ

GH Rivercourt Beeches Rd ☎(0285) 3998
Comfortable, small guesthouse, run by proprietors.
5hc (A 4hc) (1fb) B&b£9.20 Bdi£14.50 W£90 Ⱡ LDO7pm
▥ CTV 10P

GH La Ronde 52–54 Ashcroft Rd
☎(0285) 4611
An enthusiastically run comfortable guesthouse with attractive dining room.
10hc (4fb) ♞ B&b£11.25–£12.25 Bdi£17.25–£18.25 W£100–£120 Ⱡ LDO8pm
Lic ▥ CTV 1P

⊢⊣ **GH Wimborne** 91 Victoria Rd
☎(0285) 3890
A neat and modestly appointed guesthouse.
7hc (1fb) ♞ B&b£8–£9 Bdi£13–£14 W£50–£56 M LDOnoon
▥ CTV 6P nc5yrs

CLACTON-ON-SEA
Essex
Map **5** TM11

GH Chudleigh Hotel Agate Rd ☎(0255) 425407
Closed Oct
Well kept family house near sea and shops.
14rm 11hc 1→ 2⫚ (4fb) B&b£9–£10 Bdi£15–£16 W£55–£59 ⱡ LDO6.15pm
Lic 🎹 CTV 7P
Credit cards 1 2 3 Ⓥ

GH Sandrock Hotel 1 Penfold Rd ☎(0255) 428215
Closed Jan

Clacton-on-Sea

Detached house close to pier offering sound accommodation.
6rm ✱ B&b£11
Lic 🎹 CTV 6P

GH Stonar Private Hotel 19 Agate Rd ☎(0255) 426554
Small beautifully kept hotel, close to the sea and pier.
9hc (1fb) TV in 9 bedrooms Ⓡ B&b£8.50 Bdi£13.50 W£72 ⱡ LDO6pm
🎹 CTV 4P nc5yrs

GH *York House* 19 York Rd, Holland-on-Sea (2m NE B1032) ☎(0255) 814333
rs 21–31 Dec
Delightful Tudor style house with a large garden. Close to sea yet in quiet residential surroundings.
6hc (3fb)
Lic 🎹 CTV 4P 2🚗 ⌂

CLAVERDON
Warwickshire
Map **4** SP16

FH Mr & Mrs F E Bromilow **Woodside** *(SP186644)* Langley Rd (¾m S of B4095) ☎(092684) 2446

3rm 2hc 1⇌ 1⋒ (1fb) TV in 1 bedroom Ⓡ *B&b£7.50–£10 Bdi£15–£17.50 W£100–£118 Ⱡ LDO2pm

Ⲯ CTV 12P 2⌂ ⌂ 22acres non-working

CLAWDDNEWYDD
Clwyd
Map **6** SJ05

⊢⊣ **FH** Mrs G Williams **Maestyddyn Isa** *(SJ054535)* ☎(08245) 289
Apr–Nov

Old farmhouse in rural setting on the outskirts of Cleanog Forest. Situated 1m off the B5015.

3hc (1fb) ★ B&bfr£8 Bdifr£12 Wfr£80 Ⱡ

Ⲯ CTV nc3yrs 365acres mixed
Ⓥ

CLEARWELL
Gloucestershire
Map **3** SO50

FH Mrs P Jones **Tudor** *(SO569083)* ☎Dean (0594) 33046
Closed Jan

Period farmhouse situated in the Forest of Dean. 9m from M4 motorway.

3hc (2fb) B&b£9–£9.50 Bdi£14–£14.50 W£60 M LDO6.30pm

Ⲯ CTV 10P 2⌂ 15acres non-working

INN Wyndham Arms ☎Dean (0594) 33666
Closed Mon & last 2 wks Oct

A comfortable inn with good atmosphere.

3hc CTV in all bedrooms Ⓡ B&b£16 Bdi£22 L£4.85&alc D10pm £11.50alc Ⲯ 40P

Credit card 1 Ⓥ

CLEETHORPES
Humberside
Map **8** TA30

⊢⊣ **GH Stepping Stones** 59 Clee Rd ☎(0472) 696702

6hc (2fb) Ⓡ B&b£7 Bdi£10 Wfr£48 Ⱡ LDO5pm

Ⲯ CTV 6P 1⌂

CLEOBURY MORTIMER
Shropshire
Map **7** SO67

INN Talbot Hotel High St ☎(0299) 270382

Half timbered town centre inn some 400 years old.

5rm 1⇌ 4⋒ TV in 1 bedroom Ⓡ B&b£14 Bdi£20 W£75 M L£7alc High Tea £3alc D10pm £10alc

Ⲯ CTV 75P billiards

Credit cards 1 3 4 5 Ⓥ

CLEVEDON
Avon
Map **3** ST47

GH Amberley 146 Old Church Rd ☎(0272) 874402
Closed 2 wks Apr & Oct

A comfortable stone-built house enthusiastically run by proprietor.

8rm 3hc 2⇌ 1⋒ ★ Ⓡ B&b£9.50–£11.50 Bdi£14.50–£16.50 W£101.50–£115.50 Ⱡ LDO7pm

Lic Ⲯ CTV 2P

Credit card 2

CLIFTONVILLE
Kent
Map **5** TR37

See Margate

CLITHEROE
Lancashire
Map **7** SD74

INN White Lion Hotel Market Pl ☎(0200) 26955

Reputed to be the oldest alehouse in Clitheroe, now a well furnished and comfortable inn.

6hc CTV in all bedrooms ® B&b£11.50 L£3.50alc D10.15pm £5alc

CTV 9P

CLOVELLY
Devon
Map **2** SS32

FH Mrs E Symons ***Burnstone*** *(SS325233)* Higher Clovelly ☎(02373) 219

Large, comfortably furnished farmhouse with open fire in spacious lounge. Good farmhouse fare.

3hc (1fb)

CTV 4P sea 400acres arable dairy

INN *New Inn* Main St ☎(02373) 303

4hc ® LDO10.30pm

CTV sea

INN Red Lion The Quay ☎(02373) 237
Apr–Oct

9hc ® B&b£9.50 Bdi£14 L£2.75–£4.95 D8pm £3.75–£6.50

CTV 6P

Credit cards 1 0

CLUN
Shropshire
Map **7** SO38

INN *Sun* ☎(05884) 559

4hc (A 3) ® D9pm

CTV 7P nc8yrs

CLUNTON
Shropshire
Map **7** SO38

FH Mrs J Williams **Hurst Mill** *(SO318811)* ☎Clun (05884) 224
Feb–Nov

Small stone-built farmhouse in picturesque setting with a river running through, surrounded by tree-clad hills. Friendly atmosphere.

4rm 2hc (1fb) ® B&b£8–£8.50 Bdi£11–£11.50 LDO5.30pm

CTV 6P 2 85acres mixed

Ⓥ

Clitheroe — Collyweston

CLYRO
Powys
Map **3** SO24

FH Mrs J Harris **Crossway** *(SO216459)* ☎Hay-on-Wye (0497) 820567
Mar–Oct

Small farm situated in the hills, in quiet and peaceful surroundings. Clyro village 1½ miles.

2rm (1fb) B&b£6 Bdi£9.50 W£64 LDO10am

CTV 6P 3 nc5yrs 50acres mixed

Ⓥ

CLYST ST MARY
Devon
Map **3** SX99

FH Mrs A Freemantle **Ivington** *(SX985912)* ☎Topsham (039287) 3290
Closed Xmas

Large brick-built farmhouse surrounded by lawns and gardens, situated 200yds from A3052.

3hc (2fb) ® B&b£7 W£45.50 M

CTV 3P 200acres arable beef dairy

Ⓥ

CODSALL
Staffordshire
Map **7** SJ80

FH Mrs D E Moreton **Moors** *(SJ859048)* Chillington Ln ☎(09074) 2330

A much modernised and extended 200 year-old farmhouse, providing comfortable accommodation in pleasant rural location 3m from M54 at junction 3; 5 miles NW of Wolverhampton.

6rm 4hc 2 (2fb) ® B&b£10–£12 Bdi£16.50–£20 W£93–£100 LDO9pm

Lic CTV 20P nc4yrs 100acres mixed

COLEFORD
Devon
Map **3** SS70

INN New Inn (Guestaccom) ☎Copplestone (03634) 242

4rm 3hc 1 ® *B&b£10–£11 D9.30pm £4alc

56P nc14yrs

COLESHILL
Warwickshire
Map **4** SP28

INN George & Dragon 154 Coventry Rd ☎(0675) 62249

Large half-timbered roadside inn near M6 Junction 4.

4hc TV in all bedrooms ® B&b£10 Bdi£14 L£2.50–£5.75 D10pm £2.50–£5.75

40P

COLL (Island of)
Strathclyde *Argyllshire*
Map **13** NM25

Car Ferry from Oban (some services via Lochaline/Tobermory. Also linking with Tiree)

GH Tigh-na-Mara ☎(08793) 354
Mar–Oct

Modern bungalow on road between pier and village, overlooking anchorage where seals are visible.

8hc (3fb) TV in 2 bedrooms *B&b£8.50–£9 Bdi£16–£17 W£105–£112 LDO6.30pm

Lic CTV 10P

Ⓥ

COLLYWESTON
Northamptonshire
Map **4** TF00

INN Cavalier Main St ☎Duddington (078083) 288

5rm 2hc 3 CTV in all bedrooms ® *B&b£11.50–£17.25 L£5.50 D9.30pm £5.50&alc

60P

Credit card 1

Colwyn Bay

1 Cabin Hill Private Hotel
2 Grosvenor Hotel
4 Northwood Hotel
5 Southlea
6 Sunny Downs Private Hotel

Colwyn Bay

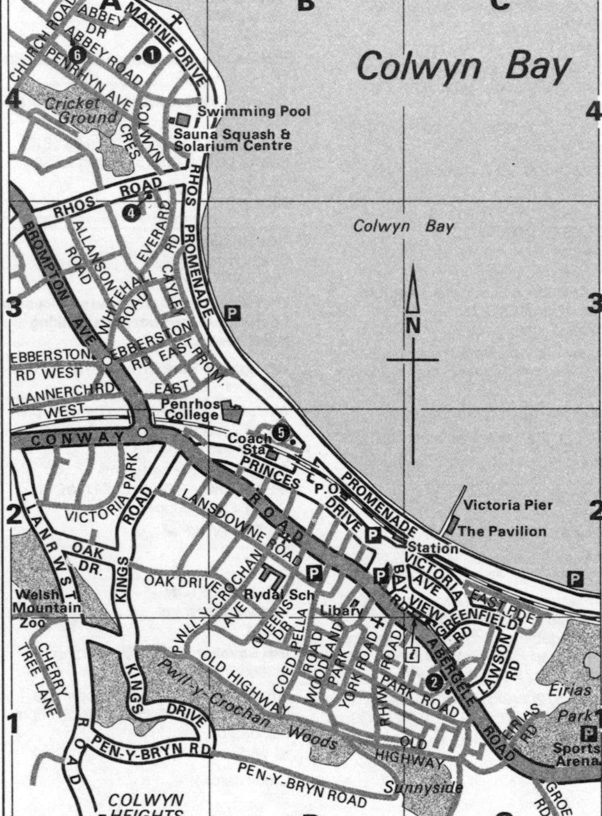

COLWYN BAY
Clwyd
Map **6** SH87
See plan

GH Cabin Hill Private Hotel College Av, Rhos-on-Sea ☎(0492) 44568 Plan **1** *A4*
Mar–mid Nov
Detached Edwardian house in residential area, off Marine Drive.
10hc 3🚿 (5fb) 🐕 Ⓡ B&b£9.50–£11.50 Bdi£11–£15 W£65–£80 M̸ LDO5pm
Lic ▥ CTV 6P
Ⓥ

GH *Grosvenor Hotel* 106–108 Abergele Rd ☎(0492) 31586 Plan **2** *C1*
Detached Victorian house set back from the A55 and adjacent to shops.
16hc 2🛁 🚿 (8fb) 🐕
Lic CTV 12P
See advertisement on page 117

GH Northwood Hotel 47 Rhos Rd, Rhos-on-Sea ☎(0492) 49931 Plan **4** *A3*
Closed Jan
Detached hotel, a short walk from shops and beach.
14rm 10hc 1🛁 3🚿 (4fb) TV in 4 bedrooms Ⓡ B&b£9–£10 Bdi£13–£14 W£73–£80 ⱡ LDO5pm
Lic ▥ CTV 12P

GH Southlea 4 Upper Prom ☎(0492) 2004 Plan **5** *B2*
Closed Xmas
Single fronted mid terrace Victorian house adjacent to beach.
9rm 7hc 1🛁 1🚿 (5fb) Ⓡ B&b£8.75–£9.50 Bdi£11.75–£13 W£75–£80 ⱡ LDO6.30pm
Lic ▥ CTV 🅿̸
Credit cards [1] [3] Ⓥ

GH Sunny Downs Private Hotel 66 Abbey Rd, Rhos-on-Sea ☎(0492) 44256 Plan **6** *A4*
Detached Edwardian house in residential area.
17rm 13hc 4🚿 (4fb) Ⓡ B&b£10.45–£11.95 Bdi£13.95–£15.45 W£97.65–£108.15 ⱡ LDO4pm
Lic ▥ CTV 12P nc3yrs

COLYTON
Devon
Map **3** SY29

GH *Old Bakehouse* ☎(0297) 52518
Closed Jan
7hc 4 (1fb) CTV available in bedrooms LDO9pm
Lic 10P

COMBE MARTIN
Devon
Map **2** SS54

GH Firs Woodlands ☎(027188) 3404
Mar–Oct
8hc (5fb) B&b£7 Bdi£12 W£65–£75 LDO5pm
Lic CTV 10P
Ⓥ

GH *Mellstock House* Woodlands ☎(027188) 2592
Closed Dec
6rm 4hc 2 (2fb) LDO6pm
Lic CTV 5P 1 nc3yrs sea

GH *Miramar Hotel* Victoria St ☎(027188) 3558
11hc (5fb)
Lic CTV 9P 2

GH Newberry Lodge Hotel
Newberry Rd ☎(027188) 3316
Closed Xmas
13rm 12hc 1 (4fb) Ⓡ B&b£7–£8 Bdi£12–£13 W£45–£52 M LDO7.30pm
Lic CTV 13P

GH The Woodlands Woodlands ☎(027188) 2769
2 Mar–4 Oct rs 5 Oct–1 Mar
8rm 4hc (2fb) B&b£7–£8 Bdi£11–£12 W£50–£57 M LDO5pm
Lic CTV 6P 2 nc3yrs
Credit card 3

FH Mr & Mrs Peacock **Longlands** *(SS614451)* Easterclose Cross ☎(027188) 3522
Mar–Oct
Situated in unspoilt woods and valleys with fine views.
6hc *B&b£7–£8 Bdi£10–£11.50 LDO6.30pm
Lic CTV 15P 27acres sheep mixed

COMPTON
Berkshire
Map **4** SU57

INN Swan Hotel ☎(063522) 269
Friendly warm atmosphere with bar and restaurant menus.
4hc Ⓡ B&b£11–£13 Bdi£16–£20 L£2.50–£4.90&alc D9pm £7alc
TV 40P
Ⓥ

COMRIE
Tayside *Perthshire*
Map **11** NN72

GH *Mossgiel* ☎(0764) 70567
Closed Nov
A homely and cosy little house on the western outskirts of town.
6hc LDO5.30pm
CTV 6P

FH Mrs J H Rimmer **West Ballindaloch** *(NN744262)* Glenlednock ☎(0764) 70282
Mar–Oct
Cosy, small farmhouse with neat garden set amid hills in secluded glen. 4m from Comrie.
2rm (1fb) B&b£6.50–£7 W£45.50 M
CTV 3P 1500acres sheep
Ⓥ

CONISTON
Cumbria
Map **7** SD39

INN Crown ☎(0966) 41243
Cheerful village inn near lake.
6hc B&b£10.50–£11.50 Bdi£16.50–£18 W£73–£83 M L£2.50–£4.50&alc D7.45pm £6–£6.50&alc
CTV 35P 3
Ⓥ

CONNOR DOWNS
Cornwall
Map **2** SW53

GH Pine Trees ☎Hayle (0736) 753249
Mar–Oct rs Nov–Feb
Small detached residence positioned adjacent to the A30.
9hc 2 (4fb) B&b£7.50–£8.50 Bdi£10.50–£12 W£65–£90 LDO4pm
Lic CTV 15P (heated)

CONSTANTINE
Cornwall
Map **2** SW72

INN *Trengilly Wartha* Nancenoy ☎Falmouth (0326) 40332
6hc 1 Ⓡ LDO9.30pm
40P
Ⓥ
See advertisement on page 151

CONWY
Gwynedd
Map **6** SH77

GH *Cyfnant Private Hotel* Henry Rd ☎(049263) 2442
Closed Jan
Edwardian semi-detached house in residential area, ½ mile from Castle.
6hc (2fb) TV in all bedrooms
Lic CTV 6P

GH Llys Gwilym 3 Mountain Rd, off Cadnant Park ☎(049263) 2351
Semi-detached house in own garden ¼m from the Castle.
6hc (3fb) B&b£7–£7.50 Bdi£10.50–£11 W£48–£50 LDO6pm
Lic CTV 3P nc2yrs Ⓥ

GH Sunnybanks Llanrwst Rd, Woodlands ☎(049263) 3845
Etr–Oct
Semi-detached house in quiet residential area.
7hc (2fb) B&bfr£6.50 Bdifr£10.50 Wfr£60 LDO8pm
TV 6P
Ⓥ

COOKLEY
Suffolk
Map **5** TM37

FH Mr & Mrs A T Veasy **Green** *(TM337772)* ☎Linstead (098685) 209
Etr–Nov
17th-century farmhouse with exposed timbers. Situated in an area of rural peace and quiet. Friendly atmosphere.
3hc (1fb) B&bfr£8.50 Bdifr£12.75 LDO4pm
CTV 3P nc8yrs 45acres arable
Ⓥ

COOMBE
Cornwall
Map **2** SW95

FH Mrs J Scott **Treway** *(SW935505)* ☎St Austell (0726) 882236
Apr–Oct
Pleasant, comfortable farmhouse in isolated rural setting approx 8m from St Austell.
3rm 2hc (2fb) B&b£7–£7.50
CTV 3P 180acres beef dairy mixed
Ⓥ

COPPLESTONE
Devon
Map **3** SS70

FH Mrs J A King ***Elston Barton*** *(SS784025)* (1m E on unclass road) ☎(03634) 397
Closed Xmas & New Year rs Jan & Feb
3rm 1hc Ⓡ
CTV 4P 1 non-working
See advertisement on page 122

CORRIE
Isle of Arran, Strathclyde *Buteshire*
Map **10** NS04

GH Blackrock House ☎(077081) 282
Closed Dec
Stone house dating from 1930 with modernised interior and good sea views.
9rm 8hc (4fb) Ⓡ B&b£8.50 Bdi£12.50 W£57.50 M LDO5pm
Lic CTV 8P

CORWEN
Clwyd
Map **6** SJ04

GH *Central Hotel* ☎(0490) 2462
In centre of village, incorporating a cafe.
10hc (5fb) CTV in 3 bedrooms TV in 3 bedrooms
Lic CTV 20P 2 river

COSHESTON
Dyfed
Map **2** SN00

INN *Hill House* ☎Pembroke (0646) 684352
rs Oct–Mar except school hols & Xmas
A comfortable inn, enthusiastically run.
6hc CTV in 1 bedroom Ⓡ D10pm
CTV 40P

COTLEIGH
Devon
Map **3** ST20

FH Mrs J Boyland **Barn Park** *(ST218050)* ☎Upottery (040486) 297
Apr–Oct
Comfortably furnished farmhouse offering tasty country fare.
2rm (1fb) B&b£7 Bdi£10 W£60 LDO5pm
CTV 2P 82acres beef dairy

COUNTISBURY *(Near Lynton)*
Devon
Map **3** SS74

FH Mrs R Pile **Coombe** *(SS766489)* ☎Brendon (05987) 236
mid Apr–Oct

5hc (3fb) ★ Ⓡ B&b£8.50–£9.25 Bdi£13.75–£14.50 W£89 Ⱡ LDO5pm

ⅢI CTV 6P 365acres hill stock

COVENTRY
West Midlands
Map **4** SP37

GH Croft Hotel 23 Stoke Gn, off Binley Rd ☎(0203) 457846

12rm 9hc 3⋔ (1fb) CTV in 2 bedrooms B&b£13–£17.50 Bdi£18–£22.50 Wfr£91 Ⱡ LDO6.15pm

Lic ⅢI CTV 22P

ⓥ

⊢⊣ **GH Fairlight** 14 Regent St ☎(0203) 24215
Closed 24 Dec–2 Jan

Victorian terraced house near city centre and railway station.

11hc (3fb) Ⓡ B&b£8–£9 W£53–£60 Ɱ

ⅢI CTV 7P

⊢⊣ **GH Northanger House**
35 Westminster Rd ☎(0203) 26780
Closed 1wk Xmas

7hc (2fb) ★ Ⓡ B&bfr£8 Wfr£56 Ɱ

ⅢI CTV

GH *Ravenswood* 31 Westminster Rd ☎(0203) 20656

7hc 1→ (1fb)

ⅢI CTV 7⌂

GH Spire View 36 Park Rd ☎(0203) 51602

Large, comfortable Victorian terraced house overlooking city centre and close to the railway station.

7rm 6hc 1⋔ (2fb) CTV in 1 bedroom ★ B&b£7.50–£8.50 Wfr£52.50 S%

ⅢI CTV 3P

GH Trinity House Hotel 28 Lower Holyhead Rd ☎(0203) 555654

Tall, bay windowed house with bright modern interior, situated in a cul-de-sac, close to the town centre.

8hc (2fb) Ⓡ B&bfr£9.25 Bdifr£15 Wfr£58 Ɱ LDO9pm

Lic ⅢI CTV 4P

ⓥ

COVERACK BRIDGES *(Near Helston)*
Cornwall
Map **2** SW63

⊢⊣ **FH** Mr & Mrs E Lawrence **Boscadjack** *(SW673311)* ☎Helston (03265) 2086
Apr–Oct

Modernised farmhouse, situated in the Cober Valley amidst delightful unspoilt countryside. 2¼m N of Helston, off B3207.

4hc (2fb) ★ B&bfr£7 Bdifr£10 Wfr£49 Ɱ (W only end Jul & Aug)

ⅢI CTV P 92acres dairy

COWDENBEATH
Fife
Map **11** NT19

GH Struan Bank Private Hotel 74 Perth Rd ☎(0383) 511057

A small pleasantly appointed hotel on outskirts of town

8hc B&b£9 Bdi£12.50 LDO8pm

Lic ⅢI CTV 8P

ⓥ

CRACKINGTON HAVEN
Cornwall
Map **2** SX19

FH Mrs M Knight **Manor** *(SX159962)* ☎St Gennys (08403) 304

Dating from the 12th century and mentioned in the Domesday Book. Attractive gardens with beautiful view, in secluded position. Guests are not permitted to smoke in the house.

4rm 2→ ★ B&b£9 Bdi£14 W£98 Ⱡ LDO5pm

ⅢI CTV 6P nc14yrs billiards 180acres arable beef dairy

CRAFTHOLE
Cornwall
Map **2** SX35

INN Finnygook ☏St Germans (0503) 30338

Well modernised, country inn with pleasant views and comfortable bedrooms.

6rm 1hc 5⇌fl CTV in 5 bedrooms ✱ Ⓡ
✱B&b£25 L£1–£5 D£8alc
30P 2 nc14yrs

CRAIL
Fife
Map **12** NO60

Crafthole — Crediton

GH Caiplie 51–53 High St
☏(0333) 50564
Etr–Oct rs Jan–Etr

Compact and neatly maintained guesthouse in main street of coastal village.

7hc (2fb) Ⓡ B&b£7.50–£10.50 Bdi£14.50–£16.50 W£77–£98 Ⱡ LDO5pm
Lic CTV
Ⓥ

CRAWLEY
West Sussex
Map **4** TQ23

For accommodation details see under Gatwick Airport

CREDITON
Devon
Map **3** SS80

FH Mr & Mrs M Pennington **Woolsgrove** *(SS793028)* Sandford
☏Copplestone (03634) 246
Apr–Oct

17th-century farmhouse overlooking grassland. 3m NW on unclass road and 1m N of A377.

3rm 2hc (1fb) ✝ B&b£7.50–£8 Bdi£9.50–£10 W£52.50 M LDO4pm
CTV P 🏠 150acres mixed
Ⓥ

CREETOWN
Dumfries & Galloway *Kirkcudbrightshire*
Map **11** NX45

INN Creetown Arms Hotel St Johns Street ☎(067182) 282
Neat, spotlessly clean village inn run by dedicated proprietor.
6hc Ⓡ B&b£9–£9.50 Bdi£12.50–£14 L£2–£5&alc D8.30pm £6&alc
CTV 15P

CRIANLARICH
Central *Perthshire*
Map **10** NN32

GH Glenardran ☎(08383) 236
Stone house in village with good accommodation.
6hc (3fb) *B&b£7.50–£8 Bdi£11.50–£12.50 W£45–£48 M LDO7pm
Lic CTV 6P nc7yrs
Ⓥ

GH Moungreenan ☎(08383) 286
Friendly little guesthouse with good views of Ben More.
5hc (1fb) ✝ B&b£8–£8.25 Bdi£11.50–£12 W£55–£56.75 M LDO9am
CTV P

Crediton — Criccieth

CRICCIETH
Gwynedd
Map **6** SH53

GH Glyn-y-Coed Private Hotel Portmadoc Rd ☎(076671) 2870
Closed Xmas & New Year
10hc (5fb) Ⓡ B&b£10 Bdi£15 W£100 M LDO6pm
Lic CTV 12P

GH Kairon Hotel Marine Ter ☎(076671) 2453
10hc Ⓡ B&b£8.50–£9 Bdi£12.50–£13.50 W£85.50–£90 L LDO7pm
Lic CTV 14P

GH Min-y-Gaer Private Hotel Porthmadoc Rd ☎(076671) 2151
Apr–Oct
Substantial Victorian semi-detached house with coastal views.
10hc (4fb) Ⓡ B&b£8.50–£9.50 Bdi£12.50–£13.50 W£83–£89 L LDO4pm
Lic CTV 12P
Credit cards 1 3 Ⓥ

GH *Moorings* Marine Ter ☎(076671) 2802
Etr–Sep
Victorian mid terrace on the front, adjacent to the castle.
8hc (2fb) TV available in 2 bedrooms Ⓡ LDO6.30pm
Lic CTV 24P sea
Ⓥ

GH Môr Heli Private Hotel Marine Ter ☎(076671) 2794
Mar–Sep
Victorian mid terrace house on the front, 1/4 mile from shops.
14hc (4fb) B&bfr£8.50 Bdifr£11.50 Wfr£80 LDO6.30pm
Lic CTV 20P
Ⓥ
See advertisement on page 124

GH Neptune Private Hotel Marine Ter (Guestaccom) ☎(076671) 2794
Mar–Sep
Victorian mid terrace house on front adjacent to the castle.
12hc (4fb) B&bfr£8.50 Bdifr£11.50 Wfr£80 L LDO6.30pm
Lic CTV 20P
Ⓥ
See advertisement on page 124

CRICKHOWELL
Powys
Map **3** SO21

GH Dragon Country House Hotel High St ☎(0873) 810362
Attractive cottage style house enthusiastically run, with cosy bar for residents.
11hc 1➡ 1⋒ (2fb) CTV in 4 bedrooms ★ ® B&bfr£9.50 Bdifr£14.50 W£89.50–£103.95 Ⱡ LDO8pm
Lic ▥ CTV 20P ⌂

CRIEFF
Tayside *Perthshire*
Map **11** NN82

⊢⊣ **GH Comely Bank** 32 Burrell St ☎(0764) 3409
Mar–Oct rs Nov–Feb
7hc (2fb) B&b£7.25 Bdi£10.50 W£66.50 Ⱡ LDO7pm
CTV ✗
Ⓥ

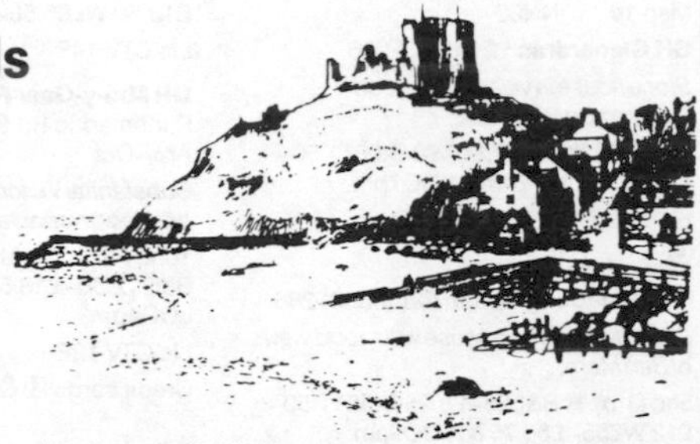

⊢⊣ **GH Heatherville** 29–31 Burrell St ☎(0764) 2825
Comfortable, privately owned house forming part of a terrace.
4hc (2fb) ★ B&b£7–£7.50 Bdi£11–£12 W£70–£75 LDO5pm
▥ CTV 4P nc2yrs

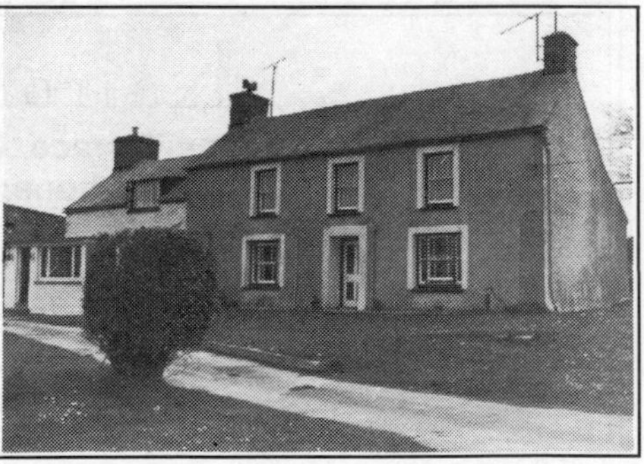

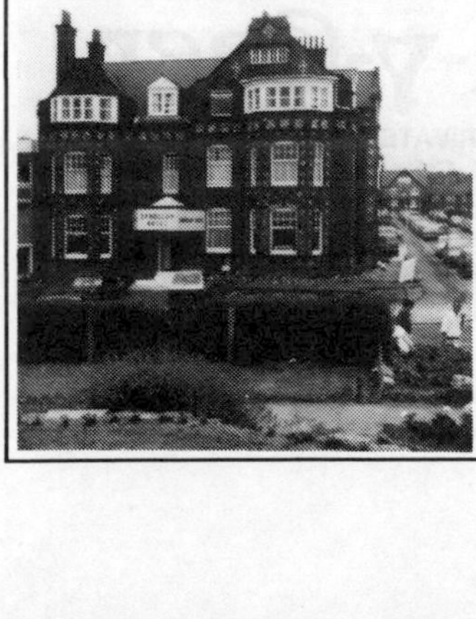

CROESGOCH
Dyfed
Map **2** SM83

GH *Cwmwdig Water* Berea ☎(03483) 434
Mar–Nov

A 200 year old converted farmhouse and barns set in country overlooking the sea and National Park.

4hc (A 7hc) (5fb) ® LDO7.30pm

Lic 🍽 CTV 15P ⌂ sea

⊢⊣ **FH** Mrs A Charles **Torbant** *(SM845307)* ☎(03483) 276

16May–Sep rs 14 Apr–15 May

Larger than average farm guesthouse in pleasant position overlooking open country.

11hc (5fb) ✦ B&b£7.50–£9 Bdi£13–£14.50 W£89–£93 Ⱡ LDO8pm

Lic 🍽 CTV 40P ⌂ 110acres dairy

See advertisement on page 298

FH Mrs M B Jenkins **Trearched** *(SM831306)* ☎(03483) 310

Farm overlooks St George's Channel. Ideal for touring Southwest Wales and coast. Off A487.

7hc (2fb) B&b£8.50–£10 Bdi£13–£15 W£56–£70 M LDO5pm

🍽 CTV P ✓ 139acres arable

Ⓥ

CROMER
Norfolk
Map **9** TG24

⊢⊣ **GH Brightside** 19 Macdonald Rd ☎(0263) 513408

Apr–Oct

7hc (3fb) ✦ B&b£7.50 Bdi£11 W£50 Ⱡ LDO3.30pm

Lic 🍽 CTV nc5yrs

GH *Chellow Dene* 23 Macdonald Rd ☎(0263) 513251

Closed Xmas wk

7hc (2fb)

Lic 🍽 CTV 6P nc3yrs

Ⓥ

GH Sandcliffe Private Hotel Runton Rd ☎(0263) 512888

Friendly run private hotel situated on the coast road, conveniently placed for access to town centre.

22rm 4hc 18➡ (8fb) B&b£11.20 Bdi£14.20 W£84 M LDO8pm

Lic CTV 10P

Credit cards 1 3

GH Westgate Lodge Private Hotel 10 Macdonald Rd ☎(0263) 512840

12rm 8hc 4⋒ (6fb) ✦ B&bfr£9.20 Bdifr£14.95 Wfr£86.25 Ⱡ LDO6.30pm

Lic 🍽 CTV 14P nc3yrs

Credit cards 1 3

CROMHALL
Avon
Map **3** ST69

⊢⊣ **FH** Mrs S Scolding **Varley** *(ST699905)* Talbot End ☎Wickwar (045424) 292

Etr–Sep

Spacious, two-storey stone-built farmhouse with garden. Well maintained and neatly decorated throughout.

3hc (3fb) ✦ B&b£7.50–£8.25 W£52.50 M

🍽 CTV 4P 75acres dairy

Ⓥ

CROOK
Cumbria
Map **7** SD49

⊢⊣ **FH** Mrs I D Scales **Greenbank** *(SD462953)* ☎Staveley (0539) 821216

Feb–Dec

Attractive farmhouse with pleasant gardens, near village centre.

5hc 1⋒ (3fb) ® B&b£9.50–£10 Bdi£16.50 £17.50 LDO2pm

Lic 🍽 CTV 7P nc12yrs 15acres mushrooms

Ⓥ

CROSSGATES
Powys
Map **3** SO06

GH Guildfa House ☎Penybont (059787) 241
Delightful country house style property prominently positioned adjacent A44 at Crossgates. Comfortable bedrooms and character lounge.
6hc 2⋔ (2fb) ★ Ⓡ B&b£9–£11 Bdi£15.50–£17.50 W£95–£105 Ⱡ LDO6.30pm
Lic ▥ CTV 10P

CROXDALE
Co Durham
Map **8** NZ23

INN Croxdale ☎Spennymoor (0388) 815727
6hc TV in 3 bedrooms B&b£11–£14 Bdi£15–£19 W£66–£84 M LDO7.30pm
CTV 6P
Ⓥ

CROYDE
Devon
Map **2** SS43

GH *Bay View Hotel* Baggy Point (1m W) ☎(0271) 890224
7hc 5⇌ CTV in 5 bedrooms TV in 2 bedrooms ★ Ⓡ LDO9.30pm
Lic ▥ 24P nc7yrs sea

GH Moorsands House Hotel Moor Ln ☎(0271) 890781
Apr–Oct
8hc (2fb) ★ B&b£8.50–£10.50 Bdi£13–£15.50 W£91–£105 Ⱡ LDO1pm
Lic ▥ CTV 8P nc4yrs
Ⓥ

GH *St Helens Priory Hotel* ☎(0271) 890757
Etr–Oct
5hc (2fb) ★
Lic CTV 15P nc12yrs

INN *Thatched Barn* ☎(0271) 890349
4rm 3hc 1⇌⋔ CTV in 1 bedroom LDO10pm
▥ 40P
Ⓥ

CROYDON
Gt London
London plan **4** D1 (pages 222–223)

GH Central Hotel 3–5 South Park Hill Rd ☎01-688 5644
rs Xmas day
Victorian brick built house offering very good rooms, in an Austrian atmosphere.
25rm 11hc 7⇌ 7⋔ CTV in all bedrooms ★ Ⓡ B&b£20–£27 LDO8pm
Lic lift ▥ CTV 20P

GH Friends 50 Friends Rd ☎01-688 6215
Victorian house run by Maltese family plainly furnished, friendly atmosphere.
11hc (3fb) ★ B&b£13–£15
▥ CTV 4P nc2yrs
Ⓥ

GH Lonsdale Hotel 158 Lower Addiscombe Rd ☎01-654 2276
9hc (3fb) CTV in all bedrooms ★ Ⓡ *B&b£16 Bdi£21.50 LDO8pm
Lic ▥ CTV 10P sauna bath

GH Markington Hotel 9 Haling Park Rd, South Croydon ☎01-688 6530
Closed Xmas
Small, family run bed and breakfast hotel.
16rm 5hc 1⇌ 10⋔ (3fb) CTV in all bedrooms ★ Ⓡ B&b£17–£25 LDO8pm
Lic ▥ CTV 7P
Credit cards 1 2 3 Ⓥ

GH Oakwood Hotel 69 Outram Rd ☎01-654 2835
Near town centre, Victorian house with bay windows, offering comfortable rooms.
15rm 9⇌ 6⋔ (3fb) CTV in all bedrooms Ⓡ *B&b£15–£24 Bdi£29.50 LDO8pm
Lic ▥ CTV 8P 3🏠 sauna bath
Credit cards 1 2 3 4 5

CRUCKTON
Shropshire
Map **7** SJ41

FH Mrs M L Birchall **Woodfield** *(SJ432108)* ☎Shrewsbury (0743) 860249
Large, modern detached farmhouse with neat gardens.
3rm ★ *B&bfr£7.50
▥ CTV P 84acres

CRYMYCH
Dyfed
Map **2** SN13

FH Mr & Mrs Hazelden **Felin Tŷgwyn** *(SN162355)* ☎Crosswell (023979) 603
Situated approx 2m from Crymych, at the foot of the Preseli Mountains, within easy reach of Newport beach, Cardigan, Carmarthen and Haverfordwest.
5hc (1fb) Bdifr£12 W£76–£88.50 Ⱡ (W only 25 May–7 Sep)
Lic ▥ CTV 5P 8acres dairy
Ⓥ

CUBERT
Cornwall
Map **2** SW75

FH J & F Whybrow **Treworgans** *(SW787589)* ☎Crantock (0637) 830200
Closed Xmas
Detached bungalow, situated approx 1m from the village.
5hc B&b£6–£6.50 Bdi£9–£9.50 W£63 Ⱡ LDO4pm
▥ CTV 6P 70acres mixed

CULLEN
Grampian *Banffshire*
Map **15** NJ56

GH Wakes Hotel Seafield Pl ☎(0542) 40251
23rm 22hc B&b£8–£9 Bdi£11–£12 W£65–£70 Ⱡ LDO7pm
Lic CTV 20P

CULLODEN MOOR
Highland *Inverness-shire*
Map **14** NH74

FH Mrs E M C Alexander **Culdoich** *(NH755435)* ☎Inverness (0463) 790628
Etr–Oct
18th-century farmhouse in isolated position near Culloden battlefield and Clava standing stones.
2rm (1fb) ★ B&b£8–£9 Bdi£11–£12 W£80 Ⱡ LDO7pm
CTV 6P 200acres mixed

CULLOMPTON
Devon
Map **3** ST00

FH Mrs A C Cole **Five Bridges** *(ST026095)* ☎(0884) 33453
Closed Xmas
Well-maintained brick-built farmhouse.
4hc (3fb) B&b£6.50 Bdi£10 W£65 Ⱡ LDO6pm
CTV 6P 1🏠 22acres non-working
Ⓥ

CURY CROSS LANES
Cornwall
Map **2** SW62

FH Mrs M F Osborne **Polglase** *(SW286213)* ☎Mullion (0326) 240469
Etr–Sep
Comfortable working farm with modern accommodation and good food. 5m from Helston.
6rm 5hc (2fb) ★ B&b£6.50–£7 Bdi£10.50–£11 W£73.50–£77 Ⱡ (W only 21 Jul–Aug)
CTV 4P 65acres mixed

CWMBACH *(Near Glasbury)*
Powys
Map **3** SO13

GH Rhydfelin Farm Builth Rd ☎Builth Wells (0982) 553678
Closed 26–30 Dec
6hc (1fb) *B&b£7.50 Bdi£13 W£50 M LDO8.45pm
Lic ▥ CTV 12P
Credit cards 1 3
See advertisement on page 96

DALMALLY
Strathclyde *Argyllshire*
Map **10** NN12

GH Orchy Bank Stronmilchan Rd ☎(08382) 370
Apr–Oct
White house in rural setting by River Orchy. Friendly proprietor is bilingual.

9rm 8hc (2fb) Ⓡ ✱B&b£8.50–£10 Bdi£12.50–£15 W£80–£100 Ⱡ LDO9pm
CTV 9P ♿

DALWOOD *(Near Axminster)*
Devon
Map **3** ST20
⊢⊣**FH** Mr & Mrs Cobley **Elford** *(ST258004)* ☎Axminster (0297) 32415
Mar–Oct
17th-century farmhouse with panoramic, pastoral views.
5rm 4hc 2➡ (2fb) ✘ B&b£8–£9 Bdi£11.50–£12.50 W£73.85–£79.85 Ⱡ LDO5pm
Lic ⩩ CTV 8P 37acres mixed

DARLINGTON
Co Durham
Map **8** NZ21
GH Raydale Hotel Stanhope Road South ☎(0325) 58993
Closed 24 Dec–1 Jan
11hc (2fb) TV in 1 bedroom B&b£14.95–£17.25 Bdi£20.70–£23 LDO3pm
Lic ⩩ CTV 12P
Credit cards 1 3 5

DARTINGTON
Devon
Map **3** SX76
INN Cott ☎Totnes (0803) 863777
Closed Xmas Day
6hc B&b£16 Bdi£23.50 W£112 M
L£6–£8alc D10pm £6–£8alc
⩩ CTV 60P
Credit cards 1 2 3 4 5

DARTMOUTH
Devon
Map **3** SX84
GH Orleans 24 South Town ☎(08043) 2967
5hc (1fb) ✘ ✱B&b£8.50–£9.50 W£57–£60 M
⩩ CTV ⚑
Credit card 3

DAVIOT
Highland *Inverness-shire*
Map **14** NH73
FH Mrs E M MacPherson **Lairgandour** *(NH720376)* ☎(046385) 207
Etr–early Oct
In a quiet location near to Culloden Moor, Loch Ness and the Cairngorms. Situated E of A9 at junction with B9154.
5rm 4hc (3fb) ✱B&b£7.50 Bdi£10 LDO 5pm
CTV 6P 1000acres mixed

DAWLISH
Devon
Map **3** SX97
⊢⊣**GH Broxmore Private Hotel** 20 Plantation Ter ☎(0626) 863602
Closed Jan & Feb rs Mar
8hc (3fb) ✘ Ⓡ B&b£7.60–£8.70 Bdi£11.60–£13 W£74.50–£86 Ⱡ LDO5pm
Lic ⩩ CTV ⚑ nc5yrs
⊢⊣**GH Lynbridge Private Hotel** Barton Villas ☎(0626) 862352
Etr–Oct
8hc (2fb) ✘ B&b£8–£8.50 Bdi£10.50–£11 W£52–£57 Ⱡ LDO6.30pm
⩩ CTV 6P nc2yrs
Ⓥ
⊢⊣**GH Mimosa** 11 Barton Ter ☎(0626) 863283
Apr–Sep
9rm 7hc 2⋒ (4fb) ✘ B&b£6.50–£7.50 Bdi£9.50–£10.50 W£41–£49 M LDO2pm
CTV 4P nc5yrs
GH *Portland House* 14 Marine Pde ☎(0626) 864040
Etr–Nov
7hc (3fb) ✘ LDO9am
CTV 6P nc5yrs sea
GH Radfords Hotel Dawlish Water ☎(0626) 863322
Mar–Nov
23➡ (23fb) B&b£15–£20 Bdi£21–£26 (W only Jul & Aug) LDO6.45pm
Lic ⩩ CTV 50P ⌂
Ⓥ

DEBDEN GREEN
Essex
Map **5** TL53
⊢⊣**FH** Mrs K M Low **Wychbars** *(TL564313)* ☎Bishop's Stortford (0279) 850362
Moated farmhouse in 3½ acres. Down unclassified Debden Green road, off B1051. Farmhouse through Scotts Farm.
2rm CTV in 1 bedroom TV in 1 bedroom B&b£8–£8.50 W£50 M
⩩ CTV 10P ♿ 600acres arable
Ⓥ

DEDHAM
Essex
Map **5** TM03
GH *Dedham Hall* ☎Colchester (0206) 323027
Mar–Nov
Beautiful timber framed house in six acres of grounds providing comfortable accommodation and good home cooking.
7rm 6hc 1➡ ✘ Ⓡ LDO4pm
Lic ⩩ CTV 10P 2⌂ nc10
Ⓥ

DENBIGH
Clwyd
Map **6** SJ06
GH Cayo 74 Vale St ☎(074571) 2686
6hc (2fb) B&b£9 Bdi£13 W£63 M LDO6.30pm
Lic ⩩ CTV ⚑
Credit cards 1 2 3 4 5

DERBY
Derbyshire
Map **8** SK33
GH *Ascot Hotel* 724 Osmaston Rd ☎(0332) 41916
20hc (2fb) LDOnoon
Lic ⩩ CTV 16P
See advertisement on page 128

⊢⊣ **GH Dalby House** 100 Radbourne St ☎(0332) 42353
9hc (2fb) CTV in 1 bedroom ★ ® B&b£8–£11 Bdi£12–£15 LDO4pm
CTV 8P 1

⊢⊣ **GH Georgian House Hotel** 32/34 Ashbourne Rd ☎(0332) 49806
Beautifully preserved Georgian town house on the A52, ½ mile north of city centre.
17rm 15hc 1 (3fb) CTV in 2 bedrooms ★ B&b£9.25–£12.50 Bdi£14.20–£17.45 W£89–£139 LDO7pm
Lic CTV 20P

Derby
—
Devil's Bridge

GH Kerrance Hotel 115 London Rd ☎(0332) 45242
Closed Xmas
12hc (1fb) B&bfr£9.50 Bdifr£13.50 Wfr£66.50
Lic CTV

DERSINGHAM
Norfolk
Map **9** TF63

GH Westdene House Hotel
60 Hunstanton Rd ☎(0485) 40395
Closed Nov
5hc 1 (1fb) ★ ® B&b£10–£12.50 Bdi£13.50–£16 LDO9.30pm
Lic CTV 12P
Ⓥ

DEVIL'S BRIDGE
Dyfed
Map **6** SN77
⊢⊣ **FH** Mrs E E Lewis **Erwbarfe**

(SN749784) ☎Ponterwyd (097085) 251
Mar–Oct

See gazetteer entry under Shottle.

A traditional stone-built farmhouse with oak beamed ceiling in the lounge. 2m NE of Devil's Bridge on A4120.
3hc (2fb) ✱ Ⓡ B&b£8–£9 Bdi£12–£15 W£58 M (W only Jul & Aug) LDO4pm
CTV 4P 400acres mixed
Ⓥ

DEVIZES
Wiltshire
Map **4** SU06
INN Castle Hotel New Park St ☎(0380) 2902
Closed Xmas
15rm 13hc 2→ CTV in all bedrooms Ⓡ B&b£9.90–£17.50 Bdi£15.90–£23.50 W£69.30–£110.25 M L£6&alc D9.30pm £6&alc
8
Credit cards 1 3 5

DEVORAN
Cornwall
Map **2** SW73
GH Driffold Hotel 8 Devoran Ln (Guestaccom) ☎(0872) 863314
Attractive small hotel overlooking Devoran Creek. Friendly, personally run and good food.
7rm 3hc 2 ✱ LDO7pm
Lic CTV 14P

DIDDLEBURY
Shropshire
Map **7** SO58
FH Mrs E Wilkes **Glebe** *(SO507856)* ☎Munslow (058476) 221
Mar–4 Nov
3hc (A 4hc 1) (1fb) ✱ Ⓡ B&b£10–£14 Bdi£18.50–£23.50 W£122.50–£143.50 L LDO6pm
Lic CTV 10P nc8yrs 123acres arable beef sheep
Ⓥ

DIRLETON
Lothian *East Lothian*
Map **12** NT58
INN Castle ☎(062085) 221
Closed Xmas & New Year
rs mid Jan–Apr

Plain but comfortable inn in attractive setting on village green.
5hc (A 4hc) Ⓡ B&b£11.50–£12.50 Bdifr£18 W£70–£80 M Bar lunch £1.35–£3.50 D8pm £6.50–£8.50
CTV 12P
Credit card 1 Ⓥ

DODDISCOMBSLEIGH
Devon
Map **3** SX88
INN Nobody ☎Christow (0647) 52394
Closed Xmas Day rs Sun & Mon (except Bank Hols)
4rm 1hc 2 ✱ Ⓡ B&b£10–£14 Bar lunch 70p–£2.50 D9.30pm £8alc
50P nc14yrs
Credit cards 1 3

DOLGELLAU
Gwynedd
Map **6** SH71
GH Clifton Private Hotel Smithfield Sq ☎(0341) 422554
6hc (2fb) ✱ B&b£8.50–£9.50 Bdi£13.50–£14.50 W£56–£60 M LDO7pm
CTV 3P
Ⓥ

FH Mrs E W Price **Glyn** *(SH704178)* ☎(0341) 422286
Mar–Jun rs Jul–Nov
Stone-built farmhouse of historical interest with oak beams, floors and doors. Well situated for coastal resorts.
4hc (2fb) B&b£6.50–£7.50 (Jul–Nov) Bdi£10–£12 (Mar–June) Wfr£70 L LDO24hrs
CTV 6P 150acres mixed

FH Mrs S J Lane **Llwyn-Yr-Helm** *(SH778191)* Brithdir ☎Rhydymain (034141) 254
Apr–Oct
3m SW off B4416.
3rm 1hc B&b£7 Bdi£10 W£48 M LDO5pm
TV 3P 56acres mixed

DOLWYDDELAN
Gwynedd
Map **6** SH75
INN Gwydyr ☎(06906) 209
rs Oct–Apr
Victorian detached inn in centre of village, set in peaceful valley.
3hc TV in all bedrooms B&b£8 W£56 M Bar lunch £1.20–£2.30 D9.30pm £5.50
CTV 6P

DORNIE
Highland *Ross & Cromarty*
Map **14** NG82
FH Mrs M Macrae **Bungalow** *(NG871272)* Ardelve ☎(059985) 231
Etr–Oct
Farmhouse situated on main A87.
3hc (1fb) ✱ B&b£7–£7.50
6P nc5yrs 10acres arable mixed

DORSINGTON
Warwickshire
Map **4** SP14
FH Mrs M J Walters **Church** *(SP132495)* ☎Stratford-upon-Avon (0789) 720471
Homely Georgian house on village outskirts.
3hc (1fb) ✱ B&b£8 Bdi£13 W£84 L LDO6pm
CTV 6P 127acres arable beef horses

DOUGLAS
Isle of Man
Map **6** SC37
GH Ainsdale 2 Empire Ter, Central Prom ☎(0624) 6695
Apr–Sep
Pleasantly furnished and personally run guesthouse.
19hc (5fb) *B&b£7–£8 Bdi£8.50–£9 LDO7pm
CTV P
Ⓥ

GH Ascot Private Hotel 7 Empire Ter ☎(0624) 5081 (due to change to 75081)
Apr–Oct rs Nov–Mar
Large, central private hotel providing good family entertainment.
40rm 30hc 10➡ 5⋒ (9fb) ★ ®
B&b£8.50–£10 Bdi£10–£12 W£59.50–£84 M̸ LDO11am
Lic CTV

GH *Beachcomber* 3 Athol Ter, Queen's Prom ☎(0624) 5551
May–Sep
Small, family run guesthouse on promenade.
12hc (5fb) TV in all bedrooms LDO6pm
Lic CTV ⚑ sea
ⓥ

GH Gladwyn Private Hotel Queen's Prom ☎(0624) 5406
Etr–Sep
19hc 2⋒ (7fb) LDO4pm
Lic CTV ⚑ sea
ⓥ

GH Holyrood Hotel 51 Loch Promenade ☎(0624) 3790
Personally supervised private hotel offering comfortable accommodation.
19hc 2⋒ (9fb) ★ ✱B&b£8 Bdi£11 LDOam
Lic CTV ⚑

GH Hydro Hotel Queen's Prom ☎(0624) 6870
Etr–Sep
71rm 64hc 7➡ (27fb) ★ B&b£9.77–£12.07 Bdi£11.50–£13.80 W£68.39–£84.49 Ł LDO6.30pm
Lic lift Ⅲ CTV ⚑ ⌂

⊢⊣ **GH Rosslyn Private Hotel** 3 Empire Ter, Central Prom ☎(0624) 6056
Near promenade, this guesthouse is personally run by owners.
17hc 2➡ 2⋒ (3fb) ★ ® B&b£7.50–£8.50 Bdi£8.50–£9.50 W£52.50–£59.50 M̸ LDO5.30pm
Lic CTV ⚑
ⓥ

Douglas — Downham Market

GH *Rothesay Private Hotel* 15–16 Loch Prom ☎(0624) 5274
May–Oct
Well furnished, family run hotel with good bedrooms.
32hc 6⋒ (4fb) CTV in all bedrooms ®
Lic lift CTV ⚑ nc5yrs sea

GH *Rutland Hotel* Queen's Prom ☎(0624) 21218
Apr–Oct
Large seafront hotel supervised by resident owners.
110hc 6➡ 7⋒ (17fb) ★
Lic lift CTV ⚑ sea

GH *Welbeck Private Hotel* Mona Dr ☎(0624) 5663
Apr–Oct
Well furnished guesthouse near promenade.
27hc 9⋒ (14fb) ★ ® LDO5.30pm
Lic Ⅲ CTV sea

DOVER
Kent
Map **5** TR34

GH Beulah House 94 Crabble Hill London Rd ☎(0304) 824615
Cosy, homely compact accommodation with limited lounge facilities. Extensive lawns and gardens to rear with open aspect.
7hc (3fb) ★ B&b£9–£10 W£56 M̸
Ⅲ 8P 2⌂

GH Dover Stop 45 London Rd, River (2m NW A256) ☎(0304) 822751
Cheerful modern accommodation with limited lounge facilities.
7hc (A 4hc) (6fb) B&b£13.50–£15.50 Bdi£20–£21.50 W£108 M̸ LDO9pm
Lic Ⅲ CTV 14P sauna bath
ⓥ

GH Number One 1 Castle St ☎(0304) 202007
Conveniently situated, simply furnished, friendly and efficient establishment complemented by a cosy Victorian atmosphere.
5rm 2hc 1➡ 3⋒ (3fb) CTV in all bedrooms ★ ® B&b£9–£10.50
Ⅲ 2P 4⌂
ⓥ

GH Peverell House Private Hotel 28 Park Av ☎(0304) 202573
Etr–Sep
Quietly situated hilltop hotel, with comfortable modern well maintained accommodation.
7hc (3fb) ★ ® B&b£8.50–£10.50 Bdi£14.50–£16.50 W£56–£70 M̸ LDOnoon
Lic Ⅲ CTV 6P nc3yrs

⊢⊣ **GH St Brelades** 82 Buckland Av ☎(0304) 206126
Family accommodation with friendly attentive service.
8hc (4fb) ★ B&b£8–£9
Lic Ⅲ CTV 7P
Credit cards 1 2

⊢⊣ **GH St Martins** 17 Castle Hill Rd ☎(0304) 205938
Closed Xmas
6hc (2fb) CTV in all bedrooms ★ B&b£7.50–£9 W£52.50–£63 M̸
Ⅲ

DOWNHAM MARKET
Norfolk
Map **5** TF60

GH Cross Keys Riverside Hotel Hilgay (Guestaccom) ☎(0366) 387777
Closed 24 Dec–22 Jan
Once a coaching inn, now a small attractive and comfortable hotel, adjacent to the A10 and on the banks of the River Wissey. 3m S off A5012.
3➡ (A 2➡) (1fb) CTV in all bedrooms ★ ® B&b£12–£13.20 Bdi£18.25–£19.95 W£109.50–£120.45 Ł LDO8.30pm
Lic Ⅲ 10P ♩
ⓥ

DOWNTON
Wiltshire
Map **4** SU12

GH Warren High St ☎(0725) 20263
Closed 15 Dec–15 Jan
7rm 6hc 1 (1fb) Ⓡ *B&b£9.50–£10.50
CTV 8P nc5yrs
See advertisement on page 305

DREFACH *(Near Llanybydder)*
Dyfed
Map **2** SN54

FH Mrs W Mellor ***Rhiwson Isaf*** *(SN504467)* ☎Llanybydder (0570) 480085
¼m N of B4338.
2rm (1fb) Ⓡ
CTV 4P 100acres dairy

DROXFORD
Hampshire
Map **4** SU61

GH Little Uplands Country Motel Garrison Hill ☎(0489) 878507
Closed Xmas & New Year
1hc (A 14rm 4hc 8) (1fb) CTV in all bedrooms Ⓡ B&b£12.50 Bdi£20–£22
Lic CTV 20P (heated) (hard) billiards sauna bath
Credit cards 1 2 3 Ⓥ

DRUMNADROCHIT
Highland *Inverness-shire*
Map **14** NH53

INN Lewiston Arms Lewiston ☎(04562) 225
A comfortable and cosy old inn with a friendly relaxed atmosphere.
4rm 3hc (A 4hc) B&b£10–£12 Bdi£15–£20 L£2.50alc D8.30pm £6.50alc
CTV 30P
Credit card 3

DULFORD
Devon
Map **3** ST00

FH Mrs M A Broom ***Nap*** *(ST069065)* ☎Kentisbeare (08846) 287
Closed Xmas
Well-appointed farmhouse set in hamlet of Dulford on main road to Cullompton.
4hc (2fb)
CTV 4P 35acres mixed

DULNAIN BRIDGE
Highland *Morayshire*
Map **14** NH92

GH Rose Grove Skye of Curr ☎(047985) 335
8hc (2fb) B&b£9.50–£11 Bdi£13–£15 W£65–£75 LDO6.30pm
CTV 12P

DUMFRIES
Dumfries & Galloway *Dumfriesshire*
Map **11** NX97

GH Fulwood Private Hotel 30 Lovers Walk ☎(0387) 52262
Compact neat homely villa lying opposite railway station.
6hc (2fb) B&b£7–£7.50 W£49 M
CTV 1
Ⓥ

GH Newall House 22 Newall Ter ☎(0387) 52676
Neatly appointed house with spacious airy bedrooms in residential area between station and town centre.
7rm 6hc (3fb) TV in 4 bedrooms Ⓡ B&b£8 Bdi£12 W£79
Lic CTV 7P

DUNBAR
Lothian *East Lothian*
Map **12** NT67

GH Marine 7 Marine Rd ☎(0368) 63315
Seaside guesthouse, in terraced row in quiet residential area on west side of town.
9hc (4fb) *B&b£7.50–£8.25 Bdi£11–£12 W£65–£70 LDO5pm
CTV

GH St Beys 2 Bayswell Rd ☎(0368) 63571
Nicely appointed house close to town centre, but with sea views.
6hc (4fb) CTV in all bedrooms Ⓡ B&b£10–£12 Bdi£16–£18 W£102–£116 LDO7.50pm
CTV
Credit card 2 Ⓥ

GH Springfield House Belhaven Rd ☎(0368) 62502
Feb–Oct
Nicely appointed house with well tended garden to rear, situated on main road, on west side of town.
7hc (2fb) CTV in all bedrooms Ⓡ B&b£10–£10.50 Bdi£17–£18 W£107–£113 LDO5pm
Lic 9P
Credit cards 1 3 Ⓥ

DUNLOP
Strathclyde *Ayrshire*
Map **10** NS44

FH Mr & Mrs R B Wilson **Struther** *(NS412496)* ☎Stewarton (0560) 84946
Large farmhouse in its own gardens. On edge of Dunlop village.
6hc (2fb) Ⓡ B&bfr£7.50 Bdifr£14.50 W£100 LDO8.30pm
CTV 12P 40acres non-working

DUNOON
Strathclyde *Argyllshire*
Map **10** NS17

GH Cedars Hotel 51 Alexandra Pde, East Bay ☎(0369) 2425
Small, seafront family hotel whose compact rooms are well equipped.
14hc 2 (2fb) Ⓡ B&b£9–£11 Bdi£15–£17 W£54–£67 M LDO6.30pm
Lic CTV
Ⓥ

DUNS
Borders *Berwickshire*
Map **12** NT75

INN Black Bull Hotel Black Bull St ☎(0361) 83379 →

Informally run hotel in side street in town centre.

4hc Ⓡ B&b£10.50 Bdi£17 W£112 Ł L£1.50–£2 D9.30pm £6.50–£9&alc

Ⅲ CTV 10P

Credit cards 1 2 3

DUNSTER
Somerset
Map **3** SS94

⊢⊣ **INN Foresters Arms** 33 West St ☎(064382) 313

10hc ✶ B&b£8 Bdi£12.50 W£56 M̸ Bar lunch£2 D9pm £4

Ⅲ CTV 3P 2⌂ billiards

Credit cards 1 3 Ⓥ

DUNSYRE
Strathclyde *Lanarkshire*
Map **11** NT04

⊢⊣ **FH** Mr L Armstrong **Dunsyre Mains** *(NT074482)* ☎(089981) 251
Mar–Oct

Two-storey stone farmhouse dating from 1800 in courtyard style with splendid views and small garden.

3rm 2hc (1fb) ✶ Ⓡ B&bfr£7.50 Bdifr£12 Wfr£84 Ł LDO7pm

CTV P ⌂ 400acres beef sheep

Ⓥ

DUNVEGAN
Isle of Skye, Highland *Inverness-shire*
Map **13** NG24

⊢⊣ **GH Roskhill** Roskhill (3m S A863) ☎(047022) 317
Closed Jan & Feb

A comfortable and friendly guesthouse situated about 3 miles from Dunvegan (A863).

5hc (2fb) Ⓡ B&b£8–£8.50 Bdi£13.75–£14.50 Wfr£96 Ł LDO6.15pm

Ⅲ CTV 8P

Ⓥ

DURSLEY
Gloucestershire
Map **3** ST79

FH Mrs E Pain **Park** *(ST745970)* Stancombe Park ☎(0453) 45345
Apr–Oct

Comfortable and attractive farmhouse in peaceful south-facing valley surrounded by 160 acres of beech woods. An ideal touring and walking area. ½m SW of Dursley. Reached from B4060 Wotton-under-Edge to Cam road. Turn at sign marked Millend/Waterly Bottom.

2hc (1fb) B&b£8.50 Bdi£16 W£59 M̸ LDOnoon

P 140acres arable beef

Ⓥ

DYMCHURCH
Kent
Map **5** TR12

GH Chantry Hotel Sycamore Gdns (Guestaccom) ☎(0303) 873137
Feb–Oct

8hc 2⇌ 1⋒ (5fb) TV in 3 bedrooms ✶ B&b£10–£11 Bdi£15.50–£16.50 W£86–£96 Ł LDO6pm

Lic Ⅲ CTV 10P

GH Waterside 15 Hythe Rd ☎(0303) 872253

7hc (3fb) ✶ B&b£8.50–£9.50 Bdi£12.50–£13.50 W£75.50–£80.50 Ł LDOam

Lic Ⅲ CTV 7P nc3yrs

EARDISLAND
Hereford & Worcester
Map **3** SO45

FH Mrs F M Johnson **The Elms** *(SO418584)* ☎Pembridge (05447) 405
rs Etr–Nov

4hc ✶ B&b£9–£10 Bdi£14–£16 W£63–£70 M̸ LDO3pm

6P nc10yrs 33acres mixed

Eastbourne

EASTBOURNE
East Sussex
Map **5** TV69
See plan

GH *Alfriston Hotel* Lushington Rd ☎(0323) 25640 Plan **1** *C1*
Jan–Oct
Friendly family run guesthouse near to shopping centre and sea.
12hc (3fb) ★ Ⓡ LDO10am
Lic CTV 3🚗 nc5yrs

⟼ **GH Beachy Rise** Beachy Head Rd, ☎(0323) 639171 Plan **2** *C1*
Closed Dec
Small but homely and friendly establishment.
7hc (2fb) Ⓡ B&b£7.50–£10.50 Bdi£10–£12 W£60–£73 Ⱡ LDO 3.30pm
CTV nc5yrs
Ⓥ

GH *Courtlands Hotel* 68 Royal Pde ☎(0323) 21068 Plan **3** *E3*
Small house with annexe 65 yards away. Overlooking gardens and the sea.
7hc 1⇌ (A 5hc) (6fb) ★ LDO5pm
Lic CTV 1P 1🚗 sea
Ⓥ

GH *Delladale Lodge* 35 Lewes Rd ☎(0323) 25207 Plan **4** *C3*
Etr–Oct
Tastefully appointed guesthouse with the accent on comfort and informal atmosphere.
10hc 4⇌ (2fb) ★ Ⓡ LDO6pm
Lic CTV 10P nc5yrs

GH *Eastbourne Health Hotel* 17 Burlington Pl ☎(0323) 23604 Plan **6** *D1*
Victorian house in centre of town. Popular with those wishing a holiday with health education interests. Well equipped with spa pool, sauna and sunbeds.
8hc (2fb) ★
CTV 2P nc10yrs
Ⓥ

GH Edmar 30 Hyde Gdns ☎(0323) 33024 Plan **7** *C2*
Mar–Oct
A homely, family run guesthouse with a bright dining room.
9rm 6hc 2⇌ 1⋒ (1fb) ★ Ⓡ
✱B&b£7.50–£12 Bdi£9–£14.70 W£59.95–£102.95 Ⱡ LDO6pm
CTV 🅿 nc5yrs

GH Ellesmere Hotel 11 Wilmington Sq ☎(0323) 31463 Plan **8** *D1*
13rm 8hc 1⇌ 4⋒ (3fb) CTV in all bedrooms Ⓡ ✱B&bfr£11.50 Bdifr£15.50 Wfr£92–£103.50 M LDO7pm
Lic lift CTV nc5yrs

GH *Fairlands Hotel* 15–17 Lascelles Ter ☎(0323) 33287 Plan **10** *D1*
late Mar–mid Oct
Warm friendly delightfully modernised guesthouse
25hc 16⇌ (2fb) Ⓡ LDO 6.15pm
Lic CTV 🅿 sea
Ⓥ

⟼ **GH Far End Hotel** 139 Royal Pde ☎(0323) 25666 Plan **9** *E3*
Etr–Oct
Large house with bright and comfortable accommodation, on sea front on eastern outskirts of town.
10hc (3fb) ★ B&b£7–£9 Bdi£9–£11.50 W£49–£63 M (W only Jun–Sep) LDO6pm
CTV 6P 2🚗 nc3yrs

GH Flamingo Private Hotel 20 Enys Rd, (Guestaccom) ☎(0323) 21654 Plan **11** *C1*
Closed Nov
Large Victorian house in residential area with comfortable rooms and friendly atmosphere.
→

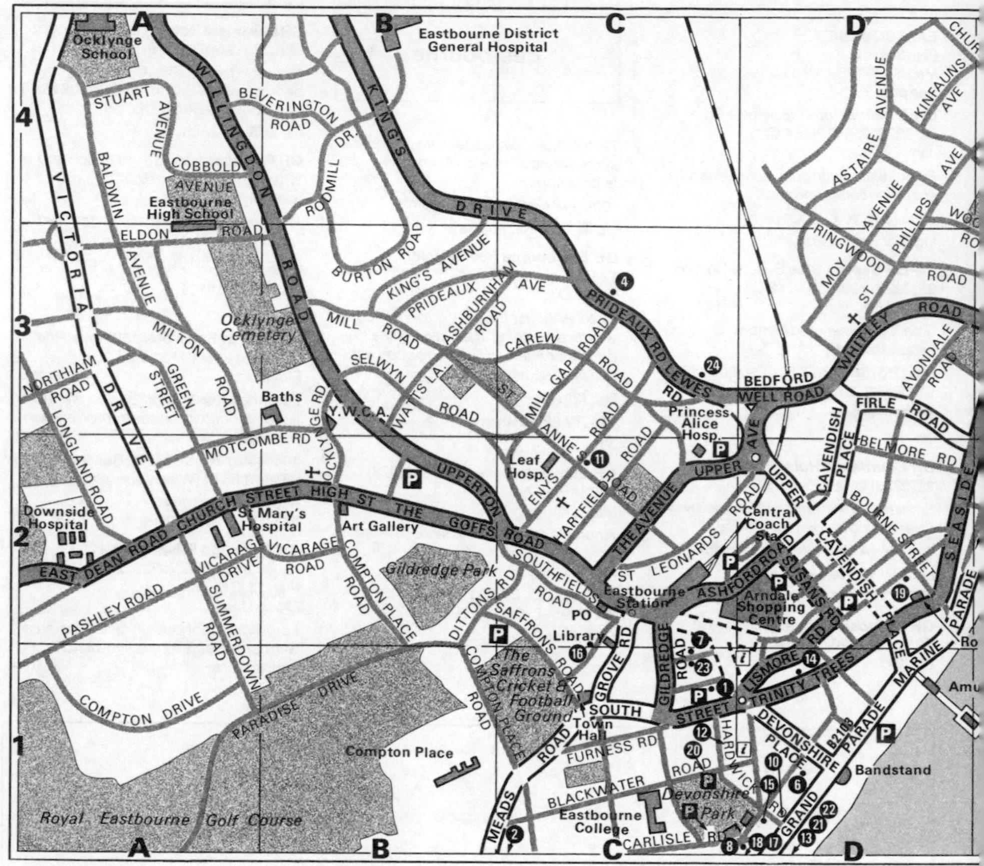

Eastbourne

1 Alfriston Hotel
2 Beachy Rise
3 Courtlands Hotel
4 Delladale Lodge
6 Eastbourne Health Hotel
7 Edmar
8 Ellesmere Hotel
9 Far End
10 Fairlands Hotel
11 Flamingo Private Hotel
12 Hanburies Hotel
13 Little Crookham
14 Mandalay Hotel
15 Mowbray Hotel
16 Orchard House
17 Rosfords Private Hotel
18 Saffrons Hotel

12rm 2hc 4→ 4⋒ (2fb) CTV in all bedrooms Ⓡ B&b£10–£14 Bdi£14.50–£18.50 W£87–£111 Ⅼ LDO4pm

Lic 🀫 CTV nc8yrs

Credit cards [1] [3] (V)

GH Hanburies Hotel 4 Hardwick Rd ☎(0323) 30698 Plan **12** *C1*

Small family run guesthouse nicely situated, near Devonshire Park, theatres and sea front.

14rm 10→ (1fb) CTV in 11 bedrooms ★ Ⓡ B&b£10.50–£13.50 Bdi£12–£15.50 W£75–£94 Ⅼ LDO6pm

Lic 🀫 CTV 4P nc12yrs

GH Little Crookham Private Hotel 16 Southcliffe Av ☎(0323) 34160 Plan **13** *D1*

May–Oct rs Jan–Feb & Nov

Small colourful guesthouse, run by friendly proprietors; five minutes walk from the sea.

7hc (1fb) Ⓡ B&b£9–£9.50 Bdi£13–£13.50 W£63 Ⅼ (W only Jun–Sep) LDO6pm

🀫 CTV P nc5yrs

GH Hotel Mandalay 16 Trinity Trees ☎(0323) 29222 Plan **14** *D1*

Closed Xmas

A comfortable house with a warm and friendly atmosphere.

12hc 1→ 7⋒ CTV in all bedrooms ★ Ⓡ B&b£14.38–£16.10 Bdi£14.95–£19.55 W£74.75–£102.35 M LDO6pm

Lic 🀫 20P nc5yrs

Credit cards [1] [3]

GH Mowbray Hotel 2 Lascelles Ter ☎(0323) 20012 Plan **15** *D1*

Apr–Nov

Large four storey Victorian house, adjacent to Devonshire Park and theatres.

16rm 12hc 4⋒ CTV in all bedrooms Ⓡ B&b£11–£12.50 Bdi£16.75–£18.25 W£110.75–£117.25 Ⅼ LDO6pm

lift CTV nc6yrs

Credit cards [1] [3]

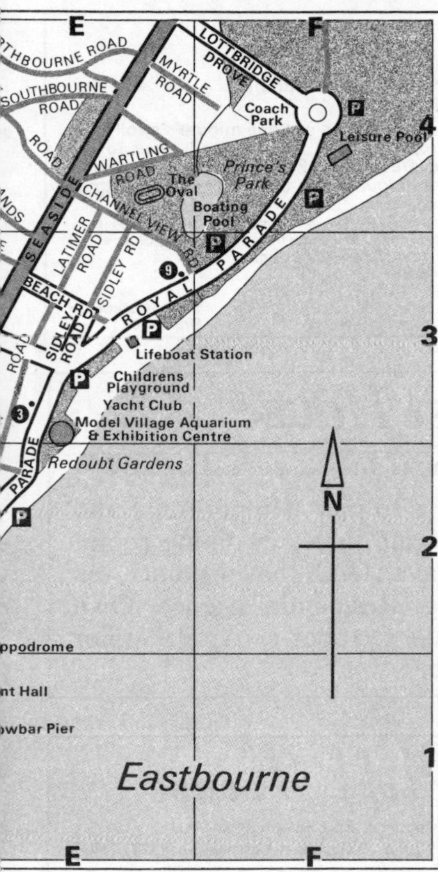

19 St Clare
20 Somerville Private Hotel
21 South Cliff House
22 Southcroft
23 Traquair Private Hotel
24 Wynstay Private Hotel

GH Orchard House 10 Old Orchard Rd ☎(0323) 23682 Plan **16** *C1*

Well appointed semi-detached Victorian house near town centre and railway station. Run by charming young couple.

8rm 5⇌ 3⋔ (2fb) CTV in all bedrooms ★ Ⓡ B&b£11–£12.50 Bdi£14–£16.50 W£89–£93 Ⱡ LDO6pm

CTV 3P nc4yrs

GH Rosforde Private Hotel 51 Jevington Gdns ☎(0323) 32503 Plan **17** *C1*

Well run, clean and comfortable accommodation.

12hc 4⋔ (4fb) ★ Ⓡ B&b£10–£12 Bdi£12.50–£15 W£63–£75 Ⱡ LDO4.30pm

Lic CTV ⚑

Ⓥ

GH Saffrons Hotel 30–32 Jevington Gdns ☎(0323) 25539 Plan **18** *D1*

Mar–Dec

Comfortable, large accommodation within this Victorian building, situated in gardens close to town centre.

25rm 14hc 7⇌ 4⋔ (1fb) CTV in all bedrooms Ⓡ B&b£11–£14 Bdi£15.50–£18.50 W£75–£82.50 Ⓜ LDO6.15pm

Lic CTV

See advertisement on page 136

⊢⊣ **GH St Clare** 70 Pevensey Rd ☎(0323) 29483 Plan **19** *D2*

Family house with friendly atmosphere, five minutes from the sea.

8hc (1fb) ★ Ⓡ B&b£7–£8 Bdi£10–£11 W£45–£52 Ⓜ LDO4pm

Ⅲ CTV ⚑

Ⓥ

See advertisement on page 136

GH Somerville Private Hotel 6 Blackwater Rd ☎(0323) 29342 Plan **20** *C1*

Closed Jan & Feb

Small homely house in quiet residential area, run by friendly proprietor.

12hc (1fb) ★ Ⓡ B&b£9.50–£11.10 Bdi£12.70–£15 W£74.50–£92.50 Ⱡ LDO5pm

Lic CTV

Ⓥ

The Saffrons Hotel

AA

30-32 JEVINGTON GARDENS, EASTBOURNE
TELEPHONE: (0323) 25539

The Saffrons Hotel is set in a quiet tree-lined avenue just one minute's stroll from the lovely Eastbourne sea front and promenades. It is situated close to the Congress Theatre, Winter Gardens and Devonshire Park Theatre. Bus services and town centre are nearby. *Large licensed lounge bar.* Open Easter to Christmas inclusive.

Some rooms with private wc and bath/shower • Colour television in all rooms • Tea- and coffee-making facilities in all rooms • Choice of menu • Unrestricted parking • Well appointed rooms with electric fires and shaver points • Separate colour TV lounge • Access to hotel at all times • Midweek bookings accepted • Conference delegates welcome

Resident Proprietors:
Mrs Joan Dick and John M. Dick

Room, Breakfast and Evening Dinner from £110 weekly

Send postage for Brochure

St Clare Guest House

70 Pevensey Road, Eastbourne, Sussex BN21 3HT Telephone: Eastboure (0323) 29483

A comfortable, friendly Guesthouse close to pier, Hippodrome and shops. We offer colour TV lounge, separate tables in dining room, good food, well cooked. All bedrooms have H&C, shaver points, tea making facilities and full central heating. Residential licence. Own keys for access at all times. Winter breaks October to April. Senior Citizens special rates May and September.

South Cliff House

19 South Cliff Avenue, Eastbourne, East Sussex BN20 7AH
***Proprietors:* Diane & Lionel John Telephone: Eastbourne (0323) 21019**

Quiet road, close to the sea, theatres, and a short walk along the seafront to the Bandstand and Pier (East). Beachy Head to the West. Noted for good home-cooked food and a friendly atmosphere. Tea and coffee-making facilities, comfortable lounge with colour TV. Own keys and access to rooms at all times. Four-course evening dinner. Separate tables in dining-room. Payphone for guests. Unrestricted parking.
Bed & Breakfast from £9 per day. From £55 per week.
Bed, Breakfast & Evening Dinner from £12.50 per day. From £70 per week.

Southcroft

GUEST HOUSE
15 South Cliff Avenue, Meads, Eastbourne, Sussex
Telephone: (0323) 29071

A small select private guesthouse, situated in a quiet residential area within easy reach of the beach, shopping centre and theatres. Well furnished bedrooms with fitted carpets, full central heating, hot and cold water. Television lounge. Residential licence. Unrestricted parking outside hotel. All year booking. Special terms for Christmas & Easter. Conference delegates and private functions catered for.

Proprietors: Mr & Mrs G P Stevens.

GH *South Cliff House* 19 South Cliff Av ☎(0323) 21019 Plan **21** *D1*

Compact, well decorated guesthouse.

6hc (1fb) ★ ® LDO5pm

Lic Ⅲ CTV ⚑

GH Southcroft 15 South Cliff Av ☎(0323) 29071 Plan **22** *D1*

Attractively appointed and well maintained guesthouse.

7hc (2fb) ® B&b£9–£9.50 Bdi£12–£12.50 W£75–£80 Ⅼ LDO5pm

Lic Ⅲ CTV nc3yrs

ⓥ

GH Traquair Private Hotel 25 Hyde Gdns ☎(0323) 25198 Plan **23** *C1*

Clean, colourful and comfortable accommodation where cooking is taken seriously.

11rm 6hc 5⫛ (3fb) CTV in 6 bedrooms ® B&b£8.50–£12 Bdi£14.50–£18 LDO6.50pm

Lic Ⅲ CTV ⚑

GH Wynstay Private Hotel 13 Lewes Rd ☎(0323) 21550 Plan **24** *C3*
Closed Xmas & New Year

Situated 1 mile from town centre this simply appointed house is run by friendly proprietors.

7rm 2hc 5⫛ (1fb) TV in all bedrooms ★ ® B&b£10–£12.50 Bdi£12–£15 W£75–£90 Ⅼ LDO2pm

Ⅲ 7P

Eastbourne — East Grinstead

EAST BUDLEIGH
Devon
Map **3** SY08

⊢⊣ **FH** Mrs M I Down **Hayes Barton** *(SY051852)* ☎(03954) 3372
Closed Xmas

1m E unclass rd.

3rm 1hc (2fb) ★ ® B&b£8 W£54 Ⓜ

Ⅲ CTV 4P ⚲(grass)

ⓥ

EAST CALDER
Lothian *Midlothian*
Map **11** NT06

⊢⊣ **FH** Mr & Mrs D R Scott **Whitecroft** *(NT095682)* 7 Raw Holdings ☎Mid Calder (0506) 881810

Compact roadside bungalow attached to small holding ½m E on B7015.

3rm (1fb) ★ B&b£6.50–£8 W£56 Ⓜ

Ⅲ CTV 4P 5acres arable

ⓥ

EAST COWTON
North Yorkshire
Map **8** NZ30

INN Beeswing ☎North Cowton (032578) 349

4⇌ CTV in all bedrooms ★ ® B&b£15 Bdi£21 W£105 Ⓜ L£1.50–£5 D10pm £5–£7

Ⅲ 17P

ⓥ

See advertisement on page 258

EAST GRINSTEAD
West Sussex
Map **5** TQ33

GH Cranfield Hotel Maypole Rd ☎(0342) 21251

Homely, comfortable private hotel in quiet residential area.

17hc 5⫛ (A 2hc 1⇌ 1⫛) (3fb) CTV in 17 bedrooms TV in 2 bedrooms ® B&b£13.80–£19.55 Bdi£19.80–£25.55 LDO8pm

Lic Ⅲ CTV 12P

EASTLEIGH
Devon
Map **2** SS42

GH Pine's Farmhouse Hotel ☎Instow (0271) 860561

Delightful, friendly, Georgian house with large gardens and glorious views. 2½m NE of Bideford off A39.

8hc (2fb) ✱ Ⓡ B&b£9–£9.50 Bdi£13.50–£14.50 W£85–£92 L LDO7pm

Lic ▥ CTV P ⌂

Ⓥ

EAST MEON
Hampshire
Map **4** SU62

FH Mrs P M Berry **Giants** *(SU696207)* Harvesting Ln ☎(073087) 205
Mar–Oct

Modern farmhouse, set in ½ acre with views from all rooms of the surrounding countryside. Queen Elizabeth Country Park of 1,400 acres, with facilities for pony-trekking and grass skiing is nearby.

3rm 1hc 2⇀ TV in 1 bedroom ✱ Ⓡ B&b£6–£7.50 Bdi£10.50–£12 W£70–£79 L LDO4pm

▥ CTV 4P 30acres arable sheep

EAST MEY
Highland *Caithness*
Map **15** ND37

FH Mrs M Morrison **Glenearn** *(ND307739)* ☎Barrock (084785) 608
Etr–Oct

Small croft situated on the main coast road; Thurso 15 miles.

1⇀ (1fb) B&b£6–£6.50 Bdi£9.50–£10 W£39 M LDO24hrs

▥ CTV 4P 7¼acres mixed

Ⓥ

EAST WITTERING
West Sussex
Map **4** SZ79

GH Wittering Lodge Hotel Shore Rd ☎Bracklesham Bay (0243) 673207
Etr–Oct

Small well appointed and comfortable hotel offering good food.

9rm 8hc 1⇀ (3fb) B&b£14–£15 Bdi£21–£22 W£120–£130 L LDO7.30pm

Lic ▥ CTV 12P 2⌂

Credit card ③ Ⓥ

EBBERSTON
North Yorkshire
Map **8** SE88

GH Foxholm Hotel (on B1258) ☎Scarborough (0723) 85550
Mar–Nov & Xmas

10rm 4hc 1⇀ 3⇀ (1fb) B&b£11–£22 Bdi£16–£20 W£100–£125 L LDO7.30pm

Lic ▥ CTV 12P 2⌂

Ⓥ

EDINBURGH
Lothian *Midlothian*
Map **11** NY27

See plan

GH Adam Hotel 19 Landsdowne Cres ☎031-337 1148 District Plan **6**
Closed Xmas & New Year

Old fashioned comfortable accommodation.

9rm 6hc (2fb) TV in all bedrooms ✱ B&b£11–£12 Bdi£16–£17 LDO10am

Lic CTV

GH *Adria* 11–12 Royal Ter ☎031-556 7875 Central plan **1** *F6*

Spacious, well decorated guesthouse.

25hc 6⇀

▥ CTV P

⊢⊣ **GH Ben Doran Hotel** 11 Mayfield Gdns ☎031-667 8488 District plan **7**
Closed 23–30 Dec
Situated in a terraced row, with modest bedrooms.
9hc (4fb) B&b£8–£10
CTV 6P
Credit card 3

GH Boisdale Hotel 9 Coates Gdns ☎031-337 1134 District plan **8**
10rm 3→ 1♨ (4fb) TV in 2 bedrooms B&b£10–£14 Bdi£14–£18 W£70–£90 M LDO3pm
Lic CTV

GH Bonnington 202 Ferry Rd ☎031-554 7610 District plan **8A**
6hc (3fb) B&b£8.50–£9 Bdi£13.50–£14 W£59.50–£63 M LDO6pm
CTV 10P
Ⓥ

GH Buchan Hotel 3 Coates Gdns ☎031-337 1045 District plan **9**
Carefully decorated and furnished Victorian guesthouse in terraced row.
9hc (6fb) B&b£10–£11 Bdi£15–£16 W£70–£77 L LDO10am
CTV
Ⓥ

Edinburgh

GH Clans Hotel 4 Magdala Cres ☎031-337 6301 District plan **10**
The hotel occupies three storeys of a residential block.
7rm 6hc 1♨ (2fb) B&b£10–£15
CTV

GH Dorstan Private Hotel 7 Priestfield Rd ☎031-667 6721 District plan **11**
Closed Xmas & New Year
A nicely maintained house situated in a residential area.
14hc 3→ 1♨ (2fb) Ⓡ B&b£9.75–£10.75 W£66–£74 M
CTV 10P
Ⓥ

GH Dunstane House 4 West Coates ☎031-337 6169 District plan **11A**
10hc (5fb) B&b£13–£16 W£82–£101 M
Lic CTV 10P
Credit card 3

GH Galloway 22 Dean Park Cres ☎031-332 3672 Central plan **2** *A6*
Compact, nicely appointed four-storey terraced house.
10rm 7hc 2→ 1♨ (6fb) B&b£9–£16 Bdi£13–£20 W£54–£116 M LDO5pm
CTV
Ⓥ

GH *Glendale Hotel* 5 Lady Rd ☎031-667 6588 District plan **12**
A compact, well decorated house.
8hc (2fb) TV in 5 bedrooms
TV 8P nc3yrs

GH Glenisla Hotel 12 Lygon Rd ☎031-667 4098 District plan **13**
Closed 2–3 wks winter
A very attractively appointed and well maintained house in a residential area.
9hc (1fb) B&b£10.50–£12 Bdi£15.50–£17.50 LDO2.30pm
CTV 5P
Ⓥ

GH Golf View Hotel 2 Marchhall Rd (off Dalkeith Rd) ☎031-667 4812 District plan **14**
Apr–Oct
11rm 5hc 3→ 3♨ (2fb) Ⓡ *B&b£9.20–£13.80
Lic CTV 10P
See advertisement on page 144

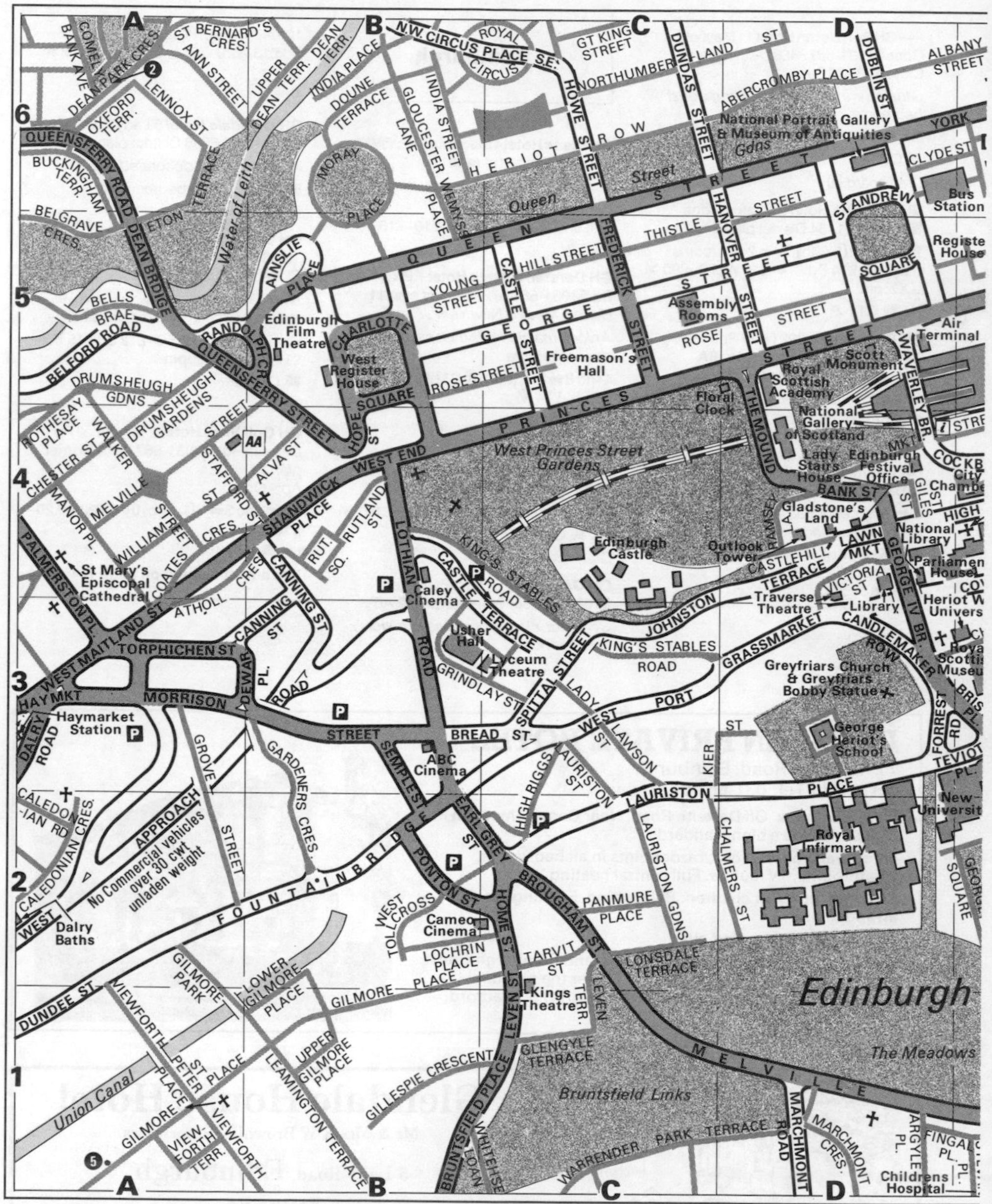

GH Greenside Hotel 9 Royal Ter ☎031-557 0022 Central plan **3** *F6*
Closed Dec
Neat and well maintained with nice spacious bedrooms.
12hc 1 (3fb) B&b£14–£18 W£98–£126 M
CTV nc5yrs

GH Grosvenor 1 Grosvenor Gdns, Haymarket ☎031-337 4143 District plan **15**
A Victorian town house with a peaceful atmosphere.
7rm 5hc 1 1 (3fb) CTV in all bedrooms B&b£9–£11

Ⓥ

See advertisement on page 144

GH Halcyon Hotel 8 Royal Ter ☎031-556 1033 Central plan **4** *F6*
Closed Feb

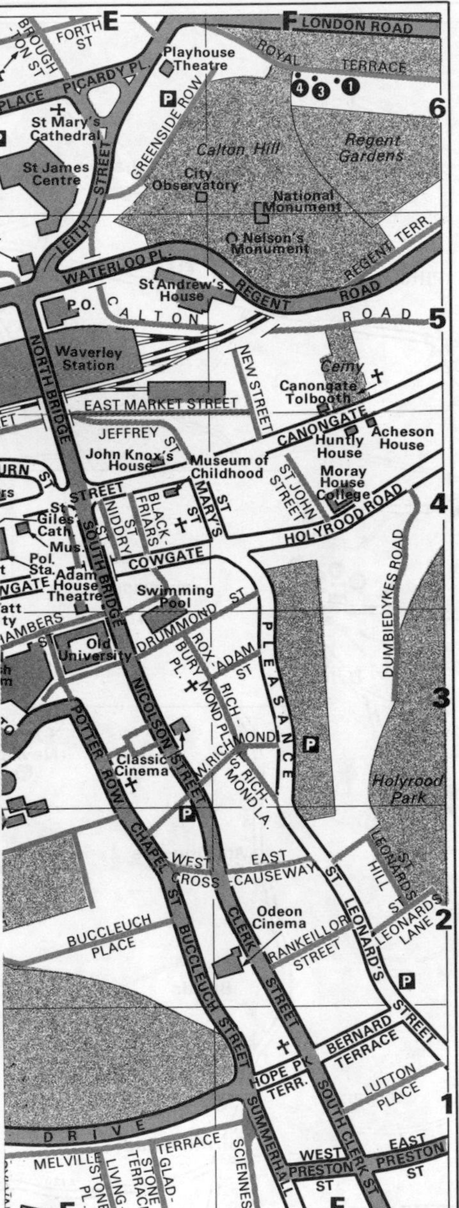

Edinburgh Central

1 Adria
2 Galloway
3 Greenside Hotel
4 Halcyon Hotel
5 Kariba

Forms part of a large Regency terraced row.

16hc (4fb) ✱B&b£11–£12 Bdi£12–£13 W£77–£91 M

ᗰ CTV

GH Hillview 92 Dalkeith Rd ☎031-667 1523 District plan **16**

Situated close to the Commonwealth swimming pool.

8rm 7hc 1 (4fb) Ⓡ B&b£8.50–£10 Bdi£14–£15.50 LDO9pm

ᗰ CTV 3P

Ⓥ

See advertisement on page 144

GH Kariba 10 Granville Ter ☎031-229 3773 Central plan **5** *A1*

7rm 2hc 1 (2fb) TV in all bedrooms B&b£9–£12 Bdi£16–£19 LDOpm

ᗰ CTV 3P

Ⓥ

GH Kildonan Lodge Hotel 27 Craigmillar Pk ☎031-667 2793 District plan **17**

The hotel incorporates a most attractive restaurant and cocktail lounge. (Residents and diners only).

9hc (5fb) CTV in all bedrooms B&b£8.50–£11.50 Bdi£15–£18 W£90–£108 LDO9.30pm

Lic ᗰ 20P

Credit card 2 Ⓥ

See advertisement on page 144

GH Marchhall Hotel 14–16 Marchhall St ☎031-667 2743 District plan **18**

11hc (3fb) CTV in all bedrooms Ⓡ B&b£10–£14 Bdi£15–£19 W£65–£95 M LDO6pm

Lic ᗰ CTV

GH Marvin 46 Pilrig St ☎031-554 6605 District plan **18A**

Neat family run guesthouse in terraced row.

7rm 5hc 1 1 (2fb) TV in 4 bedrooms Ⓡ B&b£8–£12.50 W£50–£78.75 M

ᗰ CTV 6P 1

GH *Newington* 18 Newington Rd ☎031-667 3356 District plan **19**

A house of character and appeal well appointed and thoughtfully equipped

8hc (2fb) CTV in all bedrooms Ⓡ (W only Oct–Apr)

ᗰ CTV 3P

GH St Margaret's Hotel 18 Craigmillar Pk ☎031-667 2202 District plan **19A**

A neatly maintained house in terraced row. Coach tours taken early in season.

8hc (3fb) Ⓡ B&b£7–£9

ᗰ CTV 6P

Credit card 2

GH Salisbury Hotel 45 Salisbury Rd ☎031-667 1264 District plan **20**
Closed Xmas & New Year

A neatly decorated conversion of terraced houses close to a shopping suburb.

14rm 12hc 2 (3fb) Ⓡ B&b£8–£10 W£48 M

Lic ᗰ CTV 16P

Ⓥ

GH Sharon 1 Kilmaurs Ter ☎031-667 2002 District plan **21**
Closed Dec & Jan

A compact, neatly appointed house.

9hc (2fb) Ⓡ B&b£8–£10

ᗰ CTV 5P nc5yrs

Ⓥ

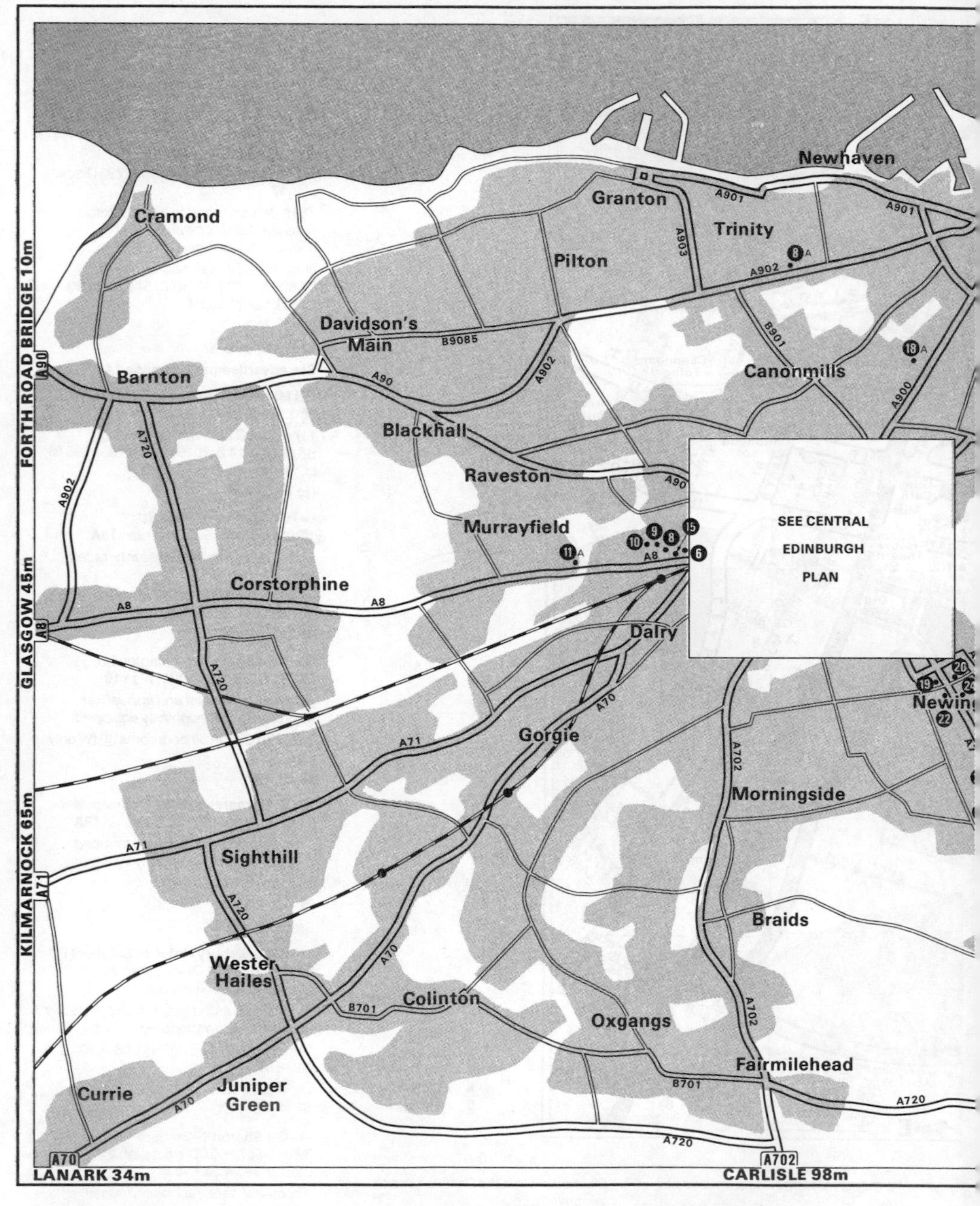

Edinburgh District

6 Adam Hotel
7 Ben Doran Hotel
8 Boisdale Hotel
8A Bonnington
9 Buchan Hotel
10 Clans Hotel
11 Dorstan Private Hotel
11A Dunstane House
12 Glendale Hotel
13 Glenisla Hotel
14 Golf View Hotel
15 Grosvenor
16 Hillview
17 Kildonan Lodge Hotel

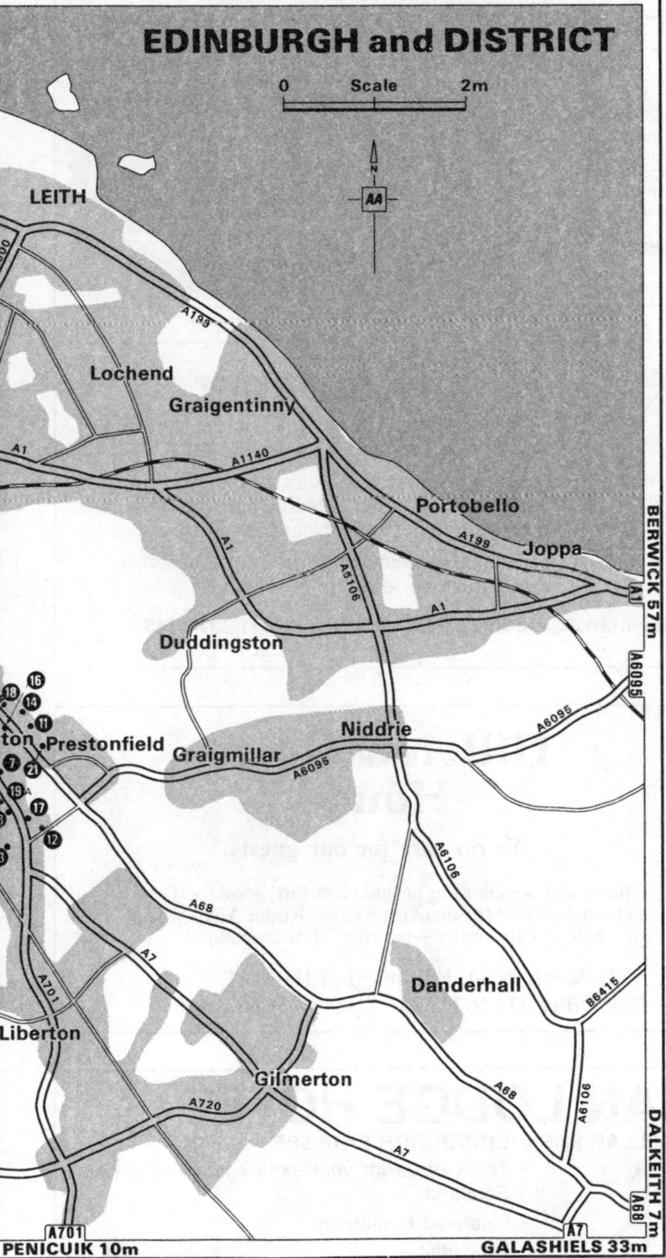

18 Marchhall Hotel
18A Marvin
19 Newington
19A St Margaret's Hotel
20 Salisbury Hotel
21 Sharon
22 Sherwood
23 Southdown
24 Thrums Private Hotel

GH Sherwood 42 Minto St ☎031-667 1200 District plan **22**
Closed Xmas & New Year
6hc (3fb) Ⓡ B&b£8–£9
CTV 3P
Ⓥ

GH Southdown 20 Craigmillar Pk ☎031-667 2410 District plan **23**
A neatly maintained house, part of a terraced row, which takes coach tours in April & May.
8hc (4fb) TV in all bedrooms Ⓡ B&bfr£7.50 LDO9am
CTV 8P
See advertisement on page 145

GH Thrums Private Hotel 14 Minto St, Newington ☎031-667 5545 District plan **24**
Closed Xmas & New Year
A neat, compact house with gardens to front and rear.
7rm 6hc 1 (2fb) CTV in 2 bedrooms TV in 2 bedrooms Ⓡ B&b£7–£8 Bdi£11–£12 W £40–£50 M LDO7pm
Lic CTV 6P
Ⓥ

EDLINGHAM
Northumberland
Map **12** NU10

FH Mrs M Oates **Lumbylaw** *(NU115096)* ☎Whittingham (066574) 277
May–Sep
Modernised farmhouse, offering good home cooking, friendly relaxing atmosphere and fine scenery.
3hc (1fb) Ⓡ B&b£9–£10 Bdi£14–£15 W£100 L (W only Jul & Aug) LDO6pm
4P 4 900acres mixed

EGERTON
Kent
Map **5** TQ94

FH Mrs D Boardman **Link** *(TQ898470)* ☎(023376) 214
Apr–Oct
1m SW off unclass rd.
3rm 1 B&b£9–£10 Bdi£13–£14.50 W£70 M LDO8pm
CTV 3P 3 nc9yrs 10acres arable

EGGLESTON
Co Durham
Map **12** NY92

INN *Moorcock* Hilltop ☎Teesdale (0833) 50395
6hc CTV available in bedrooms Ⓡ D10pm
60P
See advertisement on page 145

Golf View Hotel

EDINBURGH

Residents' licence. Adjacent to the Royal Commonwealth Swimming Pool and Tennis Courts. A short putt from the first tee of the Prestonfield Golf Course. Large private car park. All rooms hot and cold, shaver points. Full central heating. Private bathrooms and shower rooms. Under the personal supervision of Mr and Mrs D'Ambrosio.

2 Marchhall Road, Edinburgh EH16 5HR.
(off Dalkeith Road)
Tel: 031 667 4812

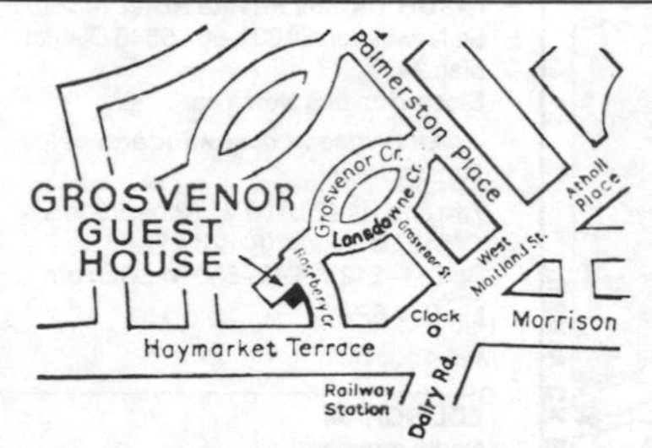

Grosvenor Guest House

Quiet cul-de-sac. Spacious rooms. All bedrooms with H&C, electric blankets, shaving points and television. Near City centre.

Special off-season rates on weekly basis. Resident proprietor: John G Gray.

1 Grosvenor Gardens, Haymarket, Edinburgh EH12 5JU. Tel: 031 337 4143

EDINBURGH

Hillview Guest House

We do care for our guests.

That is why we claim to provide comfort, good food and personal service for no extra charge. Route A68—within one mile of City centre—parking. Dinners 6.30pm.

92 Dalkeith Road, Edinburgh, EH16 5AF
Tel: Office 031 667 1523 Guests 031 667 3668

KILDONAN LODGE HOTEL

27 CRAIGMILLAR PARK, EDINBURGH EH16 5PE

Think of us for your extra special holiday in Scotland

Licensed Restaurant
Cocktail Bar
Ample Car Parking
Full Central Heating

Ask for our special **Bargain Break Brochure** for holidays in April, May and June

For reservations: phone (031) 667 2793

EGLINGHAM
Northumberland
Map **12** NU11

FH Mrs A I Easton **West Ditchburn** *(NU131207)* ☎ Powburn (066578) 337
Mar–Oct

True working farm whose key notes are hospitality, comfort and excellent home cooking.

4rm 3hc (2fb) CTV in 2 bedrooms TV in 1 bedroom ® B&b£10 Bdi£14 W£90 LDO5pm

CTV nc4yrs 1000acres beef

ELIE
Fife
Map **12** NO40

GH Elms Park Pl ☎ (0333) 330404

A neatly appointed house with garden to rear.

6hc (2fb) B&b£7.50–£8.50 Bdi£12–£13.50 W£80–£85 LDO6pm

Lic CTV

Ⓥ

ELLESMERE
Shropshire
Map **7** SJ33

GH Grange Hotel Grange Rd (Guestaccom) ☎ (069171) 2735

12rm 1hc 10 1 (A 3) (1fb) CTV in all bedrooms ® B&b£17.50 Bdi£28 W£115 LDO8pm

Lic 20P (hard)
Credit cards 1 3 5

ELSDON
Northumberland
Map **12** NY99

FH Mrs T M Carruthers **Dunns** *(NY937969)* ☎ Rothbury (0669) 40219

Old farmhouse in quiet position amongst the Cheviot Hills and Coquet Valley.

3rm 2hc (1fb) *B&b£6–£6.50 W£40

CTV P 1000acres beef sheep mixed

Ⓥ

FH Mrs J Armstrong **Raylees** *(NY926915)* ☎ Otterburn (0830) 20287

3rm 1hc (1fb) *B&b£8

CTV 6P nc3yrs 700acres mixed

ELY
Cambridgeshire
Map **5** TL58

GH Nyton 7 Barton Rd ☎ (0353) 2459

9rm 5hc 4 (2fb) TV in 1 bedroom ® B&b£10–£14 W£63–£98

Lic CTV 12P

Ⓥ

INN Castle Lodge Hotel 50 New Barns Rd ☎ (0353) 2276

8rm 5hc 1 2 CTV in all bedrooms B&b£10.50–£14 Bdi£16.50–£21 W£66.15–£88.20 Bar lunch £1–£3 D8.30pm £6–£7.50 S%

8P nc5yrs

Ⓥ

EMPINGHAM
Leicestershire
Map **4** SK90

INN White Horse High St ☎ (078086) 221

A warm and welcoming stone-built inn at the centre of the village and Europe's largest man-made lake, Rutland Water. Popular inn with tourists and local fishermen alike.

3hc CTV in all bedrooms ® B&b£15 Bdi£22.50 W£140 L£4.95&alc D9.45pm £7.50&alc

25P 5

Credit cards 1 2 5

EMSWORTH
Hampshire
Map **4** SU70

GH Jingles 77 Horndean Rd ☎ (02434) 3755

Large Victorian house with simple bedroom appointments, run by pleasant and friendly proprietors. →

9hc (1fb) ® B&b£10.35–£11 Bdi£13.80–£14.50 LDO6pm

▥ CTV 9P

Credit cards 1 3

ERLESTOKE
Wiltshire
Map **3** ST95

FH Mrs P Hampton **Longwater Park** *(ST966541)* ☎Bratton (0380) 830095
Closed Xmas

3hc ® B&b£8.50 Bdi£13 W£86.50 Ł LDO4pm

▥ CTV 6P ⌂ ♩ 166acres dairy

Ⓥ

ERWOOD
Powys
Map **3** SO04

FH N M Jones ***Ty-Isaf*** *(SO101425)* ☎(09823) 607

3hc ✗ LDO5pm

▥ TV 5P 340acres mixed

Ⓥ

ETON
Berkshire
Map **4** SU97

GH *Christopher Hotel* High St ☎Windsor (07535) 52359

Well furnished free-house, with modern, very well equipped chalets, and complemented by the well-run Peacock Restaurant.

(A 19fl) (6fb) CTV in all bedrooms ® LDO9.30pm

Lic ▥ 19P

ETTINGTON
Warwickshire
Map **4** SP24

FH Mrs B J Wakeham **Whitfield** *(SP265506)* Warwick Rd ☎Stratford-upon-Avon (0789) 740260
Mar–Aug

Pleasant house set in active farm with a wide variety of animals for interest.

3hc (1fb) ✗ B&b£6–£6.25 W£42 M

▥ CTV 3P 220acres mixed

Ⓥ

EVESHAM
Hereford & Worcester
Map **4** SP04

GH Waterside Family Hotel 56/59 Waterside ☎(0386) 2420

9rm 3hc 2→ 4fl (A 4rm 2→ 2fl) (3fb) CTV in all bedrooms ® B&bfr£13.50 Bdifr£20 Wfr£127.76 Ł LDO9.30pm

Lic ▥ 30P ♩

Credit cards 1 2 3

EWHURST GREEN
East Sussex
Map **5** TQ72

INN *White Dog* Village St (Guestaccom) ☎Staplecross (058083) 264

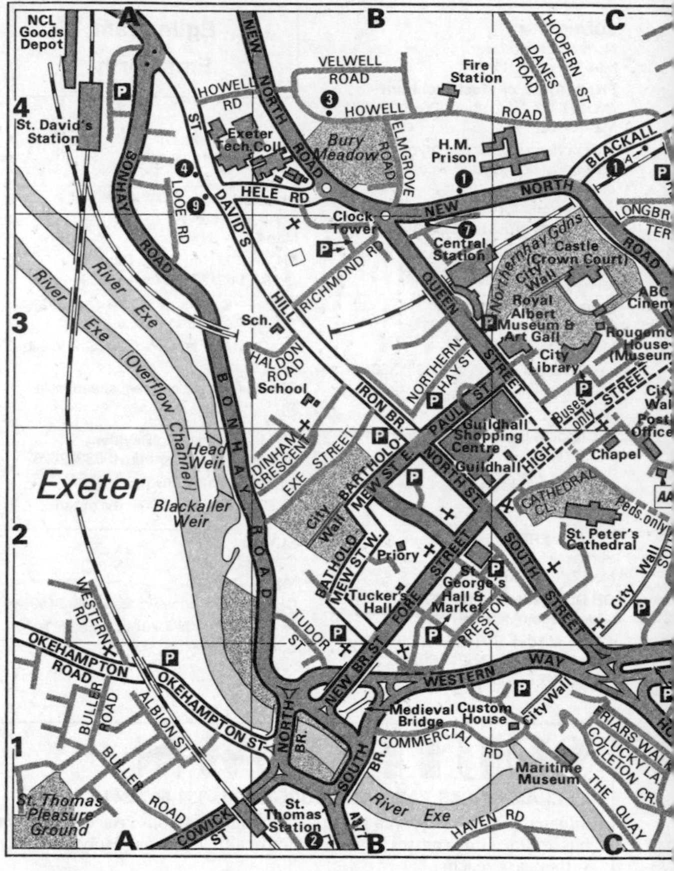

7hc 3→ ✗ ® D10pm sn

▥ CTV 80P nc8yrs

Ⓥ

EXBOURNE
Devon
Map **2** SS60

⊢⊣ **FH** Mrs S J Allain **Stapleford** *(SS580039)* ☎(083785) 277

2m SE unclass rd.

2rm 1hc ✗ ® B&b£8–£10 Bdi£12.50–£15 W£50–£60 M LDO5pm

CTV 2P 2⌂ nc12yrs ♩ 80acres beef sheep

EXETER
Devon
Map **3** SX99
See Plan

⊢⊣ **GH Braeside** 21 New North Rd ☎(0392) 56875 Plan **1** *B4*

8hc (3fb) TV in all bedrooms ✗ B&b£7.50–£9 Bdi£11–£12.50 W£45–£50 M LDO6pm

⊢⊣ **GH Dunmore** 22 Blackall Rd ☎(0392) 31643 Plan **1A** *C4*
Closed Xmas & New Year

8hc (5fb) TV in all bedrooms ® B&b£6.50–£8

▥ CTV

GH Hotel Gledhills 32 Alphington Rd ☎(0392) 71439 Plan **2** *B1*
Closed Xmas

12rm 4hc (4fb) TV in all bedrooms ✗(ex guide dogs) ® B&bfr£13 Bdifr£17.15 Wfr£78 M LDO5pm

Lic ▥ CTV 9P 3⌂

Credit cards 1 2 3

GH Park View Hotel 8 Howell Rd ☎(0392) 71772 Plan **3** *B4*
Closed Xmas

10rm 6hc 2→ 2fl (A 5rm 4hc 1fl) (3fb) CTV in all bedrooms B&b£9.78–£11.50 Bdi£14.78–£16.50 LDO9.30pm

▥ CTV 6P ⌂

Credit cards 1 3 Ⓥ

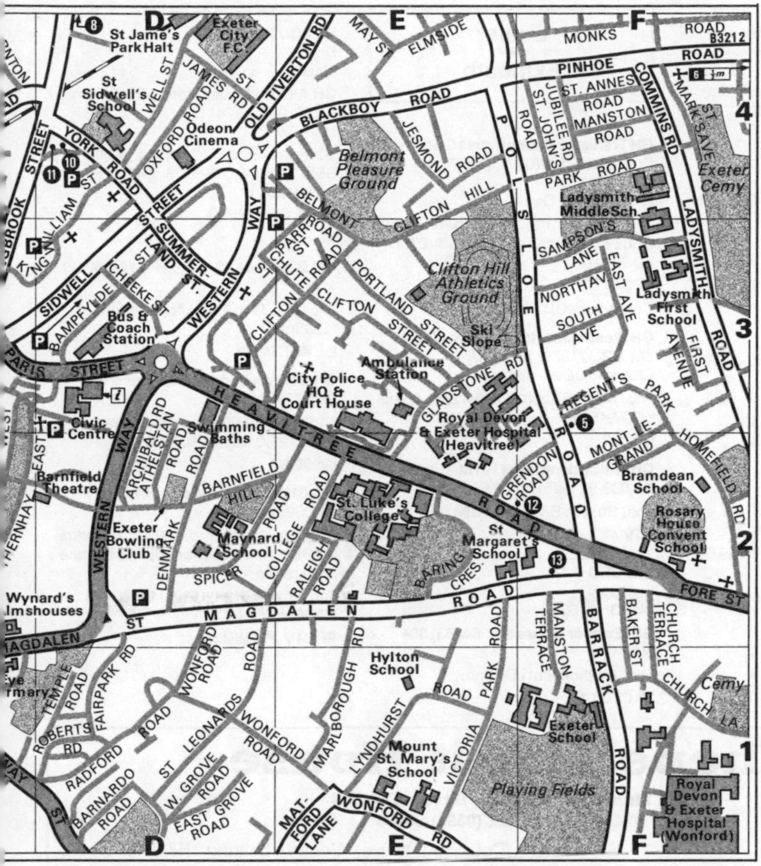

Exeter

1 Braeside
1A Dunmore
2 Hotel Gledhills
3 Park View Hotel
4 Radnor Hotel
5 Regents Park Hotel
6 Shene
7 Sunnymede
8 Sylvania House Hotel
9 Telstar Hotel
10 Trees Mini Hotel
11 Trenance House Hotel
12 Westholme Hotel
13 Willowdene Hotel

GH Radnor Hotel 79 St Davids Hill ☎(0392) 72004 Plan **4** *A4*
Closed Xmas & New Year
8hc 2⋒ (3fb) B&b£7.50–£8 Bdi£11.50–£12 LDO4pm
CTV 7P
Credit card 3

GH Regents Park Hotel Polsloe Rd ☎(0392) 59749 Plan **5** *F3*
Closed 2 wks Xmas
11hc (2fb) B&b£9.50 Bdi£15 W£66.50 M LDO6pm
CTV 16P
Credit cards 2 3

GH Shene 328 Pinhoe Rd ☎(0392) 55786 Plan **6** *F4*
7rm 6hc 1➡ (2fb) ® B&b£8–£9 Bdi£12–£13 W£54.50–£61.50 M LDO5pm
CTV 10P ♿
Credit cards 1 2 3 V
See advertisement on page 148

GH Sunnymede 24 New North Rd ☎(0392) 73844 Plan **7** *B3*
Closed Xmas
8hc (1fb) CTV in all bedrooms ★ ® B&b£8.50 Bdi£11.50 W£57.50 M
LDO4pm
CTV nc
Credit cards [2] [3]

GH Sylvania House Hotel
64 Pennsylvania Rd (Guestaccom) ☎(0392) 75583 Plan **8** *D4*
Closed 14–31 Dec
8rm 3hc 1 4 (2fb) ★ B&b£10 W£63 M
CTV 4P
Credit card [3]

GH Telstar Hotel 77 St Davids Hill ☎(0392) 72466 Plan **9** *A4*
Closed Xmas
8rm 6hc (2fb) ★ B&b£7.50–£8.50 Bdi£11.50–£12.50 W£77–£84 M
LDO1pm
CTV 5P

GH Trees Mini Hotel 2 Queen's Cres, York Rd ☎(0392) 59531 Plan **10** *D4*
12hc (1fb) ★ B&b£8.50–£9.50 W£59.50 M
CTV 1 nc3yrs
Ⓥ

Exeter — Exmouth

GH Trenance House Hotel 1 Queen's Cres, York Rd ☎(0392) 73277 Plan **11** *D4*
Closed 25–27 Dec
14rm 9hc 1 (3fb) CTV in all bedrooms ® B&b£9–£10 Bdi£14–£15 W£63–£70 M
LDO2pm
CTV 10P
Credit cards [1] [3] Ⓥ

GH Westholme Hotel 85 Heavitree Rd ☎(0392) 71878 Plan **12** *F2*
Closed mid Dec–mid Jan
7hc (1fb) ® B&b£8.50–£9 W£56–£59 M
LDO7.45pm
CTV 9P

GH Willowdene Hotel 161 Magdalen Rd ☎(0392) 71925 Plan **13** *F2*
8hc (1fb) ★ *B&b£9 W£63 M
CTV

EXFORD
Somerset
Map **3** SS83

GH *Exmoor House* ☎(064383) 304
Mar–Oct
5hc (A 12hc) (2fb) LDO6pm
CTV 12P

EXMOUTH
Devon
Map **3** SY08

GH Aliston House Hotel 58 Salterton Rd ☎(0395) 274119
Mar–Oct
10rm 6hc 4 TV in 3 bedrooms ® B&b£12.50–£14 Bdi£18.50–£19.50 W£80–£87 L
Lic CTV 16P
Ⓥ

GH *Blenheim* 30 Morton Rd ☎(03952) 4230
6hc (2fb) TV in 2 bedrooms ★ ®
LDO5pm
Lic CTV 2P

GH Carlton Lodge Hotel Carlton Hill ☎(0395) 263314
6hc 4 (4fb) CTV in all bedrooms B&b£12.50 Bdi£16.50 W£80 L
Lic 8P

GH Clinton House 41 Morton Rd ☎(0395) 271969
A house dating from the 1920's, just off the seafront, near beach and ½ mile from the town centre.
8hc (2fb) ★ B&b£8 Bdi£11 W£51 M
LDO6pm
CTV nc5yrs

GH *Dawson's* 8 Morton Rd
☎(0395) 272321
Etr–Sep
7hc (2fb) TV in 3 bedrooms ®
CTV 2P

FH Mrs A J Skinner **Maer** *(SY018803)*
Maer Ln ☎(0395) 263651
Jun–Oct
In large garden which has views of sea and Haldon Hills, 5 minutes walk to beach and 20 minutes walk to town.
3rm 1hc (2fb) ® B&b£7 W£49 M
CTV 3P 300acres mixed

FH Mrs J Reddaway ***Quentance***
(SY037812) Salterton Rd ☎Budleigh Salterton (03954) 2733
Apr–Oct
Superior-style farmhouse with bedrooms overlooking south-east Devon coastline.
3rm 2hc (3fb) ®
CTV P 260acres dairy mixed sheep

EYE
Hereford & Worcester
Map **3** SO56

FH Mrs E M Morris **Park Lodge**
(SO502643) ☎Leominster (0568) 5711
2hc (1fb) B&b£7–£8 Bdi£10–£12
W£70 L LDO6.30pm
CTV 6P 2 200acres mixed

FALFIELD
Avon
Map **3** ST69

FH Mr & Mrs Bryant **Green**
(ST687943) ☎(0454) 260319
A two-storey, colour-washed stone-built farmhouse, with lawns, tennis court and swimming pool in the grounds.
7hc (2fb) B&b£7.50–£8.50 Bdi£11–£12
W£70 L (W only Etr–Oct) LDO7pm
CTV 10P (hard) 100acres non-working

FALMOUTH
Cornwall
Map **2** SW83
See plan

GH Bedruthan 49 Castle Dr, Sea Front ☎(0326) 311028 Plan **1** *D2*
Occupying a fine seafront position, close to Pendennis Castle and offering panoramic sea views.
7rm 6hc 1 (1fb) ® B&b£7.50–£8
Bdi£11.50–£12 W£75–£78 L (W only Jun–Sep) LDO4pm
Lic CTV 4P
Ⓥ

GH Collingbourne Hotel Melvill Rd
☎(0326) 311259 Plan **2** *C1*
Closed Oct rs Nov–Apr
A small family hotel situated within its own attractive grounds, close to the seafront.
16rm 2 14 (6fb) ® B&b£9.75–£10.75 Bdi£13.75–£15 W£80–£96 L
LDO6pm
Lic CTV 14P nc3yrs
Ⓥ

GH Cotswold House Private Hotel
49 Melvill Rd ☎(0326) 312077
Plan **3** *C1*
Apr–Oct
A small, private hotel pleasantly located close to Gyllyngvase Beach and the town and harbour.
11rm 9hc 2 (1fb) B&b£7.95–£9
Bdi£12.95–£14 W£79–£85 L
LDO5.30pm
Lic CTV 12P nc10yrs

GH Hotel Dracaena Dracaena Av
☎(0326) 314470 Plan **4** *B3*
A detached, private hotel, commercially orientated.
9rm 6hc 3 (A 6rm 4hc 2) (7fb) CTV in all bedrooms ® B&b£17.25
Bdi£21.85 W£92–£100 L LDO6.30pm
Lic 15P
Credit cards 2 3 Ⓥ

⊢×**GH Evendale Private Hotel**
51 Melvill Rd ☎(0326) 314164
Plan **5** *C1*
Etr–Nov
A small hotel pleasantly located close to the beach, Princess Pavilion and Gardens.
10rm 7hc 3🛁 (3fb) B&b£8–£10 Bdi£12.50–£15 W£80–£90 Ł LDO6.30pm
CTV 10P nc3yrs
ⓥ

GH Gyllyngvase House Hotel
Gyllyngvase Rd ☎(0326) 312956
Plan **6** *C1*
The hotel stands in its own grounds ideally situated for the beaches, town, parks and pavilion.
16rm 7hc 2🛁 7🚿 (2fb) B&b£10.35–£12.65 Bdi£13.80–£16.67 W£60–£72 M̸ LDO5.30pm
Lic ꟿ CTV 15P
Credit card ③

Falmouth

GH Harbour Hotel Harbour Ter ☎(0326) 311344 Plan **7** *C3*
6rm 4hc 2🚿 (2fb) Ⓡ B&b£10–£11 Bdi£14.75–£15.75 W£58–£65 M̸ LDO7.30pm
Lic ꟿ CTV 🐕̸

⊢×**GH Langton Leigh** 11 Florence Pl
☎(0326) 313684 Plan **8** *C2*
Mar–Oct
Attractive character terraced property in an elevated position with views of Falmouth.
8rm 5hc 3🚿 (4fb) B&b£7–£9 Bdi£10.50–£12.50 W£63–£75 Ł LDO4.30pm
Lic ꟿ CTV 6P 1🚗
ⓥ

GH Maskee House Spernen Wyn Rd
☎(0326) 311783 Plan **9** *C1*
Etr–Oct
Fine, well appointed small hotel near sea, with peaceful, well-tended gardens.
6hc (4fb) CTV in all bedrooms ✱ Ⓡ B&b£9.50–£10.50 W£63–£70 M̸
ꟿ CTV 6P 3🚗

GH *Milton House* 33 Melvill Rd
☎(0326) 314390 Plan **10** *D1*
Small semi-detached residence positioned close to beaches, town and pavilion.
6hc (2fb) LDO6pm
ꟿ CTV 6P sea

⊢×**GH Penty Bryn Hotel** 10 Melvill Rd
☎(0326) 314988 Plan **11** *D2*
Feb–Oct
Small terraced residence close to beaches and town centre.
7rm 3hc 3🚿 (3fb) Ⓡ B&b£7.50–£9 Bdi£11–£13 W£50–£60 Ł LDO4.50pm
Lic ꟿ CTV 2P nc5yrs
ⓥ

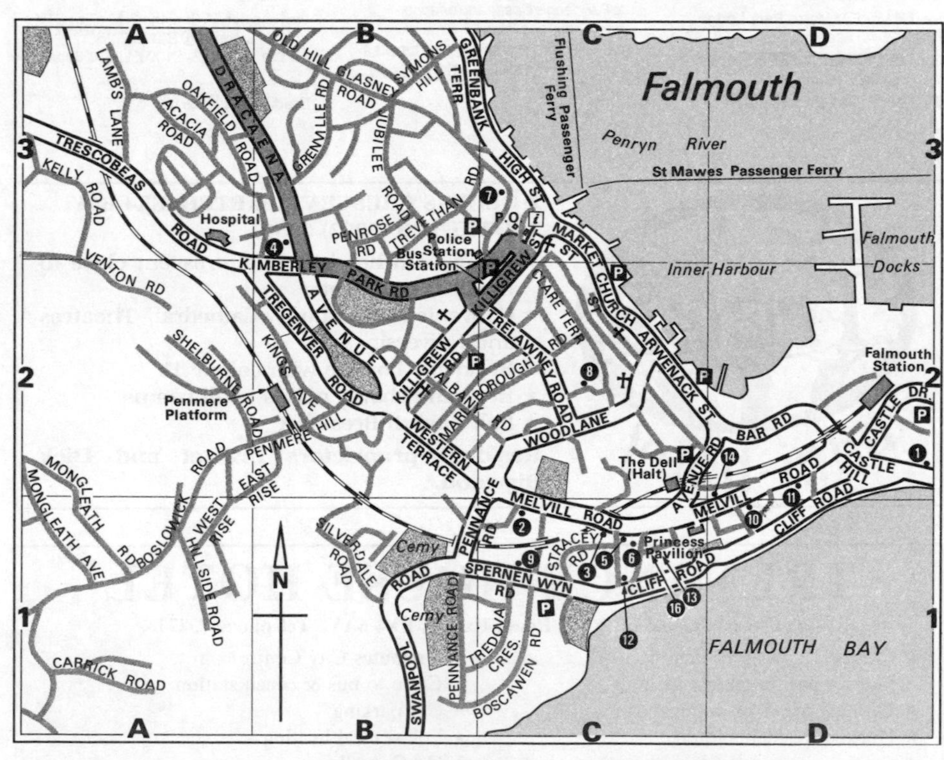

Falmouth
1 Bedruthan
2 Collingbourne Hotel
3 Cotswold House Private Hotel
4 Hotel Dracaena
5 Evendale Private Hotel
6 Gyllyngvase House Hotel
7 Harbour Hotel
8 Langton Leigh
9 Maskee House
10 Milton House
11 Penty Bryn Hotel
12 Rathgowry Hotel
13 Rosemary Hotel
14 Tregenna House
16 Wickham

GH *Rathgowry Hotel* Gyllyngvase Hill ☏(0326) 313482 Plan **12** *C1*
May–Nov
9rm 2⇌ 5⋒ (5fb) Ⓡ LDO 7.30pm
Lic CTV 12P sea

⊢⊣ **GH Rosemary Hotel**
22 Gyllyngvase Ter ☏(0326) 314669
Plan **13** *C1*
Closed Dec
Family hotel situated in a quiet road just off the sea front.
11hc (5fb) B&b£7.50–£9.50 Bdi£10.50–£13 W£49–£60 M LDOnoon
Lic ⅢⅢ CTV 3P
Credit card 1

Falmouth

⊢⊣ **GH Tregenna House** 28 Melvill Rd
☏(0326) 313881 Plan **14** *D2*
Semi-detached, friendly hotel positioned close to beaches, town and pavilion.
6hc (2fb) B&b£7–£8 ⇌£10.50–£11.50 W£49–£56 M
Lic ⅢⅢ CTV 6P
Ⓥ

⊢⊣ **GH Wickham** 21 Gyllyngvase Ter
☏(0326) 311140 Plan **16** *C1*
Apr–Oct
Small guesthouse pleasantly situated in a quiet road, close to beaches.
10hc (2fb) ✱ B&b£7.50–£8.50 Bdi£10.50–£12.50 W£49–£56 ⱡ LDO5pm
CTV 3P nc3yrs
Ⓥ

FARNHAM
Surrey
Map **4** SU84

INN Eldon Hotel 43 Frensham Rd, Lower Bourne ☎Frensham (025125) 2745

Popular, privately managed hotel with modern, well equipped bedrooms, good leisure facilities plus restaurant.

14rm 5hc 8➡ 1⋒ CTV in 10 bedrooms B&b£15–£25 Bdi£17.50–£35 L£2–£10.50&alc High Tea fr£1.50 D9.45pm £5–£12&alc

Ⅲ CTV 70P ⇆ squash

Credit cards ① ② ③ ⑤ Ⓥ

FAR SAWREY
Cumbria
Map **7** SD39

GH West Vale ☎Windermere (09662) 2817

Small, well furnished, guesthouse where home cooking is a speciality.

8rm 3hc 5⋒ (1fb) ✶ ® B&b£10.45 Bdi£17.50

Lic Ⅲ CTV 8P nc5yrs

FAZELEY
Staffordshire
Map **4** SK20

⊢⊣ **GH Buxton House Hotel** 65 Colehill St ☎Tamworth (0827) 284842
Closed Xmas

15rm 6hc 1➡ 8⋒ (4fb) CTV in 13 bedrooms TV in 2 bedrooms B&b£7.50–£16.50 Bdi£11.50–£23 LDO5pm

Lic Ⅲ CTV 16P

Credit cards ① ③ Ⓥ

FELINDRE
West Glamorgan
Map **2** SN60

⊢⊣ **FH** Mr F Jones **Coynant** *(SN648070)* ☎Ammanford (0269) 2064 & 5640

Secluded house in elevated position at head of valley. Warm welcome.

6hc 2⋒ (3fb) CTV in 3 bedrooms ✶ ® B&b£8–£8.50 Bdi£11–£12

Ⅲ CTV 10P U 150acres livestock

FELMINGHAM
Norfolk
Map **9** TG22

FH J Burton ***Felmingham Hall*** *(TG245275)* ☎Swanton Abbott (069269) 228

Large, interesting old manor house. Remote but near North Walsham. Big rooms comfortably appointed.

10hc 6➡ 2⋒ (3fb) CTV in all bedrooms ✶ ® LDO5pm

Lic Ⅲ CTV 100P nc12yrs 65acres mixed

Ⓥ

FENITON
Devon
Map **3** SY19

GH Colestocks House Colestocks (1m N unclass rd) ☎Honiton (0404) 850633
Mar–Oct rs 1 Dec–Xmas

6rm 2hc 4➡ (A 2hc) (2fb) ✶ ® B&b£9–£10.50 Bdi£13.50–£16.50 W£87.50–£108.50 Ⱡ LDO7pm

Lic Ⅲ CTV 8P nc12yrs

Ⓥ

FENSTANTON
Cambridgeshire
Map **4** TL36

INN Tudor Hotel High St ☎St Ives (0480) 62532

Mock Tudor inn situated in small village of Fenstanton off busy A604 Hunstanton–Cambridge bypass.

6➡ CTV in all bedrooms ✶ ® *B&b£18 L£7alc D10pm £7alc

Ⅲ 50P

Credit cards ① ③

FERNDOWN
Dorset
Map **4** SU00

GH Broadlands Hotel West Moors Rd ☎(0202) 877884

17rm 10hc 4➡ 3⋒ (2fb) B&b£12.50 Bdi£17.75 W£80 M LDO6.30pm

Lic Ⅲ CTV ⌂

FFESTINIOG
Gwynedd
Map **6** SH64

GH Newborough House Hotel Church Sq ☎(076676) 2682

Stone-built Georgian house on edge of village.

6hc (4fb) B&b£9–£10 Bdi£14–£15.50 W£95 Ⱡ LDO5pm

Lic Ⅲ CTV 6P nc7yrs

Ⓥ

FIDDLEFORD
Dorset
Map **3** ST81

INN Fiddleford ☎Sturminster Newton (0258) 72489
Closed Xmas Day

Situated near Sturminster Newton on main Blandford to Sherborne road, in rural setting.

4rm 3hc 1➡ 1⋒ B&b£11.50 Bdi£14 W£61 M L£4alc D10pm £7alc

Ⅲ 50P

FILEY
North Yorkshire
Map **8** TA18

GH *Beach Hotel* The Beach ☎Scarborough (0723) 513178
Apr–Oct

Substantial Victorian house overlooking bay, with clean accommodation and spacious public rooms. Specialises in family holidays.

22hc (12fb) LDO6pm

Lic CTV sea

GH Downcliffe Hotel The Beach ☎Scarborough (0723) 513310
Apr–Oct

17rm 12hc 5⋒ (9fb) CTV in 5 bedrooms B&b£10.50–£11 Bdi£12–£13 W£73.50–£77 M LDO6pm

Lic CTV 9P 1⌂

FINTRY
Central *Stirlingshire*
Map **11** NS68

FH Mrs M Mitchell **Nether Glinns** *(NS606883)* ☎(036086) 207
Apr–Oct

Well-maintained farmhouse situated among rolling hills. Access via signposted ½m gravel drive.

3rm (1fb) B&bfr£6.50

CTV 6P 150acres dairy mixed

FISHGUARD
Dyfed
Map **2** SM93

GH Glanmoy Country House Goodwick (1m NW on A40) ☎(0348) 872844

3 CTV in all bedrooms Ⓡ B&b£15–£16 Bdi£20–£25 W£126–£130 LDO9pm

Lic 40P nc10yrs

Ⓥ

FLAMBOROUGH
Humberside
Map **8** TA27

GH Flaneburgh Hotel North Marine Rd (Minotel) ☎Bridlington (0262) 850284
Mar–Oct

Three-storey building standing in its own ground on the edge of the village and near the cliffs of Flamborough Head.

16rm 10hc 6 (2fb) CTV in all bedrooms Ⓡ *B&b£10–£12 Bdi£15–£17 W£92–£105 LDO10pm

Lic CTV 20P

FLAX BOURTON
Avon
Map **3** ST56

INN Jubilee Farleigh Rd ☎(027583) 2741

4hc B&b£12 L£5–£6alc D10.30pm

CTV 51P nc

FLUSHING
Cornwall
Map **2** SW83

GH Nankersey Hotel St Peters Rd ☎Falmouth (0326) 74471

Grade II listed building beautifully positioned within character fishing village enjoying excellent river views.

7hc (3fb) Ⓡ B&b£10.50–£11.50 Bdi£21–£23 W£66.50–£73.50 LDO7pm

Lic CTV

Credit cards 1 3 Ⓥ

FOLKESTONE
Kent
Map **5** TR23
See Plan

GH Argos Private Hotel 6 Marine Ter ☎(0303) 54309 Plan **1** *E1*

Homely little house, close to the ferry terminal.

9hc (2fb) B&b£9–£10 Bdi£12.50–£13.50 W£57.50–£65 LDO10pm

Lic CTV nc3yrs

GH Arundel Hotel The Leas, 3 Clifton Rd ☎(0303) 52442 Plan **2** *B1*
Mar–Oct

Spacious, comfortable accommodation on four floors, with friendly and efficient service.

13hc (3fb) B&b£9.20–£11.50 Bdi£12.65–£16.10 W£62.10–£66.70 LDO3.30pm

Lic CTV

GH *Beaumont Private Hotel* 5 Marine Ter ☎(0303) 52740 Plan **3** *E1*

Victorian terraced house with homely accommodation.

8hc (4fb) LDO4pm

Lic CTV

GH Belmonte Private Hotel 30 Castle Hill Av ☎(0303) 54470 Plan **4** *B2*
Apr–Oct

Simple, old-fashioned, functional accommodation with homely and courteous atmosphere.

10hc (2fb) B&b£8.50–£9 Bdi£11.50–£12 W£55–£58 LDO6pm

CTV 6P nc3yrs

GH Wearbay Hotel 23/25 Wearbay Cres ☎(0303) 52586 Plan **5** *F2*

Old-fashioned, friendly accommodation.

12rm 11hc 1 (1fb) B&b£7.70–£13.31 Bdi£13.20–£19.31 W£46.20–£79.86 S% LDO11pm

Lic CTV 1

Credit cards 1 3 Ⓥ

GH Westward Ho! 13 Clifton Cres ☎(0303) 52663 Plan **6** *A1*
rs Oct–Etr

11rm 10hc 1 Ⓡ B&b£12–£13 Bdi£14–£15 W£70–£90 LDO5pm

Lic lift

FONTHILL BISHOP
Wiltshire
Map **3** ST93

INN Kings Arms ☎Hindon (074789) 523
rs Xmas & Boxing Day

3hc Ⓡ B&b£11–£11.50 W£74.50–£77 Bar lunch 65p–£4.50 D10pm

CTV 25P

Credit card 1 Ⓥ

FONTMELL MAGNA
Dorset
Map **3** ST81

GH Estyard House Hotel ☎(0747) 811460
Closed Nov & Xmas

In centre of quiet and attractive Dorset village.

6hc B&b£9.75 Bdi£14.25 W£91 LDO3pm

8P nc10yrs

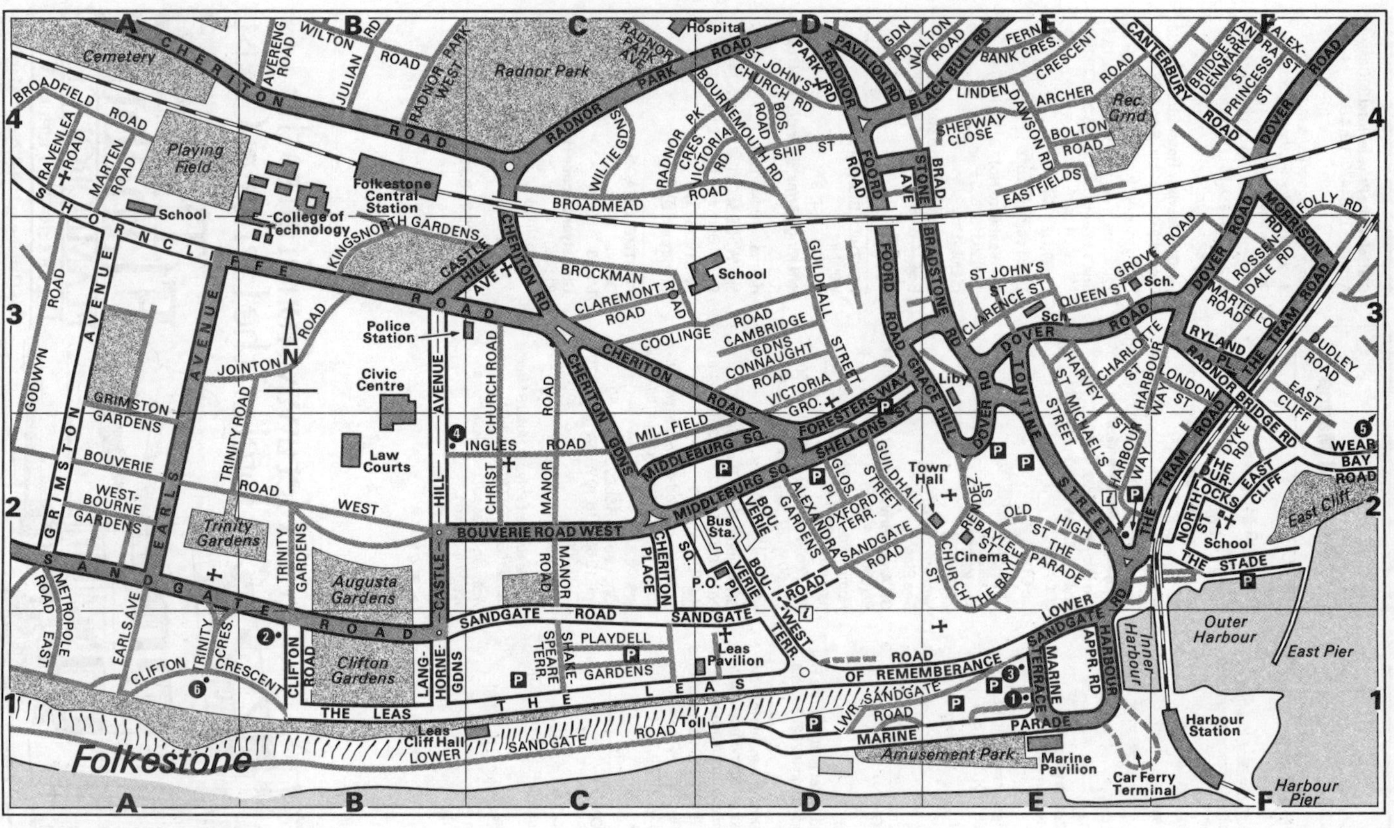

Folkestone

1 Argos Private Hotel
2 Arundel Hotel
3 Beaumont Private Hotel
4 Belmonte Private Hotel
5 Wearbay Hotel
6 Westwood Ho! Hotel

FORDEN
Powys
Map **7** SJ20

⊢⊣ **FH** Mrs K Owens **Coed-y-Brenin** *(SJ248025)* Kingswood Ln ☎(093876) 272

Modern farmhouse in lovely Border countryside, signposted Kingswood from A490 at Forden. ½m E off B4388 unclass rd.

3hc ✶ ® B&b£7.50–£8 W£50–£53.50 M

Ⅲ CTV 5P 280acres beef dairy sheep mixed

Ⓥ

FORDINGBRIDGE
Hampshire
Map **4** SU11

GH Oakfield Lodge 1 Park Rd ☎(0425) 52789
Jan–Oct

Attractive corner house with modestly priced accommodation, run by jolly proprietors.

10rm 7hc 1fl (2fb) ✶ B&b£9–£10 W£58–£65 M

CTV 10P

Ⓥ

FORDOUN
Grampian *Kincardineshire*
Map **15** NO77

⊢⊣ **FH** Mrs M Anderson **Ringwood** *(NO743774)* ☎Auchenblae (05612) 313
Mar–Oct

Small, modernised villa in open setting amidst farmland and with its own neat garden and outhouse. Very high standard of décor and furnishings. 1m NW of village on B966.

4rm 1hc (1fb) ✶ ® B&b£7.50–£9 W£50–£60 M

Ⅲ CTV 4P 16acres arable

Ⓥ

FORGANDENNY
Tayside *Perthshire*
Map **11** NO01

⊢⊣ **FH** Mrs M Fotheringham **Craighall** *(NO081176)* ☎Bridge of Earn (0738) 812415

Large bungalow-type farmhouse tastefully furnished, with friendly atmosphere. 2½m W off B935 Bridge of Earn–Forteviot road.

3hc (1fb) ✶ B&bfr£6.50 Bdifr£11.50 Wfr£45.50 M LDO9pm

Ⅲ CTV 4P ⌂ 1000acres arable beef, sheep

FORTON
Lancashire
Map **7** SD45

GH Oakfield Lancaster Rd ☎(0524) 791630

Spacious well furnished family run Victorian house on A6.

8hc (2fb) ✶ B&b£8.50 Bdi£12 W£59.50 M LDO8pm

Ⅲ CTV 15P

Ⓥ

FORT WILLIAM
Highland *Inverness-shire*
Map **14** NN17

GH *Benview* Belford Rd ☎(0397) 2966
Mar–Nov

Detached stone-built house with modern extension situated beside A82 just N of town centre.

15hc (2fb) LDO7.15pm

Ⅲ CTV 20P

Ⓥ

⊢⊣ **GH Guisachan** Alma Rd ☎(0397) 3797

Comfortable house in an elevated position at north end of town.

15hc (4fb) ✶ B&b£8–£10 Bdi£12.50–£14.50

Lic Ⅲ CTV 15P

⊢⊣ **GH Hillview** Achintore Rd ☎(0397) 4349

A friendly, comfortable and nicely appointed guesthouse situated beside the A82 overlooking Loch Linnhe.

9hc (2fb) ® B&b£6.50–£7.50 Bdi£10.50–£11.50 LDO6.30pm

Ⅲ CTV 9P

GH Innseagan Achintore Rd ☎(0397) 2452
Apr–Oct

Large stone-built house with modern extensions, situated on the A82 South of the town, overlooking Loch Linnhe.

26rm 14hc 12⇌ (2fb) ✶ Bdi£12.75–£16 LDO7pm

Lic Ⅲ CTV 30P

⊢⊣ **GH Lochview** Heathcroft, Argyll Rd ☎(0397) 3149
Etr–Oct

A comfortable modern style guesthouse.

7rm 6hc 1⇌ (2fb) B&b£7–£8 Bdi£11–£12 W£75–£82 Ł LDO6.30pm

Ⅲ CTV 8P

⊢⊣ **GH Rhu Mhor** Alma Rd ☎(0397) 2213
Etr–Sep

A traditional style guesthouse in a quiet residential area.

7hc (2fb) B&b£7–£7.50 Bdi£11–£11.50 LDO5pm

CTV 7P

Ⓥ

GH *Stronchreggan View* Achintore Rd ☎(0397) 4644
Apr–Oct

Comfortable and well appointed modern style house.

7hc (3fb) ✶ LDO6.30pm

Ⅲ 7P loch

Ⓥ

FOUR CROSSES
Powys
Map **7** SJ21

⊢✕⊣ **FH** Mrs J E Wigley **Maerdy** *(SJ259168)* (¾m SE B4393) ☎ Guilsfield (093875) 202
Apr–Oct
Warm, friendly old farmhouse full of beams and polished floors.
2hc 1⋔ (1fb) ✖ B&bfr£8 Bdifr£12 Wfr£80 ⅃ LDO3pm
TV P 157acres arable dairy mixed

FOVANT
Wiltshire
Map **4** SU02

INN Cross Keys Hotel ☎ (072270) 284
4hc B&b£10 Bdifr£14 Wfr£90 ⅃ L£4.25alc D10pm £6.70alc
▥ CTV 30P
Credit card 3

FOWEY
Cornwall
Map **2** SX15

GH Ashley House Hotel 14 Esplanade ☎ (072683) 2310
Mar–Oct
8hc (3fb) ✖ Ⓡ ✻B&b£9–£11 Bdi£14–£16 W£85–£95 ⅃ S% LDO9pm
Lic CTV ⌀

GH Carnethic House Lambs Barn ☎ (072683) 3336
Mar–Oct
8rm 3hc 4⋔ (2fb) CTV in all bedrooms ✖ Ⓡ B&b£14–£16 Bdi£19.95–£22 W£98–£133 M LDO6.45pm
Lic ▥ 20P nc12yrs ⌒ (heated)
Credit cards 1 2 3 5 Ⓥ

GH Wheelhouse 60 Esplanade ☎ (072683) 2452
15 Mar–Dec
7rm 6hc (1fb) ✖ B&b£9–£10 Bdi£15–£16 W£63–£70 M LDOnoon
Lic ▥ CTV nc12yrs

⊢✕⊣ **FH** M & H T Dunn **Trezare** *(SX112538)* ☎ (072683) 3485
Apr–Sep
Conveniently situated 1m from Fowey, pleasant atmosphere and good farmhouse fare.
3rm 2hc ✖ B&b£7.50–£8 W£52–£56 M
CTV 4P 2⌂ 230acres arable beef dairy sheep mixed

FOWNHOPE
Hereford & Worcester
Map **3** SO53

GH Bowens Farmhouse ☎ (043277) 430
Feb–Dec
9hc 2➡ 2⋔ (3fb) ✖ Ⓡ B&b£11.50–£13 Bdi£17–£20 W£109–£119 ⅃ LDO7.30pm
Lic ▥ CTV 8P 2⌂ nc10yrs
Ⓥ

FRADDON
Cornwall
Map **2** SW95

⊢✕⊣ **GH St Margaret's Private Hotel** ☎ St Austell (0726) 860375
Large detached house enjoying good position for touring north and south Cornwall.
12hc (6fb) B&bfr£8 Bdifr£10 Wfr£63.50 ⅃ S% LDO7pm
Lic ▥ CTV 20P

FRESHWATER
Isle of Wight
Map **4** SZ38

GH Blenheim House Gate Ln ☎ Isle of Wight (0983) 752858
May–Oct
Charming private house with small outdoor pool, situated less than ½ mile from the sea.

8⋔ (4fb) CTV in all bedrooms 🐕✗ Ⓡ B&b£10–£12 Bdi£14.50–£16.50 W£68–£72⋎ LDO7pm

Lic ⊞ 6P 1⌂ nc5yrs ⛱ (heated)

FRESSINGFIELD
Suffolk
Map **5** TM27

⍀ **FH** Mrs R Tomson **Hillview** *(TM264771)* ☎(037986) 443

A modern farmhouse, comfortably furnished, situated on the outskirts of the village off B1116 Diss/Framlingham rd.

3rm 2hc B&b£8 Bdi£12 W£80⋎

⊞ CTV 3P 2acres stock

FH Mrs R Willis ***Priory House*** *(TM256770)* Priory Rd ☎(037986) 254

Attractive 400-year-old brick-built farmhouse with beamed interior and quality furniture. Secluded garden.

3hc 🐕✗

⊞ CTV 6P nc8yrs 2acres

FRINTON-ON-SEA
Essex
Map **5** TM21

GH Forde 18 Queens Rd ☎(02556) 4758
Closed Dec

An old fashioned establishment with simple bedrooms and small lounge.

6hc (1fb) B&b£8.50 Bdi£12 W£59⋎ LDOnoon

⊞ CTV 1P nc5yrs

Credit cards ① ③ Ⓥ

GH Montpellier Private Hotel 2 Harold Gv (Guestaccom) ☎(02556) 4462
Closed Xmas & New Year

Situated in residential area and recently renovated, with spacious bedrooms.

6rm 1hc 4➡ 1⋔ (2fb) CTV in 2 bedrooms TV in 2 bedrooms 🐕✗ Ⓡ B&b£10.75–£13.50 Bdi£16.25–£19 W£98–£114⋎ LDO5pm

Lic ⊞ CTV 6P 1⌂

Credit cards ① ③

GH Uplands 41 Hadleigh Rd ☎(02556) 4889
Closed Jan

Small, family run hotel with good lounges and a Cordon Bleu cook.

8hc (2fb) B&b£9.95 Bdi£14.75 W£64–£66.50 Ⓜ LDO3.30pm

Lic ⊞ CTV 7P nc6yrs

GAIRLOCH
Highland *Ross & Cromarty*
Map **14** NG87

GH Horisdale House Strath ☎(0445) 2151
Jun–Sep rs May & Oct

Modern, elegant, comfortable and well-equipped guesthouse.

9hc (3fb) 🐕✗ Ⓡ B&b£9 Bdi£15 LDO9am

⊞ 12P nc7yrs

GALASHIELS
Borders *Selkirkshire*
Map **12** NT43

GH Buckholmburn Edinburgh Rd ☎(0896) 2697

Detached house sitting high above the Galawater on the A7 on the northern outskirts of the town.

8rm 4hc (3fb) B&b£11 Bdi£16 W£77 Ⓜ LDO7pm

Lic ⊞ CTV 20P

Credit cards ① ② ③ ⑤

GALSTON
Strathclyde *Ayrshire*
Map **11** NS53

⍀ **FH** Mrs J Bone **Auchencloigh** *(NS535320)* ☎(0563) 820567
Apr–Oct

5m S off B7037 towards Sorn.

2rm (1fb) 🐕✗ B&b£7–£7.50 Bdi£10–£10.50 W£72⋎ LDO6pm

⊞ CTV 6P ⛪ 240acres beef sheep mixed

Ⓥ

GARFORTH
West Yorkshire
Map **8** SE43

GH Coach House Hotel 58 Lidgett Ln ☎Leeds (0532) 862303
Closed 24 Dec–4 Jan

6hc (A 4hc) (1fb) Ⓡ *B&b£12

⊞ CTV 8P 2⌂

GARGRAVE
North Yorkshire
Map **7** SD95

GH Kirk Syke 19 High St ☎(075678) 356
Mar–Oct

Large stone house in village, with pleasant modern bedrooms.

5rm 4hc 1➡ (A 4rm 2➡ 2⋔) Ⓡ B&b£9 Bdi£14 W£63 Ⓜ LDOnoon

Lic ⊞ CTV 10P

Ⓥ

GARSTANG
Lancashire
Map **7** SD44

⍀ **FH** Mrs J Fowler **Greenhalgh Castle** *(SD501452)* Castle Ln ☎(09952) 2140
Etr–mid Oct

½m E unclass rd.

3hc 🐕✗ Ⓡ B&b£7.50–£8 W£50–£54 Ⓜ

CTV 6P 3⌂ 160acres dairy sheep

GARTHMYL
Powys
Map **7** SO19

⍀ **FH** Mrs P Jones **Trwstllewelyn** *(SO189984)* ☎Berriew (068685) 295
Etr–Oct

Spacious 17th-century farmhouse, with traditional fine furnishings and open fires in the recently-discovered and restored inglenook fireplace.

3rm 2hc 🐕✗ Ⓡ B&b£8 Bdi£13 W£84⋎ LDO4.30pm

CTV 4P ⛪ ♪ 300acres mixed

GATEHEAD
Strathclyde *Ayrshire*
Map **10** NS33

FH Mr & Mrs A Elliot **Old Rome** *(NS393360)* ☎ Drybridge (0563) 850265

Situated in a completely rural setting 300 yards off the A759 to Troon road (5m). Farmhouse has charm and character and dates from 17th century.

4hc (1fb) ✱ Ⓡ B&b£11 Bdi£16.50 W£100 Ⱡ LDO9pm

Lic 🀫 CTV 20P ✔ 10acres non-working Ⓥ

GATE HELMSLEY
North Yorkshire
Map **8** SE65

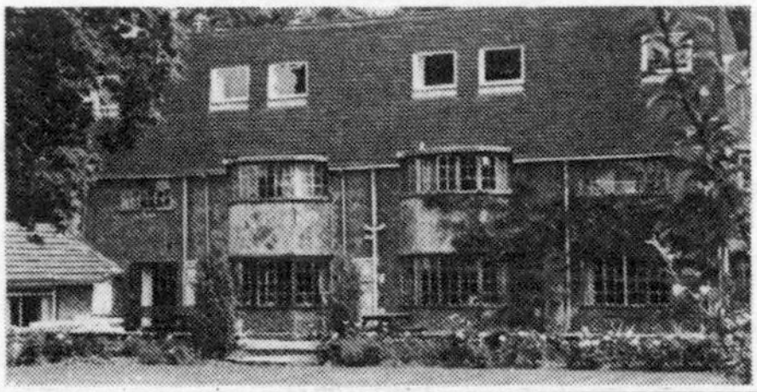

⊢⊣ **FH** Mrs K M Sykes **Lime Field** *(SE693534)* Scoreby ☎ York (0904) 489224
Mar–Oct

Quietly situated with large garden and rural views. Convenient for touring York, The Dales and Moors.

4rm 2hc (3fb) ✱ B&b£7.50–£8.50 W£52.50–£59.50 M

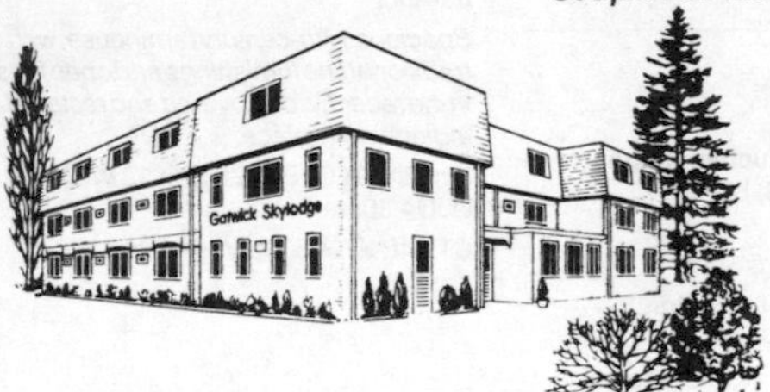

CTV 4P nc3yrs 125acres arable beef

GATWICK AIRPORT, LONDON
West Sussex
Map **4** TQ24

GH *Barnwood Hotel* Balcombe Rd, Pound Hill, Crawley ☎ Crawley (0293) 882709

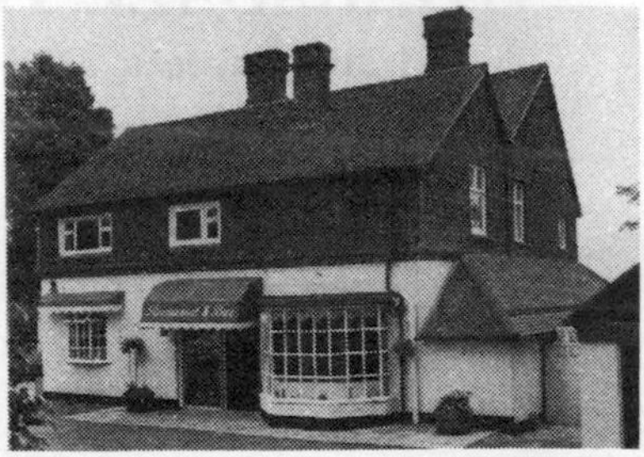

Modern private hotel with comfortable lounge and bar.

26hc 1→ 24⋒ (2fb) CTV in all bedrooms ✱ Ⓡ LDO8.45pm

Lic 🀫 40P ♿

GH Gainsborough Lodge 39 Massetts Rd, Horley (2m NE of airport adjacent A23) ☎Horley (02934) 3982
Closed 23–26 Dec
Victorian house with comfortable, compact accommodation.
9rm 3➡ 6⋒ (2fb) ✱ Ⓡ B&b£11–£15
₥ CTV 16P

GH Gatwick Skylodge Motel London Rd, County Oak, Crawley (2m S of airport on A23) ☎Crawley (0293) 544511
45➡ (7fb) CTV in all bedrooms Ⓡ
✱B&b£15.50–£24 W£168 M LDO10pm
Lic ₥ 55P
Credit cards 1 2 3

GH *Trumble's Hotel & Restaurant* Stanhill, Charlwood ☎Crawley (0293) 862212
Closed 24 Dec–2 Jan
Overlooking Gatwick and incorporating an attractive restaurant serving home made teas.
5hc 2➡ 3⋒ CTV in all bedrooms ✱ Ⓡ LDO9.15pm
Lic ₥ 30P 2🚗 nc10yrs
Ⓥ

GAYHURST
Buckinghamshire
Map **4** SP84

FH Mrs K Adams **Mill** *(SP852454)* ☎Newport Pagnell (0908) 611489
17th-century stone-built farmhouse with the River Ouse running through the grounds from which fishing is available. 1m S off B526 unclass road to Haversham.
3hc (1fb) TV in all bedrooms Ⓡ B&b£10 Bdi£15 W£100 𝒱 LDO5pm
₥ 6P 6🚗 ⌂ ⚲ U 505acres mixed
Ⓥ

GEDNEY HILL
Lincolnshire
Map **8** TF31

FH Mrs C Cave **Sycamore** *(TF336108)* ☎Holbeach (0406) 330445
Situated on the B1166 in the village. The farmhouse is over 100 years old.
3rm (1fb) TV in all bedrooms Ⓡ B&b£10 Bdi£16 W£70 M LDO4pm
₥ CTV 6P ⚲ 80acres beef mixed
Ⓥ

GIGGLESWICK
North Yorkshire
Map **7** SD86

GH Woodlands The Mains ☎Settle (07292) 2576
Closed Xmas & New Year
10hc (2fb) ✱ B&b£14.75 Bdi£22 W£147 𝒱 LDOnoon
Lic ₥ CTV 10P nc12yrs
See advertisement on page 162

FH Mrs B T Hargreaves **Close House** *(SD801634)* ☎Settle (07292) 3540
May–Sep
17th-century farmhouse with tree-lined private drive and well-kept gardens. River bathing and fishing nearby.
4hc ✱ Ⓡ B&bfr£15 Bdifr£24.50 Wfr£94.50 M LDOnoon
Lic 6P 230acres dairy sheep
Ⓥ

GLAN-YR-AFON *(Near Corwen)*
Gwynedd
Map **6** SJ04

⊢⊣**FH** Mrs G B Jones **Llawr-Bettws** *(SJ016424)* Bala Rd ☎Maerdy (049081) 224
Rambling, stone-built farmhouse with pleasant, homely atmosphere. At Druid traffic lights on A5 follow A494 Bala road for 2m.
3hc (2fb) ✱ B&b£8 Bdi£10–£12 W£70–£80 𝒱 LDO6.30pm
CTV 6P ⌂ 62acres beef sheep mixed
Ⓥ

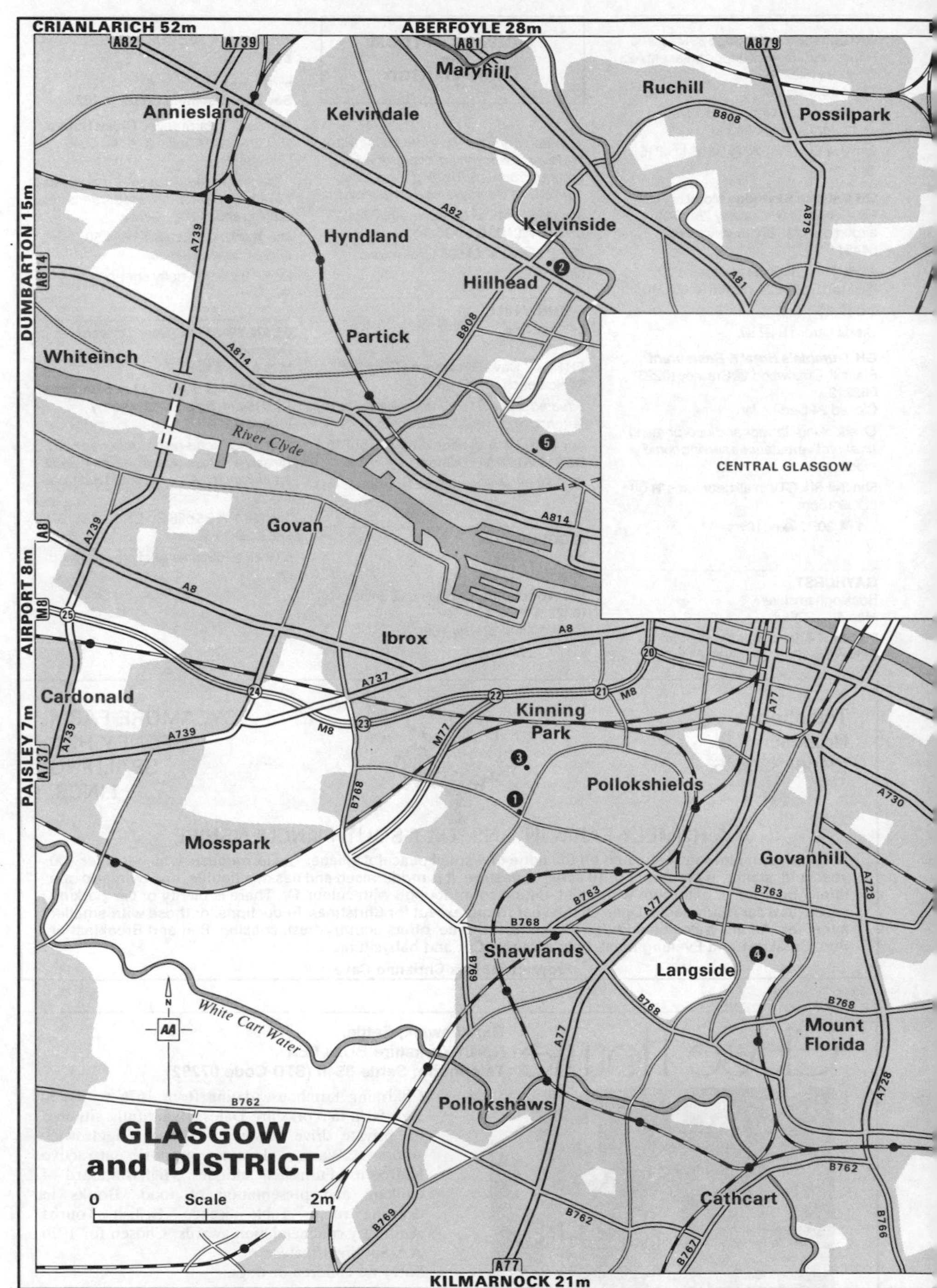
CRIANLARICH 52m
ABERFOYLE 28m
DUMBARTON 15m
AIRPORT 8m
PAISLEY 7m
KILMARNOCK 21m
Maryhill
Ruchill
Possilpark
Anniesland
Kelvindale
Hyndland
Kelvinside
Hillhead
Partick
Whiteinch
River Clyde
Govan
Ibrox
Cardonald
Kinning
Park
Pollokshields
Mosspark
Govanhill
Shawlands
Langside
Mount
Florida
White Cart Water
Pollokshaws
Cathcart
CENTRAL GLASGOW
GLASGOW
and DISTRICT
0
Scale
2m

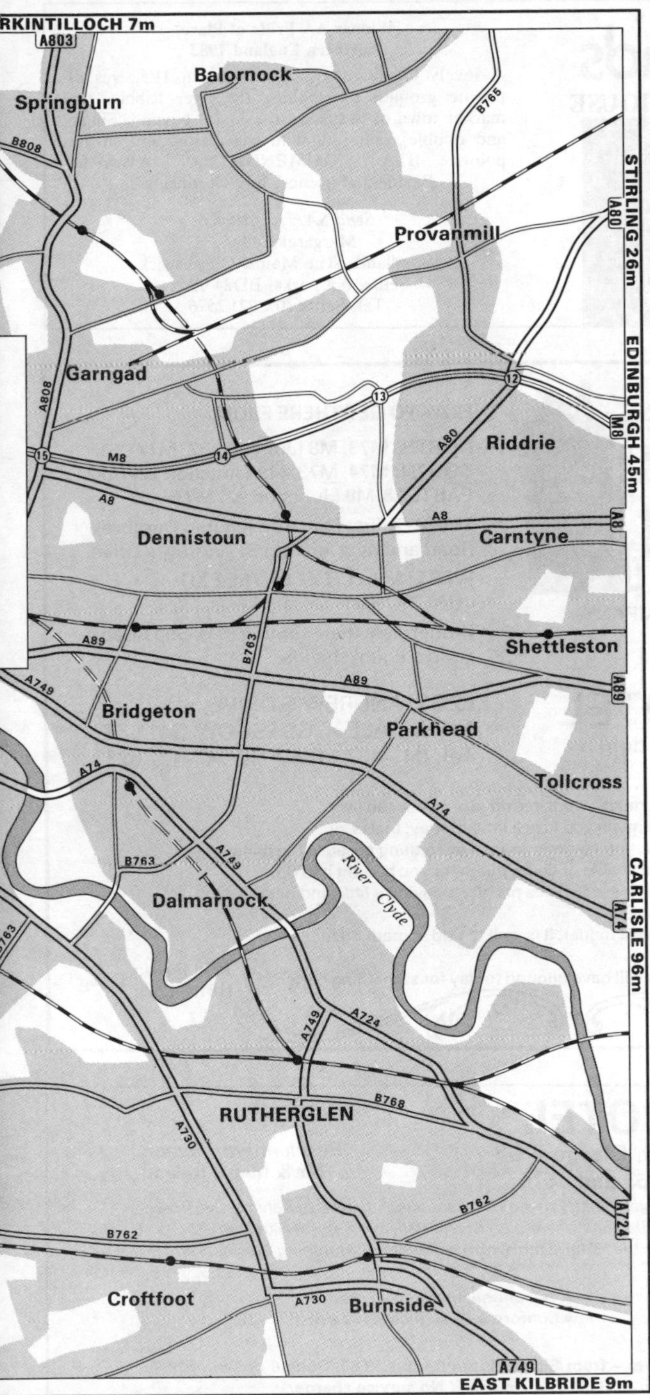

GLASBURY
Powys
Map **3** SO13

FH Mrs B Eckley **Ffforddfawr** *(SO192398)*
☎(04974) 332
Mar–Oct
17th-century farmhouse bordered by the River Wye. 3m from Hay-on-Wye.
2hc 🐕
🏴 CTV 4P nc6yrs 280acres mixed

GLASFRYN
Clwyd
Map **6** SH95

⊢⊣ **FH** Mrs C Ellis **Growine** *(SH927502)*
☎Cerrigydrudian (049082) 447
Apr–Oct
Modernised and extended farmhouse at end of drive. N of A5, E of village.
2rm 🐕 B&b£6.50 Bdi£10 W£42 M
LDO1pm
🏴 CTV 4P 70acres sheep

GLASGOW
Strathclyde *Lanarkshire*
Map **11** NS56
See plan

GH Dalmeny Hotel 62 St Andrews Dr, Nithsdale Cross ☎041-427 1106 Plan **1**
A friendly, comfortable and nicely appointed private hotel.
10hc 3⇌ 2⋔ (1fb) CTV in all bedrooms Ⓡ B&b£18.35
Lic 🏴 CTV 20P
Ⓥ
See advertisement on page 162

GH Kelvin Private Hotel
15 Buckingham Ter, Hillhead ☎041-339 7143 Plan **2**
A terrace house in West End, close to Botanic Gardens.
15hc (3fb) B&b£11–£12.50
🏴 CTV 5P

GH *Linwood Hotel* 356 Albert Dr, Pollokshields ☎041-427 1642 Plan **3**
Nicely appointed house with tidy garden, in quiet residential area.
11hc (2fb) TV in 4 bedrooms 🐕
🏴 CTV 8P

Glasgow

1 Dalmeny Hotel
2 Kelvin Private Hotel
3 Linwood Hotel
4 Marie Stuart Hotel
5 Smith's Hotel

COUNTRY GUESTHOUSE

Winner AA Pride of Place, Northern England 1983

A lovely Georgian-style house set in 1½ acres of private grounds overlooking the river Ribble, the market town of Settle, to the Dales beyond. Single and double rooms all with washbasins and shaver points. BTA COMMENDATION AWARD, Residential licence, Fire Certificate.

Send SAE for details.
Margaret Callan,
Woodlands, The Mains, Giggleswick,
Settle, N. Yorks, BD24 0AX.
Tel: Settle (07292) 2576

ENJOY THE COMFORT AND COMPANY OF YOUR ALTERNATIVE HOME

HOW TO GET THERE FROM:–

NORTH: M73, M8 (Junction 22) M77
SOUTH: M74, M73, M8 (Junction 22) M72
EAST: A8/M8 (Junction 22) M77

The M77 First Exit, turn left into Dumbrek Road and next left into St Andrew's Drive.

WEST: M8 – CITY CENTRE EXIT JUNCTION 21

Rutherglen, then Kinning Park Slip Road. Follow Pollokshields.

DALMENY HOTEL

(Nearest to Burrell Collection)

62 ST. ANDREW'S DRIVE,
NITHSDALE X, GLASGOW G41 5EZ
Tel: 041-427 1106 AND 041-427 6288

'It is unwise to pay too much — but it is unwise to pay too little.
When you pay too much you lose a little money, that is all.
When you pay too little, you sometimes lose everything because the thing you bought was incapable of doing the thing you bought it to do.
The common law of business balance prohibits paying a little and getting a lot it can't be done.
If you deal with the lowest bidder, it is well to add something for the risk you run.
And if you do that, you will have enough to pay for something better'.

John Ruskin
(1819–1900)

SMITH'S HOTEL

(Est.1928)

963 Sauchiehall Street, Glasgow G3
Telephone 041-339 6363 and 7674

Resident Proprietors:
Mr & Mrs S Ireland

Enjoy a comfortable stay in this old established Private Hotel situated adjacent to Kelvingrove Park and within short walking distance of Glasgow University, Kelvin Hall, and City Art Museum.
Being 5 minutes' from the City Centre, the Hotel is most convenient for all shopping precincts and Bus, Rail and Airport Terminals.

- Convenient Parking
- Central Heating
- Colour TV Lounge
- Telephone intercom all rooms
- Conforms to 'Higher Standard' of S.T.B.

Terms: Full Breakfast inclusive — from Single Room £9.20–£12.65. Double or Twin £18.40. Family room £23.00. **Tax inclusive. No service charge.**

GH Marie Stuart Hotel 46–48 Queen Mary Av, Cathcart ☎041-423 6363 Plan **4**

Private hotel with modern extension.

31rm 22hc 8→ 1⋔ (4fb) CTV in 8 bedrooms TV in 1 bedroom Ⓡ✱B&b£13.90–£23.25 Bdi£18.40–£27.75 W£98–£162.75 M̸ LDO7pm

Lic ▥ CTV 50P

GH Smith's Hotel 963 Sauchiehall St ☎041-339 7674 Plan **5**

A long established private hotel in the West End.

26hc (8fb) ★ B&b£9.20

▥ CTV P̸

GLASTONBURY

Somerset
Map **3** ST53

GH Hawthorns Hotel 10 Northload St ☎(0458) 31255

12hc 3⋔ (2fb) ★ Ⓡ B&b£11–£15 W£95–£110 L̸ LDO9.30pm

Lic ▥ CTV

Credit cards [1] [2] [3] [5] Ⓥ

FH Mrs H T Tinney **Cradlebridge** *(ST477385)* ☎(0458) 31827

Large, renovated farmhouse with vegetable and fruit garden.

4rm 3hc (1fb) B&b£9–£9.50 Bdi£16–£16.50 W£54–£57 M̸ LDOnoon

▥ CTV 6P 163acres dairy

Ⓥ

GLENCOE

Highland *Argyllshire*
Map **14** NN15

GH *Dunire* ☎Ballachulish (08552) 318

A comfortable modern bungalow delightfully situated amid the mountains of Glencoe.

6rm 5hc (3fb)

▥ CTV 10P 1🚗 ⌂

⊢×⊣**GH Scorrybreac** ☎Ballachulish (08552) 354
Feb–Oct

A modern style guesthouse, comfortable and well appointed.

5hc (1fb) ★ B&b£8–£9 Bdi£12.50–£14 W£84–£96 L̸ (W only Jul & Aug) LDO24hrs

▥ CTV 8P

Credit cards [2] [3]

GLENMAVIS

Strathclyde *Lanarkshire*
Map **11** NS76

⊢×⊣**FH** Mrs M Dunbar **Braidenhill** *(NS742673)* ☎Glenboig (0236) 872319

300-year-old farmhouse on the outskirts of Coatbridge. About ½m from town boundary, N off B803.

3hc (1fb) B&b£7.50

▥ CTV 4P 50acres arable

GLENRIDDING

Cumbria
Map **11** NY31

GH *Bridge House* ☎(08532) 236
Mar–Oct

6hc (5fb) Ⓡ

▥ 7P lake

GLOSSOP

Derbyshire
Map **7** SK09

GH Colliers Hotel & Restaurant 14/14A High St ☎(04574) 63409

6hc (1fb) CTV in all bedrooms ★ B&b£15–£17.50 Bdi£25–£30 W£95–£125 M̸ LDO9pm

Lic ▥ CTV P

Credit card [3]

GH Hurst Lee Hotel Derbyshire Level (off A57) Sheffield Rd ☎(04574) 3354
rs Xmas & New Year

7⋔ (2fb) ★ B&b£16 Bdi£22.50 W£112 M̸ LDO4pm

Lic ▥ CTV 12P nc7yrs

Credit card [3] Ⓥ

GLOUCESTER

Gloucestershire
Map **3** SO81

GH Alma 49 Kingsholm Rd ☎(0452) 20940

A well maintained guesthouse offering a warm welcome.

8hc (2fb) TV in 1 bedroom ★ B&b£10–£12

▥ CTV 6P 1🚗 nc10yrs

Credit card [3]

GH *Claremont* 135 Stroud Rd ☎(0452) 29450

6hc (2fb) TV in all bedrooms ★

▥ 6P

Ⓥ

⊢×⊣**GH Lulworth** 12 Midland Rd ☎(0452) 21881

8hc (2fb) CTV in all bedrooms B&b£8–£8.50

▥ CTV 8P

GH Monteith 127 Stroud Rd ☎(0452) 25369

8rm 6hc 2→ (3fb) CTV in all bedrooms ✱B&b£8–£8.50

▥ CTV 8P

See advertisement on page 164

GH Rotherfield House Hotel 5 Horton Rd ☎(0452) 410500

11hc (2fb) B&b£12.65 Bdi£18.40 W£88.55 M̸ LDO6.30pm

Lic ▥ CTV 9P

GOLSPIE

Highland *Sutherland*
Map **14** NH89

⊢×⊣**GH Glenshee** Station Rd ☎(04083) 3254

Small, homely guesthouse near beach and golf course.

6hc (3fb) B&b£7–£7.50 W£45 M̸

▥ CTV 10P ♿

INN Park House Hotel Main St ☎(04083) 3667
Mar–Oct
Small, family run establishment situated in the centre of the village backing onto the seafront.
5rm 2hc 3⋒ TV in all bedrooms Ⓡ B&b£13 Bdi£19 W£91 M L£2.70–£3&alc D8pm fr£4.50alc
CTV 5P
Ⓥ

GOMSHALL
Surrey
Map **4** TQ04
INN Black Horse ☎Shere (048641) 2242
Well maintained modern bedrooms, comfortable lounge and good bar facilities are complemented by efficient friendly service.
6hc Ⓡ B&b£16.10 Bdi£23.60 W£112.70 M L£5.75–£6.30 D9.30pm £7alc
CTV 60P nc12yrs
Credit cards 3 5 Ⓥ

GOONHAVERN
Cornwall
Map **2** SW75
GH *Reen Cross Farm* ☎Perranporth (087257) 3362
Closed Xmas
Family owned farmhouse since 1899, with views over the valley of Perranwell.
9hc (2fb) LDO10pm
Lic CTV 12P 2

GOREY
Jersey, Channel Islands
Map **16**
GH Royal Bay Hotel ☎Jersey (0534) 53318
May–Oct
18rm 5hc 11⋒ (4fb) B&b£9.40–£14.65 Bdi£11–£15.85 W£110.95 L LDO6.45pm
Lic CTV 8P nc3yrs

Golspie — Grange

GORRAN
Cornwall
Map **2** SW94
FH Mrs P A Atkins **Pentargon** *(SW985450)* High Lanes ☎Mevagissey (0726) 842227
May–14 Oct
2hc (1fb) B&b£6.50–£7.50 Bdi£10–£11 W£45–£52 L (W only 21 Jul–30 Aug)
CTV 2P

GORRAN HAVEN
Cornwall
Map **2** SX04
GH *Perhaver* ☎Mevagissey (0726) 842471
Etr–mid Oct
Situated on top of cliffs, 500yds from village.
5hc Ⓡ LDO5pm
Lic CTV nc18yrs sea

GOSPORT
Hampshire
Map **4** SZ69
GH Bridgemary Manor Hotel Brewers Ln ☎Fareham (0329) 232946
Quiet hotel in residential area, with nicely appointed restaurant and lounge area.
16hc (2fb) *B&b£10.75 Bdifr£12.75 LDO10pm
Lic CTV 20P

GOUROCK
Strathclyde *Renfrewshire*
Map **10** NS27
GH Claremont 34 Victoria Rd ☎(0475) 31687
Stone house on hillside overlooking the Clyde Estuary.
6hc (2fb) TV in all bedrooms B&b£9 W£56 M
CTV 4P

GRAMPOUND
Cornwall
Map **2** SW94
FH Mrs L M Wade **Tregidgeo** *(SW960473)* ☎St Austell (0726) 882450
May–Sep
Comfortably furnished farmhouse in a beautiful secluded and peaceful setting.
4rm 3hc (2fb) *B&b£6.50–£7 W£45.50 M
CTV 4P 216acres mixed

GRAMPOUND ROAD VILLAGE
Cornwall
Map **2** SW95
INN Midway ☎St Austell (0726) 882343
Apr–Oct
4hc Ⓡ B&b£9.25–£9.75 Bdi£13.50–£14 W£89.75–£93.25 L Bar lunch 55p–£2.25 D7pm £4.25
CTV 4P
Ⓥ

GRANDES ROCQUES
Guernsey, Channel Islands
Map **16**
GH *Hotel le Saumarez* Rue De Galad ☎Guernsey (0481) 57381
Mar–Oct rs Nov–Feb
19hc 9→ 4⋒ (8fb) LDO7pm
Lic CTV 30P
Ⓥ

GRANGE (in Borrowdale)
Cumbria
Map **11** NY21
GH Grange ☎Borrowdale (059684) 251
Mar–Nov
7hc 1→ 1⋒ (1fb) Ⓡ B&b£8.50 Bdi£13.95 W£59 M LDO6pm
8P
Credit card 3
See advertisement on page 70

GRANGE-OVER-SANDS
Cumbria
Map **7** SD47

⊢⊣ **GH Elton Private Hotel** Windermere Rd ☎(04484) 2838
Closed Nov
10hc B&b£8–£9 Bdi£11–£11.50 W£70–£75 Ⱡ LDO6pm
CTV 8P
Ⓥ

GH Grayrigge Private Hotel Kents Bank Rd ☎(04484) 2345
Large family owned hotel with spacious rooms.
27rm 24hc 3🛁 (A 12hc) (14fb)
✻B&b£9–£10 Bdi£12–£14 W£56–£70 M LDO7pm
Lic 🏛 CTV 60P 6🚗

⊢⊣ **GH Thornfield House** Kents Bank Rd ☎(04484) 2512
Apr–Oct
6hc (2fb) TV in all bedrooms 🐕 Ⓡ B&bfr£7.50 Bdifr£11 Wfr£75 Ⱡ LDO5pm
🏛 6P nc5yrs

GRANTOWN-ON-SPEY
Highland *Morayshire*
Map **14** NJ02

GH *Braemoray Private Hotel* Main St ☎(0479) 2303
Feb–Nov
Offers comfortable lounges and elegant spacious rooms.
6hc 3🛁 🚿 (1fb)
Lic 🏛 CTV 6P

⊢⊣ **GH Dar-Il-Hena** ☎(0479) 2929
Etr–Oct
This well appointed property has a friendly atmosphere, elegant lounge and comfortable bedrooms.
7hc (3fb) Ⓡ B&b£7.25 Bdi£11.75 W£78 Ⱡ LDO7pm
🏛 CTV 10P

⊢⊣ **GH Dunachton** off Grant Rd ☎(0479) 2098
Comfortable, well appointed house in a quiet residential area.
8hc 1🛁 (2fb) B&b£6.90–£7.25 Bdifr£11.25 W£45–£48.30 M
Lic 🏛 CTV 10P

⊢⊣ **GH Dunallan** Woodside Av ☎(0479) 2140
Feb–Nov
5hc (2fb) 🐕 B&b£6–£6.50 Bdi£9.50–£10 LDO4pm
🏛 CTV 6P

⊢⊣ **GH Kinross House** Woodside Av ☎(0479) 2042
Closed Xmas
Stone-built house in quiet residential part of town.
6hc (2fb) B&b£6.80–£7 Bdi£10.50–£11 W£72–£75 Ⱡ LDO7pm
🏛 6P
Ⓥ

⊢⊣ **GH Pines Hotel** Woodside Av ☎(0479) 2092
Etr–Sep
Traditional style house with spacious rooms, conveniently situated for shops.
10hc (2fb) B&bfr£8 Bdifr£13 Wfr£80.50 Ⱡ LDO5pm
CTV 4P 🏠

⊢⊣ **GH Ravenscourt** Seafield Av ☎(0479) 2286
Jan–Oct
Offers comfortable and spacious accommodation.
6hc (2fb) B&b£6.50–£7.25 Bdi£10–£11.50 W£63–£75 Ⱡ LDO7pm
🏛 CTV 15P

⊢⊣ **GH Riversdale** Grand Rd ☎(0479) 2648
Detached house with small garden at front and lawn at rear.
7hc (2fb) B&b£7–£7.25 Bdi£11–£11.50 W£73.50–£77 Ⱡ LDO6pm
🏛 CTV 8P 🏠

⊢⊣ **GH Umaria** Woodlands Ter ☎(0479) 2104

Situated on main road at the south end of town.

8hc (2fb) ✱ Ⓡ B&b£7–£7.50 Bdi£11–£12 W£75–£80 ⱽ LDO8pm

Lic CTV 8P

Ⓥ

GRASMERE
Cumbria
Map **11** NY30

GH *Beck Steps* College St ☎(09665) 348
Mar–Oct

Large, slate guesthouse overlooking green specialising in home cooked English food.

11hc 3⋔ (1fb)

Lic ▥ 8P nc4yrs river

GH Bridge House Hotel Stock Ln ☎(09665) 425
Mar–mid Nov

12rm 6hc 5⇌ 1⋔ (1fb) ✱ Ⓡ Bdi£18–£22 W£126–£147 ⱽ

Lic ▥ CTV 20P

Credit cards 1 3

GH *Chestnut Villa Private Hotel*
Keswick Rd ☎(09665) 218

8hc (2fb)

▥ CTV 12P

GH *Dunmail* Keswick Rd ☎(09665) 256

Detached house with large, pleasant garden and good views.

6hc (2fb) ✱

CTV 6P nc3yrs

GH Lake View Lake View Dr ☎(09665) 384
Apr–Oct

6rm 4hc 2⋔ Ⓡ B&b£10.25 Bdi£16.25 W£105 ⱽ LDOnoon

CTV 10P

GH Titteringdales Pye Ln ☎(09665) 439
Mar–Nov

7rm 4hc 2⋔ B&b£10–£12.50 Bdi£15.75–£18.25 W£105–£120 ⱽ LDO4pm

Lic ▥ CTV 8P

GRASSINGTON
North Yorkshire
Map **7** SE06

GH Ashfield House Hotel ☎(0756) 752584
Apr–Oct

Secluded, comfortable 17th century house, offering splendid food.

7hc (2fb) ✱ Ⓡ B&b£10–£11.50 Bdi£16–£18 W£106–£120 ⱽ LDO5pm

Lic ▥ CTV 7P

GH Lodge ☎(0756) 752518
Mar–Oct

Family run house with good furnishings, in village centre.

7hc (1fb) B&b£9.60 Bdi£15.95 W£67.20 Ⅿ LDO5pm

▥ CTV 8P nc5yrs

Credit card 3

GRAVESEND
Kent
Map **5** TQ67

GH *Cromer* 194 Parrock St ☎(0474) 61935
Closed Xmas

Victorian corner house with well furnished bedrooms and tastefully appointed restaurant.

11hc (3fb) CTV in 1 bedroom TV in 10 bedrooms ✱

▥ CTV 20P nc10yrs

GREAT

Placenames incorporating the word 'Great', such as Gt Malvern and Gt Yarmouth, will be found under the actual placename, *ie* Malvern, Yarmouth.

GREENHEAD
Northumberland
Map **12** NY66

FH Mrs P Staff **Holmhead** *(NY659661)*
☎Gilsland (06972) 402
Closed Oct & Xmas
A traditional Northumbrian farmhouse offering warmth and comfort. The Roman wall runs beneath the house and Thirlwall Castle is behind. ½m N unclass rd.
4hc ★ B&b£8.50–£9.50 Bdi£14–£15 Wfr£84 Ⱡ LDO5.30pm
▥ CTV 6P 1🚗 ⌂ 400acres non-working.
Ⓥ

GRETNA
Dumfries & Galloway *Dumfriesshire*
Map **11** NY36

GH Surrone House Annan Rd
☎(04613) 341
Nicely appointed former farmhouse with attractive modern bedrooms.
6rm 1hc 5➡ (4fb) CTV in all bedrooms Ⓡ Bdi£11 Bdi£16 W£110 Ⱡ LDO8pm
Lic ▥ CTV P ⌂

INN Crossways Annan Rd ☎(04613) 465
6ⓕ CTV in all bedrooms ★ Ⓡ *B&b£13 D9.45pm
▥ 30P
Credit cards 1 3 4

GRETNA GREEN
Dumfries & Galloway *Dumfriesshire*
Map **11** NY36

⊢⊣ **GH Greenlaw** ☎Gretna (04613) 361
Etr–Nov rs Dec–Etr
Compact homely villa. The majority of bedrooms are small.
6hc (1fb) B&b£7–£7.25
▥ CTV 8P
Credit card 2 Ⓥ

GUERNSEY
Channel Islands
Map **16**
Places with AA listed accommodation are indicated on location map 16. Full details will be found under individual placenames within the gazetteer.

GUILDFORD
Surrey
Map **4** SU94

GH Blanes Court Hotel Albury Rd
☎(0483) 573171
Quietly situated, elegant accommodation, with well equipped bedrooms and homely atmosphere.
20rm 9hc 1➡ 8ⓕ (2fb) CTV in all bedrooms Ⓡ *B&b£12.25–£24 W£73.50–£144 M
Lic ▥ 25P
Credit cards 2 3

GH Quinns Hotel 78 Epsom Rd ☎(0483) 60422
Comfortable modern accommodation with well equipped pretty bedrooms and good standard of cooking.
11rm 9hc 1➡ 1ⓕ (2fb) CTV in 9 bedrooms *B&b£14.40–£20.15 Bdi£22.90–£28.60 W£86.40–£171.60 Ⱡ LDO7.45pm
Lic ▥ CTV 14P

GUILDTOWN
Tayside *Perthshire*
Map **11** NO13

INN Anglers Rest Main St ☎Balbeggie (08214) 329
5hc ★ B&b£9 W£58 M (W only Jun–Sep) L£1–£2.85 High Tea £3.75–£5.50 D9.45pm £4–£7.50
CTV 39P 🚗 billiards

GULVAL
Cornwall
Map **2** SW43

⊢⊣ **FH** Mrs M E Osborne **Kenegie Home** *(SW481327)* ☎Penzance (0736) 2515
Apr–Oct
15th-century 'olde-worlde' farmhouse 1 mile from Penzance. Accent on good farmhouse food.
3hc (1fb) ★ Ⓡ B&b£7–£9 Bdi£12–£14 W£47–£60 M LDO4pm
CTV 4P 300acres mixed

GUNNISLAKE
Cornwall
Map **2** SX47

FH Cdr R N & Mrs R Fowler ***Whimple*** *(SX428708)* ☎Tavistock (0822) 832526
Closed Xmas
Attractive 17th-century farmhouse, with oak beams and panelling in lounge. On the banks of the River Tamar.
3hc ★ LDO4pm
CTV 6P 50acres dairy

GWYSTRE
Powys
Map **3** SO06

⊢⊣ **FH** Mrs M A Davies **Bryn Nicholas** *(SJ075658)* (½m E on N side of A44)
☎Penybont (059787) 447
Apr–Oct
3hc Ⓡ B&bfr£7 Bdifr£12 Wfr£45 M LDO4pm
▥ CTV 4P 250acres beef sheep
Ⓥ

See advertisement on page 208

⊢⊣ **FH** Mrs C Drew **Gwystre** *(SO070656)* ☎Penybont (059787) 316
Mar–Oct
Typical Welsh hill farm near to Elan Valley reservoir.
2rm Ⓡ B&b£7 Bdi£10.50 W£45 M LDO4pm
TV P 160acres beef sheep mixed

HALFORD
Warwickshire
Map **4** SP24

INN Halford Bridge ☎Stratford-upon-Avon (0789) 740382
5hc ★ B&b£10–£10.50 Bdi£15.50 L£4–£7&alc D10pm £4.85–£7.50
CTV 60P ♪

HALFWAY HOUSE
Shropshire
Map **7** SJ31

FH Mrs E Morgan ***Willows*** *(SJ342115)*
☎(074378) 233
Mar–Oct
Small farm cottage well situated for those travelling to Wales. It is surrounded by Long Mountain and Middlebar Hills.
3rm 1hc (1fb) ★ LDO3pm
▥ CTV 10P nc6yrs 35acres beef
Ⓥ

HALIFAX
West Yorkshire
Map **7** SE02

INN Stump Cross ☎(0422) 66004
Large period building beside the A58 1m from Halifax in the attractive Shipden Valley. 1m E A58/A6036 junc.
12hc 6➡ CTV in 6 bedrooms Ⓡ B&b£15–£22 L£4–£5&alc D10pm £4–£5&alc
▥ 40P 🚗
Ⓥ

HALKIRK
Highland *Caithness*
Map **15** ND15

⊢⊣ **GH Banniskirk House** ☎(084783) 609
Mar–mid Oct
3m SE on A895 1½m S of Georgemas junction station.
8hc (3fb) B&b£7.50 Bdi£12.50 W£85 M LDO7pm
▥ CTV 18P

HALSTOCK
Dorset
Map **3** ST50

FH Mrs G R Swann **Old Mill** *(ST511075)*
Higher Halstock (Guestaccom)
☎Corscombe (093589) 278
Comfortable 17th-century mill with friendly atmosphere, in peaceful rural setting. 2m W unclass rd.
3➡ (1fb) Ⓡ *B&b£12.50 Bdi£18.50 W£87.50 M LDO4pm
▥ CTV 5P 10acres dairy sheep

HALTWHISTLE
Northumberland
Map **12** NY76

⊢⊣ **GH Ashcroft** ☎(0498) 20213
Closed 23 Dec–6 Jan
8hc (4fb) ✱ B&b£7–£8 Bdi£12 W£45–£52 M LDO5pm
CTV 20P

⊢⊣ **FH** Mrs J Brown **Broomshaw Hill** *(NY706654)* Willia Rd ☎(0498) 20866
Tastefully modernised 18th-century farmhouse in beautiful location and within easy reach of many Roman sites; including Hadrians Wall.
2rm 1hc (1fb) TV in 1 bedroom ® B&b£7–£8 Bdi£11–£12 W£69–£75 L
CTV 6P 2 7acres livestock, horses, grazing

⊢⊣ **FH** Mrs J W Laidlow **White Craig** *(NY713649)* Shield Hill ☎(0498) 20565
Closed Xmas
Modernised, former croft-style farmhouse, with bright, modern bedrooms but retaining an olde worlde atmosphere in the comfortable lounge.
3rm 2hc 1 ✱ ® B&bfr£8 B&bfr£12.50 Wfr£54 M LDO9am
CTV 3P nc6yrs 50acres sheep
Ⓥ

HALWELL
Devon
Map **3** SX75

GH Stanborough Hundred Hotel
☎East Allington (054852) 236
Mar–10 Jan
6rm 7hc 1 (A 1) (4fb) ✱ ® B&b£12–£14 Bdi£15–£18 W£65–£70 L LDO8pm
Lic CTV 10P

HAMBLEDEN
Buckinghamshire
Map **4** SU78

INN Stag & Huntsman ☎(049166) 227
Small country inn offering simple but comfortable accommodation and warm, informal atmosphere.
3hc ® B&bfr£15 Bar lunch 85p–£3.50 LDO9.30pm

CTV 40P nc14yrs

HAMPTON COURT
Gt London
London plan **4** B2
(page 222)

INN *Cardinal Wolsey* Hampton Court Rd ☎01-941 3781
Old inn with comfortable bedrooms and honest home cooking.
18hc 3 CTV in all bedrooms ✱ ® D10pm sn
20P

HANMER
Clwyd
Map **7** SJ44

FH C Sumner & F Williams-Lee **Buck** *(SJ435424)* ☎(094874) 339
On the A525 Whitchurch (7m)–Wrexham (9m) road, the farmhouse is an ideal base from which to explore the area.
4hc ✱ B&b£8.50–£9.50 Bdi£14–£15 W£76.50–£85.50 M LDO4.30pm
CTV 12P 7acres small holding
Ⓥ

HARBERTON
Devon
Map **3** SX75

FH Mr & Mrs Blackler ***Belsford*** *(SX766594)* Belsford (1m NW unclass) ☎Totnes (0803) 863341
Apr–Oct
3hc (1fb) (W only Jul & Aug) LDO7pm
CTV 5P 30acres beef

FH Mrs I P Steer **Preston** *(SX777587)* ☎Totnes (0803) 862235
Apr–Oct
Old farmhouse on outskirts of quaint and attractive village. Totnes about 2½m.
3hc ✱ B&b£8.50 Bdi£13 W£85 L (W only Aug)
CTV P nc3yrs 250acres dairy mixed
Ⓥ

FH R Rose **Tristford** *(SX780594)* ☎Totnes (0803) 862418
Charming house with 'olde worlde' atmosphere. Good centre for touring the coast between Plymouth and Torbay.
3hc ✱ ✻ B&b£7.50 W£52 M
CTV 4 150acres mixed

HARLECH
Gwynedd
Map **6** SH53

⊢⊣ **FH** Mrs E A Jones **Tyddyn Gwynt** *(SH601302)* ☎(0766) 780298
2½m off B4573 (A496).
4rm 3hc (2fb) B&bfr£6.50 Bdifr£9.50 W£63 L LDO8pm
CTV 6P 40acres sheep
Ⓥ

⊢⊣ **INN Rum Hole Hotel** ☎(0766) 780477
Two-storey inn at lower end of village.
8rm 5hc 3 CTV in all bedrooms ® B&b£8–£12 Bdi£11–£15 W£52.50–£77 M Bar lunch £1.50–£2.50 LDO9pm
CTV 25P
Ⓥ

HARROGATE
North Yorkshire
Map **8** SE35

⊢⊣ **GH Abbey Lodge** 31 Ripon Rd ☎(0423) 69712
Smart, stylish house with very comfortable bedrooms and pleasant public areas.
8hc 1 3 (2fb) CTV in all bedrooms ✱ ® B&b£8 Bdi£13.50 W£47.60 M
Lic CTV 14P 2

Ⓥ

GH Alexa House Hotel & Stable Cottages 26 Ripon Rd ☎(0423) 501988
Closed Xmas wk
8rm 3hc 3 2 (A 4) (2fb) CTV in all bedrooms ® B&b£11.50–£13.50 Bdi£17.50–£19.50 W£110.25–£122.85 L LDO4pm
Lic CTV 14P

Harrogate

GH *Aston Hotel* Franklin Mount ☎(0423) 69534
Closed Xmas
25hc 15⋔ (2fb) TV in 10 bedrooms Ⓡ LDO6.30pm
Lic ▥ CTV 16P

⊢→ **GH Aygarth** 11 Harlow Moor Dr ☎(0423) 68705
Closed 2 wks Oct
7hc (3fb) CTV in 4 bedrooms TV in 3 bedrooms Ⓡ B&b£8–£16 Bdi£12.50–£21 W£54–£108 M LDO9.30am
▥ CTV
Ⓥ

GH Carlton Hotel 98 Franklin Rd ☎(0423) 64493
Comfortable accommodation in large house in tree lined street near town centre.
11hc (2fb) ✱ B&b£11 Bdi£16.50 W£70 M LDOam
Lic ▥ CTV 8P

GH Cavendish Hotel 3 Valley Dr ☎(0423) 509637
11rm 4hc 1→ 5⋔ (5fb) CTV in all bedrooms Ⓡ B&b£12.50–£16.50 Bdi£17–£21 W£89.50–£115.50 M LDO7.30pm
Lic ▥ CTV P
Credit cards 1 2 3 5 Ⓥ

GH Cheltenham Lodge Hotel Cheltenham Pde ☎(0423) 55041
Pair of terraced town houses in town centre. Small stylish accommodation with good facilities.
14hc 1→ 3⋔ (2fb) CTV in all bedrooms ✱ Ⓡ ✻B&b£13–£15 LDO9.30pm

Harrogate

GH Croft Hotel 42–44 Franklin Rd ☎(0423) 63326
16hc 3⋒ (4fb) CTV in 4 bedrooms TV in 12 bedrooms Ⓡ B&b£12.50–£14.50 Bdi£18.50–£20.50 W£115–£125 Ƚ LDOnoon
Lic ⅏ CTV 12P

GH *Franklin Private Hotel* 25 Franklin Rd ☎(0423) 69028
Closed Xmas
6hc
Lic CTV nc4yrs

GH Gillmore Hotel 98 Kings Rd ☎(0423) 503699
20rm 17hc 2⋒ (7fb) CTV in 2 bedrooms Ⓡ B&b£9.50–£10 Bdi£14–£14.50 W£90–£95 Ƚ LDO3pm
Lic ⅏ CTV 20P
Ⓥ
See advertisement on page 169

GH Grafton Hotel 1–3 Franklin Mount ☎(0423) 58491
Closed Dec
Stone town houses, restored and providing comfortable modern accommodation.
15rm 10hc 5⋒ (2fb) CTV in 5 bedrooms ⁂ Ⓡ B&b£8.50–£9.50 Bdi£13–£14 W£84–£91 Ƚ (W only Jul–Sep) LDO6pm
Lic ⅏ CTV ⁑

GH Ingleside Hotel 37 Valley Dr ☎(0423) 502088
Closed Xmas
9rm 6⋒ TV in all bedrooms Ⓡ *B&bfr£16 Bdifr£22.90 LDO2pm
Lic ⅏ CTV

GH Kingsway 36 Kings Rd ☎(0423) 62179
7rm 1⇸ 6⋒ (1fb) Ⓡ B&b£12 Bdi£16.50 W£80 Ꮇ LDO8pm
Lic ⅏ CTV 2P 1⌂
Ⓥ

GH Manor Hotel 3 Clarence Dr ☎(0423) 503916
14rm 5hc 3⇸ 6⋒ (2fb) CTV in 9 bedrooms ⁂ Ⓡ B&b£15–£20 Bdi£22–£26 W£95–£130 Ƚ LDO8.30pm
Lic ⅏ CTV

GH Moorland Private Hotel 34 Harlow Moor Dr ☎(0423) 64596
11rm 3hc 1⇸ 5⋒ (2fb) Ⓡ B&b£10–£13 Bdi£16–£19 W£66.50–£77.50 Ꮇ LDO6pm
Lic ⅏ CTV 3P
Credit card 2

GH Norman Hotel 41 Valley Dr (Minotel) ☎(0423) 502171
Closed Xmas
14rm 10hc 4⇸ (3fb) TV in 2 bedrooms B&b£12.50–£14.50 Bdi£18.75–£20.25 W£87.50–£101.50 Ꮇ LDO5pm
Lic CTV ⁑
See advertisement on page 169

GH Oakbrae 3 Springfield Av ☎(0423) 67682
Closed Xmas
6hc (1fb) CTV in 1 bedroom Ⓡ B&bfr£9 Bdifr£13.50 Wfr£60 Ƚ LDO5pm
⅏ CTV 4P 1⌂

GH Oakfield Hotel 34 Kings Rd ☎(0423) 67516
Closed Dec
Honest clean accommodation and small dining room are offered at this central guesthouse.
13hc (3fb) CTV in all bedrooms ⁂ Ⓡ B&b£10 Bdi£15 W£70 Ꮇ LDO6pm
Lic ⅏ CTV 7P
Credit card 1

GH Prince's 7 Granby Rd ☎(0423) 883469
Victorian house of style and character offering comfortable accommodation.
8rm 2hc 1⇸ 2⋒ (3fb) CTV in all bedrooms ⁂ Ⓡ B&b£9.75–£11.50 Bdi£14.55–£16.50 W£98–£111 Ƚ LDO4pm

Lic ⅢⅡ CTV 4🚗

GH Roan 90 Kings Rd ☎(0423) 503087
Closed Xmas
7rm 5hc 2⋔ (1fb) ✱ Ⓡ B&bfr£9
Bdifr£13.25 LDO4.30pm
ⅢⅡ CTV 🚫
Ⓥ

GH Shelbourne 78 Kings Rd ☎(0423) 504390
Closed Xmas wk
Good, clean, comfortable, town centre guesthouse.
7hc (2fb) ✱ Ⓡ B&b£9–£11.50 Bdi£14–£16 W£50–£54 M LDO4pm
Lic ⅢⅡ CTV 1P 1🚗
Credit card ③ Ⓥ

GH *Springfields* 80 Kings Rd ☎(0423) 67166
Closed Xmas & New Year
Comfortable, well furnished house near the conference centre.
6hc (2fb) ✱ CTV 5P

GH Strayend 56 Dragon View, Skipton Rd ☎(0423) 61700
6rm 1⇌ 5⋔ (1fb) TV in 2 bedrooms Ⓡ
B&b£9.50–£10.50 Bdi£13.50–£14.50
W£66.50–£73.50 Ł LDO9am
ⅢⅡ CTV 6P
Credit cards ① ② ③

GH Woodhouse 7 Spring Grove
☎(0423) 60081
Closed 25 Dec–1 Jan
Three-storey Victorian building with attractive elevated garden, situated in cul-de-sac near the town centre.
7rm 3hc 2⇌ 2⋔ (2fb) CTV in 5 bedrooms Ⓡ B&b£9.50–£11.50
Bdi£15.50–£17.50 W£97.50–£114 Ł
LDOnoon
Lic ⅢⅡ CTV 2P
Ⓥ

GH Youngs Private Hotel 15 York Rd (off Swan Rd) ☎(0423) 67336
Closed Xmas–New Year
16rm 9⇌ 7⋔ (2fb) CTV in all bedrooms
Ⓡ B&b£18–£21 Bdi£25–£28 W£114–£133 M LDO7.30pm

Lic ⅢⅡ CTV 18P 1🚗
Credit card ① Ⓥ

HARROP FOLD
Lancashire
Map **7** SD74

FH Mr & Mrs P Wood **Harrop Fold** *(SD746492)* (Guestaccom) ☎Bolton-by-Bowland (02007) 600
Lancashire longhouse built around 17th century. Nestling in pleasant quiet valley. Excellent accommodation, interesting meals.
6rm 4⇌ (A 2⇌) CTV in all bedrooms ✱
Ⓡ Bdi£30–£35 W£95 M LDO9pm
Lic ⅢⅡ 10P nc ⚘ 280acres sheep
Ⓥ

HARROW
Gt London
London plan **4** B5
(page 222)

GH *Hindes Hotel* 8 Hindes Rd
☎01-427 7468
Closed 2 wks Xmas
Small family run guesthouse with comfortable furnishings and a friendly, homely atmosphere.
13hc 1⋔ (2fb) CTV in all bedrooms ✱ Ⓡ
ⅢⅡ CTV 5P

GH Kempsford House Hotel 21–23 St Johns Rd ☎01-427 4983
30hc 8⋔ (6fb) CTV in 13 bedrooms TV in 11 bedrooms ✱ B&b£17.25–£18.40
W£102.65–£109.51 M
Lic ⅢⅡ CTV 30P
Credit cards ① ③

HARTLAND
Devon
Map **2** SS22

INN *West Country* Bursdon Moor
☎(02374) 475
Etr–mid Oct
Midway between Clovelly and Kilkhampton on A39, 4m S of Hartland.
10hc Ⓡ D9.30pm
CTV 70P 3🚗

HARWICH
Essex
Map **5** TM23

GH Hotel Continental 28/29 Marine Pde, Dovercourt Bay ☎(02555) 3454
Small private hotel run by friendly and hospitable owners.
14rm 9hc 5⋔ (3fb) B&b£10.50–£11
Bdi£16.50–£17.50 W£104–£113 Ł
LDO8.30pm
Lic ⅢⅡ CTV 8P 1🚗
Credit cards ① ③ Ⓥ

HASTINGS & ST LEONARDS
East Sussex
Map **5** TQ80

GH *Bryn-y-Mor* 12 Godwin Rd
☎(0424) 441755
A lovely house, built in 1863, harmonising period and modern luxury and overlooking heated swimming pool, garden and sea.
4hc 4⋔ (A 2hc 1⇌ 1⋔) (2fb) CTV in all bedrooms ✱ Ⓡ LDO8.15pm
Lic ⅢⅡ CTV 🚫 ⛺ sea
Ⓥ

GH Burlington Hotel 2 Robertson Ter
☎(0424) 424303
Closed 24 & 25 Dec
Four-storey house with sea views, adjacent to town centre.
17hc 6⇌ (2fb) CTV in all bedrooms Ⓡ
B&b£10–£19.95 Bdi£14–£22.50 W£84–£145 Ł LDO8pm
Lic ⅢⅡ 🚫
Credit cards ① ② ③ ④ ⑤

GH Chimes Hotel 1 St Matthews Gdns (Guestaccom) ☎(0424) 434041
An Edwardian house in elevated position with extensive views, run by friendly family.
10rm 7hc 3⇌ (2fb) TV in 5 bedrooms Ⓡ
B&b£9.50 Bdi£15.50 W£60 M
LDO6.30pm
Lic ⅢⅡ CTV 🚫

GH Eagle House 12 Pevensey Rd, St Leonards ☎(0424) 430535
Situated in residential area, offering comfortable modern accommodation and period bar lounge.
14rm 3hc 1➡ 9🚿 (2fb) CTV in all bedrooms Ⓡ ✱B&b£12.75–£15 Bdi£21.25–£23.50 W£89.25–£154.50 M LDO7.30pm
Lic ▥ 7P nc10yrs

GH Gainsborough Hotel 5 Carlisle Pde ☎(0424) 434010
Well maintained sea front house with modern well equipped bedrooms and comfortable public rooms.
12rm 8hc 2➡ (3fb) CTV in all bedrooms Ⓡ B&b£8.75–£11.50 Bdi£13.35–£16 W£80–£95 L LDO4pm
Lic ▥ P̸

GH Gresford 12 Devonshire Rd ☎(0424) 424745
Comfortable, Victorian house in town centre, overlooking the cricket ground.
9hc (3fb) ★ ✱B&b£7–£7.50 Bdi£10–£11 W£46–£75 L LDOnoon
CTV P̸
Ⓥ

⊢×⊣**GH Harbour Lights** 20 Cambridge Gdns ☎(0424) 423424
Closed Xmas
Small, two-storey town centre guesthouse with nicely appointed gardens.
8rm 6hc (1fb) TV in all bedrooms ★ B&b£7.20–£7.75 Bdi£10.70–£11.25 W£46–£50 M LDOnoon
▥ CTV P̸

GH *Russell Hotel* 35 Warrior Sq ☎(0424) 431990
Family run accommodation overlooking green, just off the sea front.
14hc 1➡ TV in 2 bedrooms ★ Ⓡ LDO6pm
Lic CTV nc2yrs sea

GH *Waldorf Hotel* 4 Carlisle Pde ☎(0424) 422185
Homely, friendly accommodation with nicely appointed restaurant and lounge.
12hc (4fb) TV in all bedrooms ★ Ⓡ LDOnoon
Lic CTV P̸ sea

HATHERLEIGH
Devon
Map **2** SS50

INN Bridge Bridge St ☎Okehampton (0837) 810357
4hc Ⓡ B&b£9.50–£12.50 Bdi£12.50–£16 W£85–£105 L L£4–£6 D9.30pm £7alc
▥ CTV 20P
Ⓥ

HATHERSAGE
Derbyshire
Map **8** SK28

FH Mrs T C Wain **Highlow Hall** *(SK219802)* ☎Hope Valley (0433) 50393
Etr–Oct
16th-century house of character with well furnished interior, isolated position south of Hathersage.
6hc (2fb) Ⓡ B&b£12 Bdi£18 W£114 L LDO6pm
Lic CTV 16P

HATTON
Warwickshire
Map **4** SP26

FH Mrs S M Fishwick **Northleigh** *(SP225693)* Five Ways Rd ☎Haseley Knob (092687) 203
A quiet country house with elegant rooms offering something special in comfort and convenience. Off A41 at Five Ways Island, ½m towards Shrewley.
3rm 2hc 1➡ CTV in all bedrooms Ⓡ B&b£14–£18 W£80 M
▥ CTV 6P 16acres sheep

HAUGH OF URR
Dumfries & Galloway *Kirkcudbrightshire*
Map **11** NX86

⊢×⊣**FH** Mrs G J MacFarlane **Markfast** *(NX817682)* ☎(055666) 220
A comfortable house offering a nice mix of traditional and modern, spacious bedrooms. 1m E of village.
3hc (3fb) ★ Ⓡ B&bfr£7 Bdifr£10.50 Wfr£73.50 L LDO4pm
CTV 3P 140acres mixed
Ⓥ

HAVERFORDWEST
Dyfed
Map **2** SM91

GH *Elliotts Hill Hotel* Camrose Rd ☎(0437) 2383
Comfortable accommodation in property situated in its own grounds.
20hc 1🚿 (4fb) CTV in 4 bedrooms TV in 1 bedroom Ⓡ LDO6.30pm
Lic ▥ CTV 20P 3🚗 ⌂

⊢×⊣**FH** Mrs J H Evans **Cuckoo Grove** *(SM928162)* ☎(0437) 2429
Apr–Oct
Comfortable accommodation for non-smokers only, in recently refurbished farmhouse. Swimming pool in grounds and views of the distant Prescelly Mountains.
5hc (1fb) ★ B&b£7.50 W£50 M
▥ CTV P ≋ 360acres beef dairy mixed
Ⓥ

HAWKSHEAD
Cumbria
Map **7** SD39

GH Highfield House Hotel Hawkshead Hill ☎(09666) 344
Delightful lakeland house with spacious rooms.
12rm 9hc 3➡ (3fb) CTV in 10 bedrooms B&b£10.50–£20 Bdi£15–£26 LDO6.30pm
Lic ▥ 15P
Ⓥ

GH Ivy House ☎(09666) 204
Mar–Oct
Attractive, well furnished Georgian house.
6rm 3hc 1➡ 2🚿 (A 5hc) (2fb) Ⓡ B&b£9–£12.50 Bdi£13.50–£17 W£87–£99 L (W only late May–mid Sep) LDO5pm
Lic CTV 12P
Ⓥ

GH Rough Close Country House ☎(09666) 370
Apr–early Nov rs Feb & Mar
Fine house overlooking Esthwaite Water, comfortably furnished and having good home cooking.
6hc ★ Ⓡ Bdi£18.50 W£120 L LDO6pm
Lic ▥ CTV 12P nc5yrs

INN *King's Arms Hotel* ☎(09666) 372
rs Xmas
6hc CTV in all bedrooms Ⓡ D10pm
▥ 6P 🚗

HAWNBY
North Yorkshire
Map **8** SE58

INN Hawnby House ☎Bilsdale (04396) 202
A stone-built country inn of some age and character standing on a hillside position in the centre of an unspoilt village in the North York Moors.
4➡ CTV in all bedrooms ★ Ⓡ ✱B&b£15 Bdi£15–£21 W£120 L Bar lunch £1.50–£3 D8pm £8
▥ 39P

HAWORTH
West Yorkshire
Map **7** SE03

GH Ferncliffe Hebden Rd ☎(0535) 43405
Closed Feb
Modern style house/restaurant situated in elevated position overlooking the Worth valley.
6🚿 (1fb) CTV in all bedrooms B&b£12.50–£15 Bdi£17–£19.50 W£87.50–£105 M LDO9.45
Lic ▥ CTV 15P
Credit cards 3 5 Ⓥ

HAYFIELD
Derbyshire
Map **7** SK08

INN *Lantern Pike* Glossop Rd ☎New Mills (0663) 44102

¾m N off A624.

4⇌ ✱ Ⓡ LDO9pm

♨ TV 4P

HAZLEHEAD
South Yorkshire
Map **7** SK10

INN Flouch ☎Barnsley (0226) 762037
Closed Xmas Day

Large country inn on the crossroads of the A628/A616 in a rural semi moorland area. Very good accommodation with inviting bars and a separate dining room.

5rm 4⇌ 1⋒ CTV in all bedrooms Ⓡ B&b£15 Bdi£22.50 L£3.75&alc D10pm £7–£8.50&alc

♨ 50P

Credit card 1

HEACHAM
Norfolk
Map **9** TF63

GH St Annes 53 Neville Rd ☎(0485) 70021
Feb–Oct

4rm 3hc (A 2⋒) (1fb) CTV in 2 bedrooms Ⓡ B&b£8.25–£11.75 Bdi£13.25–£16.75 W£57.75–£82.25 Ⱡ LDO2pm

Lic CTV 6P

HEASLEY MILL
Devon
Map **3** SS73

⊢⊣ **GH Heasley House** ☎North Molton (05984) 213
Mar–Oct

Georgian style building, overlooking a mill stream in beautiful hamlet.

10hc 1⇌ (2fb) B&b£7.80 Bdi£13.20 W£88 Ⱡ LDO5pm

Lic ♨ CTV 11P

Ⓥ

HEBRON
Dyfed
Map **2** SN12

FH Mrs N F Vaughan **Preseli Farm Stud** *(SN162289)* ☎(09947) 425

½m W of A478 Tenby–Cardigan road.

5rm 1hc 2⇌ (1fb) CTV in 1 bedroom TV in 3 bedrooms Ⓡ B&b£10–£16 Bdi£17–£24 W£100 Ⓜ (W only May–Sep) LDO10pm

Lic ♨ CTV 200P 6⌂ ⌂ ♩ ∪ 70acres mixed & stud farm

HEDDON'S MOUTH
Devon
Map **3** SS64

INN Hunters ☎Parracombe (05983) 230

10hc 5⇌ Ⓡ B&b£16.50 Bdi£28 W£152 Ⓜ Bar lunch £1.25alc D9pm £8alc

CTV 400P nc5yrs ♩ ∪ billiards

Credit cards 1 3 5

HELSBY
Cheshire
Map **7** SJ47

GH Poplars Private Hotel 130 Chester Rd ☎(09282) 3433
Closed 25–31 Dec

6hc (2fb) ✱ B&b£12 Bdi£17 W£77 Ⓜ LDO4pm

♨ CTV 10P

HELSTON
Cornwall
Map **2** SW62

Within a short radius of this town there are AA-listed farmhouses at the following locations: (see appropriate gazetteer entry for full details) **Coverack Bridges & Trenear**

GH *Hillside* Godolphin Rd ☎(03265) 4788

Small stone-built residence, a few minutes walk from town centre.

7hc (3fb) LDOam

Lic ♨ CTV 6P 1⌂

⊢⊣ **GH Wheal Tor Hotel** 29 Godolphin Rd ☎(03265) 61211
Closed Xmas

Situated on a main road, two minutes walk from the town centre.

8rm 7hc 1⋒ (1fb) ✱ B&b£7–£7.50 W£49–£52.50 Ⓜ LDO7.30pm

Lic ♨ CTV ⚑

HEMEL HEMPSTEAD
Hertfordshire
Map **4** TL00

GH *Southlea* 8 Charles St ☎(0442) 3061
Closed Xmas

Good accommodation in converted private house, situated in a residential area.

11hc (1fb) ✱

♨ CTV 8P 1⌂

GH Southville Private Hotel 9 Charles St ☎(0442) 51387

Modest guesthouse in residential area.

12hc (2fb) B&b£12.50 W£87.50 Ⓜ

♨ CTV 9P

Credit cards 2 3

HENFIELD
West Sussex
Map **4** TQ21

FH Mrs M Wilkin **Great Wapses** *(TQ243192)* Wineham ☎(0273) 492544

Part 16th-century and part Georgian farmhouse set in rural surroundings, with horses, calves and chickens. 3m NE off B2116.

3rm 2⇌ 1⋒ (2fb) TV in all bedrooms Ⓡ B&b£9–£12

♨ 7P 1⌂ 33acres mixed

HENLEY-IN-ARDEN
Warwickshire
Map **7** SP16

GH Ashleigh House Whitley Hill ☎(05642) 2315

A comfortable welcoming hotel in a quiet peaceful area, with interesting gardens close to tourist areas of Warwick and Stratford.

8hc TV in 7 bedrooms B&b£10–£15
CTV 8P 1 nc5yrs

HENSTRIDGE
Somerset
Map **3** ST71

FH Mrs I Pickford **Manor** *(ST692206)* Bowden ☎Templecombe (0963) 70213
Apr–Oct

16th-century, stone-built farmhouse with lattice windows. Surrounded by grassland and wooded areas.

2rm 1hc (1fb) B&b£9 W£60 M
CTV P 2 250acres arable beef dairy
Ⓥ

FH Mrs O J Doggrell **Toomer** *(ST708192)* Templecombe, ☎Milborne Port (0963) 250237

200-year-old stone-built farmhouse with large walled garden with an Elizabethan dovecote. 1½m W then S off A30.

3rm 2hc (2fb) CTV in 1 bedroom TV in 1 bedroom ® B&b£7.50–£8 W£50 M
CTV P 400acres mixed
Ⓥ

HEREFORD
Hereford & Worcester
Map **3** SO54

GH Ferncroft Hotel 144 Ledbury Rd ☎(0432) 265538 Jan–mid Nov

11hc (2fb) B&b£12–£12.50 Bdi£17.50–£18 W£115 ⱡ LDO7pm
Lic CTV 9P
Credit cards 1 3

GH Munstone House Munstone ☎(0432) 267122
Apr–Oct

2m N unclass rd off A49.

6hc (3fb) B&b£8–£9
CTV 10P
Ⓥ

GH White Lodge Hotel 50 Ledbury Rd ☎(0432) 273382

7rm 4hc 1 2 CTV in all bedrooms *B&b£11.50–£16 Bdi£17.75–£22.25 W£111.75–£143.25 ⱡ LDO9pm
Lic CTV 12P nc12yrs
Credit card 3

HERMITAGE
Dorset
Map **3** ST60

FH Mrs J Mayo **Almshouse** *(ST651082)* ☎Holnest (096321) 296
Mar–Oct

1m N unclass rd.

3hc (1fb) *B&bfr£7 Bdifr£10.50 LDO2pm
CTV 4P 140acres dairy

HERNE BAY
Kent
Map **5** TR16

GH Northdown Hotel 14 Cecil Park (Guestaccom) ☎(02273) 2051

Friendly small hotel with good bedrooms and quite spacious ground floor facilities.

5hc (2fb) ® B&b£9.50–£10.50 Bdi£14–£15 W£84–£90 ⱡ LDOam
Lic CTV 8P
Ⓥ

HERSTMONCEAUX
East Sussex
Map **5** TQ61

GH Cleavers Lyng Country Hotel (Guestaccom) ☎(0323) 833131
Closed Xmas rs Jan

Comfortable rooms and restaurant are features of this 16th-century house in rural setting near the Royal Greenwich Observatory.

8hc B&b£10.25–£10.75 Bdi£14.25–£14.95 W£91–£95 ⱡ LDO6pm
Lic CTV 15P
Ⓥ

HEWISH
Avon
Map **3** ST46

GH Kara ☎Yatton (0934) 834442

6hc (2fb) B&b£6–£7.50 Bdi£9–£10.50 W£59.75–£66 ⱡ LDO5pm
Lic CTV 5P
See advertisement on page 364

HEYSHAM
Lancashire
Map **7** SD46

GH Carr-Garth Bailey Ln ☎(0524) 51175
Etr–Oct

10hc (4fb) B&bfr£7.25 Bdifr£9.25 Wfr£59.50 ⱡ LDO4pm
CTV 7P

HICKLING
Norfolk
Map **9** TG42

GH Jenter House Town St ☎(069261) 372

10hc (2fb) *B&b£9 Bdi£13 W£56 ⱡ LDO4pm
CTV 10P

HIGH WYCOMBE
Buckinghamshire
Map **4** SU89

GH Amersham Hill 52 Amersham Hill ☎(0494) 20635

Large private house with simple but comfortable accommodation.

7hc CTV in all bedrooms B&b£12.50–£13.75 W£87.50–£96.25 M
9P

GH Clifton Lodge Private Hotel 210 West Wycombe Rd ☎(0494) 29062
Closed 10 days Xmas

Accommodation offering homely atmosphere. →

20rm 15hc 5➡ (1fb) CTV in all bedrooms ★ Ⓡ B&b£13.30 Bdi£20.70 W£96.60 M LDO8.15pm
Lic 🍴 CTV 18P
Credit cards 1 2 5

GH Drake Court Hotel London Rd ☎(0494) 23639
rs Xmas
20rm 18hc 2➡ (5fb) CTV in all bedrooms ★ B&b£18–£20 Bdi£24–£26 W£126–£140 M LDO8.30pm
Lic 🍴 CTV 30P ≈ (heated)
Credit cards 1 2 3 5

HILL HEAD
Hampshire
Map **4** SU50

GH Seven Sevens Private Hotel Hill Head Road ☎Stubbington (0329) 662408
Nice accommodation in residential area with sea views.
6hc (2fb) ★ *B&b£11–£12.50
🍴 CTV 8P ♿

HINCKLEY
Leicestershire
Map **4** SP49

GH Kings Hotel & Restaurant 13–19 Mount Rd ☎(0455) 637193
7rm 3➡ CTV in all bedrooms ★ Ⓡ B&b£13.50–£20 Bdi£20–£30 W£105–£150 L LDO10pm
Lic 🍴 20P 2🚗 sauna bath
Credit cards 1 2 3 6

HINDON
Wiltshire
Map **3** ST93

INN *Grosvenor Arms* High St ☎(074789) 253
3hc (2fb)
🍴 P

HITCHAM
Suffolk
Map **5** TL95

⊢⊣ **FH** Mrs B Elsdon **Wetherden Hall** *(TL971509)* ☎Bildeston (0449) 740412
Closed Dec
1m W of unclass road to Kettlebaston.
2rm (1fb) ★ B&b£7–£9 W£45–£55 M
🍴 CTV 6P nc12yrs 280acres arable mixed

HOLBETON
Devon
Map **2** SX65

⊢⊣ **FH** Mrs J A Baskerville **Keaton** *(SX595480)* ☎(075530) 255
Apr–Oct
Large, stone-built and well-maintained farmhouse in isolated rural position. Yachting at Newton Ferrers 3m away.
2rm (1fb) ★ B&b£8–£9 W£50–£55 M
TV 2P nc5yrs 135acres beef

HOLLYBUSH
Strathclyde *Ayrshire*
Map **10** NS31

⊢⊣ **FH** Mrs A Woodburn **Boreland** *(NS400139)* ☎Patna (0292) 531228
Jun–Sep
Two-storey farmhouse with roughcast exterior, situated on the banks of the River Doon. West off A713 south of village.
3rm (2fb) ★ Ⓡ B&b£7–£8
🍴 CTV 10P 🏠 126acres dairy

HOLMFIRTH
West Yorkshire
Map **7** SE10

⊢⊣ **INN White Horse** Scholes Rd, Jackson Bridge ☎(0484) 683940
rs Xmas
3m E A616 towards Sheffield.
5hc TV in all bedrooms B&b£8–£10 L£1–£6.10 LDO10pm
🍴 CTV 12P 1🚗
Credit cards 1 3 Ⓥ

HOLMROOK
Cumbria
Map **6** SD09

GH Carleton Green Saltcoats Rd ☎(09404) 608
Closed Xmas & New Year
A delightful house in rural setting, run by a local couple.
6rm 3hc 2➡ 1⫛ (1fb) Ⓡ B&b£9 Bdi£14.50 W£86 L
Lic 🍴 CTV P

HOLNE
Devon
Map **3** SX76

FH S Townsend **Wellpritton** *(SX716704)* ☎Poundsgate (03643) 273
Closed Xmas
Tastefully modernised farmhouse in Dartmoor National Park. There are panoramic views and the farm has its own swimming pool.
5hc 1⫛ ★ Ⓡ B&b£7.50–£10 Bdi£12.50–£15 W£68–£75 L (W only Jul & Aug) LDO7.30pm
🍴 CTV 5P nc5yrs (except out of season) ≈ billiards 15acres pig sheep mixed
Ⓥ

INN Church House ☎Poundsgate (03643) 208
7rm 5hc 1➡ 1⫛ TV in 1 bedroom Ⓡ B&b£9–£11 Bdi£13–£15 W£60–£65 M
Bar lunch £3alc D9.45pm £5alc
🍴 CTV 7P nc12yrs
Credit cards 1 3 Ⓥ

HOLSWORTHY
Devon
Map **2** SS30

GH Coles Mill ☎(0409) 253313
Etr–4 Oct
5⫛ TV in all bedrooms ★ Ⓡ B&b£9.50–£11 Bdi£14.50–£16 W£78–£91.50 L LDO5.30pm
Lic CTV 12P nc6yrs

FH Mr & Mrs E Cornish **Leworthy** *(SS323012)* ☎(0409) 253488
Low, white-fronted farmhouse with attractive garden facing open country.
10rm 8hc 3⫛ (6fb) ★ B&b£9–£10.50 Bdi£13–£15 Wfr£80 L LDO6pm
Lic CTV 20P 🏠 𝒫 ♪ U 240acres beef sheep mixed
Ⓥ

HOLT
Clwyd
Map **7** SJ35

⊢⊣ **FH** Mrs G M Evans **New** *(SJ394538)* Commonwood ☎Farndon (0829) 270358
Apr–Oct
Small, comfortable and cosy farm.
2rm ★ B&bfr£7 W£45 M
CTV 4P 92acres dairy sheep

HOLT
Norfolk
Map **9** TG03

GH Lawns Private Hotel Station Rd ☎(026371) 3390
18 Feb–Oct
10rm 8hc 1➡ (1fb) Ⓡ B&b£9–£13 Bdi£13.50–£19 W£109 L (W only Jun–Sep) LDO5pm
Lic 🍴 CTV 10P

HOLYHEAD
Gwynedd
Map **6** SH28

⊢⊣ **GH Witchingham** 20 Walthew Av ☎(0407) 2426
6rm 4hc 1⫛ (3fb) B&b£6.50–£7 Bdi£10.50–£11 LDOnoon
🍴 CTV 3P

HOLYWELL
Clwyd
Map **7** SJ17

⊢⊣ **FH** Mrs M D Jones **Green Hill** *(SJ188769)* ☎(0352) 713270
Feb–Nov
15th-century farmhouse completely modernised to provide comfortable accommodation, overlooking the Dee estuary.
5rm 3hc 1➡ (3fb) ★ B&bfr£7.50 Bdifr£11.50 W£52 L LDO5pm
TV 6P 🏠 125acres dairy mixed
Ⓥ

Honiton — Horton

HONITON
Devon
Map **3** ST10

GH Hill House Country Hotel Combe Raleigh ☎(0404) 3371
Apr–Oct
2m NE unclass rd.
6rm 5hc 1🚿 (2fb) ® B&b£11.38 Bdi£15.81 W£98.67 ℓ LDO7pm
Lic ⅢⅢ CTV 14P 🎾(grass)
Ⓥ

↦**FH** Mrs I J Underdown **Roebuck** *(ST147001)* (western end of Honiton-by-pass) ☎(0404) 2225
Modern farm 8 miles from the coast.
4rm 3hc (3fb) B&b£7 Bdi£10
ⅢⅢ CTV P 179acres dairy
Ⓥ

INN Monkton Court Monkton (2m E A30) ☎(0404) 2309
8rm 5hc 3🛁 TV in 3 bedrooms ® B&b£10.50–£18.50 L£3.25alc D10pm £3.25alc
ⅢⅢ 100P 4🚗

HOOK
Hampshire
Map **4** SU75

GH Oaklea London Rd ☎(025672) 2673
Comfortable, homely house with attractive lounge and dining room.
10rm 9hc 1🚿 (3fb) ☓ B&b£15.75 Bdi£21.50 W£99.25 Ⓜ LDO1pm
Lic CTV 10P

HOPE COVE
Devon
Map **3** SX63

↦**GH Fern Lodge** ☎Kingsbridge (0548) 561326
Mar–Oct
5hc (A 2hc) (4fb) B&b£6.50–£7.50 Bdi£11–£12.50 W£73.50–£83.50 ℓ LDO5pm
Lic ⅢⅢ CTV 4P 3🚗 ⌂

GH Sand Pebbles Hotel ☎Kingsbridge (0548) 561673
Mar–Nov
10rm 1hc 5🛁 4🚿 (2fb) ® B&b£11–£14 Bdi£18–£23 W£77–£98 Ⓜ LDO8pm
Lic CTV 10P nc5yrs sauna bath

HOPTON
Derbyshire
Map **8** SK25

GH Henmore Grange ☎Carsington (062985) 420
Good quality modern accommodation with character, created from stone-built former old farm buildings.
7rm 3hc 3🛁 1🚿 (1fb) ☓ ✱B&bfr£8 Bdifr£15.50 Wfr£105 ℓ LDO9pm
ⅢⅢ CTV 15P

HORNS CROSS
Devon
Map **2** SS32

↦**FH** Mrs B Furse **Swanton** *(SS355227)* ☎Clovelly (02373) 241
Closed Dec
Modern dormer-style bungalow pleasantly situated overlooking the Bristol Channel.
3rm 2hc (2fb) ☓ B&b£6.25 Bdi£9.50 W£40 Ⓜ LDO2pm
CTV P 50acres dairy

HORNSEA
Humberside
Map **8** TA24

↦**GH Hotel Seaforth** Esplanade ☎(04012) 2616
Charming Edwardian house overlooking bowling green and sea, with bright, spacious rooms.
7hc (3fb) ® B&b£6.75 Bdi£10.25 W£62.50 ℓ LDO4pm
ⅢⅢ CTV 4P

HORRABRIDGE
Devon
Map **2** SX56

GH Overcombe Hotel (Guestaccom) ☎Yelverton (0822) 853501
6rm 3hc 1🛁 2🚿 (2fb) CTV in all bedrooms ® B&b£12.25 Bdi£18.75 W£115–£119 ℓ LDO7.15pm
Lic ⅢⅢ CTV 11P ⌂
Credit cards 1 2 3 5 Ⓥ

HORSHAM
West Sussex
Map **4** TQ13

GH Wimblehurst Private Hotel 6 Wimblehurst Rd ☎(0403) 62319
Detached house with modern bedrooms, also catering for non smokers.
13rm 6hc 1🛁 4🚿 (2fb) CTV in 1 bedroom ® B&b£14–£19.50 Bdi£21–£26 Wfr£140 Ⓜ LDO7.30pm
ⅢⅢ CTV 14P ⌂

GH Winterpick Corner Winterpit Ln, Manning's Heath ☎(0403) 53882
2m SE A281.
4hc (1fb) ☓ ® B&b£10–£12
ⅢⅢ CTV 3P 2🚗 ≋(heated)

HORSHAM ST FAITH
Norfolk
Map **9** TG21

GH Elm Farm Chalet Hotel Norwich Rd ☎Norwich (0603) 898366
3hc 1🚿 (A 12hc 4🚿) (1fb) CTV in all bedrooms ☓ ® B&b£12.50–£16 Bdi£18.50–£22 W£84–£108.50 Ⓜ LDO6.30pm
CTV 20P ⛆(heated)
Ⓥ

HORTON
Dorset
Map **4** SU00

INN Horton Cranborne Rd ☎Witchampton (0258) 840252
5rm 3hc 2🛁 CTV in all bedrooms ☓ ® ✱B&b£16.50–£19.50 L£8alc D9.45pm £8alc
ⅢⅢ 100P 🚘
Credit cards 1 2 3 5

HORTON-IN-RIBBLESDALE
North Yorkshire
Map **7** SD87

INN Crown Hotel (Minotel/Guestaccom) ☎(07296) 209

10rm 3hc ✱B&b£10.30 Bdi£16.30 W£102.60 Ⱡ Bar lunch 45p–£5.30 D7pm £6.05

CTV 15P billiards

Credit card 5

HOVE
East Sussex
Map **4** TQ20
See Brighton

HOWEY *(Near Llandrindod Wells)*
Powys
Map **3** SO05

GH Corven Hall Country ☎Llandrindod Wells (0597) 3368

7rm 3hc 4⋒ (4fb) Ⓡ B&b£7.50–£8.50 Bdi£11.75–£12.75 W£73–£78 Ⱡ LDO6pm

Lic CTV 8P 2

Credit card 1 Ⓥ

FH Mrs C Nixon **Brynhir** *(SJ067586)* ☎Llandrindod Wells (0597) 2425 Mar–Nov

Remote 17th-century hill farm, traditionally furnished. Pony for children to ride. 1m E on unclass road.

7hc 2⋒ (1fb) Ⓡ B&b£7–£8 Bdi£10.50–£11.50 W£50 M LDO6pm

TV 12P billiards 150acres mixed

Ⓥ

FH Mrs R Jones **Holly** *(SJ045593)* ☎Llandrindod Wells (0597) 2402 Apr–Nov

18th-century building close to the A483, on the edge of the village, surrounded by open country.

3hc (1fb) B&b£7–£8 Bdi£11–£12 W£73–£80 LDO4pm

CTV P 70acres beef sheep

See advertisement on page 208

FH Mr & Mrs R Bufton **Three Wells** *(SO062586)* ☎Llandrindod Wells (0597) 2484 Closed Xmas wk

Detached farmhouse built around the turn of the century.

9rm 8hc 4⋒ (2fb) Ⓡ B&b£7–£8 Bdi£10.50–£12 W£70–£85 Ⱡ LDO5pm

Lic CTV 20P 50acres beef sheep mixed

Ⓥ

See advertisement on page 208

HOYLAKE
Merseyside
Map **7** SJ28

GH Sandtoft Hotel 70 Alderley Rd ☎051-632 2204

9rm 7hc 2⋒ (2fb) B&b£11.50–£12.50 Bdi£15–£17.50 W£75–£80 M LDO7.30pm

Lic CTV 6P 3

HUBBERHOLME
North Yorkshire
Map **7** SD97

INN George Kirk Gill ☎Kettlewell (075676) 223

Old Dales hostelry in attractive rural surroundings, offering home produced food.

3hc Ⓡ B&b£9.50–£10.50 W£59.50 M Bar lunch £3.90–£5.40 D9.30pm £10alc

20P nc8yrs

HULL
Humberside
Map **8** TA02

GH Ashford 125 Park Av ☎(0482) 492849

Well furnished, comfortable bedrooms are a feature of this end of terrace building in a tree lined street.

6hc (1fb) B&b£10.50 Bdi£15 W£70 M LDO10am

CTV 4P

GH Parkwood Hotel 113 Princes Av
☎(0482) 445610
Terraced town house on bus route with well fitted comfortable bedrooms.
7hc (1fb) ✱ B&b£9.25–£10 LDO7.30pm
Lic ⅢⅢ CTV ✗
See advertisement on page 179

HUNA
Highland *Caithness*
Map **15** ND37
⊢⊣ **GH Haven Gore** ☎John O'Groats (095581) 314
Modernised cottage with matching extension and sea views to Stroma and Orkney Isles.
5hc (3fb) B&b£7 Bdi£11 W£45.50 M
LDO6pm
ⅢⅢ CTV 8P
Credit cards 1 2 3

HUNSTANTON
Norfolk
Map **9** TF64
GH *Caley Hall Motel* ☎(04853) 33486
20➡ (4fb) CTV in all bedrooms Ⓡ
LDO9pm
Lic ⅢⅢ 40P

GH Claremont 35 Greevegate
☎(04853) 33171
Closed Dec
7hc (2fb) ✱ Ⓡ B&b£9 Bdi£13 W£91 ⅃
(W only Jul–14 Sep) LDO6.30pm
Lic ⅢⅢ CTV 6P nc3yrs
Ⓥ

GH *Deepdene Hotel* 29 Avenue Rd
☎(04853) 2460
Victorian building constructed from local Carstone stone.
6hc 1➡ (1fb)
Lic ⅢⅢ CTV 8P
Ⓥ

GH *Lincoln Lodge Private Hotel* Cliff Pde ☎(04853) 2948
Apr–Oct
14hc 2➡ (5fb) TV in all bedrooms Ⓡ
LDO8pm
Lic ⅢⅢ CTV 6P nc3yrs sea

⊢⊣ **GH Sunningdale** 3 Avenue Rd
☎(04853) 2562
Small comfortable establishment in a residential road close to the town centre.
5hc (1fb) ✱ B&b£7.50–£8.50
Bdi£10.50–£11.50 W£68–£75 ⅃
LDO3pm
ⅢⅢ CTV ✗

GH Sutton House Hotel 24 Northgate
☎(04853) 2552
10hc (2fb) ✱ Ⓡ B&b£9–£11 Bdi£14–£16 W£80–£105 ⅃ LDO1pm
Lic ⅢⅢ CTV 6P nc5yrs
Ⓥ

GH Tolcarne Private Hotel 3 Boston Sq
☎(04853) 2359
Mar–Oct
11hc 6⫛ (2fb) ✱ Ⓡ B&b£10–£12.50
Bdi£16.50–£18.50 W£70–£87 M
LDO7pm
Lic ⅢⅢ CTV 8P
Ⓥ

HUNTINGDON
Cambridgeshire
Map **4** TL27
INN Black Bull Post St, Godmanchester
☎(0480) 53310
1m S B1043.
10hc TV in 3 bedrooms B&b£12.65
Bdi£17.65 L£8alc D9.50pm £8alc
ⅢⅢ CTV 20P 8🚗

HURSLEY
Hampshire
Map **4** SU42
INN Kings Head Hotel ☎(0962) 75208
Closed Xmas Day
Country village inn, providing spacious airy bedrooms and bar or bistro style food.
6hc ✱ Ⓡ B&b£12.50 Bar lunch £1.50alc
D9pm £7alc
ⅢⅢ CTV 30P
Credit cards 1 3 Ⓥ

HUTTON-LE-HOLE
North Yorkshire
Map **8** SE79
GH Barn ☎Lastingham (07515) 311
Etr–Oct
9hc ✱ Ⓡ ✻B&b£10 W£70 M
Lic CTV 12P

ICKENHAM
Gt London
London plan **4** A4
(page 222)
GH Woodlands 84 Long Lane
☎Ruislip (08956) 34830
Warm, friendly atmosphere is found in this comfortably appointed establishment.
9rm 6hc 4⫛ ✱ Ⓡ B&b£10–£17
ⅢⅢ CTV 12P nc5yrs

ICKLESHAM
East Sussex
Map **5** TQ81
⊢⊣ **GH Snailham House** Broad St
☎Hastings (0424) 814556
Apr–Oct
Peaceful and comfortable country farm house.
7hc (1fb) ✱ Ⓡ B&b£8–£10 Bdi£12.25–£14.25 W£75.75–£89.75 ⅃ LDO5.30pm
Lic ⅢⅢ CTV 7P
Ⓥ

IDOLE
Dyfed
Map **2** SN41
⊢⊣ **FH** Mr & Mrs A Bowen **Pantgwyn** *(SN419157)* ☎Carmarthen (0267) 235859
Apr–Sep
Spacious rebuilt farmhouse, 3m S of Carmarthen.
2rm (1fb) ✱ B&bfr£7.50 Wfr£49 M
ⅢⅢ CTV P 35acres dairy

ILAM
Staffordshire
Map **7** SK15

FH Mrs J Fortnam ***Beechenhill*** *(SK129525)* ☎ Alstonefield (033527) 274
Jun–Oct

Two-storey, stone-built farmhouse with exposed beams, built around 1720. Situated in unspoilt rural area with panoramic views.

2rm (1fb)

CTV 2P nc5yrs 92acres beef dairy

ILFORD
Gt London
London plan **4** F4
(page 223)

GH Cranbrook Hotel 24 Coventry Rd
☎ 01-554 6544

Situated in residential area, near shopping centre.

16rm 3hc 11⋒ (6fb) CTV in all bedrooms
B&bfr£14.95 Bdifr£18.45 LDO9pm

Lic ꟾꟾꟾ CTV 12P 2🚗
Credit cards 2 3

GH Park Hotel 327 Cranbrook Rd
☎ 01-554 9616

Modern, family accommodation overlooking Valentines Park.

21hc 6➡ 5⋒ (3fb) CTV in all bedrooms
B&b£12–£20.95 Bdi£17–£25.95 W£84–£146.65 M LDO8pm

Lic ꟾꟾꟾ CTV 22P
Credit cards 1 2 3

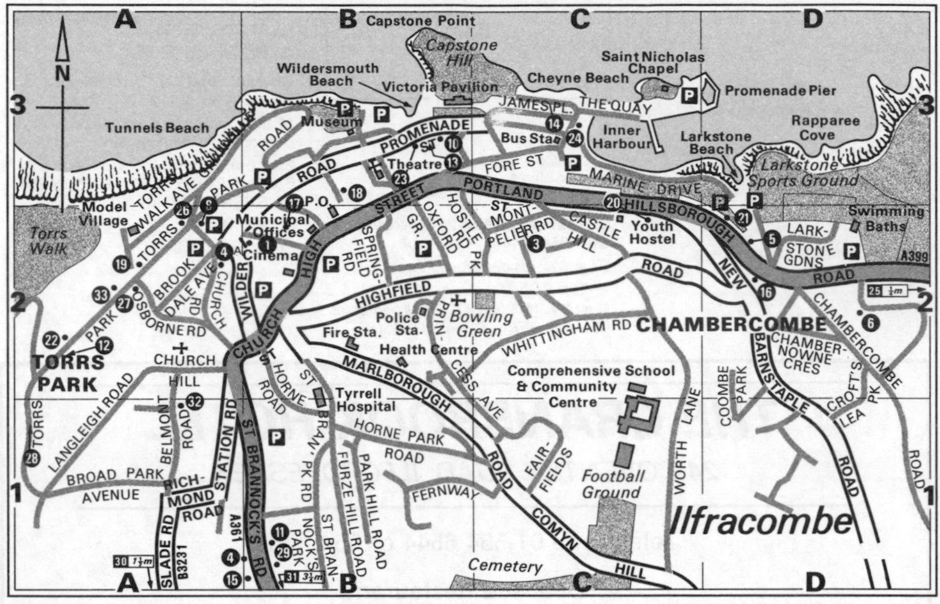

Ilfracombe

1 Avenue Private Hotel
3 Briercliffe Hotel
4 Carbis Private Hotel
4A Chalfont Private Hotel
5 Collingdale Hotel
6 Combe Lodge Hotel
8 Cresta Private Hotel
10 Dèdés Hotel
11 Earlsdale
12 Elmfield Hotel
14 Headlands Hotel
15 Lantern House Hotel
16 Laston House Private Hotel
17 Lympstone Private Hotel
18 Marlyn
19 Merlin Court Hotel
20 Merrydene Private Hotel
21 New Cavendish Hotel
22 Norbury
23 Queen's Court Hotel
24 Royal Britannia *(Inn)*
25 Rosebank Hotel
26 Seven Hills Hotel
27 Southcliffe Hotel
28 South Tor Hotel
29 Strathmore Private Hotel
30 Sunny Hill
31 Sunnymeade Country House
32 Wentworth House Private Hotel
33 Westwell Hall Private Hotel

ILFRACOMBE
Devon
Map **2** SS54
See plan

GH Avenue Private Hotel Greenclose Rd ☎(0271) 63767 Plan **1** *B2*
Apr–Oct
27rm 23hc 2⇌ 2ſ (6fb) ★ B&b£9–£10.50 Bdi£13–£14.50 W£86.50–£96 ⱡ LDO7pm
Lic CTV 11P
Credit cards [1] [3]

GH Briercliffe Hotel 9 Montpelier Ter ☎(0271) 63274 Plan **3** *C2*
10hc (5fb) B&b£9 Bdi£13 W£77–£87.50 ⱡ LDO5pm
Lic ▥ CTV 5P
Ⓥ
See advertisement on page 181

GH *Carbis Private Hotel* 50 St Brannocks Rd ☎(0271) 62943
Plan **4** *A1*
Etr–Oct
9hc (4fb) ★ LDO6pm
Lic CTV 9P

GH Chalfont Private Hotel 21 Church Rd ☎(0271) 62224 Plan **4A** *A2*
Apr–Oct
A small detached stone hotel in quiet residential area.
13rm 11hc 2ſ (6fb) ✱B&b£7–£8 Bdi£10.50–£11.50 W£63–£75 ⱡ LDO5pm
Lic ▥ CTV Ᵽ

GH Collingdale Hotel Larkstone Ter ☎(0271) 63770 Plan **5** *D2*
Jan–Oct
9hc 3ſ (6fb) ★ Ⓡ B&b£9.50–£10.50 Bdi£13–£14 W£63–£70 M̸ (W only mid Jul–Aug) LDO8pm
Lic ▥ CTV Ᵽ

⊢×⊣ **GH Combe Lodge Hotel** Chambercombe Park Rd ☎(0271) 64518 Plan **6** *D2*
9hc 1ſ (4fb) B&b£6.50–£8.50 Bdi£10.50–£12.50 W£70–£85 ⱡ LDO7pm
Lic ▥ CTV 8P ♧
Ⓥ

GH Cresta Private Hotel Torrs Park ☎(0271) 63742 Plan **8** *A2*
May–mid Oct rs Etr–May
25rm 23hc 2ſ (12fb) Ⓡ B&b£10.25–£14 Bdi£12–£16 W£70–£95 ⱡ LDO6.30pm
Lic lift CTV 30P

⊢×⊣ **GH Dèdés Hotel** 1–3 The Promenade ☎(0271) 62545 Plan **10** *B3*
Etr–Oct
17rm 10hc 7⇌ (4fb) B&b£6.50–£10.50 Bdi£10.50–£15 W£73.50–£105 ⱡ LDO9.45pm
Lic CTV 10P
Credit cards [1] [2] [3] [5] Ⓥ

⊢×⊣ **GH Earlsdale Hotel** 51 St Brannocks Rd ☎(0271) 62496 Plan **11** *B1*
12rm 7hc 4ſ (4fb) ★ B&b£6.50–£8 Bdi£10.50–£12 W£42–£52 ⱡ
Lic ▥ CTV 9P

GH Elmfield Hotel Torrs Park ☎(0271) 63377 Plan **12** *A2*
Mar–Nov

12rm 10⋔ (2fb) ★ Ⓡ B&b£13–£17 Bdi£16–£20 W£77–£99 ⅃ LDO7.30pm

Lic 𝍖 CTV 12P nc3yrs ≋ (heated)

Credit cards 1 2 3 Ⓥ

GH Headlands Hotel Capstone Cres ☎(0271) 62887 Plan **14** *C3*

Mar–Oct, Xmas & New Year

25rm 18hc 2➡ 4⋔ (6fb) CTV in 6 bedrooms B&b£9–£10 Bdi£13–£15 W£79–£99 ⅃ LDO4.15pm

Lic CTV 11🚘

Credit cards 1 3 Ⓥ

Ilfracombe

⊢⊣ **GH Lantern House Hotel** 62 St Brannocks Rd ☎(0271) 64401

Plan **15** *A1*

10hc (4fb) B&b£7.50–£8.50 Bdi£11.50–£12.50 W£52.50–£59.50 LDO5pm

Lic 𝍖 CTV 10P

Credit card 3 Ⓥ

GH Laston House Private Hotel Hillsborough Rd ☎(0271) 62627

Plan **16** *D2*

11rm 5hc 5➡ 1⋔ (4fb) Ⓡ B&b£10–£16 Bdi£12–£18 W£60–£96 ⅃ LDO7pm

Lic 𝍖 CTV 11P

See advertisement on page 184

⊢⊣ **GH Lympstone Private Hotel** 14 Cross Park ☎(0271) 63038

Plan **17** *B2/3*

Mar–Oct

16rm 14hc 2⋔ (5fb) Ⓡ B&b£6.50–£8 Bdi£9.50–£11 W£65–£75 ⅃ LDO5pm

Lic 𝍖 CTV P

See advertisement on page 184

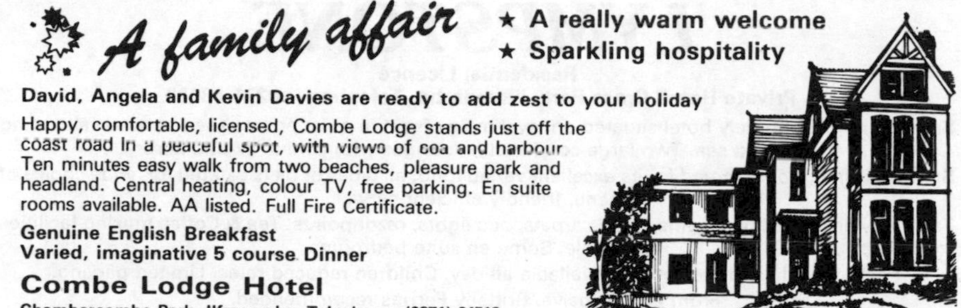

Dèdés

Licensed

1–3 The Promenade, Ilfracombe, EX34 9BD
Tel: 0271 62545

Overlooking the sea!

*Situated in superb, level position on sea front, overlooking Bristol Channel. *Good varied food a speciality, all cooked under the owning family's supervision. *Colour TV lounge with balcony.
A special feature is the unusual times of meals. Breakfast 8–10 am, Dinner 6–10 pm, with a choice of menu. This gives you complete freedom to enjoy your days out. Reduced terms early and late season. Number of rooms with private bathroom & WC. Illustrated coloured brochure from the proprietor: Mrs C J Napper.

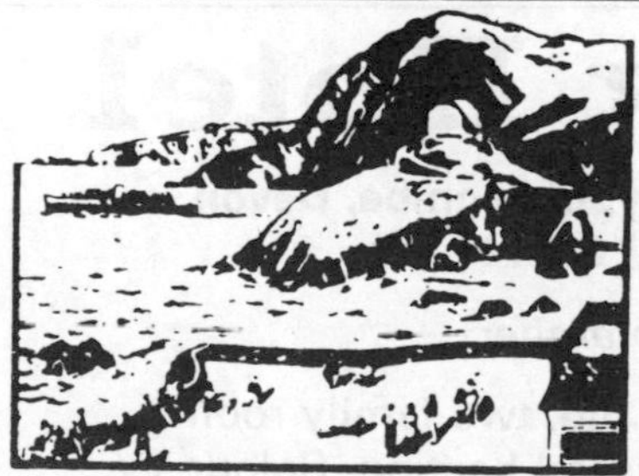

HEADLANDS HOTEL, Capstone Crescent, Ilfracombe, Devon. EX34 9BT
Telephone: 0271 62887

As featured on TV 'Wish You Were Here'

Headlands is set in a unique position right at the sea's edge with a private garden just a few steps from the picturesque old harbour. The lounge and dining room overlook the sea as do many of the well appointed bedrooms, some of which have private bath/shower, toilet and TV. Licensed Bar. Covered parking facilities are available. The hotel is open from 1st March-31st October and at Christmas and New Year.

Access/Visa/AA Wayfarer vouchers accepted

Laston House Hotel

Hillsborough Road, Ilfracombe, Devon, EX34 9NT.
Telephone: 0271 62627

The best of both worlds – a Georgian house set in its own grounds overlooking the sea but with en suite rooms, tea making facilities in bedrooms, private car park, bar lounge and putting course.
We offer a choice of menu, a high standard of housekeeping and a friendly atmosphere.
Member of WCTB
Resident Proprietors: Jim and Anne Biggin

LYMPSTONE

Residential Licence

Private Hotel, Cross Park, Ilfracombe. Telephone: 0271-63038.

Small family run homely hotel situated on level to sea front in quiet private road between shopping centre and sea. Two large comfortable lounges with colour TV and library.
Spacious dining room, noted for its excellent varied food, all types of diets catered for, wide choice of menu, friendly efficient service.
Tastefully decorated bedrooms, fitted carpets, bed lights, razor points. Tea & Coffee making facilities available. Some en suite bedrooms.
Packed lunches. Refreshments available all day. Children reduced rates. Limited parking.
From £65 inclusive. Brittany Ferries recommended.

S.A.E. please Muriel & Ken Allport.

HOTELIERS ASSOCIATION OF ILFRACOMBE
HA

New Cavendish Hotel

Larkstone Terrace, Ilfracombe, North Devon. Telephone: (0271) 63994

Family owned and managed Hotel offers you Home from Home accommodation. We are situated in the loveliest part of Ilfracombe. Breathtaking Coastal Views can be enjoyed from our Public rooms, and most of our bedrooms, which are tastefully furnished. Tea Making facilities. All bedrooms Shower and toilet en Suite, and Private Showers. Well stocked Bar. Separate TV Lounge. Games Room. Free Parking. Full English breakfast. Five course evening dinner. (No Hidden Extras.) Tariff from £80.50 to £92.00.
A real friendly welcome and a Pot of Tea on arrival from your hosts Ron and Marie Mourton.

Rosebank Hotel

26 Watermouth Road, Hele Bay, Ilfracombe, Devon
Telephone: (0271) 62814

Open March–September

Seven bedrooms all with Hot & Cold, two family rooms.
Reasonable rates. Licensed. Full central heating. Colour TV.

GH ***Marlyn*** 7 & 8 Regent Pl ☎(0271) 63785 Plan **18** *B3*
Etr–Oct
12hc (2fb) LDO4pm
Lic 🔲 CTV 12🚗

GH ***Merlin Court Hotel*** Torrs Park ☎(0271) 62697 Plan **19** *A2*
14hc 1🛁 (7fb)
Lic 🔲 CTV 12P

⟼ **GH Merrydene Private Hotel** 10 Hillsborough Ter ☎(0271) 62141 Plan **20** *C2*
May–Oct
14hc (2fb) TV in 1 bedroom B&b£8–£8.50 Bdi£11–£11.50 W£64–£74 ⱡ LDO4pm
Lic CTV 4P 3🚗 nc4yrs

GH New Cavendish Hotel 9–10 Larkstone Ter ☎(0271) 63994 Plan **21** *D2*
Apr–Oct
21rm 2hc 14🚿 (2fb) ★ Ⓡ B&b£9.20–£11.50 Bdi£13.80–£16.10 W£80.50–£92 ⱡ LDO6pm
Lic CTV 25P billiards
Ⓥ

⟼ **GH Norbury** Torrs Park ☎(0271) 63888 Plan **22** *A2*
Apr–Sep
9rm 3hc 3🚿 (3fb) B&b£7.50–£8.50 Bdi£12–£13 W£79.50–£88 ⱡ

Ilfracombe

Lic CTV 9P
Ⓥ

GH Queen's Court Hotel Wilder Rd ☎(0271) 63789 Plan **23** *B3*
Mar–Sep
16rm 13hc 1🛁 2🚿 (6fb) B&b£8.50–£9.65 Bdi£13.80–£14.95 W£59.50–£67.55 ⱡ LDO7.15pm
Lic CTV 16P
Ⓥ

GH *Rosebank Hotel* 26 Watermouth Rd, Hele Bay ☎(0271) 62814 Plan **25** *D2*
Mar–Sep
7hc (2fb) Ⓡ LDO6pm
Lic 🔲 CTV 🐕

⟼ **GH Seven Hills Hotel** Torrs Park ☎(0271) 62207 Plan **26** *A2*
Apr–Oct
15hc 5🛁 (4fb) B&b£7.50–£9.50 Bdi£11.50–£13.50 W£75.50–£90 ⱡ LDO7.30pm
CTV 12P 1🚗 nc3yrs
Credit card 3

GH Southcliffe Hotel Torrs Park ☎(0271) 62958 Plan **27** *A2*
14 May–25 Sep
19rm 9hc 8🚿 (8fb) ✱B&b£8–£10 W£72.16–£80.21 ⱡ LDO7.30pm
Lic CTV 12P 🏠

See advertisement on page 186

GH South Tor Hotel Torrs Park ☎(0271) 63750 Plan **28** *A1*
Closed Jan & Feb
15rm 9hc 6🚿 (3fb) B&b£8.50–£9.50 Bdi£13–£14.50 W£80–£89 ⱡ LDO5.30pm
Lic CTV 10P 2🚗

GH *Strathmore Private Hotel* 57 St Brannocks Rd ☎(0271) 62248 Plan **29** *B1*
10hc (6fb) LDO7pm
Lic CTV 8P

GH Sunny Hill Lincombe ☎(0271) 62953 Plan **30** *A1*
2m SW off B3231.
8rm 6hc 2🚿 (2fb) ✱B&b£9–£10.75 Bdi£13–£14.75 W£60–£70 ⱡ LDO8pm
Lic 🔲 CTV 6P nc5yrs

See advertisement on page 186

GH ***Sunnymeade Country House Hotel*** West Down ☎(0271) 63668 Plan **31** *B1*
Closed Xmas
9hc 1🚿 (3fb) ★
Lic 🔲 CTV 12P

⊢✕⊣ **GH Wentworth House Private Hotel** Belmont Road ☎(0271) 63048 Plan **32** *A1*
May–Sep
11hc (6fb) B&b£7–£8 Bdi£9–£10.25 W£57.50–£65 Ⓛ LDO5pm
CTV 11P
Ⓥ

GH Westwell Hall Hotel Torrs Park ☎(0271) 62792 Plan **33** *A2*
15rm 5hc 3→ 5⋒ (2fb) CTV in all bedrooms ® B&b£10–£13.50 Bdi£14–£17.50 W£84–£126 Ⓛ LDO7.30pm
Lic ▥ CTV 9P nc7yrs billiards
Ⓥ

INN Royal Britannia The Quay ☎(0271) 62939 Plan **24** *C3*
12rm 9hc B&b£8.50 Bdi£12.50 W£56 M Bar lunch 55p–£2&alc D10.30pm £4.50&alc
CTV
Credit cards 1 3

ILKLEY
West Yorkshire
Map **7** SE14

GH Moorview House Hotel 104 Skipton Rd (Guestaccom) ☎(0943) 600156
11rm 6hc 5⋒ (6fb) CTV in 4 bedrooms TV in 4 bedrooms ® B&b£9–£17 LDO5pm
Lic ▥ CTV 12P
Ⓥ

INGHAM
Suffolk
Map **5** TL87

INN Cadogan Arms ☎Culford (028484) 226
4hc CTV in all bedrooms ®
*B&b£10–£10.50 D9.45pm £6alc
▥ P nc10yrs

INGLEBY GREENHOW
North Yorkshire
Map **8** NZ50

FH Mrs M Bloom **Manor House** *(NZ586056)* ☎Great Ayton (0642) 722384
½m SE on private road, entrance in village.
3rm (1fb) B&b£9.50–£10 Bdi£17–£18 W£66.50 M LDOam
Lic ▥ TV 40P 3 nc8yrs 164acres arable sheep

INGLETON
North Yorkshire
Map **7** SD67

⊢✕⊣ **GH Oakroyd Private Hotel** Main St ☎(0468) 41258
Formerly the Vicarage, now a small family run hotel with comfortable accommodation and a friendly atmosphere.
7hc (4fb) CTV in all bedrooms B&b£8 Bdi£12.25 W£80 Ⓛ LDO5.15pm
Lic ▥ CTV 4P

⊢✕⊣ **GH Springfield Private Hotel** Main St ☎(0468) 41280
Closed Nov
6rm 4hc 2⋒ (4fb) CTV in all bedrooms ® B&bfr£8 Bdifr£12.25 Wfr£77 Ⓛ LDO4.30pm
Lic ▥ 12P
Ⓥ

⊢✕⊣ **FH** G W & M Bell **Langber** *(SD689709)* ☎(0468) 41587
Closed Xmas
A large detached property in open countryside in an elevated position situated in a quiet country lane about 1m south of Ingleton village.
6hc (4fb) B&b£6.75–£8 Bdi£9.75–£10.75 W£66–£72 LDO5pm
▥ CTV 6P 1 37acres sheep

INSTOW
Devon
Map **2** SS43

GH *Anchorage Hotel* The Quay ☎(0271) 860655
Apr–Oct
Semi-detached house on quay, facing boatyard, river and beach. Excellent views.
10hc 7⋒ (5fb)
Lic ▥ CTV 9P sea river

INVERGARRY
Highland *Inverness-shire*
Map **14** NH30

GH Craigard ☎(08093) 250
Apr–Oct
Detached house with spacious bedrooms and comfortable lounges.
7hc (2fb) ® B&b£8.75 Bdi£13.50 W£86.50 Ⓛ LDO7pm
Lic CTV 6P

⊢✕⊣ **GH Lundie View** Aberchalder ☎(08093) 291
Closed mid Jan–mid Dec
Modernised roadside cottage with extension overlooking pleasant hill and woodland scenery. 3m NE A82.
6hc (3fb) ® B&b£7–£7.50 Bdi£11–£12 W£75–£82 Ⓛ LDO7.30pm
Lic ▥ CTV 6P
Ⓥ

⊢✕⊣ **FH** Mr & Mrs R Wilson **Ardgarry** *(NH286015)* Faichem ☎(08093) 226
Mar–Nov
A comfortable and homely traditional farmhouse, now operating as a small holding. Located about 1m from Invergarry off the A87 – signed Faichem.
1hc (A 3hc) (1fb) ® B&b£8 Bdi£12 W£84 Ⓛ LDO3pm
▥ CTV 10P 10acres mixed

⊢✕⊣ **FH** Mrs L Brown **Faichem Lodge** *(NH286014)* ☎(08093) 314
Mar–Oct
Beautiful, modernised old stone house with cosy bedrooms and lounge. Although not a working farm the house is set in 1½ acres of farmland and owners keep ducks and hens in the garden.
3hc (1fb) ® B&b£6.30–£7.50 Bdi£10.50–£12
▥ CTV 5P 1½acres mixed
Ⓥ

INVERKEITHING
Fife
Map **11** NT18

GH Forth Craig Private Hotel 90 Hope St ☎(0383) 418440
Modern and well appointed split-level villa with river views.
5⋒ CTV in all bedrooms ® B&b£16.68 Bdi£23 W£116.73 M LDO7pm
Lic ▥ 8P

INVERNESS
Highland *Inverness-shire*
Map **14** NH64
See plan

⊢✕⊣ **GH Abermar** 25 Fairfield Rd ☎(0463) 239019 Plan **1** *A2*
Compact modern detached house with extension to rear set in residential area.
11hc 3→ (3fb) B&b£7.50–£8 W£52.50–£56 M
▥ CTV 9P
Credit cards 1 2 3 4

⊢✕⊣ **GH Ardnacoille House** 1A Annfield Rd ☎(0463) 233451 Plan **2** *D1*
Apr–Oct
Semi-detached house with lovely lounge, in own gardens. Nicely appointed and very well maintained.
6hc (2fb) B&b£7.50–£9 Bdi£11.50–£13 W£78–£88 Ⓛ LDO2pm
▥ CTV 6P nc10yrs

⊢✕⊣ **GH Arran** 42 Union St ☎(0463) 232115 Plan **3** *B2*
Set in upper floors of tenement building in central location between shops.
7hc (2fb) B&b£7.50–£8
▥ TV

GH Brae Ness Hotel 16–17 Ness Bank ☎(0463) 231732 Plan **4** *B1*
Apr–Nov
Family run accommodation, situated beside the River Ness and close to town centre.
15rm 6hc 9⋒ (3fb) ® B&b£9.50–£10.50 Bdi£14.75–£16.25 W£90–£102.50 Ⓛ LDO6.30pm
▥ CTV 8P
See advertisement on page 188

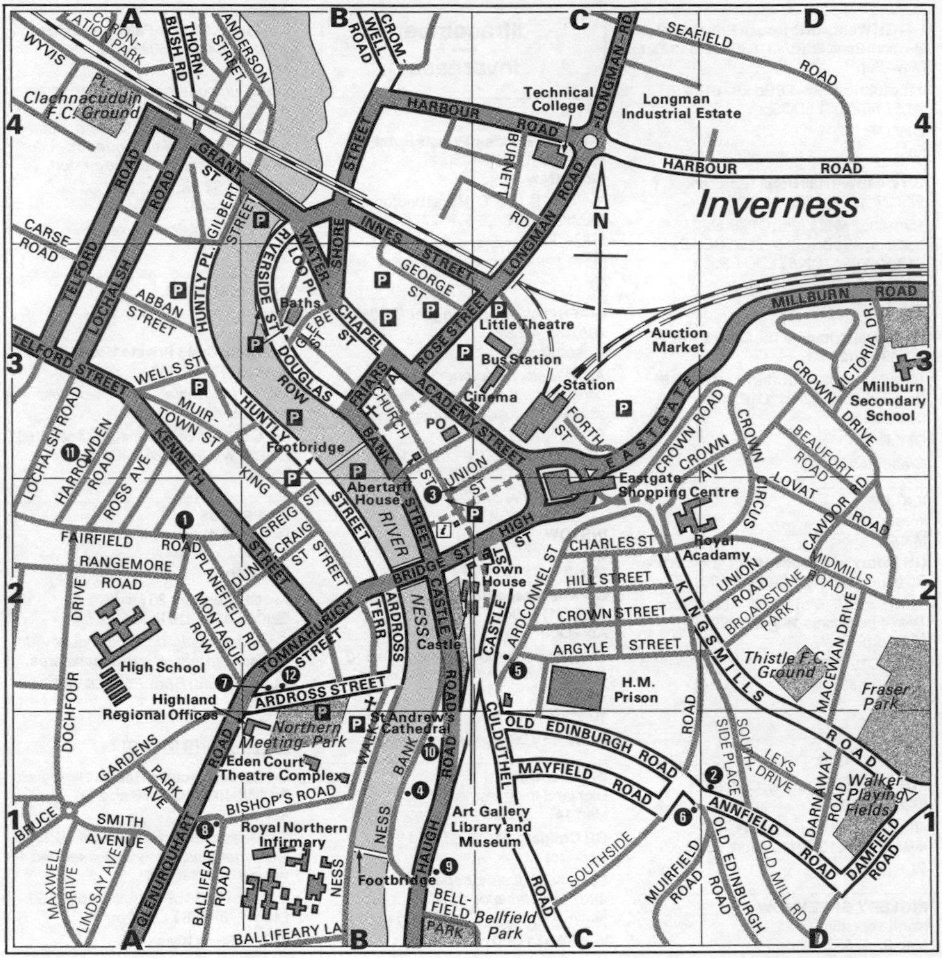

Inverness

1 Abermar
2 Ardnacoille House
3 Arran
4 Brae Ness
5 Craigside House
6 Four Winds
7 Glencairn
8 Lyndale
9 Moray Park Hotel
10 Riverside Hotel
11 St Anne's House Hotel
12 Whinpark

GH Craigside House 4 Gordon Ter (Guestaccom) ☎(0463) 231576
Plan **5** *C2*
rs Dec–Feb
Friendly, comfortable and well appointed accommodation.
6rm 2hc 1⇌ 3fi (1fb) TV in all bedrooms ✱ ® B&b£8.50–£10 Bdi£14–£16.50 W£90–£100 ⱡ LDO5pm
▥ 4P nc14yrs

GH Four Winds 42 Old Edinburgh Rd ☎(0463) 230397 Plan **6** *C1*
Closed Xmas & New Year
Detached lodge set in own grounds in residential suburb.
7hc (2fb) B&b£8.50–£9 W£56 M
▥ CTV 12P

GH *Glencairn* 19 Ardross St ☎(0463) 232965 Plan **7** *A2*
Closed Dec & Jan
Nicely appointed house in residential street.
11hc (2fb)
▥ CTV 10P 4⌂

⊢⊣ **GH Lyndale** 2 Ballifeary Rd ☎(0463) 231529 Plan **8** *A1*
Closed 23 Dec–3 Jan
Detached house set in own grounds. Some rooms are compact.
6hc (1fb) B&b£7–£8 W£45–£60 M
▥ CTV 6P
Ⓥ

GH Moray Park Hotel Island Bank Rd ☎(0463) 233528 Plan **19** *B1*
Small stone villa looking out across River Ness.
7rm 3hc 2⇌ 1fi (3fb) ✱ ®
*B&b£8.75–£10.75 Bdi£15.50–£17.50 W£103–£117 ⱡ LDO5.30pm
Lic ▥ CTV 10P nc6yrs

GH *Riverside Hotel* 8 Ness Bank ☎(0463) 231052 Plan **10** *B1*
Closed Xmas & New Year
Traditional stone villa overlooking River Ness. Attractive public rooms.
10hc (1fb) ® ✱ LDO7pm
▥ CTV ✈ river

GH St Ann's House Hotel 37 Harrowden Rd ☎(0463) 236157
Plan **11** *A3*
Apr–Oct
A small homely establishment in residential area at west end of town.
6rm 1hc 4fi (1fb) ® B&b£8.50–£11.25 Bdi£14–£16.75 W£90–£110 ⱡ LDO6pm
▥ CTV 3P nc7yrs

GH *Whinpark* 17 Ardross St ☎(0463) 232549 Plan **12** *B2*
Friendly and comfortable accommodation with nicely appointed restaurant.
9hc 4fi (4fb) CTV in all bedrooms ® LDO8pm
Lic ▥ 4P
Ⓨ

IPSTONES
Staffordshire
Map **7** SK04

⊢⊣ **FH** Mrs J Brindley **Glenwood House** *(SK006488)* ☎(053871) 294
Closed Dec
Large house approx 100 years old, built of dressed sandstone blocks in very picturesque and peaceful rural surroundings.
3rm (1fb) ✱ B&b£8–£8.50 Bdi£12–£13 W£84 ⱡ LDO2pm
▥ CTV 6P ♪(hard) U 56acres beef
Ⓥ

IPSWICH
Suffolk
Map **5** TM14

GH Gables Hotel 17 Park Rd ☎(0473) 54252
rs wknds
12hc (1fb) ® B&b£11.50 Bdi£14.50 W£77 M LDO6pm
Lic ▥ CTV 10P
Ⓥ

INN *Station Hotel* Burrell Rd ☎(0473) 52664
12hc 8fi CTV in all bedrooms ®
20P

ISLE OF MAN
Map **6**
Places with AA-listed accommodation are indicated on location map 6. Full details will be found under individual placenames in the gazetteer section.

ISLE OF SKYE
Highland *Inverness-shire*
Map **13** NG
Places with AA-listed accommodation are indicated on location map 13. Full details will be found under individual placenames in the gazetteer section.

ISLE OF WIGHT
Map **4**
Places with AA-listed accommodation are indicated on location map 4. Full details will be found under individual placenames in the gazetteer section.

ISLE OF ORNSAY
Isle of Skye, Highland *Inverness-shire*
Map **13** NG71

⊢⊣ **GH Post Office House** ☎(04713) 201
Mar–Sep
Attached to small country Post Office, with tidy garden and hill and sea views.
4rm 3hc (A 2hc) B&b£7 W£49 M
CTV 10P
Ⓥ

ISLES OF SCILLY
(No map)
See Scilly, Isles of

ISLEWORTH
Gt London
London plan **4** B3
(page 222)

GH Kingswood Hotel 33 Woodlands Rd ☎01-560 5614
11hc CTV in all bedrooms ✱ ®
B&b£13.80 →

Lic ▥ CTV 5P nc6yrs
Ⓥ

IVER HEATH
Buckinghamshire
Map **4** TQ08

GH Bridgettine Convent Fulmer Common Rd ☎Fulmer (02816) 2073
An unusual establishment, a convent run by nuns, offering simple, comfortable accommodation in a friendly, peaceful atmosphere.
22hc ✶ B&b£10 Bdi£13 W£56 M̸ LDO6pm
▥ CTV 20P

JACOBSTOWE
Devon
Map **2** SS50

⟼ **FH** Mrs J King **Higher Cadham** *(SS585026)* ☎Exbourne (083785) 647
Apr–Oct
Well decorated and comfortably furnished 16th-century farmhouse. Ideal base for touring.
4hc (1fb) ✶ B&b£6 Bdi£10 W£63 Ł LDO5pm
CTV 6P nc3yrs ♪ 139acres mixed
Ⓥ

JEDBURGH
Borders *Roxburghshire*
Map **12** NT62

GH Ferniehirst Mill Lodge ☎(0835) 63279
Closed Nov
Modern purpose built lodge in secluded position beside the River Jed. 3m S of Jedburgh off A68. Horse riding holidays are a speciality.
11rm 3hc 5⇥ 3⋒ Ⓡ B&b£12.65–£13.80 Bdi£22.65–£24.80 W£150.65–£165 Ł LDO8.30pm
Lic ▥ 16P ♪ U
Ⓥ

⟼ **GH Kenmore Bank** Oxnam Rd ☎(0835) 62369
Compact house perched high above the Jed Water and looking across to the town.
6hc (2fb) ✶ Ⓡ B&b£8 W£55 M̸ LDO8.30pm
Lic ▥ CTV 6P
Ⓥ

JERSEY
Channel Islands
Map **16**
Places with AA-listed accommodation are indicated on location map 16. Full details will be found under individual placenames in the gazetteer section.

KEITH
Grampian *Banffshire*
Map **15** NJ45

⟼ **FH** Mrs J Jackson **The Haughs** *(NJ416515)* ☎(05422) 2238
May–Oct
Traditional stone-built farmhouse, with pleasant views, 1m from Keith off A96.
4hc (1fb) ✶ Ⓡ B&b£6.80–£7.50 Bdi£12–£13 W£82–£89 Ł LDO2pm
CTV 8P 2⌂ ⌂ 220acres arable mixed
Ⓥ

⟼ **FH** Mrs E C Leith **Montgrew** *(NJ453517)* ☎(05422) 2852
Apr–Oct
Stone-built house situated in valley within easy reach of beaches, hills and the Cairngorms. 2m E off A95
4rm 1hc (1fb) B&bfr£7 Bdifr£9.50 W£66.50 Ł LDO7pm
CTV 5P 211acres arable beef

⟼ **FH** Mrs G Murphy **Tarnash House** *(NJ442490)* ☎(05422) 2728
May–Oct
Two-storey, stone farmhouse with well maintained garden to the front. 1m S off A96.
4hc (1fb) B&b£6.50–£7 W£42 M̸
▥ CTV 10P 1⌂ ♪ 100acres arable
Ⓥ

KELSO
Borders *Roxburghshire*
Map **12** NT73

⟼ **GH Bellevue** Bowmont St ☎(0573) 24588
Attractive house with good standard throughout. Ten minutes walk from the town centre.
8rm 6hc 2⋒ (2fb) ✶ B&b£8–£9 Bdi£11.50–£12.50 LDO5pm
Lic ▥ CTV 8P

KENDAL
Cumbria
Map **7** SD59

⟼ **FH** Mrs S Beaty **Garnett House** *(SD500959)* Burneside ☎(0539) 24542
Closed Xmas & New Year
15th-century stone-built farmhouse situated in an elevated position overlooking Howgill Fells, close to Windermere and Kendal.
5hc (2fb) ✶ Ⓡ B&b£7–£8 Bdi£10.50–£11.25 W£49–£55 M̸ LDO5pm
CTV 6P 270acres dairy sheep

⟼ **FH** Mrs E M Gardner **Natland Mill Beck** *(SD520907)* ☎(0539) 21122
Mar–Oct
17th-century, local-stone-built farmhouse with original beams, doors and cupboards. Large well-furnished rooms. Attractive walled garden.
3rm 2hc ✶ Ⓡ B&b£7–£8
▥ CTV 3P 100acres dairy

⟼ **FH** Mrs S Bell **Oxenholme** *(SD529905)* Oxenholme Rd ☎(0539) 27226
A delightfully furnished farmhouse dating back to 1540. Many natural beams and features an inglenook fireplace. 2m SE B6254.
2hc (1fb) ✶ B&b£7–£8
▥ CTV 4P 180acres dairy sheep

KENILWORTH
Warwickshire
Map **4** SP27

⟼ **GH Enderley** 20 Queens Rd ☎(0926) 55388
6hc Ⓡ B&b£8 W£50.40 M̸
Lic ▥ CTV 2P
Ⓥ

GH *Ferndale* 45 Priory Rd ☎(0926) 53214
Closed Xmas
7hc (1fb) ✶
▥ CTV 8P

GH Hollyhurst 47 Priory Rd ☎(0926) 53882
Closed Xmas Day
Large terraced house with well decorated bedrooms and comfortable lounge.
9hc (2fb) Ⓡ B&b£8.50–£9.50 Bdi£12–£13 W£56–£60 M̸ LDO3pm
Lic ▥ CTV 10P

GH *Kenilworth Court Hotel* 95 Warwick Rd ☎(0926) 53594
12hc (1fb) LDO7pm
Lic ▥ CTV ✶̸

KENNFORD
Devon
Map **3** SX98

⟼ **FH** Mrs R Weeks **Holloway Barton** *(SX893855)* ☎Exeter (0392) 832302
Closed Xmas
Well appointed house retaining its old charm situated 1 mile from the M5 and 1 mile from Haldon Racecourse. Well kept garden and large lawn.
4hc (1fb) ✶ Ⓡ B&b£8–£9 Bdifr£12
▥ CTV P 2⌂ ⌂ billiards 380acres arable beef dairy sheep mixed

KESWICK
Cumbria
Map **11** NY22
See plan

GH Acorn House Private Hotel Ambleside Rd ☎(0596) 72553
Plan **1** *C1/2*
10hc (4fb) Ⓡ B&b£9–£10 Bdi£13.75–£14.75 W£58–£65 M̸ LDO5pm
Lic ▥ CTV 9P

GH *Allerdale House* 1 Eskin St ☎(0596) 73891 Plan **2** *C1*
Closed Dec
6hc 2⇥ 1⋒ (3fb) Ⓡ LDO 6.15pm
Lic ▥ CTV 3P nc3yrs

GH *Bay Tree* 1 Wordsworth St ☎(0596) 73313 Plan **3** *C2/3*

Situated on main route to town centre.

6hc (2fb)

Lic CTV river

GH Clarence House 14 Eskin St ☎(0596) 73186 Plan **4** *C2*

8hc (2fb) Ⓡ ✱B&b£8.20 Bdi£12.80 W£86 LDO6pm

Lic CTV

Ⓥ

See advertisement on page 193

Keswick

GH Derwent Lodge Portinscale ☎(0596) 72746 Plan **5** *A5*

Mar–Nov rs Dec–Feb

Country house in mature gardens 1 mile from town centre.

10rm 5hc 1 (2fb) B&b£10–£12 Bdi£16–£20 W£100–£140 LDO7.30pm

Lic CTV 15P 2

Ⓥ

See advertisement on page 193

GH Foye House 23 Eskin St ☎(0596) 73288 Plan **6** *C2*

6hc (2fb) Ⓡ B&b£7.50 Bdi£12 W£80 LDO5.30pm

Lic CTV

GH Hazeldene Hotel The Heads ☎(0596) 72106 Plan **8** *B2*

10 Mar–10 Nov →

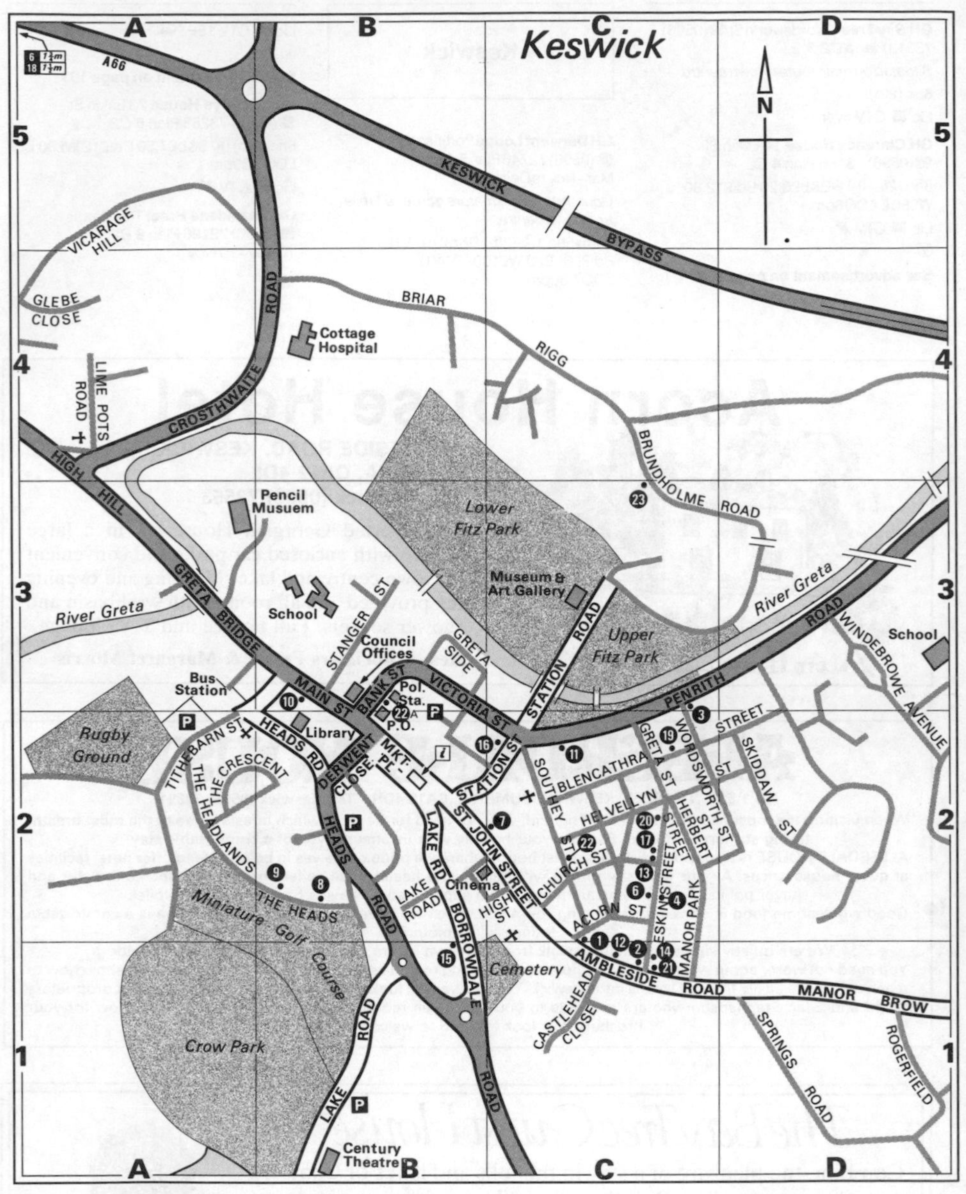

Keswick

1 Acorn House Private Hotel
2 Allerdale House
3 Bay Tree
4 Clarence House
5 Derwent Lodge
6 Foye House
7 George Hotel (*Inn*)
8 Hazeldene Hotel
9 Highfield
10 Kings Arms Hotel (*Inn*)
11 Linnett Hill Hotel
12 Lynwood Private Hotel
13 Melbreak House
14 Parkfield
15 Priorholm Hotel
16 Ravensworth Private Hotel
17 Richmond House
18 Rickerby Grange
19 Silverdale Hotel
20 Squirrel Lodge
21 Stonegarth
21 Sunnyside
22A Thornleigh
23 Woodlands

23rm 11hc 12⋒ (10fb) ® B&b£9.30–£12.90 Bdi£14.80–£18.40 W£99–£123 M LDO5pm

Lic ▥ CTV 18P

GH Highfield The Heads ☎(0596) 72508 Plan **9** *B2*
Apr–Oct

Large, Victorian semi-detached house with spacious rooms and an elevated garden.

21rm 9hc 12⋒ (3fb) B&bfr£9.90 Bdifr£16.50 Wfr£115.50 Ł LDO5pm

Lic ▥ CTV 20P nc5yrs

Keswick

GH *Lynwood Private Hotel* 12 Ambleside Rd ☎(0596) 72081
Plan **12** *C1*
Mar–Oct

9hc (5fb) ✱ LDO5pm

Lic ▥ CTV ₱ nc5yrs

⊢⊣ **GH Melbreak House** 29 Church St ☎(0596) 73398 Plan **13** *C2*
Closed Nov–30 Dec

Two large corner terrace houses carefully converted to offer comfortable accommodation.

12hc (3fb) B&b£7.75–£8.75 Bdi£11.75–£12.75 W£52–£58 M LDO4.30pm

Lic CTV ₱

GH *Parkfield* 4 Eskin St ☎(0596) 72324
Plan **14** *C1*
Mar–Dec

8hc (4fb) ✱

Lic ▥ CTV

Clarence House

14 Eskin Street, Keswick, Cumbria

A well established guest house. Fully centrally heated. Residents lounge with colour television and coal fire. Table licence.
All bedrooms have hot and cold water, security locks, electric blankets, razor points and heating.
Guests access at all times.
Pleasantly situated within easy walking distance to lake, parks and town centre. Ideal touring and walking.

Brochure from Mrs Lexie Hartley 0596 73186

Derwent Lodge

Come and stay in our Beautiful Country House overlooking Derwentwater. Ideal for touring, watersports, fellwalking or just relaxing. Warmth, comfort and good cooking. Elegant rooms, superb views of mountain and lake scenery, TV, C.H. Licensed. Ample parking, lawns and wooded grounds.

Dinner, B&B weekly £100, Daily £16.
BOOK EARLY FOR LAKE VIEW ROOMS
Colour Brochures and Bookings:
TERRY & BRENDA LANSBURY,
Derwent Lodge, Portinscale, Keswick.
Tel: (0596) 72746

Melbreak House

29 Church Street, Keswick CA12 4DX Telephone: (0596) 73398

Melbreak is a large, traditional grey-slate, Lakeland building in a peaceful yet convenient area of this lovely old market town which provides an ideal base for discovering the delights of the Lake District.
We provide all the usual amenities and a high standard of cuisine, comfort and service in an informal relaxed atmosphere.
Our emphasis is on good value for money, our rates are reasonable with generous reductions for children.
Residental Licence.
Brochure with pleasure on request.

GH Priorholm Hotel Borrowdale Rd ☎(0596) 72745 Plan **15** *B1*

9rm 5hc 3⇌ 1⋒ (2fb) CTV in 4 bedrooms ✱ Ⓡ B&b£10.70–£14.70 Bdi£13.70–£18.70 W£70–£85 ⱡ LDO11pm

Lic ▥ CTV 7P

Credit cards 1 3 Ⓥ

GH *Ravensworth Private Hotel* Station St ☎(0596) 72476 Plan **16** *C1*

Mar–Dec

9hc 1⋒ (1fb) Ⓡ LDO7.30pm

Lic ▥ CTV 5P

Keswick

⊢⊣ **GH Richmond House** 37–39 Eskin St ☎(0596) 73965 Plan **17** *C1*

Family run private hotel offering the highest standard in comfort, food and hospitality.

12rm 9hc 3⋒ (3fb) ✱ B&b£8–£10 Bdi£12.25–£14.50 W£80–£86.50 ⱡ LDO6pm

Lic ▥ CTV ✗ nc10yrs

Credit card 1

GH Rickerby Grange Portinscale (Guestaccom) ☎(0596) 72344 Plan **18** *A5*

Closed 25 & 26 Dec

Charming, comfortable house with friendly proprietors. 1m W A66.

11rm 2hc 2⇌ 5⋒ (4fb) Ⓡ B&b£10.50–£11.50 Bdi£15.60–£17 W£103–£112 ⱡ LDO5.30pm

Lic ▥ CTV 15P ⌂

GH Silverdale Hotel Blencathra St ☎(0596) 72294 Plan **19** *A2*

13hc (3fb) ✱ B&b£9.50 Bdi£14 W£87.50 ⱡ LDO6pm

Lic ▥ CTV 8P

GH *Squirrel Lodge* 43 Eskin St ☎(0596) 73091 Plan **20** *C2*

7hc TV in all bedrooms ✱ LDO4.30pm

Lic ▥ TV 2P nc5yrs

GH Stonegarth 2 Eskin St ☎(0596) 72436 Plan **21** *C1*

Mar–Oct

A large corner terrace house in residential area, which the proprietors run on a homely basis.

9rm 5hc (2fb) ® B&b£8.50 Bdi£12 W£56 M LDO5.30pm

Lic ▥ CTV 9P nc3yrs

GH Sunnyside 25 Southey St ☎(0596) 72446 Plan **22** *C2*

8hc (1fb) ✱ ® B&b£9 Bdi£13.50 W£89.50 L LDO3pm

▥ CTV 7P nc

⊢✶ **GH Thornleigh** 23 Bank St ☎(0596) 72863 Plan **22A** *B3*

A comfortable house, with very friendly proprietors who excel at providing wholesome, home made dinners.

7hc (1fb) B&b£7.50–£8.95 W£79–£95 L LDO10am

Lic ▥ CTV 3P nc8yrs

GH Woodlands Brundholme Rd ☎(0596) 72399 Plan **23** *C3*

1 wk before Etr–Oct

Charming, stone-built, country house in quiet location in own grounds.

Keswick — Keynsham

5hc (1fb) ✱ B&b£9.25–£10.25 Bdi£13.75–£14.75 W£84–£89.50 L LDO10am

▥ CTV 7P nc6yrs

Ⓥ

INN *George Hotel* St Johns Street ☎(0596) 72076 Plan **7** *C2*

17rm (2fb) D8.30pm

CTV 4P

INN Kings Arms Hotel Main St ☎(0596) 72083 Plan **10** *B3*

Feb–Dec rs Jan

19rm 11hc 1→ 7⋒ ✱ ® B&b£13–£14.50 W£91–£101.50 M Bar lunch £3.75alc LDO9.30pm

CTV ⚑

Ⓥ

KETTLEBURGH
Suffolk
Map **5** TM26

FH Mrs P Patterson ***Rookery*** *(TM273606)* Framlingham (0728) 723277

Mar–Oct

Georgian farmhouse standing in 1½ acres of well-kept gardens. Situated ¾m N of Kettleburgh on the Framlingham rd.

3hc ✱

▥ CTV 3P nc14yrs 350acres arable beef

KETTLEWELL
North Yorkshire
Map **7** SD97

GH Dale House ☎(075676) 836

Apr–Oct

6rm 3hc 3⋒ (2fb) ® Bdi£19.80 W£136 L LDO7.30pm

CTV 5P U

KEXBY
North Yorkshire
Map **8** SE75

⊢✶ **FH** Mrs K R Daniel **Ivy House** *(SE691511)* ☎York (0904) 489368

2rm (1fb) ✱ B&b£6.50–£7.50

CTV 5P 135acres mixed

KEYNSHAM
Avon
Map **3** ST66

GH Grasmere Hotel 22 Bath Rd ☎(02756) 2662

11hc ✱B&b£11–£14.50 Bdi£16.50–£20 LDO6.15pm

Lic ▥ CTV 9P ⛆(heated)

FH Mrs L Sparks **Uplands** *(ST663664)* Wellsway ☎(02756) 5764

8hc (6fb) B&bfr£11 Bdifr£17 Wfr£126 Ⅼ LDO10am

Ⅲ CTV 20P 20acres dairy

KIDLINGTON
Oxfordshire
Map **4** SP41

GH Bowood House 238 Oxford Rd ☎(08675) 2839

Friendly modern house plus extension with tastefully furnished bedrooms.

9rm 4hc 2⇌ 3⋒ (2fb) CTV in all bedrooms ✱ B&b£11–£13.50 Bdi£19.50–£22 LDO4pm

Lic Ⅲ CTV 12P ⛆(heated)

See advertisement on page 262

KILGETTY
Dyfed
Map **2** SN10

FH Mrs S A James **Little Newton** *(SN122073)* ☎Saundersfoot (0834) 812306
May–Oct

9hc (6fb) ✱ B&b£8.50–£9 Bdi£11.50–£12 W£68–£80 LDO6pm

Ⅲ CTV 10P 7acres mixed

KILKHAMPTON
Cornwall
Map **2** SS21

⊢⊣**INN London** ☎(028882) 343

3hc B&b£7.50 Bdi£11 Wfr£75 Ⅼ Bar lunch £1.50–£3.50&alc D9pm £4–£5.50&alc

CTV 4P nc10yrs

Credit card 3

KILLIECRANKIE
Tayside *Perthshire*
Map **14** NN96

⊢⊣**GH Dalnasgadh House** ☎Pitlochry (0796) 3237
Apr–Sep

Attractive house standing on the outskirts of this village.

6hc (1fb) ✱ B&b£7.75–£8.75 W£53.25–£61.25 Ⅿ

Ⅲ CTV 10P nc12yrs

Keynsham — Kingsbridge

KILMARTIN
Strathclyde *Argyllshire*
Map **10** NR89

INN Kilmartin Hotel ☎(05465) 250

A white painted inn with attractive hanging baskets, on the main A816, it is a popular eating place.

5hc B&b£11 Bdi£15–£20 W£70 Ⅿ L£2–£8&alc D9pm £8.80–£10.30

CTV 13P

Ⓥ

KILPECK
Hereford & Worcester
Map **3** SO43

⊢⊣**FH** Mrs I J Pike **Priory** *(SO446302)* ☎Wormbridge (098121) 366
Apr–Sep

2hc ✱ Ⓡ B&b£7.50 W£50 Ⅿ

TV 4P 2⌂ 9acres small holding

KILVE
Somerset
Map **3** ST14

INN Hood Arms ☎Holford (027874) 210
Closed Xmas Day

6hc 2⇌ Ⓡ B&b£12 Bdi£17 W£76 Ⅿ L£4alc D9.30pm £6alc

Ⅲ CTV 14P nc7yrs

Ⓥ

KIMBOLTON
Hereford & Worcester
Map **3** SO56

⊢⊣**FH** M J & S W Lloyd **Menalls** *(SO528611)* ☎Leominster (0568) 2605
Apr–Oct

18th-century farmhouse with old beams; set in Herefordshire valley scenery. 2½m from Leominster.

2hc (2fb) B&b£7 Bdi£10 W£40 Ⅿ LDO5pm

CTV P 40acres mixed

KINCRAIG
Highland *Inverness-shire*
Map **14** NH80

GH March House Lagganlia ☎(05404) 388
Closed Nov

6hc (1fb) ✱B&b£7.50–£8.50 Bdi£13–£14 W£87–£95 Ⅼ

Ⅲ 8P

KINGHAM
Oxfordshire
Map **4** SP22

GH Conygree Gate Church St (Guestaccom) ☎(060871) 389
Mar–Oct

Attractive Cotswold stone house situated in charming, peaceful village, with modern amenities. Kept spotlessly clean and run by two very English ladies – good home cooking.

6rm 5hc (1fb) ✱ B&b£10 Bdi£17 W£112 Ⅼ LDO5pm

Lic Ⅲ CTV 6P nc7yrs

Ⓥ

KINGHORN
Fife
Map **11** NT28

GH *Odin Villa* 107 Pettycur Rd ☎(0592) 890625

Large modern villa looking out across the Firth of Forth decorated and furnished to the highest standards.

7⋒ (2fb) CTV in all bedrooms

Ⅲ 14P sea

KINGSBRIDGE
Devon
Map **3** SX74

GH Ashleigh House Ashleigh Rd, Westville ☎(0548) 2893
Apr–Sep

8hc (1fb) Ⓡ B&b£8.75–£9.75 Bdi£13.25–£14.50 W£88–£96 Ⅼ LDO4pm

CTV 6P nc5yrs

Ⓥ

GH Hotel Kildare Balkwill Rd ☎(0548) 2451
9hc (4fb) B&bfr£12.14 Bdifr£18.35 Wfr£91.13 LDO7.15pm
Lic CTV 7P
Credit card 1 V

KINGSDOWN
Kent
Map **5** TR34
GH Blencathra Country Kingsdown Hill ☎Deal (03045) 373725
Etr–Oct
Friendly, modern, country guesthouse with use of a croquet lawn.
5hc (3fb) B&b£9 Bdi£14 W£84 LDOam
Lic CTV 7P nc3yrs

KINGSEY
Buckinghamshire
Map **4** SP70
FH Mr N M D Hooper **Foxhill** *(SP748066)* ☎Haddenham (0844) 291650
Mar–Nov
Very hospitable farmhouse offering accommodation and cooking of a high standard.
3rm 2hc (1fb) B&b£10 W£70 M
CTV 40P nc5yrs (heated) 4acres sheep small holding
V

KINGSGATE
Kent
Map **5** TR37
GH Marylands Hotel Marine Dr ☎Thanet (0843) 61259
Etr–Oct
10rm 1 (4fb) R *B&b£9–£12 Bdi£13–£16 W£55–£65 M LDO6.30pm
Lic CTV 10P

KINGSLAND
Hereford & Worcester
Map **3** SO46
FH Mrs F M Hughes **Tremayne** *(SO447613)* ☎(056881) 233
Apr–Nov

Kingsbridge — Kington

Deceptively large, two-storey building on one of the main roads to Leominster.
3hc (1fb) B&b£7 W£49 M
CTV 3P 40acres sheep mixed

KING'S LYNN
Norfolk
Map **9** TF62
GH Runcton House Hotel 53 Goodwins Rd ☎(0553) 773098
7hc 1 1 (1fb) CTV in 1 bedroom R B&b£9.50–£11.50 Bdi£14.50–£16 LDO6.30pm
Lic CTV 12P

KINGSTON
Devon
Map **2** SX64
GH Trebles Cottage Private Hotel (Guestaccom) ☎Bigbury-on-Sea (054881) 268
Mar–Oct
6rm 3hc 3 B&b£10.25 Bdi£15.25 W£98 LDO6pm
Lic CTV 10P nc8yrs

KINGSTONE
Hereford & Worcester
Map **3** SO43
FH Mrs G C Andrews **Webton Court** *(SO421365)* ☎Golden Valley (0981) 250220
Located off B4348.
6hc (2fb) *B&bfr£8 Bdifr£12.50 Wfr£84 LDO7pm
Lic CTV P 276acres arable beef sheep mixed

KINGSTON UPON THAMES
Gt London
London plan **4** B2
(page 222)
GH Hotel Antoinette 26 Beaufort Rd ☎01-546 1044
A friendly family run commercial hotel with most bedrooms en suite and attractive garden. Situated in quiet residental area.
40rm 10hc 20 10 (A 60rm 40 20) (4fb) CTV in 40 bedrooms TV in 60 bedrooms R B&b£14–£16 Bdi£20.50–£22.50 LDO9.30pm
Lic CTV 60P nc10yrs
Credit cards 1 2 3
See advertisement on page 198

GH Lingfield House Hotel 29 Beaufort Rd ☎01-546 1988
Small, corner property in quiet residential area a few minutes from the shops.
8rm 6hc 2 (3fb) CTV in 1 bedroom TV in 2 bedrooms B&b£9.20–£9.80
8P nc6yrs
Credit card 3

KINGSWELLS
Grampian *Aberdeenshire*
Map **15** NJ80
FH Mrs M Mann **Bellfield** *(NJ868055)* ☎Aberdeen (0224) 740239
Closed Dec
Modernised and extended farm cottage on quiet road set amid farmlands. 4m W of Aberdeen city centre off A944.
3hc (2fb) B&b£8–£8.50 (W only Aug)
CTV 4P 200acres arable beef dairy

KINGTON
Hereford & Worcester
Map **3** SO25
FH Mrs E E Protheroe **Bucks Head** *(SO265550)* Upper Hergest ☎(0544) 231063
2m SW on unclass Gladestry rd.
6hc (3fb) B&b£7–£7.50 Bdi£12–£12.50 W£82 LDO8.30pm
CTV 6P 290acres mixed

FH Mrs M Eckley **Holme** *(SO339553)* Lyonshall ☎(05448) 216
Etr–Oct
Fully-modernised farmhouse standing on outskirts of village, 2m E of Kington.
4rm 3hc (1fb) B&b£8.50 Bdi£12 W£56 M LDO7pm
6P nc8yrs dairy mixed

⟼FH J A Layton **Park Gate** *(SO332575)* Lyonshall ☎(05448) 243
Feb–Oct
Two-storey, stone-built farmhouse with land overlooking Wales. Offa's Dyke runs through part of the farm. 2m E of Kington.
2hc (1fb) ✱ B&b£8–£9 Bdi£14–£15 W£56 M LDO4pm
CTV P 230acres pig sheep mixed
See advertisement on page 238

KINGUSSIE
Highland *Inverness-shire*
Map **14** NH70
GH Sonnhalde East Ter ☎(05402) 266
Closed Nov
Attractive grey stone detached house located in terrace in elevated position behind main street.
7hc (2fb) *B&b£7–£7.50 Bdi£11–£12 W£77 L LDO4pm
CTV 8P
Ⓥ

KINVER
Staffordshire
Map **7** SO88
INN Kinfayre Restaurant 41 High St ☎(0384) 872565
Closed first 2 wks Jan & Aug
5 ✱ Ⓡ B&b£15 W£70 M L£4.95 D10pm £3–£8&alc
✱ CTV 13P

KIPPEN
Central *Stirlingshire*
Map **11** NS69
FH Mrs J Paterson **Powblack** *(NS670970)* ☎(078687) 260
Apr–Oct
Pleasant farmhouse near the River Forth on the Kippen to Doune road.
2hc (1fb) ✱
CTV 3P 300acres arable beef

KIRKBEAN
Dumfries & Galloway *Dumfriesshire*
Map **11** NX95
GH Cavens House ☎(038788) 234
Closed Xmas & New Year
Charming stone mansion standing in 10 acre country setting.
6rm 4 2 (1fb) Ⓡ B&b£13 Bdi£20 W£91 M
Lic CTV 12P

KIRKCONNEL
Dumfries & Galloway *Dumfriesshire*
Map **11** NS71
⟼FH Mrs E A McGarvie **Niviston** *(NS691135)* ☎(06593) 346
mid May–Sep
Pleasant, well maintained farm delightfully set overlooking River Nith. (NB washing facilities are on ground floor).
2rm (1fb) B&b£6.50 W£45 M
TV P 1 345acres sheep stock
Ⓥ

Kington — Knutsford

KIRKHILL
Highland *Inverness-shire*
Map **14** NH54
⟼FH Mrs C Munro **Wester Moniack** *(NH551438)* ☎Drumchardine (046383) 237
Small, comfortable farmhouse. Follow signs 'Highland Vineries' from A862 and watch for farm sign.
2hc (1fb) B&b£6.50–£7 Bdi£10–£11 W£45–£48 M LDO6pm
CTV 3P 600acres arable beef dairy
Ⓥ

KIRK IRETON
Derbyshire
Map **8** SK25
FH J & E Brassington **Sitch** *(SK260515)* ☎Carsington (062985) 420
rs Xmas
Large sandstone farmhouse with extensive outbuildings standing in a fairly remote but picturesque area.
7rm 2hc 3 1 (2fb) Ⓡ B&b£10 Bdi£17.50 W£70 M LDO8pm
CTV 20P 145acres arable sheep mixed
Ⓥ

KIRKOSWALD
Cumbria
Map **12** NY54
GH Prospect Hill Hotel (Guestaccom) ☎Lazonby (076883) 500
Closed Feb
Farm complex tastefully converted to retain charm and character.
9rm 5hc 2 2 ✱ Ⓡ *B&b£12.20–£17 Bdi£19.90–£24.70 LDO9pm
Lic CTV 24P
Credit cards 1 2 3 5 Ⓥ

KIRTLING
Cambridgeshire
Map **5** TL65
INN Queens Head ☎Newmarket (0638) 730253
3hc Ⓡ B&b£10–£12 Wfr£90 M Lfr£4 D9.45pm fr£4.50
CTV 40P nc
Ⓥ

KIRTON
Nottinghamshire
Map **8** SK66
GH Old Rectory Main St ☎Mansfield (0623) 861540
Closed Dec
10hc (2fb) ✱ B&bfr£10.50 Bdifr£16 Wfr£69 M LDO9pm
CTV 18P
Ⓥ

KNAPTOFT
Leicestershire
Map **4** SP68
FH Mrs J Knight **Greenway** *(SP629893)* Bruntingthorpe Rd ☎Peatling Magna (053758) 509
Closed 25 Dec
This modern bungalow is part of Knaptoft Farm but run independently. Situated in typical rolling Leicestershire farmland and within easy reach of many places of interest.
2hc Ⓡ B&bfr£9 Bdifr£13.50 Wfr£55 M LDO2pm
CTV 3P 145acres arable beef sheep mixed

KNAPTON
Norfolk
Map **9** TG33
GH *Knapton Hall Hotel* ☎Mundesley (0263) 720405
Apr–Oct
10hc (3fb) ✱ LDO7pm
Lic CTV 15P

KNIGHTON
Powys
Map **7** SO27
FH R Watkins **Heartsease** *(SO343725)* ☎Bucknell (05474) 220
Georgian, mellow-stone farmhouse with country house atmosphere and large garden.
3rm 1hc 1 (1fb) B&b£10–£15 Bdifr£15 LDO6.30pm
CTV 6P 2 billiards 700acres poultry

KNOWSTONE
Devon
Map **3** SS82
INN *Masons Arms* ☎Anstey Mills (03984) 231
3hc (A 1)
Lic CTV 8P

KNUTSFORD
Cheshire
Map **7** SJ77
GH Longview Private Hotel
55 Manchester Rd ☎(0565) 2119
Closed Xmas & New Year
Personal service is assured at this small family run hotel overlooking the common. A small menu of good home cooking is offered in the pleasant dining room.
14hc 2 (1fb) Ⓡ B&b£13.50 Bdi£19.75 LDO9pm
Lic CTV 6P
Ⓥ

KYLE OF LOCHALSH
Highland *Ross & Cromarty*
Map **13** NG72

GH Retreat ☎Kyle (0599) 4308
Apr–Oct
Stone-built house with large extension in residential area.
14hc (3fb) B&bfr£8.50 Wfr£59.50 M
CTV 10P 2 nc3yrs
Credit card 3
CTV P mixed

LAIRG
Highland *Sutherland*
Map **14** NC50

GH Carnbren ☎(0549) 2259
Apr–Oct
Modern detached house in roadside location overlooking Loch Shin.
3hc B&b£6.75–£7
CTV 3P

FH Mrs M Mackay **Alt-Na-Sorag** *(NC547123)* 14 Achnairn ☎(0549) 2058
May–Sep
Attractive farmhouse with good views of Loch Shin. Situated 100 yards off the A838 and 5m from Lairg.
3rm (1fb) B&bfr£6
CTV 3P arable beef sheep mixed

FH Mrs V Mackenzie **5 Terryside** *(NC570110)* ☎(0549) 2332
May–Sep
Two-storey stone farmhouse on roadside with distant views of Loch Shin. 3½m N off A838.
3rm *B&bfr£6
CTV P mixed

FH Mrs M Sinclair **Woodside** *(NC533147)* West Shinness ☎(0549) 2072
May–Sep
Homely house overlooking Loch Shin with Ben More in the background. Situated 7m from Lairg on the A838.
3rm B&b£6
CTV 4P 360acres cattle sheep mixed

LAMBERHURST
Kent
Map **5** TQ63

INN *Chequers* School Hill ☎Tunbridge Wells (0892) 890260
4 CTV in all bedrooms Ⓡ D10pm
30P

LAMLASH
Isle of Arran, Strathclyde *Buteshire*
Map **10** NS03

GH Glenisle Hotel ☎(07706) 258
Apr–Oct
Victorian house with extensions standing on main road in small village, with sea views. 9-hole putting green.
16hc 1 2 (4fb) Ⓡ B&b£7.20–£11 Bdi£10.58–£14 W£50.40–£98 M
LDO6pm
CTV 18P

GH Marine House Hotel ☎(07706) 298
Mar–Oct
Converted and modernised coastguard building in own grounds of ¾acre with views over to Holy Isle.
19rm 12hc 6 (6fb) Ⓡ B&bfr£9.20 Bdifr£12.65 Wfr£64.40 M
CTV 16P

LANCASTER
Lancashire
Map **7** SD46

GH Belle-Vue 1 Belle-Vue Ter, Greaves ☎(0524) 67751
6hc (3fb) TV in 4 bedrooms Ⓡ B&b£8.50–£10
CTV 6P
Ⓥ

LANCING
West Sussex
Map **4** TQ10

GH Beach House Hotel 81 Brighton Rd ☎(0903) 753368
Homely, comfortable seafront guesthouse.
6hc (2fb) Ⓡ B&b£6.50–£7.50 W£42–£49
CTV 6P

GH Seaways 83 Brighton Rd ☎(0903) 752338
Simple seafront guesthouse.
6hc (1fb) B&b£7–£8 W£45–£50 M
CTV 4P

INN Sussex Pad Hotel Old Shoreham Rd ☎Shoreham-by-Sea (07917) 4647
A modern, well-appointed inn with elegant restaurant.
9 CTV in all bedrooms Ⓡ B&b£12–£24 Bdi£20.50–£36 L£8.50–£12 D10pm £8.50–£12 S%
60P
Credit cards 1 2 3 5

L'ANCRESSE
Guernsey, Channel Islands
Map **16**

GH Lynton Private Hotel Hacsé Ln ☎Guernsey (0481) 45418
mid May–Sep
14rm 4hc 3 7 (2fb) Ⓡ B&b£9.50–£13 Bdi£13–£16.50 W£66.50–£91 L
LDO6.45pm
Lic CTV 20P nc5yrs

LANGDALE, GREAT
Cumbria
Map **11** NY30

GH New Dungeon Ghyll Hotel ☎(09667) 213
Mar–Nov
19hc (5fb) B&b£10.95–£12.95 Bdi£19.50 LDO7pm
Lic CTV 20P

INN *Three Shires* ☎(09667) 215
Little Langdale
Mar–Oct rs Winter wknds
Small, friendly, family run inn with bright, attractive bedrooms; set in peaceful lakeland valley.
8hc 1 (2fb)
Lic 20P

LANGHO
Lancashire
Map **7** SD73

GH Mytton Fold Farm Whalley Rd ☎Blackburn (0254) 48255
4 (3fb) CTV in all bedrooms Ⓡ *B&b£11–£17 Bdi£16.50–£28.50 W£77–£119 M LDO9.30pm
Lic 25P
Credit cards 1 3 Ⓥ

LANGLAND BAY
West Glamorgan
Map **2** SS68
See also Bishopston and Mumbles

GH Brynteg Hotel 1 Higher Ln ☎Swansea (0792) 66820
Closed Xmas
10rm 8hc 2 (5fb) Ⓡ B&b£9.20–£9.80 Bdi£13.80–£15 W£73.60–£86.25 L
LDO5pm
Lic CTV 9P
Ⓥ

GH Wittemberg Hotel 2 Rotherslade Rd ☎Swansea (0792) 69696
Closed Xmas
Family-run hotel a few minutes walk from Rotherslade Bay.
11rm 3hc 8 (2fb) Ⓡ B&b£10–£14.50 Bdi£15.50–£20 W£75–£110 L
LDO7pm
Lic CTV 12P nc5yrs

LANGPORT
Somerset
Map **3** ST42

GH Ashley The Avenue ☎(0458) 250386
8hc (2fb) B&bfr£8 Bdifr£12.25 Wfr£49.50 M
Lic CTV 12P

LANLIVERY
Cornwall
Map **2** SX05

FH Mr & Mrs J Linfoot **Treganoon** *(SX065589)* ☎Bodmin (0208) 872205
Etr–Oct
Farmhouse with small garden in fairly isolated position and beautiful countryside.
7rm 6hc (3fb) Ⓡ B&b£7–£7.50 Bdi£9–£10 W£45–£47 L (W only Jul & Aug)
LDO7pm
Lic CTV 8P 100acres beef
Ⓥ

LARGS
Strathclyde *Ayrshire*
Map **10** NS25

GH *Aubery* 22 Aubery Cres ☎(0475) 672330
Apr–Sep
Listed two-storey terraced house in secluded position on sea front.
6hc (2fb) LDO5.30pm
CTV 6P

GH Gleneldon Hotel 2 Barr Cres ☎(0475) 673381
Closed Feb
Victorian detached house on corner site with gardens and situated on main road near sea front.
9rm 3 (2fb) Ⓡ *B&bfr£15 Bdifr£22 W£130 LDO7.45pm
Lic CTV 18P

GH Holmesdale 74 Moorburn Rd ☎(0475) 674793
Closed Oct, Xmas & New Year
Detached house on elevated corner site located ¼m from sea front, close to Inverclyde recreational centre.
8hc (2fb) B&b£7.50 Bdi£11 W£51 LDO9am
CTV 4P

GH Sunbury 12 Aubery Cres ☎(0475) 673086
Mar–Oct
Terraced house on seafront overlooking river and islands.
6hc (2fb) Ⓡ B&b£7.50 Bdi£11.50 W£50 LDO4pm
CTV 6P
Ⓥ

LATHERON
Highland *Caithness*
Map **15** ND13

FH Mrs C Sinclair **Upper Latheron** *(ND195352)* ☎(05934) 224
May–Oct
Two-storey farmhouse in elevated position with fine views across the North sea. The farm runs its own Ponies of Britain Pony Trekking Centre.
4rm (2fb) B&b£7–£8 W£49 M
CTV 4P U 200acres arable beef mixed
Ⓥ

LAXTON
Nottinghamshire
Map **8** SK76

FH Mrs L S Rose **Moorgate** *(SK726665)* ☎Tuxford (0777) 870274
½m S unclass rd.
3rm (1fb) B&b£7–£7.50 Bdi£10–£10.50 W£45 M LDO8.30pm
CTV 8P 145acres mixed
Ⓥ

LEAMINGTON SPA (ROYAL)
Warwickshire
Map **4** SP36
See plan

GH Beech Lodge Hotel 28 Warwick New Rd ☎(0926) 22227 Plan **1** *A3*
Friendly hotel with good sized rooms, many with private facilities.
12rm 6 (1fb) Ⓡ B&b£14.75–£16.25 Bdi£22.75–£24.75 W£98–£108 M S% LDO8pm
Lic CTV 15P nc5yrs

GH Buckland Lodge Hotel 35 Avenue Rd ☎(0926) 23843 Plan **2** *C1*
Closed Xmas rs wknds
11rm 10hc 1 (2fb) B&b£9.75–£10.50 Bdi£15.50–£17 LDOnoon
Lic CTV 12P

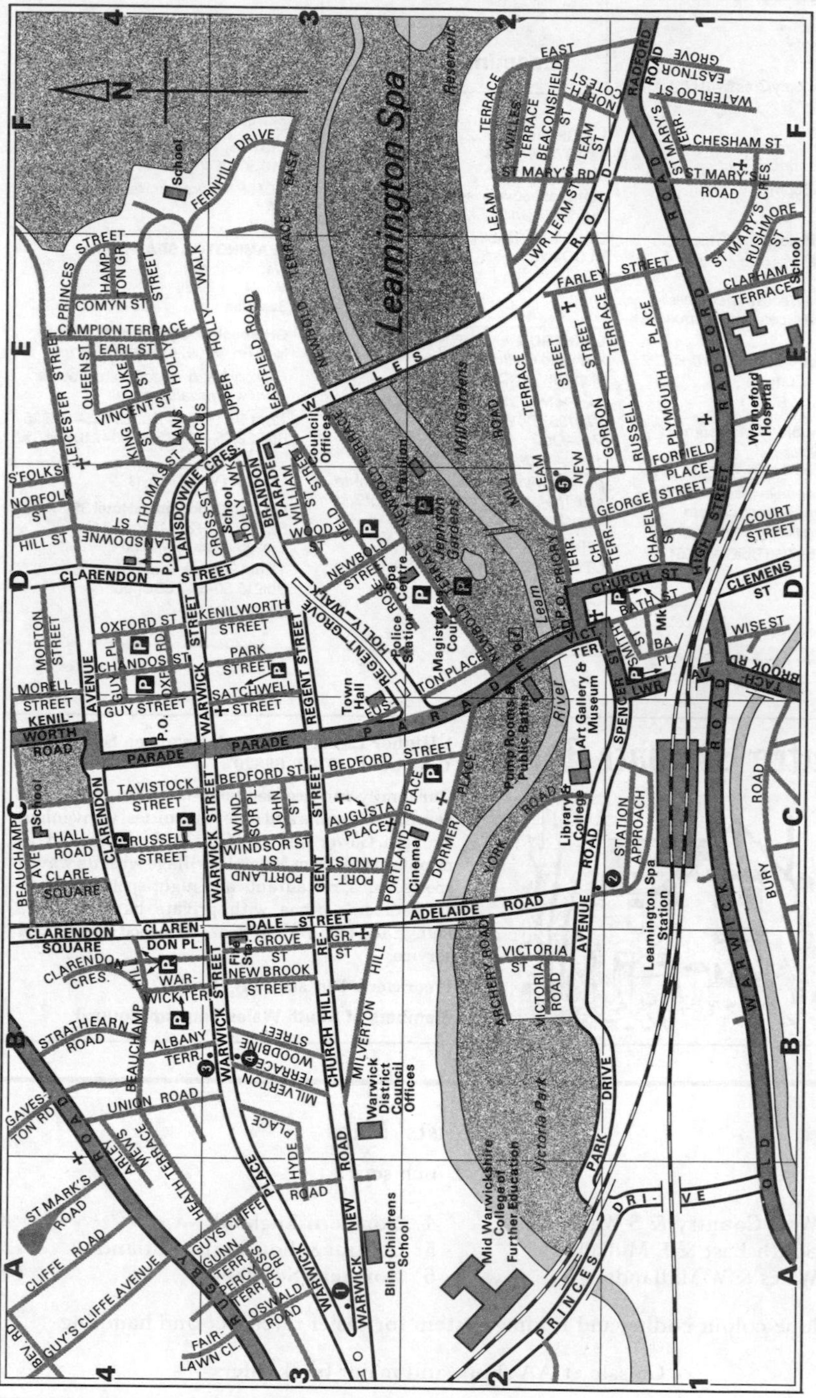

Leamington Spa

1 Beech Lodge Hotel
2 Buckland Lodge Hotel
3 Glendower
4 Poplars Hotel
5 Westella Hotel

GH Glendower 8 Warwick Pl ☎(0926) 22784 Plan **3** *B3*
Closed Xmas wk
8rm 7hc (3fb) Ⓡ B&b£8.50–£10 Bdi£12.50–£14 W£56–£65 M LDO4pm
CTV 9P 1 nc5yrs

GH Poplars Hotel 1 Milverton Ter ☎(0926) 28335 Plan **4** *B3*
Closed 25 & 26 Dec
13hc 2 3 (4fb) CTV in all bedrooms Ⓡ B&b£10.45–£11.45 Bdi£15.70–£17.70 W£69–£101 L LDO3pm
Lic CTV 11P

GH Westella Hotel 26 Leam Ter ☎(0926) 22710 Plan **5** *D2*
Large, brightly painted Georgian terraced house near town centre.
10hc (3fb) B&b£8.50–£9.50 LDO7pm
CTV 10P
Credit cards 1 3

FH Mrs R Gibbs **Hill** *(SP343637)* Lewis Rd, Radford Semele ☎(0926) 37571
Closed Xmas
Farmhouse situated in large attractive garden. 2½m SE off A425.
3hc (1fb) Ⓡ B&b£8 Bdi£13 W£50 M LDO9am
CTV 4P 350acres arable beef sheep mixed
Ⓥ

LEEDS
West Yorkshire
Map **8** SE33

GH Aragon Hotel 250 Stainbeck Ln, Meanwood ☎(0532) 759306
Closed Xmas rs Etr
11rm 6hc 3 2 (1fb) CTV in 3 bedrooms B&bfr£10.81 Bdifr£16.70 LDO7pm
Lic CTV 12P
Credit cards 1 3 5

GH Ash Mount Hotel 22 Wetherby Rd, Roundhay ☎(0532) 658164
Closed Xmas wk
Three-storey detached Victorian house in suburbs.
14hc (2fb) Ⓡ *B&bfr£11.50
CTV 12P

GH *Budapest Private Hotel* 14 Cardigan Rd, Headingley ☎(0532) 756637
13hc (2fb) LDO3pm
CTV 10P
Ⓥ

GH Clock Hotel 317 Roundhay Rd, Gipton Wood ☎(0532) 490304
22rm 19hc 1 2 (1fb) Ⓡ B&b£11.70–£15.50 Bdi£16.70–£20.50 LDO8pm
Lic CTV 15P

GH Highfield Hotel 79 Cardigan Rd, Headingley ☎(0532) 752193
10hc (1fb) B&b£10
CTV 7P

GH *Oak Villa Hotel* 57 Cardigan Rd, Headingley ☎(0532) 758439
Large Victorian semi-detached house with walled garden.
10hc (2fb)
CTV 8P

GH *Trafford House Hotel* 18 Cardigan Rd, Headingley ☎(0532) 752034
15hc (4fb) LDO3pm
CTV 9P
Ⓥ

LEEK
Staffordshire
Map **7** SJ95

GH Peak Weavers Hotel 21 King St ☎(0538) 383729
12rm 8hc 1 1 (3fb) TV in 4 bedrooms Ⓡ B&b£9.20 Bdi£14.95 W£84 L LDO7pm
Lic CTV 8P 4
Ⓥ

⊢×⊣ **FH** Mrs D Needham **Holly Dale** *(SK019556)* Bradnop ☎(0538) 383022
Apr–Oct
Two-storey, stone-built farmhouse typical of the area. 2m SE on unclass road off A523.
2hc ✱ B&b£6–£6.50 W£40 M
📺 TV 2P 72acres dairy

LEE-ON-THE-SOLENT
Hampshire
Map **4** SU50
⊢×⊣ **GH Ash House Private Hotel** 35 Marine Parade West ☎(0705) 550240
Quiet house overlooking the Solent with many antique items of interest in all rooms.
6hc (2fb) B&b£7.50–£9.50
📺 CTV 6P

LEICESTER
Leicestershire
Map **4** SK50
GH Alexandra Hotel 342 London Rd, Stoneygate ☎(0533) 703056
Closed Xmas rs Etr
18rm 10hc 3→ 5⋒ (2fb) ✱ B&b£20–£25 Bdi£26–£28 LDO4pm
Lic 📺 CTV 16P
Credit cards 1 3

GH Burlington Hotel Elmfield Av ☎(0533) 705112

Leek — Leominster

17rm 10hc 1⋒ (1fb) CTV in 10 bedrooms ✱ Ⓡ B&b£12.10 Bdi£17.50 LDO7.30pm
Lic 📺 CTV
Credit card 1

GH Daval Hotel 292 London Rd ☎(0533) 708234
Closed Xmas
14rm 10hc (2fb) CTV in 8 bedrooms TV in 6 bedrooms B&b£14.50 Bdi£21 LDO7.30pm
Lic 📺 CTV 20P
Ⓥ

GH Old Tudor Rectory Main St, Glenfield ☎(0533) 312214
3m W A50.
15hc 2→ 3⋒ (5fb) CTV in 10 bedrooms TV in 1 bedroom Ⓡ *B&b£11.50–£16.10 Bdi£18.45–£23 S% LDO9.30pm
Lic 📺 CTV 40P
Credit cards 1 3
Ⓥ

GH Scotia Hotel 10 Westcotes Dr ☎(0533) 549200
Closed Xmas wk

9hc (A 6hc) (1fb) B&b£13–£14 Bdi£19–£20 LDO5.30pm
Lic 📺 CTV 4P

GH Stanfre House Hotel 265 London Rd ☎(0533) 704294
12hc (1fb) *B&b£10.50
Lic 📺 CTV 6P
Credit card 1

LEINTWARDINE
Hereford & Worcester
Map **7** SO47
FH Mrs Y Lloyd ***Upper Buckton*** *(SO384733)* (Guestaccom) ☎(05473) 634
Mar–Nov
1½m SW off A4113.
3hc ✱ (W only Aug)
CTV P nc4yrs 285acres mixed

LEOMINSTER
Hereford & Worcester
Map **3** SO45
⊢×⊣ **GH Broadward Lodge Guesthouse & Restaurant** Hereford Rd ☎(0568) 2914
6hc 1→ (3fb) ✱ B&b£7.50–£9.50 Bdi£11–£13 W£72–£83 Ł LDO9pm
Lic 📺 CTV 20P ⌂
Credit card 1

⊢FH Mrs S J Davenport **Stagbatch** *(SO465584)* ☎(0568) 2673
Closed Xmas
14th-century, half-timbered listed building in peaceful setting. 2m W off A4112.
3⇌ B&b£7.75–£9 W£52–£60 M
CTV 6P nc12yrs (heated) 30acres sheep mixed racing stables

FH Mrs H C Davies ***Wharton Bank*** *(SO508556)* ☎(0568) 2575
Closed Xmas
Extensively modernised farmhouse. Comfortable pleasant atmosphere.
3hc 1⇌ (1fb)
CTV 4P 1 nc6yrs 212acres mixed

LERAGS
Strathclyde *Argyllshire*
Map **10** NM82

GH Foxholes Hotel Cologin ☎Oban (0631) 64982 Oban plan **4** *C1*
Apr–Oct, Xmas & New Year
Modern, hospitable guesthouse in hilly countryside 3m from Oban.
6rm 4hc 2⇌ (2fb) CTV in 6 bedrooms Ⓡ B&b£17.50–£20 Bdi£23–£25.50 W£161–£178.50 L LDO8.30pm
Lic 10P

LERWICK
Shetland
Map **16** HU44

GH Glen Orchy 20 Knab Rd ☎(0595) 2031
Conversion of church hall and adjoining manse on brow of hill in Lerwick.
6hc (1fb) B&b£9–£10 W£48–£63 M
CTV

LESLIE
Fife
Map **11** NO20

GH Rescobie Hotel (Guestaccom) ☎Glenrothes (0592) 742143
rs last 2wks Jul
Nicely appointed mansion set in own grounds in residential area of town.
8rm 5hc 3⋔ CTV in all bedrooms Ⓡ B&b£21 Bdi£29 W£203 L LDO9pm
Lic 10P
Credit cards 1 2 3 Ⓥ

LEW
Oxfordshire
Map **4** SP30

FH Mrs M J Rouse **University** *(SP322059)* ☎Bampton Castle (0993) 850297
Closed Xmas & New Year
Picturesque Cotswold farmhouse with comfortable bedrooms, good food and hospitality.
6rm 2⇌ 3⋔ (2fb) B&b£10–£12.50 Bdi£17.50–£20 W£122.50 L LDO4pm
Lic CTV 10P nc5yrs 216acres dairy

LEWDOWN
Devon
Map **2** SX48

⊢**FH** Mrs M E Horn **Venn Mill** *(SX484885)* ☎Bridestowe (083786) 288
Etr–Oct
Large modern bungalow set in peaceful surroundings with river fishing and private trout lake. 400 yards from the A30.
4rm 3hc (1fb) B&b£7–£8 Bdi£10–£11 W£70 L LDO4pm
CTV 4P 2 160acres beef sheep mixed
Ⓥ

LEWIS, ISLE OF
Western Isles *Ross & Cromarty*
Map **13**
See Stornoway

LEYBURN
North Yorkshire
Map **7** SE19

GH Eastfield Lodge St Matthews Ter ☎Wensleydale (0969) 23196
8hc (A 2hc) (2fb) CTV in 6 bedrooms Ⓡ B&b£11–£12.50 W£70–£80.50 M LDO8.30pm
Lic CTV 14P
Credit card 3

LEYSTERS
Hereford & Worcester
Map **3** SO56

FH Mrs C E Moseley ***Moor Abbey*** *(SO545633)* ☎(056887) 226
Former monastery about 400 years old with original oak staircase and upper floors. Dining room in refectory with open log fire. Access to farm is from A4112, 1m SW.
3hc (2fb)
8P nc5yrs 246acres mixed sheep

LHANBRYDE
Grampian *Morayshire*
Map **15** NJ26

INN Tennant Arms 15 St Andrews Rd ☎(034384) 2226
5rm 3hc 2⇌ CTV in 1 bedroom TV in 4 bedrooms *B&b£13 L£1.95–£3.50&alc High Tea £3.50 LDO8.30pm
20P

LICHFIELD
Staffordshire
Map **7** SK10

GH Oakleigh House Hotel 25 St Chads Rd (Guestaccom) ☎(05432) 22688
Closed 2 wks Xmas
11rm 2⇌ 9⋔ CTV in all bedrooms Ⓡ B&b£10–£17 Bdi£16–£23 LDO9.30pm
Lic 20P nc4yrs

LIFTON
Devon
Map **2** SX38

⊢**GH Mayfield House** Tinhay ☎(056684) 401
7rm 6hc 1⋔ (2fb) Ⓡ B&b£5–£6 Bdi£9–£10 LDO9pm
Lic CTV 7P

LINCOLN
Lincolnshire
Map **8** SK97

GH Brierley House Hotel 54 South Park ☎(0522) 26945
Closed Dec & Jan
Predominantly commercial trade at this large family run hotel.
12rm 6hc 2⇌ 4⋔ CTV in 10 bedrooms TV in 2 bedrooms ✱ *B&b£10 Bdi£14.50 LDO4.30pm
Lic ⅢⅢ CTV P nc5yrs
Ⓥ

GH D'Isney Place Hotel Eastgate ☎(0522) 38881
14rm 13⇌ 1⋔ (2fb) CTV in all bedrooms Ⓡ B&bfr£27.50
ⅢⅢ 5P
Credit card 1

LINDRIDGE
Hereford & Worcester
Map **7** SO66

⊢⊣**FH** Mrs J M May **Middle Woodston** *(SO673696)* ☎Eardiston (058470) 244
¾m N off A443.
3hc (1fb) ✱ B&b£8 Bdi£14 W£50 M LDO4pm
ⅢⅢ CTV 6P 10acres mixed fruit & organic
Ⓥ

LINLITHGOW
Lothian *West Lothian*
Map **11** NS97

⊢⊣**FH** Mrs A Hay **Belsyde House** *(NS976755)* Lanark Rd ☎(0506) 842098
Mar–Oct
1½m SW A706.
4rm 2hc (1fb) ✱ Ⓡ B&b£7.50–£8.50 Bdi£11–£12 W£50 M LDOnoon
ⅢⅢ CTV 10P ⌂ 106acres beef sheep mixed
Ⓥ

⊢⊣**FH** Mrs W Erskine **Woodcockdale** *(NS973760)* Lanark Rd ☎(0506) 842088
Modern two-storey house lying approximately 50 yards from farmyard and outbuildings.
3rm (1fb) ✱ B&bfr£8 W£55 M
ⅢⅢ CTV 12P ⌂ 700acres dairy sheep
Ⓥ

LISKEARD
Cornwall
Map **2** SX26

⊢⊣**FH** S A Kendall **Tencreek** *(SX265637)* ☎(0579) 43379
A well-kept 16th-century listed farmhouse set in beautiful countryside, 1m from Liskeard.
2hc ✱ Ⓡ B&b£8 W£52.50 M
CTV 2P 252acres mixed

LITTLE BREDY
Dorset
Map **3** SY58

FH Mrs D M Fry **Foxholes** *(SY582882)* ☎Long Bredy (03083) 395
Closed 20–27 Dec
2m E of village.
6rm 5hc (6fb) B&b£9–£10 Bdi£12 W£70–£75 L (W only Jul & Aug) LDO4.30pm
Lic ⅢⅢ CTV 6P ⌂ 390acres dairy mixed

LITTLE DEWCHURCH
Hereford & Worcester
Map **3** SO53

⊢⊣**FH** Mrs G Lee **Cwm Craig** *(SO535322)* ☎Carey (043270) 250
Large, spacious farmhouse next to farm buildings in quiet wooded surroundings, few minutes drive from the Wye Valley.
3rm 2hc (1fb) ✱ B&b£6–£7 W£42 M
ⅢⅢ CTV 4P 190acres arable beef dairy mixed
Ⓥ

LITTLE EVERSDEN
Cambridgeshire
Map **5** TL35

FH Mrs F Ellis **Five Gables** *(TL371535)* Bucks Ln ☎Comberton (022026) 2236
May–Sep
A listed farmhouse, parts of which date from the 15th and 17th centuries, with oak beams and inglenook fireplace.
3rm 2hc (1fb) ✱ B&b£9–£10
CTV 3P nc12yrs 240acres arable

LITTLEHAM
Devon
Map **2** SS42

INN ***Crealock Arms*** Shutta Farm ☎Bideford (02372) 77065
3hc ✱
Lic CTV 30P 🚗

LITTLEHAMPTON
West Sussex
Map **4** TQ00

GH Regency Hotel 85 South Ter ☎(0903) 717707
Closed Xmas
Simply furnished house with a friendly atmosphere.
8hc (3fb) CTV in all bedrooms Ⓡ B&b£9.50–£12 Bdi£14.50–£17 W£56–£65 M LDO7.30pm
Lic ⅢⅢ CTV
Credit cards 1 2 3 4 5

LITTLE HAVEN
Dyfed
Map **2** SM81

GH Pendyffryn Private Hotel ☎Broad Haven (043783) 337
May–Sep
Pleasant detached house in elevated position.
7hc (6fb) TV in all bedrooms ✱ Ⓡ *B&b£8.62 Bdi£14.37 W£88.55 L
Lic ⅢⅢ CTV 6P nc4yrs

LITTLEHEMPSTON
Devon
Map **3** SX86

FH Mrs E P Miller **Buckyette** *(SX812638)* ☎Staverton (080426) 638
May–Sep
7rm 6hc (4fb) ✱ B&b£8.40 Bdi£12.60 W£77.70 L LDO7pm
CTV 8P ⌂ 51acres grassland

LITTLE MILL
Gwent
Map **3** SO30

⊢⊣**FH** Mrs A Bradley **Pentwyn** *(SO325035)* ☎(049528) 249
Closed Dec & Jan
A 16th-century modernised farmhouse set in ½ acre of garden with swimming pool. Situated off A4042, ½m E of junction with A4042.
4hc (1fb) ✱ B&b£7.50 Bdi£12 W£84 L LDOnoon
Lic ⅢⅢ CTV P nc3yrs ⇌ (heated) 150acres arable beef
Ⓥ

LITTLE TORRINGTON
Devon
Map **2** SS41

⊢⊣**FH** Mrs E K Watkins **Lower Hollam** *(SS501161)* ☎Torrington (0805) 23253
Apr–Oct
Historic house situated in a peaceful, picturesque position. Good play facilities for children.
4hc (3fb) ✱ B&b£6.50–£7.50 Bdi£10.50–£12 Wfr£60 L LDO5.30pm
CTV 4P ⌂ 230acres beef sheep mixed
Ⓥ

LITTON
Derbyshire
Map **7** SK17

⊢⊣**FH** Mrs A Barnsley **Dale House** *(SK160750)* ☎Tideswell (0298) 871309
Closed Xmas
Large, stone-built Edwardian farmhouse situated on edge of picturesque village off B6049.
3rm (1fb) ✱ B&b£7–£8 W£45 M
ⅢⅢ TV P nc4yrs 100acres sheep

FH Mr & Mrs H Radford ***Hall*** *(SK159754)* ☎Tideswell (0298) 871124
100-year-old stone-built farmhouse overlooking village.
3rm 1hc (2fb) ✱
Lic ⅢⅢ TV 4P ⌂ 10acres mixed

LIVERPOOL
Merseyside
Map **7** SJ39

GH Aachen Hotel 91 Mount Pleasant ☎051-709 3477
17rm 10hc 1 (6fb) CTV in all bedrooms Ⓡ B&b£11–£12 Bdi£14–£16 W£70–£84 M LDO9.30pm
Lic CTV P
Credit cards 1 2 3 5 Ⓥ

GH New Manx Hotel 39 Catherine St ☎051-708 6171
15rm 9hc 3 (3fb) Ⓡ B&b£11 W£60 M
CTV
Credit cards 1 2 3 4 5 Ⓥ

LIZARD
Cornwall
Map **2** SW71

GH Mounts Bay Hotel Penmenner Rd ☎(0326) 290305
Closed Xmas, Jan & Feb rs Nov, Dec & Mar
Secluded family residence standing in own grounds overlooking Kynance Cove.
10rm 2hc (5fb) Ⓡ B&bfr£11 Bdifr£15 Wfr£97 L LDO6pm
Lic CTV 12P

GH Parc Brawse House ☎(0326) 290466
Mar–Oct
Comfortable character house, friendly attention from family. Property overlooks sea across farmland.
6hc Ⓡ B&b£9–£9.50 Bdi£14–£15 W£85–£90 L LDO7pm
Lic CTV 6P nc7yrs
Ⓥ

GH Penmenner House Hotel Penmenner Rd (Guestaccom) ☎(0326) 290370
Mar–Oct
Friendly family hotel. Home cooking including local produce, fresh fish, Cornish cream.
8rm 3hc 5 (2fb) Ⓡ *B&bfr£10 Bdifr£14 Wfr£70 M LDO6pm
Lic CTV 12P

LLANARTHNEY
Dyfed
Map **2** SN52

INN Golden Grove Arms Hotel ☎Dryslwyn (05584) 551
Closed 14 Jan–Feb rs 1–13 Jan
A rural inn with pleasant bars and pine-fitted bedrooms.
8rm 7hc 1 Ⓡ B&b£10 Bdi£15 W£70 M L£5alc D10pm £7.50alc
CTV 200P 3
Credit cards 1 2 3 5

FH Mrs M M Bowen **Brynheulog** *(SN533195)* ☎Dryslwyn (05584) 567
Farmhouse with large lawns, located about ½m from the village.
5rm 3hc 1 (1fb) B&b£6.50–£7 Bdi£10–£10.50 W£70 L LDOprevious evening
CTV 4P 1 21acres dairy mixed
Ⓥ

LLANBEDR (*Near Painscastle*)
Powys
Map **3** SO14

FH Mrs I M Lewis **Llanbedr Hall** *(SO144466)* ☎Painscastle (04975) 274
Apr–Oct
2rm B&b£7–£7.50 W£49 M
CTV P nc4yrs 210acres mixed

LLANBEDROG
Gwynedd
Map **6** SH33

GH Glyn Garth Hotel ☎(0758) 740268
closed Xmas Day
Detached hotel on edge of village.
10rm 7hc (3fb) Ⓡ B&b£10–£14 Bdi£16–£20 W£65–£90 L LDO10.30pm
Lic CTV 15P
Credit cards 1 3

LLWYNCELYN GUEST HOUSE

LLANDOVERY, DYFED,
SA20 0EP
Tel: 0550-20566

Proprietors:
Mr & Mrs D. C. Griffiths.

Ideal Holiday Centre. Our Guest House with its rural, riverside setting, full central heating and homely atmosphere offers Bed & Breakfast, or Dinner, Bed & Breakfast at moderate rates.

BRYN NICHOLAS FARM

Gwystre, Llandrindod Wells, Powys LD1 6RW
Tel: Penybont (059 787) 447

Enjoy peace and quiet at Bryn Nicholas Farm. A traditional Beef/Sheep farm in beautiful, tranquil Mid-Wales. A traditional house with full Central Heating offers a choice of one Double or Two Twin Bedded Rooms all with Tea/Coffee making facilities, Wash basins and Shaver Points. A comfortable Lounge with Colour TV and separate Dining Room. Your comfort and enjoyment is the main concern.

Bed & Breakfast from £7. Bed, Breakfast & Dinner from £12.

Please write or telephone to:
Proprietor: Margaret A Davies.

HOLLY FARM

Howey, LLANDRINDOD WELLS, Powys
Telephone: (0597) 2402

Holly Farm is a 70 acre working farm of sheep and cattle. 1½ miles south of the spa town of Llandrindod Wells, and ¼ mile off the A483 in quiet unspoilt countryside. Ideally situated for the holidaymaker who wishes to either motor, walk or cycle over some of the most open and beautiful countryside in mid Wales. Good home cooked food is served, using the farm's own produce whenever possible. Holders of Wales Tourist Board Farmhouse Award. The accommodation consists of 2 double and 1 family bedrooms all with H&C, bathroom with shower, sitting room, dining room. Open from April to November. Car essential, ample parking. Rates reduced for children.

Welcome to

Three Wells Farm

Howey, Llandrindod Wells, Powys LD1 5PB
Tel: 0597 2484

Licensed Farm Guesthouse. 50 acre working farm situated in the beautiful countryside 1½ miles from spa town Llandrindod Wells. Good home cooked food. Large dining room. Lounge. Sunlounge. TV room. Bar. Fully centrally heated, 8 bedrooms 4 with en suite, all with tea/coffee making. Holders of WTB Farm House award, FGH Diploma. Fire Certificate held.

Ron and Margaret Bufton

LLANBERIS
Gwynedd
Map **6** SH56

GH Lake View Hotel Tan-y-Pant
☎(0286) 870422
Cottage-style guesthouse alongside A4086 overlooking Llyn Padarn. 1m NW of town.
7rm 5hc 2⋒ (2fb) TV in 2 bedrooms ✦ Ⓡ B&b£9.50–£12.50 LDO9.30pm
Lic ▥ CTV 10P
Ⓥ

LLANBOIDY
Dyfed
Map **2** SN22

⊢⊣ **FH** Mrs B Worthing **Maencochyrwyn** *(SN181243)* Login
☎Hebron (09947) 283
Apr–Oct
Small isolated farmhouse in elevated position overlooking its own farmland and hills. 3½m WNW of Llanboidy on unclass road to East Login/Llanglydwen road.
3rm (1fb) B&b£6 Bdi£10 W£42 M LDO6pm
CTV P 80acres dairy
Ⓥ

LLANDDEINIOLWEN
Gwynedd
Map **6** SH56

FH Mrs Kettle **Ty'n-Rhos** *(SH548672)* Seion ☎Port Dinorwic (0248) 670489
Closed Xmas & New Year
½m N unclass rd.
10rm 2hc 8⇀ (3fb) CTV in 8 bedrooms ✦ Ⓡ B&b£10–£13 Bdi£15–£18 Wfr£95 Ⱡ (W only mid Jul–Aug) LDO6.30pm
Lic ▥ 10P 72acres dairy mixed
Ⓥ

LLANDDERFEL
Gwynedd
Map **6** SH93

INN *Bryntirion Hotel* ☎(06783) 205
Closed Sun
Rurally situated in peaceful Dee Valley about ½ mile from river.
3hc
Lic ▥ CTV 40P river

LLANDINAM
Powys
Map **6** SO08

FH Mrs M C Davies **Trewythen** *(SJ003901)* ☎Caersws (068684) 444
Apr–Oct
Farmhouse dating from 1820 situated 2m SW of Caersws, on unclass road off B4569.
2hc (1fb) ✦ *B&b£8–£8.50 Bdi£12–£12.50 W£58 M LDO6pm
▥ CTV P sheep mixed
Ⓥ

LLANDOGO
Gwent
Map **3** SO50

GH Brown's Hotel & Restaurant
☎Dean (0594) 530262
Feb–Nov
Proprietor-run tea rooms and guesthouse. Walking distance of the river.
8hc B&b£9.50 LDO8.30pm
Lic CTV 20P

INN Sloop ☎Dean (0594) 530291
Closed 24–26 Dec
4rm 3⇀ 1⋒ Ⓡ B&b£12–£17.50 W£72–£105 M LDO10pm
▥ 40P 2🚗 🚗
Credit cards 1 2 3 5

LLANDOVERY
Dyfed
Map **3** SN73

GH Llwyncelyn ☎(0550) 20566
Closed Xmas
Proprietor-run comfortable guesthouse with grounds running down to river.
6hc (3fb) ✦ B&b£9.90–£11 Bdi£16.50–£17.60 W£105–£111.65 Ⱡ LDO7.30pm
Lic ▥ CTV 12P ⅃

LLANDRINDOD WELLS
Powys
Map **3** SO06

GH *Griffin Lodge Hotel* Temple St (Guestaccom) ☎(0597) 2432
Closed Xmas & New Year
Detached Victorian stone-built house near centre of town.
10hc (1fb) ✦
Lic ▥ CTV 6P

FH Mrs P Lewis **Bailey Einon** *(SO078616)* Cefnllys ☎(0597) 2449
Apr–Sep
Stone-built Georgian farmhouse, part of which dates back to the 17th-century. 2m E of town on unclass road.
3hc ✦ Ⓡ B&b£7–£8 Bdi£11–£12
▥ CTV 3P nc10yrs 280acres beef sheep mixed

⊢⊣ **FH** Mrs D Evans **Dolberthog** *(SO048602)* Dolberthog Ln ☎(0597) 2255
Victorian stone farmhouse on outskirts of town.
2hc (2fb) ✦ B&b£7.50 Bdi£11 W£45 M LDO2pm
▥ TV 2P ⅃ 150acres mixed

LLANDRINIO
Powys
Map **7** SJ21

⊢⊣ **FH** Mrs G M Wigley **Newhall** *(SJ296171)* ☎Llanymynech (0691) 830384
Apr–Oct
Modernised farmhouse, partly dating from 16th century.
2rm 1hc 1⋒ (2fb) ✦ B&b£8 Bdi£13 W£56 M LDO4pm
CTV P snooker 265acres arable beef dairy

FH Mrs S M Pritchard **Rhos** *(SO276174)* ☎Llanymynech (0691) 830785
3rm 1hc 1⇀ (1fb) B&b£8.50–£9 Bdi£12.50–£13 W£75–£78 LDOam
▥ CTV 12P 265acres arable stock

LLANDUDNO
Gwynedd
Map **6** SH78
See plan

GH *Bella Vista Private Hotel* 72 Church Walks ☎(0492) 76855 Plan **1** *B4*
mid Jan–mid Dec
Victorian terraced house. 2 minutes from beach and shops.
12hc CTV in all bedrooms Ⓡ LDO5pm
Lic ▥ CTV 12P sea

⊢⊣ **GH Braemar Hotel** 5 St Davids Rd ☎(0492) 76257 Plan **2** *B3*
Edwardian house in residential area 5 minutes from beach and shops.
6hc (1fb) B&b£6.50–£7.50 Bdi£9.50–£10 W£50–£55 Ⱡ LDO6pm
▥ CTV ⅌ nc5yrs
Ⓥ

⊢⊣ **GH Brannock Private Hotel** 36 St Davids Rd ☎(0492) 77483 Plan **3** *B3*
Edwardian house in residential area 5 minutes from beach and shops.
6hc (3fb) ✦ B&b£7.50 Bdi£10.50 LDO8pm
Lic ▥ CTV 5P
Ⓥ

GH *Brigstock Private Hotel* 1 St David's Pl ☎(0492) 76416 Plan **4** *B3*
Apr–Oct
In corner position in quiet residential area 5 minutes to shops and beach.
10hc (3fb) LDO6pm
Lic CTV 7P
Ⓥ
See advertisement on page 210

⊢⊣ **GH Britannia Hotel** 15 Craig-y-Don Pde ☎(0492) 77185 Plan **5** *E3*
Closed Xmas
Single-fronted Victorian terraced house on Promenade, ¾ mile from main shopping area.
9rm 6hc 2⋒ (8fb) CTV in all bedrooms Ⓡ B&b£7–£7.50 Bdi£10–£11
CTV ⅌

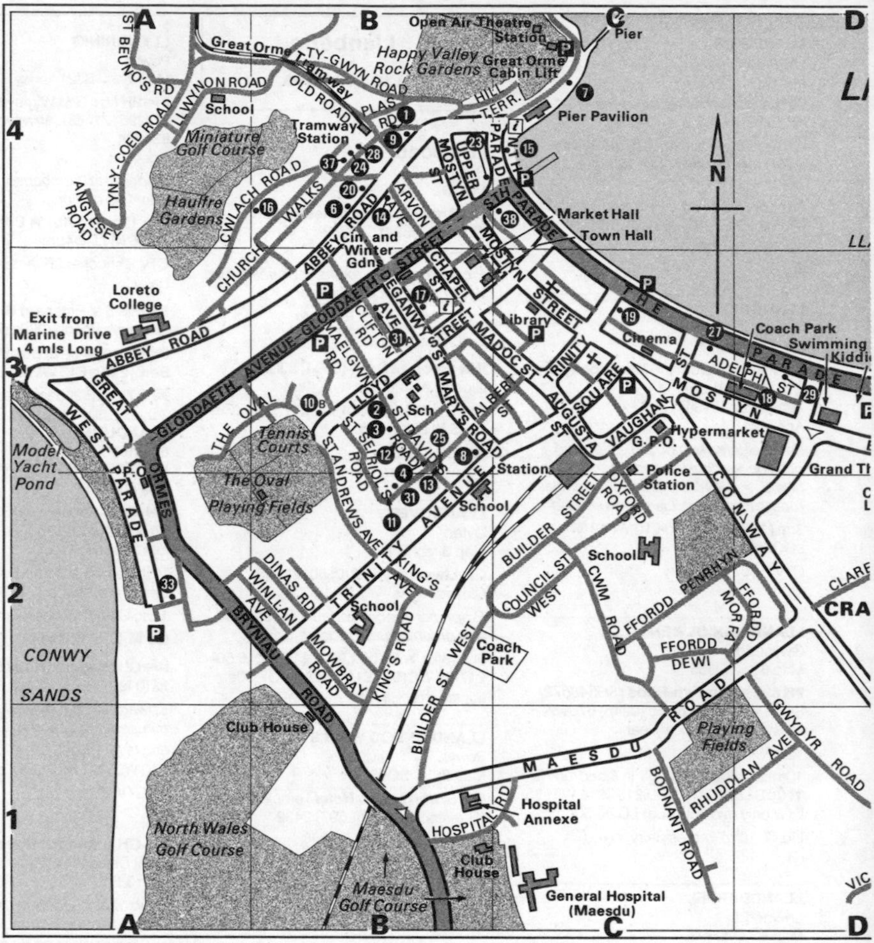

A B C D
4
3
2
1
Open Air Theatre Station
Pier
Happy Valley Rock Gardens
Great Orme Cabin Lift
Great Orme Tramway
TY-GWYN ROAD
OLD ROAD
ST BEUNO'S RD
LLWYNON ROAD
School
Tramway Station
Pier Pavilion
Miniature Golf Course
TYN-Y-COED ROAD
ANGLESEY ROAD
Haulfre Gardens
CWLACH ROAD
CHURCH WALKS
ABBEY ROAD
ARVON AVE
MOSTYN ST
UPPER MOSTYN ST
NORTH PARADE
STH PARADE
Market Hall
Town Hall
N
Cin. and Winter Gdns
GLODDAETH STREET
CHAPEL ST
MOSTYN STREET
THE PARADE
Loreto College
Exit from Marine Drive 4 mls Long
ABBEY ROAD
GLODDAETH AVENUE
DEGANWY AVE
CLIFTON RD
MAELGWYN RD
Library
Cinema
Coach Park
Swimming
ADELPHI ST
GREAT ORMES RD
WEST PARADE
Model Yacht Pond
P.O.
THE OVAL
Tennis Courts
The Oval Playing Fields
LLOYD ST
Sch
ST DAVID'S ROAD
ST SERIOL'S ROAD
ST ANDREWS AVE
ST MARY'S ROAD
ALBERT ST
MADOC ST
TRINITY SQUARE
AUGUSTA ST
VAUGHAN ST
MOSTYN ST
Hypermarket
G.P.O.
Station
Police Station
Grand Th
School
TRINITY AVENUE
OXFORD ROAD
BUILDER STREET
CONWAY
DINAS RD
WINLLAN AVE
KING'S AVE
School
COUNCIL ST WEST
CWM ROAD
FFORDD PENRHYN
MOR FA
FFORDD
CRA
CONWY SANDS
BRYNIAU ROAD
MOWBRAY ROAD
KING'S ROAD
BUILDER ST WEST
Coach Park
FFORDD DEWI
Club House
MAESDU ROAD
Playing Fields
GWYDYR ROAD
RHUDDLAN AVE
BODNANT ROAD
North Wales Golf Course
HOSPITAL RD
Hospital Annexe
Club House
Maesdu Golf Course
General Hospital (Maesdu)

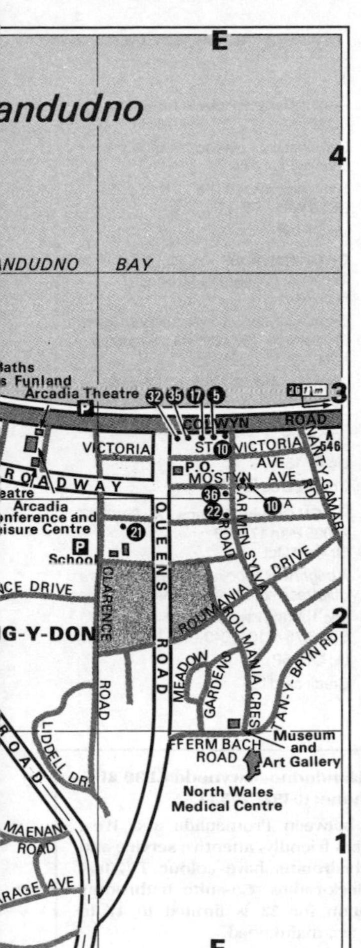

Llandudno

Llandudno

- **1** Bella Vista Private Hotel
- **2** Braemar Hotel
- **3** Brannock Private Hotel
- **4** Brigstock Private Hotel
- **5** Britannia Hotel
- **6** Bryn Rosa
- **7** Bryn-y-Mor Private Hotel
- **8** Buile Hill Private Hotel
- **9** Capri Hotel
- **10** Carmel Private Hotel
- **10A** Hotel Carmen
- **10B** Causeway Hotel
- **11** Cleave Court Private Hotel
- **12** Cliffbury Private Hotel
- **13** Cornerways Private Hotel
- **14** Craig Ard Private Hotel
- **15** Cumberland Hotel
- **16** Cwlach Private Hotel
- **17** Grafton Hotel
- **17A** Granby
- **18** Heath House Hotel
- **19** Lynwood Private Hotel
- **20** Mayfair Private Hotel
- **21** Mayfield Private Hotel
- **22** Minion Private Hotel
- **23** Montclare Hotel
- **24** Nant-y-Glyn
- **25** Oakwood
- **26** Orotava Private Hotel
- **27** Penelope Private Hotel
- **28** Plas Madoc Private Hotel
- **29** Puffin Lodge Hotel
- **31** Rosaire Private Hotel
- **31A** St Davids
- **32** St Hilary Hotel
- **33** Sandilands Private Hotel
- **35** Stratford Hotel
- **36** Tilstone Private Hotel
- **37** Warwick Hotel
- **38** Wilton Hotel

⊢×⊣ **GH Bryn Rosa** 16 Abbey Rd
☎(0492) 78215 Plan **6** *B4*
Semi-detached Victorian house in residential area. Short walk to shops and beach.
7hc (3fb) B&b£7 Bdi£10.50 W£72 Ⱳ LDO5pm
▥ CTV 6P nc2yrs
Credit card 1

GH Bryn-y-Mor Private Hotel North Pde
☎(0492) 76790 Plan **7** C4
Mar–Oct
Semi-detached Victorian house on Promenade 2 minutes from shops.
17hc (5fb) TV in all bedrooms ★ ® B&b£9–£14 Bdi£12–£17 W£72–£92 Ⱳ LDO5.30pm
CTV ⌂
Ⓥ

GH Buile Hill Private Hotel 46 St Mary's Rd ☎(0492) 76972 Plan **8** *B3*
Etr–Oct
Edwardian house in corner position in residential area. Short walk to shops and beach.
12rm 5hc 3⇥ 4⋒ (1fb) ★ ® B&bfr£10 Bdifr£13 W£88–£120 Ⱳ LDOnoon
Lic ▥ CTV 6P

⊢×⊣ **GH Capri Hotel** 70 Church Walks
☎(0492) 79177 Plan **9** *B4*
Etr–Oct
Victorian terraced house offering a warm welcome and bright comfortable bedrooms. Situated within easy reach of shops and promenade.
8hc (3fb) ★ B&b£7.50–£8 Bdi£9.75–£10.25 W£52.50–£56 Ⱳ LDO6pm
Lic ▥ CTV 3P nc6yrs
Ⓥ

⊢×⊣ **GH Carmel Private Hotel** 17 Craig-y-Don Pde, Promenade ☎(0492) 77643
Plan **10** *E3*
Etr–6 Oct
Terraced Victorian house on Promenade, ¾m from main shopping area.
10hc 5⋒ (5fb) CTV in 3 bedrooms ® B&b£7.25–£8 Bdi£10.25–£11 W£50.75–£56 M LDO6.30pm
▥ CTV 7P nc4yrs

⊢★⊣ **GH Hotel Carmen** Carmen Sylva Rd, Craig-y-Don ☎(0492) 76361 Plan **10A** *E3*

16hc 1⋒ (8fb) B&b£7.99–£8.99 Bdi£11.45–£12.50 W£54.63–£62.95 M LDO5pm

Lic ⅢI CTV ♠

GH Causeway Hotel Lloyd St ☎(0492) 75466 Plan **10B** *B3*

8hc 2⋒ (1fb) ® B&b£9–£11 Bdi£12–£14 W£73–£80 L LDO7pm

Lic ⅢI CTV 8P 1⌂ nc6yrs

⊢★⊣ **GH Cleave Court Private Hotel** 1 St Seiriol's Rd ☎(0492) 77849 Plan **11** *B2*

Apr–Oct

Edwardian house in residential area. Short walk to shops and beach.

9rm 8hc (2fb) ★ B&b£7–£8 Bdi£9–£10 W£49–£56 M

CTV 8P nc3yrs

Credit cards 1 3

⊢★⊣ **GH Cliffbury Private Hotel** 34 St Davids Rd ☎(0492) 77224 Plan **12** *B3*

May–Sep

Semi-detached house in quiet residential area, a short walk to shops and beach.

6hc (2fb) ★ B&b£6–£6.50 Bdi£8.25–£9 W£42–£45 L LDO5pm

CTV 4P nc6yrs

Credit cards 1 3

Llandudno

GH Cornerways Private Hotel 2 St Davids Pl ☎(0492) 77334 Plan **13** *B2*

Mar–mid Oct

Corner situation in quiet residential area. Short walk to beaches and shops.

10rm 6hc 2⇌ 2⋒ (3fb) CTV in 10 bedrooms ★ ® B&b£8.50–£9.50 Bdi£11.50–£12.50 W£59.50–£66.50 M LDO5pm

ⅢI CTV 5P nc7yrs

GH Craig Ard Private Hotel Arvon Av ☎(0492) 77318 Plan **14** *B4*

Closed Dec

Semi-detached Victorian house in quiet residential street adjacent to beaches and shops.

18hc (4fb) B&b£8.20–£9.20 Bdi£10.35–£11.50 W£57.20–£62.20 M LDO4pm

Lic ⅢI CTV 10P

Credit card 1

⊢★⊣ **GH Cumberland Hotel** North Parade ☎(0492) 76379 Plan **15** *C4*

Victorian mid-terrace by Central Promenade and adjacent shops.

18rm 17hc 1⋒ (10fb) CTV in all bedrooms B&b£7.50–£8.50 Bdi£10.50–£11.50 W£73.50–£80.50 L LDO6.30pm

Lic ⅢI CTV 3P

Ⓥ

⊢★⊣ **GH Cwlach Private Hotel** Cwlach Rd ☎(0492) 75587 Plan **16** *B4*

Detached Victorian house set high over town on the Orme.

10hc (4fb) B&b£6–£6.25 Bdi£8.25–£8.50 W£57.75–£59.50 L

Lic CTV ♪

GH Grafton Hotel 13 Craig-y-Don Pde ☎(0492) 76814 Plan **17** *E3*

Feb–Nov

Double-fronted Victorian mid-terrace on Promenade. ¾m from main shopping area.

20rm 2hc 4⇌ 14⋒ (4fb) CTV in all bedrooms ★ ® Bdi£11.50–£14.50 Bdi£15.50–£18.50 W£110–£130 L LDO5.30pm

Lic ⅢI 15P

Credit cards 1 3

⊢★⊣ **GH Granby** Deganwy Av ☎(0492) 76095 Plan **17A** *B3*

Etr–mid Oct

A bright well appointed guesthouse in a quiet residential area and near the shops.

9hc 1⋒ (6fb) ★ ® B&b£7–£8 Bdi£8.75–£10 W£49–£56 M LDO6pm

Lic CTV 5P

Credit card 1

GH Heath House Hotel Central Prom ☎(0492) 76538 Plan **18** *D3*
21hc (14fb) ✱ B&b£8.28–£10.35 Bdi£11.90–£14.38 W£83.32–£100.66 ⱡ LDO4pm
Lic ▥ CTV 3P
Ⓥ

⊢⊣ **GH Lynwood Private Hotel** Clonmel St ☎(0492) 76613 Plan **19** *C3*
Four-storey single-fronted mid-Victorian terrace just off Promenade near shops.
13hc (9fb) Ⓡ B&b£7.50–£10 Bdi£10–£12 W£68–£76 ⱡ LDO5pm
Lic CTV ₱
Ⓥ

⊢⊣ **GH Mayfair Private Hotel** 4 Abbey Rd ☎(0492) 76170 Plan **20** *B4*
Mar–Oct
13rm 7hc 4➡ 2⋒ (7fb) ✱ Ⓡ B&b£8–£9.50 Bdi£12–£14 W£55–£65 ⱡ
Lic ▥ CTV 3P
Credit card 1

GH *Mayfield Private Hotel* 19 Curzon Rd, Craig-y-Don ☎(0492) 77427 Plan **21** *E2*
In quiet residential area, ¾ mile from main shopping area.
8hc (5fb) CTV in all bedrooms Ⓡ LDO7pm
CTV ₱

Llandudno

⊢⊣ **GH Minion Private Hotel** 21–23 Carmen Sylva Rd, Craig-y-Don ☎(0492) 77740 Plan **22** *E2*
Etr–Oct
Detached Edwardian house in quiet residential area adjacent to beach.
16rm 12hc 4⋒ (4fb) B&b£5.75–£6 Bdi£9.50–£10.50 W£40.25–£42 ⱡ LDO4.30pm
Lic CTV 8P

⊢⊣ **GH Montclare Hotel** North Pde ☎(0492) 77061 Plan **24** *B4*
Mar–Oct rs Jan–Feb
Victorian mid-terrace overlooking North Parade adjacent to shops.
15hc (6fb) CTV in all bedrooms B&b£8–£8.50 Bdi£11–£12 W£68–£78 ⱡ LDO7.30pm
Lic ▥ CTV 4P

⊢⊣ **GH Nant-y-Glyn** 59 Church Walks ☎(0492) 75915 Plan **24** *B4*
Closed Xmas & New Year
Semi-detached Victorian house with good views over the town.
10hc (3fb) ✱ Bdi£6–£8 Bdi£9–£11 W£61.25–£75.25 ⱡ
▥ CTV nc5yrs

GH Oakwood 21 St Davids Rd ☎(0492) 79208 Plan **25** *B3*
end May–early Sep
Attractive property set in pleasant lawns some 7 minutes from sea front.
7rm 6hc 1➡ (2fb) ✱ *B&b£6.50 Bdi£9.25 W£63 ⱡ (W only Jul & Aug) LDO3.30pm
Lic ▥ CTV ₱

GH Orotava Private Hotel 105 Glan-y-Mor Rd, Penrhyn Bay ☎(0492) 49780 Plan **26** *E3*
Etr–Oct
Detached Edwardian house, 2 miles from town below Little Orme.
6hc ✱ B&b£9 Bdi£14.25 W£63 M LDO6.30pm
CTV 6P nc6yrs
Ⓥ

GH *Penelope Private Hotel* Central Prom ☎(0492) 76577 Plan **27** *C3*
Single-fronted mid-terraced Victorian house. Short walk to shops.
24hc (14fb)
Lic CTV 10P sea

⊢⊣ **GH Plas Madoc Private Hotel** 60 Church Walks ☎(0492) 76514 Plan **28** *B4*
Mar–Oct
Semi-detached Victorian house, close to shops and Promenade. →

6rm (1fb) ® B&b£7–£7.25 Bdi£9.75–£10 W£49–£50.75 M LDOnoon

Lic CTV 6P nc5yrs

Credit cards 1 2 3 ⓥ

GH Puffin Lodge Hotel Promenade ☎(0492) 77713 Plan **29** *D3*
Apr–Oct

Single-fronted Victorian mid-terrace on Central Promenade within a short walk of shops.

12rm 2⇌ 1fl (9fb) ★ ® B&b£9 Bdi£13 W£91 ⅃ LDO5pm

Lic CTV 16P

ⓥ

See advertisement on page 213

⊢×⊣ **GH Rosaire Private Hotel** 2 St Seiriol's Rd ☎(0492) 77677 Plan **31** *B2*
May–Sep

Edwardian house in quiet corner position of residential area.

12hc (3fb) ★ B&b£7–£7.50 Bdi£9.50–£10 Wfr£67 ⅃ LDO5pm

Lic CTV 5P nc5yrs

Credit cards 1 2 3 4 5

See advertisement on page 213

⊢×⊣ **GH St Davids** 32 Clifton Rd ☎(0492) 79216 Plan **31A** *B3*

Semi-detached building in central position just off sea front.

Llandudno

6hc (3fb) ★ B&b£8–£8.25 Bdi£10–£10.50 W£56–£57.75 M

Lic ▥ CTV

⊢×⊣ **GH St Hilary Hotel** 16 Promenade, Craig-y-Don Pde ☎(0492) 75551 Plan **32** *E3*

Single-fronted Victorian terraced house ¾ mile from main shopping area.

11hc 1fl (8fb) ® B&b£7–£7.50 Bdi£10–£11.60 LDO6pm

CTV ⊅

GH *Sandilands Private Hotel* Dale Rd, West Shore ☎(0492) 75555 Plan **33** *A2*
Apr–Sep

Detached Edwardian house in quiet residential area adjacent to West Shore.

11hc (5fb) LDO6pm

Lic ▥ CTV 12P sea

⊢×⊣ **GH Stratford Hotel** Promenade, Craig-y-Don ☎(0492) 77962 Plan **35** *E3*

10hc (3fb) ® Bdi£7.50 Bdi£11 W£52.50 ⅃ LDO6pm

Lic ▥ CTV ⊅

⊢×⊣ **GH Tilstone Private Hotel** Carmen Sylva Rd, Craig-y-Don ☎(0492) 75588 Plan **36** *E3*

On corner position in quiet secondary shopping area; short walk to beach.

7hc ★ B&b£8 Bdi£12.50 W£53 ⅃ LDO5pm

Lic ▥ CTV ⊅ nc12yrs

GH Warwick Hotel 56 Church Walks ☎(0492) 76823 Plan **37** *B4*
Apr–mid Oct

Semi-detached Victorian house with good views over the town.

17rm 13hc 4⇌ (10fb) ® B&b£8.50–£9.75 Bdi£11.50–£12.75 W£79.75–£86 ⅃ LDO7pm

Lic ▥ CTV

ⓥ

⊢×⊣ **GH Wilton Hotel** South Parade ☎(0492) 76086 Plan **38** *C4*
Mar–Oct

16rm 14hc 1⇌ 1fl (7fb) CTV in all bedrooms ® B&b£8–£10 Bdi£10–£13 W£75–£85 ⅃ LDO4.30pm

Lic

LLANEGRYN
Gwynedd
Map **6** SH60
FH E Pughe ***Argoed*** *(SH604057)*
☎Tywyn (0654) 710361
Etr–Sep
Homely and comfortable farmhouse with tasty country food.
3hc
TV 3P 7acres

LLANELIDAN
Clwyd
Map **6** SJ15
FH M Mosford **Trewyn** *(SJ128515)*
Rhydymeudwy ☎Clawdd Newydd (08245) 676
Mar–Oct
Homely farmhouse situated in valley of fields and trees. 2m E of B5429 and 5m from Ruthin.
2rm 1hc (1fb) ✱ *B&bfr£5.50 Bdifr£7.50 Wfr£38 M LDO6pm
CTV P 80acres mixed

LLANELLI
Dyfed
Map **2** SN50
GH Lyndhurst Private Hotel 88 Queen Victoria Rd ☎(05542) 2046
18hc (2fb) ✱ ® B&b£8.75–£9 Bdi£14 W£60–£70 M LDO6.30pm
Lic CTV 12P
Credit cards 1 3

LLANFACHRETH *(Near Dolgellau)*
Gwynedd
Map **6** SH72
FH Mrs C Tudor-Owen **Rhedyncochion** *(SH762222)* ☎Rhydymain (034141) 600
Etr–Oct
100-year-old, stone-built farmhouse with extensive views of surrounding countryside and mountains. 1m of trout fishing is available to guests.
2rm 1hc (1fb) ✱ *B&b£7 Bdi£12 W£80.50 L
CTV P 200acres mixed

LLANFAIR DYFFRYN CLWYD
Clwyd
Map **6** SJ15
FH Mrs E Jones **Llanbenwch** *(SJ137533)* ☎Ruthin (08242) 2340
Feb–Nov
Modernised farmhouse with oak beams situated on the A525, Wrexham to Ruthin road.
3hc (2fb) ✱ ® B&bfr£6 W£60 L LDO7pm
CTV P 40acres arable beef mixed
Ⓥ

LLANFAIRFECHAN
Gwynedd
Map **6** SH67
GH Plas Menai Christian Hotel Penmaenmawr Rd ☎(0248) 680346
Mar–Oct & Xmas
Victorian detached hotel alongside A55, near to shops.
32hc 1 4 (9fb) ✱ B&b£8–£9 Bdi£11.50–£12.50 W£75–£83 L (W only mid Jul–end Aug) LDO2pm
CTV 15P

LLANFAIR WATERDINE
Shropshire
Map **7** SO27
INN Red Lion ☎Knighton (0547) 528214
Closed Xmas Day
3rm 2hc 1 ✱ B&b£16.10 Bdi£24.50 L£8.10&alc D£8.10&alc LDOam
25P nc16yrs

LLANFIHANGEL-YNG-NGWYNFA
Powys
Map **6** SJ01
FH Mrs E Jenkins ***Cyfie*** *(SJ085147)*
☎Llanfyllin (069184) 451
17th-century beamed farmhouse set in peaceful undulating countryside. 2m S on unclass rd off B4382.
2hc (2fb) ®
CTV 10P 180acres mixed sheep
Ⓥ

LLANFIHANGEL-Y-PENNANT
Gwynedd
Map **6** SH60
FH Mrs M Jones ***Tynybryn*** *(SH659080)*
☎Abergynolwyn (065477) 277
1½m SW unclass rd.
3rm 1hc 1 1 (1fb) ✱ ® LDO8pm
CTV P 300acres mixed
Ⓥ

LLANGATTOCK
Powys
Map **3** SO21
GH *Park Place* The Legar
☎Crickhowell (0873) 810562
Family-run guesthouse.
7hc (2fb) ✱ ®
CTV 10P river

LLANGOLLEN
Clwyd
Map **7** SJ24
FH Mrs A Kenrick **Rhydonnen Ucha Rhewl** *(SJ174429)* ☎(0978) 860153
Etr–Nov
Large, stone-built, three-storey farmhouse, pleasantly situated with shooting on farm and trout fishing on River Dee (permit).
4hc (2fb) B&b£7–£7.50 Bdi£11–£11.50 W£75 L LDO5pm
CTV 6P 120acres dairy

LLANGRANOG
Dyfed
Map **2** SN35
INN Pentre Arms Hotel ☎(023978) 229
Simply-appointed inn situated in friendly seaside town.
10hc B&b£8.50–£9.50 Bdi£13.50–£14 W£85–£90 L Bar lunch £1.20–£3 D5.30pm fr£6&alc
CTV 7P

LLANGURIG
Powys
Map **6** SN98

INN ***Blue Bell*** ☎(05515) 254

10hc 1⇌

♨ CTV 40P ⇌ river

LLANRUG
Gwynedd
Map **6** SH56

FH Mr & Mrs D Mackinnon **Plas Tirion** *(SH524628)* ☎Caernarfon (0286) 3190
Apr–Oct

100-year-old farmhouse set in open position with traditional farm buildings and gardens.

6rm 5hc (2fb) ✱ Ⓡ ✱B&b£7 Bdi£14 W£98 Ⱡ (W only Jul & Aug)

Lic ♨ CTV P ⌂ 450acres mixed

LLANRWST
Gwynedd
Map **6** SH86

⊢⊣**FH** Mrs M Owen **Bodrach** *(SH852629)* Carmel ☎(0492) 640326
20 Apr–Nov

Situated in peaceful setting approximately 5 miles from Llanwrst

2rm (1fb) ✱ B&b£7–£7.50 Bdi£9.50–£10 W£49 M̸ LDO8pm

♨ TV 6P 184acres sheep mixed

LLANSANTFFRAID-YM-MECHAIN
Powys
Map **7** SJ22

⊢⊣**FH** Mrs M E Jones **Glanvyrnwy** *(SJ229202)* ☎Llansantffraid (069181) 258
Mar–Oct

200-year-old stone-built farmhouse, set back from main road, with pleasant lawns and orchard.

3rm 2hc (1fb) ✱ B&b£7–£8 Bdi£11–£12 W£49–£56 M̸ LDO6pm

CTV 3P nc3yrs 42acres dairy

LLANUWCHLLYN
Gwynedd
Map **6** SH83

FH Mrs D Bugby **Bryncaled** *(SH866314)* ☎(06784) 270

Closed Xmas Day

Small farmhouse with oak beamed dining room, overlooking Aran mountains. A fishing river runs through the grounds. Approximately 6 miles from Bala.

3rm 2hc ✱ Ⓡ ✱B&b£8 Bdi£12 W£80 Ⱡ LDOam

Lic ♨ CTV 6P ♩ 500acres beef sheep

LLANVAIR-DISCOED
Gwent
Map **3** ST49

⊢⊣**FH** Mrs A Barnfather **Cribau Mill** *(ST454941)* Cribau Mill, The Cwm ☎Shirenewton (02917) 528
Closed Xmas

Modern house at the head of the "cwm". (Off unclass road joining Llanvair-Discoed & Shirenewton).

2rm 2⋒ (2fb) ✱ Ⓡ B&b£7 W£49 M̸

CTV 2P 33acres mixed

Ⓥ

⊢⊣**FH** Mr & Mrs S Price **Great Llanmellyn** *(SO456923)* ☎Shirenewton (02917) 210
Apr–Sep

Charming character family farmhouse with flag-stoned floors, in pleasant location, 5 miles W of Chepstow off A48.

2hc (1fb) ✱ Ⓡ B&b£7 W£42 M̸

♨ CTV 3P 250acres dairy mixed

LLANWARNE
Hereford & Worcester
Map **3** SO52

FH Mrs I E Williams ***Llanwarne Court*** *(SO503275)* ☎Golden Valley (0981) 540385
15 Jan–15 Dec

Farmhouse, set away from the main road with large walled garden.

4hc 1⋒ (1fb) ✱ Ⓡ

♨ CTV P ⌂ 260acres mixed

Ⓥ

LLANWDDYN
Powys
Map **6** SJ01

⊢⊣**FH** R B & H A Parry **Tynymaes** *(SJ048183)* ☎(069173) 216
May–Oct

The farmhouse is situated on the edge of the nature reserve at Lake Vyrnwy.

3hc (1fb) B&b£8–£8.50 Bdi£11–£12 W£56 M̸ LDO6pm

CTV P 420acres mixed

Ⓥ

LLANWRTYD WELLS
Powys
Map **3** SN84

GH Carlton Court Hotel Dolecoed Rd ☎(05913) 494

9hc 1⇌ (3fb) ✱B&b£8.50 Bdi£15 Wfr£79.95 Ⱡ LDO9pm

Lic ♨ CTV 3P sauna bath

GH Lasswade House (Guestaccom) ☎(05913) 515

Detached Edwardian house on edge of village.

7hc (4fb) TV in 4 bedrooms Ⓡ B&b£9–£12 Bdi£15.50–£20.50 W£93–£123 Ⱡ LDO9pm

Lic ♨ 9P ⇋ sauna bath

LLECHWEDD
Gwynedd
Map **6** SH77

⊢⊣**FH** Mrs C Roberts **Henllys** *(SH767758)* ☎Conwy (049263) 3269
Apr–Oct

Large, stone-built farmhouse, signposted from main road.

2rm (1fb) B&b£6.50–£8 Bdi£9–£11 LDO7pm

CTV 3P 140acres sheep mixed

FH Mr & Mrs J A Jones ***Llechan Ucha*** *(SH755757)* ☎Conwy (049263) 2451
Etr–Oct

Modern farmhouse in isolated position, set high on mountainside with good views of the Conwy Valley.

3rm (1fb) LDO4pm

♨ CTV 3P 102acres beef mixed sheep

LOCHEYNORT' (NORTH)
Isle of South Uist, Western Isles *Inverness-shire*
Map **13** NF72

FH Mrs A MacDonald **Arinabane** *(NF787283)* 8 North Locheynort ☎Bornish (08785) 379
Apr–Oct
A modern house and croft in peaceful location on north side of a sea loch. 1½m ESE unclass road.
2hc *B&b£7 Bdi£10.50 W£70 L
LDO9pm
3P 30acres sheep mixed fish

LOCHGOILHEAD
Strathclyde *Argyllshire*
Map **10** NN10

FH Mrs J H Jackson **Pole** *(NN192044)* ☎(03013) 221
Etr–Sep
Pleasant well-kept farmhouse, 2 miles from Lochgoilhead.
3rm (1fb) B&b£6.50–£7 Bdi£10.50–£11 W£42–£45 M (W only Jun–Aug)
LDO7.30pm
CTV P 7,500acres sheep

LOCHINVER
Highland *Sutherland*
Map **14** NC02

GH Ardglas ☎(05714) 257
Closed Dec & Jan
Modern villa on elevated site overlooking the village.
8hc (3fb) B&b£7–£8 W£49–£56 M
CTV 16P

GH Hillcrest Badnaban ☎(05714) 391
Apr–Oct
Modern bungalow set in unspoilt environment, 2 miles S of the village on unclass rd.
4hc ® B&bfr£8 Bdifr£13.50
LDO6.30pm
CTV 4P

LOCHRANZA
Isle of Arran, Strathclyde *Buteshire*
Map **10** NR95

GH Kincardine Lodge ☎(077083) 267
Apr–Oct
Converted house dating from 1910, standing in own grounds overlooking the bay and castle.
6hc (4fb) ® *B&b£7.50–£8.50 Bdi£10.80–£11.80 W£52.50–£59.50 M
LDO6.30pm
CTV 6P

LOCHWINNOCH
Strathclyde *Renfrewshire*
Map **10** NS35

FH Mrs A Mackie ***High Belltrees*** *(NS377584)* ☎(0505) 842376
Situated 1m off the A737, Paisley to Largs road. Overlooks Castle Semple Loch which has an R.S.P.B. Bird Sanctuary and yachting facilities.
4rm 3hc (2fb) ® LDO9am
CTV 5P 220acres dairy mixed

LOCKERBIE
Dumfries & Galloway *Dumfriesshire*
Map **11** NY18

GH Rosehill Carlisle Rd ☎(05762) 2378
Victorian, two-storey, sandstone house with attractive garden.
5hc (3fb) B&b£7
CTV 6P

LODDISWELL
Devon
Map **3** SX74

FH Mrs A Pethybridge **Reads** *(SX727489)* ☎(054855) 317 (due to change to Kingsbridge (0548) 550317
May–Oct
Two-storey stone-built farmhouse in isolated position with fine views.
2rm 1hc (1fb) B&b£6.50–£7.50 W£45 M
TV 4P 80acres sheep mixed

LODDON
Norfolk
Map **5** TM39

FH Mrs G I Rackham **Stubbs House** *(TM358977)* ☎(0508) 20231
Feb–Nov
Fine, old Georgian farmhouse with excellent kitchen producing delicious, professional meals.
9rm 8hc 1 B&b£12 Bdi£17 W£85 L
LDO6.30pm
Lic CTV 18P nc10yrs 200acres arable
Ⓥ

LONDON
Greater London
Map **4 & 5**
See plans 1–4 pages 222–223
A map of the London postal area appears on pages 224 & 225
Places within the London postal area are listed below in postal district order commencing East then North, South and West, with a brief indication of the area covered. Detailed plans **1–3** show the locations of AA-listed hotels within the Central London postal districts which are indicated by a number. Plan **4** highlights the districts covered within the outer area keyed by a grid reference eg A5
Other places within the county of London are listed under their respective placenames and are also keyed to this plan or the main map section.

E18
South Woodford
London plan **4** E5

Grove Hill Hotel 38 Grove Hill, South Woodford ☎01-989 3344
Comfortably appointed small hotel offering good standard of service.
21hc 4 (2fb) CTV in all bedrooms ®
B&b£14.38 W£100.63 M
Lic CTV 7P 4
Ⓥ

N8
Hornsey
London plan **4** D5

Aber Hotel 89 Crouch Hill ☎01-340 2847
Converted private house offering simple accommodation and informal atmosphere.
8hc (4fb) ✯
▥ CTV ₱

NW2
Cricklewood
London plan **4** C4

⊢⊣ **Clearview House** 161 Fordwych Rd, Cricklewood ☎01-452 9773
6hc (1fb) TV in 4 bedrooms ✯ B&b£7 W£49 M
▥ CTV nc5yrs

Garth Hotel 70–76 Hendon Way, Cricklewood ☎01-455 4742
Well appointed hotel with well furnished bedrooms.
54rm 15hc 20➡ 19⋒ (10fb) CTV in all bedrooms ✯ ✻B&b£19.95–£26.95 LDO9pm
Lic ▥ CTV 36P
Credit cards 1 2 3 4 5

NW3
Hampstead and Swiss Cottage
London plan **4** D4

London N8 — London SE3

Frognal Lodge Hotel 14 Frognal Gdns, off Church Row, Hampstead (Minotel) ☎01-435 8238
Comfortable informal hotel.
17rm 10hc 7➡ (5fb) CTV in 9 bedrooms ✻B&b£17–£19 LDO9pm
Lic lift ▥ CTV ⌂
Credit cards 1 2 3 5 Ⓥ

NW6
Kilburn, West Hampstead
London plan **4** C4

Dawson House Hotel 72 Canfield Gdns ☎01-624 0079
Small, private hotel with comfortable accommodation and friendly atmosphere.
15hc ✯ B&b£9–£10.50
▥ CTV nc6yrs
Ⓥ

NW11
Golders Green
London plan **4** C5

Central Hotel 35 Hoop Ln, Golders Green ☎01-458 5636
Two modern buildings with well equipped bedrooms.
18hc (A 18➡) TV in 18 bedrooms ✯ B&b£20–£30
▥ CTV 8P
Credit cards 1 2 3 5 Ⓥ
See advertisement on page 226

Croft Court Hotel 44–46 Ravenscourt Av, Golders Green ☎01-458 3331
Modest but comfortable accommodation.
15rm 8hc 7➡ (7fb) TV in 8 bedrooms B&b£15–£24 Bdi£21.50–£30.50 W£100–£160 M LDO6pm
▥ CTV 4P
Ⓥ

SE3
Blackheath
London plan **4** E3

Bardon Lodge 15 Stratheden Rd, Blackheath ☎01-853 4051
Warm, friendly private hotel, tastefully decorated and offering good standard of accommodation.
10rm 8⋒ (3fb) CTV in 8 bedrooms TV in 2 bedrooms B&b£15–£20
▥ CTV 10P
Ⓥ

Details of the establishments shown on this map can be found under the *London Postal District* which follows the establishment name

London Plan 1

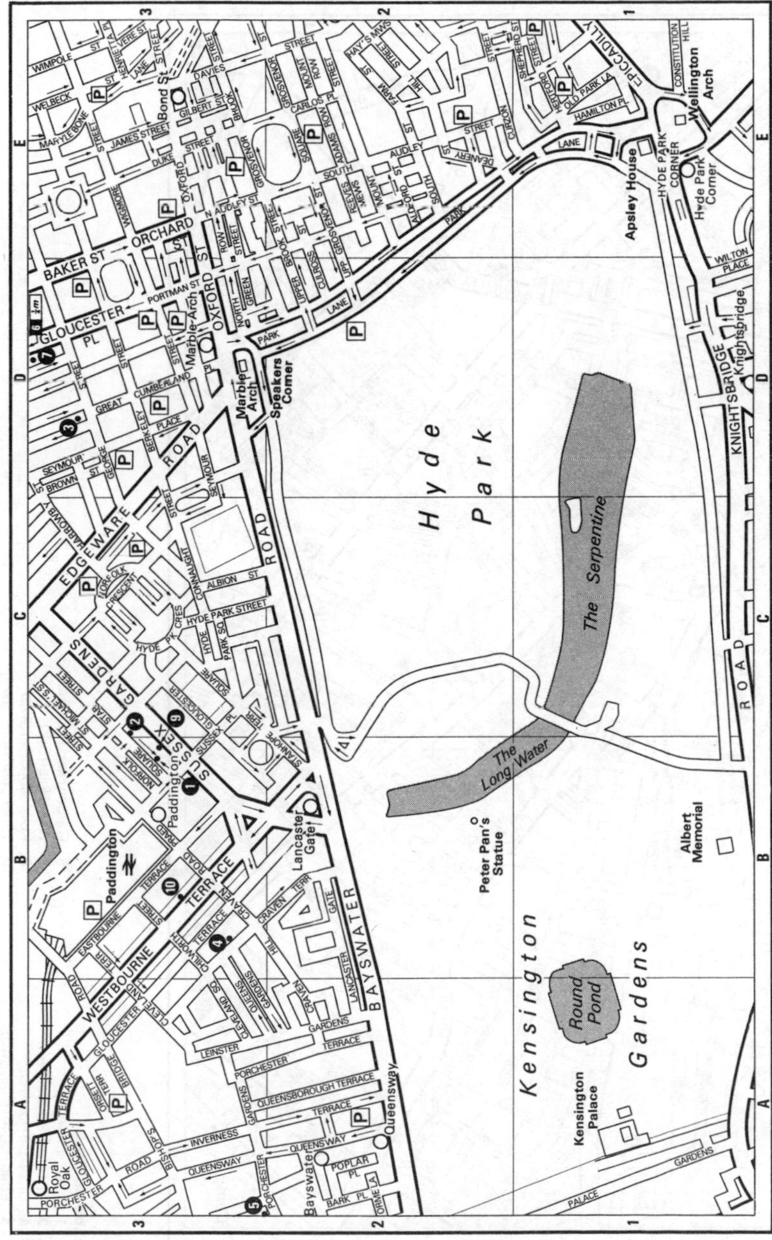

London Plan 1
1 Ashley Hotel *(W2)*
2 Camelot Hotel *(W2)*
3 Hotel Concorde *(W1)*
4 Dylan Hotel *(W2)*
5 Garden Court Hotel *(W2)*
6 Georgian House Hotel *(W1)*
7 Hart House Hotel *(W1)*
9 Nayland Hotel *(W2)*
10 Victoria Garden Hotel *(W2)*

London Plan 2

Details of the establishments shown on this map can be found under the *London Postal District* which follows the establishment name

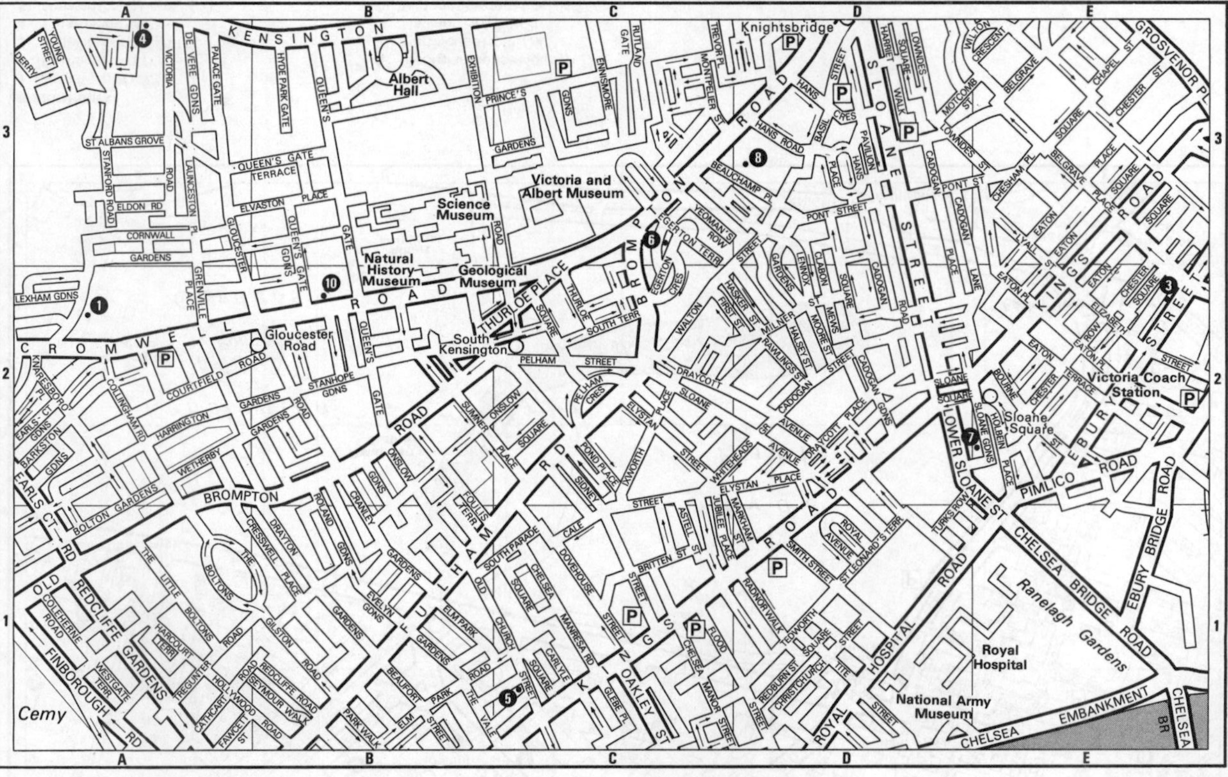

London Plan 2

- **1** Atlas Hotel *(W8)*
- **3** Chesham House *(SW1)*
- **4** Clearlake Hotel *(W8)*
- **5** Eden House Hotel *(SW3)*
- **6** Garden House Hotel *(SW3)*
- **7** Willet Hotel *(SW1)*
- **8** Knightsbridge *(SW3)*
- **10** Tudor Court Hotel *(SW7)*

Details of the establishments shown on this map can be found under the *London Postal District* which follows the establishment name

London Plan 3

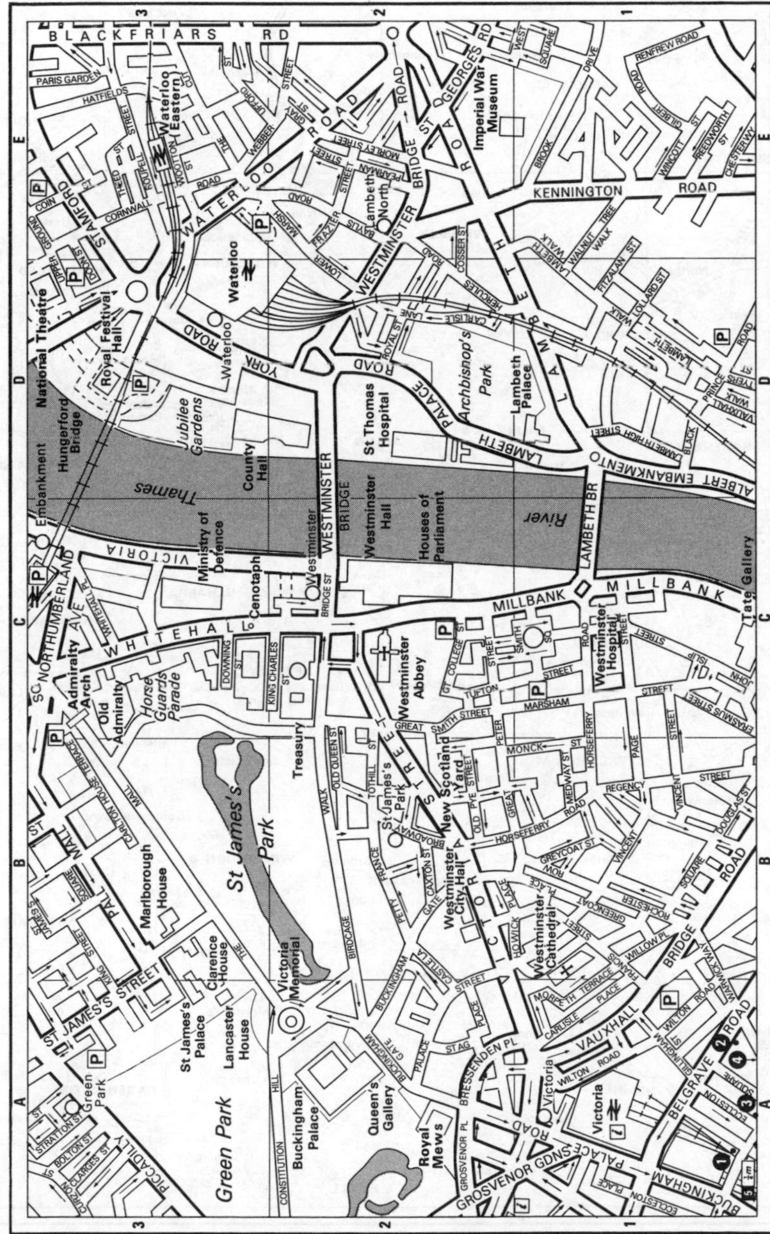

London Plan 3
1 Arden House *(SW1)*
2 Easton Hotel *(SW1)*
3 Elizabeth Hotel *(SW1)*
4 Franterré Hotel *(SW1)*
5 Hanover Hotel *(SW1)*

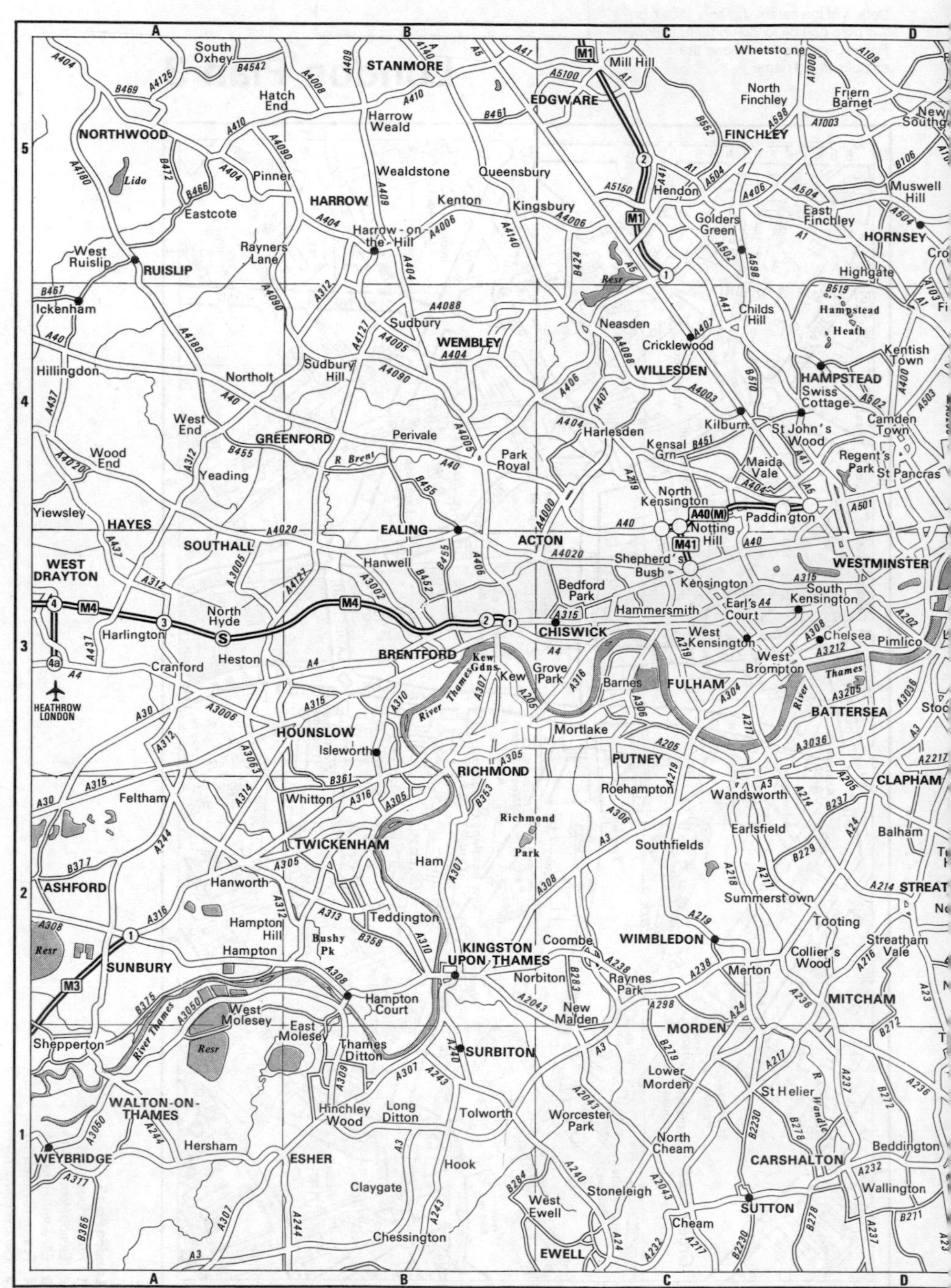

A
B
C
D
South Oxhey
STANMORE
Mill Hill
Whetstone
Hatch End
EDGWARE
North Finchley
Friern Barnet
New Southgate
Harrow Weald
NORTHWOOD
FINCHLEY
Lido
Wealdstone
Queensbury
Pinner
Hendon
Muswell Hill
HARROW
Kenton
Kingsbury
Eastcote
Golders Green
East Finchley
Harrow-on-the-Hill
HORNSEY
West Ruislip
RUISLIP
Rayners Lane
Highgate
Resr
Ickenham
Childs Hill
Hampstead Heath
Sudbury
Neasden
WEMBLEY
Cricklewood
Kentish Town
Hillingdon
Sudbury Hill
WILLESDEN
HAMPSTEAD
Northolt
Swiss Cottage
West End
Kilburn
St John's Wood
Camden Town
Perivale
Harlesden
GREENFORD
Kensal Grn
Wood End
Park Royal
Maida Vale
Regent's Park
St Pancras
R Brent
Yeading
North Kensington
Yiewsley
Paddington
HAYES
EALING
ACTON
Notting Hill
SOUTHALL
Hanwell
Shepherd's Bush
WESTMINSTER
WEST DRAYTON
Bedford Park
Kensington
South Kensington
North Hyde
Hammersmith
Earl's Court
Harlington
CHISWICK
West Kensington
Chelsea
Pimlico
Heston
BRENTFORD
West Brompton
Cranford
Kew Gdns
Kew
Grove Park
Barnes
FULHAM
HEATHROW LONDON
River Thames
BATTERSEA
HOUNSLOW
Mortlake
Isleworth
PUTNEY
RICHMOND
CLAPHAM
Feltham
Whitton
Roehampton
Wandsworth
Richmond Park
Balham
TWICKENHAM
Southfields
Earlsfield
Ham
ASHFORD
Hanworth
Summerstown
Teddington
Tooting
Hampton Hill
Bushy Pk
Coombe
WIMBLEDON
Streatham Vale
Hampton
KINGSTON UPON THAMES
Collier's Wood
SUNBURY
Norbiton
Raynes Park
Merton
Hampton Court
MITCHAM
West Molesey
New Malden
MORDEN
East Molesey
Shepperton
Thames Ditton
SURBITON
Lower Morden
St Helier
Hinchley Wood
Long Ditton
WALTON-ON-THAMES
Tolworth
Worcester Park
North Cheam
Beddington
WEYBRIDGE
Hersham
ESHER
Hook
CARSHALTON
Claygate
Stoneleigh
Wallington
West Ewell
SUTTON
Cheam
Chessington
EWELL

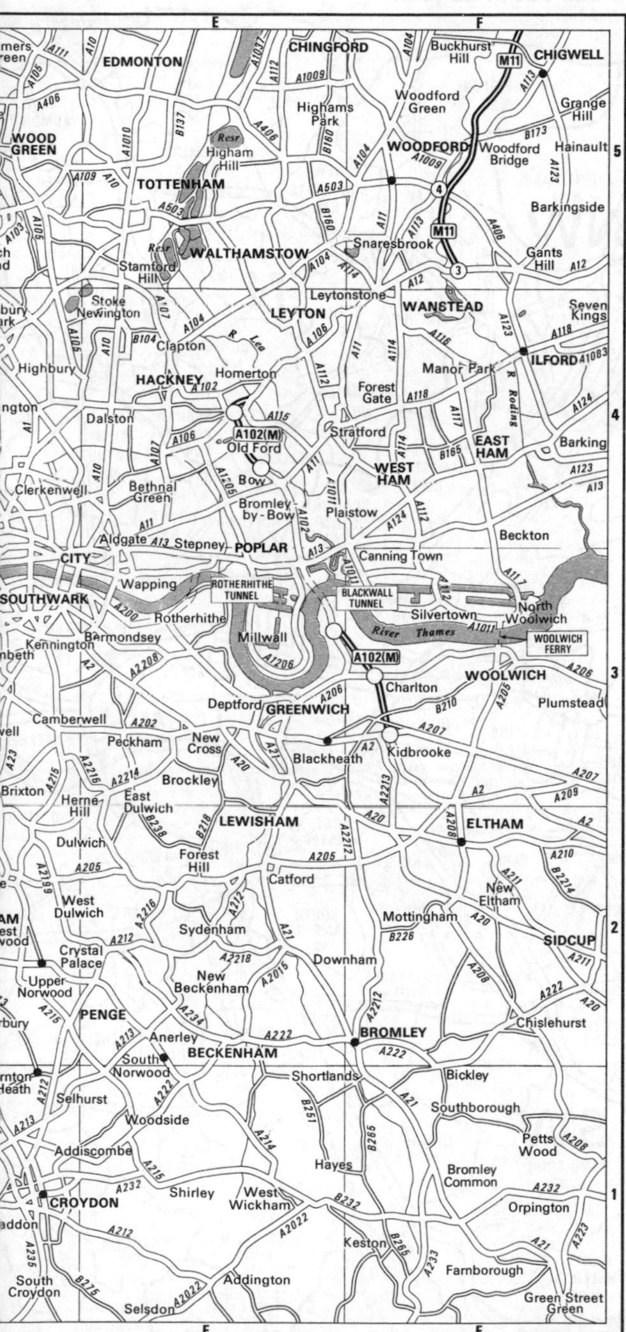

London Plan 4

The placenames highlighted by a **dot** are locations of AA listed establishments outside the Central London Plan area (Plans 1–3). Some of these fall within the London Postal District area and can therefore be found in the gazetteer under **London** in postal district order (see London Postal District map on following page). Others outside the London Postal District area can therefore be found under their respective placenames in the main gazetteer.

London Postal Districts and ways in and out of London

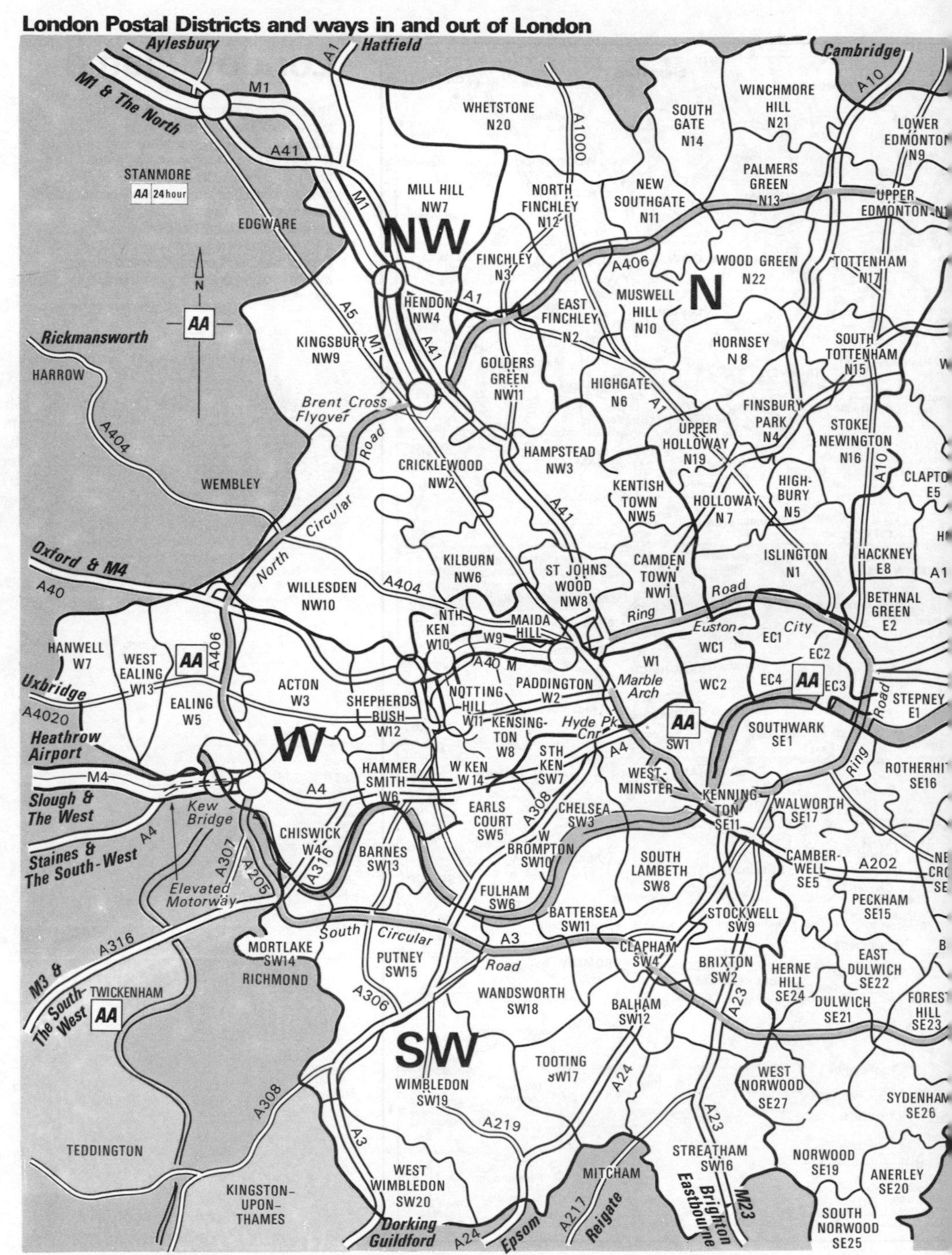

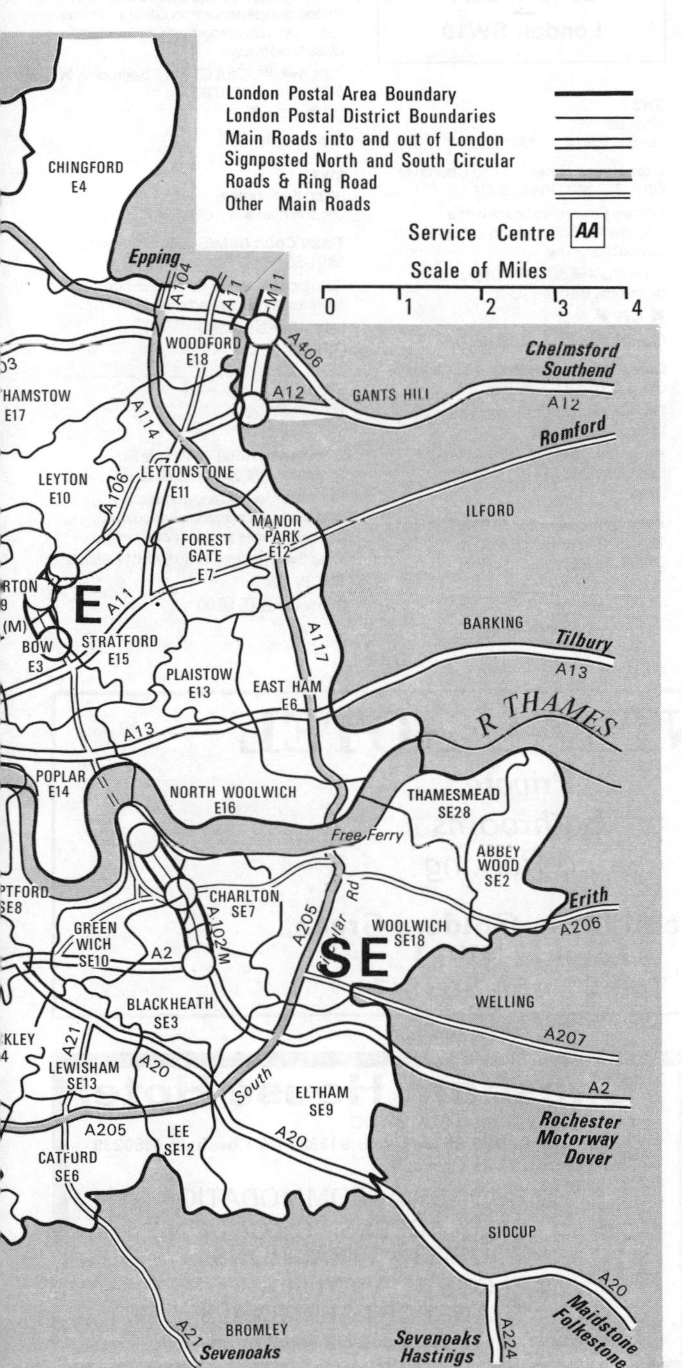

SE9
Eltham
London plan **4** F2

Yardley Court Private Hotel 18 Court Rd, Eltham ☎01-850 1850
Closed Xmas wk
Small nicely appointed guesthouse with comfortable accommodation and friendly intimate atmosphere.
9hc 3⋒ (2fb) CTV in all bedrooms ✱
B&b£15–£16 LDO9pm
▥ CTV 8P nc3yrs

SE19
Norwood
London plan **4** D2

Crystal Palace Tower Hotel
114 Church Rd ☎01-653 0176
Large Victorian house with large, comfortable bedrooms.
12hc (3fb) TV in all bedrooms
*B&bfr£8.50
▥ CTV 10P
Ⓥ

SE25
South Norwood
London plan **4** E2

Toscana 19 South Norwood Hill ☎01-653 3962
Closed Xmas
8hc CTV in 5 bedrooms TV in 1 bedroom
✱ B&b£13–£13.50 Wfr£80 M
Lic ▥ CTV 8P
Ⓥ

SW1
West End–Westminster; St James's Park, Victoria Station
London plan **4** D3

Arden House 12 St Georges Dr ☎01-834 2988 Plan 3:**1** *A1*
Simply furnished hotel with easy access to Victoria Station.
35rm 24hc 9➡ 2⋒ (A 14hc) (10fb) ✱
▥ CTV ⁄P

Chesham House 64–66 Ebury St, Belgravia ☎01-730 8513 Plan 2:**3** *E2*
Terraced house, adequately furnished and offering modest comfort.
23hc (3fb) CTV in all bedrooms ✱
*B&b£12.50–£15
▥ ⁄P
Credit cards 2 3 5
See advertisement on page 226

Easton Hotel 36–40 Belgrave Rd ☎01-834 5938 Plan 3:**2** *A1*
A transit hotel, simply furnished, close to Victoria Station.
43rm 33hc 4➡ 6⋒ (A 12rm 11hc 1➡) (10fb) ✱ B&b£13–£16
Lic ▥ CTV ⁄P

Elizabeth Hotel 37 Eccleston Sq, Victoria ☎01-828 6812 Plan 3:**3** *A1*

Simply furnished hotel situated near Victoria Station.

24rm 17hc 1⇌ 2⋒ (6fb) CTV in 4 bedrooms ✱ B&b£11.50–£21

Ⅲ CTV

Franterré Hotel 142 Warwick Way, Victoria ☎01-834 5163 Plan 3:**4** *A1*

Well maintained, small guesthouse, with comfortable bedrooms.

8hc (5fb) CTV in all bedrooms ✱ *B&b£10.66–£12.50

Ⅲ CTV ⚑ nc10yrs

Ⓥ

Hanover Hotel 30 St Georges Dr ☎01-834 0134 Plan 3:**5** *A1*

An early 19th-century terrace house with simple, comfortable accommodation.

34hc 6⇌ 12⋒ (4fb) CTV in all bedrooms

Ⅲ CTV ⚑

Ⓥ

Willet Hotel 32 Sloane Gdns, Sloane Sq ☎01-730 0634 Plan 2:**7** *E2*

Terraced house with spacious comfortably furnished bedrooms.

17hc 14⇌ (4fb) CTV in 6 bedrooms TV in 11 bedrooms ✱ Ⓡ B&b£14–£17

Ⅲ

London SW1 — London SW19

SW3
Chelsea
London plan **4** D3

Eden House Hotel 111 Old Church St ☎01-352 3403 Plan 2:**5** *C1*

Homely Edwardian house with a comprehensive room service but lacking any public rooms.

14rm 5hc 4⇌ 5⋒ (3fb) CTV in all bedrooms B&b£16–£23

Ⅲ CTV ⚑

Credit cards 1 2 3 4 5 Ⓥ

Garden House Hotel 44–46 Egerton Gdns ☎01-584 2990 Plan 2:**6** *C3*

Friendly establishment with spacious, cheerful bedrooms.

28rm 10hc 18⇌ 8⋒ (3fb) CTV in 18 bedrooms B&b£14–£18.80

lift Ⅲ

Knightsbridge Hotel 10 Beaufort Gdns ☎01-589 9271 Plan 2:**8** *D3*
Closed Xmas

Comfortable, well-equipped bedrooms, limited lounge accommodation and small basement dining room. Ideally located close to Harrods.

20hc 4⇌ 5⋒ (2fb) CTV in 2 bedrooms ✱ *B&b£19.50–£26.60

Lic Ⅲ CTV ⚑

Credit cards 2 3

SW7
South Kensington
London plan **4** C3

Tudor Court Hotel 58–66 Cromwell Rd ☎01-584 8273 Plan 2:**10** *B2*

Comfortable hotel with modern bedrooms and friendly but limited service.

89hc 42⇌ 2⋒ (13fb)

Lic lift Ⅲ CTV

SW19
Wimbledon
London plan **4** C2

Wimbledon Hotel 78 Worple Rd, Wimbledon ☎01-946 9265

Hotel has modernised compact bedrooms, with limited comfortable lounge facilities and easy car parking.

12hc 3⇌ 3⋒ (2fb) ✱ Ⓡ B&b£17.95 S%

Ⅲ CTV 10P

Credit cards 1 3 Ⓥ

London SW19 — London W2

Worcester House 38 Alwyne Rd ☎01-946 1300
Hotel has compact, well fitted bedrooms limited dining facilities and breakfast room service.
9⋔ (1fb) CTV in 9 bedrooms ✦ Ⓡ B&b£17.25–£26.45 LDO11am
▥ ⊘

W1
West End; Piccadilly Circus, St Marylebone and Mayfair
London plan **4** D3/4

Hotel Concorde 50 Great Cumberland Pl ☎01-402 6169 Plan 1:**3** *D3*
Tastefully decorated and comfortable accommodation with good lounge. Well situated in the centre of London.
28rm 5➡ 23⋔ CTV in all bedrooms ✦ B&bfr£30 LDO10.30pm
Lic lift ▥ CTV ⊘
Credit cards 1 2 3 4 5

Eros Hotel 65–73 Shaftesbury Av, Piccadilly ☎01-734 8781
Comfortable establishment, ideally situated in the West End.
63rm 40hc 23➡ (18fb) CTV in all bedrooms ✦
lift ▥ ⊘
Credit cards 1 2 3 4 5

Georgian House Hotel 87 Gloucester Pl, Baker St ☎01-935 2211 Plan 1:**6** *D3*
A terraced house in busy road just off Marble Arch.
19rm 15➡ 4⋔ (3fb) CTV in all bedrooms ✦ B&b£15–£18
Lic lift ▥ CTV ⊘ nc5yrs
Credit cards 2 3 Ⓥ

Hart House Hotel 51 Gloucester Pl, Portman Sq ☎01-935 2288 Plan 1:**7** *D3*
Imposing, five-storey terrace house with well appointed bedrooms.
15rm 9➡ (5fb) CTV in all bedrooms ✦ Ⓡ *B&bfr£12.65
▥ ⊘
Credit cards 1 2 3 Ⓥ

Milford House 31 York St ☎01-935 1935
Very small terraced house with simply appointed accommodation.
6hc 1➡ (2fb) ✦ B&b£9–£15 Wfr£50 M S%
▥ CTV ⊘
Ⓥ

Montagu House 3 Montagu Pl ☎01-935 4632
18rm 17hc 1⋔ (3fb) CTV in all bedrooms ✦ Ⓡ *B&b£11–£13
▥ CTV nc2yrs

W2
Bayswater, Paddington
London plan **4** C/D3/4

Ashley Hotel 15 Norfolk Sq, Hyde Park ☎01-723 3375 Plan 1:**1** *B3*
Closed 4 days Xmas
Situated in a quiet square close to Paddington Station.
16hc 2⋔ (1fb) CTV in all bedrooms ✦ B&b£9.50–£10.25
▥ CTV ⊘

Camelot Hotel 45 Norfolk Sq (Minotel) ☎01-723 9118 Plan 1:**2** *C3*
Friendly hotel providing modern facilities in a range of accommodation.
19rm 5hc 3➡ 1⋔ (4fb) CTV in all bedrooms ✦ Ⓡ *B&b£12.40–£16.65
▥ CTV ⊘
Credit cards 1 2 3 5 Ⓥ

Dylan Hotel 14 Devonshire Ter Lancaster Gate ☎01-723 3280 Plan 1:**4** *B3*
Traditional style guesthouse, homely and comfortable.

19hc 2➡ 5⋔ (2fb) ✱Ⓡ(W only Nov–Mar) ▥ CTV ⚑

Garden Court Hotel 30–31 Kensington Gardens Sq ☎01-727 8304 Plan 1:**5** *A3*
Friendly, family run, quietly situated hotel.
37rm 27hc 6➡ 5⋔ (3fb) ✱ B&b£12.50–£16
Lic ▥ CTV ⚑

Nayland Hotel 134 Sussex Gdns (Minotel) ☎01-723 3380 Plan 1:**9** *B3*
Small, friendly hotel with modern facilities in bedrooms including videos.
14hc (3fb) CTV in all bedrooms ✱ Ⓡ ✻B&b£12.40–£16.65
▥ CTV 2P
Credit cards 1 2 3 5 Ⓥ

Pembridge Court Hotel 34 Pembridge Gdns ☎01-229 9977
Comfortable hotel offering many facilities including a separate restaurant.
35rm 20➡ 14⋔ (4fb) CTV in all bedrooms B&b£22.71–£33.93 LDO11.30pm
Lic ▥ CTV 2🚗
Credit cards 1 2 3 4 5

Slavia Hotel 2 Pembridge Sq ☎01-727 1316
Hotel offering reasonably priced simple accommodation.
31⋔ (8fb) B&b£13–£20 W£100–£120 M LDO9pm
Lic lift ▥ CTV 2P
Credit cards 1 2 3 5 Ⓥ

Victoria Garden Hotel 100 Westbourne Ter ☎01-262 1161 Plan 1:**10** *B3*
Comfortable establishment, situated near Hyde Park and airport bus terminus.
65➡ (6fb) CTV in all bedrooms ✱ B&b£19.88–£27.75
Lic lift ▥ 4P
Credit cards 1 2 3 4 5

W4
Chiswick
London plan **4** C3

Chiswick Hotel 73 Chiswick High Rd ☎01-994 1712
A recently converted house with varying types of bedrooms.
30rm 15hc 5➡ 10⋔ (7fb) CTV in all bedrooms ✻B&b£16–£19.50 Bdi£23–£26.50 LDO8.30pm
Lic ▥ CTV 14P ▭(heated) sauna bath
Credit cards 1 2 3 5 Ⓥ

W5
Ealing
London plan **4** B4

Grange Lodge 50 Grange Rd ☎01-567 1049
Family run Edwardian house with breakfast room service.
14hc 4⋔ (3fb) LDOnoon
Lic ▥ CTV 8P ⌂

22 Grange Park ☎01-567 6984
Situated in quiet road. Room service includes full English breakfast.
11hc 2➡ (2fb) CTV in 2 bedrooms
▥ CTV 6P 1🚗

W8
Kensington
London plan **4** C3

Apollo Hotel 18–22 Lexham Gdns, Kensington ☎01-373 3236
Sister to Atlas Hotel, has many modern facilities and modest prices.
59rm 19hc 38➡ 2⋔ (10fb) B&b£12.50–£17.50 Bdi£17–£22 W£76.75–£109.25 M LDO7.45pm
Lic lift ▥ CTV ⚑
Credit cards 1 2 3 4 5

Atlas Hotel 24–30 Lexham Gdns, Kensington ☎01-373 7873 Plan 2:**1** *A2*
Modestly priced accommodation with many modern facilities.
70rm 30hc 20➡ 20⋔ (10fb) B&b£12.50–£13.50 Bdi£17–£18 W£77–£84 M LDO7.45pm
Lic lift ▥ CTV ⚑
Credit cards 1 2 3 4 5 Ⓥ

Clearlake Hotel 18–19 Prince of Wales Ter ☎01-937 3274 Plan 2:**4** *A3*
Well equipped and comfortable accommodation in the heart of Kensington.
20rm 15➡ 5⋔ (10fb) CTV in all bedrooms Ⓡ B&b£28.75–£35.65 W£140–£225 M
Lic lift ▥ CTV ⚑
Credit cards 1 2 3 5

W14
West Kensington
London plan **4** C3

Avonmore Hotel 66 Avonmore Rd ☎01-603 4296
Very comfortable accommodation offered by friendly proprietors.
9hc (1fb) CTV in all bedrooms (W only Oct–Mar) LDO8pm
Lic ▥ CTV 5P

WC1
Bloomsbury, Holborn
London plan **4** D4

Mentone Hotel 54–55 Cartwright Gdns, Bloomsbury ☎01-387 3927
Comfortable family accommodation, with public shower facilities and friendly service.
27hc (10fb) ✱ B&b£10–£15
▥ CTV ⚑ ⚲

LONG EATON
Derbyshire
Map **8** SK43

GH Camden Hotel 85 Nottingham Rd ☎(0602) 722901
Closed 23 Dec–9 Jan rs Aug Bank Hol wk
7hc (A 6hc) CTV in 3 bedrooms Ⓡ B&bfr£13.50 Bdifr£20
Lic ▥ CTV 13P nc10yrs
Credit cards 1 3

LONGFRAMLINGTON
Northumberland
Map **12** NU10

INN Granby ☎(066570) 228
Closed Xmas Day
3rm 2hc 1➡ CTV in all bedrooms ✱ Ⓡ B&b£12.50–£15.50 Bdi£21.75–£24.75 L£6.50–£8.95 D8.30pm £9.25–£11.50
▥ 30P ⚐ nc12yrs
Credit cards 1 2 3 Ⓥ
See advertisement on page 230

LONGLEAT
Wiltshire
Map **3** ST84

FH Mrs J Crossman **Stalls** *(ST806439)* ☎Maiden Bradley (09853) 323
Closed Dec
Detached house built of Bath stone, originally the home farm for Longleat House. Sun terrace with trim lawns and garden to stream. Access off A362 at Corsley Heath.
3hc (1fb) ✱ B&b£8.50 W£56 M
CTV 6P 281acres arable beef dairy Ⓥ

LONGRIDGE
Lancashire
Map **7** SD63

FH Mr F K Johnson **Falicon** *(SD629361)* Fleet Street Ln, Hothersall ☎Ribchester (025484) 583
A delightful sandstone farmhouse over 200 years old in pleasant rural surrounds with comfortably furnished bedrooms. Situated off B6245 Longbridge to Ribchester rd.
3rm 2hc 2➡ (1fb) ✱ ✻B&b£12.50–£14.50 Bdi£19–£21 LDO5pm
▥ 6P nc10yrs 13acres beef sheep

LONGSDON
Staffordshire
Map **7** SJ95

FH Mr & Mrs M M Robinson ***Bank End*** *(SJ953541)* Old Leek Rd (½m SW off A53) ☎Leek (0538) 383638
Good modern farmhouse in pleasant rural area, 2m SW of Leek.
6➡ (1fb) CTV in 5 bedrooms TV in 1 bedroom Ⓡ LDO9.30pm
Lic ▥ CTV 20P 2🚗 ⌂ 62acres beef

The Granby Inn

LONGFRAMLINGTON,
MORPETH, NE65 8DP
Tel: Longframlington 228

Formerly a coaching stop, the Inn is about 200 years old and has retained its oak beams. The Inn can cater for up to 24 diners, with a wine list available. Bar meals and sandwiches are always available. Call in for a refreshing drink or make a date for lunch and enjoy our quick friendly service or stay longer. Six bedrooms all with colour TV and tea making facilities, four with private bathroom or shower.

Centrally heated throughout.

The Inn is centrally placed in the country on the A697, north of Morpeth, and within easy reach of the beautiful North Northumbrian coast, the Cheviot Hills and the ancient town of Alnwick. Holy Island, Farne Islands, Craster and Seahouses are just some places of interest.

Holder of 'The Inn of the North' award.

Proprietors: Mr and Mrs G Hall and family

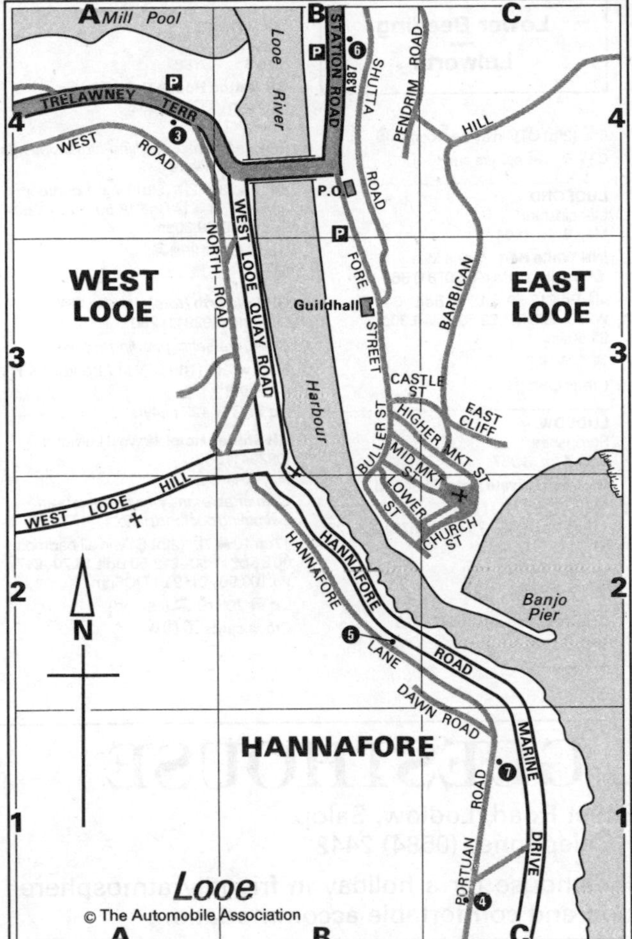

Looe
3 Kantara
4 Ogunquit
5 Panorama Hotel
6 Riverside Hotel
7 St Aubyns

LOOE
Cornwall
Map **2** SX25
See plan

⊢×⊣ **GH 'Kantara'** 7 Trelawney Ter ☎(05036) 2093 Plan **3** *A4*
Etr–Oct
6hc (3fb) B&b£6–£7
CTV
Ⓥ

⊢×⊣ **GH Ogunquit** Portuan Rd ☎(05036) 3105 Plan **4** *C1*
Apr–Oct
5rm 4hc 1⫚ (2fb) Bdi£7.50–£8.50 Bdi£12–£13 W£80–£87 L LDO24hrs
CTV P

GH *Panorama Hotel* Hannafore Rd, Hannafore ☎(05036) 2123 Plan **5** *B2*
Mar–Oct & Xmas
12hc 1⇌ 1⫚ (2fb) CTV in 6 bedrooms TV in 1 bedroom LDO7.30pm
Lic CTV 9P river sea
Ⓥ

⊢×⊣ **GH Riverside Hotel** Station Rd ☎(05036) 2100 Plan **6** *B4*
Etr–mid Oct
13hc (5fb) ★ B&b£7.50 W£52.50 M
Lic CTV

⊢×⊣ **GH St Aubyns** Marine Dr, Hannafore, West Looe ☎(05036) 4351 Plan **7** *C1*
Etr–Oct
8hc (5fb) ★ Ⓡ B&b£8–£10 W£56–£66.50 M (W only Jul & Aug)
CTV 4P

⊢×⊣ **FH** Mr & Mrs Hembrow **Tregoed** *(SX272560)* St Martins ☎(05036) 2718
Etr–Oct
Georgian-style manor house on high ground with sea view.
6hc (3fb) Ⓡ B&b£6–£8 Bdi£10–£12 LDO5pm
Lic CTV 12P 60acres dairy

LOSTWITHIEL
Cornwall
Map **2** SX15

⊢×⊣ **FH** Mrs R J Dunn **Pelyn Barn** *(SX091588)* Pelyn Cross ☎Bodmin (0208) 872451
Large farmhouse, formerly an old toll house, with large sun lounge affording scenic views. There is a well-kept lawn enclosure at rear.
3hc (1fb) ★ B&b£7–£8.50 Bdi£10–£12.50 W£55 M LDO4pm
CTV 4P 142acres dairy sheep potatoes
Ⓥ

⊢×⊣ **FH** Mrs R C Dunn **Pelyn Barn Farm Bungalow** *(SX091588)* Pelyn Cross ☎Bodmin (0208) 873062
250yds off A390 St Austell–Lostwithiel rd.
3hc 1⫚ (2fb) CTV in all bedrooms ★ B&b£8 Bdi£13 W£56 L LDO8pm
CTV 12P 2 380 acres mixed

INN Royal Oak Duke St ☎Bodmin (0208) 872552
Friendly, busy inn dating from 13th century, with large lounge bar where food is served.
6rm 2⫚ CTV in all bedrooms Ⓡ *B&b£10.50–£11.50 W£63–£69 M Lfr£2.25&alc D10pm fr£2.25&alc
16P
Credit cards 1 3

LOUGHBOROUGH
Leicestershire
Map **8** SK51

GH De Montfort Hotel 88 Leicester Rd ☎(0509) 216061
9hc (1fb) CTV in all bedrooms B&b£12 Bdi£16 W£84 M LDO4pm
Lic CTV
Credit cards 1 3

GH Sunnyside Hotel The Coneries ☎(0509) 216217
Closed 25 Dec–1 Jan
11hc B&b£10.50–£11 Bdi£15–£15.75 W£63–£66 M LDO4pm
CTV 8P 3 nc5yrs
Credit card 3 Ⓥ

LOWER BEEDING
West Sussex
Map **4** TQ22

FH Mr J Christian **Brookfield** *(TQ212282)* Winterpit Ln, Plummers Plain ☎(040376) 568
An efficiently managed farmhouse with compact bedrooms, comfortable lounge and a popular lake and lawn to the rear.
6rm 4hc (2fb) *B&b£11.50 Bdi£16.68 W£85 Ł LDO8pm
Lic CTV 50P 300acres mixed

LOWESTOFT
Suffolk
Map **5** TM59

GH Amity 396 London Road South ☎(0502) 2586
9hc 1 (5fb) CTV in all bedrooms Ⓡ B&b£9–£10 Bdi£12–£13 W£55–£60 Ł LDO4pm
Lic CTV
Credit cards 1 3 Ⓥ

GH Belmont 270 London Road South ☎(0502) 3867
6hc (3fb) Ⓡ B&b£7–£8 Bdi£10.50–£11.50 W£42–£49 M LDOnoon
Lic CTV

GH *Kingsleigh* 44 Marine Pde ☎(0502) 2513
Closed Xmas
6hc (2fb) CTV in all bedrooms Ⓡ
CTV 6P 1 nc3yrs sea

LUDFORD
Lincolnshire
Map **8** TF04

INN White Hart Magna Mile ☎Burgh-on-Bain (050781) 664
4 Bdi£12.50–£13.50 Bdi£16–£17 W£80–£85 M L£2.50alc D9.30pm £5.50alc
CTV 30P
Credit card 1

LUDLOW
Shropshire
Map **7** SO57

GH Cecil Private Hotel Sheet Rd ☎(0584) 2442
11hc (1fb) Bdi£8.75 Bdi£13.75 W£61.25 M
Lic CTV 10P
Ⓥ

GH *Croft* Dinham (0584) 2076
8hc (3fb) Ⓡ
river

LULWORTH
Dorset
Map **3** SY88

GH Gatton House Hotel ☎West Lulworth (092941) 252
Mar–Oct
Elevated position nestling into hillside with panoramic views.
9rm 4hc 3 2 (2fb) TV in 1 bedroom Ⓡ B&b£10–£14 Bdi£16.50–£22 W£60–£98 M LDO9.30pm
Lic CTV 12P 1
Ⓥ

GH *Lulworth Hotel* Main Rd ☎West Lulworth (092941) 230
Open rural setting leading to cove.
9hc 1 1 (1fb) CTV in 7 bedrooms LDO8pm
Lic CTV 12P nc4yrs

GH Shirley Hotel ☎West Lulworth (092941) 358
Mar–Oct
Comfortable family-owned hotel with swimming pool and patio.
17rm 10 7 (2fb) CTV in all bedrooms Ⓡ B&b£11.50–£12.50 Bdi£15.70–£17 W£109.90–£119 Ł LDO5pm
Lic 20P (heated)
Credit cards 1 3 Ⓥ

LUTON
Bedfordshire
Map **4** TL02

GH Arlington Hotel 137 New Bedford Rd ☎(0582) 419614
Well managed and comfortable commercial guesthouse.
17rm 13hc 2🛁 2🚿 (2fb) CTV in all bedrooms ✱B&b£12.50–£21.50 LDO7.30pm
Lic ▥ 20P
Credit cards ② ⑤ Ⓥ

GH Humberstone Hotel 618 Dunstable Rd ☎(0582) 574399
Closed 25 & 26 Dec
Very comfortable and clean guesthouse where the welcome is warm and friendly.
10rm 2🚿 (2fb) CTV in all bedrooms 🐕Ⓡ B&b£14.80 LDO7pm
Lic ▥ CTV nc7yrs

GH Lansdowne Lodge Private Hotel 31 Lansdowne Rd ☎(0582) 31411
Closed Xmas & Boxing Day
Friendly and comfortable house run by young proprietors.
14rm 5hc 9🚿 (1fb) CTV in all bedrooms Ⓡ ✱B&b£15–£31.05 Bdi£21.25–£37.30 LDO8.45pm
Lic ▥ CTV 20P

GH Stoneygate Hotel 696 Dunstable Rd ☎(0582) 582045
Small comfortable guesthouse.
11rm 6hc (2fb) CTV in 4 bedrooms TV in 7 bedrooms 🐕Ⓡ ✱B&b£14.66–£16.61 Bdi£19.36 LDO9pm
Lic ▥ CTV 25P
Ⓥ

LYDFORD
Devon
Map **2** SX58

INN *Castle* ☎(082282) 242
Closed Xmas Day
5hc Ⓡ D9.30pm
▥ 30P nc5yrs

LYDNEY
Gloucestershire
Map **3** SO60

GH Parkend House Hotel Parkend (Guestaccom) ☎Dean (0594) 562171
2½m NW B4234.
6🛁 (1fb) 🐕Ⓡ B&b£14.95 Bdi£20.70 W£120.45–£134.65 V̸ LDO9pm
Lic ▥ CTV 20P ≋(heated) sauna bath

LYME REGIS
Dorset
Map **3** SY39

⊢×⊣ **GH Coverdale** Woodmead Rd ☎(02974) 2882
Etr–Oct
Quiet location near to shops and sea.
9hc (1fb) B&b£7.50–£9 Bdi£11–£12.50 W£50–£60 M̸ LDO5pm
▥ CTV 10P

GH Kersbrook Hotel Pound Rd ☎(02974) 2596
Feb–Nov
18th-century building in 1 acre of grounds at the top of the town, a few minutes walk from the centre.
14hc 2🛁 6🚿 (2fb) Ⓡ B&bfr£13 Bdifr£20.95 Wfr£135 V̸ LDO7.30pm
Lic CTV 16P
Credit cards ① ② ③ Ⓥ

⊢×⊣ **GH Old Monmouth Hotel** Church St ☎(02974) 2456
16th-century building opposite the parish church, a few minutes walk from the harbour.
6rm 4hc 1🛁 3🚿 (2fb) 🐕Ⓡ B&b£7.50–£10.50 Bdi£12.50–£15.50 W£50–£70 V̸ LDO6.30pm
Lic ▥ CTV 6P nc3yrs
Credit cards ① ② ③ ④

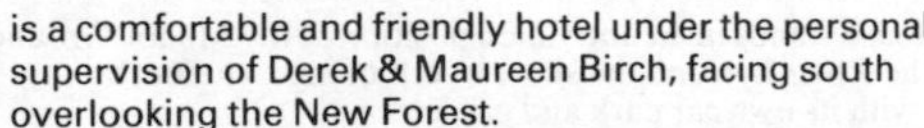

⊢⊣ **GH Rotherfield** View Rd ☎(02974) 2811
Mar–Oct rs Nov–Feb
Situated in quiet residential area with coastal and country views.
7hc (3fb) B&b£7.50–£8.50 Bdi£11.50–£12.50 W£72.50–£79.50 ⱡ LDO4pm
Lic CTV 7P

GH White House 47 Silver St ☎(02974) 3420
Mar–Oct
Main road location a few minutes walk from the harbour.
7rm 3hc 3⋔ (2fb) Ⓡ B&b£8.50–£11 Bdi£12.75–£15.25 W£53.25–£69.26 M
LDO10am
Lic ▥ CTV 7P nc3yrs
Ⓥ

LYNDHURST
Hampshire
Map **4** SU30

⊢⊣ **GH Bench View** Southampton Rd ☎(042128) 2502
Closed Dec
Large family house overlooking the New Forest.
8hc (6fb) CTV in all bedrooms ★
B&b£8–£9.50 W£55–£60 M
CTV 10P

Lyme Regis — Lynmouth

GH Ormonde House Hotel Southampton Rd ☎(042128) 2806
A friendly family run hotel, just off main road, facing the New Forest.
14rm 7hc 2→ 4⋔ (4fb) CTV in all bedrooms Ⓡ B&b£11.80–£12.80 Bdi£17.30–£18.30 W£76.40–£83.40 ⱡ LDO5pm
Lic ▥ CTV 20P
Credit cards 1 2 3
See advertisement on page 233

GH *Whitemoor House Hotel* Southampton Rd ☎(042128) 2186
Comfortable, well-appointed house overlooking the New Forest.
5hc (2fb)
Lic ▥ CTV 8P

LYNMOUTH
Devon
Map **3** SS74
See plan. See also Lynton
During the currency of this publication telephone numbers are liable to change.

GH *Countisbury Lodge Hotel* Countisbury Hill ☎Lynton (05985) 2388 Plan **3** *D2*
Mar–Oct
8hc 2→ (3fb) LDOnoon
Lic ▥ CTV 8P

GH *East Lyn* 17 Watersmeet Rd ☎Lynton (05985) 2540 Plan **5** *D2*
8hc (3fb)
CTV 4P 2⌂ river sea

⊢⊣ **GH Glenville Hotel** 2 Tors Rd ☎Lynton (05985) 2202 Plan **7** *D2*
7hc (2fb) B&b£7.50–£8 Bdi£12–£12.50 W£82 ⱡ LDO5pm
Lic CTV 8P

GH The Heatherville Tors Park (Guestaccom) ☎Lynton (05985) 2327 Plan **9** *D2*
Feb–Nov
Neat, tidy, Edwardian house with warm, comfortable atmosphere.
8rm 5hc 3⋔ (2fb) ★ B&b£10.50 Bdi£15 W£94 ⱡ LDO5.30pm
Lic ▥ CTV 8P

GH Rock House ☎Lynton (05985) 3508 Plan **18** *C3*
Mar–Oct
6hc (1fb) Ⓡ B&b£10–£12 Bdi£16–£18.50 W£65–£115 ⱡ LDO6pm
Lic ▥ CTV 6P
Credit cards 1 3

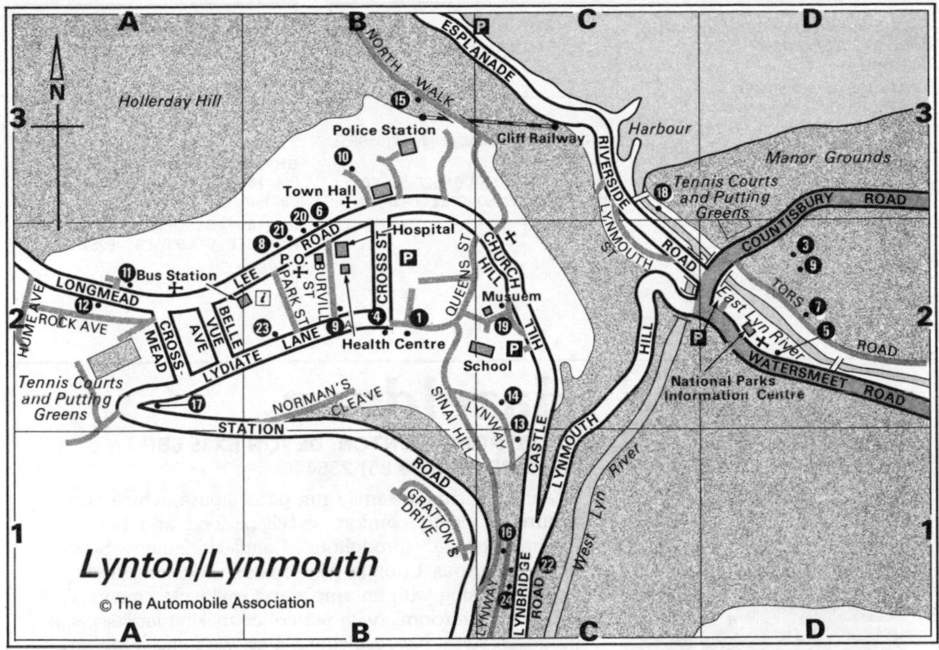

Lynmouth & Lynton
1 Alford House *(see under Lynton)*
3 Countisbury Lodge Hotel *(see under Lynmouth)*
4 Croft *(see under Lynton)*
5 East Lyn *(see under Lynmouth)*
6 Gable Lodge Hotel *(see under Lynton)*
7 Glenville Hotel *(see under Lynmouth)*
8 Hazeldene *(see under Lynton)*
9 Heatherville *(see under Lynmouth)*
9A Horwood House *(see under Lynton)*
10 Ingleside Hotel *(see under Lynton)*
11 Kingford House Private Hotel *(see under Lynton)*
12 Longmead House *(see under Lynton)*
13 Lyndhurst Hotel *(see under Lynton)*
14 Mayfair Hotel *(see under Lynton)*
15 North Cliff Hotel *(see under Lynton)*
16 Pine Lodge *(see under Lynton)*
17 Retreat *(see under Lynton)*
18 Rock House *(see under Lynmouth)*
19 St Vincent *(see under Lynton)*
20 Southcliffe *(see under Lynton)*
21 Turret *(see under Lynton)*
22 Valley House Hotel *(see under Lynton)*
23 Waterloo House Hotel *(see under Lynton)*
24 Woodlands *(see under Lynton)*

LYNTON
Devon
Map **3** SS74
See plan. See also Lynmouth

During the currency of this publication telephone numbers are liable to change.

GH Alford House 3 Alford Ter
☎(05985) 2359 Plan **1** *B2*
30 Mar–19 Oct
8rm 2hc (1fb) B&b£10.50–£12.50 Bdi£15–£17 W£90–£100 M LDO6.30pm
Lic ⅲ CTV P̸ nc5yrs
Ⓥ

GH *The Croft* Lydiate Ln
☎(05985) 2391
Plan **4** *B2*
8hc (2fb) LDO5.30pm
Lic CTV P̸
Ⓥ

GH Gable Lodge Hotel Lee Rd
☎(05985) 2367 Plan **6** *B3*
9rm 2hc 2⇌ 4⋒ (2fb) B&b£9.50–£11.70 Bdi£14–£16.70 W£89.50–£106.50 L̸ LDO7pm
Lic ⅲ CTV 9P
Ⓥ

⊢⊣ **GH Hazeldene** 27–28 Lee Rd
☎(05985) 2364 Plan **8** *B2*
Mar–Oct
8rm 6hc 2⇌ (4fb) CTV in 2 bedrooms Ⓡ B&b£7–£8 Bdi£12–£13 W£75–£85 L̸ LDO5pm
Lic ⅲ CTV 8P nc5yrs
Credit cards 1 3 Ⓥ
See advertisement on page 236

GH Horwood House Lydiate Ln
☎(05985) 2334 Plan **9A** *B2*
Apr–Oct
5hc (1fb) Ⓡ ✱B&b£7.50–£8.50 Bdi£13–£14 W£78–£84 L̸ LDOnoon
Lic CTV 6P
Ⓥ

GH Ingleside Hotel Lee Rd ☎(05985) 2223 Plan **10** *B3*
mid Mar–mid Oct
7rm 4⇌ 3⋒ (2fb) CTV in all bedrooms ✱ Ⓡ B&b£12–£15.50 Bdi£19–£22.50 Wfr£126 L̸ LDO6pm
Lic ⅲ CTV 13P ⌂
Credit card 1

⊢⊣ **GH Kingford House Private Hotel**
Longmead ☎(05985) 2361 Plan **11** *A2*
Mar–Sep
8hc 3⋒ (1fb) ✱ Ⓡ B&b£7.50–£8.50 Bdi£12–£14 W£48–£52 M LDO4.30pm
Lic CTV 8P nc5yrs

⊢⊣ **GH Longmead House** 9 Longmead ☏(05985) 2523 Plan **12** *A2*
Apr–Sep

Friendly, relaxed guesthouse, comfortable and spotlessly clean.

9hc (2fb) ★ ® B&b£7.50–£8 Bdi£12–£12.50 W£50.75–£54.25 M LDO4.30pm

Lic CTV 9P nc5yrs

Ⓥ

GH Lyndhurst Hotel Lynway ☏(05985) 2241 Plan **13** *C1*
Apr–Sep

7rm 2hc 5⇌ (1fb) ® B&b£9–£9.50 Bdi£10.50–£11.50 W£50 Ⱡ LDO5pm

Lic CTV P

Lynton

⊢⊣ **GH Mayfair Hotel** Lynway ☏(05985) 3227 Plan **14** *B1*

14rm 12hc 2⇌ (4fb) ® B&b£6.50–£8 Bdi£9.50–£11 W£60–£72 Ⱡ LDO7pm

Lic ▥ CTV 12P

Ⓥ

GH *North Cliff Private Hotel* North Walk ☏(05985) 2357 Plan **15** *B3*
Mar–Nov

21hc 1⇌ (4fb) ★

Lic CTV 15P sea

Ⓥ

GH Pine Lodge Lynway ☏(05985) 3230 Plan **16** *C1*
Etr–early Oct

9hc (1fb) ® B&b£8.75–£9.50 Bdi£13.50–£14.50 W£91–£95 Ⱡ

CTV 8P nc5yrs

Ⓥ

⊢⊣ **GH Retreat** 1 Park Gdns ☎(05985) 3526 Plan **17** *A2*
Apr–Oct
6hc (2fb) ★ Ⓡ B&b£6.50 Bdi£10 W£65 Ⱡ LDO5pm
▥ CTV 3P

⊢⊣ **GH St Vincent** Castle Hill ☎(05985) 2244 Plan **19** *C2*
6hc (2fb) ★ Ⓡ B&b£7.50–£8.50 Bdi£10.50–£11.50 W£52.50–£59.50 M LDO4pm
Lic CTV 3P

Lynton

⊢⊣ **GH Southcliffe** Lee Rd ☎(05985) 3328 Plan **20** *B2*
Mar–Dec
8rm 5hc 1 ⇌ 2 ⋒ (1fb) B&b£8–£10 Bdi£13–£15.50 W£85–£95 Ⱡ LDO6.30pm
Lic ▥ CTV 7P 1 ⌂ nc5yrs

⊢⊣ **GH Turret** Lee Rd ☎(05985) 3284 Plan **21** *B2*
Mar–Oct
6rm 1hc 2 ⇌ (1fb) ★ B&b£6.50–£7 Bdi£10.25–£10.75 W£43.75–£47.25 M LDO5pm
CTV ⁋ nc5yrs

GH Valley House Hotel Lynbridge Rd ☎(05985) 2285 Plan **22** *C1*
8rm 3hc (2fb) Ⓡ B&b£10–£12.50 Bdi£14–£16.50 W£66.50–£84 Ⱡ LDO6pm
Lic CTV 8P
Credit card 3 Ⓥ

⊢⊣ **GH Waterloo House Hotel** Lydiate Ln ☏(05985) 3391 Plan **23** *B2*

12rm 10hc (4fb) B&b£7.50–£9.50 Bdi£11.50–£14 W£75–£88 L LDO9.30pm

Lic CTV 2P

GH Woodlands Lynbridge ☏(05985) 2324 Plan **24** *C1*

Detached Victorian house in quiet position overlooking wooded valley.

8rm 6hc 2fl ★ B&b£10–£14 Bdi£15–£20 W£95–£120 L LDO7.15pm

Lic ▥ CTV 8P nc16yrs ♪

Credit cards 1 3 Ⓥ

LYTHAM ST ANNES
Lancashire
Map **7** SD32

GH *Beaumont Private Hotel* 11 All Saints Road ☏(0253) 723958

Pleasant, well furnished, family run guesthouse in quiet side road.

9hc (3fb)

Lic CTV ♪ ⌂

Ⓥ

GH Endsleigh Private Hotel 315 Clifton Drive South ☏(0253) 725622

11rm 6hc 5fl (2fb) CTV in 5 bedrooms ★ B&b£9.75–£11.75 Bdi£13.50–£15.50 W£56–£63 M LDO5pm

Lic ▥ CTV 6P

Ⓥ

Lynton — Machrihanish

GH *Ennes Court* 107 South Prom ☏(0253) 723731

10rm 5➡ 5fl (2fb) CTV in 3 bedrooms TV in 7 bedrooms ★ Ⓡ LDO6.45pm

Lic ▥ CTV 10P river

GH *Gables Hotel* 35 Orchard Rd ☏(0253) 729851

Large, attractive house with 2 comfortable lounges, bright, clean bedrooms and good home cooking.

17hc (A 2➡) (10fb)

Lic ▥ CTV 24P

GH Harcourt Hotel 21 Richmond Rd ☏(0253) 722299

early Jan–mid Dec

Small, personally run, well furnished guesthouse in quiet side road.

10hc (3fb) Ⓡ B&b£8.33–£8.62 Bdi£10.92–£11.50 W£58.31–£60.34 L LDO6pm

Lic ▥ CTV 6P

Ⓥ

⊢⊣ **GH Lyndhurst Private Hotel** 338 Clifton Drive North ☏(0253) 724343

Closed Xmas

12rm 11hc 1➡ (4fb) CTV in 3 bedrooms Ⓡ B&b£7.50–£9 Bdi£11–£12.50 W£49–£59 M LDO6pm

CTV 11P

GH Westbourne Hotel 10–12 Lake Rd, Fairhaven ☏(0253) 734736

Closed Xmas & New Year

19hc 1➡ 1fl TV in 1 bedroom ★ B&b£10.50–£11.50 Bdi£13.50–£15.50 W£85–£100 L LDOam

Lic lift ▥ CTV 6P ⌂

Ⓥ

MABLETHORPE
Lincolnshire
Map **9** TF58

GH *Auralee* ☏(05213) 7660

Closed 25 Dec

Friendly, comfortable, family-run seaside house for holiday and commercial trade.

9hc (2fb) TV in all bedrooms ★

Lic ▥ CTV 8P nc3yrs

MACHRIHANISH
Strathclyde *Argyllshire*
Map **10** NR62

GH Ardell House ☏(058681) 235

Detached house standing opposite golf course. Attractive bedrooms and friendly proprietors. Annexe rooms are in picturesque converted stables.

6rm 4hc 1⫛ (A3⫛) CTV in 1 bedroom TV in 2 bedrooms Ⓡ B&b£11–£12.50 Bdi£16–£18 Wfr£70 M LDO6.30pm
Lic CTV 12P

MAIDSTONE
Kent
Map **5** TQ75

GH Carval Hotel 56–58 London Rd ☎(0622) 62100
Comfortable homely accommodation located alongside a busy road, with basement dining room.
8hc (4fb) ✱ Ⓡ *B&b£9–£11
Lic CTV 8P
Credit cards 1 2 3 5

GH Howard Hotel 22–24 London Rd ☎(0622) 58778
Georgian terraced house with simple bedrooms, on busy hillside road.
16hc (3fb) ✱ Ⓡ B&b£12 Bdi£17 W£84 M LDO7pm
Lic CTV 17P

GH Rock House Hotel 102 Tonbridge Rd ☎(0622) 51616
Closed 24 Dec–2 Jan
Small modern guesthouse with cheerful bedrooms and limited lounge facilities.
10hc (1fb) CTV in 2 bedrooms ✱ Ⓡ B&b£10–£13.80 W£63–£89.60 M
CTV 7P
Credit cards 1 3 Ⓥ

Machrihanish — Malvern, Great

MALDON
Essex
Map **5** TL80

INN Swan Hotel Maldon High St ☎(0621) 53170
Small pub and restaurant with modestly furnished bedrooms.
6hc ✱ *B&b£13.80 W£91.77 M LDO8.30pm
CTV 20P 1
Credit cards 1 2 3

MALHAM
North Yorkshire
Map **7** SD96

GH Sparth House Hotel ☎Airton (07293) 315
10rm 9hc 1⫛ (3fb) ✱ B&b£11.50–£12.50 Bdi£17–£18 W£110–£115 ⱡ LDO5.30pm
Lic CTV 7P (grass)

MALPAS
Cheshire
Map **7** SJ44

FH Mrs N Evans **Kidnal Grange** *(SJ473493)* ☎(0948) 860344
Apr–Oct
Clean comfortable farmhouse in attractive rural surroundings; much home produce used in cooking. Large ornamental pond with ducks.
6rm (1fb) B&b£8–£8.50 W£56 M
CTV 10P 120acres arable beef pig mixed

FH Mrs D Bevin **Pitts** *(SJ459466)* ☎Threapwood (094881) 224
2m E B5069 on right.
5rm 2hc 1 (3fb) CTV in 4 bedrooms TV in 1 bedroom ✱ B&b£8 Bdi£12.50 W£75 ⱡ LDO6pm
CTV 12P 85acres dairy poultry

MALVERN, GREAT
Hereford & Worcester
Map **3** SO74

GH Bredon Hotel 34 Worcester Rd ☎(06845) 66990
Closed Xmas
9hc (2fb) B&b£13–£15 LDO6.30pm
Lic CTV 10P
Credit cards 1 2 3

GH Fromefield Hotel 147 Barnards Green Rd ☎(06845) 62466
7rm 5hc 1 1⫛ (2fb) ✱ B&b£11–£15 Bdi£17.50–£21.50 LDO5pm
Lic CTV 5P
Ⓥ

⊢⊣ **GH Sidney House Hotel** 40 Worcester Rd ☎(06845) 4994
Listed Georgian house being restored by cheerful, welcoming young owners.
6hc (2fb) B&b£7.50–£13 Bdi£11–£16.50 W£69.50–£102.50 ⱡ LDO6pm
Lic 𝍔 CTV 8P
Credit cards 1 3

MANATON
Devon
Map **3** SX78
⊢⊣ **FH** Mrs M Hugo **Langstone** *(SX747823)* ☎(064722) 266
Mar–Oct
Long, low granite farmhouse in traditional Dartmoor style with lawn and childrens swing. On the edge of the moor with fine views.
3hc ✶ B&bfr£8 Bdifr£14
CTV 3P nc5yrs 140acres beef

MANCHESTER
Gt Manchester
Map **7** SJ89
GH *Horizon Hotel* 69 Palatine Rd, West Didsbury ☎061-445 4705
A large brick built semi-detached house with attractive, modern furnishings, situated in residential area 2½m from city centre.
13hc 5⇌ 2⋒ CTV in all bedrooms ✶ Ⓡ
Lic 𝍔 CTV 20P ♿
Ⓥ

GH Imperial Hotel 157 Hathersage Rd ☎061-225 6500
Modernised, semi-detached house situated about 1½m from city centre, close to Manchester University.
20rm 1⇌ 11⋒ Ⓡ B&b£15–£18 Bdi£18–£21 W£80–£98 M LDO8pm
Lic 𝍔 CTV 40P nc3yrs
Credit cards 1 2 3 Ⓥ

GH Kempton House Hotel 400 Wilbraham Rd, Chorlton-cum-Hardy ☎061-881 8766
Closed 25 & 26 Dec
14hc (1fb) ✶ B&b£11.50 Bdi£14 LDO6.30pm
Lic 𝍔 CTV 9P
Ⓥ

GH Hotel Tara 10–12 Oswald Rd, Chorlton-cum-Hardy ☎061-861 0385
Victorian houses converted to large, modern hotel in quiet area.
18hc (2fb) ✶ Ⓡ B&b£14.95–£16.10 Bdi£21.28–£22.43 LDO4pm
Lic 𝍔 CTV 30P

MAN, ISLE OF
Map **6**
Places with AA-listed accommodation are indicated on location map 6. Full details will be found under individual placenames in the gazetteer section.

MAPPOWDER
Dorset
Map **3** ST70
⊢⊣ **FH** Mrs A K Williamson-Jones **Boywood** *(ST733078)* ☎Hazelbury Bryan (02586) 416
1½m N unclass rd towards Hazelbury Bryan.
3rm ✶ B&b£8 Bdi£13 W£50 M LDO6pm
𝍔 CTV P ▭(heated) 17acres

MARGATE
Kent
Map **5** TR37
⊢⊣ **GH Alice Springs Hotel** 6–8 Garfield Rd ☎Thanet (0843) 23543
Situated in residential cul-de-sac, near the sea with compact well equipped bedrooms.
18rm (4fb) CTV in 8 bedrooms TV in 10 bedrooms ✶ Ⓡ B&b£7–£7.50 Bdi£10–£11 W£40–£54 M LDO6pm
Lic 𝍔 CTV ₱ nc6yrs

GH Beachcomber Hotel 2–3 Royal Esplanade, Westbrook ☎Thanet (0843) 21616
Closed Oct & Xmas rs Nov–Mar
15hc (3fb) ✶ ∗B&b£9.20 Bdi£12.65–£13.80 W£63.25–£80.50 ⱡ (W only 20 Jul–25 Aug) LDO1pm
Lic CTV ₱ nc4yrs

⊢⊣ **GH Charnwood** 20 Canterbury Rd ☎Thanet (0843) 24158
Closed Nov & Dec
Old-fashioned-type accommodation.
15hc (8fb) ✶ B&b£7–£9 Bdi£10–£12 W£54–£60 ⱡ LDO6pm
Lic CTV ₱
Credit card 3 Ⓥ

GH Galleon Lights Hotel 12–14 Fort Cres, Cliftonville ☎Thanet (0843) 291703
Jun–Sep rs Oct–May
Comfortable modernised accommodation, with a basement dining room and bar, facing the Winter Gardens.
21rm 14hc 5⇌ 2⋒ (2fb) CTV in 11 bedrooms ✶ ∗B&b£7.50 Bdi£11 W£48–£51 M (W only Jun–Sep) LDO4pm
Lic 𝍔 CTV ₱ nc10yrs
Credit cards 1 3

⊢⊣ **GH Tyrella Private Hotel** 19 Canterbury Rd ☎Thanet (0843) 292746
rs Xmas & New Year
Small, family run house, close to the sea with modern, well-decorated bedrooms.
8hc (4fb) ✶ Ⓡ B&b£7–£8 Bdi£10–£11 W£38–£45 M LDO2pm
Lic 𝍔 CTV ₱ nc6yrs
Ⓥ

GH *Westbrook Bay House* 12 Royal Esplanade, Westbrook ☎Thanet (0843) 292700
Well maintained bedrooms, some with excellent sea views, and tastefully furnished public rooms.
12hc 1⇌ (4fb) ✶ LDO4pm
Lic 𝍔 CTV P sea Ⓥ

INN *Ye Olde Charles* Cliftonville ☎Thanet (0843) 21817
11hc
Lic 𝍔 CTV 40P

MARK CAUSEWAY
Somerset
Map **3** ST34
FH Mrs E Puddy **Croft** *(ST355475)*
☎Mark Moor (027864) 206
Closed Xmas Day
Comfortable and well-decorated farmhouse with traditional furnishings throughout.
4hc B&b£6.50–£7 Bdi£8.50–£9.50 W£48 LDOnoon
CTV 2 nc14yrs 130acres dairy

MARLOW
Buckinghamshire
Map **4** SU88
GH *Glade Nook* 75 Glade Rd
☎(06284) 4677
Small, modern house, family run to a very high standard.
7hc 1 1 (1fb) ®
CTV 7P

MARSDEN
West Yorkshire
Map **7** SE01
INN *Coach & Horses* Standedge
☎Huddersfield (0484) 844241
11hc 1 3 LDO10pm
TV 200P 5

Mark Causeway — Masham

MARSHGATE
Cornwall
Map **2** SX19
FH Mrs P Bolt **Carleton** *(SX153918)*
☎Otterham Station (08406) 252
Etr–Oct
Farmhouse is situated adjacent to the Boscastle road in Marshgate with views over the surrounding farmlands.
3rm (1fb) B&b£7.48 Bdi£10.92 W£48.88 (W only Jul & Aug) LDO7pm
CTV 3P 120acres dairy

MARSTOW
Hereford & Worcester
Map **3** SO51
FH Mrs S C Watson **Trebandy** *(SO544203)* ☎Llangarron (098984) 230
Apr–Oct
Large, Georgian farmhouse situated in the remote Garron Valley, well off the A4137, 1m NW unclass rd. Ideal for peaceful stay.
2hc ® B&b£7–£7.50 W£47
CTV 6P 237acres mixed

MARYBANK
Highland *Ross & Cromarty*
Map **14** NH45
FH Mrs R Macleod **Easter Balloon** *(NH484535)* ☎Urray (09973) 211
Etr–Oct
Roadside farmhouse standing in its own garden on edge of village.
5rm 4hc (2fb) B&bfr£6 Bdifr£9.50 Wfr£42 LDO8pm
CTV 12P 143acres mixed

MARY TAVY
Devon
Map **2** SX57
FH Mrs B Anning **Wringworthy** *(SX500773)* ☎(082281) 434
Apr–Sep
2m S A386.
3rm (1fb) B&b£8 Bdi£13 LDO9am
CTV 3P nc3yrs 80acres dairy

MASHAM
North Yorkshire
Map **8** SE28
GH Bank Villa (Guestaccom) ☎Ripon (0765) 89605
Mar–Oct
7rm 3hc B&b£10 Bdi£17 W£107.50 LDOnoon
Lic CTV 7P nc5yrs
Ⓥ

Mathon — Mawgan Porth

MATHON
Hereford & Worcester
Map **3** SO74

⟼ **FH** Mrs S Williams **Moorend Court** *(SO726454)* ☎ Ridgway Cross (088684) 205

Beautiful 15th-century farmhouse in secluded position with panoramic views towards Malvern. Trout fishing on farm.

7hc 1→ (4fb) TV in all bedrooms Ⓡ B&b£8–£10.50 Bdi£12.50–£15 LDO10am

20P (grass) 200acres arable beef sheep

Ⓥ

MATLOCK
Derbyshire
Map **8** SK36

GH Town Head Farmhouse 70 High St, Bonsall ☎ Wirksworth (062982) 3762
Apr–Oct

200-year-old stone-built farmhouse with attached converted barns, located on edge of village 5 miles from Matlock.

6hc Ⓡ B&b£8.50–£9.50 W£59.50 M

8P nc10yrs

FH Mrs M Brailsford **Farley** *(SK294622)* ☎ (0629) 2533
Closed Xmas & New Year

Stone-built farmhouse, parts of which date back to 1610, set high in the Derbyshire hills. 1½m NNW unclass rd.

2rm 1hc (1fb) B&b£7.50 Bdi£12 W£84 L LDO7pm

CTV 8P 225acres arable beef dairy

⟼ **FH** Mr & Mrs Groom **Manor** *(SK327580)* Dethick ☎ Dethick (062984) 246
Closed Xmas

A large beautifully preserved mid 16th-century stone-built manor house situated in a tiny hamlet.

4rm 2hc 1 B&bfr£8 Bdifr£14 W£52 M LDOnoon

CTV 10P nc5yrs 200acres dairy sheep mixed

⟼ **FH** M Haynes **Packhorse** *(SK323617)* Matlock Moor ☎ (0629) 2781

Former inn on much travelled Chesterfield to Manchester packhorse route. Tastefully furnished. Lawns and putting greens. 2m NE of Matlock off A632 at Tansley signpost.

5hc (3fb) B&b£6.50–£7 W£45.50 M

CTV 6P nc3yrs 40acres mixed

Ⓥ

⟼ **FH** Mrs J Hole **Wayside** *(SK324630)* Matlock Moor ☎ (0629) 2967
Closed Xmas day & New Years day

Pleasant, modernised, stone-built farmhouse, adjacent to A632 Matlock–Chesterfield road.

6hc (2fb) B&b£7–£7.50

CTV 6P 60acres dairy

MATTISHALL
Norfolk
Map **9** TG01

FH Mrs M Faircloth **Moat** *(TG049111)* ☎ Dereham (0362) 850288
May–Oct

Period farmhouse standing back from the road with good friendly atmosphere.

2hc (1fb) *B&b£6.50 Bdi£10 W£65 L LDO4pm

CTV 2P nc8yrs 100acres mixed

MAWGAN PORTH
Cornwall
Map **2** SW86

GH Pandora Tredragon Rd ☎ St Mawgan (06374) 412 (due to change to (0637) 860412)
Jun–mid Sep

7rm 6hc (1fb) *B&b£7.50–£8.50 Bdi£10.50–£12.50 W£49–£59 M

Lic CTV 7P nc3yrs

Ⓥ

GH White Lodge Hotel ☎St Mawgan (06374) 512 (due to change to (0637) 860512)
Mar–Oct
Large building in commanding position overlooking sea and countryside.
15rm 5hc 10🛁 (6fb) B&b£9–£13 Bdi£14–£17 W£67–£84 Ⱡ LDO7.30pm
Lic ♨ CTV 18P

MAYFIELD
Staffordshire
Map **7** SK14
INN Queens Arms ☎Ashbourne (0335) 42271
7hc CTV in 4 bedrooms B&b£9.20 Bdi£11 Bar lunch £1–£3
20P

MELBOURNE
Derbyshire
Map **8** SK32
INN Melbourne Hotel ☎(03316) 2134
6hc Bdi£12.50 W£87.50 Ⓜ L50p–£5&alc D10pm 50p–£5&alc
200P

MELKSHAM
Wiltshire
Map **3** ST96
GH Longhope 9 Beanacre Rd ☎(0225) 706737
8rm 3hc 2🚿 (3fb) CTV in 3 bedrooms B&b£10 Bdi£14 W£80 Ⓜ LDO6pm
♨ CTV 8P

GH *Regency Hotel* 10–12 Spa Rd ☎(0225) 702971
12hc 1🚿 (1fb) CTV in 1 bedroom TV in 11 bedrooms LDO6.30pm
Lic ♨ CTV 🚫
Ⓥ

GH Shaw Farm Shaw ☎(0225) 702836
Closed 24–26 Dec
1½m NW off A365.
12rm 6hc 1🛁 5🚿 (2fb) ✱ B&b£12 Bdi£18.50 W£80 Ⓜ LDOnoon
Lic ♨ CTV 20P ≈ (heated)

⊢⊣ **GH York** Church Walk ☎(0225) 702063
9hc (3fb) B&bfr£8 Bdifr£12
♨ CTV P 🏠
Ⓥ

MELTON MOWBRAY
Leicestershire
Map **8** SK71
GH Sysonby Knoll Hotel 225 Asfordby Rd ☎(0664) 63563
Closed Xmas
18rm 7🛁 4🚿 (1fb) CTV in all bedrooms Ⓡ B&b£15–£22 LDO7.30pm
Lic ♨ CTV 15P ≈
Credit cards 1 3 Ⓥ
See advertisement on page 244

GH Westbourne House Hotel 11A–15 Nottingham Rd ☎(0664) 69456
16hc (3fb) B&b£9–£9.50 LDO7pm
♨ CTV 18P

MENDHAM
Suffolk
Map **5** TM28
FH Mrs J E Holden **Weston House** *(TM292828)* ☎St Cross (098682) 206
Apr–Oct
Fine old house approximately 300 years old, in 1 acre of garden with fishing nearby.
3hc (1fb) ✱ B&bfr£8.50 Bdifr£12.50 W£80 Ⱡ LDOnoon
♨ CTV 6P 330acres arable dairy

MENHENIOT
Cornwall
Map **2** SX26

FH Mrs S Rowe **Tregondale** *(SX294643)* ☏Liskeard (0579) 42407
Farm situated 1½m N of A38, E of Liskeard.
3rm 2hc (1fb) B&b£7.50–£8 Bdi£10.50–£11 W£49 M LDO8pm
CTV 3P 180acres arable beef sheep mixed
Ⓥ

MERIDEN
West Midlands
Map **4** SP28

GH Meriden Hotel Main Rd ☏(0676) 22005
8hc (2fb) B&b£14 Bdi£20 W£70 M LDO5pm
CTV 10P

MERRYMEET
Cornwall
Map **2** SX26

FH Mrs B Cole **Merrymeet** *(SX279660)* ☏Liskeard (0579) 43231
end May–mid Sep
Small, two-storey, tile-hung farmhouse with front garden, on the A390.
2rm *B&b£5.50 W£37 M
TV 1P 1 nc2yrs 40acres mixed

MEVAGISSEY
Cornwall
Map **2** SX04

GH Headlands Hotel Polkirt Hill ☏(0726) 843453
Apr–Nov
Large detached house, standing above road with magnificent sea views.
14rm 8hc 6 (3fb) *B&b£9.75–£10.90 Bdi£13.75–£14.90 W£68.25–£76.30 M LDO7pm
Lic CTV 11P

GH Polhaun Hotel Polkirt Hill ☏(0726) 843222
Etr–Oct
Modern guesthouse with excellent sea views.
7hc 1 1 (1fb) TV in all bedrooms B&bfr£9 Bdifr£13 Wfr£89 L LDO6.30pm
Lic 9P nc10yrs

GH Valley Park Private Hotel Tregoney Hill ☏(0726) 842347
Large detached house dating back several hundred years, with several semi-tropical gardens.
8rm 5hc 3 (4fb) B&b£11.50–£12.50 Bdi£17.25–£18.30 W£103.50–£110 L LDOnoon
Lic CTV 11P

INN Ship Fore St ☏(0726) 843324
Large stone inn on corner of main shopping street.
5hc B&b£8.50 W£59.50 M
CTV

MIDDLESBROUGH
Cleveland
Map **8** NZ42

GH Chadwick Private Hotel 27 Clairville Rd ☏(0642) 245340
rs Xmas
6hc (1fb) B&b£10 Bdi£14 W£98 M LDO4pm
CTV
Ⓥ

GH Grey House Hotel 79 Cambridge Rd ☏(0642) 817485
Closed Xmas & New Year
10hc (1fb) *B&b£11 Bdi£15 LDO7pm
Lic CTV 10P 1

GH Longlands Hotel 295 Marton Rd ☏(0642) 244900
7hc (1fb) B&b£13.90 Bdi£17.40 W£72.45–£96.60 M LDO5.30pm
Lic CTV 6P 2

MIDDLETON-ON-SEA
West Sussex
Map **4** SU90

GH Ancton House Hotel Ancton Ln
☎(024369) 2482
Cosy 16th-century guesthouse set in rural surroundings.
9rm 6hc 2 1 Ⓡ B&b£12 Bdi£15.50 Wfr£95 LDO6.30pm
Lic CTV 5P 5
Credit card 3

MIDDLETOWN
Powys
Map **7** SJ21

FH Mrs E J Bebb **Bank** *(SJ325137)*
☎Trewern (093874) 260
Mar–Oct
Situated on the A458 Shrewsbury–Welshpool road at the foot of the Breidden Hills with good views.
2hc B&bfr£7 Bdifr£10.50
CTV P 30acres sheep

MIDHURST
West Sussex
Map **4** SU82
See Bepton, Rogate

MILBORNE PORT
Somerset
Map **3** ST61

FH Mrs M J Tizzard **Venn**
(ST684183) ☎(0963) 250208
Mar–Nov
Modern bungalow-type farmhouse set back off main A30, a short distance from village.
3rm 2hc (2fb) Ⓡ B&b£8 W£55 M
CTV P 300acres dairy
Ⓥ

MILFORD HAVEN
Dyfed
Map **2** SM90

GH *Belhaven House Hotel* 29 Hamilton Ter ☎(06462) 5983
12hc 5 (3fb) LDO8.30pm
Lic CTV sea

MILFORD-ON-SEA
Hampshire
Map **4** SZ29

GH Seaspray 8 Hurst Rd ☎Lymington (0590) 42627
Mar–Oct
Modern chalet-style building on the sea front, with a large garden.
6rm 4hc 2 (1fb) TV in all bedrooms B&b£10–£12 Bdi£16–£18 W£97–£112 LDO3pm
Lic 8P

MILLPOOL
Cornwall
Map **2** SW53

GH Chyraise Lodge Hotel ☎Germoe (073676) 3485
Small comfortable family residence within own grounds in secluded valley.
9hc (1fb) Ⓡ B&b£8.50–£9.50 Bdi£12–£13 W£80–£87.50 LDO5.30pm
Lic CTV 10P
Ⓥ

MILNGAVIE
Strathclyde *Dunbartonshire*
Map **11** NS57

FH Mrs L Fisken ***High Craigton***
(NS525766) ☎041-956 1384
Off A809, two-storey painted stone-built farmhouse on hilltop with views over fields towards Glasgow.
2hc (2fb)
CTV 5P 1070acres sheep

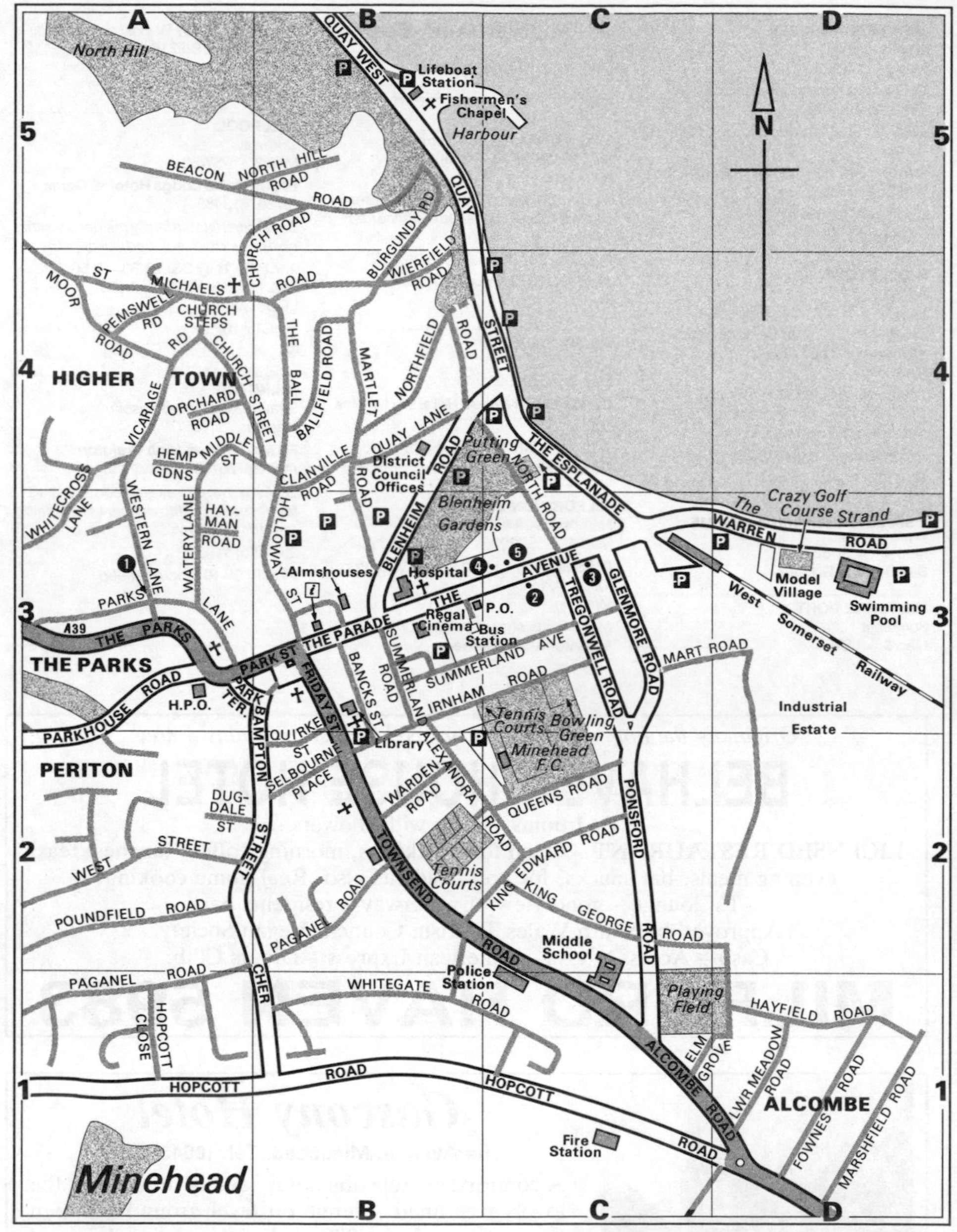

Minehead

1 Carbery
2 Dorchester Hotel
3 Gascony Hotel
4 Glen Rock Hotel
5 Mayfair Hotel

MINEHEAD
Somerset
Map **3** SS94
See plan

GH *Carbery* Western Ln, The Parks
☎(0643) 2941 Plan **1** *A3*
Etr–Oct
6hc ✈ LDO10am
Lic CTV 8P nc16yrs

GH Dorchester Hotel 38 The Avenue
☎(0643) 2052 Plan **2** *C3*
13hc (4fb) ✈ B&b£8.75 Bdi£12.75 W£75 ⱪ LDO6.30pm
Lic ▥ CTV 15P nc5yrs
Credit cards 1 3 Ⓥ

GH Gascony Hotel The Avenue
☎(0643) 2817 Plan **3** *C3*
Mar–Oct
14rm 5hc 2→ 5⋒ (6fb) ✈ Ⓡ B&b£9–£10 Bdi£13.50–£14.50 W£72–£79 ⱪ LDO6pm
Lic CTV 10P ⌂
Credit cards 1 3 Ⓥ
See advertisement on page 245

⊢⊣ **GH Glen Rock Hotel** 23 The Avenue
☎(0643) 2245 Plan **4** *C3*
Mar–Nov
12hc (2fb) B&b£8–£9 Bdi£12.50–£13.50 W£74–£80 ⱪ LDO7pm
Lic CTV 10P 1⌂ nc3yrs

GH Mayfair Hotel 25 The Avenue
☎(0643) 2719 Plan **5** *C3*
rs Mar–Oct
18hc B&b£9–£10 Bdi£13–£14 W£74–£78 ⱪ LDO7pm
Lic ▥ CTV 14P

MINSTER LOVELL
Oxfordshire
Map **4** SP31

FH Mrs K Brown **Hill Grove** *(SP334110)*
☎Witney (0993) 3120
Closed Xmas
A Cotswold stone-built farmhouse with extensive views over the Windrush Valley, with river running through. Off B4047 1½m E of village towards Crawley village.
2rm ✈ Ⓡ B&b£9–£10
u112 CTV 4P ♪ 90acres arable beef mixed
Ⓥ

MINSTERWORTH
Gloucestershire
Map **3** SO71

GH Severn Bank ☎(045275) 357
Closed Xmas day
6hc (2fb) ✈ Ⓡ B&b£8.50 Bdi£14 W£59.50 M LDOnoon
Lic ▥ CTV 12P nc5yrs ♪

MOFFAT
Dumfries & Galloway *Dumfriesshire*
Map **11** NT00

⊢⊣ **GH Arden House** High St ☎(0683) 20220
Mar–Oct
Converted sandstone bank building, attractively decorated and furnished, dating from 1738, in town centre.
8rm 4→ 4⋒ (2fb) B&b£7.50–£9 Bdi£12–£13 W£52–£63 M (W only May–Sep) LDO6.45pm
▥ CTV 9P

⊢⊣ **GH Bridge** Well Rd ☎(0683) 20383
Feb–Nov
Homely family guesthouse in residential area.
6hc (2fb) Ⓡ B&b£7–£7.50 Bdi£11–£12 W£47–£50 M LDO5pm
▥ CTV 10P

⊢⊣ **GH Buchan** 13 Beechgrove
☎(0683) 20378
Apr–Oct
An attractively decorated and furnished house.
8hc (2fb) B&b£6.50–£7.50 Bdi£11–£11.50 (W only Jun–Sep) LDO7.30pm
▥ CTV 6P

GH Hartfell House Hartfell Cres
☎(0683) 20153
Closed Jan & Feb
Converted Victorian house to rear of the town with two acres of gardens.
9hc (3fb) B&b£9.10 Bdi£15.08 W£102 ⱪ LDO7.30pm
Lic ▥ CTV 10P

GH Robin Hill Beechgrove ☎(0683) 20050
Apr–Oct
An adequately appointed house with gardens in pleasant residential road.
6rm (2fb) Ⓡ B&b£9–£9.50
▥ CTV 7P

⊢⊣ **GH Rockhill** 14 Beechgrove
☎(0683) 20283
Mar–Oct
Attractive house close to a park with bowling green and tennis courts.
10hc (3fb) B&b£8–£8.50 Bdi£13–£13.50 W£85–£89 ⱪ LDO5.30pm
▥ CTV 6P

⊢⊣ **GH St Olaf** Eastgate, Off Dickson St
☎(0683) 20001
Apr–Sep
Converted two-storey house dating from 1880 situated just off the main shopping centre.
7hc (3fb) B&b£7 Bdi£10.50 W£73.50 ⱪ LDO6.30pm
▥ 4⌂

MOLESWORTH
Cambridgeshire
Map **4** TL07

INN *Cross Keys* ☎Bythorn (08014) 283
3hc 1→ 1⋒ D10.30pm
▥ 50P nc7yrs

MOLLAND
Devon
Map **3** SS82

FH Mrs P England ***Yeo*** *(SS785266)*
☎Bishop's Nympton (07697) 312
Etr–Oct
Well-maintained farmhouse with good furnishings and décor, set in large garden.
4hc (1fb) ✈
▥ CTV 5P 200acres mixed sheep

MONEYDIE
Tayside *Perthshire*
Map **11** NO02

⊢⊣**FH** Mrs S Walker **Moneydie Roger** *(NO054290)* ☎Almondbank (073883) 239
Apr–Sep
A substantial, two-storey farmhouse situated on unclassified road signed Methven, off the B8063, 2½m W of the A9.
2rm (1fb) B&b£6.50–£6.75
2P 143acres arable sheep mixed

MONKSILVER
Somerset
Map **3** ST03

FH Mrs L R Watts ***Manor House at Rowdon Farm*** *(ST082381)* ☎Stogumber (09846) 614
Closed Xmas
Solidly built stone farmhouse overlooking Quantock Hills. 5m from sea, 10m from Minehead.
5hc (2fb) LDO4pm
CTV 8P 300acres arable beef mixed sheep

⊢⊣**FH** Mrs S J Watts **Rowdon** *(ST082381)* ☎Stogumber (09846) 280
Modern farmhouse with bright comfortable accommodation overlooking Quantock Hills. Ideal touring centre for Exmoor and West Somerset coast.
4hc CTV in 1 bedroom Ⓡ B&b£6.50–£7.50 Bdi£10.50–£11.50 W£49 M
CTV 8P 300acres mixed
Ⓥ

MONMOUTH
Gwent
Map **3** SO51

INN Queens Head St James Street ☎(0600) 2767
Attractive small inn with bar of character and pretty bedrooms. Situated by Haberdashers school.
6rm 1→ 5⋒ CTV in all bedrooms Ⓡ B&b£11 Bdi£15 W£75–£85 L L£1–£6alc D10pm £1–£6alc
6P
Credit cards 1 3

MONTROSE
Tayside *Angus*
Map **15** NO75

GH Linksgate 11 Dorward Rd ☎(0674) 72273
7hc (5fb) B&b£8.50–£9.50 Bdi£12.50–£13.50 W£83–£89.50 L LDO6pm
CTV 8P

FH Mrs A Ruxton **Muirshade of Gallery** *(NO671634)* ☎Northwaterbridge (067484) 209
Situated in beautiful countryside facing the Grampian mountain range, only 5m from the sea.
2hc (1fb) *B&b£6 Bdi£9 W£42 M LDO6pm
CTV 3P 110acres arable
Ⓥ

MORECAMBE
Lancashire
Map **7** SD46

GH Ashley Private Hotel 371 Marine Road East ☎(0524) 412034
14hc (4fb) Ⓡ B&b£8.50–£9.50 Bdi£11–£12 W£56–£63 M LDO4pm
Lic CTV 4P

GH Beach Mount 395 Marine Road East ☎(0524) 420753
Mar Nov
27rm 5hc 20→ 2⋒ (3fb) CTV in 22 bedrooms B&b£11–£11.50 Bdi£15–£16 W£90–£100 L LDO7pm
Lic CTV 6P
Credit card 2

⊢⊣**GH Ellesmere Private Hotel** 44 Westminster Rd ☎(0524) 411881
Apr–Oct
Small, friendly guesthouse with good home made food.
5hc (2fb) B&b£6–£7 Bdi£8–£9 W£52 L
CTV

GH Elstead Private Hotel 72 Regent Rd ☎(0524) 412260
12hc (2fb) *B&b£6.50–£8.50 Bdi£7.50–£9.50 W£45.50–£58 L LDO3pm
Lic CTV

GH Glendene 42 Westminster Rd ☎(0524) 416358
Etr–15 Oct
Small guesthouse offering good value for money.
5hc (1fb) *B&b£4–£5 Bdi£7–£8 W£28–£35 M LDO3pm
CTV
Ⓥ

GH New Hazelmere Hotel 391 Marine Road East ☎(0524) 417876
Apr–Nov rs Dec–Mar
22hc (7fb) TV in 3 bedrooms B&b£9.20 Bdi£12.65–£13.80 W£50–£57.50 L LDO5pm
Lic CTV 1P
Ⓥ

GH Hotel Prospect 363 Marine Road East ☎(0524) 417819
Etr & May–Oct
14rm 6hc 8→ (5fb) Ⓡ B&b£8.05–£9.20 Bdi£11.50–£12.65 W£77.05–£85.10 L LDO3pm
Lic CTV 6P

GH Rydal Mount Private Hotel 361 Marine Road East ☎(0524) 411858
Apr–Oct
14rm 11hc 3⋒ (4fb) TV in 1 bedroom Ⓡ *B&b£10–£11 Bdi£11–£12 W£58–£60 M LDO4.30pm
Lic CTV 12P nc3yrs

GH Hotel Warwick 394 Marine Road East ☎(0524) 418151
23rm 11hc 3→ 9⋒ (6fb) CTV in 4 bedrooms TV in 5 bedrooms Ⓡ B&b£9–£10 Bdi£12.50–£14 Wfr£60 M LDO5.30pm
Lic lift CTV
Credit cards 1 2 3 Ⓥ

GH Wimslow Private Hotel 374 Marine Rd East ☎(0524) 417804
Mar–Oct & 4 days Xmas
15rm 12hc 3🚿 (4fb) 🐕 ⓡ B&b£10 Bdi£13.50 W£85 ɫ LDO4.30pm
Lic ♨ CTV 9P
Credit cards 1 3

INN York Hotel Lancaster Rd ☎(0524) 418226
12hc
CTV 12P

MORETONHAMPSTEAD
Devon
Map **3** SX78

GH Cookshayes 33 Court St ☎(0647) 40374
15 Mar–Oct
Large brick detached house close to village centre, well maintained gardens.
8hc 1🛁 4🚿 (1fb) ⓡ B&b£9.50–£11 Bdi£15–£16.50 W£63–£75 M̸ LDO5.30pm
Lic ♨ CTV 15P nc8yrs
Credit cards 1 3 ⓥ

⊢×⊣ **GH Elmfield** Station Rd ☎(0647) 40327
Etr–Oct
6rm 2hc (2fb) B&b£8 Bdi£13.50 W£80 ɫ LDO6.30pm
Lic ♨ CTV 8P
ⓥ

GH *Wray Barton Manor* ☎(0647) 40246
Closed Xmas wk
7hc 2🛁 2🚿 (1fb) CTV in 5 bedrooms 🐕 ⓡ LDO6.45pm
Lic ♨ CTV 60P nc12yrs

MORFA NEFYN
Gwynedd
Map **6** SH23

GH *Erw Goch* ☎Nefyn (0758) 720539
Georgian house offering good leisure facilities for adults and children.
15hc (7fb)
Lic ♨ CTV 20P

MORNINGTHORPE
Norfolk
Map **5** TM29

FH Mrs O E Gowing ***Hollies*** *(TM212939)* ☎Long Stratton (0508) 30540
Apr–Sep
Large, Georgian house standing in own grounds, in quiet rural area, ¾m E of A140. Hard tennis court and heated swimming pool in south facing garden. Good atmosphere.
10hc 1🛁 (4fb) 🐕
♨ CTV 12P 350acres arable

MORTEHOE
Devon
Map **2** SS44

⊢×⊣ **GH Baycliffe Hotel** Chapel Hill ☎Woolacombe (0271) 870393
11rm 10hc 1🛁 (3fb) B&b£7.50–£10 Bdi£12.50–£15 W£50–£65 M̸ LDO6.30pm
Lic ♨ CTV 9P

GH Haven ☎Woolacombe (0271) 870426
Apr–Oct rs Mar
17rm 4hc 13🛁 (6fb) ⓡ B&b£10–£12 Bdi£15–£17 W£100–£117 ɫ LDO8pm
Lic ♨ CTV 20P 1🏠

GH Sunnycliffe Hotel (Guestaccom) ☎Woolacombe (0271) 870597
8rm 4🛁 4🚿 CTV in all bedrooms 🐕 ⓡ *B&b£14–£16 Bdi£20–£22 W£120–£140 ɫ LDO6.30pm
Lic ♨ 11P nc10yrs

MORTIMER'S CROSS
Hereford & Worcester
Map **3** SO46

INN Mortimer's Cross ☎Kingsland (056881) 238
4hc CTV in all bedrooms B&b£9.50 Bdi£13.50 Bar lunch £5 LDO10.30pm
♨ 20P
Credit card 3

MORVAH
Cornwall
Map **2** SW33

⊢×⊣ **FH** Mrs J Mann **Merthyr** *(SW403355)* ☎Penzance (0736) 788464
Apr–Oct
Well-appointed farmhouse with sun lounge and sea views, on B3306 NW of Penzance.
5hc (2fb) B&b£7–£8 W£45.50–£52.50 M̸
CTV 6P nc6yrs 100acres mixed

MOUNT
Cornwall
Map **2** SX16

⊢×⊣ **FH** Mrs E J Beglan **Mount Pleasant** *(SX152680)* ☎Cardinham (020882) 342
Etr–Nov
Farmhouse situated 6m E of Bodmin in open country on the edge of Bodmin Moor. Own transport essential.
6hc (2fb) B&b£7 Bdi£10 W£45 M̸ LDO4pm
Lic ♨ CTV 12P 53acres beef

MOUSEHOLE
Cornwall
Map **2** SW42

GH Tavis Vor ☎Penzance (0736) 731306
Mar–Oct
Delightful country house style residence, in own grounds running to the edge of the sea.
7hc 3🚿 (2fb) 🐕 B&b£9.50–£10.50 Bdi£14.50–£15.50 W£96.25–£103.25 ɫ LDO6pm
Lic ♨ CTV 7P

MOY
Highland *Inverness-shire*
Map **14** NH73

⊢×⊣ **GH Invermoy House** ☎Tomatin (08082) 271
Closed Nov
Formerly the local railway station, the main line still runs close by. 1½m off A9.
7hc 1🚿 ⓡ B&b£8 Bdi£13 W£77–£80 ɫ LDO6.30pm →

Lic 𝍐 CTV 11P ⌂
Ⓥ

MOYLGROVE
Dyfed
Map **2** SN14

FH Mrs J I Young **Cwm Connell** *(SN119461)* ☎(023986) 220
Charming 200-year-old farmhouse in picturesque location with lovely views of sea and coastline. Comfortable bedrooms each with its own character; there is a walled garden at rear available to guests.
3rm ✱ *B&b£7.50 Bdi£10.50 W£66.50 ⱡ (W only end Jul & Aug)
𝍐 5P 2🚗 nc9yrs 5acres mixed

FH Mrs A D Fletcher **Penrallt Ceibwr** *(SN116454)* ☎(023986) 217
A very pleasant farm off A487, ½m from Ceibwr beach.
6hc (3fb) *B&b£8–£9 Bdi£14–£15 W£87–£98 ⱡ LDO7pm
Lic 𝍐 CTV 20P ⌂ 300acres arable dairy mixed
Ⓥ
See advertisement on page 249

MULL, ISLE OF
Strathclyde *Argyllshire*
Maps **10** & **13**
See Salen & Tobermory

MULLION
Cornwall
Map **2** SW61

⊢⊣ **GH Belle Vue** ☎(0326) 240483
Etr–Sep
Small family residence, close to golf course and beaches.
8hc (1fb) ✱ B&b£7–£8.50 Bdi£11–£12.50 W£45–£80 ⱡ LDO4pm
CTV 10P
Ⓥ

GH Henscath House Mullion Cove ☎(0326) 240537
Closed Xmas–New Year
All public rooms and front bedrooms here have magnificent views, and there is good atmosphere and good food.

Moy — Mylor Bridge

6rm 2hc 2⇌ 2⋒ (1fb) ✱ Ⓡ B&b£9–£10 Bdi£14.50–£15.50 W£97–£104 ⱡ LDO7pm
Lic 𝍐 CTV 8P

GH *Trenowyth House Private Hotel* Mullion Cove ☎(0326) 240486
Mar–Oct
Family hotel well positioned offering good views.
6hc (2fb) Ⓡ LDO8pm
Lic 𝍐 CTV 7P

INN Old Inn Church Town ☎(0326) 240240
2 Jan–24 Dec
Character inn with attractive bar, comfortable rooms and good food.
5rm 2hc 3⇌ TV in all bedrooms Ⓡ B&b£9.50–£13 LDO9.30pm
10P nc12yrs

MUMBLES
West Glamorgan
Map **2** SS68
See also Bishopston and Langland Bay

GH *Carlton Hotel* 654–656 BMumbles Rd, Southend ☎Swansea (0792) 60450
Closed Xmas
Seafront hotel with modestly appointed bedrooms.
19hc 1⇌ 7⋒ (1fb) CTV in 12 bedrooms ✱ Ⓡ LDO10.15pm
Lic 𝍐 CTV nc7yrs

GH Harbour Winds Private Hotel Overland Rd, Langland ☎Swansea (0792) 69298
Apr–Oct
Well maintained comfortable detached house in own grounds.
8rm 6hc 1⇌ 1⋒ (3fb) Ⓡ B&b£10–£11 Bdi£15.50–£16.50 W£70–£77 ⱡ LDO5pm
𝍐 CTV 12P ⌂
Ⓥ

⊢⊣ **GH Shoreline Hotel** 648 Mumbles Rd, Southend ☎Swansea (0792) 66322
13rm 7hc 1⇌ 5⋒ (3fb) CTV in 6 bedrooms B&b£8–£15 Bdi£12.50–£20 W£49–£95 M LDO5.30pm
Lic 𝍐 CTV ⊁
Credit cards 1 3

⊢⊣ **GH Southend Hotel & Restaurant** 724 Mumbles Rd ☎Swansea (0792) 66329
A modestly appointed establishment.
11hc (4fb) CTV in 6 bedrooms Ⓡ B&b£8–£9 Bdi£11–£16 W£53–£60 M LDO9.30pm
Lic 𝍐 CTV ⊁
Credit cards 1 2 3 Ⓥ

MUNGRISDALE
Cumbria
Map **11** NY33

GH The Mill ☎Threlkeld (059683) 659
mid Mar–mid Nov
8rm 6hc 2⇌ (1fb) CTV in 2 bedrooms ✱ Ⓡ B&b£12–£14 Bdi£16–£19.50 LDO6pm
Lic CTV 12P 2🚗

FH Mrs J M Tiffin ***Wham Head*** *(NY373342)* ☎Skelton (08534) 289
3½m NE of unclass road to Haltcliff Bridge.
4rm 3hc (2fb) LDO4pm
CTV 6P 1🚗 ⌂ 126acres mixed

INN Mill ☎Threlkeld (059683) 632
Closed Xmas day
6hc B&b£8.50 Bdi£13 W£59.50 M L£2–£3.50 D9pm £2.25–£4.50
CTV 25P

MYLOR BRIDGE
Cornwall
Map **2** SW83

⊢⊣ **GH Penmere** Rosehill ☎Falmouth (0326) 74470
Mar–Oct
Small friendly comfortably furnished family guesthouse in attractive coastal village; views of estuary.
6hc (3fb) B&b£7.50 Bdi£12 W£52.50 ⱡ LDO5pm

🏨 CTV 6P 🏠
Ⓥ
See advertisement on page 151

NAILSWORTH
Gloucestershire
Map **3** ST89
GH Gables Private Hotel Tiltups End, Bath Rd (Guestaccom) ☎(045383) 2265
Closed Xmas
A modestly appointed establishment.
6rm 5hc (2fb) B&b£9.50–£10 Bdi£14.50–£15 W£66.50–£70 LDO8.30pm
Lic CTV 8P
Ⓥ

NAIRN
Highland *Nairnshire*
Map **14** NH85
GH Greenlawns Private Hotel 13 Seafield St ☎(0667) 52738
Charming, small guesthouse with attractive garden.
8rm 6hc 1➡ 1⋔ (1fb) CTV in all bedrooms Ⓡ B&bfr£10 Bdifr£15 Wfr£65 M LDO7pm
Lic 🏨 CTV 8P
GH Sunny Brae Marine Rd ☎(0667) 52309
Apr–Oct
10hc (2fb) Ⓡ B&b£10–£11.50 Bdi£16–£17.50 W£102–£112 ⱡ LDO5.30pm
Lic 🏨 CTV 14P
Credit card 1

NANTGAREDIG
Dyfed
Map **2** SN42
FH Mrs J Willmott **Cwmtwrch** *(SN497220)* ☎(026788) 238
Closed 2 wks Oct
Early 19th-century Welsh-stone farmhouse, carefully modernised and furnished.
3rm 2hc 1⋔ (1fb) ✶ *B&b£9–£11 Bdi£14.50–£16.50 Wfr£100 ⱡ LDO7pm
Lic 🏨 CTV 10P 30acres beef mixed
Ⓥ

NARBERTH
Dyfed
Map **2** SN11
GH *Blaenmarlais* ☎(0834) 860326
rs May–Sep
Attractive country hotel in own grounds.
11hc 1➡ (A 3hc) (5fb) ✶
Lic CTV 30P 8🚗
⊢⊣ **FH** Mrs I M Bevan **Jacob's Park** *(SN103158)* ☎(0834) 860525
Closed Dec
3hc ✶ B&b£7–£7.50 Bdi£11–£11.50 W£75–£77 ⱡ LDO7.30pm
🏨 CTV 6P 🏠 28acres beef sheep
Ⓥ

NEAR SAWREY
Cumbria
Map **7** SD39
GH High Green Gate ☎Hawkshead (09666) 296
Mar–Oct & Xmas–New Year
7hc 1⋔ (2fb) B&b£9.50 Bdi£14.25 W£93 ⱡ LDO6pm
🏨 CTV 7P 🏠
GH Sawrey House Private Hotel ☎Hawkshead (09666) 387
Closed Dec
Delightful house offering warm comfortable accommodation and good home cooking.
11rm 7hc 3➡ 1⋔ (3fb) Ⓡ B&b£10.50–£13.25 Bdi£17–£19.75 W£115–£134 ⱡ LDO4pm
Lic 🏨 CTV 20P

NEATISHEAD
Norfolk
Map **9** TG32
GH *Barton Angler Hotel* ☎Horning (0692) 630740
Apr–Oct rs Nov–Mar
8hc 3⋔ (1fb) CTV in 3 bedrooms
Lic 🏨 CTV 16P nc7yrs
FH Mr & Mrs Charlton **Allens** *(TG341202)* Three Hammer Common ☎Horning (0692) 630904
Off A1151, 1m N of Wroxham unclass rd.
3hc (1fb) ✶ Ⓡ *B&b£8 Bdi£12.50 W£56 M
🏨 CTV P 🏠 52acres arable

NEEDHAM MARKET
Suffolk
Map **5** TM05
FH Mrs R M Hackett-Jones **Pipps Ford** *(TM108537)* ☎Coddenham (044979) 208
Closed Xmas & New Year
16th-century farmhouse close to the River Gipping, with delightful old-fashiond garden, surrounded by farmland and meadows. Entrance off roundabout junction A45/A140.
3rm 2➡ 1⋔ (1fb) *B&b£10–£18 Bdi£16–£22 W£112–£154 ⱡ LDOnoon
🏨 4P 🏠 ≈ ⤴ 8acres smallholding
Ⓥ

NESSCLIFF
Shropshire
Map **7** SJ31
INN Nesscliff Hotel ☎(074381) 253
5hc Ⓡ B&b£10.90 Bdi£15 L£3.50&alc D10pm £15alc
CTV 75P 2🚗 🚫

NETHER LANGWITH
Nottinghamshire
Map **8** SK57
⊢⊣ **FH** Mrs J M Ibbotson **Blue Barn** *(SK539713)* ☎Mansfield (0623) 742248
2½m NW of Cuckney, 2nd lane on the left off A616 to Creswell.
4rm (1fb) ✶ Ⓡ B&bfr£7.50
🏨 TV 8P 2🚗 250acres arable mixed

NETLEY
Hampshire
Map **4** SU40
GH La Casa Blanca 48 Victoria Rd ☎Southampton (0703) 453718
8hc (1fb) CTV in all bedrooms ✶ Ⓡ *B&b£8.50–£10 W£47.75–£55 M
🏨

NETTLECOMBE
Dorset
Map **3** SY59

INN Marquis of Lorne ☎Powerstock (030885) 236
Closed Xmas

8rm 4hc 4⋒ ✱ Ⓡ B&b£12–£15.50 Bdi£16–£19.50 W£77–£101.50 Ⓜ L£8.95alc D10pm £8.95alc

CTV 40P

Credit card 1

NEWARK-ON-TRENT
Nottinghamshire
Map **8** SK75

GH Edgefield Hotel & Restaurant Vicarage Ln, North Muskham ☎(0636) 700313

A former mid-Victorian vicarage situated ½m west of North Muskham and adjacent to junction of A1 with A6065, 4m north of Newark.

8rm 6hc 2⇌ (2fb) CTV in all bedrooms ✱ (except guide dogs) Ⓡ B&b£15–£25 Bdi£22.50–£32 Wfr£70 Ⓜ LDO10pm

Lic ⅏ CTV 40P 2

Credit card 1

NEWBOLD-ON-STOUR
Warwickshire
Map **4** SP24

FH Mrs J Kerby **Berryfield** *(SP216483)* ☎Ilmington (060882) 248
Mar–Oct

A deceptively-large farmhouse in secluded position. Situated off the Armscote–Ilmington road.

3hc (1fb) B&b£6–£7.50 W£40 Ⓜ

CTV P 100acres mixed

Ⓥ

NEWBRIDGE
Lothian *Midlothian*
Map **11** NT17

FH Mrs & Mrs W Pollock ***Easter Norton*** *(NT157721)* ☎031-333 1279
Apr–Sep

Small homely farmhouse in excellent position for motorway and Edinburgh Airport.

Nettlecombe — Newport

3rm (2fb) ✱

CTV P 5acres poultry

NEWBURY
Berkshire
Map **4** SU46

INN *Hare & Hounds Hotel* Speen ☎(0635) 47215

Annexe contains modern accommodation with well-equipped bedrooms. 1m W A4.

(A 7⋒) (1fb) TV in all bedrooms

⅏ 50P

NEWBY BRIDGE
Cumbria
Map **7** SD38

GH Furness Fells ☎(0448) 31260
mid Jan–mid Dec

4hc (A 2hc)) (2fb) ✱ Ⓡ Bdi£8.50 Bdifr£13.50 W£56 Ⓜ LDO6.30

Lic ⅏ CTV 10P

Ⓥ

NEWCASTLE-UNDER-LYME
Staffordshire
Map **7** SJ84

GH Grove Court Hotel 100 Lancaster Rd ☎(0782) 614406
rs Xmas

9rm 2hc 1⇌ 6⋒ (A 2⇌) (1fb) CTV in 10 bedrooms Ⓡ B&b£8.63–£14.95 Bdi£17.25–£20.70

Lic ⅏ CTV 12P

FH Mrs M J Heath **Home** *(SJ823454)* Keele ☎(0782) 627227
Apr–Oct

1¾m W along A5525.

2rm (1fb) TV in 1 bedroom ✱ Ⓡ B&b£7–£7.50 Bdi£11–£11.50 W£44 Ⓜ LDO4.30pm

CTV 6P nc2yrs 250acres dairy sheep

NEWCASTLE UPON TYNE
Tyne & Wear
Map **12** NZ26

GH Avenue Hotel 2 Manor House Rd, Jesmond ☎(0632) 811396

9hc (1fb) ✱ B&b£16.67 Bdi£22.37 LDO6.45pm

Lic ⅏ CTV

Credit cards 1 5

GH Chirton House Hotel 46 Clifton Rd ☎(0632) 730407

11rm 8hc 3⋒ (1fb) ✱B&b£13.80 Bdi£20.70 W£90 Ⓜ LDO6pm

Lic ⅏ CTV 12P

Ⓥ

GH Clifton Cottage Dunholme Rd ☎(0632) 2737347

6hc (2fb) TV in all bedrooms Ⓡ B&b£7.50–£9 W£59.50 Ⓜ

⅏ CTV 6P

GH Morrach Hotel 82–86 Osborne Rd ☎(0632) 813361

34rm 22hc 8⇌ 4⋒ (1fb) CTV in all bedrooms Ⓡ B&b£11.50–£17.25 Bdifr£13.70 Wfr £86.25 Ⓜ LDO9.30pm

Lic ⅏ CTV 27P 4 billiards

Credit cards 1 2 3 Ⓥ

GH Western House Hotel 1 West Av ☎Tyneside 091-285 6812

14hc (3fb) B&bfr£11.50 Bdifr£16.10 Wfr£62.10 Ⓜ LDO8pm

Lic ⅏ CTV

Credit card 3

NEWPORT
Dyfed
Map **2** SN03

INN Golden Lion Hotel East St ☎(0239) 820321

A friendly inn in the village.

10rm 9hc 5⇌ 4⋒ CTV in 8 bedrooms ✱ Ⓡ ✱Bdi£10 W£65 Ⓜ Bar lunch £2alc High tea £4alc D9.30pm £4–£5alc

⅏ CTV 25P

Credit cards 1 3 Ⓥ

NEWPORT
Gwent
Map **3** ST38

GH Caerleon House Hotel Caerau Rd
☎(0633) 64869
Small establishment close to the town centre.
8hc (1fb) CTV in all bedrooms ★ ® B&b£12.50–£14 LDO8.45pm
Lic 🛁 8P
Ⓥ

NEWPORT
Isle of Wight
Map **4** SZ48

INN Shute Clatterford Shute, Carisbrooke ☎(0983) 523393
Feb–Nov
Georgian country residence on hillside nesting below the massive Carisbrooke Castle, with a lovely restaurant/bar. 1m W B3323.
7rm 5hc 1🛁 1🚿 ★ ® B&b£10.75 Bdi£14.75 W£98.25 ⱡ Bar lunch 70p–£3.50 D9.30pm £3.60–£5.60
🛁 CTV 25P nc5yrs
Credit cards 1 3 Ⓥ

NEWPORT PAGNELL
Buckinghamshire
Map **4** SP84

Newport — Newquay

INN Cannon 50 High St ☎(0908) 610042
Closed 24 Dec–1 Jan
Family run small high street 16th-century inn with pleasant accommodation.
5hc ★ ® B&b£15 Bdi£19.50 Bar lunch £3.50–£5 D7pm £3.95–£5.50
CTV 15P
Credit cards 1 3

NEWQUAY
Cornwall
Map **2** SW86
See plan

GH Arundell Hotel Mount Wise
☎(06373) 2481 Plan **1** *B1*
Whit–mid Sep
Large seasonal family hotel, comfortable and recently renovated.
40rm 24hc 8🛁 8🚿 (9fb) ★ ®
*B&b£5.75–£8.62 Bdi£8.05–£12.65 W£40.25–£60.34 M (W only mid Jul–3rd wk Aug) LDO6.45pm
Lic CTV 30P sauna bath

GH Barrowcliffe Hotel Henver Rd
☎(06373) 3492 Plan **1A** *E3*
May–Sep
23rm 18hc 1🛁 4🚿 (2fb) ★ ®
B&b£6.90–£10.35 Bdi£8.91–£12.65 W£46–£67.85 M LDO6.30pm
Lic 🛁 CTV 20P nc3yrs
Credit card 3

GH *Castaways Hotel* 39 St Thomas Rd
☎(06373) 5002 Plan **2** *D1*
Apr–Oct
Tudor style family hotel.
13hc (4fb) (W only mid Jul–early Sep) LDO6.30pm

GH Cherington 7 Pentire Av
☎(06373) 3363 Plan **3** *A2*
Etr–Oct
Family hotel close to Pentire beach.
22rm 7hc 6🛁 6🚿 (A rm 6hc) (7fb) ★
B&b£7–£9 Bdi£12–£15 W£55–£75 ⱡ (W only Jun–Aug) LDO7pm
Lic CTV 16P 2🚗

GH Copper Beech Hotel
70 Edgcumbe Av ☎(06373) 3376
Plan **4** *D2*
Etr–mid Oct
Well appointed family hotel in peaceful area, adjoining Trenance Gardens.
16hc (5fb) B&b£6.90–£8.05 Bdi£9.78–£12.35 W£67.85–£85.10 ⱡ (W only mid Jul–Aug) LDO6.15pm
Lic 🛁 CTV 16P
Credit cards 1 2 3 4

⊢⊣ **GH Fairlands** 107 Tower Rd
☎(06373) 2917 Plan **5** *B2*
Closed Dec
Comfortable small terraced hotel, overlooking Fistral Beach.
8hc (4fb) ✱ B&b£5.50–£7 Bdi£7.50–£9.50 W£38.50–£49 M (W only Jul & Aug) LDO4pm
CTV 10P
Ⓥ

GH Fistral Beach Hotel Esplanade Rd, Pentire ☎(06373) 3993 Plan **6** *A2*
Mar–Oct & Xmas
Modern small very comfortable family hotel, adjacent to beach.
15rm 10hc 5fi (4fb) B&b£8.50–£10.75 Bdi£10.80–£14.30 W£70–£99.80 ⱡ (W only mid Jul–end Aug) LDO7pm
Lic ꟿ CTV 12P

⊢⊣ **GH Gluvian Park Hotel**
12 Edgcumbe Gdns ☎(06373) 3133
Plan **7** *D2*
Apr–Oct
Comfortable modern family hotel close to sea front and Tolcarne beach.
23rm 12hc 1⇌ 10fi (8fb) ✱ Ⓡ B&b£7.50–£11.50 Bdi£12.25–£16.50 W£73.50–£106.75 LDO5.30pm
Lic ꟿ CTV 10P ⌂

GH Hepworth Hotel 27 Edgcumbe Av ☎(06373) 3686 Plan **8** *D2*
Etr–Sep
Modern comfortable family hotel, recently refurbished to high standards.
13rm 9hc 4fi (4fb) ✱ *B&b£6.90–£10 Bdi£10.65–£14 W£67–£89 ⱡ (W only 14 Jul–25 Aug) LDO6.30pm
Lic ꟿ CTV 10P

GH Jonel 88–90 Crantock St ☎(06373) 5084 Plan **9** *B2*
May–Sep
Small comfortable well appointed terraced hotel, close to town.
11hc (3fb) ✱ Ⓡ *B&b£7–£9.50 Bdi£10–£12.50 W£63–£85 ⱡ LDO4pm
Lic ꟿ CTV 7P

Newquay

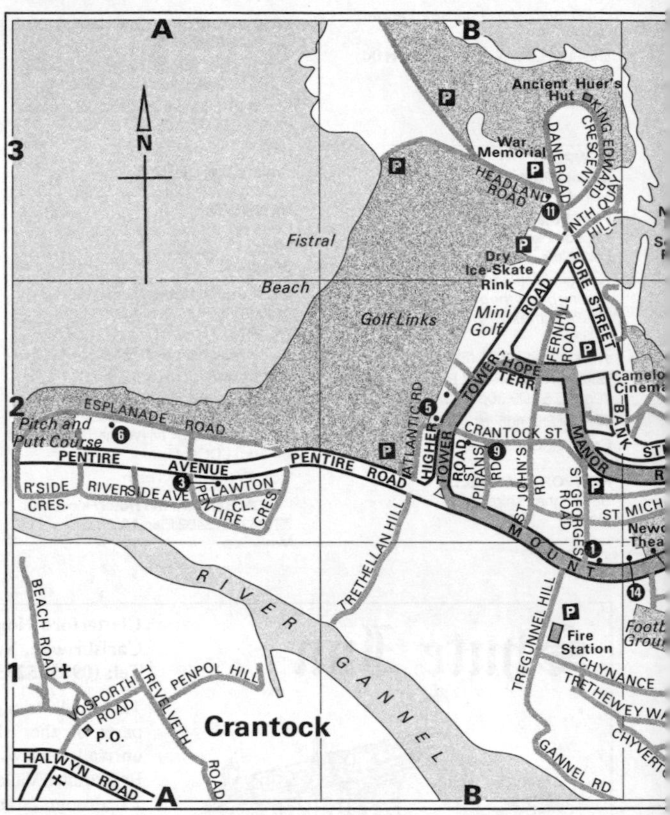

Newquay
1 Arundell Hotel
1A Barrowcliff Hotel
2 Castaways Hotel
3 Cherington
4 Copper Beech Hotel
5 Fairlands
6 Fistral Beach Hotel
7 Gluvian Park Hotel

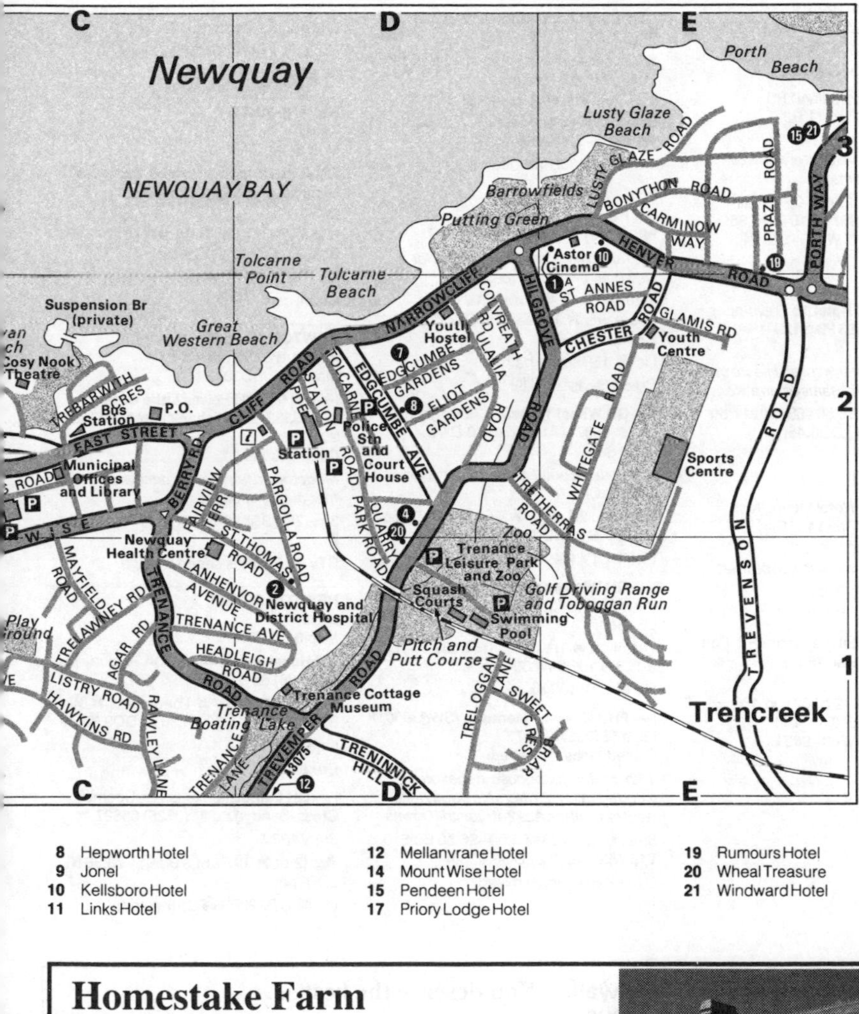

Newquay

C D E
Porth Beach
Lusty Glaze Beach
NEWQUAY BAY
Barrowfields
Putting Green
Tolcarne Point
Tolcarne Beach
Suspension Br (private)
Great Western Beach
Cosy Nook Theatre
Bus Station
P.O.
Station
Police Stn and Court House
Municipal Offices and Library
Youth Hostel
Astor Cinema
Youth Centre
Sports Centre
Newquay Health Centre
Newquay and District Hospital
Trenance Leisure Park and Zoo
Zoo
Squash Courts
Swimming Pool
Golf Driving Range and Toboggan Run
Pitch and Putt Course
Trenance Cottage Museum
Trenance Boating Lake
Play Ground
Trencreek
LUSTY GLAZE ROAD
BONYTHON ROAD
CARMINOW WAY
PRAZE ROAD
PORTH WAY
HENVER ROAD
NARROWCLIFF
HILGROVE ROAD
COLVREATH RD
ULALIA ROAD
ST ANNES ROAD
CHESTER ROAD
GLAMIS RD
EDGCUMBE GARDENS
ELIOT GARDENS
EDGCUMBE AVE
TOLCARNE ROAD
STATION PDE
CLIFF ROAD
TREBARWITH CRES
EAST STREET
BERRY RD
FAIRVIEW TERR
PARGOLLA ROAD
PARK ROAD
QUARRY
TRETHERRAS ROAD
WHITEGATE ROAD
TREVENSON ROAD
ST THOMAS ROAD
LANHENVOR AVENUE
TRENANCE AVE
HEADLEIGH ROAD
TRENANCE ROAD
TREVEMPER ROAD
MAYFIELD ROAD
TRELAWNEY RD
AGAR RD
LISTRY ROAD
HAWKINS RD
RAWLEY LANE
TRENANCE LANE
TRELOGGAN LANE
SWEET BRIAR CRES
TRENINNICK HILL
A3075
1 2 3

8 Hepworth Hotel
9 Jonel
10 Kellsboro Hotel
11 Links Hotel
12 Mellanvrane Hotel
14 Mount Wise Hotel
15 Pendeen Hotel
17 Priory Lodge Hotel
19 Rumours Hotel
20 Wheal Treasure
21 Windward Hotel

GH Kellsboro Hotel 12 Henver Rd ☎(06373) 4620 Plan **10** *E3*
Mar–Nov
Well appointed family hotel, close to beaches.
16hc 6➡ 3⋒ (8fb) B&b£10.35–£11.50 Bdi£13.80–£17.25 W£80.50–£97.75 Ⱡ (W only Jul & Aug) LDO 7pm
Lic 🅼 CTV 16P ♿ ⊡(heated)

GH Links Hotel Headland Rd ☎(06373) 3211 Plan **11** *B3*
Mar–Oct
Personally run private hotel with well equipped bedrooms.
15rm 2hc 10➡ 1⋒ (4fb) CTV in all bedrooms ✶ Ⓡ B&b£8.10–£10.35 Bdi£10.40–£12.65 W£55–£65 M LDO5.30pm
Lic lift 🅼 CTV

GH Mellanvrane Hotel 15 Trevemper Rd ☎(06373) 2593 Plan **12** *D1*
May–Oct
Large modern hotel, with facilities to cater for the tourist and businessman alike.
23hc (5fb) *B&b£6.50–£8 Bdi£11.50–£13 W£70–£80 Ⱡ LDO6.45pm
Lic 🅼 CTV P
Credit cards 1 3

GH *Mount Wise Hotel* Mount Wise ☎(06373) 3080 Plan **14** *C1*
Apr–Nov
Modern comfortable high rise property.
36hc 9➡ (A 2rm) (20fb)
Lic lift CTV 30P sea

GH Pendeen Hotel Alexandra Rd, Porth ☎(06373) 3521 Plan **15** *E3*
Mar–Oct
15rm 5hc 6➡ 4⋒ (2fb) CTV in 4 bedrooms ✶ B&b£8.60–£11 Bdi£12.50–£16 W£69–£89 Ⱡ LDO7.30pm
Lic 🅼 CTV 15P

GH Priory Lodge Hotel Mount Wise ☎(06373) 4111 Plan **17** *C1*
Exceptionally well appointed character hotel, set in own grounds.
21rm 5hc 5⋒ 11➡ (11fb) ✶ B&b£11.50–£14.37 Bdi£17.25–£23 W£79.35–£114.85 Ⱡ
Lic 🅼 CTV 30P ⊡(heated)
Ⓥ

GH Rumours Hotel 89 Henver Rd ☎(06373) 2170 Plan **19** *E3*
Well appointed hotel, convenient for Newquay and Porth beaches.
15rm 2hc 8➡ 2⋒ (1fb) CTV in all bedrooms ✶ Ⓡ B&b£15–£17 Bdi£22–£24 LDO10.30pm
Lic 🅼 15P sauna bath
Credit cards 1 2 3 5

⊢⊣ **GH Wheal Treasure** 72 Edgcumbe Av ☎(06373) 4136 Plan **20** *D1/2*
May–Sep
Comfortable hotel, close to Trenance Gardens.
10rm 8hc 2⋒ (2fb) ✶ B&b£7.50–£8.50 Bdi£11–£13 W£70–£84 Ⱡ LDO5pm
Lic 🅼 CTV 10P nc4yrs

⊢⊣ **GH Windward Hotel** Alexandra Rd, Porth ☎(06373) 3185 Plan **21** *E3*
Etr–Sep
7rm 5hc 1➡ 1⋒ (2fb) Ⓡ B&b£7.50–£9 Bdi£9–£10.50 W£60–£72 Ⱡ
Lic 🅼 CTV 10P 🏠

⊢⊣ **FH** J C Wilson **Manuels** *(SW839601)* Lane ☎(06373) 3577
Closed Xmas–New Year
17th-century farmhouse in sheltered, wooded valley, 2m from Newquay take the west road off the A392 at Quintrill Downs.
5rm 2hc (2fb) B&b£5.50–£6.50 Bdi£10–£13 W£64–£82 Ⱡ LDO6.30pm
CTV 6P 🏠 44acres mixed

NEW QUAY
Dyfed
Map **2** SN35

INN *Queens Hotel* Church St ☎(0545) 560678
A friendly little inn, with comfortable rooms and good restaurant.
8hc CTV in all bedrooms D9pm
🅼 8P 🚗

NEW ROMNEY
Kent
Map **5** TR02

GH Blue Dolphins Hotel & Restaurant Dymchurch Rd ☎(0679) 63224
rs Sun
8rm 4hc 4⋒ (2fb) ✶ B&b£9.75–£13.25 Bdi£20–£23.50 LDO9.15pm
Lic 🅼 CTV 12P 1🚗 🏠
Credit cards 1 3

NEWTON *(Near Vowchurch)*
Hereford & Worcester
Map **3** SO33

⊢⊣ **FH** Mrs J C Powell **Little Green** *(SO335337)* ☎Michaelchurch (098123) 205
Closed Xmas
Modernised farmhouse, once an inn, with friendly atmosphere.
3hc (2fb) B&b£8–£9 Bdi£10–£12 W£80 Ⱡ
CTV 3P 50acres sheep & cattle

NEWTON ABBOT
Devon
Map **3** SX87

GH Hazelwood House 33A Torquay Rd ☎(0626) 66130
6hc 3⋒ (1fb) CTV in 4 bedrooms ✶ Ⓡ B&b£12 Bdi£16.50 W£80 Ⱡ LDO9.30pm
Lic 🅼 CTV 7P
Credit card 1

⊢⊣ **GH Lamorna** Exeter Rd, Coombe Cross, Sandygate ☎(0626) 65627
3m N A380.
7hc (2fb) ✶ Ⓡ B&b£8 Bdi£14 W£56 M LDO9pm
Lic 🅼 CTV 20P 1🚗 ⊡(heated)

Newtonmore — North Berwick

NEWTONMORE
Highland *Inverness-shire*
Map **14** NN79

GH Alvey House Hotel Golf Course Rd ☎(05403) 260
Detached house in small terraced garden 50 yards from golf course.
7rm 4hc 3⋒ (2fb) ✱ *B&b£10 Bdi£15 W£98 ⱡ LDO6pm
Lic ▥ CTV 10P
Ⓥ

GH Coig Na Shee Fort William Rd ☎(05403) 216
Feb–Nov
6hc (1fb) Ⓡ B&b£9.50–£10.50 Bdi£15.50–£17.50 W£98–£112 ⱡ LDO5pm
▥ CTV 8P
Ⓥ

GH Glenquoich Glen Rd ☎(05403) 461
Closed Xmas
6rm 5hc (3fb) B&b£8.50 Bdi£14 W£53 ⱡ LDO7pm
▥ CTV 6P ⌂

NEWTON REGIS
Staffordshire
Map **4** SK20

⊢⊣ **FH** Mrs M Lasse **Newton House** *(SK278075)* ☎Tamworth (0827) 830632
Large Georgian style farmhouse in a peaceful village setting overlooking surrounding countryside.
4hc 1⋒ (2fb) ✱ B&bfr£7.50 Bdifr£12.50 Wfr£50 M LDOnoon
▥ CTV 4P nc7yrs

NEWTON STEWART
Dumfries & Galloway *Wigtownshire*
Map **10** NX46

⊢⊣ **GH Duncree House Hotel** King St ☎(0671) 2001
Stone lodge dating from 1830 standing in own grounds of 5 acres.
6hc (5fb) B&b£7.50–£8 Bdi£10.50–£11 W£73.50–£77 ⱡ LDO5.30pm
Lic CTV 30P
Credit cards 1 2 3 Ⓥ

NEWTOWN
Powys
Map **6** SO19

⊢⊣ **FH** L M & G T Whitticase **Highgate** *(SO111953)* ☎(0686) 25981
Mar–Oct
15th-century black and white timbered farmhouse, in elevated position with commanding views over valley and hills. Rough shooting, fishing and ponies available.
3hc ✱ B&b£8–£9.50 Bdi£12–£13 W£53–£63 ⱡ LDO5pm
▥ CTV P ⌂ billiards 250acres arable beef sheep mixed

⊢⊣ **FH** Mrs I Jarman **Lower Gwestydd** *(SO126934)* Llanllwchaiarn ☎(0686) 26718
Mar–Oct rs Nov & Feb
17th-century farmhouse with historical features both inside and out. 2m E off B4568.
3hc (2fb) ✱ Ⓡ B&b£8–£8.50 Bdi£12–£12.50 W£80–£84 LDO4pm
▥ TV 4P ⌂ 200acres arable beef sheep

NITON
Isle of Wight
Map **4** SZ57

GH *Windcliffe House Hotel* Sandrock Rd ☎(0983) 730215
Picturesque family house with pretty gardens and swimming pool.
12hc (7fb) LDO7pm
Lic CTV 18P ⌂ sea

NORMANBY
North Yorkshire
Map **8** NZ90

FH D I Smith **Heather View** *(NZ928062)* ☎Whitby (0947) 880451
Apr–Oct
Attractive modern farmhouse, well-appointed and comfortable. Conveniently situated for coastal visits.
4hc (2fb) ✱ Ⓡ *B&b£7–£7.50 Bdi£9.25–£9.75 ⱡ LDO4.30pm
▥ CTV 6P nc5yrs 40acres arable sheep mixed
Ⓥ

NORTHALLERTON
North Yorkshire
Map **8** SE39

GH Windsor 56 South Pde ☎(0609) 774100
Closed 1st two wks Oct & 24 Dec–2 Jan
Friendly proprietors offer hospitality and comfortable accommodation in this well managed guesthouse.
6hc (A 2rm) (3fb) Ⓡ B&bfr£10
▥ CTV

INN Station Hotel 2 Boroughbridge Rd ☎(0609) 2053
10hc Ⓡ *B&b£8–£9.50 W£49 M Bar lunch £1–£2 LDO6.30pm
▥ CTV 60P

NORTHAMPTON
Northamptonshire
Map **4** SP76

GH Poplars Hotel Cross St, Moulton ☎(0604) 43983
Closed Xmas wk
21rm 13hc 2➡ 6⋒ (4fb) TV in 10 bedrooms Ⓡ B&b£17.50 Bdi£23 W£130 ⱡ LDO6pm
Lic ▥ CTV 22P ⌂
Credit card 1

NORTH BERWICK
Lothian *East Lothian*
Map **12** NT58

⊢⊣ **GH Cragside Private Hotel** 16 Marine Pde ☎(0620) 2879
Neatly appointed guesthouse on sea front in East Bay.
6hc (2fb) ✱ B&b£8 Bdi£12 W£82 ⱡ LDO4pm
▥ CTV
Ⓥ

NORTH CADBURY
Somerset
Map **3** ST62
FH E J Keen ***Hill*** *(ST634279)* ☎(0963) 40257
Etr–Sep
Double-fronted, red-brick farmhouse in pleasant garden offering a limited amount of accommodation.
3rm 1hc (1fb) ✗
▥ TV 4P

NORTH DUFFIELD
North Yorkshire
Map **8** SE63
FH Mr & Mrs F B Arrand ***Hall*** *(SE692374)* ☎Bubwith (075785) 301
May–Sep
Farmhouse situated in low-lying area overlooking the River Derwent, ½m NE of village.
3rm 2hc (2fb) ✗
▥ CTV P 170acres mixed

NORTH HYKEHAM
Lincolnshire
Map **8** SK96
GH Loudor Hotel 37 Newark Rd ☎Lincoln (0522) 680333
Large detached house providing comfortable, modern accommodation.
10rm 3⇥ 7⋒ (2fb) CTV in all bedrooms ✗ Ⓡ B&b£15–£19.50 Bdi£21.50–£26.50 LDO9pm

Lic ▥ CTV 12P
Credit cards 1 3

NORTH PETHERTON
Somerset
Map **3** ST23
⊢×⊣**FH** Mrs C M J Howard **Balls Farm** *(ST285341)* Woolmersdon ☎(0278) 662320
Etr–Oct
1m NW unclass road. Riding stables for children.
3hc (1fb) ✗ Ⓡ B&b£8–£8.50 Bdi£13–£13.50 W£88 Ł LDO5pm
CTV P 30 acres beef sheep mixed

NORTH WALSHAM
Norfolk
Map **9** TG23
GH Beechwood Private Hotel
20 Cromer Rd ☎(0692) 403231
Closed 4 days Xmas
11rm 5hc 3⇥ 3⋒ (7fb) B&b£11.50 Bdi£17.25 W£95–£106 Ł LDO6pm
Lic ▥ CTV 12P nc3yrs
Ⓥ

NORTHWOOD
Shropshire
Map **7** SJ43
GH *Woodlands Country House*
☎Wem (0939) 33268
Closed Xmas
1m S off B5063.
8hc 1⇥ 2⋒ (2fb) LDO6.30pm
Lic ▥ CTV 12P

NORTH WOOTTON
Somerset
Map **3** ST54
FH Mrs M White **Barrow** *(ST553416)*
☎Pilton (074989) 245
Feb–Oct
15th-century stone-built farmhouse on edge of village, situated between Wells, Glastonbury and Shepton Mallet.
4hc (1fb) ✗ Ⓡ *B&b£7 Bdi£11 W£49 M̸ LDO9am
CTV 3P 156acres dairy

NORTON
Nottinghamshire
Map **8** SK57
⊢×⊣**FH** Mrs J Palmer **Norton Grange** *(SK572733)* ☎Mansfield (0623) 842666
Etr–Sep
A 200-year-old stone-built farmhouse fronted by small gardens, at edge of village.
3rm 2hc (1fb) ✗ B&b£7–£8 W£45 M̸
CTV 4P 172acres arable beef mixed

NORTON *(Near Shifnal)*
Shropshire
Map **7** SJ70

INN ***Hundred House*** Bridgnorth Rd ☎(095271) 254

A big rambling 15th-century inn at centre of village and on the busy A442. Large plain bedrooms, attractive dining room.

4hc (1fb) CTV in 1 bedroom TV in 3 bedrooms Ⓡ LDO9.30pm

NORWICH
Norfolk
Map **5** TG20

GH Grange Hotel 230 Thorpe Rd ☎(0603) 34734
Closed Xmas

38rm 8hc 30⋔ (1fb) CTV in 37 bedrooms Ⓡ B&b£14.25–£21.50 LDO8pm

Lic ▥ 48P sauna bath

Credit cards 1 2 3 5 Ⓥ

GH Marlborough House Hotel 22 Stracey Rd, Thorpe Rd ☎(0603) 28005

12hc 4⋔ (2fb) CTV in 4 bedrooms B&b£9 Bdi£12 W£56–£65 Ⱡ LDO6.30pm

Lic ▥ CTV 3P 2🚗

Credit cards 2 3

NOTTINGHAM
Nottinghamshire
Map **8** SK53

GH Balmoral Hotel 55–57 Loughborough Rd, West Bridgford ☎(0602) 818588
Closed Xmas

Converted pair of large semi-detached houses on main A60, 1 mile south of city centre.

25rm 6hc (1fb) CTV in all bedrooms B&bfr£13.85 Bdifr£20.13 LDO7.30pm

Lic ▥ CTV 36P

Credit cards 1 3

GH *Crantock Hotel* 480 Mansfield Rd ☎(0602) 623294
Closed 24 & 25 Dec

6hc 1➡ 1⋔ (2fb) Ⓡ

Lic ▥ CTV 10P

GH Grantham Commercial Hotel 24–26 Radcliffe Road, West Bridgford ☎(0602) 811373

24hc B&b£8.50–£9.50 Bdi£11.25–£12.25 W£48–£52 Ⱡ LDO7pm

▥ CTV 10P

GH Rufford Hotel Melton Rd, West Bridgford ☎(0602) 814202
Closed Xmas

1m S on A606.

31⋔ CTV in all bedrooms Ⓡ
*B&b£18.40 Bdi£25.30 LDO7.45pm

Lic ▥ CTV 36P

Credit card 1

GH Waverley 107 Portland Rd, Waverley St ☎(0602) 786707
Closed 2 wks Xmas

17hc (2fb) B&bfr£7 Bdifr£10.50 LDO4pm

▥ CTV 1🚗

GH Windsor Lodge Hotel 116 Radcliffe Rd, West Bridgford ☎(0602) 813773

1m S on A52.

43rm 4hc 3➡ 28⋔ (8fb) CTV in all bedrooms B&b£13.80 Bdi£20.70 LDO7.15pm

Lic ▥ CTV 48P billiards

Credit cards 1 3

NUNEATON
Warwickshire
Map **4** SP39

GH Abbey Grange Hotel 100 Manor Court Rd ☎(0203) 385535

9hc CTV in all bedrooms Ⓡ B&b£17.50 Bdi£22.65–£30 LDO9.30pm

Lic ▥ CTV 30P

Credit cards 1 2 3 5

GH Drachenfels Hotel 25 Attleborough Rd ☎(0203) 383030

8rm 7hc 1➡ (2fb) CTV in all bedrooms B&b£12.50–£16.50 LDO9.30pm

Lic ▥ 10P

INN *George Eliot Hotel* Market Pl, Bridge St ☎(0203) 386599

13rm TV in all bedrooms

▥ 10P

NUNNEY
Somerset
Map **3** ST74

INN George Church St ☎(037384) 458

12rm 5➡ 4⋔ CTV in 5 bedrooms Ⓡ B&b£14–£24 Bdi£16.25–£31.85 L£7.10–£12.10&alc D10pm £7.10–£12.10&alc

CTV 20P

Credit cards 1 2 3 5

OAKFORD
Devon
Map **3** SS92

FH Mr K Barnikel **Newhouse** *(SS892228)* ☎(03985) 347

2m W off A361

3hc (1fb) Ⓡ B&b£9 Bdi£13 W£80 Ⱡ LDO6pm

▥ CTV 4P 42acres beef

Ⓥ

FH Mr J R Pearce **Westcott** *(SS910214)* ☎(03985) 265

200-year-old farmhouse in secluded setting on the edge of Dartmoor. Bedrooms have four poster beds. High standard of cooking. Horse riding and fishing are available.

4rm 3➡ 1⋔ CTV in all bedrooms Ⓡ
*B&b£16.50 Bdi£27.50 W£173.25 Ⱡ LDO10pm

Lic ▥ CTV 30P nc10yrs 222acres beef dairy pigs sheep mixed horses

Oban
1 Ardblair
2 Barriemore Private Hotel
3 Crathie
4 Foxholes Hotel *(see under Lerags)*
5 Glenburnie Private Hotel
6 Heatherfield Private Hotel
7 Kenmore
8 Roseneath
9 Sgeir-Mhaol
10 Wellpark Hotel

Oban

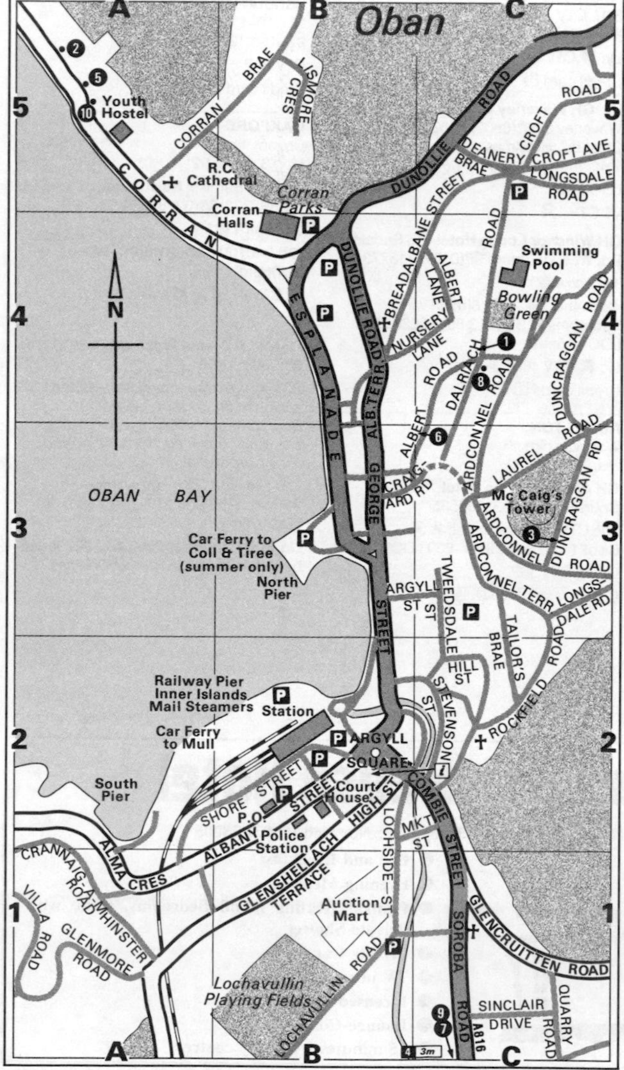

OBAN
Strathclyde *Argyllshire*
Map **10** NM83
See plan. See also **Lerags**

⊢⊣ **GH Ardblair** Dalriach Rd ☎(0631) 62668 Plan **1** *C4*
9 May–29 Sep
Behind town centre, convenient to swimming pool, bowling green and tennis courts.
16hc (A 6hc) (4fb) ★ B&b£6–£7 Bdi£10.50–£11.50 LDO6.30pm
Temperance CTV 11P
Ⓥ

GH *Barriemore Private Hotel* The Esplanade ☎(0631) 62197 Plan **2** *A5*
week before Etr–mid Oct
Attractive stone house on seafront with small garden offering simple accommodation.
14hc (4fb)
CTV 17P nc6yrs sea

⊢⊣ **GH Crathie** Duncraggen Rd ☎(0631) 62619 Plan **3** *C3*
Mar–Oct
Modern house high on hill behind McCaigs Tower.
9hc (2fb) Ⓡ B&b£6.50–£7.95 Bdi£10.50–£11.50 W£42–£52 Ⅼ LDO7pm
Lic ▥ CTV 12P

GH Glenburnie Private Hotel The Esplanade ☎(0631) 62089 Plan **5** *A5*
Apr–Oct
Grey stone-built hotel on sea front with private parking to front of hotel.
15hc 4⋒ (4fb) ✱B&b£8.63–£13.50 S%
CTV 12P 1⌂ nc4yrs
Credit card 1

⊢⊣ **GH Heatherfield Private Hotel** Albert Rd ☎(0631) 62681 Plan **6** *C3*
Pleasant house situated on hill behind town with ¾ acre of garden.
10hc (4fb) Bdi£7.50–£9 Bdi£11.50–£13.50 W£52.50–£63 Ⅼ LDO7.30pm
CTV 14P
Ⓥ

⊢⊣ **GH Kenmore** Soroba Rd ☎(0631) 63592 Plan **7** *C1*
White painted stone house situated on A816 with small modern extension.
6hc (2fb) B&b£7.50–£8.50
CTV 12P

⊢⊣ **GH Roseneath** Dalriach Rd ☎(0631) 64262 Plan **8** *C4*
Closed Xmas & New Year
Attractive sandstone house in terrace on hillside offering views across bay to Kerrera.
10hc (2fb) B&b£6.75–£9 Bdi£10.75–£13.50 W£45–£60 M LDO6.15pm
▥ CTV 10⌂
Ⓥ

⊢⊣ **GH Sgeir Mhaol** Soroba Rd ☎(0631) 62650 Plan **9** *C1*
Situated on the A816 to the south of the town centre, this small guesthouse is attractively painted in cream and yellow.
6hc (3fb) B&b£7–£8.50 Bdi£10–£12.50 LDO6pm
CTV 10P

GH Wellpark Hotel Esplanade ☎(0631) 62948 Plan **10** *A5*
Apr–Oct
Semi-detached hotel built in granite and sandstone, offering good standard of accommodation in a seafront location.
15rm 8hc 7 (3fb) B&b£9.20–£10.35 Bdi£13.80–£14.95 W£93–£100 LDO7.30pm
CTV 11P

ODDINGLEY
Hereford & Worcester
Map **3** SO95
FH Mrs P Baylis ***Pear Tree's*** *(SO909589)* ☎Droitwich (0905) 778489
Etr–Oct
Large, modern farmhouse in quiet country lane close to M5 motorway.
2hc
CTV 12P nc5yrs 17acres arable beef mixed

ODDINGTON
Gloucestershire
Map **4** SP22
INN *Fox* ☎Stow-on-the-Wold (0451) 30446
Closed Xmas
3hc
P nc4yrs

INN Horse & Groom ☎Cotswold (0451) 30584
5rm 1 4 Ⓡ *B&b£12.50–£14 L£3.25 D10pm £6&alc S%
40P

OKEHAMPTON
Devon
Map **2** SX59
FH Mrs K C Heard **Hughslade** *(SX561932)* ☎(0837) 2883
Closed Xmas
Pleasant farmhouse on the edge of the town. Ideal base for exploring Dartmoor and the north and south Devon coasts.
3hc (3fb) B&b£8.50–£10 Bdi£13.50–£14 Wfr£80 LDO5.30pm
CTV 6P U 500acres arable beef sheep mixed

OKEOVER
Staffordshire
Map **7** SK14
FH Mrs E J Harrison **Little Park** *(SK160490)* ☎Thorpe Cloud (033529) 341
Apr–Oct
200-year-old stone and brick farmhouse with oak beams in most rooms. A footpath to Dovedale and Ilam runs through the farm.
3hc (1fb) *B&bfr£7 Bdifr£11 Wfr£75 LDO4pm
CTV 3P nc3yrs 123acres dairy
Ⓥ

OLD DALBY
Leicestershire
Map **8** SK62
FH Mrs V Anderson **Home** *(SK673236)* Church Ln ☎Melton Mowbray (0664) 822622
Closed Dec
19th-century farmhouse, parts of which date from 1730, in the Vale of Belvoir. Former bailiff's house when property was part of Old Dalby estate.
3hc (2fb) *B&b£7.50–£8.50 Bdi£11.50–£12.50 Wfr£54
TV 4P 3acres non-working

ONICH
Highland *Inverness-shire*
Map **14** NN06

GH Glenmorven House ☎(08553) 247
Mar–Oct
Nicely appointed guesthouse situated on the shores of Loch Linnhe with superb outlook.
7hc (2fb) Ⓡ Bdi£14.95–£16.65 W£105–£115 Ⱡ LDO7pm
Lic Ⅲ 20P
Ⓥ

GH *Tigh-A-Righ* ☎(08553) 255
Closed 22 Dec–7 Jan
5hc (4fb) LDO8.15pm
Lic Ⅲ CTV 50P

⊢⊣**FH** Mr & Mrs A Dewar **Cuilcheanna House** *(NN019617)* (Guestaccom)
☎(08553) 226
Etr–Sep
Large Victorian house with gardens set in sloping fields leading to Loch Linnhe. Excellent views over lochs and mountains.
9rm 8hc (2fb) B&b£8–£9 Bdi£14–£15 W£90–£98 Ⱡ LDO7pm
Ⅲ 10P 🏠 120acres beef
Ⓥ

ORFORD
Suffolk
Map **5** TM44

INN King's Head Front St ☎(03945) 271
Closed 4–29 Jan
5hc ✦ B&b£13.20 W£92.40 M̸ L£9alc D9pm £9alc
100P 2🚗
Credit card [5]

OSWESTRY
Shropshire
Map **7** SJ22

GH Ashfield Country House Llwyn-y-Maen, Trefonen Rd ☎(0691) 655200
Mar–Dec
14rm 8hc 6⇌ (3fb) CTV in all bedrooms Ⓡ B&b£12.50–£25 Bdi£18–£30.50 W£105–£160 Ⱡ LDO6pm
Lic Ⅲ 20P
Ⓥ

OTTERBURN
Northumberland
Map **12** NY89
See also **Elsdon and Rochester (Northumberland)**

⊢⊣**FH** G F & M A Stephenson **Monkridge** *(NY913917)* ☎(0830) 20639
Jan–Nov
Well-cared for, comfortable farmhouse in the attractive environment of the Northumberland Moors.
2rm (1fb) ✦ Ⓡ B&bfr£7 Bdifr£12 Wfr£84 Ⱡ LDO2pm
Ⅲ CTV 3P 1400acres arable sheep mixed

OTTERY ST MARY
Devon
Map **3** SY19

⊢⊣**FH** Mrs S Hansford **Pitt** *(SY089966)*
☎(040481) 2439
Etr–Oct
4rm (1fb) ✦ B&b£7.50–£8.50 Bdi£12–£13 LDO6pm
CTV 6P 190acres mixed
Ⓥ

OVINGTON
Northumberland
Map **12** NZ06

INN Highlander ☎Prudhoe (0661) 32016
4rm 2hc 2⇌ ✦ *B&bfr£16.50 D8.30pm £8.50alc
Ⅲ CTV 30P 🚫 nc10yrs
Ⓥ

OXENHOPE
West Yorkshire
Map **7** SE03

FH Mrs A Scholes **Lily Hall** *(SE023362)* Uppermarsh Ln ☎ Haworth (0535) 43999
Jan–Nov
Pleasant farmhouse with smallholding rearing turkeys and hens. Overlooking pleasant valley in Brontë country. Horse riding, tennis, golf and bathing 4 miles.
4hc B&b£7–£7.50 Bdi£11–£12 W£49 M
CTV 12P nc5yrs 9acres beef
Ⓥ
See advertisment on page 172

OXFORD
Oxfordshire
Map **4** SP50

GH Ascot 283 Iffley Rd ☎ (0865) 240259
Small, family house, 1m from centre.
7rm 6hc (2fb) TV in all bedrooms Ⓡ B&b£8–£10.50
CTV 2P
Ⓥ

GH Brown's 281 Iffley Rd ☎ (0865) 246822
Small, family house, 1m from city.
6hc (3fb) TV in 3 bedrooms Ⓡ B&b£8–£9.50
CTV 3P

GH Burren 374 Banbury Rd ☎ (0865) 513513
Clean, well decorated family house with spacious accommodation.
7hc 2 2 (4fb) TV in all bedrooms *B&b£9–£12
CTV 5P

GH Combermere 11 Polstead Rd ☎ (0865) 56971
Apr–Oct
6hc (2fb) TV in all bedrooms Ⓡ B&b£10–£12 W£65–£80 M
3P nc8yrs

GH Conifer 116 The Slade, Headington ☎ (0865) 63055
Small, family run establishment providing clean, comfortable bedrooms.
8hc 1 2 (1fb) B&b£10–£12
CTV 8P (heated)

GH Earlmont 322–324 Cowley Rd ☎ (0865) 240236
Friendly guesthouse with modern standards.
5hc (A 7hc) (3fb) CTV in 2 bedrooms TV in 5 bedrooms B&b£8.50–£10
CTV 12P 1
Ⓥ

GH Falcon 88–90 Abingdon Rd ☎ (0865) 722995
Closed 15 Dec–15 Jan
Accommodation here is above average and the lounge is comfortable.
10hc (2fb) B&b£8–£10 W£56–£89 M
CTV 9P
Credit card 3

GH *Galaxie Private Hotel* 180 Banbury Rd ☎ (0865) 55688
Warm, friendly house offering some modern bedroom facilities.
27hc 4 (4fb)
CTV 25P

GH Micklewood 331 Cowley Rd ☎ (0865) 247328
Simple, homely accommodation.
7hc (1fb) TV in all bedrooms B&b£8.50–£9 S%
CTV 6P
Credit card 2

GH Pine Castle 290 Iffley Rd ☎ (0865) 241497
Homely guesthouse with comfortable, well-furnished rooms.
7hc (2fb) CTV in all bedrooms B&b£7–£10 Bdi£10.50–£13.50 W£47–£66 M
CTV 4P

GH Tilbury Lodge 5 Tilbury Ln, Botley
☎(0865) 862138
Closed Xmas wk
Spotlessly kept modern accommodation in quiet almost rural area away from city centre.
7rm 5hc 2⇌ 2ⓕ (3fb) B&bfr£10
ⓜ CTV 6P 2🚗
ⓥ

GH *Victoria Hotel* 180 Abingdon Rd
☎(0865) 724536
A reputable, well-appointed establishment with tastefully decorated bedrooms.

Oxford

15hc 5⇌ (2fb) ® (W only low season)
LDO9.30pm
Lic ⓜ CTV 20P

GH Westgate Hotel 1 Botley Rd
☎(0865) 726721
Closed Xmas
Small, friendly family run hotel with simple accommodation.

13rm 9hc (1fb) CTV in all bedrooms ®
*B&b£14.50
Lic ⓜ CTV 12P
Credit cards 1 2 3 5 ⓥ

GH Westwood Country Hotel Hinksey Hill Top (Minotel) ☎(0865) 735408
Closed 24 Dec–2 Jan
Small, country hotel in woodland setting on outskirts of town.
18rm 10⇌ 8ⓕ (4fb) CTV in all bedrooms
★ ® B&b£15–£24 LDO8pm
Lic ⓜ 25P 1🚗 ♿
Credit cards 1 2 3

Tilbury Lodge is situated in a quiet country lane just two miles west of the city centre, one mile from the railway station and two miles from Farmoor reservoir with its trout fishing and sailing opportunities.
Good bus service available.
Botley shopping centre is a few minutes walk away with restaurants, shops, launderette, banks, etc.

Central heating
Some rooms en suite
Ample parking
Children made welcome
Tea and coffee made free on request

TILBURY LODGE, 5 TILBURY LANE, EYNSHAM ROAD, BOTLEY, OXFORD OX2 9NB

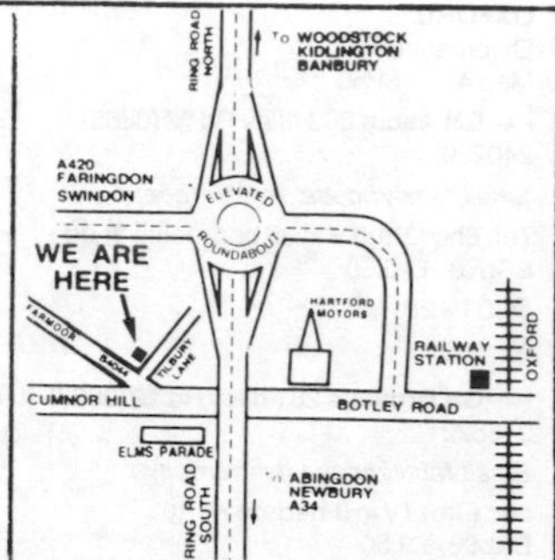

Westwood Hotel
Hinksey Hill, Oxford

Mr and Mrs Parker wish to provide a warm welcome, and comfortable accommodation with excellent food awaits the disconcerning visitor. The lounge and Restaurant and residential licensed bar and Restaurant opens out into 3½ acres of beautiful gardens and woodlands. Ideal for honeymooners and all demanding a peaceful rest.

All 17 bedrooms have private facilities along with radio-intercom Colour TV and Tea and Coffee facilities. Whilst our delux and honeymoon rooms also have a hairdryer and trouser press. During the Summer months, weather permitting, a BBQ is held usually on Tuesdays and Thursdays. Lunches are available to residents if required. Evening meals are available from 7–8pm Monday to Saturday and 6.30–7.00pm on Sundays (Winter only). BBQ's are at 6.30pm.

Amenities close at hand include golf, horse riding and boating. Brochure available on request with further details. Tel: Oxford (0865) 735408.

At second roundabout arriving from town centre take the second exit marked FARRINGDON or WOOTON, then at top of hill bear left. Hotel is 100 yards on right. From the A34 North, turn off at the MAIDENHEAD sign A423. From the A34 South turn off at the first sign for Oxford then the first exit off of roundabout up Hinksey Hill.

Proprietors: Mr & Mrs Parker

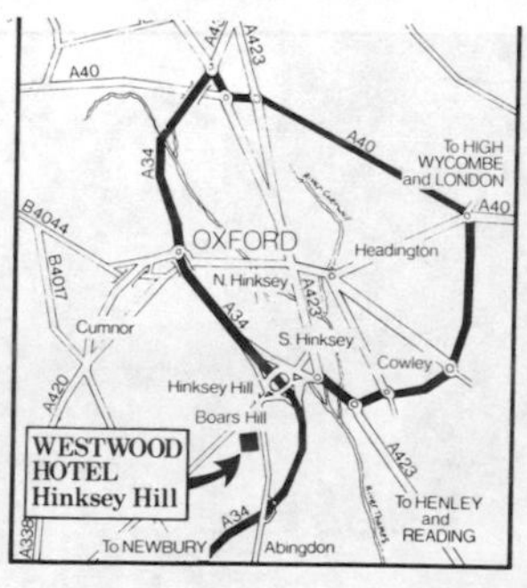

GH Willow Reaches Private Hotel 1 Wytham St ☎(0865) 721545 rs 16 Dec–Jan

Small private hotel in quiet area, offering simple accommodation.

9rm 6hc 2→ 1ⓕ (3fb) CTV in all bedrooms ✈ Ⓡ B&b£9–£17 LDO6.30pm

Lic ▥ CTV 4🚗

Credit cards 2 3 5

Oxford — Oxwich

OXHILL
Warwickshire
Map **4** SP34

⊢⊣**FH** Mrs S Hutsby **Nolands** *(SP312470)* ☎Kineton (0926) 640309

1m E Pillaton Priors on A422.

2hc (A 2hc) (1fb) ✈ Ⓡ B&b£6–£7.50 Bdi£10–£11

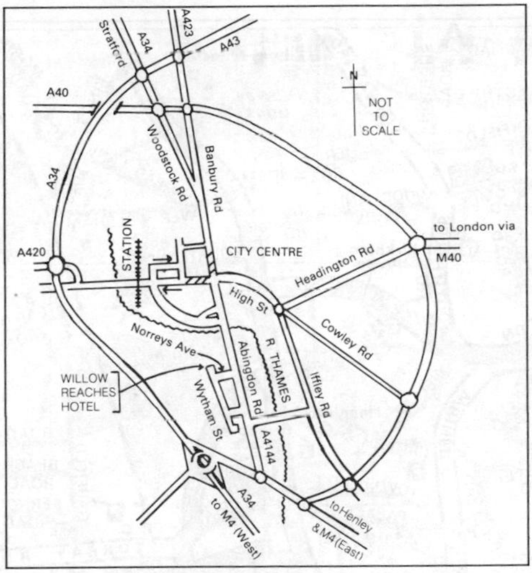

▥ CTV 5P 1🚗 nc3yrs ♪ U 300acres arable

OXWICH
West Glamorgan
Map **2** SS58

GH Oxwich Bay Hotel Gower ☎Swansea (0792) 390329 Closed Xmas & Jan rs wknds Nov–Apr

Family holiday hotel, close to the beach.

10hc (2fb) ✈ Ⓡ B&b£12–£14 Bdi£18–£20 W£75.60–£88.20 M LDO10.50pm

Lic ▥ CTV 80P

Credit cards 1 2 3 5

PADOG
Gwynedd
Map **6** SH85

⊢⊣ **FH** Mrs E A Jones **Pant Glas** *(SH846513)* Pentrefoelas Rd
☎Pentrefoelas (06905) 248
Etr–Nov

Situated ½m W of A5/B4407 junction.

3rm (1fb) ✱ ✱B&b£6–£6.60 Bdi£10–£11 W£40–£42 M

CTV 181acres beef sheep

PADSTOW
Cornwall
Map **2** SW97

⊢⊣ **GH Alexandra** 30 Dennis Rd
☎(0841) 532503
Mar–Oct

6hc (6fb) B&b£7.50–£8.50 Bdi£11–£12 W£52–£56 M LDO5pm

CTV 5P

GH *Cross House* Church St ☎(0841) 532391
rs Nov–Mar

9hc (4fb) ✱

Padog — Paignton

sea

GH Nook House Fentonluna Ln
☎(0841) 532317

10hc (4fb) B&b£12.07–£14.37 Bdi£17.82–£20.12 W£58.65–£71.30 M (W only Jun–Sep) LDOnoon

Lic ▥ CTV 10P

GH Tregea High St ☎(0841) 532455

8hc (3fb) B&b£9.20–£9.80 Bdi£13.50–£14.50 W£84.50–£94.50 L

Lic ▥ CTV 8P

GH Woodlands Treator ☎(0841) 532426

Treator 1m W B3276.

10⋒ (3fb) B&b£8.62–£10 Bdi£13.62–£15 W£60.34–£70 M LDO5pm

Lic ▥ CTV 15P

PAIGNTON
Devon
Map **3** SX86
See plan

⊢⊣ **GH Amaryllis Hotel** 14 Sands Rd
☎(0803) 559552 Plan **1** *B2*

11rm 8hc (6fb) B&b£7–£9.50 Bdi£10.50–£13 W£45–£65 L LDOnoon

Lic CTV 10P nc3yrs

⊢⊣ **GH Beresford Private Hotel**
1 Adelphi Rd ☎(0803) 551560
Plan **1A** *C2*
Closed Xmas & New Year

9rm 7hc 2⋒ (1fb) ✱ Ⓡ B&b£7.50–£11 Bdi£12–£16 W£65–£90 L LDO10am

Lic CTV 3P

GH Cambria Hotel Esplanade Rd, Sea Front ☎(0803) 559256 Plan **2** *C3*

24hc (7fb) Ⓡ B&b£8.50–£12.50 Bdi£9.50–£15.50 W£58–£98 L LDO6pm

Lic ▥ CTV

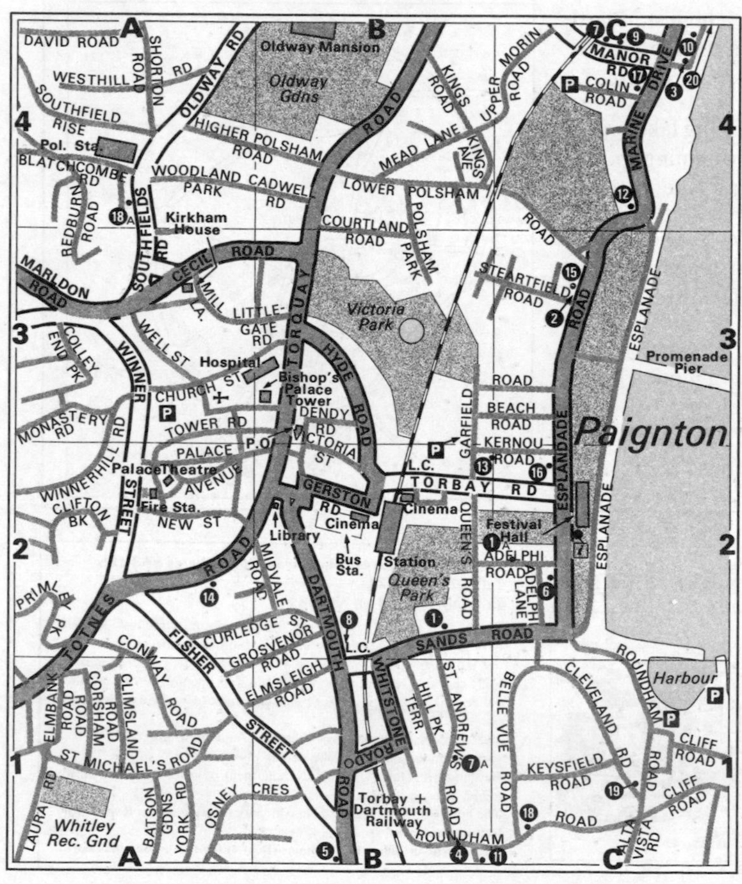

Paignton

1 Amaryllis Hotel
1A Beresford Hotel
2 Cambria Hotel
3 Channel View Hotel
4 Cherra Hotel
5 Clennon Valley Hotel
6 Commodore Hotel
7 Cornerways Hotel
7A Danethorpe
8 Nevada Private Hotel
9 Orange Tubs Hotel
10 Preston Sands Hotel
11 Radford Hotel
12 Redcliffe Lodge Hotel
13 St Weonard Private Hotel
14 San-Remo Hotel
15 Sattva Hotel
16 Sealawn Hotel
17 Sea Verge Hotel
18 Shorton House Hotel
18A South Mount Hotel
19 Sunnybank Private Hotel
20 Torbay Sands Hotel

GH *Channel View Hotel* 8 Marine Pde
☎(0803) 522432 Plan **3** *C4*
10hc 1🛁 2⋔ (2fb) CTV available in bedrooms LDO9am
Lic 🔥 CTV 12P sea
Ⓥ

⊢⊣ **GH Cherra Hotel** 15 Roundham Rd
☎(0803) 550723 Plan **4** *C4*
Etr–Oct
12rm 9hc 3⋔ (3fb) CTV in all bedrooms
Ⓡ B&b£7–£9 Bdi£10–£12 W£60–£80 LDO5.30pm
Lic 🔥 CTV 12P nc5yrs
Ⓥ

Paignton

GH Clennon Valley Hotel 1 Clennon Rise
☎(0803) 550304 Plan **5** *B1*
Closed Xmas
11rm 3hc 1🛁 7⋔ (3fb) CTV in 8 bedrooms
Ⓡ B&b£8.50–£11 Bdi£13.50–£15 W£75–£95 LDO5pm
Lic 🔥 CTV 12P
Credit card 3 Ⓥ

See advertisement on page 268

⊢⊣ **GH Commodore Hotel**
14 Esplanade Rd ☎(0803) 553107
Plan **6** *C2*
Closed Xmas & New Year
15rm 14hc 1⋔ (6fb) B&b£6.90–£9.77
Bdi£9.77–£12.65 W£48.30–£68.39 M
LDO4.30pm
Lic CTV 8P
Ⓥ

GH *Cornerways Hotel* 16 Manor Rd
☎(0803) 551207 Plan **7** *C4*
Etr–Oct
30hc 14⋔ (6fb)
Lic 🔥 CTV 26P sea

Paignton

⊢⊣ **GH Danethorpe** 23 St Andrews Rd ☎(0803) 551251 Plan **7A** *B1*
Etr–Sep
11hc 3⋔ (1fb) B&b£7.50–£8.50 Bdi£10.50–£12.75 W£75–£85 L LDO5pm
Lic ▥ CTV 10P
Credit card 3

GH *Nevada Private Hotel* 16 Dartmouth Rd ☎(0803) 558317 Plan **8** *B2*
Apr–Oct
12hc (3fb) ✱
Lic ▥ CTV 12P

⊢⊣ **GH Orange Tubs Hotel** 14 Manor Rd ☎(0803) 551541 Plan **9** *C4*
Apr–Oct
11rm 5hc 6⋔ (2fb) ✱ Ⓡ B&b£7–£11 Bdi£10–£15 W£49–£77 M LDO6.30pm
Lic ▥ CTV 7P nc2yrs
Credit card 1 Ⓥ

⊢⊣ **GH Preston Sands Hotel** 12 Marine Pde, Preston ☎(0803) 558718 Plan **10** *C4*
15hc 9⋔ (5fb) CTV in 7 bedrooms B&b£7–£11 Bdi£11.50–£15 W£49–£70 L LDO6pm
Lic ▥ CTV 12P nc2yrs
Ⓥ

⊢⊣ **GH Radford Hotel** 28–30 Youngs Park Rd ☎(0803) 559671 Plan **11** *B1*
14hc (4fb) B&b£6.45–£8.30 Bdi£9.30–£10.75 W£45–£58 M LDO4pm
Lic ▥ CTV 4P

GH Redcliffe Lodge Hotel 1 Marine Dr ☏(0803) 551394 Plan **12** *C4*
Mar–Nov
19rm 7→ 6⋒ (3fb) CTV in 13 bedrooms ★ Ⓡ B&b£10.50–£15.50 Bdi£15.50–£20.50 LDO7pm
Lic 🏨 CTV 20P 🏠
Credit card 3

↦ **GH St Weonard Private Hotel** 12 Kernou Rd ☏(0803) 558842 Plan **13** *B2*
Mar–Nov
9hc (4fb) ★ Ⓡ *B&b£6–£8 Bdi£9–£12 W£64–£78 Ⱡ LDO6pm
Lic CTV 2P
Ⓥ

Paignton

GH *San-Remo Hotel* 35 Totnes Rd ☏(0803) 557855 Plan **14** *A2*
Mar–Nov & Xmas
18hc (A 4hc) (7fb)
Lic CTV 8P

GH Sattva Hotel 29 Esplanade Rd ☏(0803) 557820 Plan **15** *C3*
Apr–mid Oct
24rm 10hc 3→ 11⋒ (4fb) ★ B&b£11–£13 Bdi£14.50–£17 W£70–£90 M LDO6pm
Lic 🏨 CTV 6P 🏠

↦ **GH Sealawn Hotel** Sea Front ☏(0803) 559031 Plan **16** *C2*
Semi-detached Victorian holiday hotel opposite sea front.
14rm 4hc 6→ 4⋒ (4fb) ★ B&b£7.50–£11.50 Bdi£11–£14 W£60–£106 Ⱡ (W only Jul–Aug)
Lic CTV 14P nc2yrs
Ⓥ

⊢×⊣ **GH Sea Verge Hotel** Marine Dr, Preston ☎(0803) 557795 Plan **17** *C4*

12rm 7hc 5⋔ (2fb) CTV in all bedrooms B&b£7.50–£12.50 Bdi£12–£17 W£52.50–£87.50 M LDOnoon

Lic ▥ 12P

Credit cards 1 3

⊢×⊣ **GH Shorton House Hotel** 17 Roundham Rd ☎(0803) 557722 Plan **18** *C1*
Mar–Nov

21rm 18hc 3⋔ (A 2hc) (9fb) ® B&b£7.50–£10 Bdi£9.85–£12 W£49–£63 M LDO4pm

Lic ▥ CTV 10P billiards

Credit card 1

GH South Mount Hotel 7 Southfield Rd ☎(0803) 557643 Plan **18A** *A4*
20 Mar–20 Oct

9hc (2fb) ✱B&b£7 Bdi£10.50 W£65–£73.50 ⱡ LDO10am

Lic CTV 7P

⊢×⊣ **GH Sunnybank Private Hotel** 2 Cleveland Rd ☎(0803) 525540 Plan **19** *C1*

12rm 10hc (5fb) B&b£7–£9 Bdi£11–£13.20 W£42–£60 ⱡ LDO7pm

Lic ▥ CTV 6P ⌂ Credit cards 1 3 Ⓥ

⊢×⊣ **GH Torbay Sands Hotel** Sea Front, 16 Marine Pde, Peston ☎(0803) 525568 Plan **20** *C4*

Closed Nov–Xmas

12hc (3fb) ★ B&b£7.50–£11.50 Bdi£11–£15 W£66–£90 ⱡ LDO6pm

Lic CTV 5P

Ⓥ

PAISLEY
Strathclyde *Renfrewshire*
Map **11** NS46
For accommodation details see under Glasgow Airport

PANTYGELLI (*Near Abergavenny*)
Gwent
Map **3** SO31

FH Mrs M E Smith **Lower House** *(SO314159)* Old Hereford Rd ☎Abergavenny (0873) 3432
Etr–Oct

Isolated stone-built farmhouse with mountain views, 3m from Abergavenny.

3hc (1fb) ✱B&b£7–£7.50 Wfr£49 M

CTV 4P 200acres arable beef sheep

PARKMILL (*Near Swansea*)
West Glamorgan
Map **2** SS58

FH Mrs D Edwards **Parc-le-Breos House** *(SS529896)* ☎Penmaen (044125) 636

1½m NW off A4118.

4hc (4fb) ★ ✱B&b£8–£11.50 Bdi£11–£12 W£77 ⱡ

▥ CTV P ∪ billiards 45acres mixed

Ⓥ

PARRACOMBE
Devon
Map **3** SS64

FH Mr H Bearryman **Lower Dean** Trentishoe ☎(05983) 215

3m W unclass rd & ½m N off A399.

9rm 2➜ (6fb) ★ B&b£8.50 Bdi£12.50 Wfr£77 ⱡ (W only mid Jul–Aug) LDO7pm

Lic ▥ CTV 9P ∪ billiards 20acres mixed

Ⓥ

PATELEY BRIDGE
North Yorkshire
Map **7** SE16

GH Grassfields Country House Hotel ☎Harrogate (0423) 711412
Apr–Oct

Elegant Georgian country house in 4 acres, with rooms of character and hospitable proprietors.

9rm 3hc 3➜ 3⋔ (3fb) ® B&b£14.50 Bdi£20 W£136 ⱡ LDO7pm

Lic ▥ CTV 20P 2⌂

PEEBLES
Borders *Peeblesshire*
Map **11** NT24

⊢⋆⊣ **GH Lindores** Old Town ☎(0721) 20441
Neat house with combined lounge and dining room.
5hc (3fb) 🐕 B&b£7.50–£8.00 W£52.50–£56 M
Ⅲ CTV 3P
Ⓥ

⊢⋆⊣ **GH Whitestone House** Innerleithen Rd ☎(0721) 20337
Neat, well maintained guesthouse to E of town.
5hc (2fb) 🐕 B&b£7.50–£8.00
Ⅲ CTV 6P

PELYNT
Cornwall
Map **2** SX25

FH Mrs Tuckett ***Trenderway*** *(SX214533)* ☎Polperro (0503) 72214
Etr–Oct
3hc (1fb) 🐕 LDOnoon
Ⅲ CTV 4P 600acres arable beef sheep

PEMBROKE
Dyfed
Map **2** SM90

GH High Noon Lower Lamphey Rd ☎(0646) 683736
Small comfortable guesthouse just north of town centre. Personally managed, hospitable and attentive service.
9hc (2fb) 🐕 B&b£8–£10 Bdi£10.50–£12.50 W£70–£85 L
Lic Ⅲ CTV 6P

PENARTH
South Glamorgan
Map **3** ST17

GH *Alanleigh Hotel* 14 Victoria Rd ☎Cardiff (0222) 701242
Stone-built house in quiet road with residents bar.
13hc 1➡ (3fb) CTV in all bedrooms 🐕 LDO6pm
Lic Ⅲ CTV 8P

PENMACHNO
Gwynedd
Map **6** SH75

⊢⋆⊣ **FH** M Jones **Tyddyn Gethin** *(SH799514)* ☎(06903) 392
Feb–Nov
Farm situated high on mountainside with panoramic views of the surrounding country.
3hc (1fb) 🐕 B&b£7–£7.50 Bdi£10.50–£11 W£70–£76 L LDO5pm
CTV P 80acres mixed
Ⓥ

PENNAN
Grampian *Aberdeenshire*
Map **15** NJ86

INN Pennan ☎New Aberdour (03466) 201
Friendly little inn with many interesting features, set on the water's edge.
6rm Ⓡ B&b£14.50 Bdi£23 Bar lunch £2.30 D9pm £8.50
Ⅲ CTV 6P ⤴
Credit cards 1 3 5 Ⓥ

PENNANT
Dyfed
Map **2** SN56

FH Mrs S M Goddard **Bikerehyd** *(SN520635)* (Guestaccom) ☎Nebo (09746) 365
3hc CTV in all bedrooms 🐕 Ⓡ B&bfr£9.50 Bdifr£16.50 W£104 L LDO10am
Lic CTV P nc5yrs 15acres mixed
Ⓥ

PENRITH
Cumbria
Map **12** NY53

⊢⋆⊣ **GH Brandelhow** 1 Portland Pl ☎(0768) 64470
A mid-terrace house close to town centre.
6hc (4fb) Ⓡ B&b£6.50–£7.50 Bdi£10–£11 W£42–£49 M LDO4.30pm
Ⅲ CTV 3P

⊢⋆⊣ **GH Pategill Villas** Carleton Rd ☎(0768) 63153
12hc (A 1hc) (6fb) B&b£7.50–£8.50 Bdi£12.50–£13.50 LDO6.30pm
Lic Ⅲ CTV 16P
Credit cards 2 3

GH *Woodland House Hotel* Wordsworth St ☎(0768) 64177
8hc (2fb) LDO6pm
Lic Ⅲ CTV 12P
See advertisement on page 273

PENRUDDOCK
Cumbria
Map **12** NY42

⊢⋆⊣ **FH** Mrs S M Smith **Highgate** *(NY444275)* ☎Greystoke (08533) 339
Feb–Nov
250-year old stone-built farmhouse with beamed ceilings: tastefully modernised. Good base for touring and recreational facilities. Situated on the A66 Penrith to Keswick road.
4rm 3hc (1fb) 🐕 Ⓡ B&b£8–£8.50 Bdi£12–£12.50 W£75 L LDO6pm
CTV 4P nc10yrs 400acres mixed

PENYBONT
Powys
Map **3** SO16

⊢⋆⊣ **FH** Mrs S F Fox **Neuadd** *(SO092618)* Cefnllys ☎Llandrindod Wells (0597) 2571
Mar–Oct
Two-storey, isolated farmhouse situated in elevated position with fine views.
3hc (1fb) *B&b£7 Bdi£10.50 W£70 L LDO5pm
Ⅲ CTV 6P ⌂ ⤴ 329acres mixed
See advertisement on page 273

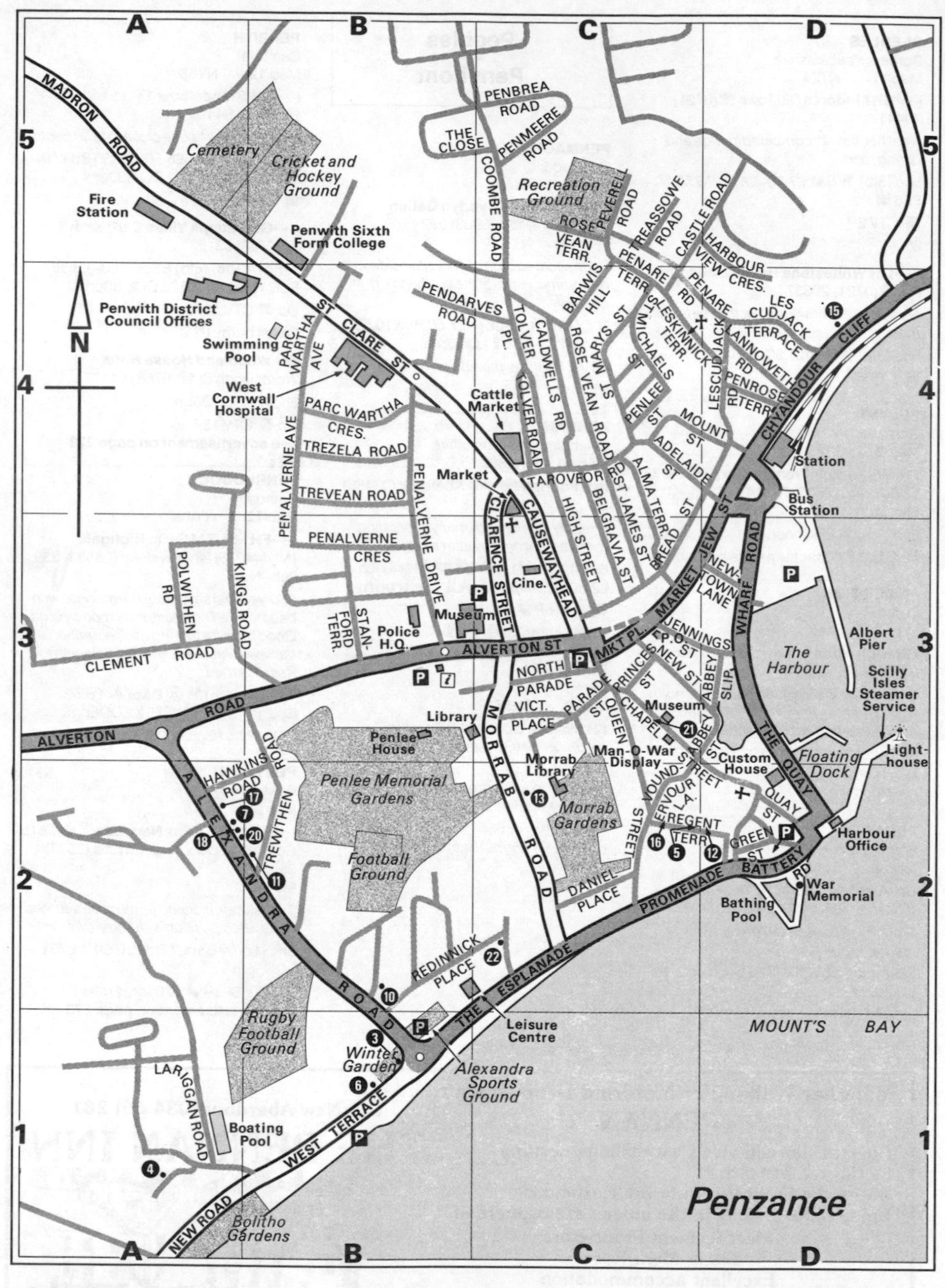

Penzance

3 Beachfield Hotel
4 Bella-Vista Private Hotel
5 Camilla Hotel
6 Carlton Private Hotel
7 Dunedin
10 Glencree Private Hotel
11 Holbein House Hotel
12 Kilindini Private Hotel
13 Kimberley House
15 Mount Royal Hotel
16 Old Manor House Private Hotel
17 Penmorvah Hotel
18 Pentrea Hotel
20 Trenant Private Hotel
21 Trevelyan Hotel
22 Willows

PENZANCE
Cornwall
Map **2** SW43
See plan
Penzance telephone numbers are due to change during the currency of this guide.

GH Beachfield Hotel The Promenade ☎(0736) 2067 Plan **3** *B1*
Mar–Nov
32hc 12⋒ (2fb) Ⓡ B&b£10.03–£12.18 Bdi£14.67–£16.82 W£67.41–£80.34 Ⓚ LDO7pm
Lic ▥ CTV ⊁

Penzance

⊢⊣ **GH Bella-Vista Private Hotel** 7 Alexandra Ter, Lariggan ☎(0736) 62409 Plan **4** *A1*
Apr–Oct
Modest terraced property overlooking promenade.
10hc (6fb) ✱ B&b£6.50–£8.50 Bdi£10.50–£12.50 W£65–£87 Ⓚ LDO5pm
CTV 8P nc3yrs

⊢⊣ **GH Camilla Hotel** Regent Ter ☎(0736) 3771 Plan **5** *C2*
Jan–Nov
Character Regency residence with comfortable friendly family atmosphere, positioned close to promenade.
10hc (2fb) B&b£7–£7.50 Bdi£10–£11 W£49–£52 Ⓜ LDO5.30pm
CTV
Ⓥ

GH Carlton Private Hotel ☎(0736) 2081 Plan **6** *B1*
Mar–Sep rs Oct & Feb
Small modest family hotel, personally run, and positioned on sea front offering commanding views.
12rm (4fb) CTV in 3 bedrooms ✱ B&b£9–£10.50 Bdi£15–£16.50 W£78–£90 V̸ (W only Jun–Aug) LDO5pm
Lic CTV ⚑ nc10yrs

⊢⊣ **GH Dunedin** Alexandra Rd ☎(0736) 2652 Plan **7** *A2*
Feb–Dec
Very comfortable small personally run guesthouse positioned close to sea front.
9hc (4fb) CTV in all bedrooms Ⓡ B&b£7–£9 Bdi£10.50–£12.50 W£70–£85 V̸ LDO5.30pm
Lic ∭ CTV ⚑
Ⓥ

⊢⊣ **GH Glencree Private Hotel**
2 Mennaye Rd ☎(0736) 2026 Plan **10** *B2*
Apr–Sep
Modest small family 'holiday orientated' guesthouse. Positioned close to sea front.
9hc (3fb) ✱ B&b£7.50–£8.50 Bdi£12–£13 W£52.50–£59.50 M̸ S% LDOnoon
CTV

GH Holbein House Hotel Alexandra Rd ☎(0736) 5008 Plan **11** *B2*

Penzance

Small comfortable family hotel, personally run and positioned in quiet area leading to sea front.
8rm 7hc 1→ (3fb) B&b£8.50–£10 Bdi£13.50–£15.50 W£82–£101 V̸ LDO5pm
Lic ∭ CTV ⚑
Credit card 3

GH Kilindini Private Hotel 13 Regent Ter ☎(0736) 4744 Plan **12** *D2*
Closed Xmas
Regency terraced house, comfortably appointed offering friendly service.
12rm 8hc 1→ 3⋒ (4fb) ✱ B&b£8.50–£10.50 Bdi£12–£14 W£59.50–£72.50 M̸ LDO3.30pm
Lic ∭ CTV 10P nc3yrs
Ⓥ

GH Kimberley House 10 Morrab Rd (Guestaccom) ☎(0736) 2727 Plan **13** *C2*
Small tastefully furnished residence offering warm and friendly welcome from resident proprietors.
9hc (2fb) ✱ Ⓡ B&b£8–£8.50 Bdi£12.75–£13.25 W£84–£87 V̸
LDO5pm
Lic ∭ CTV 4P nc5yrs
Credit cards 1 3

GH Mount Royal Hotel Chyandour Cliff ☎(0736) 2233 Plan **15** *D4*
Apr–Oct
Small family hotel facing sea and harbour.
8rm 5hc 3→ (1fb) *B&b£10.50–£12 W£70–£80.50 M̸
∭ CTV 8P 4⌂
Ⓥ

GH Old Manor House Private Hotel Regent Ter ☎(0736) 3742 Plan **16** *C2*
Closed Xmas
Regency terraced small friendly family hotel, convenient to beach.
12hc 7⋒ (4fb) CTV in 12 bedrooms ✱ B&b£12–£14 Bdi£17–£20 W£130 V̸ LDO7pm
Lic ∭ CTV 12P nc3yrs ≋(heated)
Credit cards 1 3 5

GH Penmorvah Hotel Alexandra Rd ☎(0736) 3711 Plan **17** *B2*
Very comfortable friendly small family hotel.
11rm 5→ 6⋒ (4fb) CTV in all bedrooms Ⓡ B&b£12.50–£13.50 Bdi£18.50–£20 W£82–£89 M̸ LDO7.30pm
Lic ∭ 2P
Credit cards 1 2 3 5 Ⓥ

⊢⊣ **GH Pentrea Hotel** Alexandra Rd ☎(0736) 69576 Plan **18** *A2*
10hc (3fb) Ⓡ B&b£7.50–£9 Bdi£12–£13.50 W£45–£55 M LDO7pm
Lic CTV 1
Credit cards 1 3 Ⓥ

⊢⊣ **GH Trenant Private Hotel** Alexandra Rd ☎(0736) 2005 Plan **20** *B2*
May–6 Oct
Conveniently positioned for both promenade and town centre.
7hc B&b£6.50–£8 Bdi£9.80–£11.30 W£45–£54 M LDO5pm
TV nc6yrs

⊢⊣ **GH Trevelyan Hotel** 16 Chapel St ☎(0736) 2494 Plan **21** *C3*
Feb–Nov
17th-century property offering comfortable accommodation within town centre.
8rm 7hc 1 (4fb) B&bfr£7 Bdifr£11 Wfr£49 M LDOnoon
Lic CTV 9P

GH Willows Cornwall Ter ☎(0736) 3744 Plan **22** *C2*
Closed Oct
Victorian corner house with attractive gardens.
7rm 4hc (1fb) Ⓡ *B&bfr£8.50 Bdifr£13.50 Wfr£83.50 L LDOnoon
CTV 6P nc5yrs

PERRANPORTH
Cornwall
Map **2** SW75

GH Cellar Cove Hotel Droskyn Point ☎(087257) 2110 (due to change to Truro (0872) 572110)
Closed Nov
14hc (4fb) B&b£10–£12 Bdi£13.50–£18 W£90–£120 L LDO6.30pm
Lic CTV 18P

⊢⊣ **GH Fairview Hotel** Tywarnhayle Rd ☎(087257) 2278
Mar–Oct
Good views from this comfortable family hotel.
15hc Ⓡ B&b£7–£9 Bdi£10–£13 W£49–£60 M S% LDO5pm
Lic CTV 4P

⊢⊣ **GH Lake House Private Hotel** Perrancombe ☎(087257) 3202
late Mar–early Oct
Pleasant friendly family hotel, adjoining Boscawen gardens and lake.
10hc (2fb) B&b£8–£10 Bdi£10–£12.50 W£56–£70 M LDO6.30pm
Lic CTV 7P 1
Credit cards 1 3

GH Lamorna Private Hotel Tywarnhayle Rd ☎(087257) 3398 (due to change to Truro (0872) 573398)
Closed Xmas
Comfortable personally run small family hotel.
10hc (4fb) Ⓡ B&b£10.50 Bdi£14 W£85 L LDO6.30pm
Lic CTV

GH *Lynton* Cliff Rd ☎(087257) 3457
Feb–Nov
Overlooking beach, small family hotel.
8hc (3fb)
Lic CTV 6P sea

GH *Park View Private Hotel* 42 Tywarnhayle Rd ☎(087257) 3009
Mar–Oct
Friendly service from owners of this comfortable family hotel.
9hc (4fb) LDO5pm
Lic CTV 10P

GH Villa Margarita Private Hotel Bolingey ☎(087257) 2063
Exceptionally well appointed colonial style villa offering a good standard of food 1m S off B3284.
5rm 3hc 2 (A 2) (3fb) Ⓡ B&b£10.85–£12 Bdi£17.85–£19 W£110–£118 L
Lic CTV 8P nc8yrs

PERTH
Tayside *Perthshire*
Map **11** NO12

GH *Clark Kimberley* 57–59 Dunkeld Rd ☎(0738) 37406
8hc (2fb)
CTV 12P

GH *Clunie* 12 Pitcullen Cres ☎(0738) 23625
Closed Dec & Jan
7hc 1 1 (2fb)
CTV 7P

⊢⊣ **GH Darroch** 9 Pitcullen Cres ☎(0738) 36893
Friendly house in convenient location with well equipped bedrooms.
6hc (2fb) CTV in all bedrooms Ⓡ B&b£8 Bdi£12.50 LDO6.15pm
CTV 12P

⊢⊣ **GH Gables** 24–26 Dunkeld Rd ☎(0738) 24717
Two adjoining houses on a busy junction N of the town.
8hc (4fb) B&b£7–£8
CTV 8P
Ⓥ

⊢⊣ **GH Pitcullen** 17 Pitcullen Cres ☎(0738) 26506
6hc (2fb) Ⓡ B&b£8–£8.50 Bdi£12–£12.50
CTV 6P
Ⓥ

PETERSFIELD
Hampshire
Map **4** SU72

GH Concorde Hotel 1 Weston Rd ☎(0730) 63442
8hc (2fb) TV in 2 bedrooms Ⓡ *B&b£14.38–£20.70 Bdi£21.28–£27.60 LDO5pm
Lic CTV 12P
Credit cards 1 3

PICKERING
North Yorkshire
Map **8** SE88

⊢⊣ **GH Bramwood** 19 Hallgarth
☎(0751) 74066

6hc (2fb) ✱ B&b£8–£9 Bdi£12–£13 W£56–£63 M LDOnoon

CTV 6P nc6yrs

GH Cottage Leas Country Middleton
☎(0751) 72129

11rm 5hc 6⋒ (3fb) CTV in 1 bedroom TV in 10 bedrooms ® B&b£8.50–£12 Bdi£15–£18 W£59.50–£84 M LDO9.30pm

Lic 50P (hard)

Credit cards 1 5

PILSDON
Dorset
Map **3** SY49

FH K B Brooks **Monkwood** *(SY429986)*
☎Broadwindsor (0308) 68723

Thatched farmhouse in rural setting with pleasant views. Charmouth 6m, Bridport 5m.

2rm (1fb) ✱ *B&b£6–£8

CTV P 160acres beef dairy sheep mixed

PILTON
Somerset
Map **3** ST54

GH Long House ☎(074989) 283
rs Nov–Feb

7rm 1hc 3➡ 3⋒ (1fb) B&b£14 Bdi£21 W£116 L LDO6.30pm

Lic 8P nc6yrs

Credit cards 1 2 3 5 Ⓥ

PITLOCHRY
Tayside *Perthshire*
Map **14** NN95
See plan

GH Adderley Private Hotel 23, Toberargan Rd ☎(0796) 2433
Plan **1** *C3*
Etr–mid Oct

Small family run hotel, close to town centre.

10hc (2fb) ® B&b£8.50–£9.25 Bdi£13.45–£14.45 W£89.80–£95.50 L LDO6.30pm

CTV 10P nc5yrs

Ⓥ

GH Balrobin Private Hotel Higher Oakfield ☎(0796) 2901 Plan **2** *D3*
Apr–Oct

Neatly appointed guesthouse.

8hc 1➡ 3⋒ (1fb) ® B&b£9–£10 Bdi£14–£15 W£93–£100 L LDO7.30pm

Lic CTV 8P

Ⓥ

GH Duntrune 22 East Moulin Rd
☎(0796) 2172 Plan **3** *D3*
Etr–Oct

Pleasantly furnished house.

7hc 2➡ 2⋒ (1fb) ✱ ® B&b£8.50–£9.50 Bdi£13.50–£14.50 W£88–£94 L LDO6.30pm

8P nc5yrs

Ⓥ

GH *Fasganeoin Hotel* Perth Rd
☎(0796) 2387 Plan **4** *D2*
Etr–Oct

Attractive large house standing in its own grounds at southern entrance to the town.

9hc (4fb) ✱ LDO7.20pm

Lic 20P river

GH *Faskally Home Farm* ☎(0796) 2007 Plan **5** *A4*
Apr–Oct

Pleasant 'U' shaped building with popular caravan site attached. Set on west side of A9 on northern outskirts of Pitlochry. Sheltered from Loch Faskally by trees.

8rm 6hc (2fb)

P

GH Torrdarach Hotel Golf Course Rd
☎(0796) 2136 Plan **6** *B4*
Mar–Oct

7rm 6hc 1➡ (1fb) ✱ ® B&b£10 Bdi£16 W£105 L LDO7pm

Lic CTV 7P

⊢⊣ GH Wellhouse Private Hotel
11 Toberargan Rd ☎ (0796) 2239
Plan **7** *C3*

Pitlochry

7rm 6hc (2fb) ✱ B&b£7.50–£8.50
Bdi£14–£15 W£52.50 M LDO8pm
Lic CTV 8P

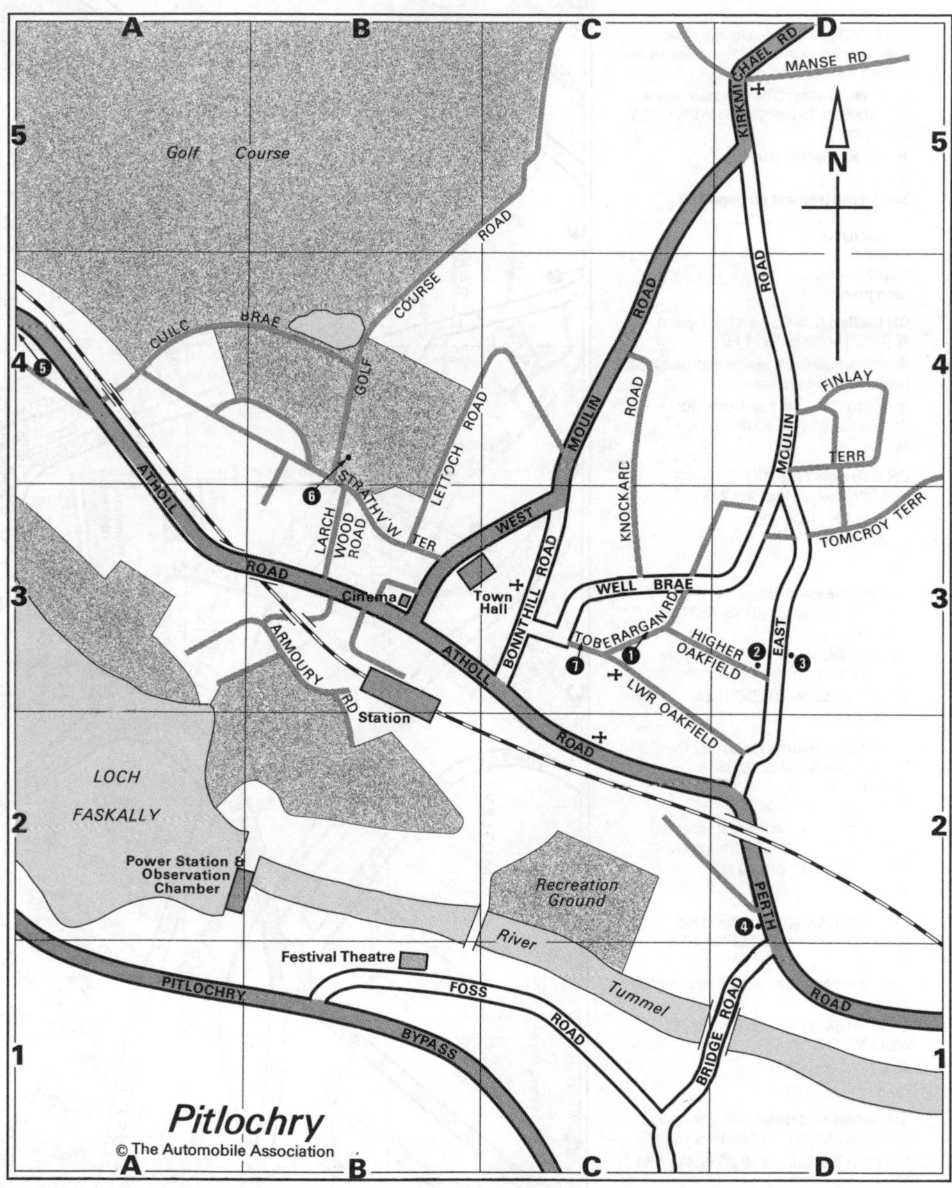

Pitlochry

1 Adderley Private Hotel
2 Balrobin Private Hotel
3 Duntrune
4 Fasganeoin Hotel
5 Faskally Home Farm
6 Torrdarach Hotel
7 Wellhouse Private Hotel

PLUCKLEY
Kent
Map **5** TQ94

FH Mrs F Harris **Elvey** *(TQ916457)*
☎(023384) 442
rs Xmas
Detached converted oasthouse with extensive views over the Weald. Meals are served in the farmhouse.
8rm 5⇌ 3⋒ (6fb) CTV in all bedrooms Ⓡ B&bfr£10.75 Bdifr£16.25 W£106.75 Ʋ LDO7pm
✈ 12P ⌂ 75acres mixed
Ⓥ
See advertisement on page 280

PLYMOUTH
Devon
Map **2** SX45
(See plan)

GH Cadleigh 36 Queens Rd, Lipson ☎(0752) 665909 Plan **1** *F8*
Redbrick building in residential road, near park, 1m from city centre.
9hc (4fb) CTV in all bedrooms Ⓡ B&b£8.50–£9.50 LDOam
ⅢⅢ CTV

GH *Carnegie Hotel* 172 Citadel Rd, The Hoe ☎(0752) 25158 Plan **2** *B3*
9hc (2fb) ✈ LDO6.30pm
Lic ⅢⅢ CTV ⱣⱣ
Ⓥ

⊢⊣ **GH Chester** 54 Stuart Rd, Pennycomequick ☎(0752) 663706 Plan **3** *A7*
Large white stone detached house in small garden, 1m from city centre.
8hc (1fb) B&b£8–£9 LDO10am
Lic ⅢⅢ CTV 9P

⊢⊣ **GH Cranbourne Hotel** 282 Citadel Rd, The Hoe ☎(0752) 263858 Plan **3A** *C3*
Closed last 2 wks Dec
An end of terrace Georgian property, personally run by resident proprietors.
10hc (7fb) B&b£7.50–£9.50
ⅢⅢ CTV P

⊢⊣ **GH Dudley** 42 Sutherland Rd, Mutley ☎(0752) 668322 Plan **4** *D8*
rs Xmas
Double fronted house in quiet residential street.
6hc (5fb) B&b£7–£9.50 Bdi£12–£14.50 W£45 Ɱ LDO9am
ⅢⅢ CTV
Credit cards 1 3

GH Gables End Hotel 29 Sutherland Rd, Mutley ☎(0752) 20803 Plan **5** *D7*
7hc (3fb) ✈ B&b£9–£10.35 W£60–£69 Ɱ
ⅢⅢ CTV 2⌂

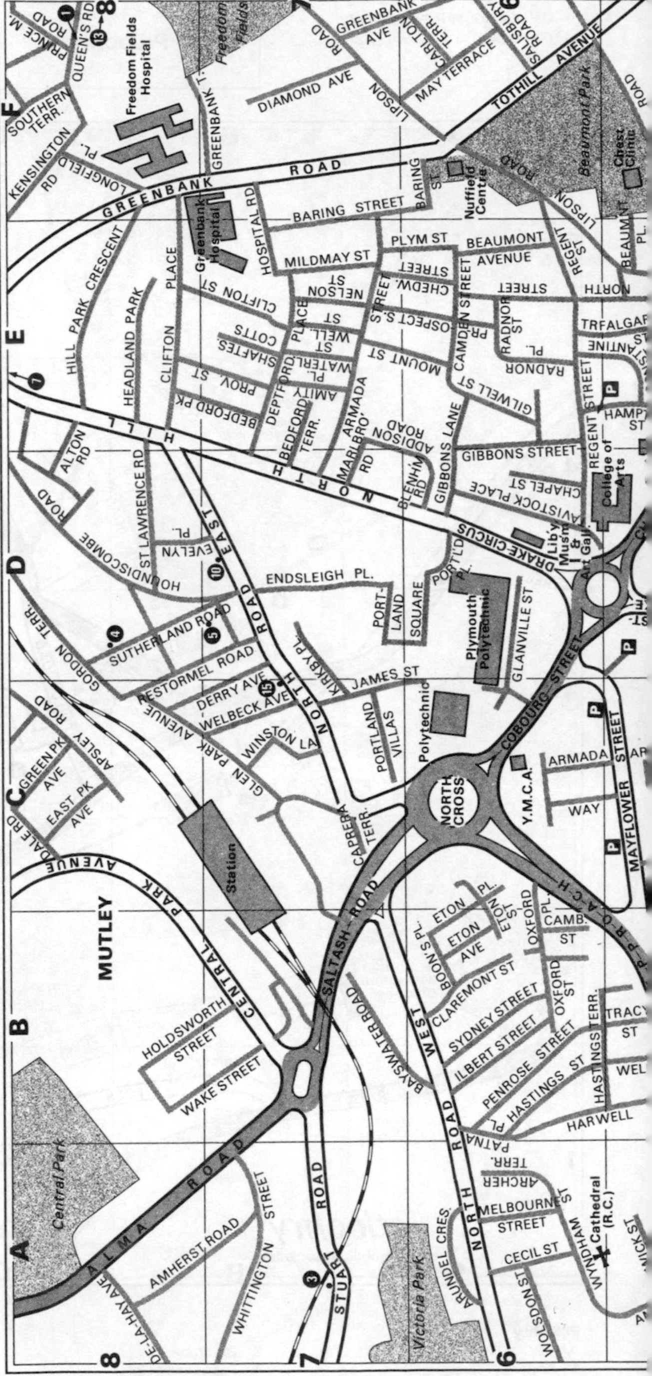

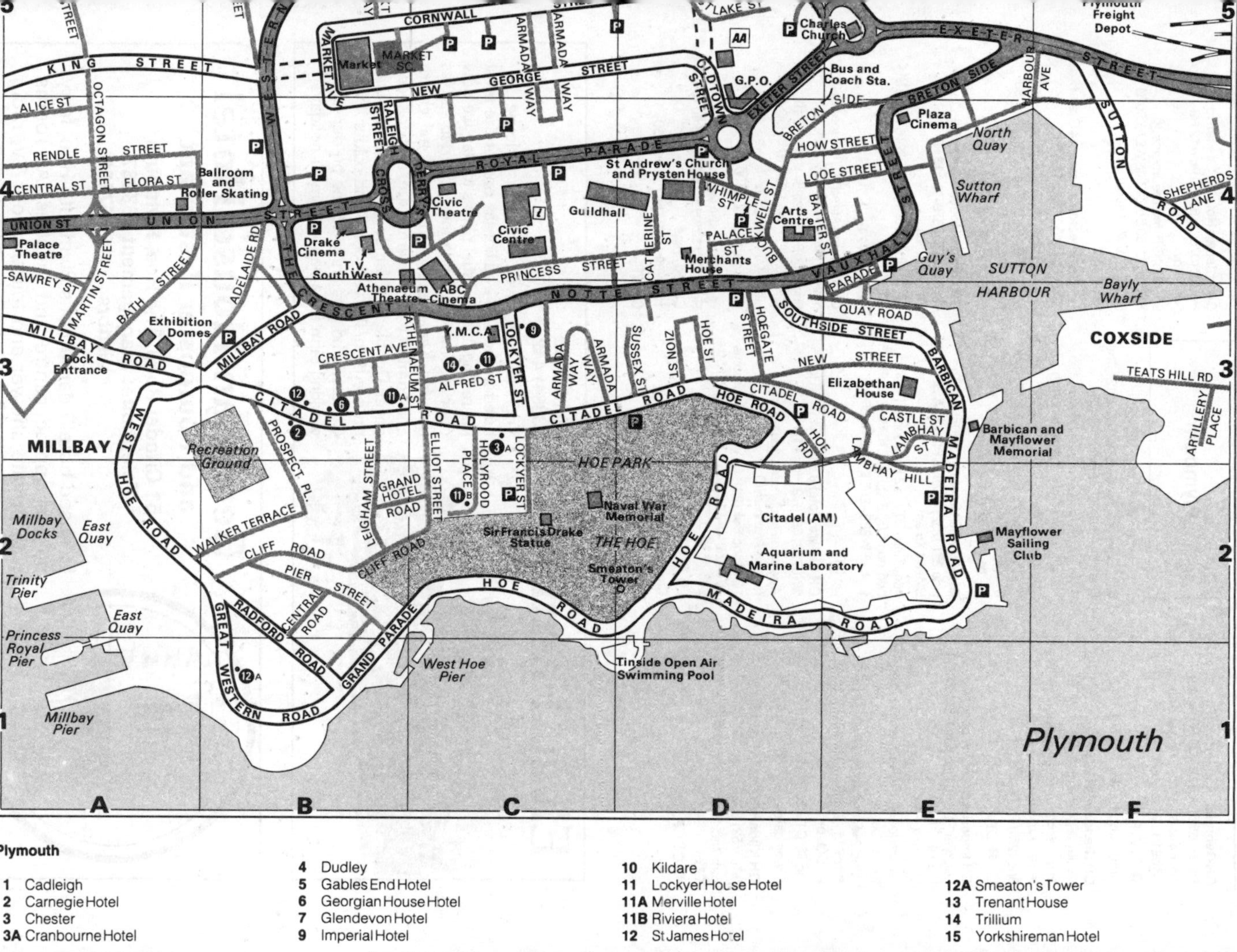

Plymouth

1 Cadleigh
2 Carnegie Hotel
3 Chester
3A Cranbourne Hotel
4 Dudley
5 Gables End Hotel
6 Georgian House Hotel
7 Glendevon Hotel
9 Imperial Hotel
10 Kildare
11 Lockyer House Hotel
11A Merville Hotel
11B Riviera Hotel
12 St James Hotel
12A Smeaton's Tower
13 Trenant House
14 Trillium
15 Yorkshireman Hotel

GH Georgian House Hotel 51 Citadel Rd, The Hoe ☎(0752) 663237 Plan **6** *B3*

10rm 4⇌ 6⋔ (1fb) CTV in all bedrooms Ⓡ B&b£19 LDO9.30pm

▥ CTV 2P

Credit cards 1 2 3

GH *Glendevon Hotel* 20 Ford Park Rd, Mutley ☎(0752) 663655 Plan **7** *E8*

In residential area, a large double fronted terraced house.

8hc (2fb)

Lic ▥ CTV

GH Imperial Hotel 3 Windsor Villas, Lockyer St, The Hoe ☎(0752) 27311 Plan **9** *C3*
Closed Xmas

Large double fronted building very close to the Hoe.

22hc 2⇌ 11⋔ (6fb) CTV in 18 bedrooms B&b£15–£18 Bdi£21–£24 W£99–£123 Ⓛ LDO7pm

Lic ▥ CTV 20P 1🚗

Credit cards 1 2 3 Ⓥ

GH Kildare 82 North Road East ☎(0752) 29375 Plan **10** *D7*

8rm 7hc 1⇌ (3fb) ✱ Ⓡ *B&b£6.95–£7.50

▥ CTV ℙ

Plymouth

GH Lockyer House Hotel 2 Alfred St, The Hoe ☎(0752) 665755 Plan **11** *C3*

An end of terrace Georgian house situated in quiet side street, although close to city centre.

6hc (1fb) B&b£8.80 Bdi£14.46 W£61.60 Ⓜ S% LDO6pm

Lic ▥ CTV ℙ

GH Merville Hotel 73 Citadel Rd, The Hoe ☎(0752) 667595 Plan **11A** *B3*
Closed Xmas

10hc (2fb) CTV in 2 bedrooms TV in 2 bedrooms Ⓡ B&b£9–£10 Bdi£13.95–£14.95 W£88–£95 Ⓛ LDO12.30pm

Lic CTV 2P

GH Riviera Hotel 8 Elliott St, The Hoe ☎(0752) 667379 Plan **11B** *C2*

A personally run hotel situated on the famous Plymouth Hoe.

10rm 4hc 6⇌ (2fb) CTV in all bedrooms Ⓡ B&b£10–£13 Bdi£15–£18 W£66.50–£86.45 Ⓜ LDO5.30pm

Lic ▥ CTV ℙ

Credit cards 1 2 3

GH St James Hotel 49 Citadel Rd, The Hoe ☎(0752) 661950 Plan **12** *B3*
Feb–Nov

9⋔ (3fb) CTV in all bedrooms Ⓡ *B&b£11.50 Bdi£17.45 W£75.50 Ⓜ

Lic ▥ CTV ℙ nc6yrs

Ⓥ

⊢⊣ **GH Smeaton's Tower** 44 Grand Pde ☎(0752) 21007 Plan **12A** *B1*

6rm 4hc (2fb) CTV in all bedrooms ✱ Ⓡ B&b£6.50–£7.50 Bdi£10.50–£11.50 W£45–£50 Ⓜ LDO8pm

Lic ▥ CTV ℙ

GH Trenant House Queens Rd, Lipson ☎(0752) 663879 Plan **13** *F8*
Closed Xmas

21hc (1fb) B&b£10.50 Bdi£15 W£63 Ⓜ LDO4pm

Lic ▥ CTV 24P

GH Trillium 4 Alfred St, The Hoe ☎(0752) 670452 Plan **14** *C3*

6hc ✱ Ⓡ B&b£12.25–£14 Bdi£19.15–£20.90 W£77.20–£88.20 Ⓜ LDO4pm

Lic ▥ CTV 3P nc5yrs

Credit cards 1 2 3 Ⓥ

⊢⊣ **GH Yorkshireman Hotel** 64 North Road East ☎(0752) 668133 Plan **15** *C7*
Closed Xmas

12hc (3fb) ✱ B&b£7.25–£7.50

CTV 7P

POLBATHIC
Cornwall
Map **2** SX35
GH *Old Mill* ☎St Germans (0503) 30596
8hc (2fb) LDO4.30pm
Lic Ⅲ CTV 12P river

POLMASSICK
Cornwall
Map **2** SW94
GH Kilbol House ☎Mevagissey (0726) 842481
7rm 3hc 3🛁 1🚿 (2fb) B&b£10.50–£12.50 Bdi£15.50–£17.50 W£105–£119 ⱡ LDO5pm
Lic Ⅲ CTV 12P ≋
Credit cards 1 2 3 Ⓥ

POLPERRO
Cornwall
Map **2** SX25
GH Kit Hill Talland Hill ☎(0503) 72369
6hc (1fb) CTV in 1 bedroom TV in 2 bedrooms ✗ ✱B&b£7.50–£10 W£52.50–£70 M̸
Lic Ⅲ CTV 10P nc6yrs

GH Landaviddy Manor Landaviddy Ln ☎(0503) 72210
Apr–Oct
Charming stone country house in peaceful setting, tastefully furnished and decorated.
9rm 6hc 3🚿 ✗ Ⓡ B&b£9–£13 Bdi£16–£20 W£60–£80 M̸ LDO4pm
Lic Ⅲ CTV 12P

GH Lanhael House ☎(0503) 72428
Mar–Oct
6rm 4hc 1🚿 ✗ B&b£9.50
Ⅲ CTV 7P nc ≋

⊢⊣**GH Penryn House Hotel** The Coombes ☎(0503) 72157
14rm 9hc 5🛁 (5fb) B&b£7–£9.50 Bdi£10–£13 W£49–£91 ⱡ LDO6pm
Lic Ⅲ CTV 15P
Ⓥ

GH *Sleepy Hollow Private Hotel* Brentfields ☎(0503) 72288
Mar–Sep
6hc 2🚿 (1fb) ✗ (W only Jul & Aug)
CTV 6P nc12yrs sea

POLZEATH
Cornwall
Map **2** SW97
GH White Lodge Old Polzeath ☎Trebetherick (020886) 2370
7hc (2fb) B&b£8.50–£10 Bdi£12–£14 W£55–£65 M̸
Lic Ⅲ CTV 10P

PONSWORTHY
Devon
Map **3** SX77
FH Mr & Mrs Fursdon **Old Walls** *(SX697745)* ☎Poundsgate (03643) 222
Mar–Oct
Farmhouse standing in its own small estate in isolated position, near Dartmoor. Pleasant atmosphere.
3rm B&b£8.80–£9.35
Ⅲ TV 4P 36acres beef

PONTARDULAIS
West Glamorgan
Map **2** SN50
⊢⊣**FH** Mr & Mrs G Davies **Croft** *(SN612015)* Heol-y-Barna ☎(0792) 883654
Situated in elevated position with open aspect to the Gower Peninsula and the Loughor Estuary. Approx ½m from A48.
3hc ✗ B&b£7.50–£9 Bdi£11–£12.50 W£52–£60 M̸ LDO2.30pm
Ⅲ CTV 4P nc5yrs 5acres beef small holding

PONTFAEN
Dyfed
Map **2** SN03

FH Mrs S Heard **Tregynon** *(SN054345)* ☎Newport (0239) 820531

A comfortable, beamed 17th-century farmhouse in the foothills of the Preseli mountains. Vegetarian meals are a speciality. 3m E of village, off unclass road joining B4313 and Newport. 5m from Newport sands.

5hc (3fb) ✱ B&b£8.60 Bdi£13.80 W£95 Ł LDO6.30pm

Lic 𝍐 CTV P 10acres sheep mixed

PONTHIRWAUN
Dyfed
Map **2** SN24

⊢⊣ **FH** Mr & Mrs J Moine **Penwernfach** *(SN266437)* ☎Newcastle Emlyn (0239) 710694
Apr–Oct

18th-century stone farmhouse with two inglenook fireplaces and a stone circular stairway. Animals on the farm may be fed by visitors. Salmon and trout fishing 1½ miles away. Situated 1m SE B4570.

3hc (1fb) CTV in all bedrooms ✱ Ⓡ B&b£7.50–£8.50 W£52.50–£59.50 M

𝍐 6P 6acres non-working

Ⓥ

PONTLLYFNI
Gwynedd
Map **6** SH45

GH Bron Dirion Hotel ☎Clynnogfawr (028686) 346
Mar–Sep

Detached country house in quiet rural situation.

9hc (4fb) B&b£8.50 Bdi£12 W£75 Ł LDO6.30pm

Lic 𝍐 CTV 10P

POOLE
Dorset
Map **4** SZ09
For locations and additional guesthouses see **Bournemouth**

GH Avalon Private Hotel 14 Pinewood Rd, Branksome Park ☎(0202) 760917
Branksome & Westbourne plan **83** *A2*
Closed Xmas

In quiet select area near Branksome beach.

14rm 11hc 3⇌ (2fb) Ⓡ B&b£9.78–£14.49 Bdi£13.22–£19.66 W£60–£92 Ł LDO2.30pm

Lic 𝍐 CTV 14P nc6yrs

GH Blue Shutters Hotel 109 North Rd, Parkstone ☎(0202) 748129

In quiet area near to Branksome beach.

12hc (2fb) ✱ B&b£10–£11.50 Bdi£14.50–£16 W£63–£77 M LDO6.30pm

Lic 𝍐 CTV 10P

GH Dene Hotel 16 Pinewood Rd, Branksome Park ☎(0202) 761143
Branksome & Westbourne plan **87** *B2*
Closed Xmas

Comfortable and tastefully appointed in quiet location near to Branksome beach.

18rm 6hc 1⇌ 7⋒ (4fb) CTV in 8 bedrooms ✱ Ⓡ B&b£14–£16.50 Bdi£19.50–£24 W£78.20–£120.20 Ł LDO7pm

Lic 𝍐 CTV 20P
Credit cards 1 2 3 5 Ⓥ

GH Ebdon House Hotel 21 St Clair Rd ☎(0202) 707286

8hc 3⋒ (3fb) TV in 3 bedrooms ✱ Ⓡ B&b£9.50–£10.50 Bdi£15–£16 W£89–£98 Ł LDO7pm

Lic 𝍐 CTV 5P

GH Fairlight Hotel 1 Golf Links Rd, Broadstone ☎(0202) 694316

3m NW B3074.

10rm 3hc 7⇌ (1fb) B&bfr£13 Bdifr£19 Wfr£112 Ł

Lic 𝍐 CTV 10P

Poole — Pooley Bridge

⊢ GH Lewina 225 Bournemouth Rd, Parkstone ☎(0202) 742295
Closed Nov & Dec
Short distance from town centre.
6hc (1fb) Ⓡ B&b£7–£8 Bdi£10.50–£11.50 W£47–£54 M LDO10am
CTV 6P

GH Ormonde House Hotel 18 Ormonde Rd, Branksome Park ☎(0202) 761093
Branksome & Westbourne plan **94** *A2*
In quiet residential area with pleasant walk to Branksome beach.
8hc (2fb) Ⓡ *B&b£6.85–£9.35 Bdi£10.25–£12.50 W£84.50 L LDO4pm
Lic CTV 5P
Ⓥ

GH Redcroft Private Hotel
20 Pinewood Rd, Branksome Park ☎(0202) 763959 Branksome & Westbourne plan **95** *D1*
Opposite entrance to Branksome Dene Chine in quiet location.
10hc 3→ 1⋒ (3fb) TV in 1 bedroom ★ Ⓡ B&b£12.65 Bdi£18.37 W£75.90–£79.20 M LDO4pm
Lic CTV 12P nc5yrs

GH *Sandbourne Hotel* 1 Sandcotes Rd, Parkstone ☎(0202) 747704
Corner site on main road, short distance from town centre.
7hc (3fb) ★ LDO4pm
CTV 8P

GH Sheldon Lodge 22 Forest Rd, Branksome Park ☎(0202) 761186
Branksome & Westbourne plan **97** *A2*
Detached guesthouse in quiet area with attractive public rooms and good bedrooms.
14rm 3hc (2fb) Ⓡ B&b£12–£14 Bdi£15–£18 W£70–£85 L LDO7pm
Lic CTV 3P
Ⓥ

GH Twin Cedars Hotel 2 Pinewood Rd, Branksome Park ☎(0202) 761339
Branksome & Westbourne plan **100** *A2*
Closed Nov
Set in own grounds in quiet area near Branksome beach.
9hc 3→ 3⋒ (A 2⋒) (7fb) CTV in all bedrooms Ⓡ B&b£12–£15 Bdi£15–£18 Wfr£70 M LDO7pm
Lic CTV P nc10yrs

GH Wayside Lodge Hotel
179 Bournemouth Rd, Parkstone ☎(0202) 732328
On main road between Poole and Bournemouth.
12rm 6hc 2→ 4⋒ (4fb) B&b£9.20 Bdi£13.23 W£86.25 L LDO3pm
Lic CTV 15P
Credit cards 1 2 3

GH *Westminster Cottage Hotel*
3 Westminster Road East, Branksome Park ☎(0202) 765265
Branksome & Westbourne Plan **102** *A2*
In quiet location of select Branksome area.
12hc 4→ ⋒
Lic CTV 14P

POOLEY BRIDGE
Cumbria
Map **12** NY42

⊢ **FH** Mrs A Strong **Barton Hall** *(NY478251)* ☎(08536) 275
Etr–Oct
Attractive farmhouse, well furnished and decorated; large garden with summer house. Boating, fishing and golf nearby.
2hc (1fb) ★ B&b£7.50
P nc8yrs 72acres dairy

PORLOCK
Somerset
Map **3** SS84

GH Gables Hotel ☎(0643) 862552
Mar–Nov rs Dec
7rm 6hc 1➡ Bdifr£9 Bdifr£15 Wfr£100 V̸
LDO10am
Lic ▥ CTV Ᵽ nc12yrs

GH Lorna Doone Hotel High St ☎(0643) 862404
11hc 1➡ 1⌂ (3fb) ★ B&b£9.75 Bdi£14.75 W£99.75 V̸ LDO7pm
Lic ▥ CTV 8P
Ⓥ

⊢×⊣ **GH Overstream** Parson St ☎(0643) 862421
Closed Xmas
8hc (3fb) ★ B&b£8–£12 Bdi£12–£16 W£50–£65 M̸ LDO5pm
Lic lift 12P nc3yrs

PORTESHAM
Dorset
Map **3** SY68

GH Millmead Country Goose Hill ☎Abbotsbury (030587) 432
Feb–Nov
Short distance from Abbotsbury and Hardy's Monument, in quiet hamlet.
7hc (3fb) CTV in all bedrooms
B&b£11.50 Bdi£18.50 W£72 V̸
LDO5.30pm
Lic ▥ CTV 12P nc10yrs
Credit cards [1] [3] Ⓥ

PORTHCAWL
Mid Glamorgan
Map **3** SS87

⊢×⊣ **GH Collingwood Hotel** 40 Mary St ☎(065671) 2899
Modestly appointed small establishment.
8hc (2fb) B&b£8 Bdi£11.50 W£50 M̸
LDO5pm
Lic ▥ CTV Ᵽ

GH Minerva Private Hotel
52 Esplanade Av ☎(065671) 2428
8rm 6hc 2➡ (3fb) CTV in 1 bedroom
B&b£8.50–£11 Bdi£12–£14.50 W£55–£72 M̸ LDO5pm
▥ CTV Ᵽ
Ⓥ

PORTHCOTHAN BAY
Cornwall
Map **2** SW87

⊢×⊣ **GH Bay House** ☎Padstow (0841) 520472
Apr–6 Oct
17hc (1fb) B&b£8–£12 Bdi£12–£16 W£76–£103 V̸ LDO6.30pm
Lic CTV 17P

PORTHCURNO
Cornwall
Map **2** SW32

GH Mariners Lodge ☎St Buryan (073672) 236
Apr–Oct
Well appointed hotel on headland.
7hc 1⌂ (1fb) ★ *B&b£16–£18 Bdi£22–£24 W£112–£126 LDO8pm
Lic CTV 12P

⊢×⊣ **FH** Mrs D M Jeffrey **Corniché Trebehor** *(SW376244)* ☎Sennen (073687) 424
Closed Xmas
Well appointed, modern farmhouse designed by owner. Situated 2m from village, 2m from Lands End and 8m from Penzance. Ideal for touring.
4hc ★ B&b£8–£8.50 Bdi£12–£13 W£89 V̸ (W only Jul & Aug) LDO6pm
Lic ▥ CTV 5P nc6yrs 200acres dairy mixed

PORTHMADOG
Gwynedd
Map **6** SH53

GH Oakleys The Harbour ☎(0766) 2482
Apr–Nov
Detached Victorian house in quiet town position.
8hc 1➡ (2fb) ✱ B&b£8.50–£9.50 Bdi£13.50–£15 W£90–£100 ⅃ LDO5pm
Lic CTV 18P

GH Owen's Hotel High St ☎(0766) 2098
Mar–Oct
A guesthouse attached to cafe/bakers in centre of town.
12rm 8hc 1⋒ (4fb) CTV in 6 bedrooms Ⓡ B&b£10–£11 Bdi£16–£17 Wfr£72 M S% LDO6.45pm
Lic ₩ CTV 4P 5🚗
Ⓥ

PORTHTOWAN
Cornwall
Map **2** SW64

⊢⊣ **FH** Mrs M R Honey **Torvean** *(SW704483)* Coast Rd ☎(0209) 890536
Mar–Oct
3hc (1fb) CTV in all bedrooms ✱ Ⓡ B&b£7–£9 Bdi£11–£12 W£49 M
CTV 6P 250acres arable

PORT ISAAC
Cornwall
Map **2** SW98

GH Archer Farm Hotel Trewetha ☎(020888) 522
Apr–Dec
Attractive, detached, converted farmhouse set in own grounds. 1m E B3267.
8rm 2hc 1➡ 2⋒ (1fb) B&b£9.50–£11 Bdi£16–£17.50 W£63–£73.50 M LDO7.30pm
Lic ₩ CTV 8P
Ⓥ

GH Bay Hotel 1 The Terrace ☎(020888) 380
Etr–Oct
Double fronted building in elevated position overlooking sea.
11rm 9hc (5fb) B&b£8.50–£11.50 Bdi£13–£16 W£52–£68 M LDO8pm
Lic CTV 10P

⊢⊣ **GH Fairholme** 30 Trewetha Ln ☎(020888) 397
Detached double fronted building on main road leading to Port Isaac.
6hc (2fb) ✱ B&b£6.50–£7 Bdi£11–£11.50 W£42–£45 M LDO10am
₩ CTV 8P

GH Trethoway Hotel 98 Fore St ☎(020888) 214
Apr–Oct
9hc (3fb) B&b£9–£12.50 Bdi£13.50–£17 W£60–£70 ⅃ LDO3pm
Lic CTV 6P

PORTLOE
Cornwall
Map **2** SW93

INN Ship ☎Truro (0872) 501356
Feb–Oct
6hc B&b£10 W£70 M L£2alc D9.30pm £6alc
CTV 25P 🚫

PORTPATRICK
Dumfries & Galloway *Wigtownshire*
Map **10** NX05

⊢⊣ **GH Blinkbonnie** School Brae ☎(077681) 282
Apr–Oct
Pleasantly appointed bungalow in elevated position with fine views seaward from dining room and lounge.
5hc (1fb) Ⓡ B&b£7.35–£7.50 Bdi£12–£12.50 W£51.45–£52.40 M LDO5.30pm
₩ CTV 6P

PORTREE
Isle of Skye, Highland *Inverness-shire*
Map **13** NG44

GH Bosville Bosville Ter ☎(0478) 2846
Apr–mid Oct
Well maintained rough cast building overlooking harbour and Raasay.
14rm 12hc 2⋒ (3fb) Ⓡ B&b£9–£10.50 Bdi£13.50–£15.50 LDO8pm
Lic ₩ CTV P
Credit card 1

GH Craiglockhart Beaumont Cres ☎(0478) 2233
Closed Dec
Comfortable house in pleasant seafront location overlooking the harbour and Raasay.
4rm 2hc 2⋒ (A 6hc) (1fb) Ⓡ ✻B&b£8.50–£10.50 Bdi£14.80–£16.80 W£95–£110 ⅃ LDO7pm
₩ CTV 6P
Ⓥ

FH Mrs M Bruce ***Cruachanlea*** *(NG513373)* Braes ☎Sligachan (047852) 233
Situated 5m SE of Portree on B883, overlooking sea to the Isle of Raasay. Hill views all around.
3hc (1fb) Ⓡ LDO6.30pm
₩ CTV 6P 5acres sheep

⊢⊣ **FH** Sylvia P MacDonald **Upper Ollach** *(NG518362)* Braes ☎Sligachan (047852) 225
Apr–Oct
Grey, stone crofting farm in hilly farmland with gardens and trees screening the house. Close to coastline, 6½m SE of Portree on B883.
3rm (1fb) ✱ B&b£7 Bdi£11
CTV 4P 7acres arable sheep poultry
Ⓥ

PORT ST MARY
Isle of Man
Map **6** SC26

GH Mallmore Private Hotel The Promenade ☎(0624) 833179
Etr–Sep
Delightfully situated hotel overlooking the bay.
43hc (10fb) Ⓡ ✻B&b£8 Bdifr£8.75 Wfr£56 M
CTV P billiards

PORTSMOUTH & SOUTHSEA
Hants
Map **4** SZ69
See plan

GH Amberley Court 97 Waverley Rd, Southsea ☎(0705) 735419 Plan **1** *F3*
Pleasant family-run guesthouse of some quality.
9hc 1⋒ (3fb) ✱ B&b£9 Bdi£15 W£56 M
₩ CTV 🅿

⊢⊣ **GH Astor House** 4 St Andrew's Rd, Southsea ☎(0705) 755171 Plan **2** *E1*
Very comfortable and homely establishment with antique furniture.
6hc (3fb) CTV in 5 bedrooms TV in 1 bedroom Ⓡ B&b£7–£8.50 W£39–£48 M
₩ CTV
Ⓥ

GH Beaufort Hotel 71 Festing Rd, Southsea ☎(0705) 823707 Plan **4** *F3*
Closed Xmas
Smart, homely, comfortable hotel close to gardens and seafront.
16hc (4fb) ✱ B&b£10.50–£12.50 W£65–£85 M
₩ CTV 8P nc4yrs
Credit Cards 1 3 Ⓥ

GH Birchwood 44 Waverley Rd, Southsea ☎(0705) 811337 Plan **5** *F3*
Simple yet comfortable and homely house in city centre.
6hc (4fb) ✱ B&bfr£8.50 Bdifr£12.50 W£50 M
₩ TV 🅿 nc8yrs

GH Bristol Hotel 55 Clarence Pde, Southsea ☎(0705) 821815 Plan **6** *E2*
Four-storey Victorian house with excellent sea views.
14rm 5hc 9⋒ (6fb) CTV in 9 bedrooms TV in 5 bedrooms ✱ Ⓡ B&b£11–£13 Bdi£15.50–£17.50 W£72–£76 M LDO5pm
Lic ₩ CTV 7P
See advertisement on page 288

Fratton
Fratton Station
Portsea
Portsmouth Harbour
H.M. Naval Base
H.M.S. Victory
Admiralty House
Royal Naval Barracks (H.M.S. Nelson)
Tricorn Shopping Centre
Pedestrians only
Cathedral R.C.
H.P.O.
Portsmouth and Southsea Station
Victoria Park
Swimming Pool
Guildhall
Civic Offices
Central Library
Portsmouth Polytechnic
Police Sta. and Courts
College of Art
Coach Station
United Service Rec. Gnd. (officers)
RN Sports Centre
Portsmouth Grammar School
City Record Office
City Museum and Art Gallery
Buckingham House
Ravelin House
Cathedral
Garrison Church
Govenors Green
Pembroke Gardens
Statue
Garrison Rec. Gnd.
King's Bastion
Long Curtain
Square Tower
Round Tower and Point Battery
Vernon Shore Establishment
Bus Station
Portsmouth Harbour Sta.
Donegal Pier
Marlborough Pier
Passenger Ferry to Gosport
Passenger Ferry to Ryde (I of W)
to Fishbourne (I of W)
Kings Theatre
Pol. Sta.
St John's College
FRATTON ROAD
FAWCETT ROAD
LAWRENCE ROAD
VICTORIA ROAD NORTH
ALBERT ROAD
ELM GROVE
KING'S ROAD
ANGLESEA ROAD
COMMERCIAL ROAD
ARUNDEL STREET
WINSTON CHURCHILL AVENUE
HAMPSHIRE TERR.
LANDPORT TERR.
BELLEVUE TERR.
MUSEUM ROAD
CAMBRIDGE ROAD
ST GEORGE'S ROAD
GUN WHARF ROAD
BURNABY RD
PARK ROAD
QUEEN STREET
THE HARD
HIGH STREET
BROAD STREET
WHITE HART RD
EAST ST
PEMBROKE ROAD
MARKETWAY
ALFRED RD
EDINBURGH ROAD
STANHOPE ROAD
LAKE ROAD
CHURCH STREET
CHARLES ST
NORTHAM STREET
ST JOHN'S ROAD
CLARENDON STREET
COBOURG STREET
SOMERS RD
CANAL WALK
RAILWAY VIEW
SYDENHAM TERR
CUMBERLAND RD
FRODDINGTON ROAD
ABINGDON RD
BRADFORD ROAD
GREETHAM ST
HYDE PARK RD
BLACKFRIARS ROAD
RAGLAN ST
ISAMBARD BRUNEL ROAD
GROSVENOR ST
ST JAMES'S ROAD
GREEN ROAD
BELMONT STREET
COTTAGE GROVE
MARGATE ROAD
HUDSON ROAD
ST ANDREW'S ROAD
ST DAVID'S ROAD
OUTRAM ROAD
CASTLE ROAD
SOUTHSEA TERR.
GORDON ROAD
ST MARY'S RD
CLIVE ROAD
NEWCOME RD
PENHALE RD
ARIEL ROAD
WALMER RD
ORCHARD ROAD
MANNERS ROAD
PERCY ROAD
JESSIE ROAD
BRAM. ROAD
HAROLD ROAD
BOULTON ROAD
OXFORD ROAD
GOODWOOD ROAD
ALBANY ROAD
CURZON HOWE RD
HAVANT ST
COLLEGE ST
CROSS ST
CUMBERLAND ST
FLATHOUSE ROAD
UNICORN RD

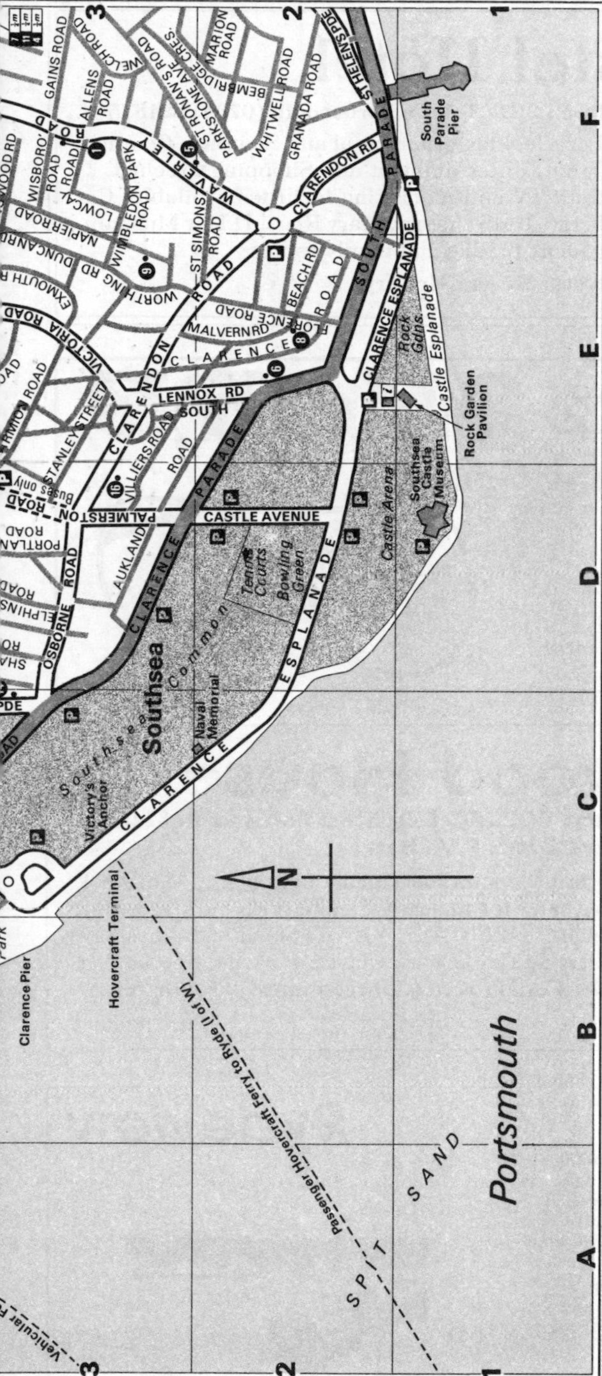

Portsmouth

1 Amberley Court
2 Astor House
4 Beaufort Hotel
5 Birchwood
6 Bristol Hotel
7 Chequers Hotel
8 Gainsborough House
9 Goodwood House
11 Lyndhurst
12 Ryde View
13 St Andrew's Lodge
14 Somerset Private Hotel
15 Tudor Court Hotel
16 Upper Mount House

GH Chequers Hotel Salisbury Rd, Southsea ☎(0705) 735277 Plan **7** *F3*
Comfortable hotel in quiet residential area with simple accommodation and good public areas.
13rm 11hc (3fb) TV in 2 bedrooms B&b£15 Bdi£21 LDO6.30pm
Lic Ⅲ CTV 12P
Credit cards 1 3 Ⓥ
See advertisement on page 288

⊢⊣ **GH Gainsborough House** 9 Malvern Rd, Southsea ☎(0705) 822604 Plan **8** *E2*
Closed Xmas
Victorian terraced house with red brick exterior, quietly situated.
7hc (1fb) ★ Ⓡ B&b£7–£8 Bdi£10.50–£11.50 W£63–£67 Ⱡ LDO3pm
Ⅲ CTV Ᵽ nc3yrs

GH Goodwood House 1 Taswell Rd, Southsea ☎(0705) 824734 Plan **9** *E3*
Closed 22 Dec–3 Jan
Comfortable accommodation in a friendly informal atmosphere, within easy reach of shopping centre and promenade.
8hc (1fb) TV in 8 bedrooms ★ Ⓡ B&b£8.50–£10.50 Bdi£14–£15 LDO5pm
Ⅲ CTV Ᵽ nc2yrs
See advertisement on page 288

⊢⊣ **GH Lyndhurst** 8 Festing Gv, Southsea ☎(0705) 735239 Plan **11** *F3*
Closed Xmas
A homely house set in quiet residential area.
7hc (2fb) Ⓡ ✱B&b£8 Bdi£11 W£68 Ⱡ LDO2pm
Ⅲ CTV

GH *Ryde View* 9 Western Pde, Southsea ☎(0705) 820865 Plan **12** *C4*
Closed Xmas
Comfortable establishment overlooking the common with excellent sea views.
14hc (7fb) TV in all bedrooms LDOnoon
Lic Ⅲ CTV sea
See advertisement on page 288

⊢⊣ **GH St Andrews Lodge**
65 St Andrews Rd, Southsea ☎(0705) 827079 Plan **13** *E5*
Closed 20 Dec–5 Jan
10hc (4fb) TV in 2 bedrooms CTV in 1 bedroom B&b£7–£8 Bdi£9.50–£11 W£49–£56 M LDOnoon
ꟾꟾꟾ CTV
Ⓥ

GH *Somerset Private Hotel* 16 Western Pde, Southsea ☎(0705) 822495 Plan **14** *C3*
Closed Xmas
Well maintained and efficiently managed with a friendly atmosphere. Some bedrooms on the top floors have extensive views of the harbour.
16hc (7fb)
CTV ⊘ nc3yrs sea
Ⓥ

GH Tudor Court Hotel 1 Queen's Gv, Southsea ☎(0705) 820174 Plan **15** *D4*
Centrally situated well appointed hotel with quality tudor style restaurant and bar.
11hc 2➡ (2fb) CTV in 3 bedrooms B&b£12 Bdi£18 W£72 M LDO1pm
Lic ꟾꟾꟾ CTV 9P
Credit card [3]

GH Upper Mount House Hotel The Vale, Clarendon Rd, Southsea ☎(0705) 820456 Plan **16** *D3*

Red brick three-storey building set to the rear of a main road in a quiet lane.
9rm 2hc 2➡ 4⋔ (2fb) CTV in all bedrooms ® B&b£13.50–£16 Bdi£19.45–£21.95 W£88–£112 ⱡ LDO7pm
Lic ꟾꟾꟾ CTV 7P
Credit cards [1] [3]

POSTBRIDGE
Devon
Map **3** SX67
GH *Lydgate House Hotel* ☎Tavistock (0822) 88209
8hc 2➡ (1fb) ® LDO9.30pm
Lic ꟾꟾꟾ CTV 12P river

POUNDSGATE
Devon
Map **3** SX77
GH *Leusdon Lodge* (Guestaccom) ☎(03643) 304
rs Nov–Mar
150-year-old granite-built house on edge of Dartmoor, offering traditional English fare.
8hc 2➡ (2fb) LDO9pm
Lic ꟾꟾꟾ CTV 20P

PRAA SANDS
Cornwall
Map **2** SW52
⊢⊣ **GH La Connings** ☎Germoe (073676) 2380
Etr–Oct
Chalet-style guesthouse surrounded by farm land and adjacent coast.
6hc (3fb) ✱B&b£8–£10 Bdi£11–£14 W£77–£90 ⱡ LDO6pm
Lic ꟾꟾꟾ CTV 11P ⛱

PRESTATYN
Clwyd
Map **6** SJ08
GH Bryn Gwalia Hotel 17 Gronant Rd ☎(07456) 2442
Closed 1 wk Xmas
Edwardian house in residential area, short walk to shops.
8rm 4hc 1➡ 3⋔ (2fb) CTV in 7 bedrooms TV in 1 bedroom ✶ ® B&b£12–£16 Bdi£15–£20 W£80–£100 M LDO9pm
Lic ꟾꟾꟾ 15P
See advertisement on page 290

GH Hawarden House 13 Victoria Rd ☎(07456) 4226
6hc (2fb) CTV in 4 bedrooms ✶ ✱B&b£7–£7.50 Bdi£10–£10.50 W£46–£49 M LDO5.30pm
Lic ꟾꟾꟾ CTV 8P
Ⓥ

PRESTON
Lancashire
Map **7** SD52

GH Fulwood Park Hotel 49 Watling Street Rd ☎(0772) 718067
rs Xmas
Extensively modernised family-run hotel.
21rm 6hc 7⇌ 8⋒ (A 4rm 3hc 1⋒) (2fb) ✱ (except guide dogs) Ⓡ *B&b£11 Bdi£15.25
Lic ∰ CTV 24P ♿
Credit cards 1 2 3 4 5

GH Lauderdale Hotel 29 Fishergate Hill ☎(0772) 555460
18hc (3fb) B&b£9.20–£10 Bdi£12.70–£13.50 LDO6pm
Lic ∰ CTV 8P 6⌂

GH Tulketh House 209 Tulketh Rd, Ashton ☎(0772) 728096
Closed Xmas
Comfortable modern accommodation is provided in this Victorian-style hotel.
7rm 6hc 1⋒ (1fb) CTV in 1 bedroom TV in 3 bedrooms Ⓡ B&b£18.40 Bdi£26.45 W£185.15 Ⱡ LDO8pm
Lic ∰ CTV 20P ⌂
Ⓥ

GH Withy Trees 175 Garstang Rd, Fullwood ☎(0772) 717693
Closed Xmas day
2m N on A6.

10hc (2fb) ✱ B&b£9–£10 W£63–£70 M
∰ CTV 20P

PRESTWICK
Strathclyde *Ayrshire*
Map **10** NS32

⊢⊣ **GH Kincraig Private Hotel** 39 Ayr Rd ☎(0292) 79480
Attractive red sandstone villa on main road with neatly appointed good-sized rooms.
6hc (1fb) ✱ Ⓡ B&b£7.50 Bdi£12 W£79 Ⱡ LDO5pm
Lic ∰ CTV 8P nc3yrs

GH *Villa Marina Hotel* 19 Links Rd ☎(0292) 70396
Large semi-detached stone house near to beach.
5hc (1fb) ✱ LDO10am
Lic ∰ CTV 8P

PWLLHELI
Gwynedd
Map **6** SH33

FH Mrs M Hughes **Bryn Crin** *(SH379358)* ☎(0758) 612494
Apr–Sep
Large spacious farmhouse situated on hillside with panoramic views of Cardigan Bay and Snowdonia. Situated off unclass rd.
3rm 2hc (2fb) ✱ *B&b£6–£7 W£40–£45 M
TV 3P 80acres mixed
Ⓥ

⊢⊣ **FH** Mrs J E Ellis **Gwynfryn** *(SH364357)* ☎(0758) 612536
Closed 15–30 Dec
Large granite-built farmhouse, surrounded by 2 acres of gardens and woodland, bordered to the south by a stream. 1m NW.
2hc ✱ B&b£6–£7.50 W£40 M
∰ TV 2P nc5yrs 96acres dairy
Ⓥ

QUEEN CAMEL
Somerset
Map **3** ST52

INN Mildmay Arms ☎Yeovil (0935) 850456
6hc 2⋒ *B&b£10–£15 Bdi£14–£20 W£70–£95 M L£2–£8&alc D10pm £2–£8&alc
∰ 25P
Credit card 3

RAGLAN
Gwent
Map **3** SO40

GH Grange Old Abergavenny Rd ☎(0291) 690260
A well run, attractive house in 1½ acres, approximately ¼m outside Raglan.
4rm 3hc 1⋒ B&bfr£13 Bdifr£19 LDO9pm
Lic 𝍷 CTV 10P ⌂
Ⓥ

RAMSGATE
Kent
Map **5** TR36

⊢⊣ **GH Jalna Hotel** 49 Vale Sq ☎Thanet (0843) 593848
Feb–Nov
Located in a quiet residential part of the town, with well maintained bedrooms and a basement dining room.
9rm 4hc 3⋒ (5fb) ★ B&b£7.50–£9 Bdi£11.50–£13 Wfr£60 Ⳑ LDOnoon
Lic CTV 3P
Ⓥ

GH Piper Lodge Hotel 26 Victoria Rd, East Cliff ☎Thanet (0843) 591661
12rm 6hc 4⋒ (4fb) TV in 6 bedrooms ★ Ⓡ ✱B&b£9.50–£10.50 Bdi£15–£16 W£54–£60 M LDO7.30pm
Lic 𝍷 CTV 20P ⛆ (heated)

GH St Hilary Private Hotel 21 Crescent Rd ☎Thanet (0843) 591427
Closed Xmas
Cheerful compact bedrooms, basement dining room, situated in residential area.
7hc (4fb) ★ ✱B&b£7.50–£8.50 Bdi£10.50–£11.50 W£59.50–£65 Ⳑ LDO3.30pm
Lic CTV ⚑ nc4yrs
Credit card 1 Ⓥ

RASKELF
North Yorkshire
Map **8** SE47

GH Old Farmhouse ☎Easingwold (0347) 21971
16 Jan–15 Dec
A converted farmhouse of around 1700 in quiet country village.
10hc 5➡ 5⋒ ✱B&b£10.25 Bdifr£15.75 W£105 Ⳑ LDOnoon
𝍷 CTV 15P

RAVENSCAR
North Yorkshire
Map **8** NZ90

GH Smugglers Rock Country ☎Scarborough (0723) 870044
Mar–Nov
Converted and restored farmhouse, close to moors and sea.
8hc (2fb) ★ B&b£9 Bdi£12.50 W£60 M LDO1pm
𝍷 CTV 8P billiards
Ⓥ

RAVENSTONEDALE
Cumbria
Map **12** NY70

INN Fat Lamb Country Cross Bank (Guestaccom) ☎Newbiggin-on-Lune (05873) 242
17th-century farmhouse, now an inn, has comfortable accommodation and well appointed restaurant.
9rm 6hc 3➡ Ⓡ B&b£11.50–£12.50 Bdi£18–£19.25 W£113.40–£121.27 Ⳑ L£6.50–£6.75&alc D9.30pm £6.50–£6.75&alc
𝍷 CTV 50P
Ⓥ

READING
Berkshire
Map **4** SU77

GH Aeron 191 Kentwood Hill, Tilehurst ☎(0734) 24119
Closed 2 wk Xmas & New Year
Professionally run clean and friendly establishment. 3m W off A329.
9hc (A 9hc) (1fb) CTV in all bedrooms Ⓡ B&b£11–£14.50 LDO8.15pm
Lic 𝍷 18P
Credit cards 1 3

GH Private House Hotel 98 Kendrick Rd ☎(0734) 874142
Closed Xmas
Comfortable and cheerful establishment offering good accommodation, run by friendly proprietors.
7hc ★ B&b£13–£14 Bdi£18–£20 LDOnoon
Lic 𝍷 CTV 7P nc12yrs

REDCAR
Cleveland
Map **8** NZ62

GH *Claxton House Private Hotel* 196 High St ☎(0642) 486745
Closed 24 Dec–2 Jan
Accommodation here is clean and comfortable and there is an interesting lounge dining room.
14hc 5⋒ (1fb) ★ LDO5.30pm
Lic 𝍷 CTV 10P sea

REDDITCH
Hereford & Worcester
Map **7** SP06

GH Old Rectory Ipsley Ln ☎(0527) 23000
A very hospitable hotel set in a new town, within peaceful surroundings.
6rm 3hc 1➡ 2⋒ ★ B&b£14–£21 Bdi£21–£28 W£98–£147 M LDOnoon
Lic 𝍷 CTV 10P 2⌂
Credit card 1 Ⓥ

REDHILL
Surrey
Map **4** TQ25

GH Ashleigh House Hotel 39 Redstone Hill ☎(0737) 64763
Closed Xmas
Very comfortable homely accommodation with outstanding hospitality.
9rm 6hc 1⋒ (1fb) ★ B&b£13–£14.50
𝍷 CTV 9P ⛆ (heated)
See advertisement on page 292

REDMILE
Leicestershire
Map **8** SK73

FH Mrs A Barton **Olde Mill House** *(SK789358)* ☎Bottesford (0949) 42460
A beautiful house approx 250 years old, which has been considerably modernised; set in the peaceful Vale of Belvoir.
3hc ★ B&b£9 Bdi£15 W£98 Ⅼ LDO6pm
Ⅲ CTV 4P 2🚗 nc10yrs 5acres non-working

FH Mr & Mrs P Need **Peacock** *(SK791359)* ☎Bottesford (0949) 42475
Modernised 250-year-old farmhouse situated in the Vale of Belvoir, close to Castle. Hunter stud farm with paddocks.
5hc (2fb) ★ B&bfr£8.50 Bdifr£14 W£95 Ⅼ LDO8.30pm
Lic Ⅲ CTV 20P ⌂ U 5acres mixed
Ⓥ

REIGATE
Surrey
Map **4** TQ25

GH Cranleigh Hotel 41 West St ☎(07372) 40600
An efficient, well managed hotel, with well equipped modern bedrooms, an outdoor heated swimming pool and rear garden.
12hc 4➡ (3fb) CTV in 4 bedrooms TV in 2 bedrooms ★ Ⓡ ✱B&b£15–£18 Bdi£22–£25 LDO7pm
Lic Ⅲ CTV 5P ⌂ ≋(heated)
Credit cards 1 2 3 4 5 Ⓥ

GH Priors Mead Blanford Rd ☎(07372) 48776
Comfortable family-run hotel with good size bedrooms. Quietly located.
9rm 8hc 1➡ (3fb) B&b£10–£13
Ⅲ CTV 6P
Ⓥ

RHANDIRMWYN
Dyfed
Map **3** SN74

FH Mrs G A Williams **Galltybere** *(SN772460)* ☎(05506) 218
Isolated farmhouse 9m N of Llandovery amid splendid scenery. Ideal for birdwatching and hikers.
2rm (A 2hc) (1fb) ★ ✱B&bfr£8 Bdifr£14 W£56 M LDO6pm
CTV 6P nc7yrs ♪ 320acres sheep

RHES-Y-CAE
Clwyd
Map **7** SJ17

INN Miners Arms ☎Halkyn (0352) 780567
rs Nov–mid Mar
Part 16th-century village inn in quiet rural situation.
8hc ★ B&b£12.50–£13.50 Bdi£17.50 W£110 Ⅼ L£2.75–£7 D10.30pm £6.50alc
Ⅲ 150P
Ⓥ

RHOS-ON-SEA
Clwyd
Map **6** SH88
See Colwyn Bay

RHUALLT
Clwyd
Map **6** SJ07

INN *White House* ☎St Asaph (0745) 582155
Roadside inn in rural situation.
6rm 5hc D10.30pm
CTV 100P

RHYL
Clwyd
Map **6** SJ08

GH Hafod-y-Mor 18–20 Palace Av ☎(0745) 2566
10rm 8hc 2⋒ (4fb) TV in 8 bedrooms ★ Ⓡ B&b£9–£12.50 Bdi£11–£15 LDOnoon
Lic Ⅲ CTV 6P
Ⓥ

⟼**GH Pier Hotel** 23 East Pde ☎(0745) 50280
Closed Dec
Mid terrace, on seafront, short walk to shops.
11rm 8hc 1⋒ (3fb) B&b£7.50–£10 Bdi£11–£13.50 W£60–£75 Ⱡ
Lic 𝍖 CTV P
Credit card ③ Ⓥ

⟼**GH Toomargoed Private Hotel** 31–33 John St ☎(0745) 4103
Double fronted mid terrace in residential area off Marine Parade.
15hc (8fb) ✱ B&b£7–£9 Bdi£9–£11.50 W£60–£70 Ⱡ
Lic CTV

RICKINGHALL
Suffolk
Map **5** TM07
INN *Hamblyn House* The Street ☎Diss (0379) 898292
4hc CTV in 2 bedrooms ✱ Ⓡ D10.30pm
𝍖 CTV 12P 2🚗

RIEVAULX
North Yorkshire
Map **8** SE58
⟼**FH** Mrs M E Skilbeck **Middle Heads** *(SE584869)* ☎Bilsdale (04396) 251
Apr–Nov
Old stone farmhouse of character, comfortably furnished and with a homely atmosphere, 1m E of B1257 and 3m NW of Helmsley.
3rm (1fb) ✱ B&b£7 W£49 M
𝍖 CTV P 170acres arable beef dairy sheep mixed

RINGWOOD
Hampshire
Map **4** SU10
GH Little Forest Lodge Poulner Hill ☎(04254) 78848
30 Mar–15 Oct
4hc 2⇌ 2⋒ (2fb) TV in all bedrooms Ⓡ ✱B&b£10–£14 Bdi£15–£18 W£70–£98 M LDO6.30pm
𝍖 CTV 10P 2🚗
Credit cards ① ③

GH Little Moortown House Hotel ☎(04254) 3325
Georgian house with comfortable accommodation and an attractively furnished dining room.
6rm 2hc 4⋒ (1fb) CTV in 4 bedrooms B&b£13–£17 Bdi£19.50–£23.50 W£78–£102 M LDO7pm
Lic 𝍖 CTV 8P nc12yrs
Credit cards ① ③

RIPLEY
Derbyshire
Map **8** SK45
GH Britannia 243 Church St, Waingroves ☎(0773) 43708
Modern detached house, 1½ miles south of Ripley.
6rm 5hc 1⋒ (1fb) ✱ Ⓡ B&b£11
𝍖 CTV 10P

RIPON
North Yorkshire
Map **8** SE37
GH Nordale 1 & 2 North Pde ☎(0765) 3557
Accommodation here is simple, but clean and the lounge is comfortable.
12rm 10hc (4fb) B&b£8.50–£11 Bdi£13–£17 W£60–£75 M LDO5pm
Lic CTV 14P
⟼**GH Old Country** 1 The Crescent ☎(0765) 2162
7hc (4fb) ✱ B&b£7.50–£8.50 W£50–£60 M
𝍖 CTV 7P 2🚗

ROCHE
Cornwall
Map **2** SW96
GH Greystones Mount Pleasant ☎(0726) 890863
A newly constructed property, which has been tastefully furnished with many antique items giving it a more olde worlde atmosphere, while still offering modern facilities. On A30.
7rm 2hc 2⇌
CTV

ROCHESTER
Kent
Map **5** TQ76
GH Greystones 25 Watts Av ☎Medway (0634) 47545
Closed Xmas Day
Homely atmosphere with comfortable bedrooms and facilities complemented by friendly personal supervision.
6hc (2fb) ✱ B&b£9–£12
𝍖 CTV 3P 1🚗

ROCK
Cornwall
Map **2** SW97
GH Roskarnon House Hotel ☎Trebetherick (020886) 2785
Mar–mid Oct
16rm 10hc 4⇌ 1⋒ (4fb) CTV in 5 bedrooms ✱ B&b£9–£15 Bdi£15–£20 W£70–£100 Ⱡ (W only mid Jul–mid Sep) LDO8pm
Lic CTV 12P 2🚗
Ⓥ

RODBOURNE *(Near Malmesbury)*
Wiltshire
Map **3** ST98
⟼**FH** Mrs C M Parfitt **Angrove** *(ST949842)* ☎Malmesbury (06662) 2982
Apr–Sep
A typical Cotswold-style farmhouse backed by woodland and bordered by the River Avon where trout and course fishing is available. 1m NW unclass.
3hc ✱ Ⓡ B&b£7–£10 Bdi£11–£15 W£78 Ⱡ
𝍖 CTV 10P ⤴ 204acres beef
Ⓥ

ROGART
Highland *Sutherland*
Map **14** NC70

⊢→ **FH** Mrs J S R Moodie **Rovie** *(NC716023)* ☎(04084) 209
Apr–Oct
Lodge-style farmhouse in lovely surroundings with river flowing through. Rabbit shooting on farm and fishing locally in River Fleet. 4m from sea and S off A839.
6hc (1fb) ✱ B&b£7 Bdi£12.50 W£49 M
LDO6.30pm
CTV 6P 120acres arable beef sheep

ROGATE
West Sussex
Map **4** SU82

FH Mrs J C Fracis **Mizzards** *(SU803227)* ☎(073080) 656
A beautiful old farmhouse, skilfully modernised in a peaceful setting by a small river. On A272 between Petersfield and Midhurst.
3rm 1⇌ 2⋒ (1fb) CTV in 1 bedroom ✱ B&b£9–£12 W£63–£72 M
▥ CTV 10P nc7yrs ⊡ 13½acres sheep

ROMFORD
Gt London
Map **5** TQ58

GH Repton Private Hotel 18 Repton Dr, Gidea Park ☎(0708) 45253
8hc ✱ B&b£11.50–£16.10 Bdi£16–£20.60 LDO10am
▥ CTV

ROMSEY
Hampshire
Map **4** SU32

⊢→ **GH Adelaide House** 45 Winchester Rd ☎(0794) 512322
Small homely house on the edge of the town.
5hc (1fb) ✱ B&b£7.95–£9.50 W£53–£63 M
▥ CTV 5P
Ⓥ

⊢→ **GH Chalet** Botley Rd, Whitenap ☎(0794) 514909
Comfortable house set in quiet residential area.
4hc (A 1⇌) (1fb) TV in 1 bedroom ✱ B&b£8–£8.50
▥ CTV 6P nc4yrs

ROSEDALE ABBEY
North Yorkshire
Map **8** SE79

FH Mrs D J Rawlings **High House** *(SE698974)* ☎Lastingham (07515) 471
18th-century stone-built farmhouse with oak beams, log fires and panoramic views over dale. 2m from Rosedale Abbey.
3hc (1fb) B&b£9–£10 Bdi£14–£15 W£98 L LDO6pm
▥ 6P 100acres beef dairy sheep

ROSS-ON-WYE
Hereford & Worcester
Map **3** SO52
For details of farmhouse accommodation in the vicinity, see Marstow and St Owen's Cross

GH Arches Country House Walford Rd ☎(0989) 63348
Closed Xmas & New Year
6hc 1⇌ (2fb) ✱ Ⓡ ✻ B&b£8 Bdi£12.95 W£87.60 L LDO6.30pm
Lic ▥ CTV 8P
Ⓥ

GH Bridge House Hotel Wilton ☎(0989) 62655
Closed Xmas
9rm 7hc 1⇌ 1⋒ (1fb) B&b£9.25–£10.50 Bdi£14.75–£16.50 W£80–£90 M
LDO9pm
Lic CTV 15P

⊢→ **GH Ryefield House** Gloucester Rd ☎(0989) 63030
Jan–Oct
7rm 5hc 1⇌ 1⋒ (3fb) Ⓡ B&b£8–£8.40 Bdi£12.80–£13.50 W£84.50 L
LDO4.30pm
Lic ▥ CTV 9P
Ⓥ

GH Sunnymount Hotel Ryefield Rd (Guestaccom) ☎(0989) 63880
6hc (1fb) Ⓡ B&bfr£10 Bdifr£14.75 W£90 L
Lic ▥ CTV 6P ⌂
Credit cards 1 3 Ⓥ

ROSTON
Derbyshire
Map **7** SK14

⊢→ **FH** Mrs E K Prince **Roston Hall** *(SK133409)* ☎Ellastone (033524) 287
May–Sep
Former manor house, part Elizabethan and part Georgian, in centre of quiet village. Ideal for touring the Peak District.
2rm 1hc (1fb) ✱ B&b£7–£8.50 Bdi£10–£12 LDO10am
TV 4P nc13yrs 100acres arable beef
Ⓥ

ROTHBURY
Northumberland
Map **12** NU00

GH Orchard High St ☎(0669) 20684
Closed Xmas
6hc (2fb) ✱ B&b£9–£9.50 Bdi£15–£16 W£60–£63 M LDO7pm
Lic ▥ ⌿
Ⓥ

ROTHESAY
Isle of Bute, Strathclyde *Buteshire*
Map **10** NS06

GH *Alva House Private Hotel*
24 Mountstuart Rd ☎(0700) 2328
May–Sep
Neat semi-detached Victorian terraced house.
6hc (1fb)
CTV ⌿ sea

ROTTINGDEAN
East Sussex
Map **5** TQ30

⊢→ **GH Braemar House** Steyning Rd ☎Brighton (0273) 34263
Family-run comfortable and homely accommodation, near the Downs.
14hc (3fb) B&b£8–£9 W£56 M
▥ CTV ⌿
Ⓥ

GH Corner House Steyning Rd ☎Brighton (0273) 34533
In a beautiful village, this small guesthouse offers comfortable accommodation.
6hc (1fb) TV in all bedrooms B&b£8.50–£9.50 Wfr£63 M
▥ ⌿ nc4yrs

ROWLEY REGIS
West Midlands
Map **7** SO98

GH Highfield House Hotel Holly Rd ☎021-550 1066
12hc ✱ B&b£11 Bdi£15.50 W£108.50 L
S% LDOnoon
Lic ▥ CTV 12P

RUDGWICK
West Sussex
Map **4** TQ03

INN Goblins Pool Hotel Bucks Gn ☎(040372) 2446
Very attractive two-storey period cottage, set in own gardens.
4hc ✱ Ⓡ B&b£18–£30 Bdifr£30 W£126–£210 L LDO9.30pm
Lic ▥ 20P nc6yrs
Credit cards 1 3

RUDYARD
Staffordshire
Map **7** SJ95

FH Mrs E J Lowe **Fairboroughs** *(SJ957609)* ☎Rushton Spencer (02606) 341
May–Nov rs Apr
4½m NW of Leek off A523 then off unclass rd.
3hc (1fb) B&bfr£8.50 Bdifr£13.50 W£88 L LDOnoon
CTV 4P 140acres beef sheep
Ⓥ

RUGBY
Warwickshire
Map **4** SP57

GH Grosvenor House Hotel 81 Clifton Rd ☎(0788) 3437
8hc (1fb) B&b£11 Bdifr£15 LDO7pm
Lic 🍽 CTV 6P
Ⓥ

GH Mound Hotel 17–19 Lawford Rd ☎(0788) 3486
Closed 5 days Xmas
18rm 14hc 4🚿 (5fb) CTV in 17 bedrooms TV in 1 bedroom 🐕 B&b£12.65–£13.80 Bdi£18.40–£19.55 LDO3pm
Lic 🍽 CTV 16P

RUISLIP
Gt London
London plan **4** A5
(page 222)

GH 17th Century Barn Hotel West End Rd ☎(08956) 36057
Closed 23 Dec–2 Jan
17th-century house with relaxed friendly atmosphere offering comfortable period or modern bedrooms.
56hc 27🛁 (6fb) CTV in all bedrooms Ⓡ B&b£28.50–£36.50 Bdi£36–£43.50 W£252–£304.50 Ⓛ S% LDO9.30pm
Lic 🍽 CTV 70P
Credit cards 1 2 3

RUSHTON SPENCER
Staffordshire
Map **7** SJ96

⊢✕⊣ **FH** Mrs J Brown **Barnswood** *(SJ945606)* ☎(02606) 261
Mar–Dec except Xmas
Large stone-built farmhouse with grounds stretching to the edge of Rudyard Lake, with splendid views to distant hills.
4rm 2hc (2fb) 🐕 B&b£7.50 W£49 Ⓜ
CTV 100acres beef dairy

RUSKIE
Central *Perthshire*
Map **11** NN60

⊢✕⊣ **FH** Mrs S F Bain **Lower Tarr** *(NN624008)* ☎Thornhill (078685) 202
Closed Xmas & New Year
Large, well-maintained 200-year-old farmhouse, fully moderised and with good views over rolling hill land.
2rm 1hc (1fb) 🐕 Ⓡ B&b£6–£6.50 Bdi£9.50–£10 W£65 Ⓛ LDO3pm
CTV P 🏠 ⛳ 210acres arable beef sheep mixed
Ⓥ

RUSTINGTON
West Sussex
Map **4** TQ00

⊢✕⊣ **GH Kenmore** Claigmar Rd ☎(09062) 4634
rs Xmas
Close to shops and sea front with modern well-appointed rooms.
5hc 1🛁 (3fb) TV in all bedrooms Ⓡ B&b£6.95–£10.20 W£55.15–£62.90 Ⓜ
🍽 5P

GH Mayday Hotel 12 Broadmark Ln ☎(09062) 71198
Closed Oct
A delightful large detached building with extension, set in quiet residential area close to sea front.
8hc 4🚿 (1fb) CTV in 7 bedrooms TV in 1 bedroom 🐕 Ⓡ B&b£14–£16 Bdi£18–£21 W£86–£94.50 Ⓛ LDO7.30pm
Lic 🍽 CTV 12P nc6yrs

RUTHIN
Clwyd
Map **6** SJ15

FH Margaret E Jones **Pencoed** *(SJ107538)* Pwllglas ☎Clawdd Newydd (08245) 251
Closed Xmas
Isolated stone-built farmhouse with timbered ceilings. Set on high ground with extensive views.
3hc (2fb) ✱B&bfr£6.50 Bdifr£0 Wfr£60 Ⓛ
🍽 TV P 160acres mixed

⊢✕⊣ **FH** Mrs T Francis **Plas-Y-Ward** *(SJ118604)* Rhewl ☎(08242) 3822
May–Sep
Period farmhouse, dating back to 14th-century, set beside River Clwyd and looking towards the Clwydian range. 1½m from Ruthin.
2rm 1hc 🐕 B&b£8 W£54 Ⓜ
TV 6P nc5yrs ⛳ 215acres arable dairy sheep

RYDAL
Cumbria
Map **11** NY30
See Ambleside

RYDE
Isle of Wight
Map **4** SZ59

GH Dorset Hotel 33 Dover St ☎(0983) 64327
Feb–Nov
Friendly hotel with good lounge facilities and simple, adequately furnished bedrooms.
25rm 1🛁 6🚿 (4fb) 🐕 B&b£15 Bdi£20 W£78 Ⓛ LDO6.45pm
Lic CTV 24P nc5yrs ≋ (heated)
Credit cards 1 2 3 5

GH Teneriffe 36 The Strand ☎(0983) 63841
Large house close to the sea, with large bar and dance floor, two lounges and basement restaurant.
30rm 11hc 17🛁 2🚿 (4fb) 🐕 Ⓡ B&b£8.05–£8.65 Bdi£11–£12 W£49–£52.50 Ⓜ LDO6pm
Lic 🍽 CTV 9P
Ⓥ

FH Mrs S Swan **Aldermoor** *(SZ582906)* Upton Rd ☎(0983) 64743
Apr–Oct
Modernised old stone and brick farmhouse.
3hc 🐕 ✱B&b£7–£8 Bdi£10–£11 W£45–£55 Ⓜ LDO6pm
CTV 20P 2🏠 nc7yrs U (children only) 27acres beef
Ⓥ

RYE
East Sussex
Map **5** TQ92

⊢✕⊣ **GH Little Saltcote** 22 Military Rd ☎(0797) 223210
Victorian house with tastefully decorated rooms.
6hc 1🛁 (2fb) TV in all bedrooms Ⓡ B&b£7.50–£8
🍽 3P

GH Mariner's Hotel High St ☎(0797) 223480
17th-century house retaining some of its old world charm including original beams. Comfortable rooms.
14hc 13🛁 CTV in all bedrooms Ⓡ B&b£20.70–£28.50 LDO10.30pm
Lic 🍽 CTV 🐕
Credit cards 1 2 3 4 5 Ⓥ

GH *Monastery Hotel & Restaurant* 6 High St ☎(0797) 223272
Closed Xmas & New Year
A former 14th-century monastery, reputed to have two ghosts.
8hc 1🚿 (1fb) LDO9.30pm
Lic 🍽 CTV nc5yrs
Ⓥ

GH Old Borough Arms The Strand ☎(0797) 222128
The lack of any lounge or dining room is compensated for by well equipped comfortable bedrooms, where breakfast is served.
9🚿 (4fb) TV in all bedrooms Ⓡ B&b£10.50–£12.50
Lic 🍽 CTV 2🏠

GH *Playden Oasts Hotel* Playden ☎(0797) 223502
200-year-old oasthouse with considerable character and charm.
8hc 5🛁 3🚿 (2fb) CTV available in bedrooms Ⓡ LDO9.30pm
Lic 🍽 CTV 12P 🏠

⊢✕⊣ **FH** Mrs P Sullivan **Cliff** *(TQ933237)* Iden Lock ☎Iden (07978) 331
Mar–Oct
Elevated farmhouse run by charming young proprietors. Extensive views of Romney Marsh; also free coarse fishing available on River Rother within walking distance of house. 2m E off Military rd.
3hc (1fb) Ⓡ B&b£7.50–£8 Wfr£48 Ⓜ
🍽 CTV 6P 6acres small holding
Ⓥ

ST AGNES
Cornwall
Map **2** SW75

GH Glen Hotel Quay Rd ☎(087255) 2590
7rm 6hc 1⋒ (1fb) Ⓡ B&b£8.50–£10.95 Bdi£12–£15.75 W£85–£102.50 ⱡ LDO6pm
Lic 🕮 CTV 10P

⊢⊣ **GH Penkerris** Penwinnick Rd ☎(087255) 2262
A pleasant peaceful detached house, set at the edge of village in attractive garden, close to leisure park.
6hc (1fb) TV in all bedrooms Ⓡ B&b£5–£7.50 Bdi£7.50–£11.50 W£45–£75 ⱡ LDO4.30pm
CTV 8P

⊢⊣ **FH** W R & K B Blewett **Mount Pleasant** *(SW722508)* Rosemundy ☎(087255) 2387
May–Oct
Spacious bungalow set in the farm meadows and standing in its own large garden with beautiful views.
11hc (3fb) B&b£6–£7 Bdi£9–£10
CTV 12P 35acres dairy

ST ALBANS
Hertfordshire
Map **4** TL10

GH Ardmore House 54 Lemsford Rd ☎(0727) 59313
Comfortable, modern accommodation in large detached house with pleasant garden.
14hc 3⋒ (3fb) CTV in all bedrooms ✱ Ⓡ B&b£12
🕮 CTV 24P

GH Glenmore House 16 Woodstock Road North ☎(0727) 53794
Detached family house with large well kept secluded garden. Sited in quiet residential area.
8hc (2fb) Ⓡ B&b£12–£15.50 W£84–£108.50 M
🕮 CTV 5P
Ⓥ

GH Melford 24 Woodstock Road North ☎(0727) 53642
Converted house tastefully furnished with pleasant, relaxing décor.
12hc 4⋒ (3fb) Ⓡ B&b£14.95 W£89.70 M
Lic 🕮 CTV 12P

St Agnes — St Andrews

ST ANDREWS
Fife
Map **12** NO51

GH *Argyle* 127 North St ☎(0334) 73387
Apr–Oct
Large private hotel on prominent corner site, with spacious bedrooms and good lounge accommodation.
19hc 1⋒ (4fb) Ⓡ LDO6pm
Lic 🕮 CTV nc2yrs

⊢⊣ **GH Arran House** 5 Murray Park ☎(0334) 74724
Small guesthouse with combined dining room/lounge and very pleasant bedrooms.
11hc 1➡ (6fb) B&b£8–£10 Bdi£13–£15 W£50–£65 M LDOnoon
🕮 CTV ⚲
Ⓥ

GH *Beachway House* 4–6 Murray Pk ☎(0334) 73319
Etr–Oct rs Nov–mid Apr
Conversion of three adjoining houses in between town centre and sea.
18hc (6fb) Ⓡ LDO2pm
🕮 CTV ⚲

GH Cleveden House 3 Murray Pl ☎(0334) 74212
Nicely decorated house in side street between town centre and sea.
6hc (2fb) ✱ B&b£9–£9.50
🕮 CTV 16P

GH *Kerelaw House* 5 Playfair Ter, North St ☎(0334) 75906
Feb–Nov
A modestly appointed but homely guesthouse in terraced row.
6hc 1→ (2fb) Ⓡ LDO6.30pm
▥ CTV ⁋ ⌂ sea

GH Number Ten 10 Hope St ☎(0334) 74601
Closed Dec
Attractively decorated house in terraced row off town centre.
10hc (4fb) Ⓡ B&b£8.50–£10 Bdi£14.50–£15.50 W£92–£98.50 ⱡ LDO4.30pm
▥ CTV
Ⓥ

GH Yorkston Hotel 68 & 70 Argyle St ☎(0334) 72019
Neatly appointed house on roadside leading into town from east.
12hc (2fb) ✱ Ⓡ ✱B&bfr£9.25 Bdifr£14.75 Wfr£98.70 ⱡ LDO6.30pm
Lic ▥ CTV ⁋

ST AUBIN
Jersey, Channel Islands
Map **16**
⊢ **GH Panorama Private Hotel** High St ☎Jersey (0534) 42429
Mar–Nov
17rm 14hc 2→ 1⋒ (2fb) CTV in 4 bedrooms ✱ B&b£7.50–£16
▥ CTV ⁋ nc5yrs
Credit cards 1 2 3 5 Ⓥ

ST AUSTELL
Cornwall
Map **2** SX05
GH *Alexandra Hotel* 52–54 Alexandra Rd ☎(0726) 4242
14hc 4⋒ (2fb) LDO5pm
Lic ▥ CTV 16P

GH Cornerways Penwinnick Rd ☎(0726) 61579
Closed Xmas
6hc (2fb) B&b£8.50–£9.50 Bdi£11.50–£13.50 W£54–£58 M LDO5pm
Lic ▥ CTV 12P

St Andrews — St Clears

⊢ **GH Lynton House Hotel** 48 Bodmin Rd ☎(0726) 3787
6hc (2fb) ✱ B&b£7.50–£8.50 Bdi£11–£12 W£50–£57 M LDOnoon
Lic CTV 6P

⊢ **GH Pen-Star** 20 Cromwell Rd ☎(0726) 61367
Apr–Oct
6hc (4fb) B&b£6.50–£8 Bdi£9.50–£11 W£42–£52.50 ⱡ (W only Jul & Aug) LDO5pm
Lic ▥ CTV 9P ⌂

GH *Selwood House Hotel* 60 Alexandra Rd ☎(0726) 65707
12hc (4fb) LDO5pm
Lic ▥ CTV 10P 2🚗

⊢ **GH Treskillon** 26 Woodland Rd ☎(0726) 2920
10hc (2fb) ✱ B&b£8–£11 Bdi£11–£13 W£66–£78 ⱡ LDO6.30pm
Lic ▥ CTV 10P ⌂

GH Wimereux 1 Trevanion Rd ☎(0726) 2187
14rm 5→ 3⋒ (3fb) ✱ B&b£9–£13 Bdi£14–£16 W£78–£85 ⱡ LDO6.30pm
Lic ▥ CTV 15P
Credit card 3

⊢ **INN Holmbush** 101 Holmbush Rd ☎(0726) 3217
Large public house on roadside leading into town from east.
3hc TV in 2 bedrooms B&b£7 W£42 M Bar lunch£1.50–£2.50 LDO10pm
50P
Credit card 3

ST BLAZEY
Cornwall
Map **2** SX05
⊢ **GH Moorshill House Hotel** Rosehill ☎Par (072681) 2368
Closed Xmas
17th-century house situated along private drive.
5hc (2fb) ✱ B&b£6.50 Bdi£10 W£60–£65 ⱡ LDO9pm
Lic ▥ CTV 6P
Ⓥ

ST BURYAN
Cornwall
Map **2** SW42
⊢ **FH** Mr & Mrs W Hosking **Boskenna Home** *(SW423237)* ☎(073672) 250
Etr–Sep
Farmhouse with pleasant spacious rooms and traditional furniture. In a convenient position with beaches a few miles away.
3rm 1hc ✱ B&b£6 Bdi£9 W£42 M
CTV P ⌂

⊢ **FH** Mrs M R Pengelly **Burnewhall** *(SW407236)* ☎(073672) 200
mid May–mid Oct rs Wed
Spacious former 'gentleman's residence' with all bedrooms having sea views. A footpath from the farmhouse leads to the beach affording safe bathing.
3hc (1fb) ✱ B&b£6–£7 Bdi£10.50–£11.50 W£68–£75 ⱡ LDO4pm
CTV 3P 150acres dairy

ST CATHERINE'S
Strathclyde *Argyllshire*
Map **10** NN10
GH Thistle House ☎Inveraray (0499) 2209
May–Sep
Spacious detached Victorian house on Loch Fyne with attractive rooms and loch views.
6hc (1fb) B&bfr£10.50
▥ 10P

ST CLEARS
Dyfed
Map **2** SN21
⊢ **INN Black Lion Hotel** ☎(0994) 230700
Modestly appointed village inn.
11hc B&b£8–£9.50 W£55–£66.50 M Bar lunch £1.30–£4alc D8.30pm £6.50alc
▥ CTV 25P billiards

ST CLEMENT
Jersey, Channel Islands
Map **16**

GH Belle Plage Hotel Green Island
☎Jersey (0534) 53750
Apr–Oct
19rm 4→ 15⋒ (2fb) ★ B&b£15–£19 Bdi£16–£21 LDO7.45pm
Lic CTV 20P nc8yrs
Credit cards 1 3

ST DAVIDS
Dyfed
Map **2** SM72

GH Alandale 43 Nun St ☎(0437) 720333
Closed Dec
6hc (1fb) B&b£8–£8.50 Bdi£14–£15 W£56–£59.50 ⱡ (W only Jul & Aug) LDO6.30pm
CTV nc9yrs
Credit cards 1 2 3 Ⓥ

GH *Belmont House* 12 Cross Sq ☎(0437) 720264
Well maintained house facing the Old Cross.
8hc (4fb) ★ LDO4pm
Lic CTV 8P
Ⓥ

See advertisement on page 297

GH Pen-y-Daith 12 Millard Pk ☎(0437) 720720
Mar–Oct
Comfortable modern house, neat and well maintained.
8hc (3fb) ★ B&bfr£8 Bdifr£13 Wfr£85 ⱡ
Lic CTV 8P
Ⓥ

GH Y Glennydd 51 Nun St ☎(0437) 720576
Closed Dec
Traditional, proprietor run guesthouse.
10hc (3fb) ★ B&b£7.50 Bdi£12.50 W£75 ⱡ LDO5pm
Lic CTV

GH The Ramsey Lower Moor ☎(0437) 720321
7hc (2fb) Ⓡ B&b£7–£7.50 Bdi£12–£12.50 W£80 ⱡ
CTV P
Ⓥ

ST DOGMAELS
Dyfed
Map **2** SN14

GH *Glanteifi* ☎Cardigan (0239) 612353
A country hotel overlooking the estuary. Riding and sailing instruction are arranged.
12hc 5→ 1⋒ (4fb)
Lic CTV 20P sea

FH Mrs M Cave **Granant Isaf** *(SN126473)* Cipyn ☎Moylegrove (023986) 241
Apr–Oct
The Pembrokeshire Coastal Path runs along the boundary of this farm which enjoys spectacular views of the sea and cliffs.
2rm (1fb) B&b£6.50–£7 Bdi£10–£10.50 W£63–£66 ⱡ LDO5pm
CTV 4P 400acres dairy
Ⓥ

ST ERME
Cornwall
Map **2** SW85

FH Mrs F Hicks **Pengelly** *(SW856513)* Trispen ☎Mitchell (087251) 245
Etr–Oct
Attractive, well-built farmhouse. Good central base for touring Cornwall.
4hc (1fb) ★ B&b£6–£6.75 W£30 M
CTV 4P nc10yrs 230acres dairy mixed

FH Mrs B Dymond ***Trevispian Vean*** *(SW850502)* Trispen ☎Truro (0872) 79514
Apr–Sep
Extensively modernised farmhouse, clean and well maintained. Large sun lounge at the front.
7rm 6hc (3fb) ★ (W only end May–Sep) LDO6pm
CTV P 400acres arable beef sheep
Ⓥ

ST EWE
Cornwall
Map **2** SW94

FH Mrs J G Kent **Lanewa** *(SW983457)* ☎Mevagissey (0726) 843283
Comfortable farmhouse situated in the small village of St Ewe. 6m from St Austell.
3hc (1fb) ★ B&bfr£6.50 Bdifr£8.50
CTV 3P 60acres arable beef sheep mixed

ST FLORENCE
Dyfed
Map **2** SN00

GH *Greenhills Hotel* ☎Manorbier (083482) 291
Comfortable hotel in its own lawned garden.
15hc (5fb) TV in 4 bedrooms ★
Lic CTV 20P

GH *Ponterosa* Eastern Ln ☎Manorbier (083482) 378
May–Sep
Bright, well appointed split level house on outskirts of village.
6hc (2fb) ★ Ⓡ LDO6.30pm
Lic CTV 6P

ST HELIER
Jersey, Channel Islands
Map **16**

GH Almorah Hotel La Pouquelaye ☎Jersey (0534) 21648
Apr–Oct
16rm 11→ (5fb) ★ B&b£9–£14 Bdi£11–£16 LDO7.30pm
Lic CTV 10P
Ⓥ

GH Cliff Court Hotel St Andrews Rd, First Tower ☎Jersey (0534) 34919
Mar–Nov rs Dec–Feb

11rm 2hc 9➡ (9fb) ★ B&b£12–£17.50 Bdi£14–£19.50 W£84–£122.50 M LDO7pm

Lic ▥ CTV 10P ⌂ ≈ (heated) billiards

⊢✕⊣ **GH Runnymede Court Hotel** 46–52 Roseville St ☎Jersey (0534) 20044

mid Mar–Nov

51rm 4hc 35➡ 12⋒ (7fb) B&b£7–£11.50 Bdi£9–£15 W£49–£80.50 L (W only mid Jun–mid Sep) LDOnoon

Lic CTV nc5yrs

ST IVES
Cambridgeshire
Map **4** TL37

GH *The Firs Hotel* 50 Needingham Rd ☎(0480) 63252

5rm 4hc (2fb) TV in all bedrooms Ⓡ LDO9.30pm

Lic ▥ 8P

ST IVES
Cornwall
Map **2** SW54
See plan

⊢✕⊣ **GH Bay View** Headland Rd, Carbis Bay ☎Penzance (0736) 796469 Plan **1** *B1*

9rm 7hc 2⋒ (3fb) B&b£6–£10.50 Bdi£10–£14.75 W£69.50–£102 M (W only Jul & Aug) LDO6pm

Lic ▥ CTV 9P U

Ⓥ

GH Blue Mist The Warren ☎Penzance (0736) 795209 Plan **2** *B4*

Apr–Oct rs Mar

A comfortable small hotel close to town centre and Porthminster beach.

8hc (3fb) ✱B&b£6.90–£9.20 Bdi£10.35–£12.65 W£48.30–£64.40 L LDO5pm

4P nc3yrs

⊢✕⊣ **GH Chy-an-Creet Private Hotel** Higher Stennack ☎Penzance (0736) 796559 Plan **3** *A5*

mid Mar–mid Oct

Soundly appointed personally run residence with small grounds and gardens. Close to town centre.

13rm 12hc 1⋒ (3fb) B&b£7.95–£10.95 Bdi£10.95–£15.95 W£55–£77 M LDO6pm

Lic CTV 17P ⌂

Credit cards 1 3 Ⓥ

GH *Cottage* The Valley, Carbis Bay ☎Penzance (0736) 797405 Plan **4** *B2*

7hc 4➡ 3⋒ (2fb) ★ Ⓡ LDO5pm

Lic ▥ CTV 10P ⌂ sea

GH *Cottage Hotel* Carbis Bay ☎Penzance (0736) 796351 Plan **5** *B2*

May–Sep

Modern hotel in four acres of wooded grounds, overlooking St Ives Bay.

59➡ (50fb) ★ Ⓡ LDO7pm

Lic lift ▥ CTV 100P ⌂ sea

GH Dean Court Hotel Trelyon Av ☎Penzance (0736) 796023 Plan **6** *B4*

Mar–Oct

Comfortable friendly residence overlooking St Ives Bay.

12rm 5➡ 7⋒ CTV in all bedrooms ★ Ⓡ B&b£15–£20 Bdi£19–£25 W£110–£130 L LDO5pm

Lic ▥ CTV 12P

⊢✕⊣ **GH Hollies Hotel** Talland Rd ☎Penzance (0736) 796605 Plan **7** *B4*

Family hotel affording good views of St Ives Bay.

12hc (5fb) ★ B&b£7.50–£13 Bdi£10.50–£18 W£53–£90 L LDO6pm

Lic ▥ CTV 12P ⌂

GH *Island View* 2 Park Av ☎Penzance (0736) 795111 Plan **8** *B4*

Mar–Oct

Victorian terraced house, overlooking harbour.

10hc (4fb) ★ Ⓡ LDO6.30pm

CTV P sea

⊢✕⊣ **GH Kandahar & Cortina** 26 The Warren ☎Penzance (0736) 796183 Plan **8A** *B4*

Closed Xmas & New Year

11rm 10hc 1⋒ (1fb) CTV in all bedrooms B&b£7.50–£10

▥ CTV 6P

Ⓥ

GH *Longships* 2 Talland Rd ☎Penzance (0736) 798180 Plan **9** *B4*

Etr–mid Oct rs mid Oct–mid Apr

Spacious, comfortable friendly guesthouse.

23hc 3➡ 12⋒ (10fb) TV available in bedrooms LDO6pm

Lic lift ▥ CTV 18P sea

GH Lyonesse Hotel 5 Talland Rd ☎Penzance (0736) 796315 Plan **10** *B4*

Comfortable family hotel in good position with views of bay.

15rm 10hc ★ B&b£10–£13 Bdi£13 £17.50 W£59–£78 L LDOnoon

Lic ▥ CTV 5P

Credit card 1 Ⓥ

⊢✕⊣ **GH Monowai Private Hotel** Headland Rd, Carbis Bay ☎Penzance (0736) 795733 Plan **11** *B1*

May–Sep

Family hotel, friendly and comfortable, with pleasant gardens and unrestricted views of St Ives Bay.

10hc (2fb) B&bfr£6.50 Bdifr£9.50 Wfr£65 L LDO6.30pm

Lic ▥ CTV 7P nc5yrs ≈ (heated)

Ⓥ

⊢✕⊣ **GH Pondarosa** 10 Porthminster Ter ☎Penzance (0736) 795875 Plan **12** *B4*

Apr–Oct

Conveniently positioned close to Porthminster beach, friendly relaxed atmosphere.

10rm 9hc 1➡ (2fb) ★ B&b£7.50–£9.50 Bdi£12–£14.50 W£75–£90 L LDO6.30pm

▥ CTV 8P nc5yrs

Ⓥ

GH Primrose Valley Hotel Primrose Valley ☎Penzance (0736) 794939 Plan **13** *B4*

Apr–Oct →

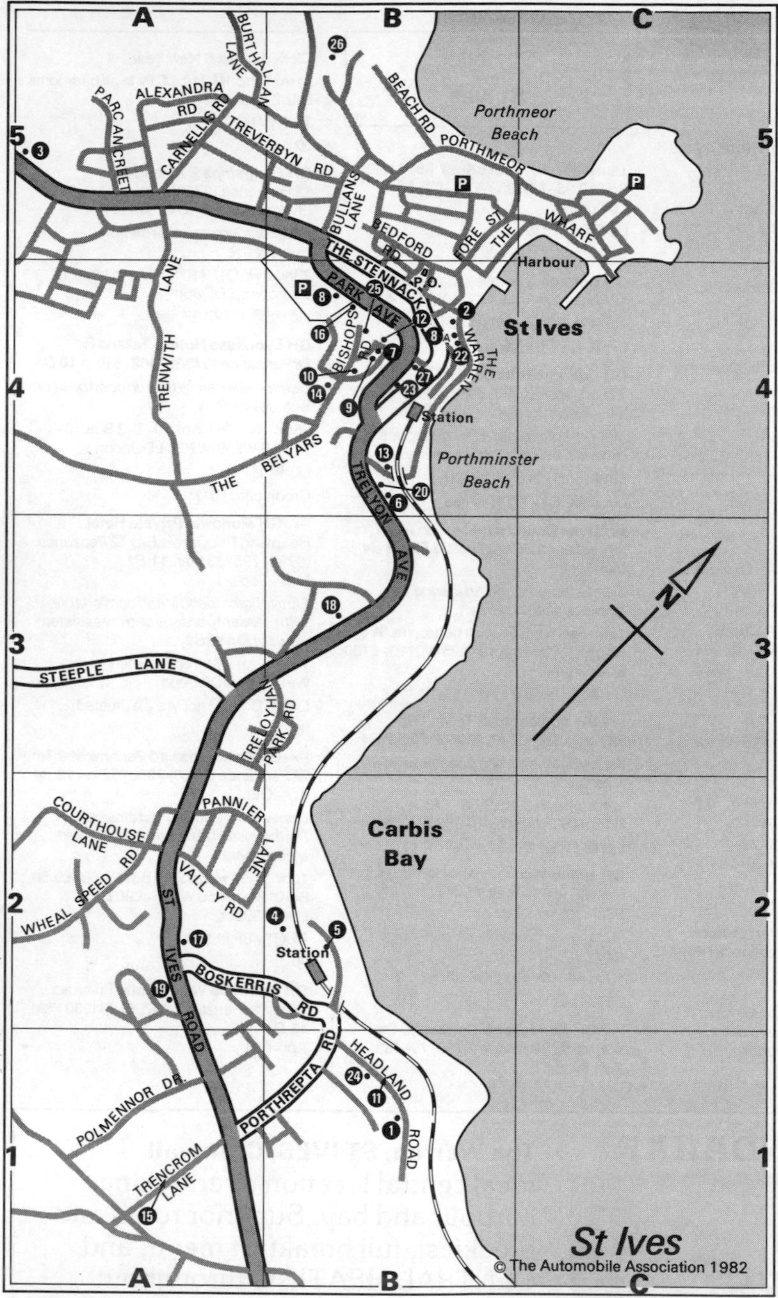

St Ives

1 Bay View
2 Blue Mist
3 Chy-an-Creet Private Hotel
4 Cottage Guesthouse
5 Cottage Hotel
6 Dean Court Hotel
7 Hollies Hotel
8 Island View
8A Kandahar & Cortina
9 Longships
10 Lyonesse Hotel
11 Monowai Private Hotel
12 Pondarosa
13 Primrose Valley Hotel
14 Rosemorran Private Hotel
15 Hotel Rotorua
16 St Margarets **3 Park Av**
17 St Margarets Hotel **Carbis Bay**
18 St Merryn Hotel
19 Sherwell
20 Shun Lee Private Hotel
22 Sunrise
23 27 The Terrace
24 Tregorran
25 Trelissick Hotel
26 Verbena
27 Windsor Hotel

Pleasant, small family hotel ideally positioned about 100yds from Porthminster beach.

11rm 5hc 5⇌ 1⋒ (4fb) ✱ B&b£8.37–£12.68 Bdi£13.37–£17.68 W£86.25–£112.70 Ⅴ (W only Jul & Aug) LDO6pm

Lic CTV 11P ⌂

⊢⊣ **GH Rosemorran Private Hotel** The Belyars ☎Penzance (0736) 796359 Plan **14** *B2*
Mar–Oct

Small comfortably furnished family hotel set in own grounds, close to beaches and town.

14rm 2hc 2⇌ 10⋒ (4fb) ✱ B&b£7–£11.50 Bdi£10–£15.80 W£48–£80 Ⅴ LDOnoon

Lic ▥ CTV 14P

Credit card ①

GH Hotel Rotorua Trencrom Ln, Carbis Bay ☎Penzance (0736) 795419 Plan **15** *A1*
Mar–Oct rs Nov–Feb

Purpose built in quite lane just off St Ives rd, close to Carbis Bay.

13rm 10⇌⋒ (10fb) B&b£8.90–£11.37 Bdi£12.06–14.53 W£62.30–£78.48 M LDO6pm

Lic ▥ CTV 12P ⌂ ≋ billiards

GH *St Margarets* 3 Park Av ☎Penzance (0736) 795785 Plan **16** *B4*

St Ives

Closed Xmas

Victorian house overlooking the harbour and having simply appointed bedrooms.

6hc (3fb) ✱ LDO6.30pm

Lic ▥ CTV ⅌ sea

GH *St Margarets Hotel*, St Ives Rd, Carbis Bay ☎Penzance (0736) 796453 Plan **17** *A2*
May–Oct

14hc (4fb) LDO7.30pm

Lic ▥ CTV 18P nc3yrs sea

GH *St Merryn Hotel* Trelyon ☎Penzance (0736) 795767 Plan **18** *B3*
Mar–Nov

12hc 1⇌ 1⋒ (A 3hc) (6fb) ✱

Lic ▥ CTV 20P sea

⊢⊣ **GH Sherwell** St Ives Road, Carbis Bay ☎Penzance (0736) 796142 Plan **19** *A2*
Jan–20 Dec

Friendly intimate guesthouse, personally run with views of Carbis Bay.

8hc (2fb) ✱ B&b£6.75–£7.75 Bdi£10–£11 W£65–£75 Ⅴ LDO6.30pm

▥ CTV 8P nc2yrs

Ⓥ

GH Shun Lee Private Hotel Trelyon Av ☎Penzance (0736) 796284 Plan **20** *B4*
23 Mar–2 Nov

Friendly hotel superbly located and built by Capt. Paynter during 19th century.

11rm 3hc 2⇌ 5⋒ (1fb) ✱ B&b£9–£13 Bdi£13.75–£17 W£62–£89 Ⅴ LDO6.30pm

Lic ▥ CTV 10P nc5yrs

⊢⊣ **GH Sunrise** 22 The Warren ☎Penzance (0736) 795407 Plan **22** *B4*
Spring Bank Hol–Oct

Character cottage property under ownership of charming proprietress. Positioned right at waters edge.

8rm 7hc 1⇌ TV in all bedrooms ✱ Ⓡ B&b£7–£9

CTV 4P

Ⓥ

See advertisement on page 302

⊢⊣ **GH '27 The Terrace'** 27 The Terrace ☎Penzance (0736) 797450 Plan **23** *B4*
rs Sep–Apr Closed Xmas & New Year

6⋒ (2fb) CTV in all bedrooms ✱ Ⓡ B&b£8–£10 Bdi£14 LDOnoon

Lic ▥ 3P ⌂ nc5yrs

Credit cards ① ③

GH Tregorran Hotel Headland Rd, Carbis Bay ☎Penzance (0736) 795889 Plan **24** *B1*
Apr–Oct →

Small, well appointed family-run hotel with attractive bedroom annexe and good sports facilities.

15rm 8hc 7⋔ (3fb) Ⓡ B&b£9.50–£12.50 Bdi£13–£16.50 W£59.50–£80.50 M LDO5pm

Lic Ⅲ CTV 20P ⌂ ≈ (heated)

GH Trelissick Hotel Bishop's Rd ☎Penzance (0736) 795035 Plan **25** *B4* Apr–Oct

Comfortable family hotel set in own grounds overlooking harbour and St Ives Bay.

15rm 11hc 3➡ 1⋔ (2fb) B&b£10 Bdi£14.50 W£65–£110 Ⱡ LDO6.45pm

Lic CTV 12P

Credit cards 1 3

⊢⊣ **GH Verbena** Orange Ln ☎Penzance (0736) 796396 Plan **26** *B5* Etr–Sep

Comfortable personally run guesthouse in elevated position with good views over Porthmeor Beach.

7rm 5hc (2fb) Ⓡ B&b£6–£6.75 Bdi£9.50–£10.25 W£42–£47.25 M LDO5pm

Temperance CTV 8P

Ⓥ

GH Windsor Hotel The Terrace ☎Penzance (0736) 798174 Plan **27** *B4*

Pleasant small family hotel with good views, offering friendly warm atmosphere.

10hc (4fb) CTV in 4 bedrooms ✈ ✱B&b£7.50–£12 Bdi£10.50–£14.40 W£50–£83 LDO9am

Lic Ⅲ CTV 4P ⌂

ST JOHN'S IN THE VALE

Cumbria
Map **11** NY32

⊢⊣ **FH** Mrs M E Harrison **Shundraw** *(NY308236)* ☎Threlkeld (059683) 227 Etr–Oct

Large, well-maintained, stone-built farmhouse, parts of which date from 1712. In elevated position with views across valley.

3rm (1fb) ✈ B&b£6 W£38.50 M

TV 4P 52acres sheep

ST JUST

Cornwall
Map **2** SW33

GH Boscean Country Hotel (Guestaccom) ☎Penzance (0736) 788748 Mar–Oct

Well appointed charming country house. Peaceful location, just a short walk from sea.

9rm 3hc 6➡ (3fb) ✈ B&b£9.75–£11.75 Bdi£15–£17 W£95–£112 Ⱡ LDO7pm

Lic Ⅲ CTV 12P 2⌂ ⌂

ST JUST-IN-ROSELAND

Cornwall
Map **2** SW83

GH Rose-Da-Mar Hotel ☎St Mawes (0326) 270450 Apr–Oct & Xmas

9rm 4hc 4➡ 1⋔ (2fb) B&b£14–£15.50 Bdi£23.50 W£98–£108.50 Ⱡ LDO7.30pm

Lic Ⅲ CTV 9P nc7yrs

⊢⊣ **FH** Mrs W Symons **Commerrans** *(SW842375)* ☎Portscatho (087258) 270 Etr–Oct

Pleasant modernised farmhouse, attractively decorated throughout, and situated in a large garden.

4rm 3hc (1fb) ✈ B&b£8–£8.50 Bdi£11.50–£12.50 W£75–£80 Ⱡ LDO9am

Ⅲ CTV 6P nc1yr 61acres beef sheep

ST KEW HIGHWAY

Cornwall
Map **2** SX07

FH Mrs S Harris ***Kelly Green*** *(SX047758)* ☎Bodmin (0208) 850275 Closed Xmas

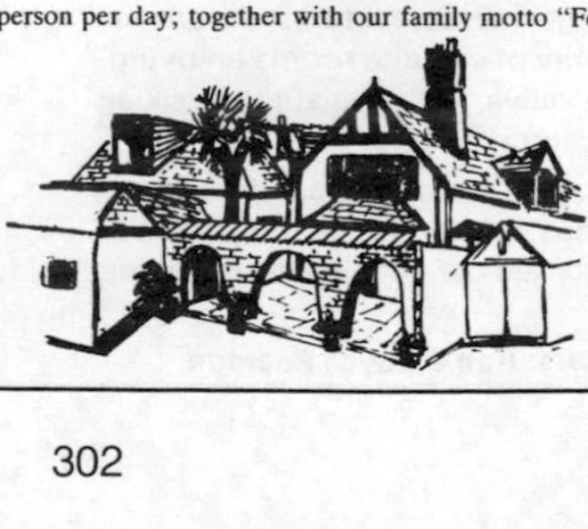

Old, two-storey farmhouse with lawn at the front.

5rm 4hc (4fb) ✱

CTV 6P 257acres mixed

ST KEYNE
Cornwall
Map **2** SX26

FH Mrs & Mrs P Cummins **Badham** *(SX249590)* ☎Liskeard (0579) 43572
Mar–Dec

5hc (2fb) ✱ B&b£9–£10 Bdi£14–£15 W£84–£90 ⱸ LDO6pm

Lic ♨ CTV 20P 🎣 4acres small holding

🅥

⊢⊣ **FH** Mr V R Arthur **Killigorrick** *(SX228614)* ☎Liskeard (0579) 20559

Pleasant farmhouse in peaceful surroundings. 3½m from Liskeard, 1m W off Duloe–Dobwalls Rd.

4hc (2fb) ✱ B&bfr£6 Bdifr£9 Wfr£60 ⱸ

CTV 6 P nc5yrs 21acres mixed

ST LAWRENCE
Isle of Wight
Map **4** SZ57

GH Woody Bank Hotel Undercliff Dr
☎Ventnor (0983) 852610
Mar–Oct

9rm 5hc 4🚿 (1fb) B&b£11–£13 Bdi£17.50–£19.50 W£122–£129 ⱸ LDO7.30pm

Lic ♨ CTV 9P nc5yrs

ST MARGARET, SOUTH ELMHAM
Suffolk
Map **5** TM38

FH Mrs H B Custerson **Elms House** *(TM310840)* ☎St Cross (098682) 228
rs Oct–Apr closed Xmas & New Year

Delightful period farmhouse in extremely quiet location: friendly atmosphere.

2hc ✱ B&bfr£10 Bdifr£20 Wfr£90 ⱸ LDO5pm

♨ CTV 4P nc10yrs 200acres arable sheep

🅥

ST MARGARET'S AT CLIFFE
Kent
Map **5** TR34

FH C & L Oakley **Walletts Court** *(TR347446)* West Cliff ☎Dover (0304) 852424
Closed Xmas

A restored 17th-century farmhouse with large beamed bedrooms, inglenooks and oak staircase. Situated on the white cliffs of Dover, 3m from harbour. 1m W B2058.

3hc (A 4🚿) (3fb) ✱ Ⓡ B&b£10–£12 Wfr£63 M

♨ CTV 12P 🏠 4acres arable

ST MARTIN
Guernsey, Channel Islands
Map **16**

GH Triton Les Hubits ☎ Guernsey (0481) 38017

14hc 4🛁 (2fb) ✱ B&b£9.50–£11 LDO6.60pm

CTV 10P nc4yrs

ST MARTIN
Jersey, Channel Islands
Map **16**

GH St Martin's House ☎Jersey (0534) 53271
Mar–Oct

11rm 7hc 2🛁 3🚿 (2fb) ✱ Ⓡ B&b£9.50–£12 Bdi£12.50–£17.50 LDO11am

Lic ♨ CTV 15P ♿ nc3yrs 🏠 🏊

ST OWEN'S CROSS
Hereford & Worcester
Map **3** SO52

⊢⊣ **FH** Mrs F Davies **Aberhall** *(SO529242)* ☎Harewood End (098987) 256
Mar–Nov

200-year-old farmhouse situated 4m from Ross-on-Wye on the B4521. Hard tennis courts for guests use and a cellar with table tennis, pool table etc.

3hc (2fb) ✱ Ⓡ B&b£7.50–£8 Bdi£11–£11.50 W£75 ⱸ LDO4pm

♨ CTV 3P 🎾(hard) billiards 132acres arable dairy

🅥

ST PETER PORT
Guernsey, Channel Islands
Map **16**

⊢⊣ **GH Baltimore House Hotel** Les Gravees ☎(0481) 23641
Mar–Oct

Pleasant Georgian house with walled garden. Bright and clean with comfortable, well furnished rooms.

12rm 7hc 1🛁 4🚿 (3fb) Ⓡ B&b£7.50–£11 Bdi£9.75–£14.75 W£52.50–£77 ⱸ LDO7pm

Lic CTV 7P

Credit cards 1 2 3 4 5

GH Midhurst House Candie Rd
☎Guernsey (0481) 24391
Mar–Oct

4rm 1🛁 3🚿 (2fb) ✱ Ⓡ B&b£11–£13 Bdi£15–£17 W£77–£91 M LDO7pm

Lic ♨ CTV 🍸 nc5yrs

ST PETER'S VALLEY
Jersey, Channel Islands
Map **16**

GH Midvale Private Hotel ☎Jersey (0534) 42498
Apr–Oct

20rm 9hc 7🛁 4🚿 (4fb) ✱ B&b£9.25–£11.25 Bdi£12.25–£14.25 (W only Jul & Aug) LDO6.30pm

Lic CTV 15P nc1yr

ST SAMPSON'S
Guernsey, Channel Islands
Map **16**

GH Ann-Dawn Private Hotel Route Des Capelles ☎ Guernsey (0481) 25606
Etr–Oct

14rm 1🛁 6🚿 (1fb) ✱ Ⓡ B&b£9.50–£10.50 Bdi£11.50–£15.50 W£80.50–£108.50 ⱸ LDO6pm

Lic ♨ CTV 12P nc5yrs

ST SAVIOUR
Guernsey, Channel Islands
Map **16**

GH La Girouette House Hotel
☎Guernsey (0481) 63269
Feb–Oct rs Dec
14rm 4hc 2⇌ 8⋔ (6fb) CTV in all bedrooms ✱ ® B&b£11–£15 Bdi£15–£19.80 W£77–£105 M LDO7.30pm
Lic 🍴 14P nc3yrs
Credit cards [1] [2] [3] Ⓥ

SALCOMBE
Devon
Map **3** SX73

GH Bay View Hotel Bennett Rd
☎(054884) 2238
Mar–Oct
11hc 1⇌ 1⋔ (3fb) ✱ *B&b£12–£16 W£84–£112 M
Lic 🍴 CTV 8P nc2yrs
Ⓥ

GH Charborough House Hotel Devon Rd ☎(054884) 2260
mid Mar–Oct
9rm 1hc 1⇌ 7⋔ (2fb) CTV in all bedrooms ✱ ® B&b£11.50–£15 Bdi£18.50–£22 W£98–£135 L LDO8pm
Lic 🍴 CTV 9P
Credit cards [1] [3] Ⓥ

GH Lyndhurst Hotel Bonaventure Rd
☎(054884) 2481
Closed Xmas
8rm 2hc 4⋔ (2fb) TV in 6 bedrooms ✱ ® B&b£10 Bdi£15 W£96 L LDO5.30pm
Lic 🍴 CTV 8P nc7yrs
Credit cards [1] [3] Ⓥ

GH Stoneycroft Hotel Devon Rd
☎(054884) 2218
Closed Dec
10rm 9⋔ (2fb) ✱ *B&b£10–£12 Bdi£15.50–£17.50 W£63–£73.50 M LDO7pm
Lic 🍴 CTV 10P 1🚗 nc5yrs
Ⓥ

GH Trennels Private Hotel Herbert Rd
(054884) 2500
Jan–Nov
11hc ✱ B&b£8.50–£9.50 Bdi£12.50–£14.50 W£48–£52 M
🍴 CTV 8P 1🚗 nc12yrs

GH Woodgrange Private Hotel Devon Rd ☎(054884) 2439
Apr–Oct
12rm 6hc 5⇌ 1⋔ (2fb) CTV in all bedrooms ® Bdi£10–£12 Bdi£16–£18 W£91–£120 L LDO10am
Lic 🍴 10P 🏠
Credit cards [1] [2] [3]

SALEN
Isle of Mull, Strathclyde *Argyllshire*
Map **10** NM54

GH Craig Hotel ☎Aros (06803) 347
Closed Xmas
Painted roadside hotel offering comfortable accommodation and friendly atmosphere.
7hc B&b£11.50–£13.50 Bdi£16.50–£19.50 W£110 L LDO5.30pm
Lic 7P

SALFORD
Bedfordshire
Map **4** SP93

INN *Red Lion Country Hotel* Wavendon Rd ☎Milton Keynes (0908) 583117
8hc 2⇌ TV in 8 bedrooms D9.30pm
🍴 CTV 22P 🎳

SALFORD
Gt Manchester
Map **7** SJ89

GH Hazeldean Hotel 467 Bury New Rd
☎061-792 6667
21hc 11⇌ 6⋔ (2fb) CTV in all bedrooms ® B&bfr£21.81 LDO8pm
Lic 🍴 CTV 21P 🏠
Credit cards [1] [2] [3] [5]

SALISBURY
Wiltshire
Map **4** SU12

GH Byways House 31 Fowlers Rd
☎(0722) 28364
17rm 11hc 6⫛ (3fb) ✱ B&b£9–£10 W£63–£70M
CTV 12P 1🚗

GH Hayburn Wyke 72 Castle Rd
☎(0722) 24141
6hc 1⫛ (2fb) ✱ B&bfr£17
CTV 5P 1🚗 nc6yrs

GH Holmhurst Downton Rd
☎(0722) 23164

Detached brick-built villa situated on main A338 adjacent to Cathedral.
8rm 5hc 3⫛ (1fb) B&b£7.50–£8
CTV 8P nc5yrs
See advertisement on page 306

INN White Horse Hotel Castle St
☎(0722) 27844
12hc 4⫛ CTV in all bedrooms ®
B&b£16–£18 Bdi£23–£25 W£161–£175 L£2.25–£3.50&alc D9.15pm £6.50–£7&alc
CTV 12P 10🚗
Credit cards 1 3 5
See advertisement on page 306

SALTDEAN
East Sussex
Map **5** TQ30
See also **Brighton & Hove**

GH Linbrook Lodge 74 Lenham Av (Guestaccom) ☎Brighton (0273) 33775
Closed 2 wks Nov →

House built on a slope in quiet residential area, all rooms have bright and colourful décor.

8hc 4⋒ (3fb) CTV in 2 bedrooms TV in 1 bedroom Ⓡ B&b£9–£10 Bdi£12.50–£14 W£56–£60 M LDO4pm

Lic 🍽 CTV 8P

Ⓥ

GH *White House Private Hotel* 1 Chichester Drive West ☎Brighton (0273) 32465

8hc 2→ 5⋒ (2fb) CTV in all bedrooms ★ Ⓡ LDO7pm

Lic 🍽 CTV sea

Saltdean — Sandown

SANDOWN
Isle of Wight
Map **4** SZ58

GH Chester Lodge Hotel Beachfield Rd ☎(0983) 402773

Closed mid Dec–mid Jan

Small, comfortable, family-run guesthouse near to beach, five minutes walk to town centre.

17hc (6fb) B&b£8.05–£8.63 Bdi£11.50–£12.65 W£56.35–£60.41 M LDO6.15pm

Lic CTV 15P nc3yrs

GH Cliff House Hotel Cliff Rd ☎(0983) 403656

Etr–mid Oct

Nicely appointed, comfortable house, overlooking the sea.

16rm 8hc 3→ 5⋒ (5fb) Ⓡ B&b£11.50–£16 Bdi£16.50–£21.50 W£113–£126.50 ⱡ LDO6.30pm

Lic 🍽 CTV 20P ♿

Credit card 3

GH *St Catherine's Hotel* 1 Winchester Pk ☎(0983) 402392
Closed mid Dec–mid Jan
18hc 5⇌ 4⋒ (1fb) CTV available in bedrooms ✱ Ⓡ LDO7pm
Lic ⅢⅢ CTV 8P

GH *Trevallyn Hotel* 32 Broadway ☎(0983) 402373
Mar–Oct rs Nov & Dec
Clean, simple accommodation is provided here, with entertainment in the oriental bar.
25hc (5fb) ✱ Ⓡ LDO6pm
Lic CTV 30P

SANDPLACE
Cornwall
Map **2** SX25

GH Polraen Country House Hotel ☎Looe (05036) 3956
Closed 15 Dec–Jan
6rm 1⇌ 5⋒ (3fb) Ⓡ B&b£12.50–£15 Bdi£18.50–£21 W£120–£140 Ⅼ LDO6pm
Lic ⅢⅢ CTV 12P
Credit cards 1 3

SANDWICH
Kent
Map **5** TR35

INN Fleur De Lis Delf St ☎(0304) 611131
4hc TV in all bedrooms Ⓡ B&b£12 Bdi£16.95 L£5.50alc D9.30pm £6.50alc
CTV
Credit cards 1 2 3 5 Ⓥ

SANNOX
Isle of Arran, Strathclyde *Buteshire*
Map **10** NS04

GH Cliffdene ☎Corrie (077081) 224
Closed Oct & Nov
Stone house built in 1900 on main road overlooking beach and sea.
5hc (A 2hc) (3fb) B&b£7.50 Bdi£10.50 W£52.50 LDO6.30pm
CTV 5P

SANQUHAR
Dumfries & Galloway *Dumfriesshire*
Map **11** NS71

INN Blackaddie House Hotel
Blackaddie Rd ☎(06592) 270
Detached country house, near River Nith, popular with businessmen.
6rm 5hc CTV in all bedrooms ® *B&bfr£10 Lfr£5.50&alc D8.30pm fr£7.50&alc
25P

SARISBURY GREEN
Hampshire
Map **4** SU50

GH Dormy ☎Locks Heath (04895) 2626
Small, homely guesthouse with friendly, family service.
7rm 3hc 2 (1fb) TV in all bedrooms ® B&b£8.50–£10.50 Bdi£13.50–£15.50 LDO5pm
CTV 10P
Credit card 3 V

SAUNDERSFOOT
Dyfed
Map **2** SN10

GH Claremont Hotel St Brides Hill
☎(0834) 813231
Apr–Oct
21rm 17hc 4 (5fb) CTV in 5 bedrooms ® B&b£9–£12 Bdi£12–£16 W£63–£84 (W only mid Jul–Aug) LDO7pm
Lic CTV 16P
Credit card 3 V

GH Harbour Light Private Hotel
2 High St ☎(0834) 813496
Closed Dec
Cheerful small hotel with residents bar. A few minutes from harbour and beach.
11hc (6fb) ® *B&b£8–£10.50 Bdi£11.50–£13.50 W£56–£72 LDO4pm
Lic CTV 9P
Credit cards 1 2 3 V

GH *Jalna Hotel* Stammers Rd ☎(0834) 812282
Mar–Oct
Purpose built well maintained hotel. Few minutes walk to beach and harbour.
14hc 6 4 (10fb) TV in all bedrooms ® LDO6.45pm
Lic CTV 14P

GH Malin House Hotel St Brides Hill
☎(0834) 812344
Family hotel standing in its own grounds in elevated position. Bar for residents.
11rm 4 7 (4fb) CTV in all bedrooms ® B&b£10–£12 Bdi£15–£16 W£98–£112 (W only Jul & Aug) LDO7pm
Lic CTV 20P (heated)

GH Merlewood Hotel St Brides Hill
☎(0834) 812421
Etr–Sep
Modern family run hotel standing in elevated position overlooking the bay.
14rm 3 11 (11fb) CTV in all bedrooms ® *B&b£10–£13 Bdi£14–£18 LDO7pm
Lic CTV 30P (heated)
Credit card 3

GH Rhodewood House St Brides Hill
☎(0834) 812200
Family holiday hotel with friendly atmosphere.
34rm 25hc 17 2 (10fb) CTV in 21 bedrooms ® B&b£13–£19 Bdi£19.50–£25.50 W£125–£163 LDO9.30pm
Lic CTV 50P billiards solarium
Credit cards 1 2 3 V

GH Sandy Hill Sandy Hill Rd
☎(0834) 813165
Mar–Oct
5hc (3fb) CTV in all bedrooms ® B&b£8–£9 Bdi£11–£12.50 W£77–£87.50 ⅃ (W only Jul & Aug) LDO6pm
Lic 7P nc5yrs
Ⓥ

SAWLEY
Lancashire
Map **7** SD74

GH Spread Eagle Hotel ☎Clitheroe (0200) 41202
9rm 6➡ 3⋔ (2fb) CTV in all bedrooms ® *B&b£17.50–£32.50 Bdi£27–£42 S% LDO9pm
Lic 80P sauna bath
Credit cards 1 2 3 5

SAXELBY
Leicestershire
Map **8** SK62

FH Mrs M A Morris **Manor House** *(SK701208)* ☎Melton Mowbray (0664) 812269
Etr–Oct
The manor house, parts of which date back to the 12th and 15th-centuries, is situated on the edge of the village. 5m from Melton Mowbray.
2hc (2fb) ® B&bfr£8.50 Bdifr£14 W£90 ⅃ LDOnoon
CTV 6P 125acres dairy sheep

SCARBOROUGH
North Yorkshire
Map **8** TA08
(See plan)

GH Avoncroft Hotel Crown Ter ☎(0723) 372737 Plan **1** *C2*
Mar–Oct rs Dec–Feb
31hc 1➡ (13fb) CTV in all bedrooms ® B&b£9.50–£12.40 Bdi£12.20–£15.20 W£74.20–£98.50 ⅃ LDO6pm
Lic
Ⓥ

GH Bay Hotel 67 Esplanade, South Cliff ☎(0723) 373926 Plan **2** *D1*
27hc (3fb) B&b£7–£8.50 Bdi£9.50–£11.50 LDO5.45pm
CTV

GH Sefton Hotel 18 Prince of Wales Ter ☎(0723) 372310 Plan **8** *C2*
Mar–Oct & Xmas
Victorian town house with spacious public rooms and some charming bedrooms.
16rm 13hc 3➡ (3fb) B&b£9.20–£9.75 Bdi£10.92–£11.50 W£64.40–£68.25 M LDO6pm
Lic lift CTV nc4yrs
Ⓥ

Stone-built house overlooking sea, with comfortable public rooms and smart basement dining area.
18rm 6hc 12⋔ (3fb) CTV in all bedrooms ® B&b£14–£17 Bdi£18–£21 W£126–£140 ⅃
Lic

GH *Burghcliffe Hotel* 28 Esplanade, South Cliff ☎(0723) 61524 Plan **3** *C2*
13hc 2➡ 4⋔ (2fb) TV in 2 bedrooms LDO6pm
Lic CTV sea

GH *Church Hills Private Hotel* St Martins Av, South Cliff ☎(0723) 363148 Plan **4** *C2*
Sturdy Victorian building with comfortable lounge and bar, and cosy basement dining room.
16hc (1fb)
Lic CTV nc9yrs

GH Geldenhuis Hotel 145–147 Queens Pde ☎(0723) 361677 Plan **5** *B4*
Mar–Oct & Xmas
Terraced houses overlooking North Bay with spacious dining room and comfortable lounge.
23hc (2fb) ® LDO5.30pm
Lic CTV 18P

GH *Park Hotel* 21–23 Victoria Park, Peasholm ☎(0723) 375580 Plan **6** *B4*
Closed Dec–Feb
Hotel has cheerful, spacious public rooms and attractive dining area.
16hc 1➡ 3⋔ (6fb) LDO5pm
Lic CTV 2P
Ⓥ

GH Ridbech Private Hotel 8 The Crescent ☎(0723) 361683 Plan **7** *C3*
May–Oct
In Georgian terrace, hotel has charming, spacious lounge and character dining room.

SCILLY, ISLES OF
No map

ST MARY'S
Hugh Town

GH *Brantwood* Rocky Hill ☎Scillonia (0720) 22531
Etr–mid Oct
Small bungalow in rural area with comfortable lounge and good bedrooms.
6hc LDO6.15pm
Lic CTV nc10yrs sea
Ⓥ

SCOTCH CORNER
North Yorkshire
Map **8** NZ20

INN Vintage Hotel ☎Richmond (0748) 4424
rs Sun Closed Xmas & New Year
8rm 3hc 4➡ 1⋔ CTV in all bedrooms ® B&b£14.50–£18.50 Bdi£22–£27.50 W£95.50–£123.50 M L£4.75–£5.50&alc D9.15pm £7.50–£8.50&alc
50P
Credit cards 1 3 Ⓥ

SEAFORD
East Sussex
Map **5** TV49

GH Avondale Hotel 5 Avondale Rd ☎(0323) 890008
Closed Xmas
Small, family run house with friendly atmosphere.

6hc (2fb) ★ B&b£8–£9.25 Bdi£12.50–£13.75 W£54–£87 M̸ LDO4pm

CTV

SEATON *(Near Looe; 7m)*
Cornwall
Map **2** SX35

GH Blue Haven Hotel Looe Hill
☎Downderry (05035) 310

6rm 4hc 2⋔ (1fb) B&b£8–£9.50 Bdi£12.25–£13.75 W£78–£83 L̸ LDO8pm

Lic CTV 6P

SEATON
Devon
Map **3** SY29

GH Check House Beer Rd ☎(0297) 21858
Etr–Oct

9rm 6hc 1 2⋔ (1fb) ★ B&b£9.50–£11 Bdi£14–£15.50 W£60–£73 M̸ LDO6.30pm

Lic CTV 12P 1 nc8yrs

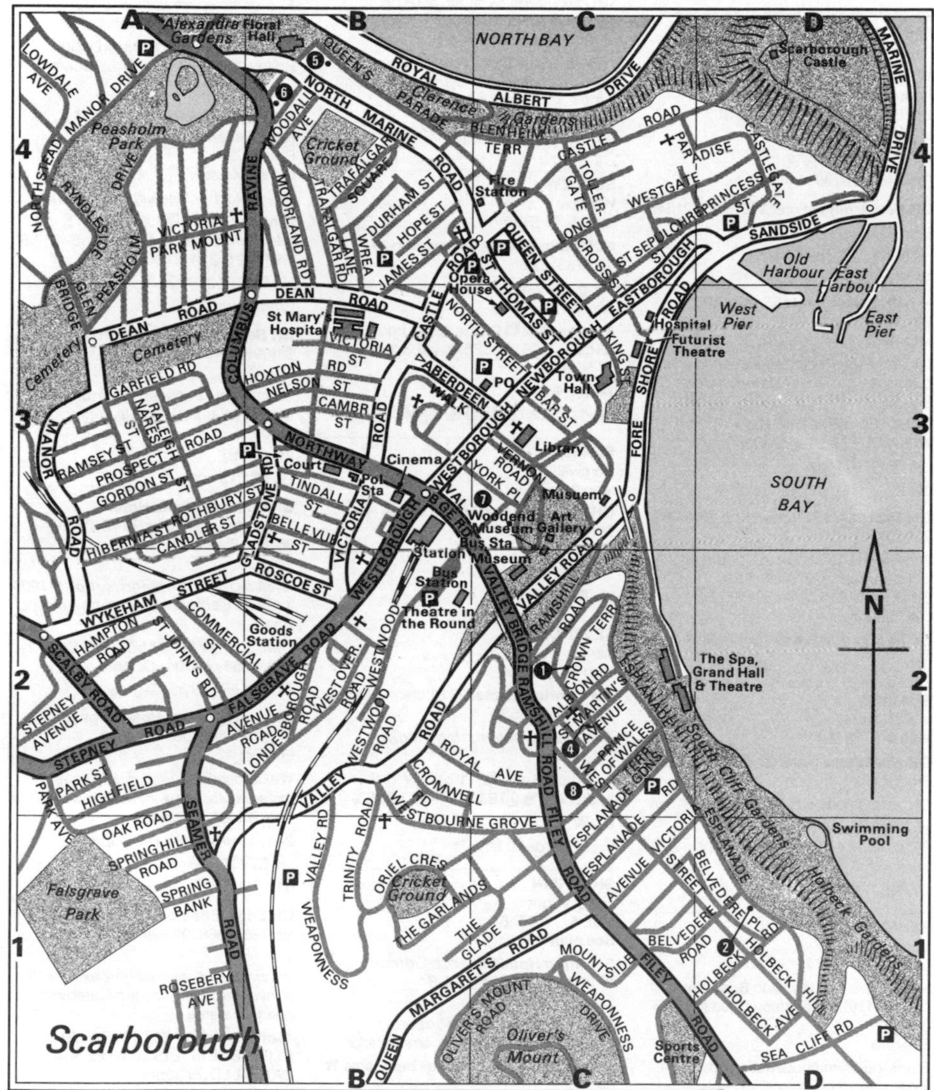

Scarborough
1 Avoncroft Hotel
2 Bay Hotel
3 Burghcliffe Hotel
4 Church Hills Private Hotel
5 Geldenhuis
6 Park Hotel
7 Ridbech Private Hotel
8 Sefton Hotel

GH Eyre House Queen St ☎(0297) 21455
9hc (4fb) Ⓡ B&b£8.50–£9.50 Bdifr£12.50 Wfr£59.50 M̸ LDOnoon
Lic ▥ CTV 10P ≈

⊢⊣ **GH Harbourside** 2 Trevelyan Rd ☎(0297) 20085
7hc (3fb) Ⓡ B&b£7.50–£8 Bdi£12.50 W£50–£52.50 M̸ LDO8pm
▥ CTV 10P
Credit cards [1] [2] [3]

GH Mariners Homestead Esplanade ☎(0297) 20560
Feb–Nov
11rm 7hc 1→ 3⌂ (1fb) CTV in 1 bedroom TV in 1 bedroom Ⓡ B&b£11–£12 Bdi£17–£18 W£70–£75 M̸ LDO4.30pm
Lic ▥ CTV 9P nc3yrs
Credit card [3] Ⓥ

GH *Netherhayes* Fore St ☎(0297) 21646
Etr–Sep
10hc (3fb) ✱ LDO6.30pm
Lic CTV 10P nc3yrs

⊢⊣ **GH St Margarets** 5 Seafield Rd ☎(0297) 20462
Mar–Nov
Large double fronted house overlooking playing fields. Close to town centre.
9hc 4⌂ (2fb) CTV in all bedrooms Ⓡ B&b£7.50–£8.50 Bdi£12.25–£13.25 W£52.50–£59.50 M̸ LDO9pm
Lic ▥ CTV 6P ⌂
Ⓥ

GH Thornfield 87 Scalwell Ln ☎(0297) 20039
9hc 3→ 1⌂ (3fb) CTV in 2 bedrooms TV in 1 bedroom Ⓡ B&b£9–£11 Bdi£13.50–£15.50 W£63–£77 M̸ LDO5.30pm
Lic ▥ CTV 10P 2⌂ ⌂ ≈(heated)
Ⓥ

SEAVIEW
Isle of Wight
Map **4** SZ69

GH *Northbank Hotel* ☎(098371) 2227
Etr–Oct
Large traditional family house with excellent sea views.
20hc (4fb) CTV in 2 bedrooms TV in 2 bedrooms Ⓡ LDO8pm
Lic ▥ CTV 10P 10⌂ ⌂ sea

SEBERGHAM
Cumbria
Map **11** NY34

⊢⊣ **FH** Mrs E M Johnston **Bustabeck** *(NY373419)* ☎Raughton Head (06996) 339
Etr–Sep
Stone-built farmhouse dating from 1684. Extensively modernised.
3rm (1fb) ✱ B&b£6 Bdi£10 W£60 Ł
TV 4P 72acres dairy mixed
Ⓥ

SELBY
North Yorkshire
Map **8** SE63

GH Hazeldene 34 Brook St (A19) ☎(0757) 704809
Closed Xmas wk
Friendly guesthouse near town centre with homely fittings and furnishings and simple accommodation.
7hc (2fb) ✱ B&b£8.50–£10
CTV 5P

SEMLEY
Wiltshire
Map **3** ST82

INN Bennett Arms ☎East Knoyle (074783) 221
Delightfully set on village green opposite church.
3rm 1hc (A 3⌂) CTV in all bedrooms Ⓡ B&b£13 W£91 M̸ L£5alc D9.30pm £7.50alc
▥ 30P ⌂
Credit cards [1] [2] [3] [4] [5] Ⓥ

SENNEN
Cornwall
Map **2** SW32

GH *Sunny Bank Hotel* Sea View Hill ☎(073687) 278
Mar–Dec
10hc (3fb)
Lic ▥ CTV 12P

SEVENOAKS
Kent
Map **5** TQ55

GH Moorings Hotel 97 Hitchin Hatch Ln ☎(0732) 452589
Cosy homely hotel run by friendly proprietor.
9rm 4hc 1⌂ (A 2⌂) (1fb) CTV in all bedrooms ✱ Ⓡ B&b£11–£13.25 S%
Lic ▥ 25P
Credit cards [1] [3]

SHANKLIN
Isle of Wight
Map **4** SZ58
See plan

GH *Afton Hotel* Clarence Gdns ☎(098386) 3075 Plan **1** *B4*
Feb–Nov
Luxurious guesthouse with period furniture and colourful accommodation.
9rm 3hc 6⌂ (2fb) CTV in all bedrooms ✱ Ⓡ
Lic ▥ P nc5yrs

⊢⊣ **GH Aqua Hotel** The Esplanade ☎(0983) 863024 Plan **2** *C2*
Etr–Oct
Modern house with small but comfortable accommodation.
24rm 22hc 2→ (8fb) ✱ B&b£6.90–£11.50 Bdi£10.88–£16.68 W£69–£115 Ł LDO6pm
Lic CTV 2P
Credit card [3]

GH Avenue Hotel 35 Victoria Av ☎(0983) 862386 Plan **3** *B1*
Apr–Sep
Friendly hotel with well furnished bedrooms and comfortable lounge.
10rm 2hc 2⌂ (1fb) ✱ B&bfr£8.50 Bdifr£12.50 Wfr£59.50 M̸ LDO6pm
Lic ▥ CTV 10P

GH Bay House Hotel 8 Chine Av, off Keats Green ☎(0983) 863180 Plan **4** *C2*
Closed Xmas
Overlooks the chine with lovely sea views.
20rm 4hc 13→ 3⌂ (3fb) CTV in 5 bedrooms B&b£11–£16 Bdi£15–£17.50 W£77–£112 M̸ LDO6.30pm
Lic ▥ CTV 25P 2⌂ ♿
Credit card [3] Ⓥ

GH *Berry Brow Hotel* Popham Rd ☎(0983) 862825 Plan **5** *C1*
May–Nov
Country house atmosphere in quiet residential area, with pleasant secluded gardens.
21hc (4fb)
Lic ▥ CTV 10P

GH Culham Private Hotel 31 Landguard Manor Rd ☎(0983) 862880 Plan **7** *A3*
Apr–Oct
Small red brick private house built in 1900, in residential area with heated swimming pool.
10rm 3hc 1→ 6⌂ B&b£9–£10 Bdi£12–£13 W£63–£70 M̸ LDO4pm
▥ CTV 8P nc9yrs ≈(heated)

GH *Curraghmore Hotel* Hope Rd ☎(0983) 862605 Plan **8** *C3*
Etr–Oct
Well appointed, in delightful garden facing south, and within a short walk of the beach and town centre.
24hc 10→ 5⌂ (8fb) LDO5pm
Lic CTV 20P ⌂ sea
Ⓥ

GH Edgecliffe Hotel Clarence Gdns ☎(0983) 866199 Plan **9** *B4*
Jan–Nov
A warm friendly atmosphere exists in this converted private house situated in quiet residential area.
11rm 7hc 1→ 3⌂ (3fb) ✱ B&b£9.20–£11.50 Bdi£13–£15.20 W£82.80–£90.85 Ł LDO6.30pm
Lic ▥ CTV ⚑ ⌂
Credit cards [1] [2] [3] Ⓥ

Shanklin

GH Fawley Hotel 12 Hope Rd ☎(0983) 862190 Plan **10** *B3*
May–Oct
A small tastefully appointed hotel with a friendly atmosphere.
13hc (3fb) ★ B&b£9.50–£10.50 Bdi£11.50–£13.50 W£75–£85 ⱡ LDO4.30pm
Lic CTV 12P nc5yrs

GH Leslie House Hotel 10 Hope Rd ☎(0983) 862798 Plan **12** *B3*
Large, detached house, set in residential area near esplanade and seafront.
10hc (4fb) B&b£11.50–£13.50 Bdi£14.50–£16.50 W£74–£95 ⱡ LDO6pm
Lic ▥ CTV 8P

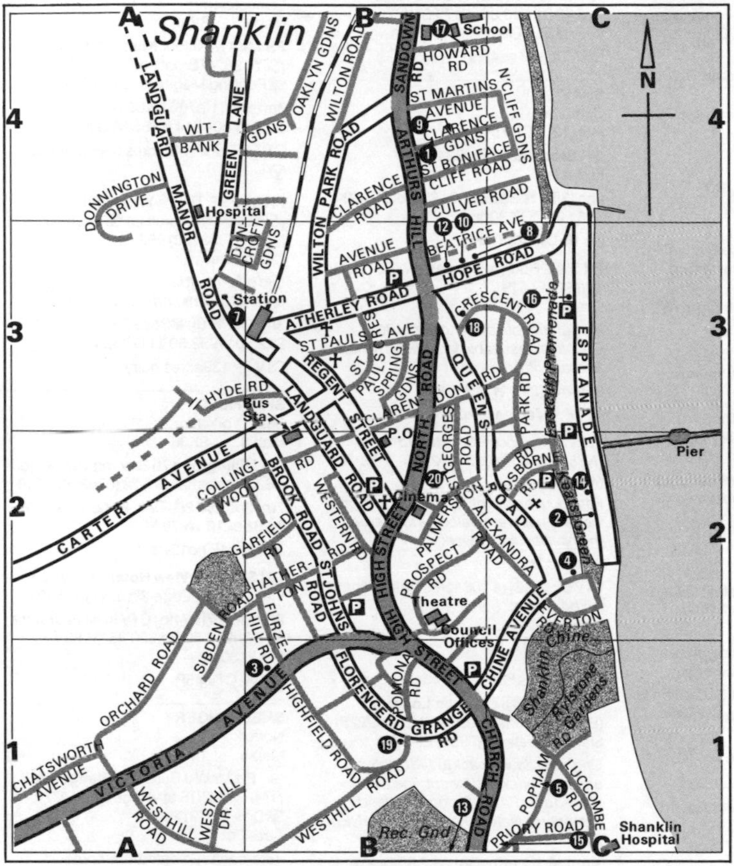

Shanklin

1 Afton Hotel
2 Aqua Hotel
3 Avenue Hotel
4 Bay House Hotel
5 Berry Brow Hotel
7 Culham Private Hotel
8 Curraghmore Hotel
9 Edgecliffe Hotel
10 Fawley Hotel
12 Leslie House Hotel
13 Luccombe Chine House Country Hotel
14 Meyrick Cliffs
15 Monteagle Hotel
16 Ocean View Hotel
17 Overstrand Private Hotel
18 Perran Lodge
19 Soraba Private Hotel
20 Swiss Cottage Hotel

GH *Luccombe Chine House Country Hotel* ☎(0983) 862037
Plan **13** *B1*
Secluded old manor house in 10acres, overlooking sea.
6➡ ⋔ CTV in all bedrooms ✱ Ⓡ
LDO9pm
Lic Ⅲ 12P nc18yrs sea

⊢⊣**GH Meyrick Cliffs** The Esplanade ☎(0983) 862691 Plan **14** *C2*
May–Oct
Nicely appointed seafront house with Victorian atmosphere.
20rm 19hc 1➡ 1⋔ (7fb) ✱ B&b£8 Bdi£12 W£80 Ⱡ LDO6.30pm
Lic CTV 5P nc5yrs

GH Monteagle Hotel Priory Rd ☎(0983) 862854 Plan **15** *C1*
Etr–Oct
Large hotel with many facilities including snooker table and outdoor swimming pool.
40rm 13hc 18➡ 9⋔ (4fb) ✱ B&b£10–£14 Bdi£12–£17 W£76–£130 Ⱡ
LDO8pm
Lic Ⅲ CTV 30P nc5yrs ⛰(heated) billiards

GH *Ocean View Hotel* 38 The Esplanade ☎(0983) 862602 Plan **16** *C3*
Feb–Nov
Seafront hotel with excellent sun lounge and attractive wood panelled dining room.
36hc 4➡ 9⋔ (12fb)
Lic CTV 25P ⌂ sea

GH Overstrand Private Hotel Howard Rd ☎(0983) 862100 Plan **17** *B4*
Et–Oct rs Nov–Mar
Stone-built house in attractive gardens. Rooms have character and comfort.
15hc 4➡ 7⋔ (8fb) CTV in 4 bedrooms ✱ Ⓡ B&b£10–£15 Bdi£14–£19 W£89–£114 Ⱡ LDO6.30pm
Lic Ⅲ CTV 20P ⌂ ⚲(grass)
Credit card 1 Ⓥ

GH Perran Lodge 2 Crescent Rd ☎(0983) 862816 Plan **18** *B3*
Etr–Oct
Red-brick two-storey south-facing house with lawn and verandah.
20rm 11hc 5➡ 4⋔ (6fb) ✻B&b£9–£11.35 Bdi£11.50–£13.85 W£46.75–£66.50 M LDO6pm
Lic CTV 10P nc3yrs

GH Soraba Private Hotel Paddock Rd ☎(0983) 862367 Plan **19** *B1*
Near the famous chine and within 10 minutes walk of beach and shops. Home comfort and friendly atmosphere.
6hc (4fb) ✱ B&b£8.20 Bdi£12.50 W£70–£80 Ⱡ LDO3pm
Lic Ⅲ CTV 3P ⌂

GH Swiss Cottage Hotel 10 St Georges Rd ☎(0983) 862333 Plan **20** *B2*
Closed 15 Dec–10 Jan
Attractive compact house with friendly proprietors.
13rm 7hc 3⋔ (2fb) ✱ B&b£10.35–£13.80 Bdi£13.80–£17.25 W£75.90–£87.92 Ⱡ LDO6pm
Lic CTV 10P nc4yrs

SHAP
Cumbria
Map **12** NY51

GH Brookfield ☎(09316) 397
Feb–Dec
6hc (3fb) ✱ B&b£8.50–£9 Bdi£15.50–£16.50 LDO7.30pm
Lic Ⅲ CTV 25P 6⌂

FH E & S Hodgson **Green** *(NY551121)* ☎(09316) 619
Etr–Sep
Large farmhouse dating from 1705. Countryside suitable for walking holidays. Set back off A6
3rm 2hc (2fb) ✱ ✻B&b£7
TV 4P 167acres mixed

FH S J Thompson ***Southfield*** *(NY561184)* ☎(09316) 282
Mar–Oct
Farmhouse set in pleasant area with good views. Guests are welcome to interest themselves in farm work.
2rm 1hc ✱
CTV 3P nc12yrs 108acres beef dairy mixed sheep

SHAWBURY
Shropshire
Map **7** SJ52

⊢⊣**FH** Mrs S J Clarkson **Longley** (Braggs Country Suppers) *(SJ602228)* Stanton Heath ☎(0939) 250289
Originally dating back to 1710, this attractive brick and tile cottage was named after Paul C Bragg, the world authority on Natural Farming. 2¼m NE off A53.
3rm 1➡ 1⋔ (1fb) B&bfr£7.50 Bdifr£11 W£48 M
Ⅲ CTV 6P 15acres arable beef sheep mixed
Ⓥ

⊢⊣**FH** G C Evans **New** *(SJ586215)* Muckleton ☎(0939) 250358
Modern farmhouse with large, newly furnished and extremely comfortable rooms. 2m NE of Shawbury off A53 on unclass rd.
4rm 3hc 1⋔ (1fb) ✱ Ⓡ B&b£7.50–£8.50 Bdi£12–£13 Wfr£75 Ⱡ
Ⅲ CTV 10P nc2yrs 70acres arable beef

⊢⊣**FH** Mrs M R Griffiths **Sowbath** *(SJ576230)* ☎(0939) 250417
Large Victorian farmhouse on A53, 1½m north of Shawbury and midway between Shrewsbury and Market Drayton.
2hc (1fb) B&b£6–£7 W£40 M
Ⅲ CTV 6P ⤴ 200acres arable dairy mixed
Ⓥ

SHEARSBY
Leicestershire
Map **4** SP69

FH Mr A M Knight **Knaptoft House** *(SP619894)* Bruntingthorpe Rd, Knaptoft ☎Peatling Magna (053758) 388
3rm 1hc (1fb) Ⓡ B&b£9–£9.50 Bdi£13.50–£14 W£55 M LDO2pm
CTV 6P ⌂ ⤴ 145acres sheep mixed
Ⓥ

FH Mrs S E Timms **Wheathill** *(SP622911)* Church Ln ☎Peatling Magna (053758) 663
Closed Dec
Old brick-built farmhouse retaining original beams and inglenook fireplaces.
3rm 2hc ✱ Ⓡ ✻B&b£7.50–£8 Bdi£12–£12.50 W£52.50 Ⱡ LDO5pm
CTV 3P 133acres dairy

SHEFFIELD
South Yorkshire
Map **8** SK38

GH Millingtons 70 Broomgrove Rd (off A625 Eccleshall Rd) ☎(0742) 669549
7rm 3hc 2➡ 2⋔ TV in all bedrooms ✱ Ⓡ B&b£10 W£70 M
Ⅲ CTV 4P nc12yrs

GH Sharrow View Hotel 13 Sharrow View, Nether Edge ☎(0742) 51542
26rm 4➡ 7⋔ (4fb) CTV in all bedrooms Ⓡ B&b£15.50 Bdi£20.45 W£85 Ⱡ LDO9.30pm
Lic Ⅲ CTV 45P

SHELFANGER
Norfolk
Map **5** TM18

⊢⊣**FH** Mr W J Butler **Shelfanger Hall** *(TM102832)* (S of village off B1077) ☎Diss (0379) 2094
Apr–Oct
16th-century moated farmhouse, in peaceful setting of 2 acres of wooded grounds. Set back 1 mile from the road, S of village off B1077.
3hc (1fb) ✱ B&b£7.50–£8 W£49 M
Ⅲ CTV 10P nc5yrs 450acres dairy

SHEPTON MALLET
Somerset
Map **3** ST64

INN Kings Arms Leg Sq ☎(0749) 3781
rs Xmas eve Closed Xmas day
3hc Ⓡ B&b£11–£13.50 W£69.30–£85.05 M Bar lunch £1.85–£6 D9.30pm £1.85–£6
Ⅲ CTV P nc10yrs
Ⓥ

INN Wine Vaults & Shambles Restaurant ☎(0749) 2436
3hc ✱ Ⓡ B&b£9 Bdi£12.50 Lfr£1.80 D9.30pm fr£4

SHERBOURNE
Warwickshire
Map **4** SP26
See Warwick

SHERFIELD ON LODDON
Hampshire
Map **4** SU65
GH Wessex House Hotel
☎Basingstoke (0256) 882243
Closed 10 days Xmas
Attractive, smart well-equipped hotel in neat grounds.
8➡ (2fb) CTV in all bedrooms ✱ Ⓡ B&b£27–£35 LDO9.30pm
Lic CTV 12P nc3yrs

SHERIFF HUTTON
North Yorkshire
Map **8** SE66
GH Rangers House Sheriff Hutton Park ☎(03477) 397
Interesting and unusual building with minstrel's gallery and ornate marble fireplace, as well as attractive garden.
6rm 5hc 1➡ (1fb) ✱ B&b£14.50–£16 Bdi£20–£26.50 W£91.35–£100.80 M LDO10.30pm

Shepton Mallet — Shipston-on-Stour

Lic CTV 50P
Ⓥ

SHERINGHAM
Norfolk
Map **9** TG14
GH Beacon Hotel Nelson Rd ☎(0263) 822019
Apr–Oct rs Nov–Mar
8hc ✱ Ⓡ B&b£12 Bdi£12.50–£15 W£95 L LDO7pm
Lic CTV 7P nc12yrs
Credit cards 1 3 Ⓥ

GH Beeston Hills Lodge 64 Cliff Rd ☎(0263) 822615
Etr–Oct
7hc 2➡ ✱ Ⓡ B&bfr£8 Bdifr£11 W£75 L LDO6.30pm
CTV 10P nc8yrs

GH *Camberley House Hotel* 62 Cliff Rd ☎(0263) 823101
May–Oct
9hc (3fb) Ⓡ LDO7pm
Lic CTV 10P sea
See advertisement on page 316

GH *Melrose Hotel* 9 Holway Rd ☎(0263) 823299
Family owned and run hotel near town centre.
10hc (1fb) LDO6pm
TV 10P nc8yrs
Ⓥ

SHETLAND
Map **16**
See Lerwick

SHIPSTON-ON-STOUR
Warwickshire
Map **4** SP24
FH Mr J C Soar ***Portobello*** *(SP234399)* ☎(0608) 61618
1½m W at B4035/A429 junction.
2hc ✱ Ⓡ LDO4pm
TV 12P 2 6acres mixed

INN Bell Sheep St ☎(0608) 61443
8rm 5hc 2➡ Ⓡ B&bfr£15.53 Bdifr£21.78 Wfr£95 M L£1.95–£6.25&alc D9.45pm £2.75–£6.25&alc
CTV 24P
Credit cards 1 2 3 4 5

INN White Bear High St (Guestaccom) ☎(0608) 61558
Friendly town centre inn with comfortable attractive bedrooms.
9rm 2➡ 1 Ⓡ B&b£12 Bdi£17–£23 W£75 M L£8.50alc D9.30pm £10.50alc
CTV 20P
Credit cards 1 2 3 5

SHIRWELL
Devon
Map **2** SS53
⊢⊣ **FH** Mrs G Huxtable **Woolcott** *(SS600388)* ☎(027182) 216
Mar–Nov
Situated in a quiet picturesque area on the foothills of Exmoor. The bedrooms overlook the unspoilt Devon countryside 1½m NE off A39.
3rm (2fb) B&bfr£5.25 Bdifr£8 Wfr£56 M LDO4pm
CTV 3P 85acres beef sheep

SHOREHAM-BY-SEA
West Sussex
Map **4** TQ20
GH Pende-Shore Hotel 416 Upper Shoreham Rd ☎(07917) 2905 (due to change to 452905)
Closed 24 Dec–1 Jan
Very smart private hotel with added personal touches. There is a bistro style restaurant and a bar.
14hc 1 (2fb) TV in 6 bedrooms ® B&b£15.64–£17.60 Bdi£22.40–£24.40 W£109.48–£123.20 M LDO7pm
Lic CTV 8P

SHOTTLE
Derbyshire
Map **8** SK34
GH Shottle Hall Farm ☎ Cowers Lane (077389) 276
Closed Xmas, New Year & last 2 wks Jul
9hc (3fb) ® B&B£12.80–£14 Bdi£18.75–£20 W£89 M LDO8pm
Lic CTV 30P
Ⓥ

SHREWSBURY
Shropshire
Map **7** SJ41
GH Cannock House Private Hotel 182 Abbey Foregate ☎ (0743) 56043
6hc (1fb) B&Bfr£8.50
CTV 5P nc5yrs

SIDMOUTH
Devon
Map **3** SY18
GH Canterbury Salcombe Rd ☎(03955) 3373
Mar–Nov
7rm 2hc 1 4 (3fb) ® B&b£9.50–£13 Bdi£13–£16.50 Wfr£94.30 L LDO5pm
CTV 6P

GH Mount Pleasant Private Hotel Salcombe Rd ☎(03955) 4694
Mar–Oct
15rm 2hc 5 8 (2fb) ® B&b£13.50–£15 Bdi£18–£20 W£95–£100 M LDO7.30pm
Lic CTV 20P

GH *Ryton House* 52–54 Winslade Rd ☎(03955) 3981
Closed Nov
Victorian converted semis in residential road. Well situated for town centre and seafront.
9hc (4fb) LDO6pm
CTV 8P

SITTINGBOURNE
Kent
Map **5** TQ96
GH Hillcroft Boarding House 94 London Rd ☎(0795) 71501
Closed 2–16 Jan
Modern well equipped bedrooms and friendly personal service in very comfortable surroundings.
12rm 6hc (2fb) CTV in all bedrooms ® B&b£10.35–£13.80 W£62.45–£86.60 M LDO8pm
CTV 20P (heated)
Credit cards 1 3

SKEGNESS
Lincolnshire
Map **9** TF56
GH Chatsworth Hotel North Pde ☎(0754) 4177
Jun–Sep rs Mar–May & Oct

22rm 9hc 8➡ 5⋒ (4fb) Ⓡ B&bfr£11.50 Bdifr£15.50 Wfr£93 Ⱡ LDO7.30pm
Lic 🎹 CTV 8P 4🚗

GH Crawford Hotel South Pde ☎(0754) 4215
Etr–Oct & Xmas rs Jan–Mar
Small, comfortable, very well equipped hotel with good modern facilities.
20rm 8hc 10➡ 2⋒ (8fb) B&b£12–£14 Bdi£16–£20 W£109.25–£115.50 Ⱡ LDO5pm
Lic lift 🎹 CTV 8P ⛆(heated)
Ⓥ

SKIPTON
North Yorkshire
Map **7** SD95

GH Craven House 56 Keighley Rd ☎(0756) 4657
8hc (2fb) Ⓡ B&bfr£8.50 Bdifr£13.50 W£94.50 Ⱡ
🎹 CTV 2P
Credit card 2

GH *Fairleigh* 24 Belle Vue Ter, Broughton Rd ☎ (0756) 4153
5hc (2fb) ✯
🎹 CTV 🅿

GH Highfield Hotel 58 Keighley Rd ☎ (0756) 3182
Closed Xmas & New Year
10rm 3➡ Ⓡ B&b £10.25–£11 Bdi£16.50–£17.25 W£104–£119.50 Ⱡ LDO7pm
Lic CTV
Ⓥ

GH Unicorn Hotel Keighley Rd ☎ (0756) 4146
Closed Xmas & New Year
Town centre hotel with good bedrooms.
9➡ (5fb) CTV in all bedrooms ✯ Ⓡ B&b£12–£15 W£90 M
🎹 CTV 🅿
Credit card 3

INN Red Lion Hotel High St ☎(0756) 60718
Cosy well furnished Inn (the oldest building in Skipton).
4rm 2hc 2➡ CTV in 4 bedrooms Ⓡ B&b£9–£10.50 Bar lunch £1.50–£5 LDO7.30pm
🎹 TV 6P
Ⓥ

SKIPTON-ON-SWALE
North Yorkshire
Map **8** SE37

GH Skipton Hall ☎Thirsk (0845) 567457
Stone-built Georgian farmhouse with comfortable spacious rooms of character; standing in own grounds by the village centre.
7hc Ⓡ B&b£9 Bdi£14 W£60 M S% LDO7.30pm
CTV 12P

SKYE, ISLE OF
Highland *Inverness-shire*
Map **13** NG
Refer to location atlas for details of places with AA-listed establishments.

SLAIDBURN
Lancashire
Map **7** SD75

FH Mrs P M Holt **Parrock Head** *(SD697527)* Woodhouse Ln ☎(02006) 614
Closed 18–30 Dec
Modernised farmhouse dating back to 1677, set in the Bowland Fells.
3➡ (A 7➡) (3fb) CTV in all bedrooms Ⓡ B&b£15–£16 Bdi£21–£22 W£105 M LDO8pm
Lic 🎹 10P 200acres beef sheep mixed
Ⓥ

SLEAFORD
Lincolnshire
Map **8** TF04

GH The Mallards 6 Eastgate ☎(0529) 303062
11hc 2⋒ CTV in 3 bedrooms Ⓡ
✱B&b£13 Bdi£18 LDO8.45pm
Lic 🎹 CTV
Credit cards 1 2 3 5

SLOUGH
Berkshire
Map **4** SU97

GH *Francis House Hotel* 21 London Rd, Langley ☎(0753) 22286
Closed Xmas wk
Comfortable modern hotel, well run by friendly proprietors.
17hc ✯ LDO4.30pm
Lic 🎹 CTV 16P nc10yrs

SMEATON, GREAT
North Yorkshire
Map **8** NZ30

FH Mrs N Hall **Smeaton East** *(NZ349044)* ☎(060981) 336
May–Oct rs Nov–Apr
A 17th-century working farm on the edge of the village. Spacious rooms of period character; clean, well-furnished and comfortable. Situated in rural surroundings.
3hc ✯ B&b£8.50–£10 Bdi£14.50–£16 W£60 M LDO10am
🎹 CTV 4P nc7yrs 120acres dairy mixed
Ⓥ

SNAPE
Suffolk
Map **5** TM35

INN *Crown* ☎(072888) 324
4hc CTV in all bedrooms D8.30pm
🎹 100P nc14yrs

SOMERTON
Somerset
Map **3** ST42

GH Church Farm School Ln, Compton Dundon ☎(0458) 72927
Mar–Oct
4rm 3hc (A 2rm 1➡ 1⋒) (1fb) CTV in 2 bedrooms TV in 1 bedroom Ⓡ
✱B&b£9.50–£11.50 Bdi£16.50–£18.50 W£57–£69 M LDO5pm
Lic CTV 6P 2🚗 nc4yrs
Ⓥ

Sopworth — Southampton

SOPWORTH
Wiltshire
Map **3** ST88

FH Mr D M Barker **Manor** *(ST826865)* ☎Didmarton (045423) 676
Apr–Oct

3rm (1fb) B&b£7.50–£8 W£45 M

TV 4P 300acres arable beef sheep mixed

SOUTHAMPTON
Hampshire
Map **4** SU41
See plan

GH Banister House Hotel 11 Brighton Rd, off Banister Rd ☎(0703) 21279 (due to change to 221279) Plan **1** *B4*
Closed Xmas

Terraced house in city centre with well decorated, comfortably furnished accommodation.

20rm 19hc 1 (4fb) CTV in all bedrooms B&b£12.25–£13.50 Bdi£16.50–£17.75 W£85.75–£94.50 M LDO8.15pm

Lic CTV 15P

Credit cards 1 3 V

GH Claremont 33 The Polygon ☎(0703) 23112 (due to change to 223112) Plan **3** *B3*

Small, homely house within walking distance of city centre.

14rm 11hc 3 (5fb) B&b£7.50–£9 W£42–£45 M

CTV 10P

GH Cliffden 43 The Polygon ☎(0703) 24003 (due to change to 224003) Plan **4** *B3*

Well-maintained guesthouse with relaxed informal atmosphere.

8hc (2fb) B&b£6.50–£7.50 Bdi£9.50–£10.50 W£42–£49 M LDO10am

CTV 3P

GH Eaton Court Hotel 32 Hill Ln ☎(0703) 23081 (due to change to 223081) Plan **5** *A3*
Closed 1 wk Xmas

Modest yet homely house with good range of evening meals.

12rm 10hc 2 (2fb) B&b£10.75–£12.75 LDO7pm

Lic CTV 12P

Credit cards 1 3

GH *Elizabeth House Hotel* 43/44 The Avenue ☎(0703) 24327 (due to change to 224327) Plan **6** *B5*
rs wknds in winter

Well maintained house offering modern facilities.

25hc 5 9 (3fb) CTV in 12 bedrooms

Lic CTV 22P

GH Hunters Lodge Hotel 25 Landguard Rd, Shirley ☎(0703) 27919 (due to change to 227919) Plan **7** *A4*
Closed Xmas

Quietly situated, this proprietor run hotel combines modern and traditional standards.

17hc 2 2 (1fb) CTV in 2 bedrooms B&b£11.50 Bdi£16.10 W£80 M LDO6.30pm

Lic CTV 15P 4

Credit card 3

GH Linden 51 The Polygon ☎(0703) 25653 (due to change to 225653) Plan **8** *A3*

Two terraced houses set in the heart of the city centre. Well decorated and comfortably furnished.

12hc (4fb) B&b£7.50–£8.50

CTV 7P

GH Lodge 1 Winn Rd, The Avenue ☎(0703) 557537 Plan **9** *B5*

Comfortable well managed accommodation with spacious lounge amenities.

13rm 11hc 2 (2fb) CTV in 2 bedrooms TV in 1 bedroom Ⓡ B&b£12 Bdi£17 LDO9pm

Lic CTV 10P

Credit cards 1 3

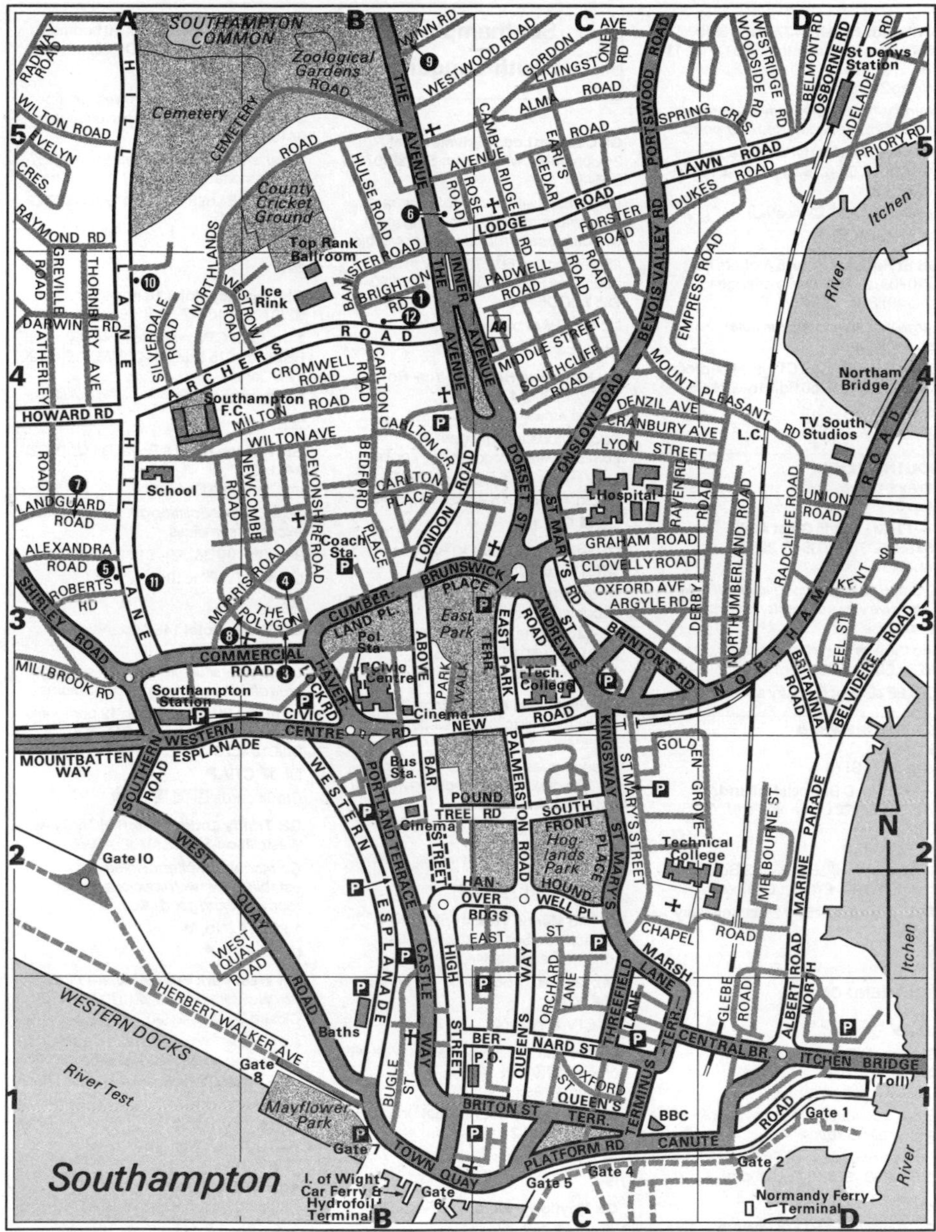

Southampton

1 Banister House Hotel
3 Claremont
4 Cliffden
5 Eaton Court Hotel
6 Elizabeth House Hotel
7 Hunters Lodge Hotel
8 Linden
9 Lodge
10 Madison
11 Rosida Hotel
12 St Regulus Hotel

GH Madison 137 Hill Ln ☎ (0703) 333374
Plan **10** *A4*
Homely house in residential area.
8hc (3fb) TV in all bedrooms ★ Ⓡ
B&b£9
CTV 6P

GH Rosida Hotel 25–27 Hill Ln ☎(0703) 28501 (due to change to 228501) Plan **11** *A3*
Closed 24 Dec–1 Jan
Friendly, hospitable family run hotel with well equipped modernised bedrooms.
36hc 4→ 5⋔ (7fb) CTV in 9 bedrooms Ⓡ B&b£15.50–£16.50 W£99–£104 Ⅿ LDO7.30pm
Lic 🅼 CTV 30P ≈(heated)
Credit cards 1 3

GH St Regulus Hotel 5 Archers Rd ☎(0703) 24243 (due to change to 224243) Plan **12** *B4*
Large Victorian hotel set in quiet residential area.
27rm 24hc 3⋔ (1fb) CTV in all bedrooms B&b£13.25–£18.50 Bdi£16–£21.25 LDO7.30pm
Lic 🅼 CTV 30P 9🚗

SOUTH BRENT
Devon
Map **3** SX66
⊢⊣**FH** M E Slade **Great Aish** *(SX689603)* ☎(03647) 2238
Jan–Nov
Situated near Dartmoor National Park. Extensive views of countryside from farmhouse.
5hc (3fb) 🏃 B&bfr£6.50 Bdifr£9.50 W£66.50 Ł LDO5.30pm
CTV 6P ⌂ 60acres dairy sheep mixed

SOUTH BREWHAM
Somerset
Map **3** ST73
⊢⊣**FH** Mrs D Dabinett **Holland** *(ST732357)* ☎Upton Noble (074985) 263
Apr–mid Sep
4rm 3hc (1fb) Ⓡ B&b£8–£9 Bdi£13–£14.50 W£90–£100 Ł LDOnoon
🅼 CTV 8P 2🚗 nc5yrs 250acres dairy sheep
ⓥ

SOUTHEND-ON-SEA
Essex
Map **5** TQ88

GH Argyle Hotel 12 Clifftown Pde ☎(0702) 339483
Closed 2 wks Xmas
Small, comfortable house overlooking sea and public gardens.
11hc (4fb) B&b£9–£9.50 Bdi£12.50–£13 W£63–£66.50 Ł LDO6pm
Lic 🅼 CTV Ᵽ nc5yrs

GH *Camelia Hotel* 178 Eastern Esplanade, Thorpe Bay ☎(0702) 587917
Caring proprietors and many extra facilities make this private hotel rather special.
12hc 1→⋔ 🏃
Lic 🅼 CTV sea

GH Cobham Lodge Private Hotel 2 Cobham Rd, Westcliff-on-Sea ☎(0702) 346438
Larger hotel with much to offer, attractive modern bedrooms, smart dining room, two lounges and a full size snooker table.
28rm 17hc 2→ 6⋔ (7fb) CTV in all bedrooms B&b£12.50 Bdi£18 W£90–£95 Ł LDO6.30pm
Lic 🅼 CTV ⌂ billiards
Credit cards 1 3

GH Ferndown Hotel 136 York Rd ☎(0702) 68614
Closed Xmas
Accommodation is modern and comfortable and food is home cooked.
13hc (1fb) TV in 2 bedrooms 🏃 Ⓡ B&bfr£10 Bdifr£15 Wfr£65 Ⅿ LDO4pm
Lic 🅼 CTV 10P

GH Gladstone Hotel 40 Hartington Rd ☎(0702) 62776
A comfortable hotel providing modern accommodation.
7hc (4fb) 🏃 B&b£9–£9.50 Bdi£12–£13 W£81–£84.50 Ł LDO8.30pm
Lic 🅼 CTV Ᵽ nc3yrs

GH Maple Leaf Private Hotel 9–11 Trinity Av, Westcliff-on-Sea ☎(0702) 346904
Friendly guesthouse offering compact, old fashioned accommodation with well equipped bedrooms.
16hc (2fb) 🏃 Ⓡ B&b£12 Bdi£17 LDO8.30pm
Lic 🅼 CTV 4P
Credit cards 1 2 3 5

⊢⊣**GH Marine View** 4 Trinity Av, Westcliff-on-Sea ☎(0702) 44104 (due to change to 344104)
6hc (2fb) 🏃 Ⓡ B&b£7.50–£8 W£49–£52.50 Ⅿ
🅼 CTV Ᵽ nc4yrs

GH Mayfair 52 Crowstone Av, Westcliff-on-Sea ☎(0702) 340693
Closed Xmas
6hc (1fb) 🏃 *B&b£7.50–£8 Bdi£10.50–£11 W£58–£62 Ł LDO4pm
🅼 CTV 4P nc5yrs
ⓥ

GH Mayflower Hotel 5–6 Royal Ter ☎(0702) 340489
Listed Regency terraced house with well equipped bedrooms.
22rm 21hc (3fb) CTV in 13 bedrooms B&bfr£9.20
🅼 CTV Ᵽ

GH *Norfolk Hotel* 21 The Leas, Westcliff-on-Sea ☎(0702) 351069
Mainly commercial sea front hotel.
17hc 2→ 1⋔ (6fb) CTV in 10 bedrooms TV in 3 bedrooms Ⓡ LDO7.30pm
Lic 🅼 CTV 10P sea

GH Pavilion 1 Trinity Av, Westcliff-on-Sea ☎(0702) 41007 (due to change to 341007)
Quiet terraced house offering homely accommodation.
8hc (1fb) B&b£8.50 Bdi£11.50 W£70 Ł LDOnoon
🅼 CTV Ᵽ
ⓥ

GH Regency Hotel 18 Royal Ter ☎(0702) 340747
11hc (5fb) CTV in all bedrooms Ⓡ B&b£13–£15 Bdi£18–£20 W£115–£120 Ł LDOam
Lic 🅼 CTV 1P 1🚗
ⓥ

GH Terrace Hotel 8 Royal Ter ☎(0702) 348143
mid Jan–mid Dec
Small, homely, clifftop guesthouse with excellent sea views.
9hc (3fb) Ⓡ B&b£9–£10
Lic 🅼 CTV Ᵽ nc10yrs
ⓥ

GH Tower Hotel 146 Alexandra Rd ☎(0702) 348635
Large hotel situated in a quiet residential area offering well equipped bedrooms.
13rm 3hc 2⋔ (2fb) CTV in 12 bedrooms TV in 1 bedroom Ⓡ B&b£11–£20 Bdi£16–£25 W£112–£175 Ł LDO10pm
Lic 🅼 CTV Ᵽ
Credit cards 1 2 3 5 ⓥ

GH *Trinity Lodge Hotel* 6–8 Trinity Av, Westcliff-on-Sea ☎(0702) 46066
Comfortable, well appointed establishment with spacious public rooms offering good value.
15hc 3⋔ (1fb) 🏃
Lic 🅼 CTV Ᵽ

GH West Park Private Hotel 11 Park Rd, Westcliff-on-Sea ☎(0702) 330729
Closed 24 Dec–2 Jan
Larger hotel with many modern bedroom facilities and welcoming service.
21hc 12→ 4⋔ CTV in all bedrooms Ⓡ B&b£18.50 Bdi£24.75 LDO6.30pm
Lic 🅼 CTV 18P ⌂
Credit cards 1 2 3 ⓥ

SOUTH LAGGAN
Highland *Inverness-shire*
Map **14** NN29
⊢⊣**GH Forest Lodge** ☎Invergarry (08093) 219
Feb–Nov
Modern bungalow standing in own ground on edge of wooded area.
7hc (2fb) Ⓡ B&b£7 Bdi£12 W£78.75 Ł LDO7pm
🅼 CTV 9P

SOUTH LUFFENHAM
Leicestershire
Map **4** SK90

INN Boot & Shoe ☎Stamford (0780) 720177

4hc B&b£9–£10 Bdi£14–£15 W£56–£60 M LDO10.30pm

20P

SOUTHMOOR
Oxfordshire
Map **4** SU39

FH Mrs A J Crowther **Fallowfields** *(SU393979)* Fallow Field ☎Longworth (0865) 820416
mid Apr–Sep rs Wed

On W side of village S of A420.

4rm 3hc 1 (1fb) Ⓡ B&b£12–£16 Bdi£21–£25 Wfr£84 M LDO6.30pm

Lic CTV 15P nc10yrs (heated) 12acres sheep

SOUTH PETHERTON
Somerset
Map **3** ST41

FH Mrs M E H Vaux **Rydon** *(ST427173)* Compton Durville ☎(0460) 40468
Closed Xmas–New Year rs Nov–Mar

3hc (1fb) Ⓡ B&b£9 Bdi£13 W£88 L LDO4.30pm

CTV 5P 85acres pig horticulture

Ⓥ

South Luffenham — Southport

SOUTHPORT
Merseyside
Map **7** SD31
See plan

GH Crimond Hotel 28 Knowsley Rd (Guestaccom) ☎(0704) 36456 Plan **3** *D3*

12rm 6hc 4 (3fb) CTV in all bedrooms Ⓡ B&b£11–£14 Bdi£17–£20 LDO7pm

Lic CTV 15P (heated) sauna bath

Credit cards 1 3

GH Fairway Private Hotel 106 Leyland Rd ☎(0704) 42069 Plan **4** *E3*
Mar–Oct

9rm 7hc 2 (4fb) Ⓡ B&b£8–£9 Bdi£11–£12 W£56–£64 M LDO5pm

Lic CTV 20P

GH *Fernley Private Hotel* 69 The Promenade ☎(0704) 35610 Plan **5** *D3*

22hc (4fb)

Lic CTV 16P lake sea

GH *Franklyn Hotel* 65 The Promenade ☎(0704) 40290 Plan **6** *D4*

28hc (6fb)

CTV 20P sea

GH Fulwood Private Hotel 82 Leyland Rd ☎(0704) 30993 Plan **7** *D3*

Large detached family house situated in a quiet side road.

11hc (1fb) B&bfr£9.50 Bdifr£13 Wfr£86 L LDOnoon

Lic CTV 9P

GH Garden Hotel 19 Latham Rd ☎(0704) 30244 Plan **8** *E3*

Friendly guesthouse in quiet side road.

10hc CTV in 7 bedrooms TV in 3 bedrooms Ⓡ B&b£10–£11 Bdi£13.50–£14.50 W£65–£72 M LDO5pm

Lic CTV

See advertisement on page 322

GH *Glenwood Private Hotel* 98–102 King St ☎(0704) 35068 Plan **9** *B2*

16hc (3fb)

Lic CTV 6P nc5yrs

See advertisement on page 323

GH *Golf Links Hotel* 85 The Promenade ☎(0704) 30405 Plan **10** *D4*

11hc (3fb)

Lic CTV 20P nc7yrs

GH *Hollies Hotel* 7 Mornington Rd ☎(0704) 30054 Plan **11** *C2*

15hc 3 4 (4fb) TV available in 6 bedrooms LDOnoon

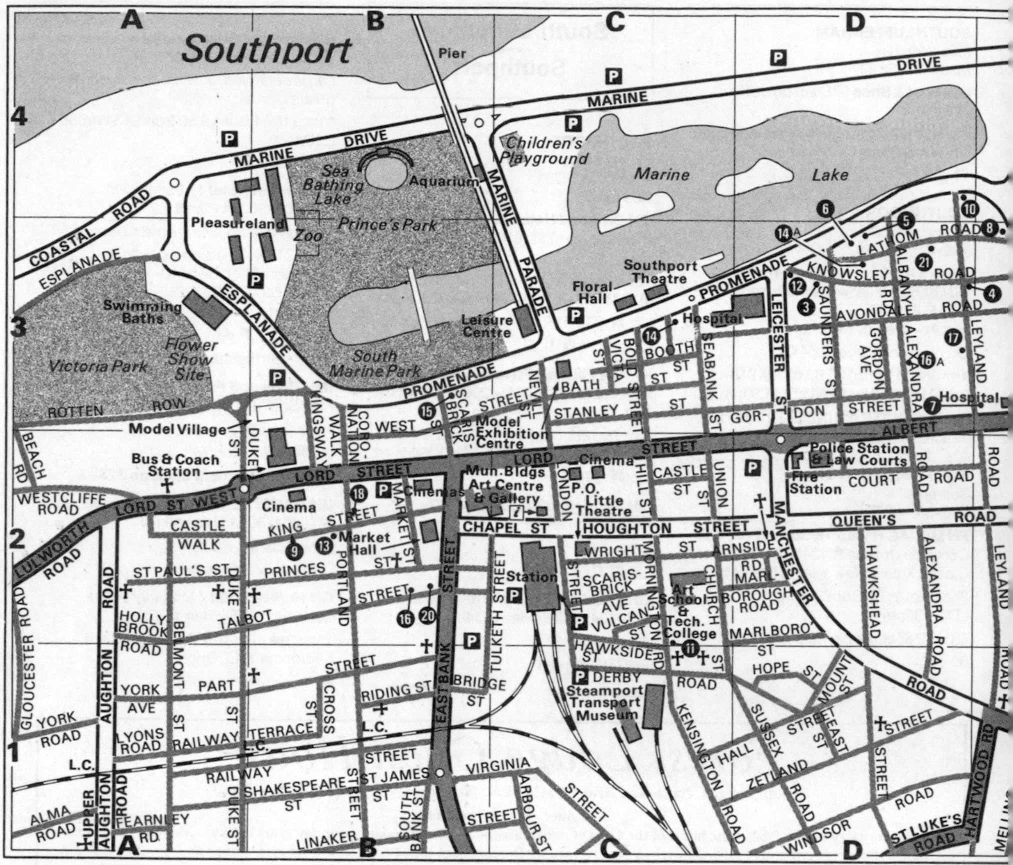

CTV 15P
See advertisement on page 324

GH Knowsley Private Hotel Promenade, 2 Knowsley Rd ☎ (0704) 30190 Plan **12** *D3*
Closed Oct
15hc (4fb) B&b£9–£9.50 Bdi£11.50–£12.50 W£60–£63.50 Ⓜ LDO3pm
Lic CTV 15P

GH Newholme 51 King St ☎ (0704) 30425 Plan **13** *B2*
Closed Xmas
6hc (3fb) Ⓡ B&b£7.50–£8 Bdi£10–£11 W£52.50–£55 Ⓜ LDOnoon
CTV 2P nc3yrs
Ⓥ

GH *Ocean Bank* 16 Bank Sq, Central Promenade ☎ (0704) 30637 Plan **14** *C3*
9hc (3fb) LDO4pm
CTV 2P nc16yrs

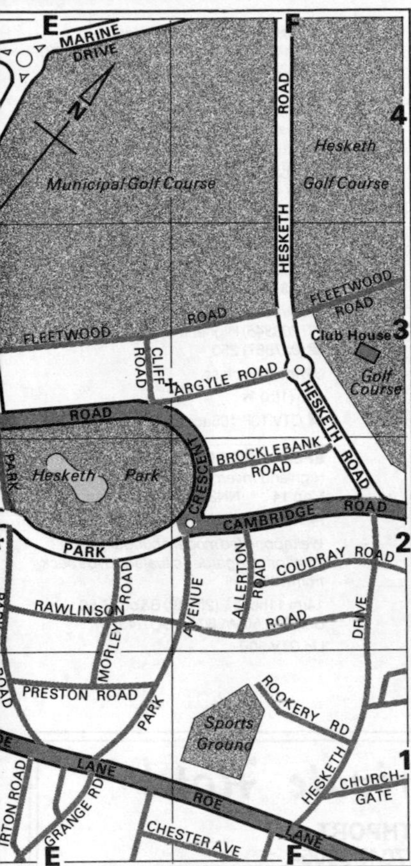

Southport

3	Crimond Hotel
4	Fairway Private Hotel
5	Fernley Private Hotel
6	Franklyn Hotel
7	Fulwood Private Hotel
8	Garden Hotel
9	Glenwood Private Hotel
10	Golf Links Hotel
11	Hollies Hotel
12	Knowsley Private Hotel
13	Newholme
14	Ocean Bank
14A	Orleans Christian Hotel
15	Richmond Hotel
16	Sidbrook Hotel
16A	Stutelea
17	Sunningdale Hotel
18	Talbot Hotel
20	White Lodge Private Hotel
21	Whitworth Falls Hotel
22	Windsor Lodge Hotel

GH Orleans Christian Hotel 6–8 Lathom Rd ☎(0704) 38430 Plan **14A** *E3*

A no smoking rule applies throughout the house.

34hc (6fb) B&b£10 Bdi£14 W£70–£85 Ⱡ LDO6pm

Ⅲ CTV 15P

Ⓥ

GH *Richmond Hotel* 31 The Promenade ☎(0704) 30799 Plan **15** *B3*

Jan–Oct

11hc 1➡ (4fb) (W only Jun–Aug)

Lic Ⅲ CTV 8P lake

GH Sidbrook Hotel 14 Talbot St ☎(0704) 30608 Plan **16** *B2*

Closed Xmas

9hc (4fb) Ⓡ B&b£8–£9 Bdi£10–£12.50 W£68–£75 Ⱡ LDO6pm

Lic CTV 10P sauna bath

GH Stutelea Alexandra Rd ☎(0704) 30080 Plan **16A** *D2*

Large house set in a quiet side road, offering inexpensive yet quality accommodation personally supervised by owner.

15hc 4➡ 1⋔ (2fb) CTV in all bedrooms ✱ Ⓡ B&b£11.50 Bdi£15 W£90 Ⱡ LDO7pm

Lic Ⅲ 9P

GH Sunningdale Hotel 85 Leyland Rd ☎(0704) 38673 Plan **17** *D3*

15rm 3hc (6fb) ✱ Ⓡ B&b£12.50–£13.25 Bdi£17–£18.25 W£71–£80 M LDO4.30pm

Lic Ⅲ CTV 10P

Ⓥ

GH Talbot Hotel Portland St ☎(0704) 33975 Plan **18** *B2*

Closed Xmas & New Year rs Jan

Corner sited house in residential area close to Lord St.

26hc (5fb) Ⓡ *B&b£9.50–£14.75 Bdi£11.75–£17.60 W£86.25–£100 Ⱡ LDO4pm

Lic CTV 30P

Credit cards 1 3

GH White Lodge Private Hotel 12 Talbot St ☎(0704) 36320 Plan **20** *B2*

10hc (3fb) ✱ B&b£8.50–£9.50 Bdi£11.50–£12.50 W£55–£62 M LDO6pm

Lic CTV 6P ⌂

Ⓥ

GH Whitworth Falls Hotel 16 Lathom Rd ☎(0704) 30074 Plan **21** *D3*

Comfortable, homely, small hotel in quiet area.

14hc (4fb) TV in 1 bedroom B&b£9.20–£9.78 Bdi£13.22–£13.80 W£79.35–£82.80 Ⱡ LDO7pm

Lic CTV 14P

Ⓥ

GH Windsor Lodge Hotel 37 Saunders St ☎(0704) 30070 Plan **22** *D3*

12rm 11hc 1⇌ (2fb) ✱ *B&b£9.50 Bdi£13.25 W£79.50 ⅃ LDO6pm

Lic ▥ CTV 10P ⌂

SOUTHSEA
Hampshire
see **Portsmouth & Southsea**

SOUTH SHIELDS
Tyne & Wear
Map **12** NZ36

GH *Sir William Fox Private Hotel* 5 Westoe Village ☎(0632) 554554

An elegant Georgian house situated in a sedate terrace and offering comfortable accommodation and friendly service.

13hc 1⇌ 4⋔ (2fb) ✱ LDO8.15pm

Lic ▥ CTV 14P nc3yrs

SOUTH TAWTON
Devon
Map **3** SX69

INN Seven Stars ☎Sticklepath (083784) 292

Attractive village inn with beams and stone walls in lounge bar.

3hc ® B&b£10 W£63 M L£1–£5 D9.30pm £5.50

▥ ⛟

Southport — Spean Bridge

SOUTHWOLD
Suffolk
Map **5** TM57

GH Mount North Pde ☎(0502) 722292 Closed Xmas

7hc (5fb) ✱ B&b£8.75–£9.75 W£59.15–£66.15 M

▥ CTV ⊘

Ⓥ

SOUTH ZEAL
Devon
Map **3** SX69

GH Poltimore ☎Sticklepath (083784) 209 (due to change to Okehampton (0837) 840209)

7hc 2⇌ 2⋔ ® B&b£11–£13.50 Bdi£16.50–£18.50 W£105–£126 ⅃ LDO11am

Lic ▥ CTV 20P nc12yrs

Ⓥ

SPARROWPIT
Derbyshire
Map **7** SK08

⊢⊣ **FH** Mrs E Vernon **Whitelee** *(SK099814)* ☎ Chapel-en-le-Frith (0298) 812928
Apr–Oct

Modernised farmhouse, part built in 1600, in pleasant hillside setting. Good centre for hill walking or touring.

3hc ® B&b£7.50–£8 Bdi£11–£11.50 W£77 ⅃ LDO4.30pm

▥ TV 3P 42acres beef

SPAXTON
Somerset
Map **3** ST23

FH Mrs D M Porter ***Headford*** *(ST208345)* Higher Merridge ☎(027867) 250

3½m SW unclass.

3rm (1fb) ✱

▥ CTV 10P 105acres mixed

SPEAN BRIDGE
Highland *Inverness-shire*
Map **14** NN28

⊢⊣ **GH Coire Glas** ☎(039781) 272

Well appointed modern bungalow with small private garden situated 50yds back from A86.

14rm 11hc 3⋔ (2fb) ® B&bfr£7.50 Bdifr£12.50 W£80 ⅃ LDO7.45pm

Lic CTV 30P

GH *'Lesanne'* ☎(039781) 231
Mar–Oct
A bungalow style house standing in an elevated position beside the A82.
5hc (1fb) ★ LDO7pm
CTV 6P nc5yrs

SPITTAL
Dyfed
Map **2** SM92
⊢⊣**FH** Mrs N M Thomas **Lower Haythog** *(SM996214)* ☎Clarbeston (043782) 279
2m SE off B4329.
3hc (1fb) B&b£7–£9 Bdi£10.50–£12.50 LDO6.30pm
▥ CTV P ⌂ ♪ 250acres dairy sheep

STAFFORD
Staffordshire
Map **7** SJ92
GH Abbey Hotel 65–68 Lichfield Rd ☎(0785) 58531
Closed Xmas & New Year
21rm 14hc 7⋔ (2fb) ★ Ⓡ B&b£10–£14 LDO8.15pm
Lic ▥ CTV 20P 7🚗
ⓥ

GH Leonards Croft Hotel 80 Lichfield Rd ☎(0785) 3676
Closed Xmas wk
12hc (A 6hc) (1fb) Ⓡ *B&b£6.90–£7.48
▥ CTV 16P

STAINTON
Cumbria
Map **12** NY42
⊢⊣**GH Limes Country Hotel** Redhills ☎Penrith (0768) 63343
Closed Xmas
8hc (2fb) ★ B&b£7.50–£9 Bdi£12.50–£14 Wfr£50.75 M LDO5pm
▥ CTV 12P

STAMFORD
Lincolnshire
Map **4** TF00
GH *St Martins Garden House Hotel* ☎(0780) 63359

10hc (2fb) CTV in all bedrooms LDO9.30pm
Lic ▥ 8P

INN Bull & Swan St Martins ☎(0780) 63558
Traditional old inn dating from 14th century, ½m S on B1081.
6rm CTV in all bedrooms ★ Ⓡ B&b£15–£22 L£1.50–£3.70&alc LDO9.30pm
▥ CTV 25P 🚜
Credit card 3

STANDLAKE
Oxfordshire
Map **4** SP30
FH Mr & Mrs W J Burton **Church Mill** *(SP396038)* Downs Rd ☎(086731) 524
Mar–Oct
A grade II listed 17th-century Mill House with adjoining water mill, on mixed farm. Private fishing is available on the River Windrush. Off Downs Rd between A415 and B4449, N of Standlake.
2hc ★ B&b£9–£10
4P 11acres mixed

⊢⊣**FH** Mrs S R Pickering **Hawthorn** *(SP373048)* ☎(086731) 211
A renovated old Costwold stone building on a working farm primarily cultivating soft fruit but with some livestock. Facilities nearby for various watersports. 2m NW off A415 towards Yelford.
2hc B&b£8–£9 W£56 M
▥ CTV 3P 25acres dairy sheep

STANFORD-LE-HOPE
Essex
Map **5** TQ68
GH Homesteads 216 Southend Rd ☎(0375) 672372
rs Xmas wk
15hc (3fb) Ⓡ *B&b£8.50–£10 Bdi£11–£12.50 LDO3pm
Lic ▥ CTV 8P 2🚗

STAPLE FITZPAINE
Somerset
Map **3** ST21
⊢⊣**FH** Mrs D M Jee **Ruttersleigh** *(ST261164)* ☎Buckland St Mary (046034) 392
Small, very pleasant farmhouse off A303.
3rm (1fb) Ⓡ B&b£6.50–£7.50 Bdi£9.50–£10.50 LDOam
CTV 3P 69acres dairy

STAUNTON
Gloucestershire
Map **3** SO51
⊢⊣**FH** Mrs S Fairhead **Upper Beaulieu** *(SO530118)* ☎Monmouth (0600) 5025
Mar–Nov
Situated on the Gloucester/Gwent border, near the Forest of Dean off A4136 SW of village. Riding facilities can be arranged.
3rm (2fb) ★ B&b£8 W£48 M
▥ CTV 8P 1🚗 nc12yrs 50acres beef

STEEPLE ASTON
Oxfordshire
Map **4** SP42
GH *Westfield Farm Motel* The Fenway ☎(0869) 40591 (Guestaccom)
Clean, well kept motel style accommodation grouped around a farm yard.
6⋔ CTV in all bedrooms Ⓡ LDO9pm
Lic ▥ CTV 20P
ⓥ

See advertisement on page 326

INN Hopcrofts Holt Hotel ☎(0869) 40259
Charming olde worlde Cotswold inn on busy main road with simple clean accommodation.
25hc 18→ 19⋔ (A 2→) CTV in all bedrooms Ⓡ B&b£13.50–£16 Bdi£20.50–£22.95 L£3.75–£6.95 D10pm £6.95&alc
▥ 100P
Credit cards 1 2 3 5

STEPASIDE
Dyfed
Map **2** SN10

GH Bay View House Pleasant Valley ☎Saundersfoot (0834) 813417
Apr–Oct

Modern proprietor run hotel catering for family holidays.

12hc (5fb) ★ B&b£8–£11 Bdi£11.50–£13.75 W£56–£70 M (W only mid Jun–Aug) LDO5.30pm

Lic CTV 16P (heated)

STEVENAGE
Hertfordshire
Map **4** TL22

GH Archways Hotel 11 Hitchin Rd ☎(0438) 316640
Closed Xmas day

Friendly and comfortable detached Victorian residence with tastefully furnished, spacious accommodation.

10rm 5hc 1 1 (A 8) (1fb) CTV in all bedrooms Ⓡ B&b£14.75–£26.50 Bdi£20.25–£32 LDO9pm

Lic CTV 22P

Credit cards 1 2 3

GH Northfield Private Hotel Stevenage Old Town ☎(0438) 314537
Closed 24 Dec–1 Jan

Small family run homely hotel situated in residential area near town centre.

10rm 5hc 2 2 (2fb) ★ Ⓡ B&b£11.50–£22 Bdi£17–£27 W£80.50–£189 M LDO6pm

Lic CTV 10P 1

Ⓥ

STEYNING
West Sussex
Map **4** TQ11

GH Down House King's Barn Villas ☎(0903) 812319
rs Xmas

A large family run Edwardian house set in large well tended gardens, overlooking the South Downs.

7rm 6hc (2fb) Ⓡ B&b£9–£11 Bdi£15–£17 W£54–£66 L LDO9am

CTV 8P nc5yrs

Ⓥ

GH *Lands Down* ☎(0903) 812065

Small, friendly guesthouse in quiet area.

5hc (1fb) LDO9am

CTV 6P nc5yrs

GH Nash Hotel Horsham Rd ☎(0903) 814988

Remotely situated and skilfully extended country house, surrounded by paddocks and a pond.

8hc (3fb) CTV in 1 bedroom TV in 6 bedrooms Ⓡ B&b£12 Bdi£16 W£84 M LDO8pm

Lic CTV 20P (hard)

Cretit cards 1 2 3 4 5

STINCHCOMBE
Gloucestershire
Map **3** ST79

FH Mrs C M St John-Mildmay **Drakestone House** *(ST734977)* ☎Dursley (0453) 2140
Apr–mid Oct

Elegant country house set in formal gardens on edge of Cotswolds off B4060.

3hc 1 Ⓡ B&b£10 Bdi£16.50 W£70 M LDO3pm

6P 10acres mixed

Ⓥ

STIPERSTONES
Shropshire
Map **7** SJ30

GH Tankerville ☎Minsterley (074374) 401 (due to change to Shrewsbury (0743) 791401)

4hc ★ B&b£10 Bdi£15 W£100 LDO2pm

TV 4P

Ⓥ

STOCKBRIDGE
Hampshire
Map **4** SU33

GH Carbery Salisbury Hill ☎Andover (0264) 810771
Closed 2 wks Xmas

Comfortable house with many facilities including pool, croquet, badminton, and swimming pool.

11hc (3fb) ★ B&b£10.92 Bdi£16.10 W£74.75 M LDO6pm

Lic CTV 14P

GH Old Three Cups Private Hotel ☎Andover (0264) 810527
Feb–Dec

15th-century coaching inn with comfortable bedrooms and popular well-managed restaurant.

8rm 5hc 3 (2fb) ★ B&b£13.80–£23 LDO9.45pm

Lic 12P

Credit cards 1 3 Ⓥ

STOCKPORT
Greater Manchester
Map **7** SJ98

GH Ascot House Hotel 195 Wellington Rd North, Heaton Norris ☎061-432 2380
Closed Xmas wk

A large family run house situated on the A6 north of Stockport.

14rm 8hc 6 CTV in 8 bedrooms TV in 6 bedrooms ★ Ⓡ B&b£10–£20 LDO7.15pm

Lic CTV 15P

Credit cards 1 2

STOCKTON
Warwickshire
Map **4** SP46

FH Mr & Mrs J Bankes-Price ***New Zealand*** *(SP453628)* ☎Southam (092681) 4604
Apr–Sep

1½m SE unclass rd.

3rm 1hc ★

CTV P 45acres arable

STOCKTON-ON-TEES
Cleveland
Map **8** NZ41

GH Claireville Hotel 517–519 Yarm Rd, Eaglescliffe ☎(0642) 780378
Closed Xmas Day & New Years Day
3m S A19.
21hc (1fb) B&bfr£12.75 Bdifr£17 Wfr£89.25 M LDO7pm
Lic CTV 20P
Credit card 3 V

GH Court Private Hotel 49 Yarm Rd ☎(0642) 604483
Three-storey, mid terrace property near the town centre with small dining room and comfortable sitting room.
7hc (3fb) CTV in all bedrooms ® B&b£9–£10.50 Bdi£12.50–£13.50 W£63–£73.50 M LDO6pm
Lic nc2yrs

GH Grange Hotel 91 Yarm Rd ☎(0642) 65908
15hc
Lic CTV 20P

STOKE HOLY CROSS
Norfolk
Map **5** TG20

FH Mr & Mrs Harrold **Salamanca** *(TG235022)* ☎Framingham Earl (05086) 2322
Closed Xmas & Etr
Old house with large garden on city outskirts. Simple but comfortable.
3hc (A 1hc) (1fb) B&b£8–£10 Bdi£12–£14.50 LDO24hrs
CTV 10P nc6yrs 165acres arable dairy
V

STOKEINTEIGNHEAD
Devon
Map **3** SX97

GH Bailey's Farm ☎Shaldon (062687) 3361
Apr–Oct
10hc (3fb) B&b£6.50–£7.50 Bdi£9.50–£11 W£70–£80 L LDO7pm
CTV P

GH Rocombe House Hotel ☎Shaldon (062687) 3367
12hc (10fb) B&b£8.50–£9 Bdi£13–£14 W£85–£90 L LDO10am
Lic CTV 20P

STOKE-ON-TRENT
Staffordshire
Map **7** SJ84

GH The White House Stone Rd, Trent Vale ☎(0782) 642460
Closed 1 wk Xmas
Comfortable, modern accommodation is offered at this guesthouse 2 miles SW of city.
8hc (2fb) ® B&b£13–£15 Bdi£20.75–£21.75 W£120–£136.50 L LDO7.15pm
Lic CTV 8P 2

STOKE ST GREGORY
Somerset
Map **3** ST32

GH Meare Green ☎North Curry (0823) 490250
6hc B&b£9–£11.50 W£60–£78 M S% LDO7pm
Lic CTV 9P nc10yrs

STONE *(Near Berkeley)*
Gloucestershire
Map **3** ST69

GH The Elms ☎Falfield (0454) 260279
A well appointed small hotel set in garden, alongside the A38.
10hc (3fb) B&b£11 Bdi£17 LDO3.30pm
Lic CTV 15P

STONE (in Oxney)
Kent
Map **5** TQ92

FH Mrs E I Hodson **Tighe** *(TQ937268)* Tighe ☎Appledore (023383) 251
May–Oct
Late-16th-century farmhouse with panoramic views of Romney Marsh, situated in spacious gardens with a pond. The rooms have antique furniture, with residents lounge having an inglenook fireplace and historic dining room with exposed beams.
3hc B&b£8.50 W£51 M
CTV 4P nc8yrs 100acres sheep

STON EASTON
Somerset
Map **3** ST65

FH Mrs J Doman **Manor** *(ST626533)* ☎Chewton Mendip (076121) 266
Closed Dec
Well-kept and attractively-furnished farmhouse. Lawn at the front and a fruit and vegetable garden. Situated in quiet minor road.
2rm 1hc (1fb) B&bfr£7 Bdifr£10.50
CTV P 300acres dairy mixed

STONEHOUSE
Gloucestershire
Map **3** SO80

FH Mrs D A Hodge **Welches** *(SO813065)* Standish ☎(045382) 2018
3rm 1hc (2fb) B&b£7.50
CTV 12P 101acres dairy

STORNOWAY
Isle of Lewis, Western Isles
Ross & Cromarty
Map **13** NB43

GH Ardlonan 29 Francis St ☎(0851) 3482
Closed Xmas & New Year
A pleasantly appointed house just off town centre. Communal breakfast tables.
5rm 4hc (1fb) B&b£7.50–£8
CTV P

STOURBRIDGE
West Midlands
Map **7** SO98

GH Limes 260 Hagley Rd, Pedmore ☎Hagley (0562) 882689
10hc (1fb) B&bfr£12.50 Bdifr£18 LDO7pm
CTV 12P

STOW-ON-THE-WOLD
Gloucestershire
Map **4** SP12

GH Limes Evesham Rd ☎(0451) 30034
Cheerful and friendly family run hotel within walking distance of the town centre.
5hc (A 1hc) (1fb) CTV in 2 bedrooms TV in 1 bedroom B&b£8–£8.50 W£56–£60 M
CTV 6P

GH Grapevine Hotel (formerly Parkdene) Sheep St ☎(0451) 30344
Closed Xmas & Jan
A comfortable well appointed small hotel offering a warm welcome and sound cooking.
15rm 4hc 8 2 (2fb) CTV in 2 bedrooms TV in 1 bedroom B&b£9.75–£13 Bdi£12–£19.50 W£68.25–£91 M LDO9.30pm
Lic CTV
Credit cards 1 3 V

STRAITON
Lothian *Midlothian*
Map **11** NT26

FH Mrs A M Milne **Straiton** *(NJ273667)* Straiton Rd ☎031-440 0298
Mar–Oct
Georgian farmhouse with garden, situated on southern outskirts of Edinbuirgh. Swing, climbing frame and lots of pets for the children.
4hc (3fb) B&b£8.50
CTV 10P 200acres arable beef mixed

STRANRAER
Dumfries & Galloway *Wigtownshire*
Map **10** NX05

GH Lochview 52 Agnew Cres ☎(0776) 3837
Stone-built terraced house overlooking park and Stranraer Bay.
6hc (2fb) B&b£7–£7.50 Bdi£11–£11.50 W£45.50–£49 M LDO10.30am
CTV 6P

STRATFORD-UPON-AVON
Warwickshire
Map **4** SP25
See plan

GH Ambleside 41 Grove Rd ☎(0789) 297239 Plan **1** *A3* →

Closed Xmas Day
6hc (3fb) TV in 3 bedrooms Ⓡ B&b£7.50–£10 W£50–£65 M
CTV 12P
Credit cards 1 3 Ⓥ

GH Avon House 8 Evesham Pl
☎(0789) 293328 Plan **2** *A2*
Closed 4 days Xmas
Friendly hotel with comfortable well-equipped bedrooms.
10hc (2fb) B&b£7–£8 W£49–£56 M
CTV 2P
Ⓥ

Stratford-upon-Avon

GH Avon View Hotel 121 Shipston Rd
☎(0789) 297542 Plan **3** *C1*
10rm 1→ 6⋔ (5fb) CTV in 9 bedrooms Ⓡ B&b£12–£18 Bdi£17.50–£23.50 LDO7.45pm
Lic 20P
Credit cards 1 2 3

GH Brook Lodge 192 Alcester Rd
☎(0789) 295988 Plan **4** *A3*
8rm 6hc 2→ (4fb) Ⓡ B&b£7–£12
CTV 10P
Ⓥ

GH Coach House 17 Warwick Rd (Guestaccom) ☎(0789) 204109 Plan **5** *C3*
12rm 8hc 1→ 3⋔ (3fb) CTV in all bedrooms Ⓡ B&b£10.50–£12.50 Bdi£14.75–£17.50 W£94.75–£110.50 L
LDO4.30pm
10P
Credit cards 1 2 3 Ⓥ

GH Glenavon Private Hotel Chestnut Walk ☏(0789) 292588 Plan **6** *A2*
Closed Xmas
11hc (3fb) B&b£8.50–£9.50
TV

GH Hardwick House 1 Avenue Rd ☏(0789) 204307 Plan **7** *C3*
Closed Xmas
12rm 9hc 2 (5fb) CTV in 6 bedrooms TV in 6 bedrooms Ⓡ B&b£7–£12.50 W£40–£84 M
10P
Ⓥ

Stratford-upon-Avon

GH Hunters Moon 150 Alcester Rd ☏(0789) 292888 Plan **8** *A3*
8rm 3hc 2 (3fb) Ⓡ *B&b£8–£12
CTV 6P
Ⓥ

GH Hylands Hotel Warwick Rd ☏(0789) 297962 Plan **9** *C3*
Closed Xmas & New Year
15 (2fb) CTV in all bedrooms Ⓡ *B&b£12–£17 W£75.60–£107 M
Lic lift 15P
Credit cards 1 3 Ⓥ
See advertisement on page 330

GH Kawartha House 39 Grove Rd ☏(0789) 204469 Plan **10** *A2*
Closed 1 wk Xmas
Semi-detached house on busy road just out of town centre in area of hotels, opposite a small park. Family atmosphere.
6hc (2fb) B&b£8–£10.50 W£56–£73.50 M
CTV

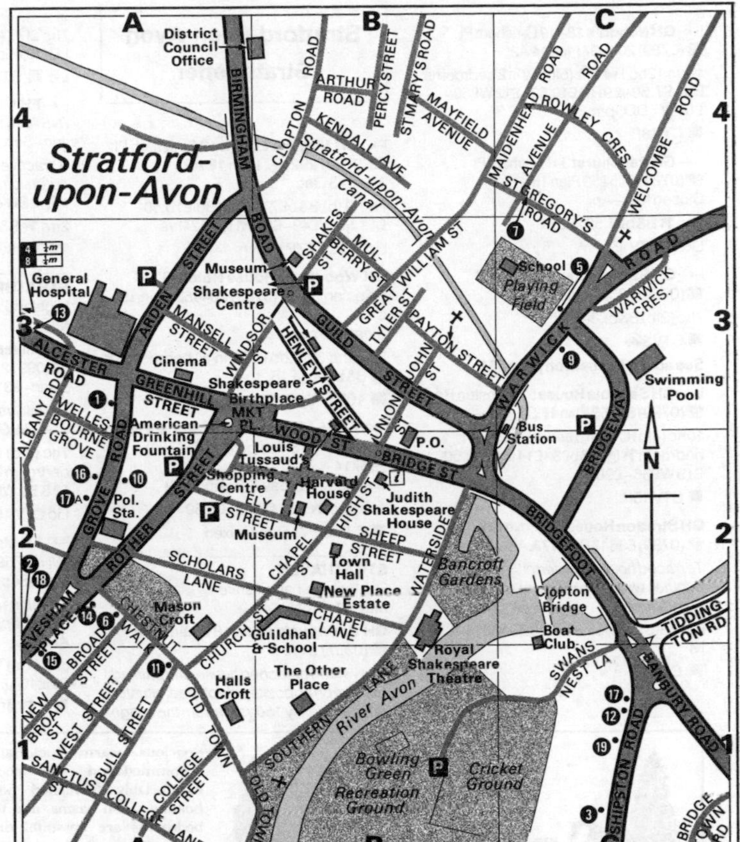

Stratford-upon-Avon

1 Ambleside
2 Avon House
3 Avon View Hotel
4 Brook Lodge
5 Coach House
6 Glenavon Private Hotel
7 Hardwick House
8 Hunters Moon
9 Hylands Hotel
10 Kawartha House
11 Marlyn
12 Melita Private Hotel
13 Moonraker House
14 Nando's
15 Penshurst
16 Salamander
17 Sequoia
17A Stretton House
18 Virginia Lodge
19 Woodburn House Hotel

GH Marlyn 3 Chestnut Walk ☎(0789) 293752 Plan **11** *A1*
Closed Xmas
8hc (2fb) ★ Ⓡ ✻B&b£7.95–£9.95 W£47.70–£59.70M
TV

GH Melita Private Hotel 37 Shipston Rd ☎(0789) 292432 Plan **12** *C1*
13rm 7hc 6→ (4fb) CTV in 7 bedrooms ★ Ⓡ B&b£11–£18
Lic CTV 12P 2

↔ **GH Moonraker House** 40 Alcester Rd ☎(0789) 67115 Plan **13** *A3*
6 (A 9rm 2→ 7) (4fb) CTV in all bedrooms Ⓡ B&b£7.50–£9.50 Bdi£12–£13.50 LDOnoon
10P 5

↤↦ **GH Nando's** 18–19 Evesham Pl ☎(0789) 204907 Plan **14** *A2*

14rm 12hc 1⇀ 1⋔ (5fb) TV in 2 bedrooms B&b£7.50–£9 Bdi£10.50–£12 W£50–£62 M̸ LDO5pm

Ⅲ CTV 8P

↤↦ **GH Penshurst** 34 Evesham Pl ☎(0789) 205259 Plan **15** *A1*
Closed Mar–Apr

8rm ✱ B&b£7.50–£8.50

Lic Ⅲ CTV 4P

↤↦ **GH Salamander** 40 Grove Rd ☎(0789) 205728 Plan **16** *A2*

7hc (2fb) B&b£8–£9

Ⅲ CTV 3⌂

See advertisement on page 331

↤↦ **GH Sequoia House** 51 Shipston Rd ☎(0789) 68852 Plan **17** *C1*

10hc (4fb) CTV in 3 bedrooms TV in 1 bedroom ✱ Ⓡ B&b£8–£14 Bdi£12.50–£19 W£56–£98 M̸

Ⅲ CTV 15P

GH Stretton House 38 Grove Rd ☎(0789) 68647 Plan **17A** *A2*

Terraced house situated only a few minutes walk from Stratford and its amenities.

6hc (3fb) B&b£8.50–£10.50 W£56–£70 M̸

Ⅲ CTV

↤↦ **GH Virginia Lodge** 12 Evesham Pl ☎(0789) 292157 Plan **18** *A2*
3 Jan–3 Dec

7hc (1fb) B&b£7–£8.50 Bdi£10.50–£11.50 W£49–£56 M̸ LDO24hrs

Lic Ⅲ CTV 7P nc3yrs

GH Woodburn House Hotel 89 Shipston Rd ☎(0789) 204453 Plan **19** *C1*
Closed Xmas

7rm 4hc 3⋔ (2fb) CTV in all bedrooms ✱ Ⓡ B&b£10–£18

Ⅲ 10P nc5yrs

↤↦ **FH** Mrs M K Meadows **Monk's Barn** *(SP206516)* Shipston Rd ☎(0789) 293714
Closed Xmas day & Boxing day

4rm 3hc ✱ B&b£6.25–£6.50

Ⅲ CTV 5P 75acres mixed

STRATHAVEN
Strathclyde *Lanarkshire*
Map **11** NS74

GH *Springvale Hotel* 18 Letham Rd ☎(0357) 21131

Grey stone detached house with painted annexe on opposite side of road, situated approximately 150 yards from the village.

7hc 2⋔ (A 7hc) (3fb) TV in 5 bedrooms LDO6.45pm

Lic Ⅲ CTV 8P

↤↦ **FH** Mrs E Warnock **Laigh Bent** *(NS701413)* ☎(0357) 20103
Jun–Sep

Attractive stone-built farmhouse with outbuildings surrounding the courtyard. 1½m SW of Strathaven on the A71.

2rm ✱ B&b£6.50

TV P nc8yrs 100acres beef

STRATHPEFFER
Highland *Ross & Cromarty*
Map **14** NH45

GH Kilvannie Manor Fodderty ☎(09972) 389
3 Jan–23 Dec

Country manor house situated 1 mile east of A834. Dinners served to non-residents.

7hc (1fb) CTV in 1 bedroom TV in 1 bedroom Ⓡ B&b£9–£10 Bdi£15–£16.50 W£100–£110 Ⱡ LDO6.30pm

Lic CTV 10P nc14yrs

↤↦ **FH** Mrs M Tait **Beechwood House** *(NH497594)* Fodderty ☎(09972) 387
May–Sep

Spacious and comfortable two-storey house, approx 1m NE of the village on A834.

3hc (1fb) ✱ Ⓡ B&b£6.50–£7.50 Bdi£10–£11 W£45.50 M̸ LDO4pm

Ⅲ CTV 10P 18acres mixed

STREET
Somerset
Map **3** ST43

FH Mrs B D Tucker ***Marshalls Elm*** *(ST485348)* ☎(0458) 42878

Old, well-preserved farmhouse with back and front gardens, set in country surroundings. Street 1½ miles.

3rm

CTV 3P 200acres arable beef sheep

STRETE
Devon
Map **3** SX84

GH Highcliff ☎Stoke Fleming (0803) 770307
Apr–Oct

10rm 9hc 1➡ (4fb) B&b£9 Bdi£12 W£63 M LDO5pm

Lic CTV 10P ⌂

GH Tallis Rock Private Hotel ☎Stoke Fleming (0803) 770370
Etr–Oct

9hc (4fb) ✱B&b£8–£8.50 Bdifr£11.50 Wfr£70 L LDOam

CTV 10P

Credit card [1] (V)

STROUD
Gloucestershire
Map **3** SO80

GH Downfield Private Hotel Cainscross Rd ☎(04536) 4496
Closed 2wks Xmas

Proprietor run hotel.

22rm 16hc 3➡ 3⋒ (3fb) B&b£9–£11 W£60–£65 M LDO8pm

Lic ⚓ CTV 26P

STURMINSTER NEWTON
Dorset
Map **3** ST71

⊢⊣**FH** Mrs S Wingate-Saul **Holbrook** *(ST743117)* Lydlinch ☎Hazelbury Bryan (02586) 348
Closed Xmas Day

3m W off A357 Stalbridge Rd.

2rm 1hc TV in 2 bedrooms ✗ (R) B&b£7.50–£9 Bdi£12–£13.50 W£56 M LDO5pm

⚓ CTV 8P ⌂ ≋ ♪ 126acres mixed

STURTON BY STOW
Lincolnshire
Map **8** SK88

FH Mrs S Bradshaw **Village** *(SK889807)* ☎Gainsborough (0427) 788309
Mar–Oct

W off B1241.

4rm 3hc ✗ B&b£9–£10

⚓ CTV 6P nc12yrs ♪(hard) ♪

(V)

SUDBURY
Suffolk
Map **5** TL84

GH Hill Lodge Private Hotel 8 Newton Rd ☎(0787) 77568
Closed Xmas wk

16rm 11hc 5⋒ CTV in all bedrooms ✗ B&b£8.25–£12 LDOnoon

⚓ CTV 20P 2⌂

INN Black Boy Hotel Market Hill ☎(0787) 79046

5hc ✗ B&b£9.50 LDO9pm

⚓ CTV 10P

Credit card [2] (V)

SUMMERCOURT
Cornwall
Map **2** SW85

⊢⊣**FH** Mr & Mrs J A Mingo **Burthy** *(SW911565)* ☎St Austell (0726) 860018
Apr–Oct

3hc (1fb) ✗ B&b£7.50 Bdi£9 W£60 L LDO5pm

CTV P 1⌂ ⌂ 200acres beef sheep mixed

⊢⊣**FH** Mrs W E Lutey **Trenithon** *(SW895553)* ☎St Austell (0726) 860253
Mar–Nov

Modern farmhouse situated in quiet location in open countryside a few miles from the coast.

4hc (2fb) B&b£5.50–£6 Bdi£8.50–£9 W£60 L LDO3pm

⚓ CTV 6P 150acres arable beef sheep mixed

(V)

SUNDERLAND
Tyne & Wear
Map **12** NZ35

GH *St Annes Hotel* 1 North Cliff, Roker Ter ☎(0783) 672649

Simple sea front hotel with spacious bedrooms and a good restaurant.

13hc 1➡ (3fb) ✗ LDO9.30pm

Lic ⚓ CTV 12P sea

SURBITON
Gt London
London plan **4** B1
(page 222–223)

GH Holmdene 23 Cranes Dr ☎01-399 9992
Closed Dec

Attractive two-storey house in residential area, peaceful and comfortable, near to town centre.

6hc (1fb) ✗ ✱B&b£10–£12 W£56–£70 M

⚓ CTV nc5yrs

(V)

GH *Warwick* 321 Ewell Rd ☎01-399 5837

Personally supervised guesthouse offering simple but comfortable accommodation.

9hc 1➡⋒ (3fb)

⚓ CTV 5P

SUTTON
Gt London
London plan **4** C1
(page 222–223)

GH Dene Hotel 39 Cheam Rd ☎01-642 3170

Set in peaceful surroundings, this hotel offers good service in an informal and friendly atmosphere.

18rm 11hc 4➡ 2⋒ (2fb) CTV in 8 bedrooms TV in 10 bedrooms ✗ (R) B&b£12.65–£29.90

⚓ 8P nc5yrs

(V)

GH Eaton Court Hotel 49 Eaton Rd ☎01-642 6766

Charming Victorian house, well positioned in quiet residential area.

13hc 2⋒ (2fb) CTV in 5 bedrooms ✗ ✱B&b£15 W£105 M

Lic ⚓ CTV 6P

Credit cards [1] [2] (V)

GH Thatched House Hotel 135 Cheam Rd ☎01-642 3131

Small hotel with a lot of character and the comforts of a family home.

18rm 1hc 6⋒ CTV in 12 bedrooms B&b£18.50 Bdi£26.50 LDO9pm

Lic ⚓ CTV 12P

Credit card [3]

SUTTON COLDFIELD
West Midlands
Map **7** SP19

GH Cloverley Hotel 17 Anchorage Rd ☎021-354 5181

18rm 1➡ 17⋒ (2fb) CTV in all bedrooms ✗ (R) B&b£20.24 LDO8pm

Lic ⚓ CTV 14P ⌂

Credit cards [1] [3] (V)

GH *Standbridge Hotel* 138 Birmingham Rd ☎021-354 3007 Birmingham plan **12**

8hc (A 1hc) CTV in 1 bedroom TV in 1 bedroom (R) LDOnoon

Lic ⚓ CTV 11P

See advertisement on page 61

SWANAGE
Dorset
Map **4** SZ07

GH Boyne Hotel 1 Cliff Av ☎(0929) 422939
Apr–Sep

Corner sited guesthouse in quiet area, a short distance from front.

15hc 1➡ (3fb) B&b£9.50–£10.50 Bdi£14.50–£15.50 W£75–£85 L LDO4.30pm

Lic CTV 8P

(V)

Swanage

↦ **GH Burlington Hotel** 7 Highcliffe Rd ☎(0929) 422422
2 Mar–2 Nov
Views of Swanage Bay and located in quiet cul de sac.
9rm 4hc 2➡ 3⋔ (4fb) CTV in 2 bedrooms TV in 6 bedrooms B&b£6.50–£10.50 Bdi£10.50–£14.50 W£69.50–£96.45 Ⱡ LDO5.30pm
Lic ⅢⅢ CTV 9P
Ⓥ

GH Byways 5 Ulwell Rd ☎(0929) 422322
mid May–Sep
Well appointed and comfortable guesthouse a short distance from the beach.
11hc (4fb) B&b£9.50–£10.50 Bdi£12.50–£13.50 W£72–£77 Ⱡ (W only mid Jul–Aug)
CTV 3P nc5yrs

GH Castleton Private Hotel Highcliffe Rd ☎(0929) 423972
Feb–Oct
Corner sited guesthouse just 100yds from beach.
12rm 7hc 1➡ 3⋔ (4fb) ★ Ⓡ B&b£8.05–£9.78 Bdi£11.50–£13.80 W£52.90–£64.40 M LDO5pm
Lic ⅢⅢ CTV 12P nc3yrs

GH *Eversden Private Hotel* Victoria Rd ☎(0929) 423276
rs Nov–Mar
Private hotel with good views, a few minutes walk from the beach.
12hc 2➡ 3⋔ (4fb) ★ LDO6pm
Lic ⅢⅢ CTV 12P

↦ **GH Firswood** 29 Kings Rd ☎(0929) 422306
Closed Dec rs Oct–Mar
7hc (4fb) ★ B&b£8–£10 Bdi£12–£14 W£51–£55 M LDOnoon
ⅢⅢ CTV 7P nc5yrs
Credit cards 1 3 Ⓥ

GH Golden Sands Private Hotel 10 Ulwell Rd ☎(0929) 422093
Mar–Nov
Well appointed Purbeck stone hotel situated 100yds from the beach.
15rm 2hc 11➡ 2⋔ (10fb) CTV in all bedrooms ★ Ⓡ *B&b£8.50–£11 Bdi£11.50–£15.50 W£55–£73 M LDO6.30pm
Lic ⅢⅢ CTV 14P
Ⓥ

GH Havenhurst Hotel 3 Cranbourne Rd ☎(0929) 424224
Mar–Oct
Pleasant guesthouse in quiet area with neat bedrooms.
16rm 9hc 1➡ 6⋔ (4fb) Ⓡ B&b£10–£12 Bdi£15–£17 W£88–£105 Ⱡ (W only 14 Jul–Aug) LDO6.30pm
Lic ⅢⅢ CTV 16P
Ⓥ

GH Ingleston Private Hotel 2 Victoria Rd ☎(0929) 422391
Apr–Oct
Corner sited villa in quiet position 250yds from the beach.
10hc (4fb) ★ B&b£9.20–£11.60 Bdi£18.40–£23.20 W£86.25–£92 Ⱡ LDO5pm
Lic CTV 8P

↦ **GH Kingsley Hall Hotel** 8 Ulwell Rd ☎(0929) 422872
Closed Dec rs Jan–Apr
Situated a short distance from the beach with uninterrupted views across bay.
13rm 4hc 3➡ 4⋔ (5fb) CTV in all bedrooms B&b£6–£10 Bdi£8.50–£15 W£42–£70 M LDO6pm
Lic ⅢⅢ CTV 14P

GH Nethercourt Hotel 62 Park Rd ☎(0929) 423518
Mar–Oct
6rm 2hc (4fb) ★ Ⓡ B&b£9–£12 W£60–£70 M
Lic ⅢⅢ CTV 6P nc10yrs
Credit cards 1 2 3 5

GH *Nethway Hotel* Gilberts Rd ☎(0929) 423909
Mar–Oct
Near to shops and sea front.
12hc (3fb) ® LDO6.30pm
Lic 10P nc2yrs

GH *Oxford Hotel* 3 & 5 Park Rd ☎(0929) 422247
Mar–Oct
Located on the rise of hill leading from town centre and sea front.
14hc (4fb) LDOam
Lic CTV sea

GH St Michael Hotel 31 Kings Rd ☎(0929) 422064
Feb–Dec
6rm 3hc 3 (4fb) ® B&bfr£9 Bdifr£13 Wfr£60 M LDOnoon
Lic CTV 6P
Ⓥ

GH Tower Lodge Private Hotel 17 Ulwell Rd ☎(0929) 422887
Mar–Nov
200yds from beach with level approach.
11rm 5hc 6 (6fb) ® B&b£12.14 Bdi£15.03 W£90 M LDO5pm
Lic CTV 9P
Credit cards 1 3

Swanage — Swansea

SWANSEA
West Glamorgan
Map **3** SS69
See also Bishopston, Langland Bay and Mumbles

GH Alexander Hotel 3 Sketty Rd, Sketty ☎(0792) 470045
Proprietor run commercial guesthouse in city.
7rm 4 2 (2fb) TV in all bedrooms ® B&b£12–£12.50 Bdi£18–£19 W£95 L (W only Jun–Aug)
Lic CTV nc2yrs
Credit cards 1 2 3 5 Ⓥ

GH Channel View 17 Bryn Rd, Brynmill ☎(0792) 466834
Stone-built house overlooking St Helens cricket and rugby ground.
8hc B&b£7–£7.50 W£46–£48 M
CTV

GH Crescent 132 Eaton Cres, Uplands ☎(0792) 466814
Closed Xmas & New Year
Family run guesthouse.
8rm 6hc 2 (2fb) ® B&b£8.50–£10 Bdi£13.50–£15 W£86–£93 L LDO4pm
CTV 4P
Credit cards 1 3
See advertisement on page 336

GH Parkway Hotel 253 Gower Rd, Sketty ☎(0792) 201632
Closed Xmas–31 Dec
Proprietor run hotel on outskirts of the city, with residents' bar.
12rm 8hc 4 (A 1) (1fb) ® B&b£10.50–£14 Bdi£16.50–£20 W£64.50–£86 L LDO10.30pm
Lic CTV 15P
Credit cards 2 3
See advertisement on page 336

GH St Davids Private Hotel 15 Sketty Rd, Uplands ☎(0792) 473814
Commercial city guesthouse with cosy bar for residents.
11rm 7hc 2 2 (3fb) CTV in all bedrooms B&b£10–£12.50 Bdi£15.50–£18 W£82–£92 L LDO4pm
Lic CTV 2P nc5yrs
Credit cards 1 3
See advertisement on page 337

GH St Helens House St Helens Cres
☎(0792) 460065
Closed Xmas

A proprietor run guesthouse near the Civic Buildings with modestly appointed bedrooms.

6hc (2fb) Ⓡ
CTV 2P
Credit card 3

GH Tregare Hotel 9 Sketty Rd, Uplands
☎(0792) 470608

Small commercial hotel.

11rm 3hc 3 5 (1fb) CTV in 9 bedrooms TV in 2 bedrooms B&b£10 Bdi£14.75 W£70 M LDO6.30pm

Swansea

Lic CTV 5P nc12yrs
Credit cards 1 3 Ⓥ

GH Uplands Court 134 Eaton Cres
☎(0792) 473046
Closed 25 & 26 Dec

Proprietor run guesthouse in residential area.

8rm 5hc 3 (2fb) TV in all bedrooms Ⓡ B&b£9–£11 Bdi£14–£16 W£55 M LDO4pm
Lic CTV nc3yrs

GH Westlands 34 Bryn Rd, Brynmill
☎(0792) 466689

Commercial guesthouse within walking distance of the city centre.

6hc (2fb) Ⓡ *B&b£6.50–£7.50 Bdi£10–£11.50 W£45–£52 M LDO10am
CTV
Ⓥ

SWINESHEAD
Bedfordshire
Map **4** TL06

FH D Marlow **Manor** *(TL057659)*
☎Riseley (023063) 8126
Closed Xmas wk

Beautiful farmhouse, recently renovated and comfortably furnished.

3rm (1fb) ✶ B&b£10–£12

𝌆 CTV 6P nc10yrs 3acres mixed small holding

SWYNNERTON
Staffordshire
Map **7** SJ83

Swineshead — Symonds Yat, East

INN Fitzherbert Arms ☎(078135) 241
Closed 25–31 Dec

5hc (A 7hc 2⇌) (2fb) B&b£10–£13 Bdi£13.75–£16.75 W£70–£85 M
LDO10pm

Lic 𝌆 CTV 60P 2🚗⌂

Credit cards 1 3

SYMONDS YAT, EAST
Hereford & Worcester
Map **3** SO51

GH Garth Cottage Hotel ☎(0600) 890364
Mar–Oct

7rm 4hc 3⋒ ✶ B&b£10–£11 Bdi£16–£17 W£105–£110 L LDO5pm

Lic 𝌆 CTV 9P nc7yrs

Credit card 1

INN Saracens Head ☎(0600) 890435

Well restored inn on banks of River Wye with good accommodation. →

6rm 3hc 3⋒ ✱ Ⓡ B&b£10–£13.50 Bdi£16.50–£20 W£103.95–£126 Ⱡ LDO9.30pm

Lic ▥ CTV P

Credit cards 1 2 Ⓥ

SYMONDS YAT, WEST *(Near Ross-on-Wye)*
Hereford & Worcester
Map **3** SO51

GH Woodlea ☎(0600) 890206
Closed Xmas

10hc 3⋒ (3fb) B&b£10.25 Bdi£16 W£105 Ⱡ LDO6pm

Lic ▥ CTV 9P ⩰

Ⓥ

TADCASTER
North Yorkshire
Map **8** SE44

GH Shann House 47 Kirkgate ☎(0937) 833931

Charming, well restored Georgian house with spacious, well fitted bedrooms and attractive lounge.

8rm 6➡ 2⋒ (1fb) CTV in all bedrooms Ⓡ ✻B&b£11 W£70 Ⓜ

Lic ▥ 8P

Credit cards 1 3 4 Ⓥ

TALGARTH
Powys
Map **3** SO13

FH Mrs B Prosser **Upper Genffordd** *(SO171304)* ☎(0874) 711360

Comfortable, character farmhouse offering good farmhouse cooking, hospitality and warm welcome. Situated within the scenic location of Brecon Beacons with views of Black Mountains. 3m S by A479.

2rm (1fb) ✱ ✻B&b£6.50–£7.50 Bdi£10 W£70–£80 Ⱡ (W only Jul) LDO5pm

▥ CTV 5P 200acres dairy mixed

TAPLOW
Buckinghamshire
Map **4** SU98

GH *Norfolk House* Bath Rd
☎Maidenhead (0628) 23687

A small, well-appointed house with comfortable rooms and a friendly atmosphere. It has an open-air swimming pool.

6hc CTV in bedrooms ✱ Ⓡ

CTV 10P

TARPORLEY
Cheshire
Map **7** SJ56

GH Perth Hotel High St ☎(08293) 2514
Feb–Dec

8rm 6hc 1➡ 1⋒ (2fb) TV in 4 bedrooms Ⓡ B&b£13.50–£17 Bdi£19–£25 W£85–£108 Ⓜ LDO9.30pm

Lic ▥ CTV 12P nc5yrs

Credit cards 1 3 5 Ⓥ

TAUNTON
Somerset
Map **3** ST22

GH Brookfield 16 Wellington Rd
☎(0823) 72786

8hc (2fb) ✱ B&b£11.50 Bdi£15.50 W£76.50 Ⓜ LDO8.30pm

Lic ▥ CTV 8P

Credit cards 1 3

GH Meryan House Hotel Bishop's Hull Rd ☎(0823) 87445

Georgian house in own grounds, personally run with friendly relaxed atmosphere and comfortable, attractive public rooms, situated outside Taunton, off A38.

8hc (3fb) ✱ B&b£13 Bdi£18 LDO7pm

Lic ▥ CTV 30P

Credit card 3

GH Ruishton Lodge Ruishton ☎(0823) 442298

Large detached house in own grounds, personally run with country house atmosphere and sound cooking. Situated a short distance from M5 junction, on A358.

6hc (2fb) TV in 2 bedrooms ✻B&b£8 Bdi£12 W£50–£56 Ⓜ LDO10pm

Lic ▥ CTV 10P

Ⓥ

GH Rumwell Hall Rumwell ☎(0823) 75268
Closed Xmas day

Elegant and spacious Georgian mansion set in 10 acres of gardens with swimming pool. The large, comfortable bedrooms and attractive public rooms are complemented by the warm friendly atmosphere.

10hc 4➡ (7fb) CTV in 4 bedrooms Ⓡ B&b£10 Bdi£15 LDO7pm

Lic ▥ CTV 100P ⩰ (heated) ⚲

Ⓥ

GH White Lodge Hotel 81 Bridgwater Rd ☎(0823) 73287

10rm 6⋒ (3fb) CTV in 6 bedrooms ✱ Ⓡ B&b£20 Bdi£26 W£150 Ⱡ LDO7pm

Lic ▥ CTV 14P

Credit cards 1 2 3

TAVISTOCK
Devon
Map **2** SX47

GH *Cherry Trees* 40 Plymouth Rd
☎(0822) 3070

Large double fronted house in terrace, situated ½ mile from the town centre.

5hc (1fb) TV in 1 bedroom ✱

▥ CTV 1P 3⌂ river

⟼**FH** Mrs E C Blatchford **Parswell Farm Bungalow** *(SX464731)* Parswell
☎(0822) 2789
Etr–Oct

Well situated bungalow on the Callington road, commanding good views of surrounding countryside.

2rm ✱ B&b£6.50–£7

TV 2P 106acres mixed

TEIGNMOUTH
Devon
Map **3** SX97

GH Baveno Hotel 40 Higher Brimley Rd
☎(06267) 3102

15hc(8fb)®*B&b£6.50–£8.75 Bdi£8.50–£10.75W£45–£60M LDO4pm

Lic 🍽 CTV10P

GH Bay Cottage Hotel 7 Marine Pde, Shaldon ☎Shaldon (062687) 2394

Mar–Nov

8hc ★*B&b£9.75 Bdi£16.25 W£110L LDO4.30pm

Lic 🍽 CTV3P

Ⓥ

GH Glen Devon 3 Carlton Pl ☎(06267) 2895

8rm 6hc 2⫪ (4fb) ★®B&b£7.50–£9 Bdi£10–£12.50 W£70–£86L LDO5pm

Lic 🍽 CTV6P

Ⓥ

GH Hillrise Winterbourne Rd ☎(06267) 3108

8hc (4fb) B&b£6–£7 Bdi£8.50–£9.50 W£45–£68L LDO6.30pm

Lic 🍽 CTV5P

GH Hillsley Upper Hermosa Rd ☎(06267) 3878

May–Sep

11hc (4fb) B&b£7.50–£9 Bdi£11.50–£12.50 W£60–£69L LDO6.30pm

Lic CTV 10P nc3yrs

GH Lyme Bay House Hotel Den Promenade ☎(06267) 2953

12rm 8hc 3⫪ (3fb) CTV in 1 bedroom ®

Teignmouth — Temple Cloud

B&b£10–£12.85 Bdi£14.50–£17.60 W£55–£72.95M LDO7pm

Lic lift 🍽 CTV P

GH Rathlin House Hotel Upper Hermosa Rd ☎(06267) 4473

Etr–Oct

10hc (5fb) ★®Bdi£10.75–£11.95 W£56–£79L (W only end Jul–Aug) LDO5.30pm

Lic 🍽 CTV12P

GH *Ravensbourne Hotel* High Woodway Rd ☎(06267) 3415

12hc (6fb)

Lic 🍽 CTV20P

GH Teign Holiday Inn Hotel Teign St ☎(06267) 2976

11hc (6fb) *B&b£6.50–£8.50 Bdi£10.50–£12.50 W£70–£80L LDO4pm

Lic 🍽 CTV11P

GH Thornhill Hotel Sea Front ☎(06267) 3460

Etr–Sep

12hc (4fb) ®B&b£9.20–£10.35 Bdi£12.65–£13.80 W£69–£89.70L LDO6pm

Lic CTV 4P nc2yrs

TELFORD

Shropshire

Map **7** SJ60

INN Cock Hotel 148 Holyhead Rd, Wellington ☎(0952) 4495

Comfortable well equipped bedrooms in a former coaching inn standing at the junction of A442 with B5061.

6hc CTV in all bedrooms ® B&b£11.50 L£2.25–£6.50alc D9pm £2.25–£6.50alc

🍽 30P 3🚗

Credit cards 1 2

INN *Swan Hotel* Watling St, Wellington ☎(0952) 3781

10hc ® D10pm

🍽 CTV 150P

TEMPLE CLOUD

Avon

Map **3** ST65

FH Mr J Harris **Cameley Lodge** *(ST609575)* Cameley ☎(0761) 52590

Newly-converted farmhouse barn into small country residence, attractively designed in keeping with the area. Overlooking 13th century church and trout lakes. 1m W unclass rd.

4rm 2hc 2⫪ TV in 4 bedrooms ★®

*B&b£11.50 W£80.50M LDO9.30pm

Lic 🍽 30P 60acres non-working

TENBURY WELLS
Hereford & Worcester
Map **7** SO56

INN *Crow Hotel* Teme St ☎(0584) 810503
4hc CTV in all bedrooms ✱ ® D10pm
▥ 50P 2⌂

TENBY
Dyfed
Map **2** SN10

GH Belvedere Private Hotel Serpentine Rd ☎(0834) 2549
Mar–Oct
A family run guesthouse where children are welcome.
14rm 13hc 1⇥ (10fb) B&b£9–£12 Bdi£13–£16 W£63–£84 M LDO6.30pm
Lic ▥ CTV 20P

GH Hotel Doneva The Norton ☎(0834) 2460
Mar–Oct
Attractive house situated a few minutes walk from town and harbour.
14rm 11hc 3⇥ (6fb) ® B&b£10–£11 Bdi£13.50–£15 W£75–£98 ⱡ (W only Jul & Aug)
Lic lift CTV 20P
Credit card 3

GH Heywood Lodge Heywood Ln ☎(0834) 2684
Closed Oct–Apr
Attractive house in own grounds, proprietor run and well appointed throughout.
14rm 9hc 5⇥ (4fb) B&b£9.55–£11 Bdi£15.50–£17.85 W£98.90–£103.50 ⱡ LDO8.30pm
Lic ▥ CTV 20P ⌂

⊢→ **GH Hildebrand Hotel** Victoria St ☎(0834) 2403
Closed Dec–Jan rs Feb–Mar & Nov
11rm 5hc 1⇥ 5⋒ (4fb) ✱ ® B&b£7.25–£10.50 Bdi£12–£14.60 W£84–£99 ⱡ LDO5pm
Lic ▥ CTV ⚑
Credit cards 1 2 3 Ⓥ

GH Myrtle House Hotel St Mary's Street ☎(0834) 2508
Feb–Nov
A well maintained and comfortable small hotel offering good hospitality.
9hc (4fb) ✱ B&b£9–£11 Bdi£13–£15 W£58–£70 M LDO6.30pm
Lic ▥ CTV ⚑
Credit cards 1 3

GH *Penally Manor Hotel* Penally ☎(0834) 2668
rs Nov–Mar
16hc 8⋒ (5fb) CTV in 4 bedrooms
Lic ▥ CTV 30P sea

GH Red House Hotel Heywood Ln ☎(0834) 2770
Apr–Oct
Well maintained house in own grounds.
29rm 9hc 17⇥ 3⋒ (10fb) ✱ B&b£10–£11.50 Bdi£14.50–£16 W£95–£107 ⱡ LDO7pm
Lic ▥ CTV 30P nc3yrs ⇌(heated) ℘ Ⓥ

GH Richmond Hotel The Croft, North Beach ☎(0834) 2533
Etr–Oct
18hc (11fb) ✱ ® B&b£9.50–£11 Bdi£12.50–£15.50 LDO6.30pm
Lic CTV ⚑
Credit cards 1 2 3 Ⓥ

GH Ripley St Marys Hotel St Mary's Street ☎(0834) 2837
Mar–Oct rs Nov–Feb
14rm 8hc 6⇥⋒ (7fb) ® B&b£9–£10.50 Bdi£14–£16 W£95–£110 ⱡ LDO5.30pm
Lic CTV ⚑
Credit cards 1 3 Ⓥ

GH Sea Breezes Hotel 18 The Norton ☎(0834) 2753
Mar–Nov
Proprietor run guesthouse with residents bar, near harbour and town.

26rm 9⇌ 1⋔ (5fb) TV in 10 bedrooms ✱ Ⓡ B&b£9–£14 Bdi£12–£17.50 W£75–£95 ⱡ LDO4.30pm
Lic ⅢⅢ CTV
Ⓥ

TEWKESBURY
Gloucestershire
Map **3** SO83

GH Ancient Grudge Hotel 15 High St
☎(0684) 292204
Closed 1st 2 wks Jan
Refurbished town centre hotel with comfortable rooms and popular restaurant.
4rm (1fb) TV in 1 bedroom Ⓡ
✱B&bfr£14 LDO9pm
Lic ⅢⅢ CTV 4P nc5yrs
Credit cards 1 2 3 5

GH South End House 67 Church St
☎(0684) 294097
rs Xmas
Comfortable town house with walled garden to the rear.
8hc (2fb) CTV in all bedrooms
B&b£20.50–£22.50 W£115–£125 Ṁ
Lic ⅢⅢ CTV 10P
Credit card 3

THORNHILL
Dumfries & Galloway *Dumfriesshire*
Map **11** NX89

Tenby — Thorpe

⊢⊣ **FH** Mrs J Mackie **Waterside Mains** *(NS870971)* ☎(0848) 30405
Mar–Oct
Farmhouse with nice bedrooms, set on banks of River Nith, catering for fishing parties. 1m N off A76.
3hc (1fb) B&b£7–£7.50 Bdi£10–£10.50 LDO4pm
ⅢⅢ CTV 4P ♩ 160acres arable dairy
Ⓥ

THORNTHWAITE *(Near Keswick)*
Cumbria
Map **11** NY22

GH Ladstock Country House Hotel
☎Braithwaite (059682) 210
mid Mar–Nov
Attractive country house, filled with period furnishings.
17hc 2⇌ (2fb) ✱ Ⓡ B&bfr£11
Bdifr£17.50 W£105 ⱡ LDO6pm
Lic ⅢⅢ CTV 20P

THORNTON CLEVELEYS
Lancashire
Map **7** SD34

⊢⊣ **GH Lyndhope** 2 Stockdove Way, Cleveleys ☎Cleveleys (0253) 852531
Small comfortable private hotel convenient for the town and Blackpool trams.
6rm 5hc B&b£6.50 Bdi£8.50 W£59.50 ⱡ LDO6pm
ⅢⅢ CTV 8P

THORNTON HEATH
Gt London London plan **4** D1 (page 222–223)

GH Dunheved Hotel 639–641 London Rd ☎01-684 2009
rs Xmas
Family run hotel situated on A233, close to Croydon town centre. Central London easily accessible.
15hc 2⋔ (4fb) TV in 1 bedroom ✱
✱B&b£15
Lic ⅢⅢ CTV 8P

THORPE (Dovedale)
Derbyshire
Map **7** SK15

GH Hillcrest House ☎Thorpe Cloud (033529) 436
Large detached house on edge of village, enjoys good views of Dovedale.
7hc (2fb) B&b£9.50–£10 Bdi£14.45–£14.95 W£62–£67 Ṁ LDO8 30pm
Lic ⅢⅢ CTV 12P
Ⓥ

THORPE BAY
Essex
See Southend-on-Sea

THRAPSTON
Northamptonshire
Map **4** SP97

INN Court House Hotel
☎(08012) 3618
7rm 5hc 2⋔ TV in all bedrooms ✱ Ⓡ B&b£10.50–£13 Bdi£14.50–£18.50 W£73.50 M Lfr£4.75&alc D9.30pm £5alc
6P
Credit cards 1 3 Ⓥ

THRINGSTONE
Leicestershire
Map **8** SK41

FH Miss J F White **Talbot House** *(SK423173)* ☎Coalville (0530) 222233
Large old farmhouse and former coaching inn on B587 between Whitwick and Swanington, 2½ miles from Coalville.
4rm (2fb) ✱ B&bfr£8 Bdifr£13 W£42 M LDO11am
4P 150acres dairy

THROWLEIGH
Devon
Map **3** SX69

FH Mr & Mrs C R Mosse **East Ash Manor** *(SX680911)* ☎Whiddon Down (064723) 244
17th-century thatched, oak-beamed farmhouse situated in beautiful countryside. 1 mile E on Whiddon Down road.
3rm 2hc (1fb) ✱ Ⓡ B&b£9
CTV 4P 160acres dairy mixed
Ⓥ

THURLESTONE SANDS
Devon
Map **3** SX64

GH *La Mer* ☎Galmpton (0548) 561207
28 May–mid Sep
9hc (6fb)
Lic CTV 10P nc3yrs sea

THURNING
Norfolk
Map **9** TG02

FH Mrs A M Fisher **Rookery** *(TG078307)* ☎Melton Constable (0263) 860357
Apr–Oct
Off B1235 onto unclassified road at Briston.
2rm (1fb) ✱ B&b£6.50 B&b£10 W£70 L LDOam
CTV 4P 400acres arable
Ⓥ

THURSBY
Cumbria
Map **11** NY35

FH Mrs M G Swainson **How End** *(NY316497)* ☎Wigton (0965) 42487
Apr–Oct
A conveniently situated farmhouse on A595 between Carlisle and Wigton.
2rm (1fb) ✱ B&b£7–£8 Bdi£11.50–£12.50 W£50 M LDOnoon
CTV 4P 170acres dairy mixed

TICEHURST
East Sussex
Map **5** TQ63

INN Bell Hotel The Square ☎(0580) 200234
Well kept old inn with beamed accommodation.
3hc ✱ B&b£9.50 L£5alc D9.30pm £5alc
12P nc3yrs

TIDEFORD
Cornwall
Map **2** SX35

FH Mrs B A Turner **Kilna House** *(SX353600)* ☎Landrake (075538) 236
Apr–Oct
Stone-built house set in a large pleasant garden on A38, ¼ mile outside village. Overlooking the River Tiddy Valley.
5hc (2fb) B&b£7.50–£8 W£49–£52.50 M
CTV 6P 12acres poultry

TIMSBURY
Avon
Map **3** ST65

GH Old Malt House Hotel & Licensed Restaurant Radford ☎(0761) 70106
Quietly situated family run hotel offering a welcoming atmosphere with personal service.
8rm 3➡ 5⋔ CTV in all bedrooms ✱ B&b£16–£17 Bdi£23.50–£25 W£94.50–£101.50 M LDO9pm
Lic 23P nc3yrs
Credit cards 1 2 3 5

TINTAGEL
Cornwall
Map **2** SX08

GH *Belvoir House* Tregatta ☎Camelford (0840) 770265
6hc (A 1⋔) (1fb) Ⓡ LDO7pm
Lic CTV 12P sea
Ⓥ

GH Penallick Hotel Treknow ☎Camelford (0840) 770296
10rm 3hc 1⋔ (3fb) Ⓡ B&b£6–£8.25 Bdi£8.75–£11 W£55–£72 L LDO6.30pm
Lic CTV 12P
Credit cards 1 3

GH Trebrea Lodge Trenale ☎Camelford (0840) 770410
Etr–Oct
7rm 3➡ 4⋔ (3fb) CTV in all bedrooms *B&b£13 Bdi£17 W£110 L LDO7pm
Lic 10P

GH Trevervan Hotel Trewarmett ☎Camelford (0840) 770486
2m S B3263.
6hc (4fb) B&b£8.50–£9 Bdi£12.50–£13 W£75–£78 L LDO7.30pm
Lic CTV 8P
Ⓥ

GH Willapark Manor Hotel Bossiney ☎Camelford (0840) 770782

9rm 2hc 5⇥ 1fi (2fb) CTV in 2 bedrooms B&b£11–£11.50 Bdi£16–£16.50 Wfr£110 LDO9.30pm

Lic CTV 20P

Ⓥ

TINTERN
Gwent
Map **3** SO50

GH Parva Farmhouse ☎(02918) 411

A comfortable 17th-century house just 50yds from the banks of the River Wye with beamed sitting room and pretty bedrooms.

Tintagel — Tissington

5hc 1⇥ 1fi (A 2⇥) (3fb) Ⓡ B&b£9–£11 Bdi£14.50–£17 W£95–£115 LDO6.30pm

Lic CTV 10P 2

Ⓥ

INN Fountain Trellech Grange
☎(02918) 303
rs Mon Closed Dec–Feb

Attractive rural inn with restaurant providing à la carte menu.

5hc CTV in 1 bedroom TV in 4 bedrooms Ⓡ B&b£9.75 Bdi£14 W£98 L£4.50–£5.80&alc D9.30pm £4.50–£5.80&alc

60P

Ⓥ

TISSINGTON
Derbyshire
Map **7** SK15

FH Mrs B Herridge **Bent** *(SK187523)*
☎Parwich (033525) 214
mid Mar–mid Nov

Traditional stone-built farmhouse situated in the Peak District National Park. →

2hc (1fb) ★ Ⓡ B&b£7–£8 Bdi£11.50–£12.50 W£77 Ⱡ LDO5pm
▥ CTV 10P nc4yrs 280acres dairy

TIVERTON
Devon
Map **3** SS91

GH Bridge 23 Angel Hill ☎(0884) 252804
11hc (2fb) TV in 6 bedrooms B&b£9–£9.50 Bdi£13–£13.50 W£84 Ⱡ LDO6.30pm
Lic ▥ CTV 5P 1🚗 ⌂ ⚲
Ⓥ

FH Mr L Heywood **Lodge Hill** *(ST945112)* Ashley ☎(0884) 252907
Large rendered farmhouse on hillside in the Exe Valley, situated 1 mile S of town, 400yds off A396.
7hc (1fb) Ⓡ B&b£8.25 Bdi£11 W£54 M LDO7pm
Lic ▥ CTV 14P ⌂ 40acres mixed

FH R Olive **Lower Collipriest** *(SS953117)* ☎(0884) 252321
Apr–Oct
Lovely thatched farmhouse with attractive courtyard offering speciality traditional cooking.
3rm 1hc 2➡ ⋒ ★ Ⓡ ✱B&b£10–£11 Bdi£12–£14 W£85–£90 Ⱡ LDOnoon
▥ CTV 6P 3🚗 nc12yrs ⚲ 220acres beef dairy

TIVETSHALL ST MARGARET
Norfolk
Map **5** TM18

GH ***Glenhaven*** ☎(037977) 238
5hc (1fb)
▥ TV 8P

TOBERMORY
Isle of Mull, Strathclyde *Argyllshire*
Map **13** NM55

GH Tobermory 53 Main St ☎(0688) 2091
early Apr–Oct
Double-fronted three-storey building with two lounges and comfortable accommodation.
14rm 13hc 1➡ (2fb) Ⓡ B&b£12.50 Bdi£19 W£130 Ⱡ LDO5pm
Lic CTV

TODMORDEN
West Yorkshire
Map **7** SD92

⊢⊣ **FH** Mrs R Bayley **Todmorden Edge South** *(SD924246)* Parkin Ln, Sourhall Rd ☎(070681) 3459
Converted 17th-century farmhouse on hillside. Clean, comfortable rooms and a cosy residents lounge 1m from town centre.
3hc (1fb) ★ B&b£8–£10.50 Bdi£13.50–£16 W£53 M LDO7.30pm
▥ CTV 10P nc8yrs 1acre non-working
Ⓥ

TOMDOUN
Highland *Inverness-shire*
Map **14** NH10

⊢⊣ **FH** Mrs H Fraser **No 3 Greenfield** *(NH201006)* ☎(08092) 221
mid May–early Oct
Small modern bungalow set in isolated position in rugged, hilly countryside. 2m E on S side of Loch Garry.
3rm (1fb) ★ B&b£6.50–£7 Bdi£10.50–£11 W£72 Ⱡ LDO7pm
CTV 6P 172acres arable mixed

TORBAY
Devon
See under Brixham, Paignton and Torquay

TORCROSS
Devon
Map **3** SX84

GH Cove House ☎Kingsbridge (0548) 580448
Mar–Nov
12rm 8hc 1➡ (1fb) CTV in 1 bedroom TV in 11 bedrooms ★ B&b£10.50–£12.50 Bdi£17.60–£19.60 W£105–£125 M (W only 16 May–Aug) LDO11am
Lic 12P nc8yrs

TORQUAY
Devon
Map **3** SX96
See Central & District plans

⊢⊣ **GH Allandene Seapoint Hotel** 5 Clifton Gv, Old Torwood Rd ☎(0803) 211808
Central plan **30** *F3*
Mar–Nov
10hc (3fb) ★ B&b£6–£8 Bdi£8–£10.50 LDO6.30pm
Lic CTV 4P 1🚗

GH Ashwood Hotel 1 St Margarets Rd ☎(0803) 38173 District plan **45**
May–Oct
9hc (2fb) TV in 1 bedroom ✱B&b£8–£9 Bdi£12.50–£13.50 W£84–£89 Ⱡ LDO5.30pm
Lic CTV 10P 1🚗 ♿ ⌂

GH Aston Hotel Belgrave Rd ☎(0803) 22407 Central plan **1** *B3*
21hc 2⋒ (4fb) CTV in 4 bedrooms Ⓡ B&bfr£8.50 Bdifr£11 Wfr£55 M
Lic ▥ CTV 4P

GH Avron Hotel 70 Windsor Rd ☎(0803) 24182 District plan **46**
May–Sep
14rm 7hc 6⋒ (2fb) TV in all bedrooms Ⓡ W£53–£59 M LDO6.30pm
CTV 6P

⊢⊣ **GH Aylwood House Hotel** 24 Newton Rd ☎(0803) 23501
Central Plan **1A** *A4*
Etr–Oct
10rm 7hc 2➡ 1⋒ (2fb) B&b£6–£8 Bdi£9–£12 W£42–£56 M LDO5pm
▥ CTV 10P ⌂

⊢⊣ **GH Beechmoor Hotel** Vansittart Rd ☎(0803) 22471 Central plan **2** *B3*
Mar–Oct rs Nov–Feb
16hc 2➡ 1⋒ (2fb) ★ B&b£6.50–£7.50 Bdi£8.50–£12 W£55–£84 Ⱡ LDO6.30pm
Lic ▥ CTV 26P 1🚗
Ⓥ

⊢⊣ **GH Blue Waters Hotel** 58 Bampfylde Rd ☎(0803) 26410
Central plan **2A** *B2*
Etr–Oct
8rm 5hc 1⋒ (1fb) ★ B&b£7–£9.50 Bdi£10.50–£14 W£70–£85 Ⱡ LDO6pm
Lic CTV 8P nc5yrs
Ⓥ

⊢⊣ **GH Braddon Hall Hotel** Braddons Hill Road East ☎(0803) 23908
Central plan **3** *F3*
Jan–Oct & Xmas
13rm 12hc 1➡ (5fb) Ⓡ B&b£6.75–£9.50 Bdi£9.10–£12.50 W£46–£65 M LDO6.30pm
Lic ▥ CTV 10P

⊢⊣ **GH Brandize Hotel** 19 Avenue Rd ☎(0803) 27798
Central plan **4** *A3*
Etr–Oct
12rm 11hc 1⋒ (4fb) B&b£6–£8 Bdi£9–£13 Wfr£45 M (W only 23 Jun–10 Sep) LDO5pm
Lic CTV 12P

GH Burley Court Hotel Wheatridge Ln, Livermead ☎(0803) 607879
District plan **47**
Etr–15 Oct
21hc 2➡ 19⋒ (7fb) ★ Ⓡ B&b£10.50–£12.50 Bdi£12.50–£16 W£68–£85 M LDO6.30pm
Lic ▥ CTV 21P ♒ (heated)
Ⓥ

GH Carn Brea 21 Avenue Rd ☎(0803) 22002 Central plan **5** *B3*
Closed Dec
21hc 7⋒ (4fb) Ⓡ ✱B&b£7–£10 Bdi£10.50–£14.50 W£70–£95 Ⱡ LDO7pm
Lic ▥ CTV 17P 2🚗
Ⓥ

⊢⊣ **GH Casey's Court Motel** 127 Newton Rd ☎(0803) 63909
District plan **48**
Apr–Oct
6hc (2fb) TV in all bedrooms Ⓡ B&b£6–£7.50 W£40–£45 M
▥ 6P 1🚗 nc2yrs
Ⓥ

Torquay

⊢×⊣ **GH Castle Mount Hotel** 7 Castle Rd ☎(0803) 22130 Central plan **6** *D4*
Feb–Oct
9hc B&bfr£7 Bdifr£11.50 Wfr£45.50 M̸
LDO1pm
CTV 7P nc7yrs
Ⓥ

GH Castleton Private Hotel Castle Rd ☎(0803) 24976 Central plan **7** *D3*
15hc ✶ LDO4pm
Lic ▥ CTV 8P nc4yrs
Ⓥ

GH *Chelston House Hotel* Chelston Rd ☎(0803) 605200 Central plan **8** *B1*
18hc 3⇌ 1⋔ (3fb) LDO5.30pm
Lic ▥ CTV 25P

⊢×⊣ **GH Cheltenham Hotel** Rousdown Rd ☎(0803) 605488 Central plan **8A** *A2*
Etr–Oct
23rm 15hc 6⇌ 2⋔ (6fb) ✶ B&b£8–£12 Bdi£11.60–£16.30 W£50–£75 Ɫ
LDO7pm
Lic CTV 17P nc4yrs ≋ (heated)

⊢×⊣ **GH Chesterfield Hotel** 62 Belgrave Rd ☎(0803) 22318 Central plan **9** *B3*
Mar–Oct
14hc (6fb) B&b£7–£8.50 Bdi£10–£12 W£45–£55 M̸
CTV 3P

GH Clairville 1 Teignmouth Rd, Brunswick Square, Torre ☎(0803) 24540 Central plan **9A** *B4*
10hc (3b) ✶ *B&b£5–£7 Bdi£7–£9 W£35–£49 M̸ (W only 14 Jul–18 Aug)
LDO6.30pm
▥ CTV ₱̸

GH Clevedon Private Hotel Meadfoot Sea Rd ☎(0803) 24260 District plan **49**
Apr–Oct
15rm 14hc 1⇌ (2fb) B&b£8.75–£10.64 Bdi£10–£15 W£70–£103.50 Ɫ S%
LDO7.30pm
Lic CTV 10P nc6yrs

GH *Clovelly Hotel* 89 Avenue Rd ☎(0803) 22286 Central plan **10** *A4*
Closed 20 Dec–3 Jan
13hc (6fb) ✶ LDO5.30pm
Lic ▥ CTV 7P

⊢×⊣ **GH Hotel Concorde** 26 Newton Rd ☎(0803) 22330 Central plan **11** *A4*
Etr–Oct
10hc 5⋔ (7fb) B&b£7–£9.50 Bdi£11–£13.50 W£42–£60 M̸ (W only Jul & Aug)
LDO6pm
Lic ▥ CTV 12P ≋ (heated)

⊢×⊣ **GH Craig Court Hotel** 10 Ash Hill Rd, Castle Circus ☎(0803) 24400 Central plan **12** *D4*
Etr–Oct
10rm 6hc 4⋔ (3fb) ✶ B&b£6.25–£9.75 Bdi£9.25–£12.75 W£43.75–£68.25 Ɫ
LDO5.30pm
Lic CTV 10P ⌂

See advertisement on page 346

⊢×⊣ **GH Cranborne Hotel** 58 Belgrave Rd ☎(0803) 28046 Central plan **12A** *B3*
15rm 7hc 5⇌ (5fb) ✶ B&b£6.50–£9.50 Bdi£11–£14 W£45–£63.50 M̸ LDO3pm
CTV 3P
Credit cards ① ③ Ⓥ

See advertisement on page 347

GH Daphne Court Hotel Lower Warberry Rd ☎(0803) 212011 Central plan **12B** *F4*
15rm 6hc 9⇌⋔ Ⓡ B&b£8.50–£9.50 Bdi£13–£15.25 W£55–£60 M̸ (W only mid Jul–mid Aug) LDO5.30pm
▥ CTV 12P ≋ (heated) billiards

GH Devon Court Hotel Croft Rd ☎(0803) 23603 Central plan **13** *C3*
Feb–Nov →

Friendly hotel with well-maintained gardens, bright bedrooms and comfortable public rooms.

14rm 1⋒ (2fb) ✗ Ⓡ B&b£5–£14 Bdi£8–£17 W£56–£98 Ⱡ LDO5pm

Lic ☗ CTV 15P ⛆(heated)

Credit cards ① ②

⊢✕⊣ **GH El Marino Hotel** Lower Warberry Rd ☎(0803) 26882 Central plan **13A** *F4*
Etr–Oct

22rm 2⇾ 21⋒ (6fb) ✗ B&b£8–£10 Bdi£10.50–£14.50 W£80–£110 Ⱡ (W only Jul & Aug) LDO6.30pm

Lic ☗ CTV 22P ⛆(heated)

GH *Elm Court* Cary Av, Babbacombe ☎(0803) 37828 District Plan **50**
Etr–Nov

16hc 2⋒ (4fb)

Lic ☗ CTV 12P nc4yrs

⊢✕⊣ **GH Erin Hotel** Avenue Rd ☎(0803) 27844 Central plan **14** *A3*

15hc (2fb) ✗ B&b£7–£9 Bdi£9.50–£13.50 W£47–£60 Ⱡ LDO6pm

Lic ☗ CTV 12P

⊢✕⊣ **GH Exmouth View Hotel** St Albans Rd, Babbacombe Downs ☎(0803) 37307 District plan **51**
Etr–Oct & Xmas

36rm 27hc 6⋒ (7fb) B&b£8–£11.50 Bdi£11.25–£15 W£78.75– £105 Ⱡ

Lic ☗ CTV 25P

⊢✕⊣ **GH Fluela Hotel** 15–17 Hatfield Rd ☎(0803) 27512 District plan **52**

16⋒ (4fb) CTV in 1 bedroom TV in 4 bedrooms Ⓡ B&b£8–£10.50 Bdi£10–£12.50 W£60–£85 Ⱡ LDO7pm

Lic ☗ CTV 24P ⌂

GH *Forest Hotel* Haldon Rd ☎(0803) 24842 District plan **53**
Etr & mid May–mid Oct

34hc 12⇾ (6fb)

Lic CTV 20P sea

⊢✕⊣ **GH Fretherne Hotel** St Lukes Road South ☎(0803) 22594
Central plan **15** *D2*
Etr–Oct

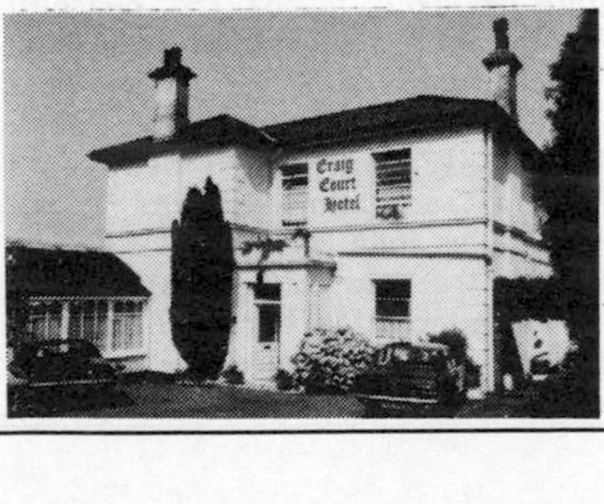

24hc B&b£7–£8 Bdi£11.50–£12.60 W£49–£56 M LDO5pm

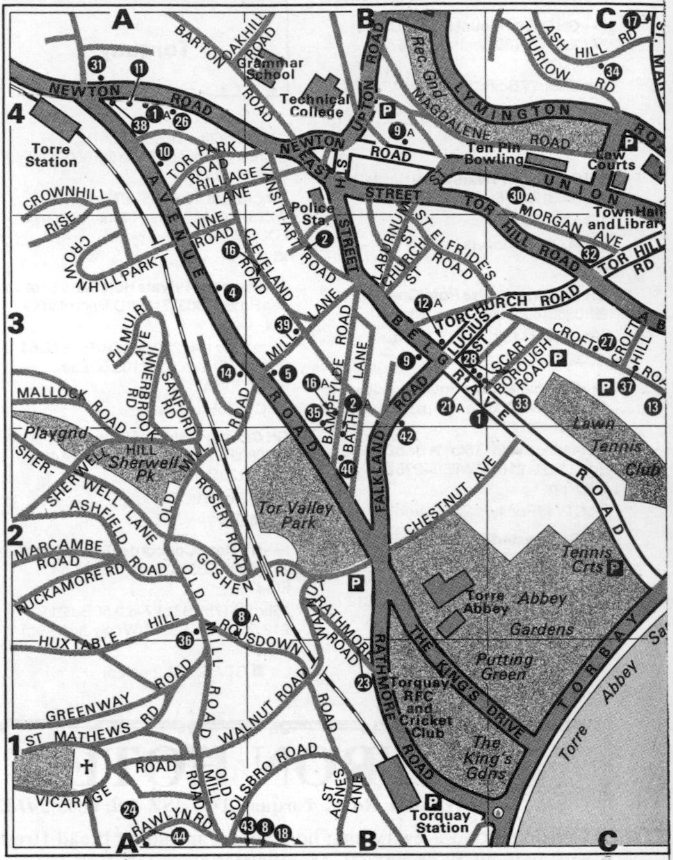

Lic CTV 20P

GH Glenorleigh Hotel 26 Cleveland Rd ☎(0803) 22135 Central plan **16** *A3*
Closed Xmas

16hc 7⋒ (5fb) ✗ Ⓡ B&b£10.35–£13.80 Bdi£11.50–£17.25 W£74.75–£119.60 M LDO6pm

Lic ☗ CTV 10P ⛆(heated)

Ⓥ

See advertisement on page 348

⊢✕⊣ **GH Glenwood Hotel** Rowdens Rd ☎(0803) 26318 Central plan **16A** *B3*

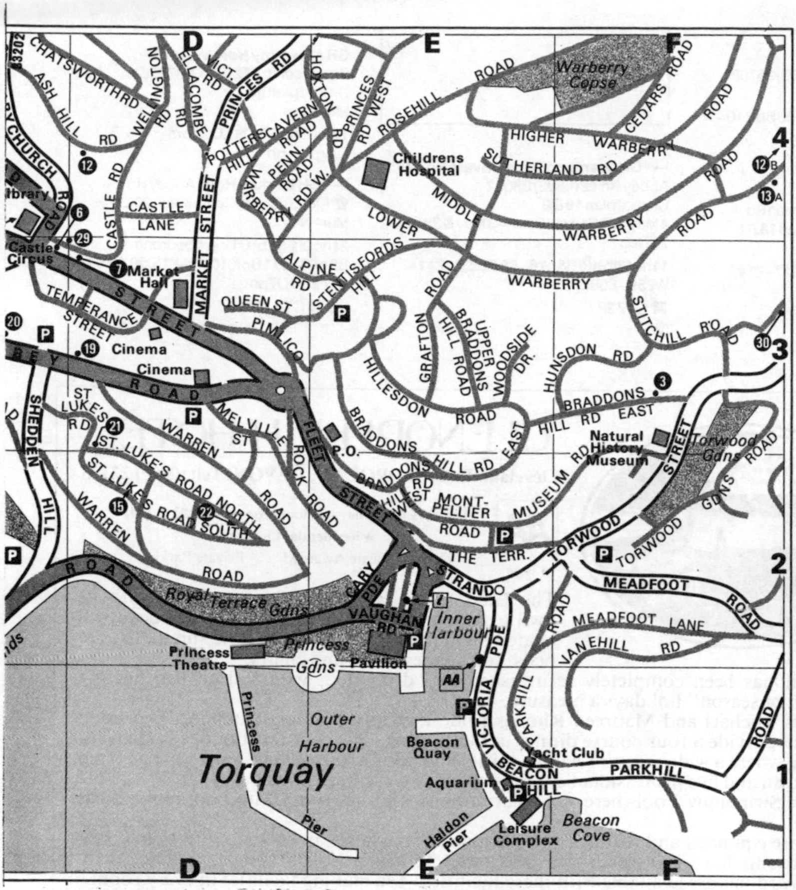

Torquay Central

1 Aston Hotel
1A Aylwood House Hotel
2 Beechmoor Hotel
2A Blue Waters Hotel
3 Braddon Hall Hotel
4 Brandize Hotel
5 Carn Brea
6 Castle Mount Hotel
7 Castleton Private Hotel
8 Chelston House Hotel
8A Cheltenham Hotel
9 Chesterfield Hotel
9A Claireville
10 Clovelly Hotel
11 Hotel Concorde
12 Craig Court Hotel
12A Cranborne Hotel
12B Daphne Court Hotel
13 Devon Court Hotel
13A El Marino Hotel
14 Erin Hotel
15 Fretherne Hotel
16 Glenorleigh Hotel
16A Glenwood Hotel
17 Hatherleigh Hotel
18 Ingoldsby Hotel
19 Jesmond Dene Private Hotel
20 Lindum Hotel
21 Mapleton Hotel
21A Marlow Hotel
22 Mount Nessing Hotel
23 Normanhurst Hotel
24 Rawlyn House Hotel
26 Richwood Hotel
27 Riva Lodge
28 Rothesay Hotel
29 St Bernards Private Hotel
30 Allandene Seapoint Hotel
30A Sevens Hotel
31 Silverlands Hotel
32 Skerries Private Hotel
33 Southbank Hotel
34 Stephen House Hotel
35 Sun Court Private Hotel
36 Torbay Rise
37 Torcroft Hotel
38 Tormohun Hotel
39 Trafalgar House Hotel
40 Tregantle Hotel
42 Westgate Hotel
43 Westowe Hotel
44 White Gables Hotel

10hc (5fb) B&b£7.50–£9 Bdi£13–£15 W£79–£88 L LDOnoon
Lic CTV 9P

GH Hart-Lea 81 St Marychurch Rd
☎(0803) 312527 District plan **53A**

A comfortable house offering a very good standard of accommodation and an interesting menu.
6hc (2fb) ® B&b£5–£6.50 Bdi£7–£9 W£35–£45 L LDO6pm
CTV

Torquay

⊢⊣ **GH Hatherleigh Hotel**
56 St Marychurch Rd ☎(0803) 25762
Central plan **17** *C4*
18hc (4fb) ★ Ⓡ B&b£6–£8.50 Bdi£10–£11.50 W£63–£82 ⱡ LDO4pm
Lic CTV 18P
Ⓥ

GH Ingoldsby Hotel 1 Chelston Rd
☎(0803) 607497 Central plan **18** *B1*
Mar–Oct
16hc (5fb) B&b£9–£11 Bdi£11–£14 W£55–£65 M LDO4.50pm
Lic CTV 14P

⊢⊣ **GH Jesmond Dene Private Hotel** 85 Abbey Rd ☎(0803) 23062
Central plan **19** *D2*
4 May–27 Sep rs 10 Jan–3 May & 28 Sep–21 Dec
11hc (3fb) Ⓡ B&b£6–£8 Bdi£9–£11 W£59–£68 ⱡ
CTV 3P
Ⓥ

GH ***Kilworthy Hotel*** Westhill Rd, Babbacombe ☎(0803) 37236
District plan **55**
Mar–Dec
12hc 2 (4fb) ★ LDO6pm
Lic CTV 10P

⊢⊣ **GH Lindum Hotel** Abbey Rd
☎(0803) 22795 Central plan **20** *C3*
Mar–Nov
21hc 9 (2fb) CTV in 4 bedrooms
B&b£8–£11 Bdi£10.50–£15.50 W£64–£77 ⱡ LDO7pm
Lic CTV 14P

Torquay

GH *Mapleton Hotel* St Lukes Rd North ☎(0803) 22389 Central plan **21** *D3*
Apr–Oct
9hc (3fb) ★ LDO6pm
Lic CTV 8P

⊢⊣ **GH Marlow Hotel** 23 Belgrave Rd ☎(0803) 22833 Central plan **21A** *B3*
14hc (3fb) B&b£7–£9 Bdi£10–£12.50 W£49–£63⊮ LDOnoon
Lic ▥ CTV 2P
ⓥ

GH Mount Nessing Hotel St Lukes Rd North ☎(0803) 22970 Central plan **22** *D2*
Etr–Oct & Xmas
13hc (5fb) *B&b£6.50–£10 Bdi£10–£14 W£59–£91⊮ S% LDO4pm
Lic ▥ CTV 10P

GH *Normanhurst Hotel* Rathmore Rd ☎(0803) 22420 Central plan **23** *B1*
May–Oct rs Apr
13hc (6fb) ★
Lic CTV 10P

GH Parkfield Hotel Claddon Ln, Maidencombe ☎(0803) 38952 District plan **55A**
29 Mar–19 Oct
13rm 10hc 3⋔ (4fb) *B&b£7–£9.50 Bdi£11–£14 W£49–£66.50⊮ LDO1pm
Lic CTV 20P

GH Pembroke Hotel Meadfoot Sea Rd ☎(0803) 22837 District plan **56**
Apr–Oct
18hc 1⋔ (3fb) ★ B&b£8.80–£9.78 Bdi£14.95–£16.10 W£75.90–£107.53⊮ LDO5.30pm
Lic CTV 8P ≋ (heated)

⊢⊣ **GH Pencarrow Hotel** 64 Windsor Rd ☎(0803) 23080 District plan **57**
mid May–early Oct
13rm 8⋔ (2fb) CTV in all bedrooms Ⓡ B&b£6.75–£8.25 Bdi£10–£12.50 W£68.50–£85⊮ (W only mid Jul–mid Aug) LDO6.30pm
Lic CTV 8P nc5yrs

⊢⊣ **GH Pines Hotel** St Marychurch Rd ☎(0803) 38384 District plan **58**
22rm 21hc 1→ (6fb) ★ Ⓡ B&b£7.25–£9 Bdi£11–£13.75 W£49.50–£62⊮
Lic CTV 15P

⊢⊣ **GH Porthcressa Hotel** 28 Perinville Rd, Babbacombe ☎(0803) 37268 District plan **58A**
13rm 10hc (3fb) B&b£7.50–£8.50 Bdi£10.50–£11.50 W£68–£85⊮
Lic CTV

GH Rawlyn House Hotel Rawlyn Rd, Chelston ☎(0803) 605208 Central plan **24** *A1*
Mar–Oct & Xmas
15rm 10hc 5⋔ (A 2hc) (5fb) ★ B&bfr£8.50 Bdifr£10 Wfr£70⊮ LDO6.55pm
Lic ▥ CTV 12P ⌂ ≋ (heated)

GH *Richwood Hotel* 20 Newton Rd ☎(0803) 23729 Central plan **26** *A4*
Etr–Oct
23hc 11⋔ (8fb) LDO4pm
Lic CTV 10P

GH *Riva Lodge* Croft Rd ☎(0803) 22614 Central plan **27** *C3*
Mar–Oct
18hc 7→⋔ (5fb) ★
Lic CTV 18P nc10yrs

GH Rosewood Teignmouth Rd, Maidencombe ☎(0803) 38178 District plan **59**
Mar–Sep rs Oct, Nov & Feb
8hc 1⋔ (3fb) ★ *B&b£7–£8 Bdi£10.30–£11.50 W£49–£56M LDO4.30pm
▥ CTV 14P nc2yrs

GH Rothesay Hotel Scarborough Rd ☎(0803) 23161 Central plan **28** *B3*
Mar–Oct
38hc (10fb) ★ *B&b£8–£11 W£77–£99 ⊮ LDO5pm
Lic CTV 35P ⌂
See advertisement on page 351

⊢⊣ **GH St Bernards Private Hotel** Castle Rd ☎(0803) 22508
Central plan **29** *B3*
Closed Xmas
14rm 3⋒ (5fb) ✱ B&b£6–£10.50 Bdi£12–£21 W£60–£85L (W only Jul & Aug)
LDO10am
Lic ▥ CTV 8P

GH Sevens Hotel 27 Morgan Av ☎(0803) 23523 Central plan **30A** *C4*

Torquay

13hc 3⋒ (4fb) ✱ ✻ B&b£6.32–£8.62 Bdi£9.80–£12.80 W£44.24–£60.34L
LDO4pm
Lic ▥ CTV 11P

GH Silverlands Hotel 27 Newton Rd ☎(0803) 22013 Central plan **31** *A4*
Closed Xmas
12hc (1fb) ✻ B&b£6–£7 W£42–£49M
▥ CTV 12P

⊢⊣ **GH Skerries Private Hotel** 25 Morgan Av ☎(0803) 23618
Central plan **32** *C3*

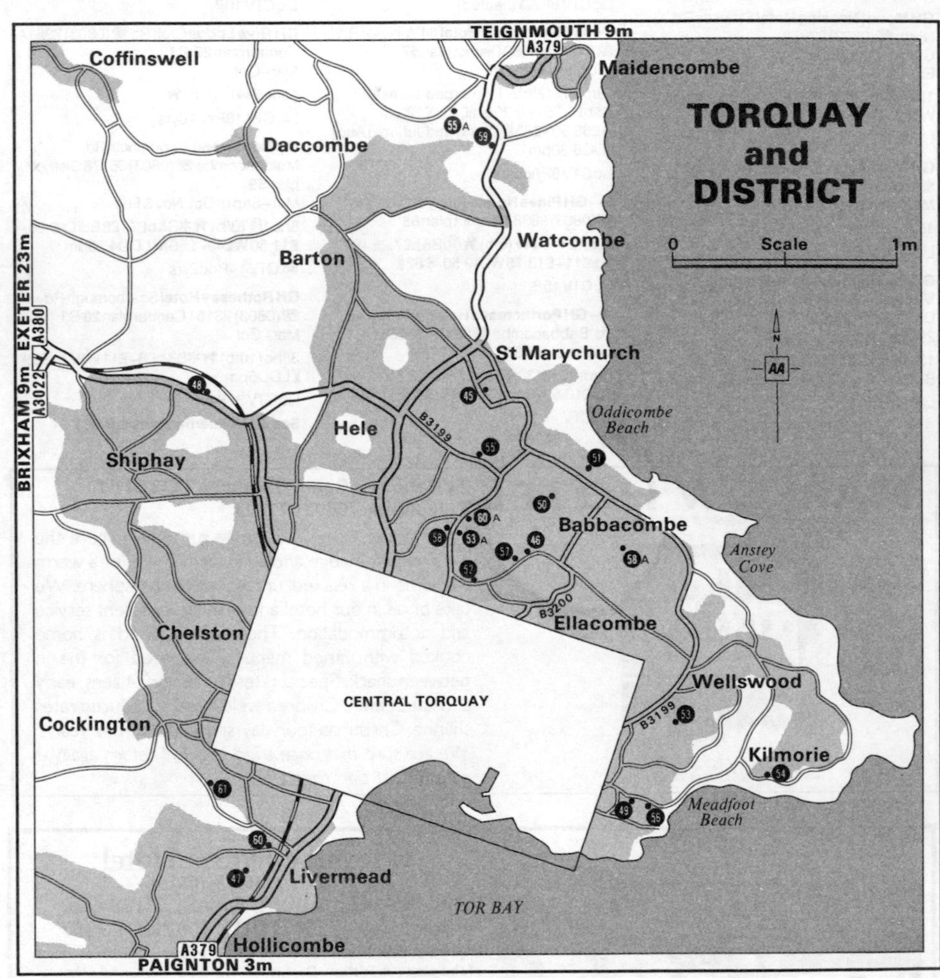

Torquay District

45 Ashwood
46 Avron Hotel
47 Burley Court Hotel
48 Casey's Court Motel
49 Clevedon Private Hotel
50 Elm Court
51 Exmouth View Hotel
52 Fluela Hotel
53 Forest Hotel
53A Hart-Lea
55 Kilworthy Hotel
55A Parkfield Hotel
56 Pembroke Hotel
57 Pencarrow Hotel
58 Pines Hotel
58A Porthcressa
59 Rosewood
60 Sunleigh Hotel
60A Ventnor
61 Villa Marina Hotel

12hc (3fb) ® B&b£6.50–£8.50 Bdi£9.50–£11.50 W£63–£77 L LDO10.30am
CTV 7P
Ⓥ

GH Southbank Hotel 15/17 Belgrave Rd ☎(0803) 26701 Central plan **33** *C3*
Apr–Nov rs Mar
20hc (7fb) ® B&b£9–£11 Bdi£12.50–£14.50 W£61–£75 M LDO5pm
Lic CTV 14P

Torquay

GH Stephen House Hotel 50 Ash Mill Rd ☎(0803) 25796
Central plan **34** *C4*
Etr–Oct
15rm 12hc 1 2 (6fb) B&b£5–£10 Bdi£9–£14 W£34–£70 (W only mid Jul–Aug) LDO5.30pm
Lic CTV 11P (heated)
Ⓥ

GH *Sun Court Private Hotel* Rowdens Rd ☎(0803) 27242 Central plan **35** *B3*
Mar–Nov
12hc (2fb) LDO5.30pm
Lic CTV 12P nc7yrs

GH Sunleigh Hotel Livermead Hill ☎(0803) 607137 District plan **60**
Etr–Oct
23rm 8hc 12 (3fb) ® B&b£8.75–£9.75 Bdi£11.50–£14.50 W£72.62–£90.50 L LDO6pm
Lic CTV 18P

GH Torbay Rise Old Mill Rd ☎(0803) 605541 Central plan **36** *A2* Etr–Oct & 4 days Xmas
16rm 14hc 2⋔ (3fb) Ⓡ B&b£8.50–£12.50 Bdi£12–£16 W£70–£105 Ⱡ LDO5.30pm
Lic CTV 10P ⩸ (heated)
Credit cards 1 3

GH Torcroft Hotel Croft Rd ☎(0803) 28292 Central plan **37** *C3* Mar–Oct
21hc 6⋔ (6fb) ✶ B&b£7.50–£10.50 Bdi£10–£14 W£65–£92 Ⱡ LDO5pm
Lic CTV 15P
Ⓥ

GH Tormohun Hotel 28 Newton Rd ☎(0803) 23681 Central plan **38** *A4*
23rm 10hc 4⇌ 4⋔ (2fb) CTV in all bedrooms ✻ B&b£6.90–£8.62 Bdi£11.96–£14 W£48.30–£60.37 Ⱡ LDO7.30pm
Lic ▥ 23P ⩸ (heated)
Credit cards 1 2

GH Trafalgar House Hotel Bridge Rd ☎(0803) 22486 Centrl plan **39** *B3*
13rm 11hc 2⋔ (3fb) B&b£6.50–£8 Bdi£10–£11.50 W£40–£56 Ⱡ LDO3pm
Lic CTV 7P
Ⓥ

GH Tregantle Hotel 64 Bampfylde Rd ☎(0803) 27494 Central plan **40** *B2*
11hc (2fb) B&b£7–£9 Bdi£11–£13.50 W£49–£60 M LDOnoon
Lic ▥ CTV 10P
Credit card 3 Ⓥ

GH Ventnor 85 St Marychurch Rd ☎(0803) 39132 District plan **60A** 25 May–28 Sep
6hc (2fb) ✶ Ⓡ B&b£5.90–£6.95 Bdi£9.10–£10.10 W£41.30–£48.65 Ⱡ (W only Jul & Aug) LDO10am
▥ CTV P
Ⓥ

GH Villa Marina Hotel Cockington Ln, Livermead ☎(0803) 605440 District plan **61** Apr–Sep
26rm 6hc 18⇌ 2⋔ (5fb) ✻ Bdi11.50–£14.65 LDO6.45pm
▥ CTV 25P

GH *Westgate Hotel* Falkland Rd ☎(0803) 25350 Central plan **42** *B2* Etr–Nov
14hc (5fb)
Lic CTV 12P ⌂

GH Westowe Hotel Chelston Rd ☎(0803) 605207 Central plan **43** *B1* Mar–Oct
Hotel exclusively for non-smokers.
12rm 10hc (1fb) CTV in 2 bedrooms ✶ B&b£10.50–£13.50 W£73.50–£94.50 Ⱡ
Lic ▥ CTV 8P nc5yrs
Ⓥ

GH White Gables Hotel Rawlyn Rd ☎(0803) 605233 Central plan **44** *A1*
10hc (4fb) ✶ B&b£6–£10 Bdi£9–£13 W£60–£90 Ⱡ LDO4pm
Lic ▥ CTV 10P

TORRINGTON, GREAT
Devon
Map **2** SS41

GH Smytham ☎(0805) 22110 May–Oct rs Nov–Apr
12hc (2fb) B&b£6.50 Bdi£10 W£70 Ⱡ LDO4pm
Lic CTV 12P ⩸

TORTHORWALD
Dumfries & Galloway *Dumfriesshire*
Map **11** NY07

INN Torr House Hotel ☎Collin (038775) 214
Small village hotel, a converted manse, which looks across farmland to Dumfries and the Solway coast.

6hc (3fb) Ⓡ B&b£10.50 Bdi£15.50 W£52.50 M LDO9.45pm
Lic 𝍔 CTV 120P ✓

TOTLAND BAY
Isle of Wight
Map **4** SZ38

GH Garrow Hotel Church Hill ☎Isle of Wight (0983) 753174
mid May–mid Sep
Large, Victorian house with clean accommodation and attractive gardens.
16rm 10hc 1➡ 5fi (7fb) B&b£10 Bdi£13 W£70 L LDO7pm
Lic 𝍔 CTV 16P nc3yrs

GH Hermitage Hotel Cliff Rd ☎Isle of Wight (0983) 752518
Small, family run hotel with comfortable lounges and nicely appointed bedrooms.
12rm 5hc 2➡ 2fi (4fb) B&b£10.50–£12 Bdi£16–£23 W£97–£146 M LDO7pm
Lic CTV 12P ⌂ ≈
Credit cards 1 3

⊢ **GH Hilton House Private Hotel** Granville Rd ☎Isle of Wight (0983) 754768
Mar–Oct
Set in a residential area in a peaceful house offering comfort and a touch of class.
6rm 5hc 1fi (2fb) Ⓡ B&b£7.50–£8 Bdi£12.50–£13 W£47.50–£50 M LDO8pm
Lic 𝍔 CTV 4P

GH Lismore Private Hotel 23 The Avenue ☎Isle of Wight (0983) 752025
Closed Dec
Small, friendly, well-kept accommodation.
8rm 4hc 4fi (4fb) ✱ Ⓡ B&b£8.50–£10 Bdi£12.50–£14 W£77–£86 L LDOnoon
Lic 𝍔 CTV 8P nc5yrs
Ⓥ

GH Nodes Country Hotel Alum Bay Old Rd ☎Isle of Wight (0983) 752859
Apr–Oct
A country house set in 2½ acres of downland countryside, with modern compact well-appointed bedrooms.
11hc 2➡ 6fi (6fb) Ⓡ B&b£10–£14 Bdi£15–£19 W£90–£120 L LDO7pm
Lic 𝍔 CTV 16P ⌂
Ⓥ

GH Sandford Lodge Private Hotel 61 The Avenue ☎Isle of Wight (0983) 753478
Mar–Sep
The bedrooms here are colourful, well-appointed and the cooking style is continental.
6rm 5hc 1➡ (2fb) ✱ Ⓡ B&b£8.50–£9 Bdi£13.50–£14.50 W£58–£60 M (W only Jul–Sep) LDO4.30pm
Lic 𝍔 CTV 7P nc3yrs

GH Westgrange Country Hotel Alum Bay Old Rd ☎Isle of Wight (0983) 752227
15 Apr–Oct
Small, friendly country hotel with comfortable bedrooms and good cooking.
13hc 8fi (8fb) ✱ B&b£9.50–£11.50 Bdi£14–£15.50 W£65–£75 M LDO7pm
Lic 𝍔 CTV 15P
See advertisement on page 354

TOTNES
Devon
Map **3** SX86

GH Four Seasons 13 Bridgetown ☎(0803) 862091
6hc (3fb) ✱ Ⓡ B&b£8.50 Bdi£12.50 W£84 L LDOam
Lic CTV
Ⓥ

FH Mrs G J Veale **Broomborough House** *(SX793601)* ☎(0803) 863134
Mar–Oct

Spacious, country-manor style house in hilly parkland with views of Dartmoor and the surrounding countryside. Games room and local game fishing.

3hc (2fb) ★ Ⓡ ✱B&b£9.50–£10.50 Bdi£16–£17 W£62.50–£69.50 M LDOnoon

CTV P

TOTTENHILL
Norfolk
Map **9** TF61

GH Oakwood House Private Hotel ☎Kings Lynn (0553) 810256
Closed 24–28 Dec

9rm 7hc 1⋔ (1fb) CTV in all bedrooms ★ Ⓡ ✱B&b£11.50 Bdi£18–£19 Wfr£98 L LDO9pm

Lic 20P

Credit cards 1 2 3 5

TOWCESTER
Northamptonshire
Map **4** SP64

INN Brave Oak Watling St ☎(0327) 50533

12rm 8hc 1⇌ CTV in all bedrooms Ⓡ B&bfr£15.50 Bdifr£23.45 L£2.10–£4.50 D9.30pm £3–£4.50&alc

12P

Credit cards 1 2 3 5

TRAPP
Dyfed
Map **3** SN61

⊢⊣ **FH** N & J Card **Llwyndewi Farm Guesthouse** *(SN658177)* ☎Llandybie (0269) 850362
Closed Xmas

Delightful 200 year old character small farm guesthouse overlooking the Black Mountains. A warm hospitable welcome from the proprietors who ensure comfortable accommodation and good home cooking.

4rm 1hc (1fb) ★ B&b£7–£8 Bdi£10.25–£11.50 W£70–£77 L

Lic CTV 12P 6acres mixed

TREARDDUR BAY
Gwynedd
Map **6** SH27

GH *High Ground* Lon Penrhyn Garw, Ravenspoint Rd ☎(0407) 860078

Built in 1922 this imposing detached house is set on a rocky outcrop, adjacent to sandy beach.

7hc (4fb)

Lic CTV 14P 2 sea

⊢⊣ **GH Moranedd** ☎(0407) 860324
May–Dec

7hc (1fb) Ⓡ B&bfr£7 Bdifr£10 Wfr£49 M LDO6pm

CTV 8P

Ⓥ

TREBARWITH
Cornwall
Map **2** SX08

INN Mill House ☎Camelford (0840) 770200
Closed 24 Dec–2 Jan

9rm 3hc 1⇌ 5⋔ CTV in all bedrooms Ⓡ B&b£12–£17.10 Bdi£19–£24.10 W£84–£119.70 M Bar lunch £3.25alc D9pm £9alc

50P nc10yrs

TREFEGLWYS
Powys
Map **6** SN99

⊢⊣ **FH** Mrs J Williams **Cefn-Gwyn** *(SO993923)* ☎(05516) 648

Clean and homely farmhouse, situated on B4569.

2hc (1fb) B&b£7–£8 Bdi£10–£11 W£70 L LDO6pm

CTV 12P 2 56acres mixed

TREFIN (TREVINE)
Dyfed
Map **2** SM83

FH Mrs B C Morgan **Binchurn** *(SM843313)* ☎Croesgoch (03483) 264
Apr–Nov
1m S unclass rd.
6hc ★ ® B&b£10 Bdi£14–£15 W£70 M
LDO6pm
CTV P beef dairy mixed sheep

TREFRIW
Gwynedd
Map **6** SH76

FH Mr & Mrs D E Roberts **Cae-Coch** *(SH779646)* ☎Llanrwst (0492) 640380
Etr–Oct rs Nov–Etr
Pleasant farmhouse in elevated position on side of Conwy Valley.
3rm B&b£7.25 W£48 M
TV 3P 1 nc3yrs 50acres mixed

TREGARON
Dyfed
Map **3** SN65

GH Aberdwr Abergwesyn Rd ☎(09744) 255
Apr–Oct
Farm guesthouse in rural location 1 mile from the village.
3hc (1fb) ★ B&b£8–£9 Bdi£13–£14 W£56–£63 M LDO5.30pm
CTV 12P
Credit card 2

FH Mrs M J Cutter **Neuaddlas** *(SN663620)* ☎(09744) 380
4hc 1 ® Bdi£13.50–£15.50 W£94.50 L LDO6pm
CTV 8P 40acres mixed Ⓥ

TREGONY *(Near Truro)*
Cornwall
Map **2** SW94

GH Tregony House 15 Fore St ☎(087253) 671
Mar–Oct
Double fronted stone house in village dating back to 17th century.
6hc Bdi£15.50 W£101 L
Lic CTV 6P nc5yrs Ⓥ

TRENEAR *(Near Helston)*
Cornwall
Map **2** SW63

FH Mrs G Lawrance **Longstone** *(SW662319)* ☎Helston (03265) 2483
Jan–Nov
Well appointed farmhouse set in beautiful countryside. Facilities include a playroom and sun lounge. From the Helston–Redruth road, B3297, take unclass road SW–Helston 1½m; Trenear 1m, thence via Coverack Bridges.
5hc (3fb) B&b£6–£7.50 Bdi£9–£10.50 Wfr£42 M LDO6pm
CTV 6P 62acres dairy Ⓥ

Trefin (Trevine) — Truro

TRESILLIAN
Cornwall
Map **2** SW84

GH Manor Cottage ☎(087252) 212
mid Mar–mid Oct
Large cottage type building on main road, attracting large cream tea trade.
5hc (1fb) *B&bfr£8.50 W£57 M
Lic CTV 10P

TRETOWER
Powys
Map **3** SO12

INN *Tretower Court* ☎Bwlch (0874) 730204
rs Dec–Feb
Family run character inn with good bars and modestly appointed bedrooms.
4hc ★ D9.30pm
CTV 100P

TREVEIGHAN
Cornwall
Map **2** SX07

FH Mrs M Jory **Treveighan** *(SX075795)* ☎Bodmin (0208) 850286
Mar–Oct
Two-storey, stone built farmhouse with farm buildings attached. Situated in isolated village with views over valley.
3hc (1fb) ★ B&b£6.50–£7 Bdi£10–£11 W£45.50 M LDO4pm
CTV 3P 170acres beef dairy

TREVONE
Cornwall
Map **2** SW87

GH Coimbatore Hotel ☎Padstow (0841) 520390
Apr–Oct
11hc (4fb) ★ B&b£8 Bdi£11.50 W£70–£80 L (W only Jul & Aug) LDO24hrs
Lic CTV P

GH Green Waves Pivate Hotel ☎Padstow (0841) 520114
Closed Oct–Mar
Substantial terraced building close to sea with own sun lounge.
22hc 10 (5fb) B&b£7.48 Bdi£14.38 W£78.20–£80.50 L LDO6.30pm
Lic CTV 15P 5 nc3yrs
Credit card 3

TRINITY
Jersey, Channel Islands
Map **16**

GH Highfield Country Hotel Route du Ebenezer ☎Jersey (0534) 62194
25hc 14 (4fb) B&b£12.50–£20.50 Bdi£14.50–£22.50 LDO9.30pm
Lic CTV 30P 1

TROON
Cornwall
Map **2** SW63

FH Mrs H Tyack **Sea View** *(SW671370)* ☎Praze (0209) 831260
Farmhouse has been modernised, yet still retains atmosphere of family-run farm. Tastefully furnished with extensive pinewood décor.
8rm 7hc (4fb) B&b£6 Bdi£9 W£40 M
LDO3pm
CTV 10P 10acres mixed

TROON
Strathclyde *Ayrshire*
Map **10** NS33

GH Glenside Darley Pl, off Bentwick Dr ☎(0292) 313677
Red sandstone house in residential area of this seaside town.
5hc (2fb) *fr£7.50 Wfr£49 M
CTV 5P

TROUTBECK *(Near Penrith)*
Cumbria
Map **11** NY32

FH Mrs R Bird **Askew Rigg** *(NY371280)* ☎Threlkeld (059683) 638
Closed Xmas
17th-century stone-built farmhouse, attractively modernised to retain original character. Entrance to drive is situated only a few yards from the A66.
4rm 2hc (2fb) ® B&b£6.50–£7 Bdifr£10
Lic CTV 6P 200acres mixed

FH Mr P Fellows **Lane Head** *(NY375271)* ☎Threlkeld (059683) 220
Mar–Oct
2½m NW of Troutbeck on south side of A66.
6rm 5hc 1 (2fb) ★ B&b£9.50 Bdifr£15.50 W£103 L LDO5.30pm
Lic CTV 10P 110acres mixed Ⓥ
See advertisement on page 356

TRURO
Cornwall
Map **2** SW84

GH Colthrop Tregolls Rd ☎(0872) 72920
Small, friendly guesthouse convenient to city, and good base for touring.
7rm 2hc (3fb) ★ B&b£8–£11 Bdi£12–£15 W£84–£100 M LDO4pm
CTV 8P nc7yrs

GH Farley Hotel Falmouth Rd ☎(0872) 70712
Closed 4 days Xmas
Comfortable, well positioned hotel for both business and tourist clientèle.
21hc (4fb) *B&b£12–£12.50 Bdi£16.50–£17 W£75.60–£84 M
LDO7pm
Lic CTV 20P
Credit card 3

TUNBRIDGE WELLS (ROYAL)
Kent
Map **5** TQ53

GH Firwood 89 Frant Rd (Guestaccom) ☎(0892) 25596
Closed 20 Dec–14 Jan
10hc 7→ 3⋒ (2fb) CTV in all bedrooms ✻ B&bfr£20 Bdifr£26
CTV 12P
Credit cards 1 2 3 5 V

TWO BRIDGES
Devon
Map **2** SX67

GH Cherrybrook Hotel ☎Tavistock (0822) 88260
Closed Xmas
Large detached house in pleasant grounds in the middle of Dartmoor.
8rm 2hc 5⋒ (1fb) ® B&b£11–£12.50 Bdi£17.50–£19 W£122.50 L LDO7.15pm
Lic 12P

TYWARDREATH
Cornwall
Map **2** SX05

GH Elmswood Tehidy Rd, Tywardreath Park ☎Par (072681) 4221
7hc (3fb) B&b£7.50–£8 Bdi£11–£11.50 W£52–£56 M LDO5pm
Lic CTV 7P

TYWYN
Gwynedd
Map **6** SH50

GH Min-y-Mor Private Hotel 7 Marine Pde ☎(0654) 710139
9hc 3⋒ (5fb) ✻ B&b£8–£9.50 Bdi£12

£14 W£56–£66.50 M LDO5pm
Lic CTV 2P

⊢×⊣ **GH Monfa** Pier Rd ☎(0654) 710858
Feb–Nov
Semi detached Victorian house adjacent to the beach, a short walk from the shops.
8rm 2hc 3⋔ (3fb) ✗ B&b£8–£10
Bdi£12–£14 W£80–£90 ⊻ LDO5pm
CTV 1P

UFFCULME
Devon
Map **3** ST01
⊢×⊣ **FH** Mrs M D Farley **Houndaller** *(ST058138)* ☎Craddock (0884) 40246
rs Oct–Mar
Very old attractive farmhouse standing in beautiful garden. Quiet, though only 800 yards from A38 at Waterloo Cross, close to M5 junction 27.
2hc (2fb) Ⓡ B&b£7–£8.50 Bdi£12–£14
Wfr£60 ⊻ (W only Apr–Oct) LDO4.30pm
CTV 4P 1⚭ 176acres mixed Ⓥ

FH Mrs C M Baker **Woodrow** *(ST054107)* ☎Craddock (0884) 40362
Farmhouse set in pleasant lawns and gardens with meadowland stretching to River Culm. Trout fishing available.
3rm 2hc (A 3rm) (2fb) ✗ *B&b£6.50–£7
Bdi£11.50–£12 W£84 ⊻ LDO9pm
CTV 10P 200acres arable dairy sheep mixed

UFFINGTON
Shropshire
Map **7** SJ51
⊢×⊣ **FH** Mr & Mrs D Timmis **Preston Boats** *(SJ530118)* Preston on Severn ☎Upton Magna (074377) 240
Closed Xmas
17th-century farmhouse with beams and inglenook fireplace. 1½m S on unclass road joining B5062 and A5.
3rm 1hc (1fb) TV in 1 bedroom B&b£7–£8 W£49 M
CTV 8P 150acres mixed

UIST (SOUTH), ISLE OF
Western Isles *Inverness-shire*
Map **13** NF
See Locheynort (North)

ULLINGSWICK
Hereford & Worcester
Map **3** SO54
FH Mrs P A Howland **The Steppes** *(SO586490)* ☎Burley Gate (043278) 424
Closed Xmas & New Year
17th-century listed building, being noted for its many points of historical and architectural interest and although it retains its original features, including a wealth of exposed beams throughout, it has been sympathetically modernised.
3⋔ CTV in all bedrooms Ⓡ B&b£12–£14 Bdi£22.50–£25 W£155 ⊻ LDO7pm
Lic CTV 6P nc12yrs 1½acres Ⓥ

UMBERLEIGH
Devon
Map **2** SS62
FH Mrs J C May ***Weir Marsh Farm Guest House*** *(SS618218)* (½m SE unclass) ☎High Bickington (0769) 60338
Closed Xmas
3hc (2fb) LDO6.30pm
CTV 4P 320acres mixed

UPLYME
Devon
Map **3** SY39
INN Black Dog Hotel Lyme Rd ☎Lyme Regis (02974) 2634
Mar–Oct
Roadside inn with garden offering simply appointed comfortable accommodation.
5hc Ⓡ B&b£10 W£63 M LDO9.30pm
CTV P 2⚭

UPOTTERY
Devon
Map **3** ST20
⊢×⊣ **FH** Mrs M M Reed **Yarde** →

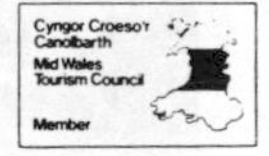

(ST193045) ☎(040486) 318
Feb–Nov
17th-century farmhouse with interesting oak panelling and beams, overlooking the Otter Valley. Near Monkton on the A30.
3rm 2hc (1fb) ★ B&b£7–£8 Bdi£10–£11 W£45 M̸
CTV 3P 1🏠 ♪ billiards 94acres beef dairy sheep

UPPER HULME
Staffordshire
Map **7** SK06
⟼**FH** Mrs J Lomas **Keekorok Lodge** *(SK005616)* ☎Blackshaw (053834) 218
Etr–Oct
Modernised stone built house with views over Tittesworth Reservoir, well known locally for fishing, situated 1m NW of village towards The Roaches (Landmark).
3rm 2hc (1fb) ★ B&b£6.50–£8 Bdi£11.50–£13 W£55 M̸ LDO10am
▥ CTV 10P nc2yrs 15acres arable

UPTON PYNE
Devon
Map **3** SX99
⟼**FH** Mrs Y M Taverner **Pierce's** *(SX910977)* ☎Stoke Canon (039284) 252
Etr–Sep
Large farmhouse about 1 mile north of A377 Exeter–Barnstaple road.
1hc (1fb) ★ B&b£7.50 W£50 M̸
▥ CTV 2P 300acres mixed Ⓥ

UPTON UPON SEVERN
Hereford & Worcester
Map **3** SO84
GH Pool House ☎(0686) 2151
Jan–Nov
Early 18th century country house, standing on the banks of the River Severn with typical English garden and a homely atmosphere.
9rm 4hc 4⇌ 1⋒ (3fb) TV in 2 bedrooms ★ ✻B&b£11.50–£17.50 Bdi£16–£21.50 W£60–£78 M̸ LDO6.30pm
Lic CTV 14P ♪
Credit card 1

USK
Gwent
Map **3** SO30
FH J Arnett **Ty Gwyn** *(SO391045)* ☎(02913) 2878
Closed Xmas day
Large modernised farmhouse situated between Raglan and Usk at Gwehelog, 3m NE off Raglan road unclass.
3hc (1fb) ★ Ⓡ ✻B&b£7.50–£8 Bdi£11.50–£12 W£79 L̸ LDO2pm
▥ CTV 5P nc4yrs 25acres mixed Ⓥ

UTTOXETER
Staffordshire
Map **7** SK03
⟼**FH Popinjay** *(SK074322)* Stafford Rd ☎(08893) 66082
1m SW off A518.
2rm B&b£7–£7.50 Bdi£10.50–£11 W£46 M̸
CTV 2🏠 10acres beef Ⓥ

VENN OTTERY
Devon
Map **3** SY09
GH Venn Ottery Barton Country Hotel ☎Ottery St Mary (040481) 2733
Mar–Oct
13rm 5hc 4⇌ 4⋒ (4fb) Ⓡ B&b£11–£15 Bdi£14–£21 W£77–£105 M̸ LDO7.15pm
Lic ▥ CTV 14P nc6yrs Ⓥ

VENTNOR
Isle of Wight
Map **4** SZ57
GH *Channel View Hotel* Hambrough Rd ☎(0983) 852230
late Mar–Oct
Set on a cliff between the sea and town.
14hc (4fb) ★ Ⓡ LDO7pm
Lic ▥ CTV sea

GH *Delamere* Bellevue Rd ☎(0983) 852322
Apr–Sep
Small, well-kept, friendly house.
9hc (3fb) LDO2pm
CTV 8P sea

GH Hillside Private Hotel Mitchell Av ☎(0983) 852271
Mar–Oct
11rm 6hc 3⇌ 3⋒ (6fb) CTV in all bedrooms Ⓡ B&b£10.75–£12.25 Bdi£12.25–£13.75 W£99.75–£120.75 L̸
Lic ▥ CTV 16P

GH Lake Hotel Shore Rd, Bonchurch ☎(0983) 852613
Apr–Oct
Set in 2½ acres of gardens close to beach and countryside.
11rm 2hc 9⋒ (A 14rm 7hc 7⋒) (7fb) B&b£9.50–£11.50 Bdi£12.50–£14.25 W£59.50 M̸ LDO6.30pm
Lic CTV 20P Ⓥ

GH Macrocarpa Mitchell Av ☎(0983) 852428
Etr–mid Oct
Large house in own grounds with good sea views.
20rm 9hc 6⇌ 5⋒ (7fb) Ⓡ B&b£10.50–£12.50 Bdi£13.50–£16.50 W£85–£115 L̸ LDO7.30pm
Lic CTV 20P

GH *Picardie Hotel* Esplanade ☎(0983) 852647
Apr–Oct
Small, comfortable house, close to the beach.
15hc Ⓡ LDO6pm
Lic CTV ⚑ sea

GH Richmond Private Hotel The Esplanade ☎(0983) 852496
Apr–Oct
Friendly and comfortable accommodation, well situated on the edge of the Esplanade.
12rm 6hc 6⋒ (3fb) Ⓡ ✻B&b£8.50–£9.50 Bdi£12.50–£14.50 W£59.50–£66.50 L̸ LDO5.30pm
Lic CTV 8P
Credit card 3 Ⓥ

GH St Maur Hotel Castle Rd ☎(0983) 852570
Closed Dec
Well kept house run by friendly family; in quiet residential area.
16rm 7hc 4→ 5⋔ (4fb) ✶ B&b£9.50–£12 Bdi£13.50–£16 W£88–£100 ⱡ LDO6.45pm
Lic 𝍖 CTV 12P nc3yrs
Credit card 1

GH Under Rock Hotel Shore Rd, Bonchurch (1m E) ☎(0983) 852714
Mar–Oct

7hc CTV in all bedrooms ✶ B&b£14 Bdi£18 W£126 ⱡ LDO5pm
Lic 𝍖 12P nc8yrs Ⓥ

VOWCHURCH
Hereford & Worcester
Map **3** SO33
FH Mrs J Howarth ***The Croft***
☎Peterchurch (09816) 226
Closed Xmas
4rm 2hc (1fb) LDO5pm
𝍖 CTV 6P 7acres small holding

WADHURST
East Sussex
Map **5** TQ63
INN Fourkeys Station Rd ☎(089288) 2252
Small old house with friendly proprietor and comfortable bedrooms most with modern facilities. →

8hc CTV in 2 bedrooms TV in 6 bedrooms Ⓡ B&b£8 Bdi£15 W£56 M Bar lunch 95p–£1.75 S% LDO10pm

Ⅲ 16P ⇼

Credit cards 1 3

WALLASEY
Merseyside
Map **7** SJ29

GH Divonne Hotel 71 Wellington Rd, New Brighton ☎051-639 4727
Closed 24 Dec–7 Jan

15rm 9hc 6⋒ (2fb) TV in all bedrooms Ⓡ B&b£9.50–£10.50 Bdi£14–£15 W£98–£105 Ⱡ LDO8pm

Lic Ⅲ CTV 6P

GH Sandpiper Private Hotel 22 Dudley Rd, New Brighton ☎051-639 7870

7hc (2fb) CTV in all bedrooms ✶ Ⓡ B&b£10 Bdi£14 W£59.50 M LDO6pm

Ⅲ 6P Ⓥ

WANSFORD
Cambridgeshire
Map **4** TL09

INN Cross Keys ☎Stamford (0780) 782266

3hc (A 3hc) TV in all bedrooms Ⓡ B&bfr£9 LDO9.30pm

Ⅲ

Credit cards 1 3

WARCOP
Cumbria
Map **12** NY71

FH Mrs E Collinson ***Highwood Holme Farm Bungalow*** *(NY760150)* Flitholme ☎Brough (09304) 304
Apr–Sep

Modern bungalow of local stone adjacent to original farmhouse. Well decorated and comfortable.

2rm ✶

Ⅲ CTV 2P

WAREHAM
Dorset
Map **3** SY98

FH Mrs J Barnes ***Redcliffe*** *(SY932866)* ☎(09295) 2225

Modern farmhouse in quiet, rural surroundings. Pleasant location adjacent to River Frome and overlooking hills and fields. ½ mile from Wareham.

5rm 4hc (2fb) ✶

Ⅲ CTV 2⌂ 250acres arable dairy

WARREN STREET *(Near Lenham)*
Kent
Map **5** TQ95

INN Harrow ☎Maidstone (0622) 858727

6rm 2hc 3➡ ✶ *B&b£18–£24 Bdi£27–£33 W£158–£195 M Bar lunch £4.50–£7.70 High tea £2.50–£3.50 D9pm £9–£14

Ⅲ CTV 30P ⇼

Credit cards 1 3 Ⓥ

WARWICK
Warwickshire
Map **4** SP26

GH Austin House 96 Emscote Rd ☎(0926) 493583

7rm 1hc (3fb) Ⓡ B&b£8.50–£9.50 Bdi£13–£14 W£87.50–£94.40 Ⱡ

Ⅲ CTV 5P 2⌂

⊢⊣ **GH Avon** 7 Emscote Rd ☎(0926) 491367
Closed Xmas Day

7hc (4fb) ✶ Ⓡ B&b£8

Ⅲ CTV 6P

GH Cambridge Villa Private Hotel 20A Emscote Rd ☎(0926) 491169
Closed Xmas

16rm 12hc 4⋒ (4fb) CTV in all bedrooms ✶ Ⓡ B&b£11–£15 LDOnoon

Ⅲ 15P

GH Guys Cross Hotel 122 Coventry Rd ☎(0926) 491208

9rm 7hc (3fb) CTV in 1 bedroom TV in 8 bedrooms B&b£10.35 Bdi£14.50 LDO5pm

Lic Ⅲ CTV 7P

Credit cards 1 2 5 Ⓥ

GH Old Rectory Sherbourne ☎(0926) 624562
2 Jan–22 Dec

Tastefully restored house offering very comfortable accommodation and home cooked food. Off A46 2m SW

5rm 1hc 1➡ 3⋒ (1fb) TV in 1 bedroom Ⓡ B&b£8.50–£11 Bdi£15–£17 W£50–£70 M LDO5.30pm

Ⅲ CTV 8P

WASHFORD
Somerset
Map **3** ST04

⊢⊣ **GH Washford House** ☎(0984) 40484
Closed Xmas

Substantial stone built house offering spacious airy accommodation. Conveniently situated for Blue Anchor seafront (1½m) and touring the Exmoor National Park.

8rm 7hc 1⋒ (2fb) B&b£7–£8 Bdi£11.50–£12.50 W£42–£49 M LDO4.30pm

Ⅲ CTV 12P

WATERLOO
Isle of Skye, Highland *Inverness-shire*
Map **13** NG62

GH *Ceol-na-Mara* ☎Broadford (04712) 323
Etr–Sep

6hc (1fb) Ⓡ LDO9pm

CTV 8P sea

WATERLOOVILLE
Hampshire
Map **4** SU60

GH Far End Private Hotel 31 Queens Rd ☎(07014) 3242
Closed 23 Dec–1 Jan

Large detached house set in well kept gardens in quiet residential area.

10hc 1➡ 1⋒ (1fb) B&b£18.50–£19.50 Bdi£24–£25 W£98–£112 Ⱡ LDO4pm

Lic Ⅲ CTV 20P 2⌂ ⊠

WATERPERRY
Oxfordshire
Map **4** SP60

⊢⊣ **FH** S Fonge **Manor** *(SP628064)* ☎Ickford (08447) 263

Stone farmhouse standing in large garden, in centre of village. Coarse fishing available.

3rm 2hc (1fb) B&b£7.50–£9 Bdi£14–£15.50 W£94.50 Ⱡ LDOam

Ⅲ TV P ⌐ 140acres arable beef sheep mixed poultry Ⓥ

WATERROW
Somerset
Map **3** ST02

INN Rock ☎Wivellscombe (0984) 23293

7rm 6➡ B&b£12 W£70 M Bar lunch £2alc D9pm £7alc

Ⅲ CTV 14P

FH Mr J Bone **Hurstone Farmhouse Hotel** *(ST056252)* ☎Wiveliscombe (0984) 23441

5hc 1➡ (1fb) B&b£10.50–£12.50 Bdi£15.50–£17.50 W£85–£95 Ⱡ LDO8.30pm

Lic CTV 8P ⌐ 65acres dairy Ⓥ

WATFORD
Hertfordshire
Map **4** TQ19

GH White House Hotel 26–29 Upton Rd ☎(0923) 37316

Close to town centre, offers well equipped bedrooms. Ideal for business people.

63rm 2hc 31➡ 29⋒ (6fb) CTV in all bedrooms Ⓡ Bdi£25–£33 Bdi£32.95–£40.95 W£150–£198 M LDO10pm

Lic Ⅲ 35P

Credit cards 1 2 3

WEDMORE
Somerset
Map **3** ST44

⊢⊣ **FH** Mr & Mrs I D Leavy **Overbrook** *(ST402476)* Blackford ☎(0934) 712081
Closed Dec & Jan

3⋒ (1fb) ✶ B&b£8 Bdi£15.50 W£52 M LDO24hrs

Ⅲ CTV 6P ⊟(heated) ⚲(hard) billiards sauna bath 4½acres small holding

WEEDON LOIS
Northamptonshire
Map **4** SP64

FH Mrs C Raven **Croft** *(SP600465)* Milthorpe ☎ Blakesley (0327) 860475
Feb–Nov

New detached house, built of Cotswold stone, in rural surroundings on edge of delightful Northamptonshire village.

2rm ★ B&b£10 Bdi£14 LDO6.30pm

𝍖 CTV P 25acres pigs turkeys

WEEK ST MARY
Cornwall
Map **2** SX29

⊢⋆⊣ **GH Lambley Park** ☎ (028884) 368

6rm 5hc 1⋔ (3fb) B&b£6.50–£8.50 Bdi£10–£14 W£73–£82 Ⱡ LDOnoon

Lic 𝍖 CTV 8P ⌂

WEETON
Lancashire
Map **7** SD33

⊢⋆⊣ **FH** Mrs T Colligan **High Moor** *(SD388365)* ☎ (039136) 273
Closed Xmas & New Years Day

Compact, homely farmhouse, clean and tidy. Much farm produce used in cooking.

2rm (1fb) ★ B&b£7–£8 W£50 M

CTV P 7acres mixed

WELLINGBOROUGH
Northamptonshire
Map **4** SP86

GH Oak House Private Hotel 9 Broad Green ☎ (0933) 71133
Closed Xmas

6rm 5⋔ ® B&b£14.50 Bdi£19 W£101.50 M LDO4pm

𝍖 CTV 6P

WELLINGTON
Shropshire
Map **7** SJ61
See under Telford

WELLS
Somerset
Map **3** ST54

GH Bekynton House 7 St Thomas Street ☎ (0749) 72222

10rm 8hc 2⋔ (2fb) ★ ® B&b£8.60–£9.25 Bdi£13.80–£15 W£54.35–£60 M LDO11am

𝍖 CTV 6P Ⓥ

GH Tor 20 Tor St ☎ (0749) 72322

9hc (7fb) B&b£8.50–£9.25 W£56.50–£61.50 M

CTV 10P

⊢⋆⊣ **FH** Mrs P Higgs **Home** *(ST538442)* Stoppers Ln, Upper Coxley ☎ (0749) 72434
Closed Xmas rs Oct–Apr
2m SW off A39.

7hc (3fb) B&b£7.25–£7.50 Bdi£12–£12.50 W£75–£85 Ⱡ LDO24hrs

Lic 𝍖 CTV 10P 12acres pigs

⊢⋆⊣ **FH** Mr & Mrs L J Law **Honeycroft** *(ST509453)* Worth ☎ (0749) 78971
Mar–Oct

3rm 1hc (1fb) ★ B&bfr£7.50 Wfr£49 M

𝍖 CTV 6P nc4yrs 40acres beef pigs

WELSHPOOL
Powys
Map **7** SJ20

⊢⋆⊣ **FH** Mrs E Jones **Gungrog House** *(SJ235089)* Rhallt ☎ (0938) 3381
Apr–Oct

300-year-old farmhouse in quiet situation high on hillside, commanding superb views of the Severn Valley 1m NE off A458.

3hc 2⋔ (1fb) ★ B&b£8 Bdi£13 W£80 Ⱡ LDO6.30pm

𝍖 CTV 6P ⌂ 21acres mixed

FH Mr & Mrs W Jones **Moat** *(SJ214042)* ☎ (0938) 3179
Apr–Oct

16th century farmhouse with timbered dining room and canopied stone fireplace. The gardens have a tennis lawn, and lead down to the river. Situated in the Severn Valley.

3hc (1fb) ★ ® *B&b£8–£8.50 Bdi£12–£12.50 W£52 M LDO2pm

CTV 3P billiards 160acres dairy

FH Mr & Mrs J Emberton **Tynllwyn** *(SJ215085)* (0938) 3175

Peaceful 19th century farmhouse offering good, modern accommodation. On A490 N of Welshpool.

6hc (3fb) B&b£8 Bdi£13 W£82 LDO6.30pm

CTV P 150acres dairy mixed

WEST BAGBOROUGH
Somerset
Map **3** ST13

GH Higher House Bishops Lydeard (0823) 432996
Feb–Dec

5hc (1fb) B&b£9–£10 Bdi£14–£15 W£90–£100 LDO5pm

Lic CTV 12P (heated)

WESTBOURNE
West Sussex
Map **4** SU70

FH Mr & Mrs E D Edgell ***Tibbalds Mead*** *(SU750873)* White Chimney Row Emsworth (02434) 4786
Feb–Nov

Elizabethan farmhouse with recent addition, some beamed ceilings. Situated on the south side of the village.

1hc (A 1) TV in all bedrooms

10P 70acres mixed

WEST CHARLETON
Devon
Map **3** SX74

INN Ashburton Arms Frogmore (054853) 242
Closed 23–31 Dec

5hc B&b£9.66–£10.14 W£63.60–£66.98 Bar lunch £1.50alc LDO9.30pm

CTV 20P nc7yrs

WEST CHILTINGTON
West Sussex
Map **4** TQ01

FH A M Steele **New House** *(TQ091186)* (07983) 2215
Jan–Nov

Listed 15th century farmhouse with oak beamed rooms and inglenook fireplace, surrounded by beautifully kept grounds.

3hc (1fb) B&b£9–£10 Bdi£12.50–£16 W£100

CTV 4P 2 nc10yrs 150acres mixed

WESTCLIFF-ON-SEA
Essex
See Southend-on-Sea

WEST LULWORTH
Dorset
See Lulworth

WESTON-SUPER-MARE
Avon
Map **3** ST36
See plan

GH Baymead Hotel Longton Grove Rd (0934) 22951 Plan **1** *C4*

34rm 32hc 2 (12fb) Ⓡ B&b£10–£12 Bdi£12.50–£15 W£70–£90 LDO6.15pm

Lic lift CTV

GH Fourways 2 Ashcombe Rd (0934) 23827 Plan **3** *C3*
rs winter

6hc (A 3hc) B&b£6–£8

CTV 7P nc10yrs

GH Glenelg 24 Ellenborough Park South (0934) 20521 Plan **4** *B1*
Closed Nov–Apr

15hc (4fb) B&b£8.50–£9.50 Bdi£11.50–£12.50 Wfr£65

Lic CTV 15P
Credit card 5

GH Kew Dee 6 Neva Rd (0934) 29041 Plan **6** *C2*

8hc (1fb) *B&b£6.50–£8 Bdi£9–£10 W£45.50–£56 LDO4pm

CTV 5P

GH Kinclaven Hotel 5 Park Pl (0934) 21723 Plan **7** *B5*
Apr–Sep

20hc (6fb) Ⓡ B&bfr£7.50 Bdi£11–£13.80 W£74.75–£80.50 LDO6pm

Lic CTV 15P nc3yrs
Credit card 3

GH Lydia 78 Locking Rd (0934) 25962

6hc (2fb) B&b£7–£8.50 Bdi£10–£12 W£63–£75 LDO4pm

Lic CTV 5P
Credit card 3

GH Milton Lodge 15 Milton Rd (0934) 23161 Plan **8A** *C4*

Proprietors have painstakingly created this comfortable new guesthouse.

6rm 3 3 (2fb) TV in all bedrooms Ⓡ B&b£10 Bdi£14 W£63 LDO4pm

CTV 5P

GH Newton House 79 Locking Rd (0934) 29331 Plan **9** *C3*

8hc 1 (4fb) CTV in 1 bedroom Ⓡ B&b£7–£10 Bdi£11–£15 W£70–£80 LDO9pm

Lic CTV 9P

See advertisement on page 364

GH Scottsdale Hotel 3 Ellenborough Park North (0934) 26489 Plan **11** *B2*
Apr–Sep rs Oct, Nov & Mar

13hc Ⓡ B&b£10 Bdi£13 W£75–£82 LDO4.30pm

CTV 13P nc12yrs

See advertisement on page 364

GH Shire Elms 71 Locking Rd (0934) 28605 Plan **12** *C3*
Closed 23 Dec–2 Jan

11rm 10hc 1 (A 3hc) (5fb) *B&b£9.50 Bdi£13.75 W£63.50

Lic CTV 10P

See advertisement on page 364

GH Southmead 435 Locking Rd (0934) 29351 Plan **13** *C3*
Closed Xmas

6hc (2fb) B&b£6.50–£7.50 Bdi£11.50–£12.50 W£45–£52 LDO5.30pm

CTV 6P

GH *Tra-Bon Private Hotel* 4 Neva Rd (0934) 29536 Plan **15** *C2*

12rm (3fb) LDO5pm

CTV 4P nc3yrs

⊢×⊣ **GH Willow** 3 Clarence Road East
☎(0934) 413736 Plan **16** *B1*
Etr–Sep
8rm 4hc 3⇥ 1⋒ (3fb) ✱ Ⓡ B&b£7–£9
Bdi£10–£12 W£45–£58 Ⓜ S%
LDO9.30am
Ⅲ CTV 8P ◫ (heated)

⊢×⊣ **GH Wychwood Hotel** 148 Milton Rd
☎(0934) 27793 Plan **17** *C4*
10hc (4fb) B&b£7.50–£8.50 Bdi£11.50–

Weston-super-Mare — West Taphouse

£13.50 W£51.75–£60 Ⓜ LDO4pm
Lic Ⅲ CTV 12P ⩳ (heated)

WEST TAPHOUSE
Cornwall
Map **2** SX16

⊢×⊣ **FH** Mrs K V Bolitho **Penadlake**
(SX144636) Two Waters Foot
☎Bodmin (0208) 872271
Apr–Oct
Old world farmhouse with large garden situated in the picturesque Glynn Valley.
2rm ✱ B&b£7–£8
CTV 2P 250acres arable beef sheep mixed

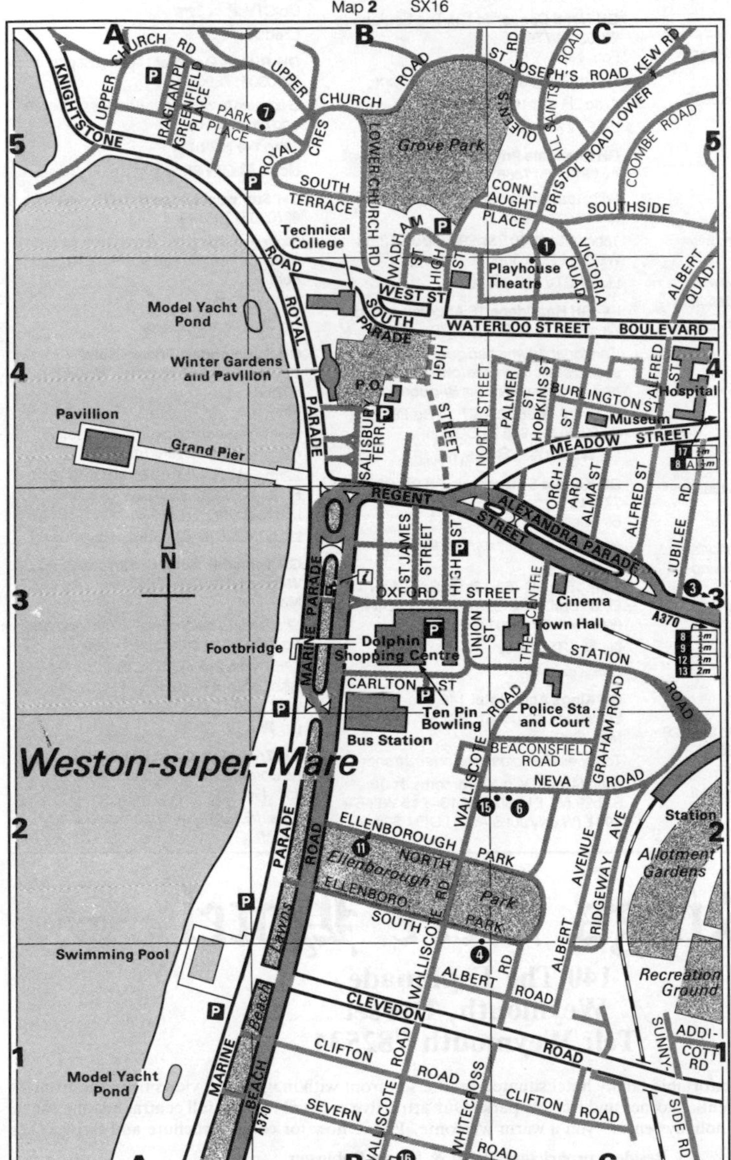

Weston-super-Mare

- **1** Baymead Hotel
- **3** Fourways
- **4** Glenelg
- **6** Kew Dee
- **7** Kinclaven Hotel
- **8A** Milton Lodge
- **9** Newton House
- **11** Scottsdale Hotel
- **12** Shire Elms
- **13** Southmead
- **15** Tra-Bon Private Hotel
- **16** Willow
- **17** Wychwood Hotel

WESTWARD HO!
Devon
Map **2** SS42

⊢⊣ **GH Buckleigh Lodge** 135 Bayview Rd ☎Bideford (02372) 75988
Apr–Sep rs Oct–Mar

6rm 5hc 1 (1fb) CTV in 1 bedroom B&b£7.50 Bdi£11.50 W£75 LDO8pm

Lic CTV 7P Ⓥ

WEST WOODBURN
Northumberland
Map **12** NY88

INN Bay Horse ☎Bellingham (0660) 60218

4hc CTV in all bedrooms Ⓡ B&b£10–£12 LDO10pm

CTV 30P billiards

WETHERBY
West Yorkshire
Map **8** SE44

GH Prospect House 8 Caxton St ☎(0937) 62428

Bright and cheerful guesthouse with comfortable, clean accommodation.

6hc (1fb) B&b£9–£9.50 W£63–£66.50 M

CTV 6P

WEYBRIDGE
Surrey
London plan **4** A1
(page 222–223)

GH Warbeck House Hotel 46 Queens Rd ☎(0932) 48764
Closed 25 Dec–1 Jan

Fine Edwardian house with comfortable, modernised bedrooms and relaxing atmosphere.

10rm 5hc 1 (1fb) Ⓡ B&b£19.50

Lic CTV 18P nc3yrs

WEYMOUTH
Dorset
Map **3** SY67

GH Beechcroft Private Hotel 128–129 The Esplanade ☎(0305) 786608
Apr–Oct

Located on sea front with continental awnings.

29rm 9hc 2 8 (7fb) Ⓡ B&b£11.04–£11.73 Bdi£15.18–£15.87 W£85.10–£90.85

Lic CTV 3P

Credit cards 1 3

GH *Hotel Concorde* 131 The Esplanade ☎(0305) 776900
Feb–Nov

End of Georgian terrace on sea front.

17hc 2 (7fb) LDO6pm

Lic CTV 4P sea

GH Ellendale Private Hotel 88 Rodwell Av ☎(0305) 786650

Within easy walking distance of harbour and town centre.

18hc (4fb) Ⓡ B&b£9.50 Bdi£12.50 W£72 LDO6.30pm

Lic CTV 12P 3

⊢⊣ **GH Hazeldene** 16 Abbotsbury Rd, Westham ☎(0305) 782579

Comfortably furnished guesthouse, a short distance from the town centre and harbour, situated on the Bridport road.

7hc (4fb) B&b£7–£7.50 Bdi£8.50–£9.50 W£52–£65 LDO2pm

Lic CTV 6P 1 nc5yrs

GH Kenora 5 Stavordale Rd ☎(0305) 771215
Etr–Oct rs Mar & Nov

In quiet cul-de-sac a short distance from the harbour.

18rm 15hc 3 (6fb) Ⓡ B&b£8.57–£9.68 Bdi£12–£13.18 W£52–£60 M (W only Jul & Aug) LDO4pm

Lic CTV 16P

Credit card 1

GH Kings Acre Hotel 140 The Esplanade ☎(0305) 782534
Mar–Oct

Terraced Georgian hotel on sea front.

14hc (4fb) CTV in 4 bedrooms Ⓡ B&b£9.50–£11.50 Bdi£13–£15 W£66–£90 (W only Jul & Aug) LDO4.30pm

Lic CTV 9P

Credit cards 1 3 Ⓥ

GH Leam Hotel 102–103 The Esplanade ☎(0305) 784127
Apr–Oct

Sea front hotel with wrought iron balconies situated opposite the Jubilee clock.

19hc (10fb) B&b£9.77–£10.35 Bdi£13.87–£14.95 W£56–£70 LDO4.30pm

Lic CTV nc3yrs

Credit card 1

GH *Richmoor Hotel* 146 The Esplanade ☎(0305) 785087

Georgian terraced hotel opposite the pier and bandstand.

22hc 1 (12fb)

Lic lift CTV 8P sea

GH *Sou'west Lodge Hotel* Rodwell Rd ☎(0305) 783749

Modern building on Portland road a short distance from the harbour and town centre.

10hc (3fb)

Lic CTV 16P nc3yrs

GH Sunningdale Private Hotel 52 Preston Rd, Overcombe ☎(0305) 832179
Mar–Nov

Guesthouse set back off main Preston road enjoying elevated position.

22rm 6 1 (7fb) Ⓡ B&b£11.75–£14 Bdi£14.75–£17.75 W£92–£113 LDO6.30pm

Lic CTV 22P (heated) billiards Ⓥ

GH Tamarisk Hotel 12 Stavordale Rd, Westham ☎(0305) 786514
Mar–Oct

Situated in a quiet cul-de-sac a short walk from the town centre and harbour.

17rm 11hc 2 4 (7fb) Ⓡ B&b£8.50–£10.25 Bdi£11–£12.50 W£71–£83 LDOnoon

Lic CTV 19P Ⓥ

GH Treverbyn Court Hotel 65 Dorchester Rd ☎(0305) 786170
Jan–Nov

Small friendly hotel close to safe sandy beach.

14rm 10hc 3⋔ (6fb) CTV in 3 bedrooms B&b£9–£14 Bdi£12.50–£17 W£54–£84 M LDO6pm

Lic CTV 14P

Credit card 3

INN Golden Lion Hotel Stedmonds St ☎(0305) 786778
Closed winter

19hc 1 ✱ B&b£10–£12 W£70–£84 M
CTV nc5yrs

WHEDDON CROSS
Somerset
Map **3** SS93

GH Higherley ☎Timberscombe (064384) 582

6hc 1⋔ CTV in 3 bedrooms ® B&b£8.25 Bdi£13.25 W£92 L LDO8.30pm

Lic CTV 30P

Credit cards 1 3 Ⓥ

WHIDDON DOWN
Devon
Map **3** SX69

FH Mrs J S Robinson **South Nethercott** *(SX688947)* ☎(064723) 276
Mar–Nov

Most attractive cob and brick farmhouse in large gardens in quiet backwater in Dartmoor National Park.

2rm 1hc 1 ✱ B&b£9.50–£10 Bdi£15.50–£16

CTV 3P nc12yrs 170acres arable dairy Ⓥ

WHITBY
North Yorkshire
Map **8** NZ81

GH Beach Cliff Hotel North Prom, West Cliff ☎(0947) 602886
Etr & Jun–Sep

Comfortable private house with spacious public areas.

12hc 1⋔ ✱ B&b£9.50–£10.50 Bdi£13–£14 W£64–£70 M LDO4pm

Lic CTV 6P nc8yrs

GH Esklet 22 Crescent Av ☎(0947) 605663
Closed Nov & Jan

Weymouth — Whitestone

7hc (3fb) B&b£7–£8 Bdi£10–£11 W£65–£70 L LDO5.30pm

CTV

GH Europa Private Hotel
20 Hudson St ☎(0947) 602251
Etr–Oct

Pleasant small guesthouse near harbour, well furnished and with good, comfortable accommodation.

7hc (2fb) ✱ B&b£7–£7.50 Bdi£10.50–£11 W£65 L LDO4.30pm

CTV nc2yrs Ⓥ

GH Hudsons Hotel 24 Hudson St ☎(0947) 605277

6rm (2fb) TV in all bedrooms ® B&b£11–£12 Bdi£16–£17 Wfr£77 M LDO7pm

Lic CTV

GH Old Hall Hotel Ruswarp ☎(0947) 602801
Apr–Oct rs Nov & Feb–Mar
1½m SW B1410.

20rm 13hc 3 4⋔ (2fb) ✱ B&b£10.50–£13.50 Bdifr£16 LDO6pm

Lic CTV 20P Ⓥ

See advertisement on page 368

GH Prospect of Whitby 12 Esplanade ☎(0947) 603026
Mar–Oct

Terraced house offering simple accommodation and spacious public areas.

16hc (3fb) ✱B&b£8.50 Bdi£12 W£55 M LDO4pm

Lic CTV

GH Sandbeck Hotel Crescent Ter, West Cliff ☎(0947) 604012
Apr–7 Oct

19rm 15hc (4fb) ✱ ® Bdi£9.75 Bdi£13.17–£13.75 W£95 L LDO5.30pm

Lic CTV

GH Seacliffe Hotel North Prom, West Cliff ☎(0947) 603139

Converted private house on North Cliffs with good lounges and bar.

20hc (4fb) B&b£10.50–£11 Bdi£15 W£98 M S% LDO6.30pm

Lic CTV 8P

See advertisement on page 368

WHITCHURCH
Hereford & Worcester
Map **3** SO51

GH Portland ☎Symonds Yat (0600) 890757

7hc (1fb) TV in all bedrooms ® Bdi£10–£11.50 Bdi£14.50–£16.25 W£70–£80.50 M LDO8pm

Lic CTV 6P

INN Crown Hotel ☎Symonds Yat (0600) 890234
Closed Xmas Day

5hc ✱B&b£9–£10 Bdi£13–£14 W£84–£90 L L£3.50–£6 D9pm

CTV 40P

Credit cards 1 2 3 5

WHITECROSS *(Near Wadebridge)*
Cornwall
Map **2** SW97

FH Mrs E L D Nicholls ***Torview*** *(SW966722)* ☎Wadebridge (020881) 2261

Modern farmhouse on main A39. Wadebridge 1½ miles.

4hc

CTV 6P 22acres mixed

WHITE CROSS *(Near Indian Queens)*
Cornwall
Map **2** SW85

GH Ambleside Manor ☎St Austell (0726) 860515

6rm 5hc 1⋔ (2fb) ✱ ® B&b£7–£9 Bdi£12–£14 W£65–£79 L LDO7pm

Lic CTV 8P nc6yrs

WHITESTONE
Devon
Map **3** SX89

FH Mrs S K Lee **Rowhorne House** *(SX880948)* ☎Exeter (0392) 74675 →

Feb–Nov

Farmhouse set in attractive gardens and lawns.

3hc (2fb) ✱ ✱B&b£7 Bdi£10 W£49 M

CTV 3P 90acres dairy Ⓥ

WHITHORN
Dumfries & Galloway *Wigtownshire*
Map **10** NX44

⊢⊣**FH** Mrs E C Forsyth **Baltier** *(NX466429)* ☎Garlieston (09886) 241

Modernised, stone built farmhouse situated 2m NW on B7004.

2hc (1fb) ✱ Ⓡ B&b£7.50 Bdi£11 W£52 M LDO4pm

CTV 6P 220acres dairy sheep mixed

WHITLAND
Dyfed
Map **2** SN21

FH C M & I A Lewis ***Cilpost*** *(SN191184)* ☎(0994) 240280
Apr–Sep

Well appointed 300 year old farmhouse offering good meals and a warm welcome. 1½ miles north of the village.

7hc 3➡ 3⋒ (3fb)

20P 160acres dairy

WHITLEY BAY
Tyne & Wear
Map **12** NZ37

Whitestone — Widegates

GH York 30 Park Pde ☎(0632) 528313

A family run guesthouse offering comfort, good home cooking and a friendly atmosphere.

8rm 1hc 7⋒ Ⓡ ✱B&b£7.50 Bdi£10 W£70 ⱢLDO6pm

CTV 4P

WHITNEY-ON-WYE
Hereford & Worcester
Map **3** SO24

INN Rhydspence ☎Clifford (04973) 262
Closed Mon & 2 wks Nov

3rm 1hc 1➡ CTV in all bedrooms ✱ Ⓡ B&b£16 Bdi£23.50 W£148 Ⱡ L£7&alc D9.30pm £7&alc

60P nc10yrs

WICKFORD
Essex
Map **5** TQ79

GH Wickford Lodge 26 Ethelred Gdns ☎(03744) 62663

Tudor style detached house in quiet residential area, offering modern, comfortable accommodation.

6hc (2fb) ✱ B&b£12–£12.50

CTV 6P

WICKHAM
Berkshire
Map **4** SU47

INN Five Bells ☎Boxford (048838) 242

4hc CTV in all bedrooms Ⓡ B&b£17 Bdi£20 L£4–£7&alc D10pm £5–£6&alc

CTV 50P

WIDDINGTON
Essex
Map **5** TL53

FH Mrs L Vernon **Thistley Hall** *(TL556311)* ☎Saffron Walden (0799) 40388
Closed Dec–mid Jan

The historic farmhouse is pleasantly surrounded by gardens and pastureland with beautiful views of the countryside.

3rm 2hc (1fb) ✱ ✱B&b£7.50–£9 Bdi£12–£15 W£50 M

CTV 4P nc5yrs 30acres mixed

WIDEGATES
Cornwall
Map **2** SX25

⊢⊣**GH Coombe Farm** ☎(05034) 223
Mar–Oct

Attractive 1920's detached house affording superb views.

8hc (7fb) B&b£6.80–£13.50 Bdi£14.25–£17 W£89–£110 ⅃ LDO7pm
Lic ⅢⅢ CTV 12P

WIDEMOUTH BAY
Cornwall
Map **2** SS20

GH *Beach House Hotel* ☎(028885) 256
Etr–Sep
13hc 2⋒ (6fb) ✱ Ⓡ LDO7.45pm
Lic CTV 20P sea

WIGAN
Gt Manchester
Map **7** SD50

INN Th'old Hall 240A Warrington Rd, Lower Ince, Ince in Makerfield ☎(0942) 866330
4hc ✱ B&bfr£9 Bdi£10.50–£15 Wfr£63 M Bar lunch £1–£2.50 D9.45pm
ⅢⅢ CTV 50P billiards

WIGHT, ISLE OF
Map 4
Places with AA-listed accommodation are indicated on location map 4. Full details will be found under individual placenames within the gazetteer section.

WIGMORE
Hereford & Worcester
Map **7** SO46

INN Compasses Hotel ☎(056886) 203
Stone built inn in small village 12 miles from Leominster.
3hc CTV in all bedrooms ✱ B&b£10 Bdi£15 W£52.50 M L£4.50–£6.50&alc D10.15pm £4.50–£6.50&alc
ⅢⅢ CTV 70P
Credit cards 1 2 3 5 Ⓥ

WILBERFOSS
Humberside
Map **8** SE75

⊢⊣ **FH** Mrs J M Liversidge **Cuckoo Nest** *(SE717510)* ☎(07595) 365
Closed Xmas
1m W of village on south side of A1079.
2hc (1fb) ✱ B&b£7.50–£8
ⅢⅢ TV P nc2yrs 150acres arable beef dairy sheep mixed

WILLAND
Devon
Map **3** ST01

FH Mrs J M Granger **Doctors** *(ST015117)* Halberton Rd ☎Tiverton (0884) 820525
Mar–Oct
Farmhouse situated in garden and farmland. Tiverton and Cullompton 4 miles.
2rm (1fb) ✱ B&b£6 Bdi£9 W£55 ⅃ LDO3pm
CTV 5P ⤻ 95acres dairy Ⓥ

WILLERSEY
Gloucestershire
Map **4** SP13

GH Old Rectory Church St ☎Evesham (0386) 853729
5rm 2➡ 3⋒ CTV in all bedrooms ✱ Ⓡ B&b£17.50–£22.50 W£110–£141 M
ⅢⅢ 6P 2🚗 nc10yrs
Credit cards 1 2 3

WILMINGTON
East Sussex
Map **5** TQ50

GH Crossways Hotel ☎Polegate (03212) 2455
Set in 2 acres of garden with pond. Colourful rooms and log fires in lounge.
10rm 7hc 2➡ 1⋒ (2fb) Ⓡ B&b£9.50–£10.50 W£63–£70 M
Lic ⅢⅢ CTV P 6🚗

WILSHAMSTEAD (WILSTEAD)
Bedfordshire
Map **4** TL04

GH *Old Manor House Hotel* Cotton End Rd ☎Bedford (0234) 740262
Beautiful old manor house with lovely garden and comfortable accommodation. There are antiques for sale.
9hc (1fb) LDO6.30pm
Lic ⅢⅢ CTV 10P

WIMPSTONE
Warwickshire
Map **4** SP24

⊢⊣ **FH** Mrs J E James **Whitchurch** *(SP222485)* ☎Alderminster (078987) 275
Lovely Georgian farmhouse built 1750, set in park-like surroundings on edge of Cotswolds, 4½ miles from Stratford-upon-Avon.
3hc (3fb) ✱ B&b£7–£8
ⅢⅢ TV 6P 208acres arable beef sheep Ⓥ

WINCLE
Cheshire
Map **7** SJ96

GH Four Ways Diner Motel Cleulow Cross (1m N of A54) ☎(02607) 228
rs Xmas
6rm 1➡ 5⋒ (2fb) CTV in all bedrooms Ⓡ B&b£11–£16 Bdi£16–£26 W£66–£96 M LDO8.30pm
Lic ⅢⅢ 30P
Credit cards 1 3 Ⓥ

WINDERMERE
Cumbria
Map **7** SD49
See plan

⊢⊣ **GH Archway** College Rd ☎(09662) 5613 Plan **1** *B5*
6hc (2fb) B&b£7.50–£8 Bdi£12–£12.75 W£79–£85 ⅃ LDO4pm
ⅢⅢ CTV 3P

GH Biskey Howe Villa Hotel Craig Walk, Bowness ☎(09662) 3988 Plan **2** *B2*
11rm 5hc (3fb) B&b£11.50–£13.75 W£70–£95 M S% LDO7pm
Lic ⅢⅢ CTV 12P ⩱ (heated) U
Credit cards 1 3

GH Brooklands Ferry View, Bowness ☎(09662) 2344 Plan **3** *B1*
6rm 3hc 3⋒ (1fb) Ⓡ Bdi£16.95–£17.85 W£115–£122 ⅃ LDO5.30pm
Lic ⅢⅢ CTV 6P Ⓥ

GH *Crag Brow Cottage Private Hotel* Helm Rd, Bowness ☎(09662) 4080 Plan **5** *B2*
Closed Dec
5hc 4➡ 1⋒ ✱
ⅢⅢ CTV 12P lake

GH Craig Foot Hotel Lake Rd ☎(09662) 3902 Plan **6** *B3*
Mar–Nov
11rm 3hc 2➡ 6⋒ (A 1➡) CTV in 2 bedrooms ✱ Ⓡ B&b£13.50–£14.50
Lic ⅢⅢ CTV nc12yrs
Credit card 1
See advertisement on page 370

GH Cranleigh Hotel Kendal Rd, Bowness ☎(09662) 3293 Plan **6A** *B2*
Mar–17 Nov
11rm 3hc 4➡ (1fb) ✱ Ⓡ B&b£12.50–£16.50 Bdi£19.50–£23.50 W£123–£148 ⅃ LDO5.30pm
Lic CTV 11P nc12yrs Ⓥ
See advertisement on page 370

GH Eastbourne Hotel Biskey Howe Rd ☎(09662) 3525 Plan **7** *B3*
9hc (3fb) B&b£8.95–£9.95 Bdi£14.90–£15.90 LDO7pm
Lic ⅢⅢ CTV 9P
Credit cards 1 3
See advertisement on page 370

GH Elim Bank Hotel Lake Rd, Bowness ☎(09662) 4810 Plan **8** *B3*
Closed Dec
7hc (2fb) CTV in 2 bedrooms ✱ B£7–£8 (room only) W£49–£56 (room only) LDO9pm
Lic ⅢⅢ CTV 7P
Credit cards 1 2 3 Ⓥ
See advertisement on page 370

GH Fairfield Country House Hotel Brantfell Rd, Bowness ☎(09662) 3772 Plan **9** *B2*
Closed Xmas & Jan rs Dec & Feb
8rm 1hc 1➡ 6⋒ (4fb) CTV in all bedrooms Ⓡ B&b£12–£15.50 Bdi£19–£23 W£127–£148 ⅃ LDO5pm
Lic ⅢⅢ 10P
Credit cards 1 2 3 5 Ⓥ
See advertisement on page 371

The Cranleigh Hotel

Kendal Road, Bowness-on-Windermere

Family run, licensed hotel in quiet location only three minutes walk from lake and village. All rooms have tea/coffee making facilities and some private baths/showers. Excellent home cooking. Two lounges and bar. Ample car park. Ideal centre for touring or take advantage of local excursions by road or water (details from reception).

Telephone: Windermere (09662) 3293

Craig Foot Country House Hotel

Lake Road, Windermere. Tel: 3902

Craig Foot was built in 1848, for SIR THOMAS PASLEY, a retired Admiral.
It is an original Lakeland country house situated in its own grounds, with beautiful views of the lake and the surrounding mountains. Most bedrooms overlook the lake, some with private facilities, all have tea and coffee.

The hotel is elegantly furnished and has a cosy cocktail bar. Full central heating, quiet peaceful garden. Car park.

EASTBOURNE HOTEL

Biskey Howe Road, Bowness on Windermere, Cumbria, Windermere 3525

FIRE CERTIFICATE RESIDENTIAL LICENCE

This charming, friendly, hotel offers you all that is best in comfort and service. Situated in a quiet position just off the main road down to the Lake and the shops, the hotel has hot and cold water in all bedrooms, varied home fare menus, a delightful lounge (with Colour TV) and a comfortable bar in which to relax.
Children are welcomed at reduced rates and everything is done to ensure that you enjoy your holiday in Lakeland.

Please send S.A.E. for your brochure to:

Michael and Lee Pointer

Elim Bank Hotel

Phone: Windermere 4810 (STD 09662)
Lake Road, Windermere,
Cumbria LA23 2JJ

Residential & Restaurant Licence.
Private Car Park.
Fire Certificate. Central heating.

À LA CARTE RESTAURANT
Open from 7–9.30 p.m.

Written recommendations of excellence are normal.

GH Glenville Hotel Lake Rd ☎(09662) 3371 Plan **10** *B3*

Elegant house with comfortable lounges, attractive dining room and neat bedrooms.

9rm 8hc 1⋒ (1fb) ★ Ⓡ B&b£9.50–£10.50 Bdi£16.50–£17.50 W£66.50–£73.50 M̸ LDO4pm

Lic Ⅲ CTV 12P

⊢×⊣ **GH Greenriggs** 8 Upper Oak St ☎(09662) 2265 Plan **11** *C4*
Mar–Oct

Friendly, conveniently situated hotel offering simple, clean accommodation.

6hc (2fb) Ⓡ B&b£7 W£45 M̸

Ⅲ CTV 3P Ⓥ

GH Haisthorpe Holly Rd ☎(09662) 3445 Plan **12** *C4*
Mar–Oct

6hc (3fb) ✱B&b£7.50 Bdi£11 W£73.50 Ł LDO4.30pm

Ⅲ CTV

⊢×⊣ **GH Hawksmoor** Lake Rd ☎(09662) 2110 Plan **12A** *B3*
mid Feb–mid Nov

An attractive house offering a cosy atmosphere. It stands in its own grounds, backed by woodland, half-way between Bowness and Windermere.

6hc (2fb) ★ B&b£7–£10.50 Bdi£12.25–£15.50 W£84–£96 Ł LDO5.30pm

Windermere

Lic CTV 10P

GH *Hilton House Hotel* New Rd ☎(09662) 3934 Plan **13** *C4*

Detached Edwardian house in elevated position within easy reach of shops and lake.

7hc 2⋒ (2fb) CTV in 1 bedroom Ⓡ LDO6.30pm

Lic Ⅲ CTV 14P

GH *Hollythwaite* Holly Rd ☎(09662) 2219 Plan **14** *C4*

Comfortable, old fashioned house whose friendly proprietors provide good home cooking.

7hc (2fb)

CTV

⊢×⊣ **GH Kenilworth** Holly Rd ☎(09662) 4004 Plan **15** *C4*
Mar–Oct

7hc (1fb) ★ B&bfr£7.75 Bdifr£12.25 Wfr£79 Ł LDO2pm

Ⅲ CTV Ⓥ

GH Lynwood Broad St ☎(09662) 2550 Plan **16** *C5*
Feb–Nov

Situated in a quiet residential area, this house offers simple but very clean accommodation.

6hc (2fb) ★ B&b£7.50–£8.50 W£49–£56 M̸

Ⅲ CTV 2P 1🚘

GH *Myine Bridge Private Hotel* Brookside, Lake Rd ☎(09662) 3314 Plan **17** *C4*
Feb–Nov

Very comfortable, friendly house with good choice of dishes at dinner.

12hc 4⋒ (1fb) ★ LDO5.30pm

Lic Ⅲ CTV 12P nc5yrs

⊢×⊣ **GH Oakfield** 46 Oak St ☎(09662) 5692 Plan **18** *C5*

5hc TV in all bedrooms Ⓡ B&b£8 Bdi£11.50–£12.50 W£49–£56 M̸ LDOnoon

Lic Ⅲ CTV P̸ nc15yrs Ⓥ

GH Oakthorpe Hotel High St ☎(09662) 3547 Plan **18A** *C5*
15 Jan–23 Dec

Personally supervised, comfortable hotel with Continental and English dishes served at dinner.

21rm 14hc (5fb) Ⓡ B&b£11–£14 Bdi£19–£22 W£123–£140 Ł LDO8.30pm

Lic CTV 18P

Credit cards 1 3

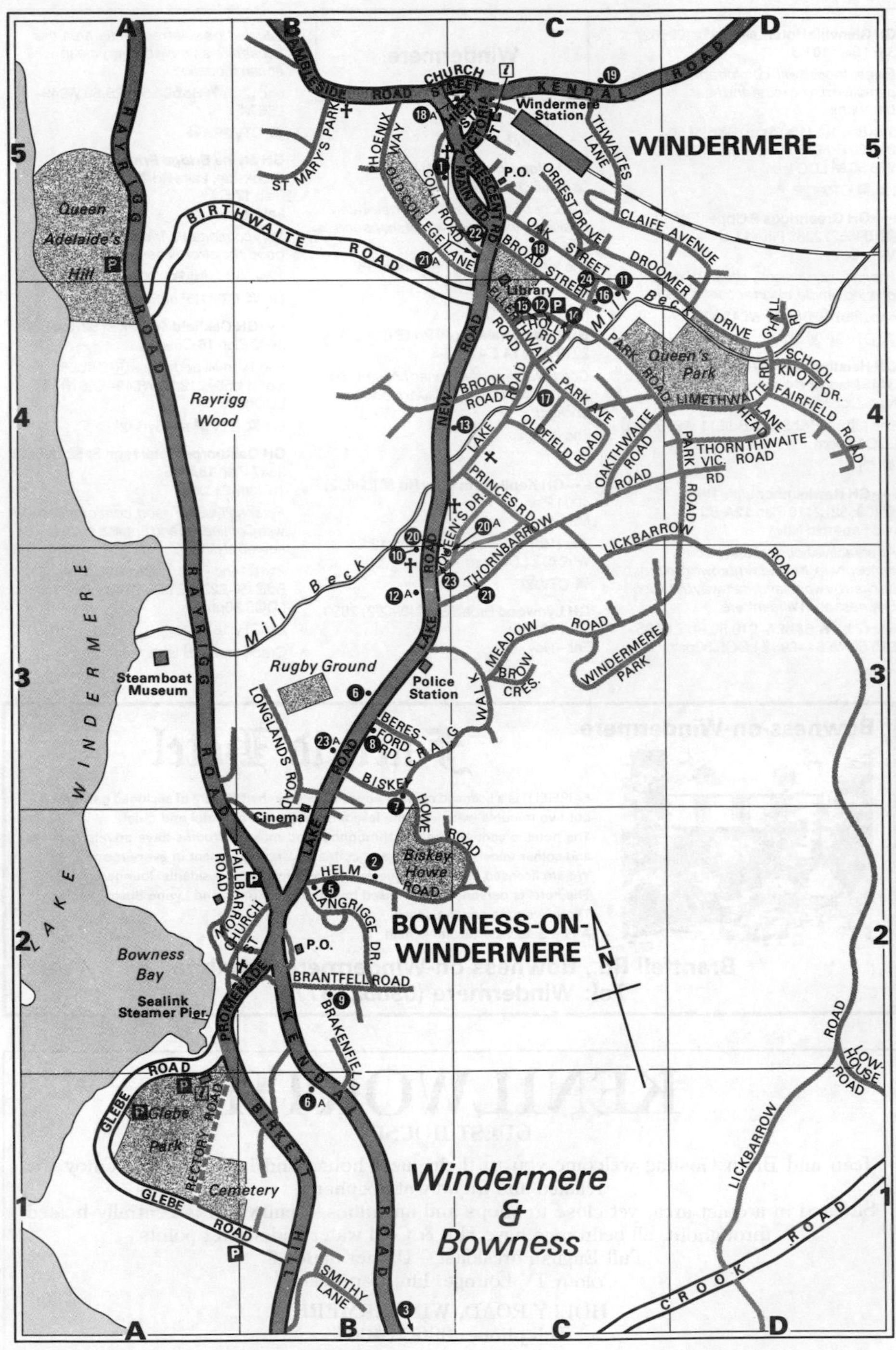
Windermere
&
Bowness
WINDERMERE
BOWNESS-ON-WINDERMERE
N
Queen Adelaide's Hill
Rayrigg Wood
LAKE WINDERMERE
Steamboat Museum
Rugby Ground
Police Station
Cinema
Biskey Howe
Bowness Bay
Sealink Steamer Pier
Glebe Park
Cemetery
Queen's Park
Windermere Station
Library
P.O.
RAYRIGG ROAD
BIRTHWAITE ROAD
AMBLESIDE ROAD
KENDAL ROAD
NEW ROAD
LAKE ROAD
CHURCH STREET
HIGH STREET
VICTORIA STREET
CRESCENT RD
MAIN RD
COLLEGE ROAD
OLD COLLEGE LANE
PHOENIX WAY
ST MARY'S PARK
ORREST DRIVE
OAK STREET
BROAD STREET
ELLERTHWAITE ROAD
HOLLY RD
CLAIFE AVENUE
THWAITES LANE
DROOMER DRIVE
GHYLL RD
SCHOOL KNOTT DR.
FAIRFIELD ROAD
LIMETHWAITE RD
HEAD LANE
THORNTHWAITE ROAD
VIC. RD
PARK ROAD
PARK AVE
OLDFIELD ROAD
OAKTHWAITE ROAD
BROOK ROAD
LAKE ROAD
PRINCES RD
QUEEN'S DR
THORNBARROW
LICKBARROW ROAD
MEADOW ROAD
WINDERMERE PARK
BROW CRES.
WALK
CRAIG
BERESFORD RD
BISKEY HOWE ROAD
HELM ROAD
LANGRIGGE DR.
LONGLANDS ROAD
FALLBARROW ROAD
CHURCH ST
PROMENADE
BRANTFELL ROAD
BRAKENFIELD
BIRKETT HILL
GLEBE ROAD
RECTORY ROAD
SMITHY LANE
LOW HOUSE ROAD
CROOK ROAD
LICKBARROW
Mill Beck
A
B
C
D
1
2
3
4
5

Windermere

1 Archway
2 Biskey Howe Villa Hotel
3 Brooklands
5 Crag Brow Cottage Private Hotel
6 Craig Foot Hotel
6A Cranleigh Hotel
7 Eastbourne Hotel
8 Elim Bank Hotel
9 Fairfield Country House Hotel
10 Glenville Hotel
11 Greenriggs
12 Haisthorpe
12A Hawksmoor
13 Hilton House Hotel
14 Hollythwaite
15 Kenilworth
16 Lynwood
17 Mylne Bridge Private Hotel
18 Oakfield
18A Oakthorpe Hotel
19 Orrest Head House
20 Rosemount
20A St Johns Lodge
21 Thornleigh
21A Tudor
22 Waverley Hotel
23 Westlake
23A White Lodge Hotel
24 White Rose

Windermere

GH Orrest Head House Kendal Rd ☎(09662) 4315 Plan **19** *C5*
Apr–Oct
7hc B&b£8.50–£9.50 W£57–£60 M
Lic CTV 12P nc5yrs

GH Rosemount Lake Rd ☎(09662) 3739 Plan **20** *B4*
Traditional lakeland house offering warm hospitality and good cuisine.
8rm 6hc 2⋔ (2fb) B&b£9–£10 Bdi£15.50–£17 W£101–£112 Ł LDO5pm
Lic ▥ CTV 6P 2🚗
Credit cards 1 3 V

GH *St Johns Lodge* Lake Rd ☎(09662) 3078 Plan **20A** *B3*
Closed Dec
A charming private hotel with comfortable accommodation.
10hc 7⋔ (3fb) CTV in 3 bedrooms TV in 1 bedroom Ⓡ LDO6pm
Lic ▥ CTV 10P

⊢⊣ **GH Thornleigh** Thornbarrow Rd, Bowness ☎(09662) 4203 Plan **21** *C3*
Etr–Oct
6hc (4fb) ★ B&b£7.50–£9 Bdi£13–£14.50 W£50–£60 M
Lic ▥ CTV 5P
See advertisement on page 374

⊢⊣ **GH Tudor** 60 Main St ☎(09662) 2363 Plan **21A** *C5*
Apr–Oct
6hc CTV in 4 bedrooms B&b£7–£8.50 Bdi£10.50–£12.85 LDO9.30pm
Lic ▥ CTV 10P nc6yrs
Credit card 1

⊢⊣ **GH Waverley Hotel** College Rd ☎(09662) 5026 Plan **22** *C5*
Mar–Nov
10hc (4fb) B&b£7.50–£10 W£50–£65 M
Lic ▥ CTV 8P nc4yrs
Credit card 1

⊢⊣ **GH Westlake** Lake Rd ☎(09662) 3020 Plan **23** *B3*
Closed New Year
7rm 2hc 1⋔ (3fb) CTV in 2 bedrooms ★ Ⓡ B&b£8–£9.50 Bdi£13.50–£16 W£56–£66.50 M LDO2pm
Lic ▥ CTV 5P
See advertisement on page 374

GH White Lodge Hotel Lake Rd, Bowness ☎(09662) 3624 Plan **23A** *B3*
Etr–Oct
12rm 4hc 6🛁 2⋔ (3fb)
CTV 20P
See advertisement on page 374

GH *White Rose* Broad St ☏(09662) 5180 Plan **24** *C4*
6hc (3fb) LDO6pm
▥ CTV

WINDSOR
Berkshire
Map **4** SU97
GH Clarence Hotel Clarence Rd ☏(07535) 64436
Comfortable and nicely appointed rooms with good public areas run by friendly management.
20rm 11hc 11⋒ (6fb) CTV in all bedrooms ✱B&b£9.75–£10.75

Lic ▥ CTV 2P
Credit cards 1 2 3 Ⓥ

WINFRITH NEWBURGH
Dorset
Map **3** SY88
FH Mrs H Cox **Wynards** *(SY802846)* ☏Warmwell (0305) 852817
Apr–Oct
Small modern farm on the outskirts of the village, with pleasant views over surrounding countryside. 1½m W off unclass rd.
6rm 3hc (1fb) B&b£9.50–£11 Bdi£14–£16.50 W£80 ⱡ LDO4.30pm
▥ CTV 8P 11acres mixed

WINTERBOURNE ABBAS
Dorset
Map **3** SY69
GH Church View ☏Martinstown (030588) 296
10hc (2fb) Ⓡ ✱B&b£7.50–£8 Bdi£11–£12 W£70–£80 ⱡ
Lic ▥ CTV 6P 2 Ⓥ

GH Whitefriars Hotel ☎Martinstown (030588) 206
Apr–Oct
Manor house situated on main road.
8rm 1hc 7⇌ (4fb) ✶ *B&b£10–£14 Bdi£15–£19 W£95–£110 ⱡ LDO9pm
Lic ⅢⅢ CTV 18P
Credit cards 1 3

WISBECH
Cambridgeshire
Map **5** TF40

GH Glendon Sutton Rd ☎(0945) 584812
Mar–Oct
18hc (2fb) B&b£13.80 Bdi£17.80 W£80.50
Lic CTV 60P ♿ ⌂

WITHAM
Essex
Map **5** TL81

INN Spread Eagle Newland St ☎(0376) 512131
Olde worlde inn with bedrooms in the main building and smaller more modest ones in the annexe.
6rm 5hc 1⇌ (A 5rm 4hc 1⇌) CTV in 2 bedrooms ✶ Ⓡ B&b£12.50–£15 W£75 Ⓜ L£6alc D10pm £6alc
CTV 40P
Credit cards 1 3 5

WITHIEL
Cornwall
Map **2** SW96

FH Mr & Mrs P U G Sharp ***Tregawne*** *(SX002662)* ☎Lanivet (0208) 831303
Closed Xmas
Charming, carefuly modernised farmhouse with antiques. Stands in Ruthern valley away from the farm.
4rm 2hc 1⇌ (1fb) Ⓡ
ⅢⅢ 8P (heated) 160acres dairy

WITTON *(Near North Walsham)*
Norfolk
Map **9** TG33

GH Witton Old Rectory ☎Walcott (0692) 650370
Comfortable, early Victorian house in own grounds situated in remote countryside.
7rm 2hc 4⇌ CTV in 1 bedroom TV in 1 bedroom Ⓡ B&b£8–£10 Bdi£13–£15 W£89–£99 ⱡ LDO9pm
Lic CTV 20P

WIVELISCOMBE
Somerset
Map **3** ST02

FH B M & P E Ferguson **Deepleigh** *(ST079294)* Langley Marsh ☎(0984) 23379
16th century farmhouse converted into small hotel having comfortable lounge with original beams, panelling and log fire. 1m N unclass rd.
8hc 1⇌ 7⋒ (6fb) ✶ B&b£12 Bdi£18 W£115 ⱡ (W only Jul & Aug) LDO6pm
Lic ⅢⅢ CTV 6P ⌂ U 16acres mixed

Winterbourne Abbas — Woolley

FH Mrs E M Wyatt ***Hillacre*** *(ST104275)* Crowford ☎(0984) 23355
Traditional farmhouse set back about 200 yds to the north of A361.
2hc (1fb) ✶
CTV P 1 800acres mixed

INN *Bear* 10 North St ☎(0984) 23537
6rm 5hc Ⓡ D9pm
CTV 6P

WIX
Essex
Map **5** TM12

FH Mrs H P Mitchell **New Farmhouse** *(TM165289)* ☎(025587) 365
A modern farmhouse with open views and self contained well equipped kitchen. ½m N on right off Wix/Bradfield rd.
5hc (2fb) ✶ B&b£8.50–£9.50 Bdi£14–£17.50 W£51–£54 Ⓜ LDO6pm
ⅢⅢ CTV 10P ⌂ 110acres arable Ⓥ

WOLSELEY BRIDGE
Staffordshire
Map **7** SK02

FH Mrs A Evans **Taft** *(SK026205)* ☎Little Haywood (0889) 881326
mid Apr–mid Oct
Farm is situated on N side of River Trent and ½m E of river bridge.
1hc (A 2rm) (1fb) Ⓡ *B&b£8–£10 W£55 Ⓜ
ⅢⅢ CTV 6P 110acres beef sheep mixed Ⓥ

WOMENSWOLD
Kent
Map **5** TR25

GH Woodpeckers Country Hotel ☎Canterbury (0227) 831319
Feb–23 Dec
Converted 19th century Rectory standing in 3 acres of grounds, complemented by good home cooking.
15rm 10hc 5⋒ (4fb) CTV in 10 bedrooms TV in 3 bedrooms Ⓡ B&b£15–£16 Bdi£19–£10 W£119–£126 ⱡ LDO9pm
Lic ⅢⅢ CTV 22P 2 ⌂ (heated) Ⓥ

WOODY BAY
Devon
Map **3** SS64

GH The Red House ☎Parracombe (05983) 255
Apr–Oct
6hc 3⇌ (1fb) B&b£9–£10.75 Bdi£14.10–£15.85 W£89–£99 ⱡ LDO5pm

WOOLACOMBE
Devon
Map **2** SS44

GH Barton House Hotel Barton Rd ☎(0271) 870548
May–Sep
12rm 4hc 6⇌ 2⋒ (5fb) Ⓡ *B&b£7.50–£10 Bdi£11.75–£14.25 W£82–£103.50 ⱡ LDO7pm
Lic ⅢⅢ CTV 12P

GH Castle The Esplanade ☎(0271) 870788
Etr–Oct
9rm 8hc 1⋒ (3fb) B&b£10.50–£13.50 Bdi£16–£19 W£67–£92 Ⓜ LDO4.30pm
Lic ⅢⅢ CTV 9P Ⓥ

GH Combe Ridge Hotel The Esplanade ☎(0271) 870321
8hc (3fb) B&b£8–£10.50 Bdi£11–£14 W£75–£90 ⱡ (W only Jul & Aug) LDO5.30pm
Lic CTV 8P Ⓥ

GH Holmesdale Hotel Bay View Rd ☎(0271) 870335
15⋒ (12fb) ✶ B&b£11–£16 Bdi£15–£20 W£61–£91 Ⓜ LDO10.30pm
Lic CTV 10P ⌂
Credit cards 1 2 3 5
See advertisement on page 376

GH *Springside Country Hotel* Mullacott Rd ☎(0271) 870452
Mar–Oct
7hc 2⇌ (4fb) ✶ LDO5pm
Lic ⅢⅢ CTV 10P

WOOLFARDISWORTHY
Devon
Map **2** SS32

FH R C & C M Beck **Stroxworthy** *(SS341198)* ☎Clovelly (02373) 333
Tastefully decorated and set in beautiful countryside offering a variety of farm produce on menu. Herd of Guernsey cows.
9hc (3fb) B&b£8–£9 Bdi£10.70–£11.70 W£52.50 Ⓜ (W only Jul & Aug) LDO7.30pm
Lic CTV 20P 90acres dairy

FH Mrs P I Westaway **Westvilla** *(SS329215)* ☎Clovelly (02373) 309
Mar–Oct
4hc (1fb) ✶ B&b£7–£8 Bdi£12–£13 W£70–£75 ⱡ
CTV 4P 22acres sheep

WOOLHOPE
Hereford & Worcester
Map **3** SO63

INN Butchers Arms ☎Fownhope (043277) 281
3hc TV in all bedrooms ✶ Ⓡ B&b£11.50–£12.50 W£69–£75 Ⓜ Bar lunch £4.15alc D9pm £7.75alc
ⅢⅢ 80P nc14yrs Ⓥ
See advertisement on page 376

WOOLLEY
Cornwall
Map **2** SS21

⊢⊣ **FH** G Colwill **East Woolley** *(SS254167)* ☎ Morwenstow (028883) 274
Etr–Nov
Farm set in undulating pastureland, close to A39. Homely atmosphere. Play areas with swings, see-saw and pony for children.
3rm (1fb) B&b£6.50–£7.50 Bdi£10.50–£11.50 W£65–£70 Ⅼ (W only Jun–Aug) LDO6pm
CTV 6P ⌂ U 117acres arable beef Ⓥ

WOOLSTASTON
Shropshire
Map **7** SO49

FH Mrs J A Davies ***Rectory*** *(SO452985)* ☎ Leebotwood (06945) 306
Mar–Nov
3 ✱
CTV 10P 170acres mixed

WOOTTON BASSETT
Wiltshire
Map **4** SU08

INN Angel Hotel 47 High St ☎ Swindon (0793) 852314
Standing in High St this semi-detached inn is built of red brick and has a good bar and restaurant menu.
6hc CTV in 1 bedroom TV in 4 bedrooms ✱ Ⓡ ✱B&b£11.50 L£3.50alc D9.30pm £5alc
CTV 8P nc12yrs
Credit cards 1 2 3 5

WORCESTER
Hereford & Worcester
Map **3** SO85

GH Lock Ryan Hotel 119 Sidbury Rd ☎ (0905) 351143

14rm 13hc 1⋒ (A 4rm 3hc 1⋒) (2fb) ✱
B&b£10.50–£11.50
Ⅲ CTV ✗ ⌂ sauna bath

WORKINGTON
Cumbria
Map **11** NY02

GH *Morven* Siddick ☎(0900) 2118
8hc 2➡ (2fb) TV in 6 bedrooms ✱
Lic Ⅲ CTV 30P sea

WORMBRIDGE
Hereford & Worcester
Map **3** SO43

FH Mrs J T Davies ***Duffryn*** *(SO415319)*
☎(098121) 217
4hc (1fb) Ⓡ LDO5pm
Ⅲ CTV 12P ⌂ 184acres arable dairy sheep Ⓥ

WORTHING
West Sussex
Map **4** TQ10

GH Blair House 11 St Georges Rd
☎(0903) 34071
Three-storey Victorian house close to sea front in quiet residential area.
7rm 1hc 2➡ 4⋒ Ⓡ B&b£9–£12
Bdi£13.50–£16.50 W£63–£84 Ⅼ
Lic Ⅲ CTV 5P Ⓥ

GH Camelot House 20 Gannon Rd
☎(0903) 204334
Closed Xmas
6rm 5hc 1⋒ (1fb) CTV in 5 bedrooms TV in 1 bedroom ✱ Ⓡ B&b£8.50–£10
Bdi£12.50–£14 W£78–£85 Ⅼ LDO10am
Lic Ⅲ CTV 3P Ⓥ

⊢⊣ **GH Meldrum House** 8 Windsor Rd
☎(0903) 33808
Closed Dec
Small terraced house with friendly atmosphere offering simple yet comfortable accommodation.
6hc (2fb) ✱ Ⓡ B&b£7–£10 Bdi£11–£14
W£46–£65 M LDO5pm
Ⅲ CTV ✗ nc3yrs

GH Osborne 175 Brighton Rd ☎(0903) 35771
Two storey terraced house facing the sea, run by friendly, helpful proprietors.
7rm 6hc 1⋒
CTV

GH St George's Lodge Hotel
46 Chesswood Rd ☎(0903) 208926
Large well equipped hotel with comfortable accommodation and well tended gardens.
16rm 8hc 7➡ (8fb) CTV in 8 bedrooms TV in 1 bedroom Ⓡ ✻B&b£8.95–£12.95
Bdi£12.95–£16.95 W£60–£90 M
LDO8.45pm
Lic Ⅲ CTV 8P 1⌂
Credit cards 1 2 3

GH Southdene 41 Warwick Gdns
☎(0903) 32909
Apr–Sep
Comfortable three-storey terraced house in residential area.
6hc 1➡ 2⋒ ✱ B&b£9 W£58 M
Lic CTV ✗

GH Wansfell Hotel 49 Chesswood Rd (Guestaccom) ☎(0903) 30612
Town house close to sea front.
12rm 6hc 2➡ 4⋒ (2fb) CTV in 9 bedrooms TV in 3 bedrooms ✱ Ⓡ
B&b£11.50–£13.25 Bdi£17.25–£19
W£94–£112 Ⅼ LDO7.30pm
Lic Ⅲ 8P nc4yrs

GH *Williton* 10 Windsor Rd ☎(0903) 37974
Small house situated very close to seafront with antique furnishings in dining room.
4hc (3fb) ✱
TV 2P

GH Windsor House Hotel
14–20 Windsor Rd ☎(0903) 39655
Large house in quiet residential area with some spacious homely bedrooms.
27rm 3➡ 6⋒ (4fb) CTV in 15 bedrooms
Ⓡ B&b£9.50–£12 Bdi£13.50–£17.50
W£99–£109 LDO6pm
Lic Ⅲ CTV 16P Ⓥ

GH *Windsor Lodge* 3 Windsor Rd
☎(0903) 200056
Family run house close to sea front with comfortable lounge and pleasant dining room.
6hc Ⓡ LDO10pm
Ⅲ CTV ✗ nc2yrs

GH *Wolsey Hotel* 179–181 Brighton Rd
☎(0903) 36149
Closed Xmas
Two terraced houses on the sea front simply but prettily furnished.
14hc (3fb) TV in all bedrooms
Lic Ⅲ CTV ✗ sea Ⓥ

WOTTON-UNDER-EDGE
Gloucestershire
Map **3** ST79

⊢⊣ **FH** Mrs K P Forster **Under-the-Hill House** *(ST758937)* Adey's Ln
☎Dursley (0453) 842557
Apr–Oct
An attractive, quietly situated small farmhouse within walking distance of the town centre.
4hc (1fb) ✱ Ⓡ B&b£7.70–£8.80
Bdi£12–£13.10 LDO10am
CTV 4P 46acres beef

WYE
Kent
Map **5** TR04

INN New Flying Horse Upper Bridge St
☎(0233) 812297
Comfortable and well managed inn with well equipped bedrooms, an à la carte dining room and a rear patio garden.
6hc (A 4➡) CTV in all bedrooms Ⓡ
B&b£13–£19 Bdi£21–£27 W£136–£150
Ⅼ Lfr£8.50&alc D9.30pm fr£8.50&alc
Ⅲ 100P
Credit cards 1 2 3 5 Ⓥ

YARCOMBE
Devon
Map **3** ST20

INN Yarcombe ☎Upottery (040486) 218
→

7hc ® B&b£10.55–£11 L£4.25alc D9.30pm£6
Ⅲ CTV 76P
Credit cards 1 2 3

YARMOUTH, GREAT
Norfolk
Map **5** TG50

⊢→ **GH Frandor** 120 Lowestoft Rd, Gorleston-on-Sea (2m S A12) ☎(0493) 662112
6hc (3fb) 🐕 B&b£7–£10 Bdi£9–£12 W£55–£75 ⱡ LDO6pm
Lic Ⅲ CTV 10P ⌂ Ⓥ

GH Georgian House Private Hotel 16–17 North Dr ☎(0493) 842623
Closed Xmas rs winter
25hc 9➡ (4fb) CTV in 14 bedrooms 🐕 B&b£9–£18 W£55–£90 M (W only Jul & Aug)
Lic Ⅲ CTV 24P nc5yrs Ⓥ

GH Hazlewood House 57 Clarence Rd, Gorleston-on-Sea ☎(0493) 662830
8hc (4fb) TV in 4 bedrooms ® *B&b£7–£8.75 Bdi£8.50–£10 W£46–£65 M LDO4.30pm
Lic Ⅲ CTV ⚑
Credit cards 1 3

GH Palm Court Hotel 10 North Dr ☎(0493) 844568
Etr–Oct
47hc 12➡ 19⋔ (8fb) CTV in all bedrooms ® B&b£14–£20 Bdi£17.50–£24 W£99–£150 ⱡ S% LDO8pm
Lic lift CTV 40P ▭(heated) sauna bath
Credit cards 1 3

YATTON
Avon
Map **3** ST46

INN Prince of Orange High St ☎(0934) 832193
6rm 1hc 5⋔ CTV in all bedrooms ® B&b£15.20 Bar lunch £1–£3 D9.45pm £3.50–£6.50
Ⅲ 40P
Credit cards 1 3 Ⓥ

YEALMPTON
Devon
Map **2** SX55

⊢→ **FH** Mrs A German **Broadmoor** *(SX574498)* Plymouth (0752) 880407
Stone-built farmhouse and outbuildings, situated in open countryside enjoying distant views of Dartmoor.
3hc 🐕 B&b£7.50–£8
CTV P nc7yrs 200acres mixed

YEAVELEY
Derbyshire
Map **8** SK14

FH Mrs J Potter ***Eddishes*** *(SK179396)* ☎Great Cubley (033523) 486
Etr–Nov
2hc (1fb) 🐕 ®
Ⅲ TV 3P nc6yrs 72acres dairy

YELVERTON
Devon
Map **2** SX56

GH Harrabeer Country House Hotel Harrowbeer Ln ☎(0822) 853302
7rm 6hc 1➡ (1fb) 🐕 B&b£12 Bdi£18.50 W£110–£116.50 ⱡ LDO6.45pm
Lic Ⅲ CTV 8P ▭

YEOVIL
Somerset
Map **32** ST51

⊢→ **GH Wyndham** 142 Sherborne Rd ☎(0935) 21468
6hc (2fb) B&bfr£7 Bdifr£11 Wfr£77 ⱡ LDO4pm
Lic Ⅲ CTV 6P

⊢→ **FH** Mrs M Tucker **Carents** *(ST546188)* Yeovil Marsh ☎(0935) 76622
Feb–Oct
Clean, pleasant traditional-style farmhouse on outskirts of Yeovil 2m N of A37.
3rm 1hc (1fb) 🐕 ® B&b£7.50–£7.75 Bdifr£13 LDO2pm
CTV P 350acres arable beef

YORK
North Yorkshire
Map **8** SE65

⊢→ **GH Abingdon** 60 Bootham Cres, Bootham ☎(0904) 21761
Feb–Nov
6rm 2hc 4⋔ (2fb) TV in 2 bedrooms 🐕 ® B&b£7.50–£8.50 W£49–£56 M
Ⅲ CTV 6P Ⓥ

GH Acomb Rd 128 Acomb Rd ☎(0904) 792321
14rm 9hc (4fb) CTV in all bedrooms ® B&b£9–£10 Bdi£12–£13 W£63–£70 M LDO8pm
Lic CTV 20P

GH Albert Hotel The Mount ☎(0904) 32525
Closed 23 Dec–3 Jan
10rm 3hc 1➡ 6⋔ (3fb) CTV in 9 bedrooms 🐕 ® *B&b£11.50–£15 Bdi£16.50–£21 W£69–£90 M LDOnoon
Lic Ⅲ CTV 6P
Credit cards 1 2 3 5 Ⓥ

⊢→ **GH Alcuin Lodge** 15 Sycamore Pl, Bootham ☎(0904) 32222
Three-storey brick built Edwardian mid-terraced property in quiet residential area approx 1m from city centre.
6hc (2fb) TV in all bedrooms 🐕 ® B&b£7–£8.50 Bdi£12–£13.50 W£49–£59.50 M LDO9.30am
Lic Ⅲ CTV 3P nc3yrs
Credit cards 1 2 3

GH Alhambra Court Hotel 31 St Marys, Bootham ☎(0904) 28474
Two combined Victorian town houses near the city centre, with spacious dining room and comfortable lounge.
22rm 20➡ 2⋔ (3fb) CTV in all bedrooms 🐕 ® B&b£10–£14.50 Bdi£16–£20.50 W£66.50–£96 M LDO3pm
Lic Ⅲ TV 20P
Credit cards 1 3

⊢⊣ **GH Amblesyde** 62 Bootham Crescent ☎(0904) 37165
2nd wk Jan–end Nov
Hospitable guesthouse in residential area offering clean, comfortable accommodation.
7hc (1fb) CTV in all bedrooms Ⓡ B&bfr£8 Bdifr£12.50 LDOam
CTV

GH Ascot House 80 East Pde ☎(0904) 25782 (due to change to 424852)
Closed Xmas
Attractive Victorian house with unusual oriel staircase window. Bedrooms have modern fittings.
9rm 3⇌ 6⋒ (2fb) TV in all bedrooms Ⓡ B&b£10 Bdi£16 W£70 M LDO5pm
CTV 10P 1 sauna bath

⊢⊣ **GH Avenue** 6 The Avenue, Clifton ☎(0904) 20575
Feb–Nov
Three-storey, late Victorian house with attractive small forecourt garden, in quiet tree lined street, near city centre.
6hc (2fb) TV in all bedrooms Ⓡ B&b£7.50–£8.50 Bdi£11.50–£12.50 W£47–£54 M LDOnoon
CTV 6P
See advertisement on page 380

⊢⊣ **GH Beech House** 6–7 Longfield Ter, Bootham ☎(0904) 34581
Closed Xmas & New Year

York

A pair of Victorian terraced houses converted into very smart and comfortable accommodation.
7rm 5hc 2⋒ (3fb) CTV in all bedrooms B&b£7–£12.50 Bdi£13–£18.50 LDOam
Lic CTV 5P nc5yrs Ⓥ

GH Bootham Bar Hotel 4 High Petergate ☎(0904) 58516
Interesting house dating from 1743 with compact accommodation.
8hc (2fb) B&b£12
lift CTV
See advertisement on page 380

GH Cavalier Private Hotel 39 Monkgate ☎(0904) 36615
10hc 2⇌ 2⋒ (4fb) CTV in 8 bedrooms Ⓡ B&b£9–£12.50 Bdi£13.50–£18 W£98–£120 L LDO4pm
Lic CTV sauna bath Ⓥ
See advertisement on page 380

GH Clifton Bridge Hotel Water End ☎(0904) 53609
Closed Xmas week
Comfortable hotel with spacious lounge and separate small oak lined bar and dining room. 1 mile from city centre.
10rm 9hc 1⋒ (1fb) Ⓡ *B&b£11–£13.50 LDO7.45pm
Lic CTV 12P
Credit cards 1 3 Ⓥ
See advertisement on page 381

GH *Coach House Hotel* Marygate ☎(0904) 52780
13hc 2⇌ (W only Nov–Feb) LDO9.30pm
CTV 14P

GH Coppers Lodge 15 Alma Ter, Fulford Rd ☎(0904) 39871
8hc (5fb) *B&b£7–£8 Bdi£11–£12 LDO2pm
CTV 6P
Credit cards 1 3

⊢⊣ **GH Craig-y-Don** 3 Grosvenor Ter, Bootham ☎(0904) 37186
7rm 6hc 1⋒ (3fb) Ⓡ B&b£7–£10.50
CTV 5P

GH Cranleigh House Hotel 28–29 East Mount Rd (Guestaccom) ☎(0904) 20837
11hc (2fb) Ⓡ *B&b£9–£10 Bdi£13.50–£14.50 W£60–£70 M LDOnoon
Lic CTV 10P

⊢⊣ **GH Crescent** 77 Bootham ☎(0904) 23216
Closed Nov & Dec
8hc (2fb) Ⓡ B&b£8–£10 →

Avenue Guest House

6 THE AVENUE, CLIFTON, YORK YO3 6AS

Telephone: 0904/20575

Beautiful Victorian house in quiet street just off the A19 York to Thirsk. Yet only ten minutes walk to the Minster and city centre. Easy access to Yorkshire moors and coast

Fully centrally heated.

Full fire certificate.

Comfortable lounge with dining area.

All bedrooms with own T.V.

All home cooked food.

Open all year, with personal attention of resident proprietors.

Bedroom and house keys giving access to rooms at all times.

Bootham Bar Hotel

The hotel is a delightful 18th-century house rebuilt in 1743, just within Bootham Bar, one of the fortified gateways into the City of York. Close to the Minster, City Walls, and many other local buildings of interest.

The Bootham bar has 10 bedrooms, 2 bathrooms, lounge with colour TV, lift and Fire Certificate.

The hotel is run by its owners and complies with the York and District Hotel and Restaurant Association Standards.

AA recommended.

Refreshments available all day in the lounge.

Price includes bed and full English Breakfast.

4 HIGH PETERGATE, YORK YO1 2EH Telephone (0904) 58516

Bootham Bar

A small Private Hotel open all year and offering every modern comfort in a beautiful old building only a 100 yards from the ancient city walls and five minutes from the Minster and City centre.

Bed and breakfast – evening meals available – colour TVs, coffee and tea facilities in all rooms – Central Heating – Sauna, some rooms with Private Bath/Shower.

Sue and Grant Henderson
The Cavalier Private Hotel, 39 Monkgate,
York YO3 7PB
Telephone: (0904) 36615

CTV nc10yrs

GH Croft Hotel 103 Mount Rd ☎(0904) 22747
Feb–Dec

10hc (1fb) ® B&b£10–£12 Bdi£16–£18 W£70–£84 M LDO4pm

CTV nc2yrs

Credit cards 1 3 V

GH Dairy 3 Scarcroft Rd ☎(0904) 39367

5hc 1 (A 1) (2fb) B&b£7.50–£8.50

CTV V

GH Fairmount Hotel 230 Tadcaster Rd, Mount Vale ☎(0904) 38298

Situated opposite the racecourse, this mellow brick built house comprises spacious comfortable accommodation of charm.

8rm 2hc 1 4 (4fb) CTV in 4 bedrooms ® B&bfr£13.25 Bdifr£19 Wfr£92.75 M LDOnoon

Lic CTV 7P 2

Credit cards 1 2 3 5

GH Field House Hotel 2 St George's Pl ☎(0904) 39572
Closed Xmas

York

17rm 1 10 CTV in all bedrooms ® B&b£16–£23 Bdi£23.50–£30.50 W£105–£161 M

Lic 22P

Credit cards 1 2 3

GH Gables 50 Bootham Cres, Bootham ☎(0904) 24381

5hc (2fb) ® B&b£7–£10

CTV

GH Georgian 35 Bootham ☎(0904) 22874

14hc 2 1 (1fb) CTV in 3 bedrooms ® B&b£8.50–£12.50

CTV 12P

See advertisement on page 382

GH Grasmead House Hotel 1 Scarcroft Hill, The Mount ☎(0904) 29996

Large, corner guesthouse with very comfortable accommodation, featuring four poster bed.

6 CTV in all bedrooms ®

*B&b£15.50–£18 Bdi£20–£23 W£106–£120 M LDO4pm

Lic CTV 1P nc5yrs

Credit card 3

GH Greenside 124 Clifton ☎(0904) 23631

6rm 5hc 1 (2fb) TV in 2 bedrooms B&b£8.50–£9.50

CTV 5P 1 V

See advertisement on page 382

GH Hazelwood 24–25 Portland St, Gillygate ☎(0904) 26548
Closed Dec & Jan

15rm 10hc 2 3 (4fb) CTV in 5 bedrooms ® B&b£7.50–£10.50 W£49.90–£69.90 M

CTV 6P

GH Heworth 126 East Pde ☎(0904) 26384 (due to change to 426384)

7hc (1fb) B&b£7–£9.50 Bdi£11–£13 W£45–£65 M LDOnoon

Lic CTV 1P 1

GH *Hobbits Hotel* 9 St Peters Gv ☎(0904) 24538
Closed 2wks Xmas →

9hc 5fl TV available in bedrooms
Lic ⊞ CTV 4P

⊢⊣ **GH Inglewood** 7 Clifton Gn ☎(0904) 53523
7hc 3fl (2fb) CTV in all bedrooms ★
B&b£8–£9.50 W£56–£66.50 M
⊞ 1🚗 Ⓥ

GH *Linden Lodge* Nunthorpe Av, Scarcroft Rd ☎(0904) 20107
Closed Dec & Jan
7hc (2fb) ★ Ⓡ LDO10am
Lic ⊞ CTV ⁋ nc7yrs

GH Mayfield Hotel 75 Scarcroft Rd ☎(0904) 54834

York

Late Victorian three storey terraced house with original features sympathetically restored to a good standard.
7rm 2⇨ 5fl (4fb) CTV in all bedrooms ★
B&b£17.50 Bdi£24 W£122.50 M
LDO8.30pm
Lic ⊞
Credit cards 1 2 3 Ⓥ

GH Moat Hotel Nunnery Ln ☎(0904) 52926
Interesting Victorian style house beneath medieval walls, with comfortable, suitably furnished accommodation.
9hc 6fl (1fb) ★ B&b£9–£13
CTV 10P
Credit cards 2 3 5

GH Orchard Court Hotel 4 St Peters Gv ☎(0904) 53964
Closed Dec
An elegant Victorian house in quiet cul-de-sac, close to city centre. The lofty public rooms are tastefully decorated.

10rm 3hc 1→ 6⋒ (4fb) CTV in 7 bedrooms Ⓡ B&b£9–£16 Bdi£15–£22 W£60–£104 M LDO7.30pm

Lic CTV 10P

Credit cards 1 3

GH Priory Hotel 126 Fulford Rd ☎(0904) 25280
Closed Xmas

A pair of large double fronted Victorian town houses with rear gardens, near city centre.

20rm 17hc 3⋒ (4fb) ✱ Ⓡ B&b£11.50–£13.80

CTV 25P

Credit cards 1 2 3 5 Ⓥ

⊢⊣ **GH St Denys Hotel** St Denys Rd ☎(0904) 22207
Closed Xmas

Former vicarage offers comfortable spacious accommodation and cosy lounge.

10rm 3hc 7→ (3fb) CTV in all bedrooms Ⓡ B&b£8–£16 Bdi£13–£21 LDO1pm

Lic CTV 10P

GH St Raphael 44 Queen Ann's Rd, Bootham ☎(0904) 54187

Comfortable and friendly guesthouse near Minster.

7hc (1fb) TV in 1 bedroom ✱ B&b£8.50–£9.50

CTV nc10yrs

⊢⊣ **GH Sycamore Hotel** 19 Sycamore Pl ☎(0904) 24712

6hc (2fb) CTV in all bedrooms ✱ Ⓡ B&b£7–£9 Bdi£12–£14 W£47–£61 M LDOnoon

Lic 4P nc5yrs

YOULGRAVE
Derbyshire
Map **8** SK26

⊢⊣ **INN Bulls Head** Church St ☎(062986) 307

4hc TV in 4 bedrooms ✱ Ⓡ B&b£7 Bdi£10 W£42 M Bar lunch £2.45–£3.95 D9.30pm £5alc

7P nc8yrs Ⓥ

YSBYTY IFAN
Gwynedd
Map **6** SH84

⊢⊣ **FH** Mrs F G Roberts **Ochr Cefn Isa** *(SH845495)* ☎Pentrefoelas (06905) 602
Etr–Oct

Farm set in elevated position with good views high above A5.

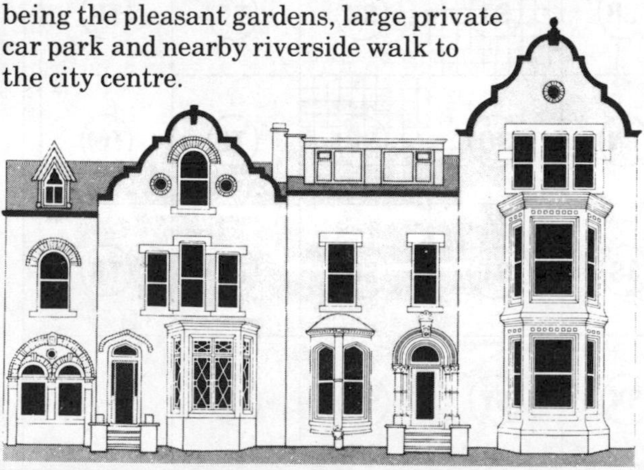

2hc (1fb) ✱ B&b£7.50 Bdi£10–£11 W£52.50 M LDO5pm

CTV 2P nc5yrs 123acres mixed

ZENNOR
Cornwall
Map **2** SW43

FH Mrs M C Osborne **Osborne's** *(SW455385)* Boswednack ☎Penzance (0736) 796944
Etr–Oct

2hc (1fb) ✱ *B&b£7

CTV 3P 2⌂ 50acres beef

The National Grid

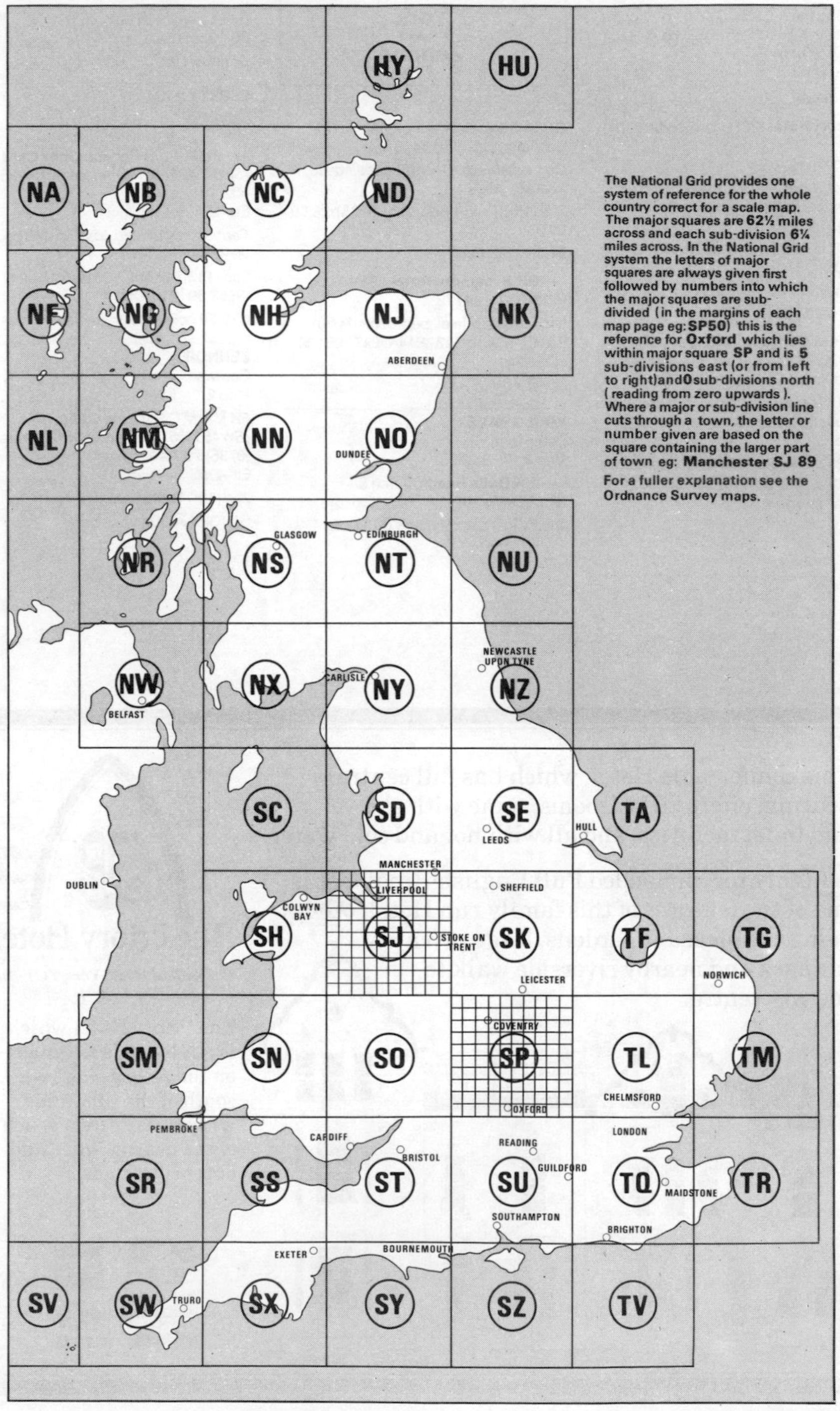

The National Grid provides one system of reference for the whole country correct for a scale map. The major squares are **62½** miles across and each sub-division **6¼** miles across. In the National Grid system the letters of major squares are always given first followed by numbers into which the major squares are sub-divided (in the margins of each map page eg: **SP50**) this is the reference for **Oxford** which lies within major square **SP** and is **5** sub-divisions east (or from left to right) and **0** sub-divisions north (reading from zero upwards). Where a major or sub-division line cuts through a town, the letter or number given are based on the square containing the larger part of town eg: **Manchester SJ 89**

For a fuller explanation see the Ordnance Survey maps.

Key to Atlas

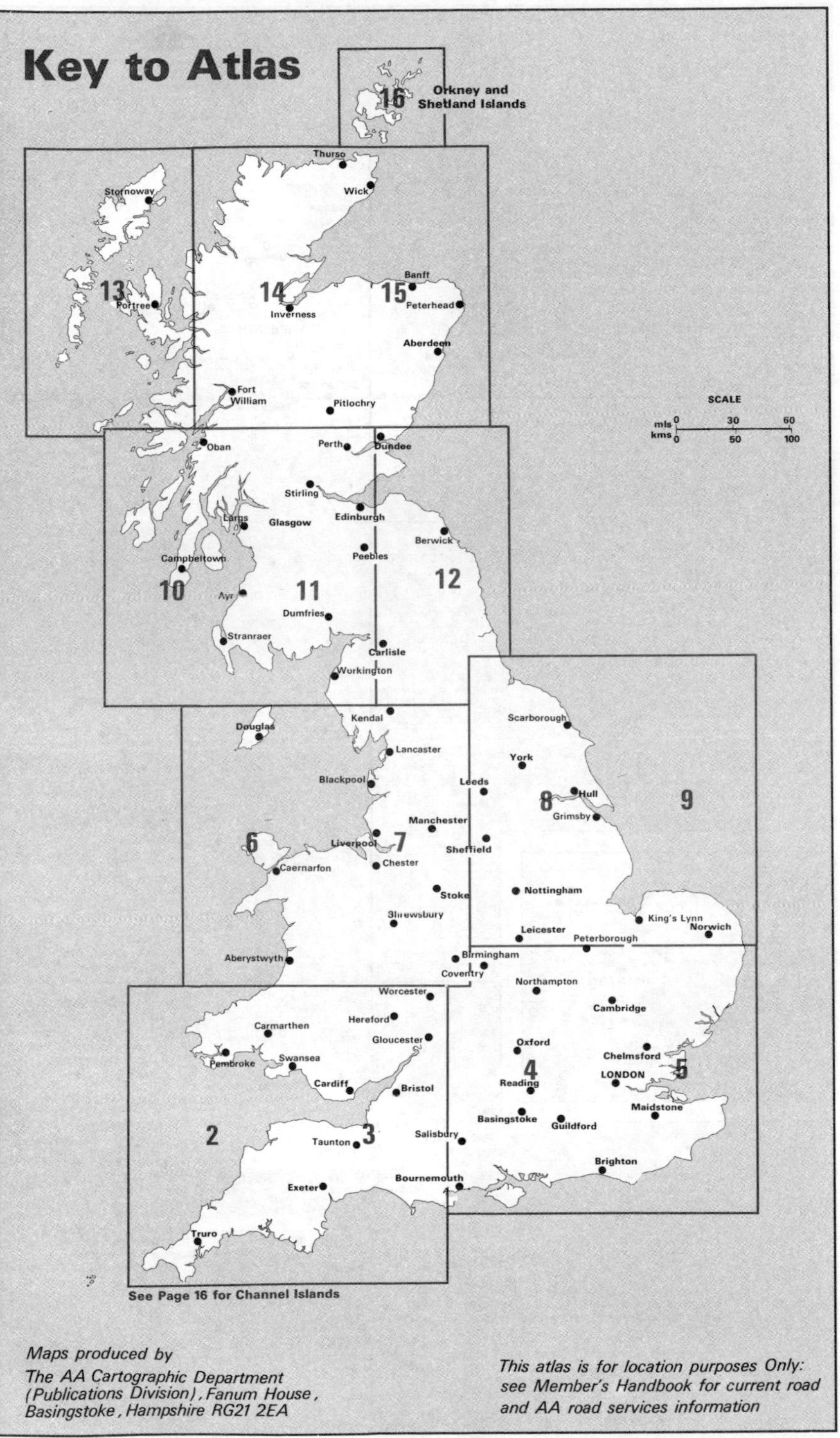

See Page 16 for Channel Islands

Maps produced by
The AA Cartographic Department (Publications Division), Fanum House, Basingstoke, Hampshire RG21 2EA

This atlas is for location purposes Only: see Member's Handbook for current road and AA road services information

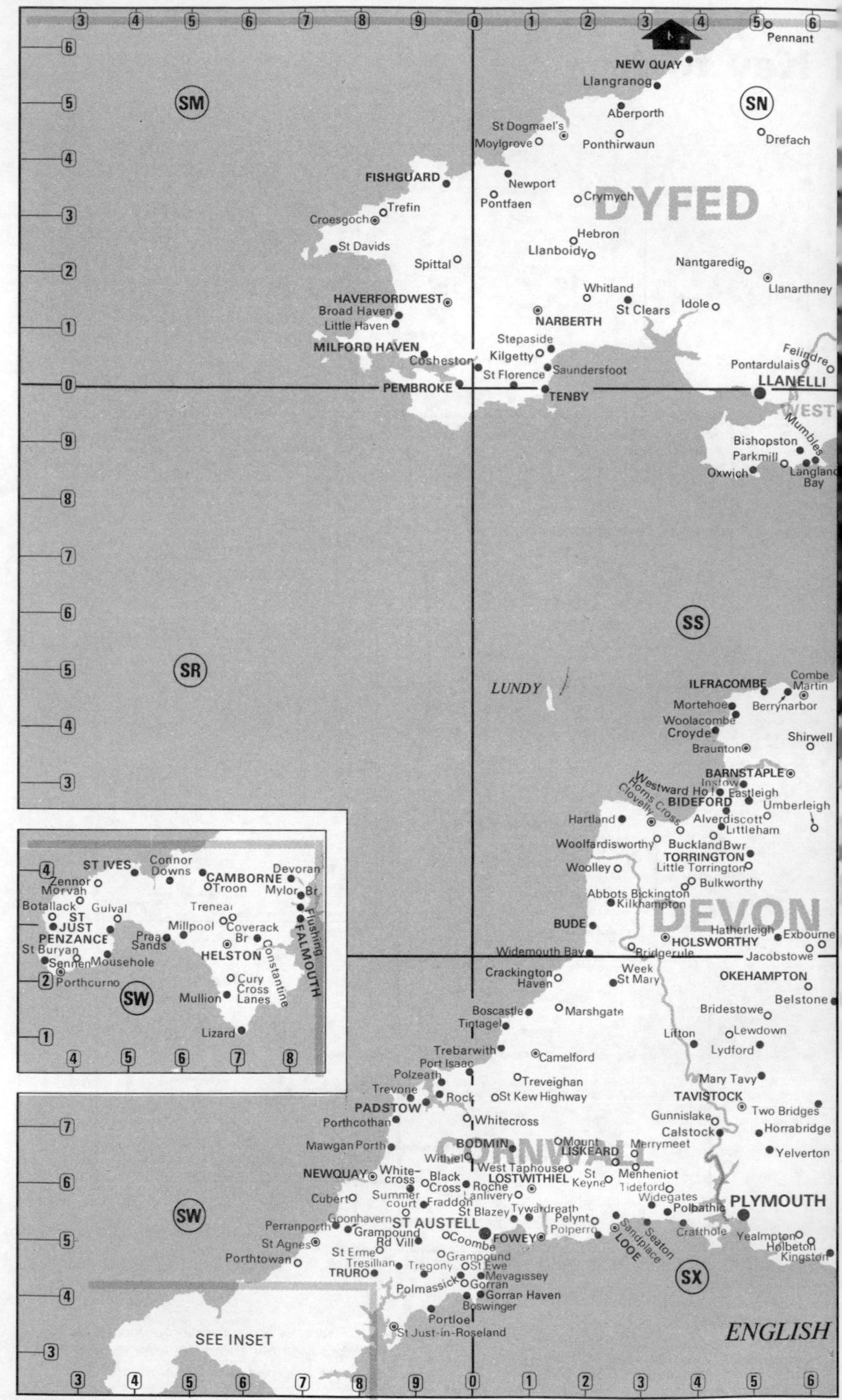

For continuation pages refer to numbered arrows

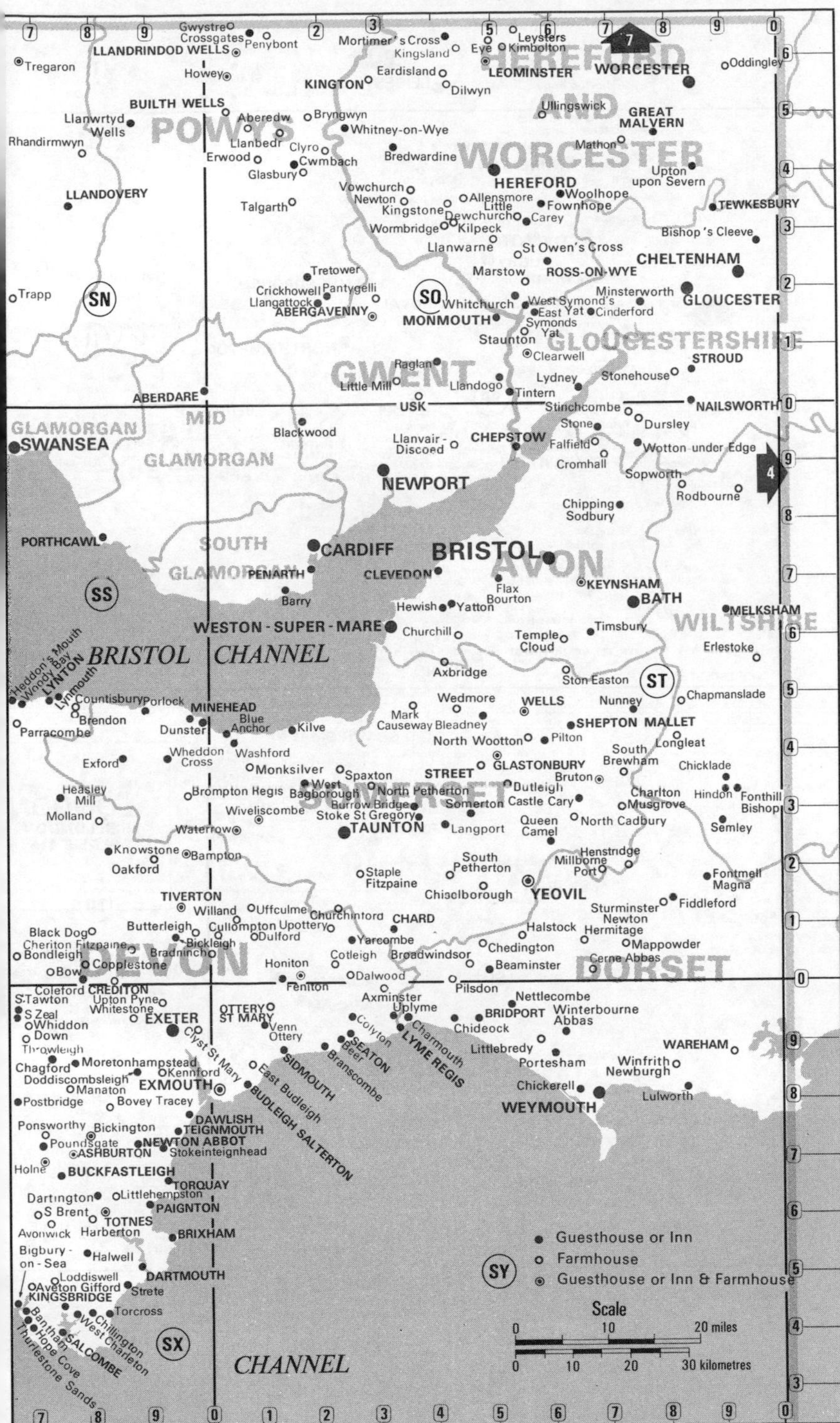

POWYS
HEREFORD AND WORCESTER
GLOUCESTERSHIRE
GWENT
MID GLAMORGAN
SOUTH GLAMORGAN
AVON
WILTSHIRE
SOMERSET
DEVON
DORSET
BRISTOL CHANNEL
CHANNEL
LLANDRINDOD WELLS
BUILTH WELLS
LLANDOVERY
KINGTON
LEOMINSTER
WORCESTER
GREAT MALVERN
HEREFORD
TEWKESBURY
CHELTENHAM
GLOUCESTER
ROSS-ON-WYE
ABERGAVENNY
MONMOUTH
STROUD
NAILSWORTH
ABERDARE
USK
SWANSEA
CHEPSTOW
NEWPORT
PORTHCAWL
CARDIFF
BRISTOL
PENARTH
CLEVEDON
KEYNSHAM
BATH
MELKSHAM
WESTON - SUPER - MARE
LYNTON
MINEHEAD
WELLS
SHEPTON MALLET
STREET
GLASTONBURY
TAUNTON
YEOVIL
TIVERTON
CHARD
CREDITON
EXETER
OTTERY ST MARY
SIDMOUTH
SEATON
LYME REGIS
BRIDPORT
WEYMOUTH
EXMOUTH
BUDLEIGH SALTERTON
DAWLISH
TEIGNMOUTH
NEWTON ABBOT
ASHBURTON
BUCKFASTLEIGH
TORQUAY
PAIGNTON
TOTNES
BRIXHAM
DARTMOUTH
KINGSBRIDGE
SALCOMBE
SN
SO
SS
ST
SX
SY
Guesthouse or Inn
Farmhouse
Guesthouse or Inn & Farmhouse
Scale
0 10 20 miles
0 10 20 30 kilometres

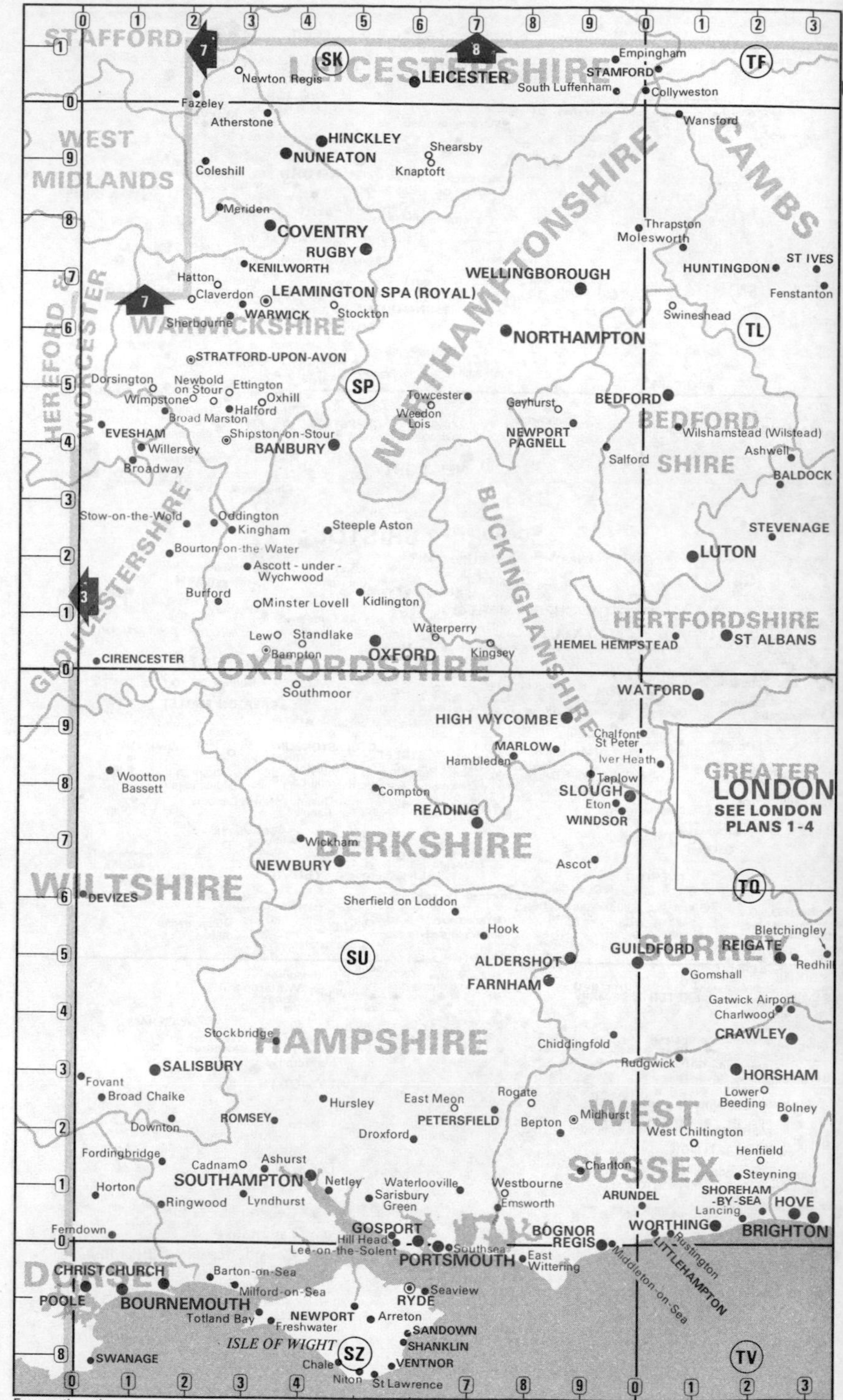

For continuation pages refer to numbered arrows

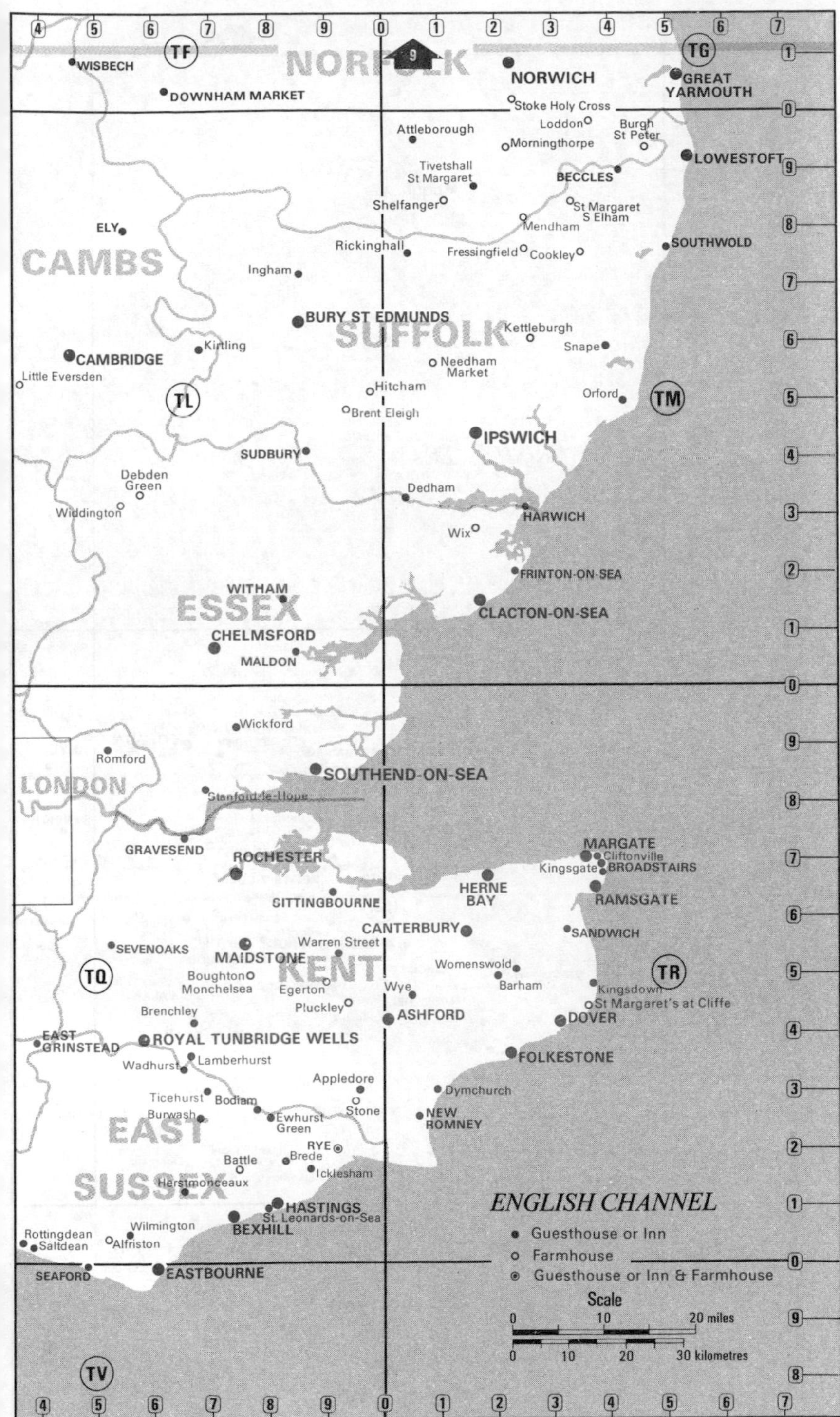

NORFOLK
9
NORWICH
GREAT YARMOUTH
WISBECH
DOWNHAM MARKET
Stoke Holy Cross
Loddon
Burgh St Peter
Attleborough
Morningthorpe
LOWESTOFT
Tivetshall St Margaret
BECCLES
Shelfanger
St Margaret S Elham
Mendham
ELY
CAMBS
Rickinghall
Fressingfield
Cookley
SOUTHWOLD
Ingham
BURY ST EDMUNDS
SUFFOLK
Kettleburgh
Snape
CAMBRIDGE
Kirtling
Needham Market
Little Eversden
Hitcham
Orford
Brent Eleigh
IPSWICH
SUDBURY
Debden Green
Dedham
Widdington
HARWICH
Wix
FRINTON-ON-SEA
WITHAM
ESSEX
CLACTON-ON-SEA
CHELMSFORD
MALDON
Wickford
Romford
LONDON
SOUTHEND-ON-SEA
Stanford-le-Hope
MARGATE
Cliftonville
GRAVESEND
ROCHESTER
Kingsgate
BROADSTAIRS
HERNE BAY
RAMSGATE
SITTINGBOURNE
CANTERBURY
SANDWICH
SEVENOAKS
Warren Street
MAIDSTONE
KENT
Womenswold
Boughton Monchelsea
Egerton
Barham
Kingsdown
Wye
St Margaret's at Cliffe
Pluckley
Brenchley
ASHFORD
DOVER
EAST GRINSTEAD
ROYAL TUNBRIDGE WELLS
Wadhurst
Lamberhurst
FOLKESTONE
Appledore
Dymchurch
Ticehurst
Bodiam
Stone
Burwash
Ewhurst Green
NEW ROMNEY
EAST
RYE
Brede
Battle
Icklesham
SUSSEX
Herstmonceaux
ENGLISH CHANNEL
HASTINGS
St. Leonards-on-Sea
BEXHILL
Wilmington
Rottingdean
Saltdean
Alfriston
SEAFORD
EASTBOURNE
TF
TG
TL
TM
TQ
TR
TV
Guesthouse or Inn
Farmhouse
Guesthouse or Inn & Farmhouse
Scale
0 10 20 miles
0 10 20 30 kilometres

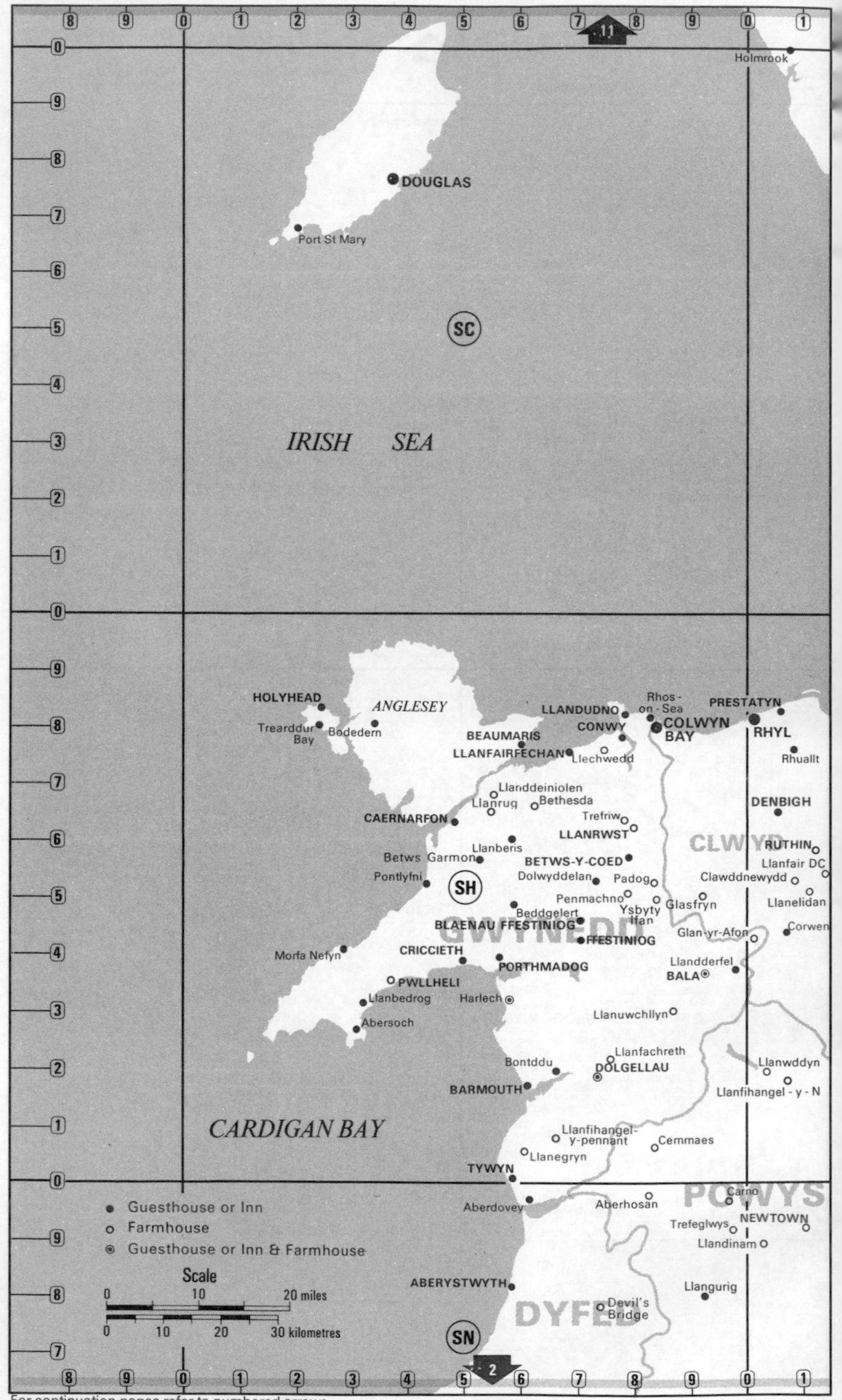

For continuation pages refer to numbered arrows

CUMBRIA
NY
12
Boot
AMBLESIDE
Hawkshead
Coniston
WINDERMERE
Bowness-on-Windermere
Crook
KENDAL
Near Sawrey
Far Sawrey
Brigsteer
Newby Bridge
NORTH
Leyburn
YORKSHIRE
Arnside
GRANGE-OVER-SANDS
Hubberholme
Ingleton
Horton-in-Ribblesdale
Kettlewell
BARROW-IN-FURNESS
Austwick
Grassington
Pateley Bridge
MORECAMBE
Caton
Giggleswick
Malham
HEYSHAM
LANCASTER
Burnsall
Bell Busk
Gargrave
SD
Slaidburn
SKIPTON
SE
Forton
Cabus
Harrop Fold
Sawley
ILKLEY
THORNTON CLEVELEYS
Garstang
CLITHEROE
BLACKPOOL
LANCASHIRE
LONGRIDGE
Haworth
BINGLEY
Weeton
Langho
Oxenhope
WEST
BRADFORD
LYTHAM ST ANNE'S
PRESTON
Todmorden
HALIFAX
Bacup
YORKSHIRE
SOUTHPORT
Marsden
Holmfirth
GREATER
WIGAN
Hazlehead
SOUTH
MANCHESTER
SALFORD
MANCHESTER
WALLASEY
MERSEYSIDE
GLOSSOP
YORKSHIRE
HOYLAKE
LIVERPOOL
STOCKPORT
ALTRINCHAM
Hayfield
8
KNUTSFORD
Sparrowpit
HOLYWELL
Helsby
BOLLINGTON
Babell
BUXTON
Litton
Rhes-y-cae
DERBYSHIRE
CHESTER
CHESHIRE
Wincle
Upper Hulme
Tarporley
Rushton Spencer
Pudyard
CLWYD
LEEK
Tissington
Holt
SJ
Longsdon
SK
NOTTS
Ipstones
Ilam
Thorpe
Blore
Okeover
Malpas
NEWCASTLE-UNDER-LYME
Mayfield
LLANGOLLEN
STOKE-ON-TRENT
Hanmer
Roston
Alkmonton
ELLESMERE
Swynnerton
UTTOXETER
Northwood
OSWESTRY
STAFFORDSHIRE
STAFFORD
Abbots Bromley
Llansantffraid-ym-Mechain
Shawbury
Blithbury
LEICESTERSHIRE
Nesscliff
Wolseley Bridge
Four Crosses
Llandrinio
SHREWSBURY
Uffington
Middletown
Wellington
Halfway House
LICHFIELD
WELSHPOOL
Cruckton
TELFORD
SHROPSHIRE
Forden
Codsall
Stiperstones
Woolstaston
Norton
Garthmyl
CHURCH STRETTON
WEST
SUTTON COLDFIELD
Church Stoke
BRIDGNORTH
4
MIDLANDS
Rowley Regis
Diddlebury
STOURBRIDGE
BIRMINGHAM
Kinver
Clun
Clunton
Cleobury Mortimer
Llanfair Waterdine
Bucknell
Leintwardine
LUDLOW
BROMSGROVE
SO
SP
KNIGHTON
Tenbury Wells
Lindridge
REDDITCH
Wigmore
Abberley
WARWICKSHIRE
Henley-in-Arden
HEREFORD AND WORCESTER
3

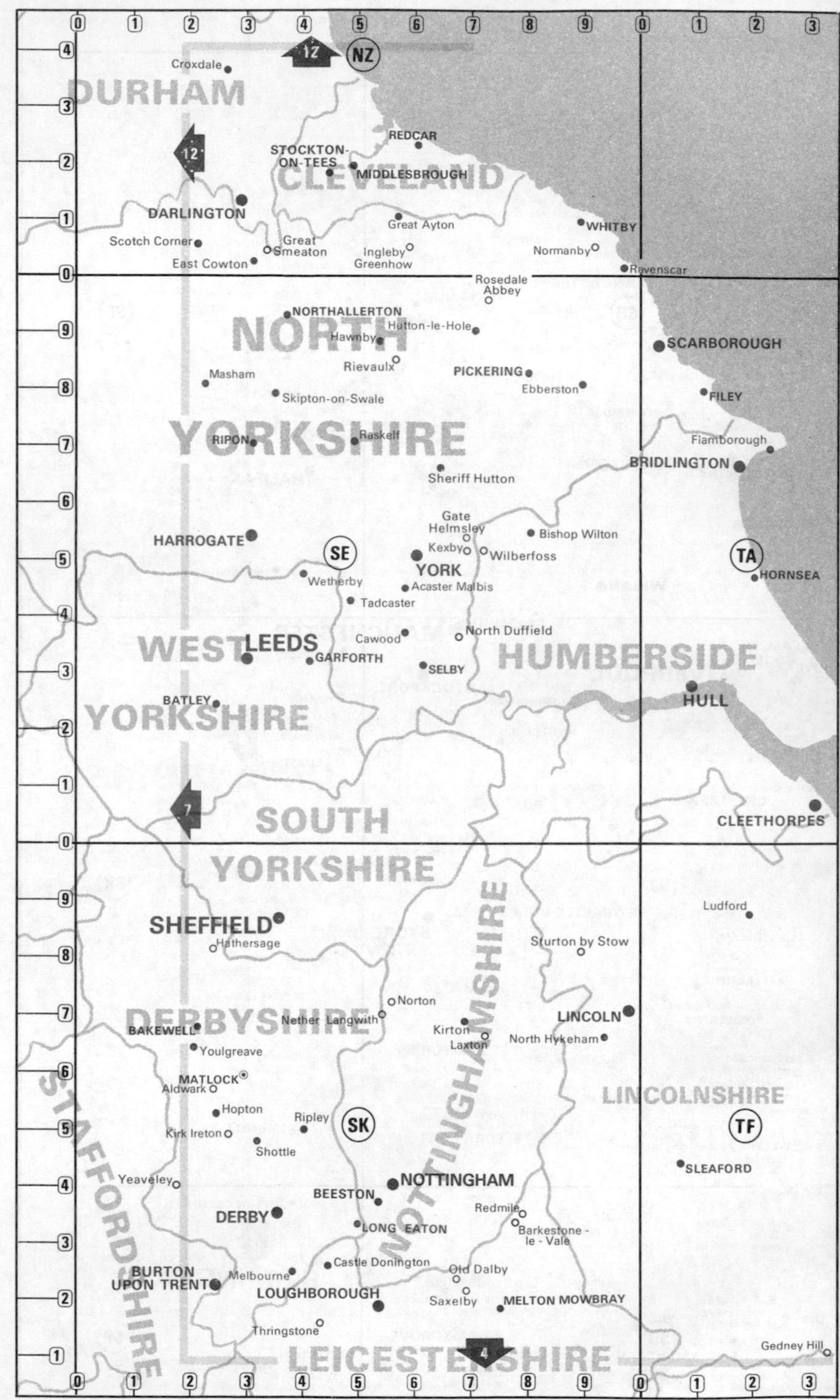

For continuation pages refer to numbered arrows

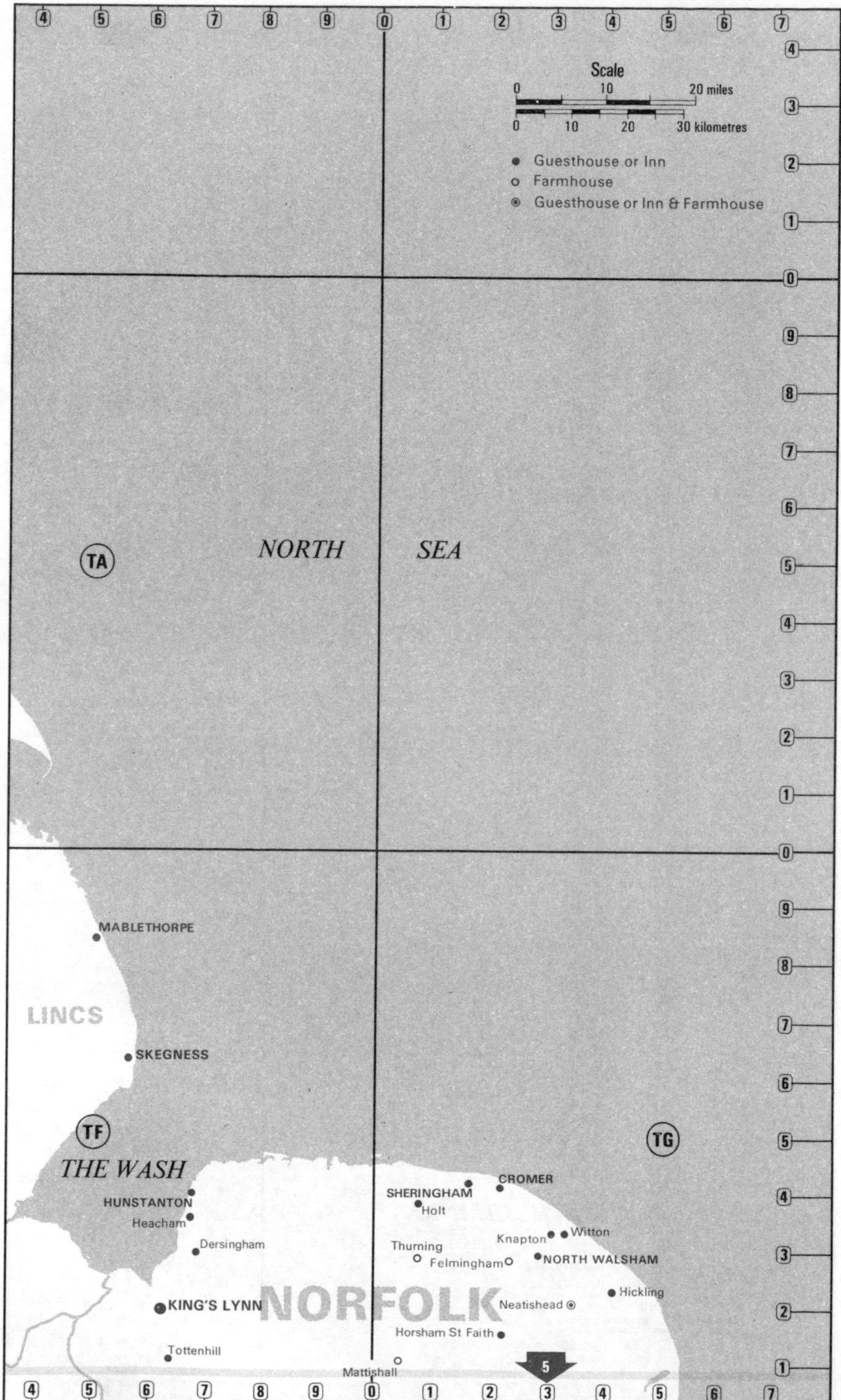
Scale
0
10
20 miles
0
10
20
30 kilometres
Guesthouse or Inn
Farmhouse
Guesthouse or Inn & Farmhouse
TA
NORTH
SEA
MABLETHORPE
LINCS
SKEGNESS
TF
TG
THE WASH
HUNSTANTON
Heacham
Dersingham
KING'S LYNN
NORFOLK
Tottenhill
SHERINGHAM
CROMER
Holt
Thurning
Felmingham
Knapton
Witton
NORTH WALSHAM
Neatishead
Hickling
Horsham St Faith
Mattishall
5

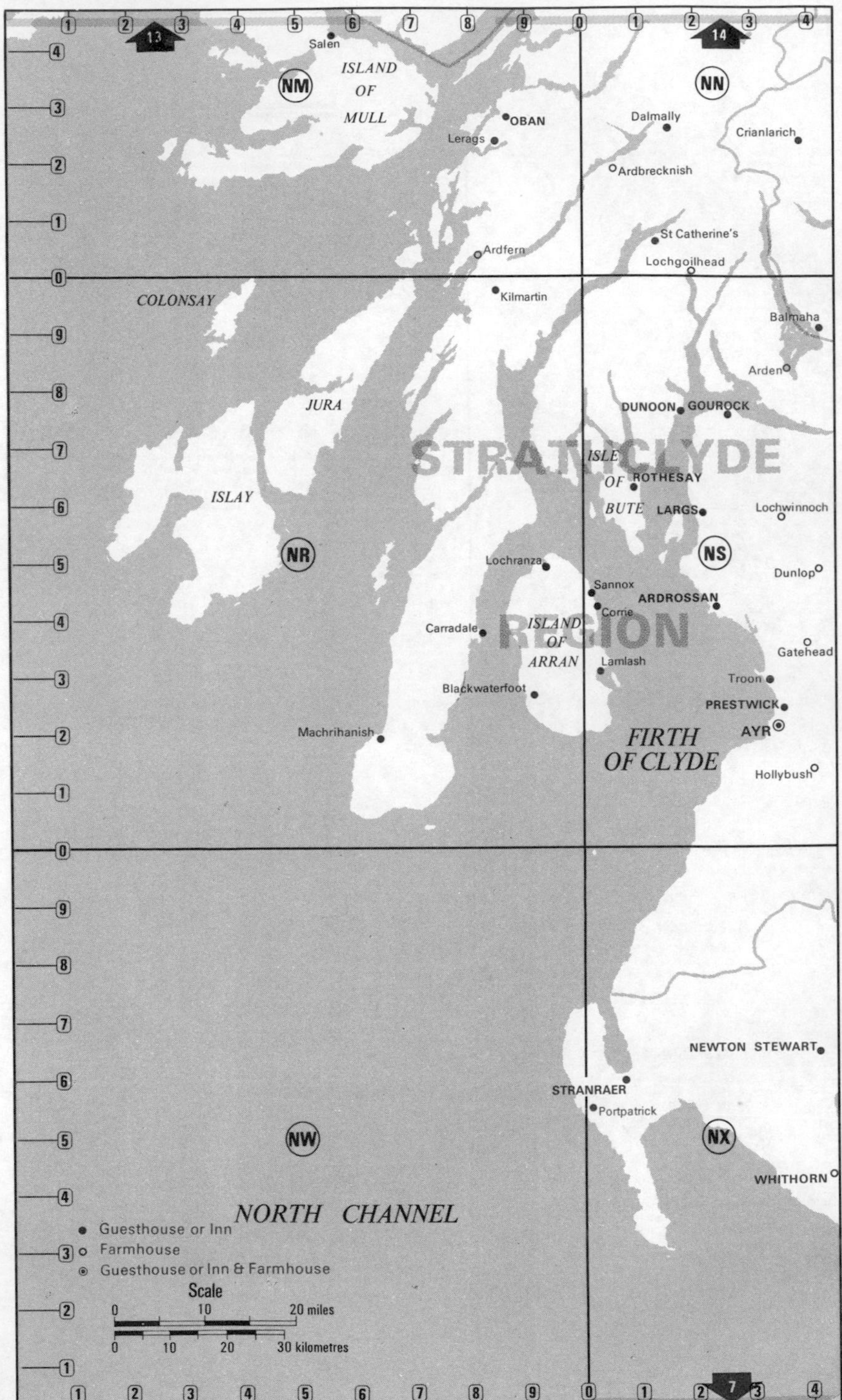

13
14
7
NM
NN
NR
NS
NW
NX
Salen
ISLAND OF MULL
OBAN
Lerags
Dalmally
Crianlarich
Ardbrecknish
St Catherine's
Lochgoilhead
Ardfern
Kilmartin
COLONSAY
Balmaha
Arden
JURA
DUNOON
GOUROCK
STRATHCLYDE REGION
ISLE OF BUTE
ROTHESAY
LARGS
Lochwinnoch
ISLAY
Lochranza
Dunlop
Sannox
Corrie
ARDROSSAN
Carradale
ISLAND OF ARRAN
Gatehead
Lamlash
Troon
Blackwaterfoot
PRESTWICK
AYR
Machrihanish
FIRTH OF CLYDE
Hollybush
NEWTON STEWART
STRANRAER
Portpatrick
WHITHORN
NORTH CHANNEL
Guesthouse or Inn
Farmhouse
Guesthouse or Inn & Farmhouse
Scale
0 10 20 miles
0 10 20 30 kilometres

For continuation pages refer to numbered arrows

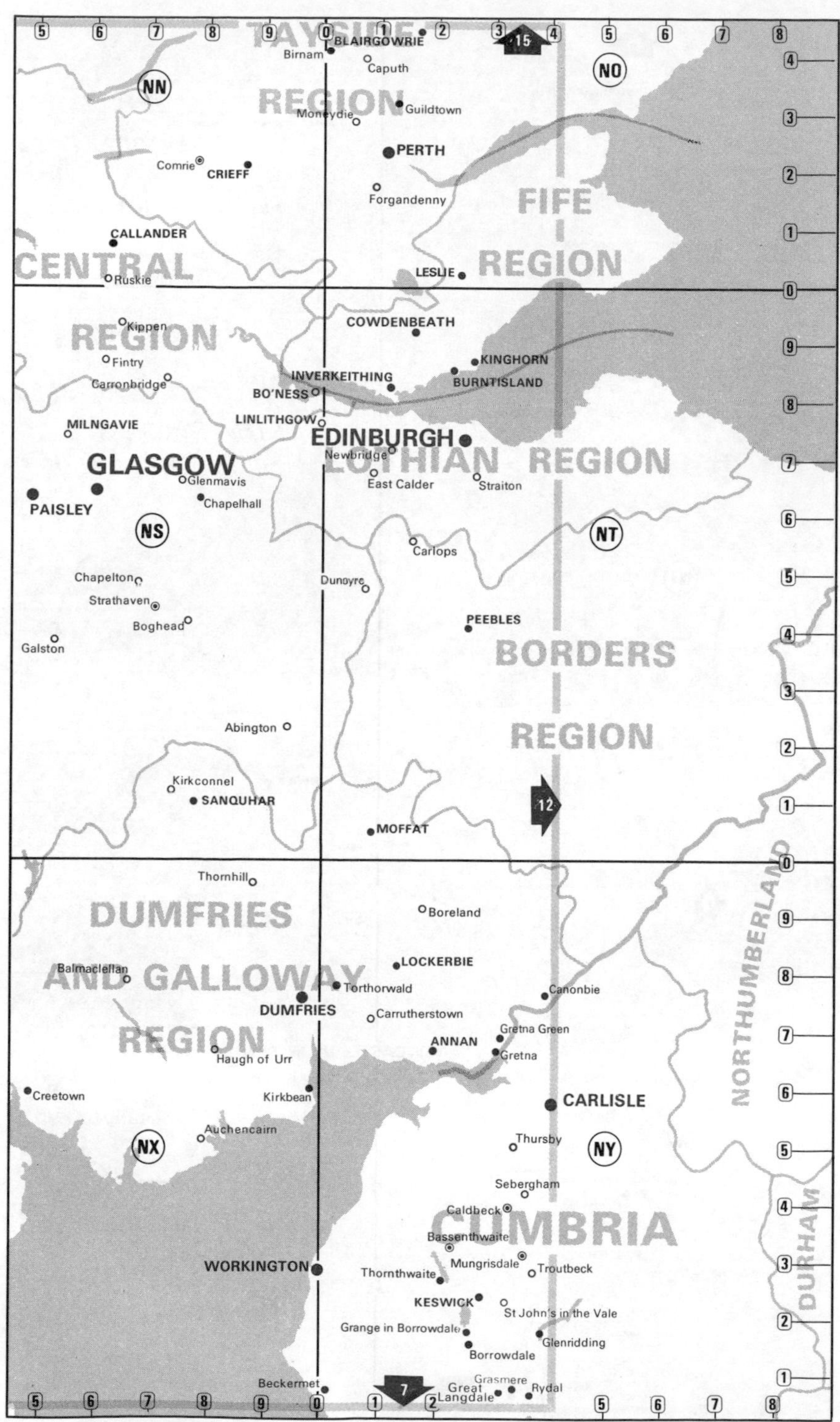
TAYSIDE REGION
NN
NO
BLAIRGOWRIE
Birnam
Caputh
Guildtown
Moneydie
PERTH
Comrie
CRIEFF
Forgandenny
FIFE REGION
CALLANDER
CENTRAL REGION
Ruskie
LESLIE
COWDENBEATH
Kippen
KINGHORN
Fintry
INVERKEITHING
BURNTISLAND
Carronbridge
BO'NESS
LINLITHGOW
MILNGAVIE
EDINBURGH
Newbridge
LOTHIAN REGION
GLASGOW
Glenmavis
East Calder
Straiton
PAISLEY
Chapelhall
NS
NT
Carlops
Chapelton
Dunsyre
Strathaven
PEEBLES
Boghead
Galston
BORDERS REGION
Abington
Kirkconnel
SANQUHAR
MOFFAT
Thornhill
DUMFRIES AND GALLOWAY REGION
Boreland
LOCKERBIE
Balmaclellan
Torthorwald
Canonbie
DUMFRIES
Carrutherstown
Gretna Green
ANNAN
Gretna
Haugh of Urr
NORTHUMBERLAND
Creetown
Kirkbean
CARLISLE
Auchencairn
Thursby
NX
NY
Sebergham
Caldbeck
CUMBRIA
Bassenthwaite
Mungrisdale
Troutbeck
WORKINGTON
Thornthwaite
DURHAM
KESWICK
St John's in the Vale
Grange in Borrowdale
Glenridding
Borrowdale
Beckermet
Grasmere
Great Langdale
Rydal
15
12
7

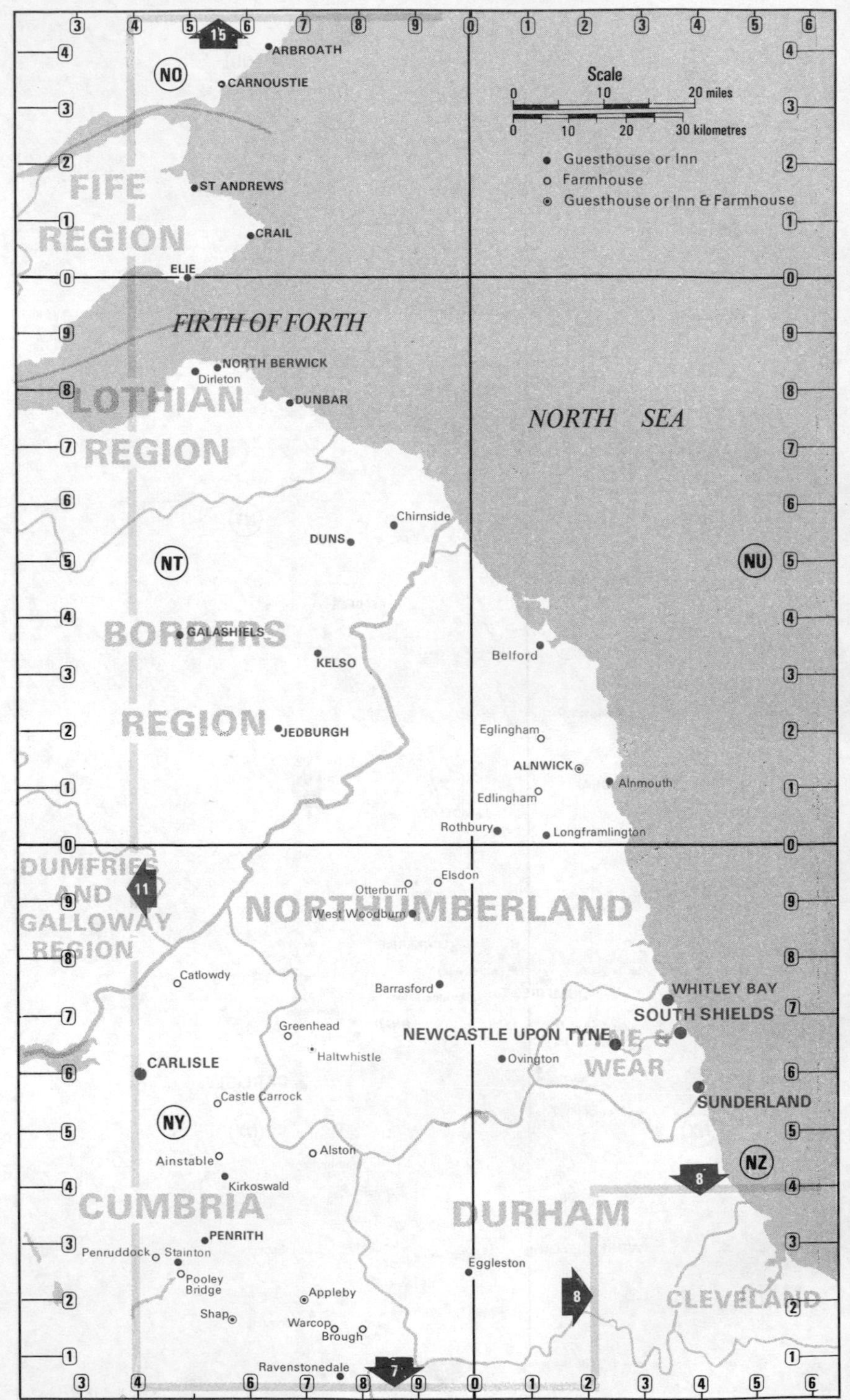

NO
ARBROATH
CARNOUSTIE
Scale
0 10 20 miles
0 10 20 30 kilometres
Guesthouse or Inn
Farmhouse
Guesthouse or Inn & Farmhouse
FIFE REGION
ST ANDREWS
CRAIL
ELIE
FIRTH OF FORTH
NORTH BERWICK
Dirleton
LOTHIAN REGION
DUNBAR
NORTH SEA
Chirnside
DUNS
NT
NU
BORDERS REGION
GALASHIELS
KELSO
Belford
JEDBURGH
Eglingham
ALNWICK
Alnmouth
Edlingham
Rothbury
Longframlington
DUMFRIES AND GALLOWAY REGION
Elsdon
Otterburn
NORTHUMBERLAND
West Woodburn
Catlowdy
Barrasford
WHITLEY BAY
SOUTH SHIELDS
Greenhead
NEWCASTLE UPON TYNE
TYNE & WEAR
Haltwhistle
CARLISLE
Ovington
SUNDERLAND
Castle Carrock
NY
Alston
NZ
Ainstable
Kirkoswald
CUMBRIA
DURHAM
PENRITH
Penruddock
Stainton
Eggleston
Pooley Bridge
Appleby
CLEVELAND
Shap
Warcop
Brough
Ravenstonedale
15
11
8
7

For continuation pages refer to numbered arrows

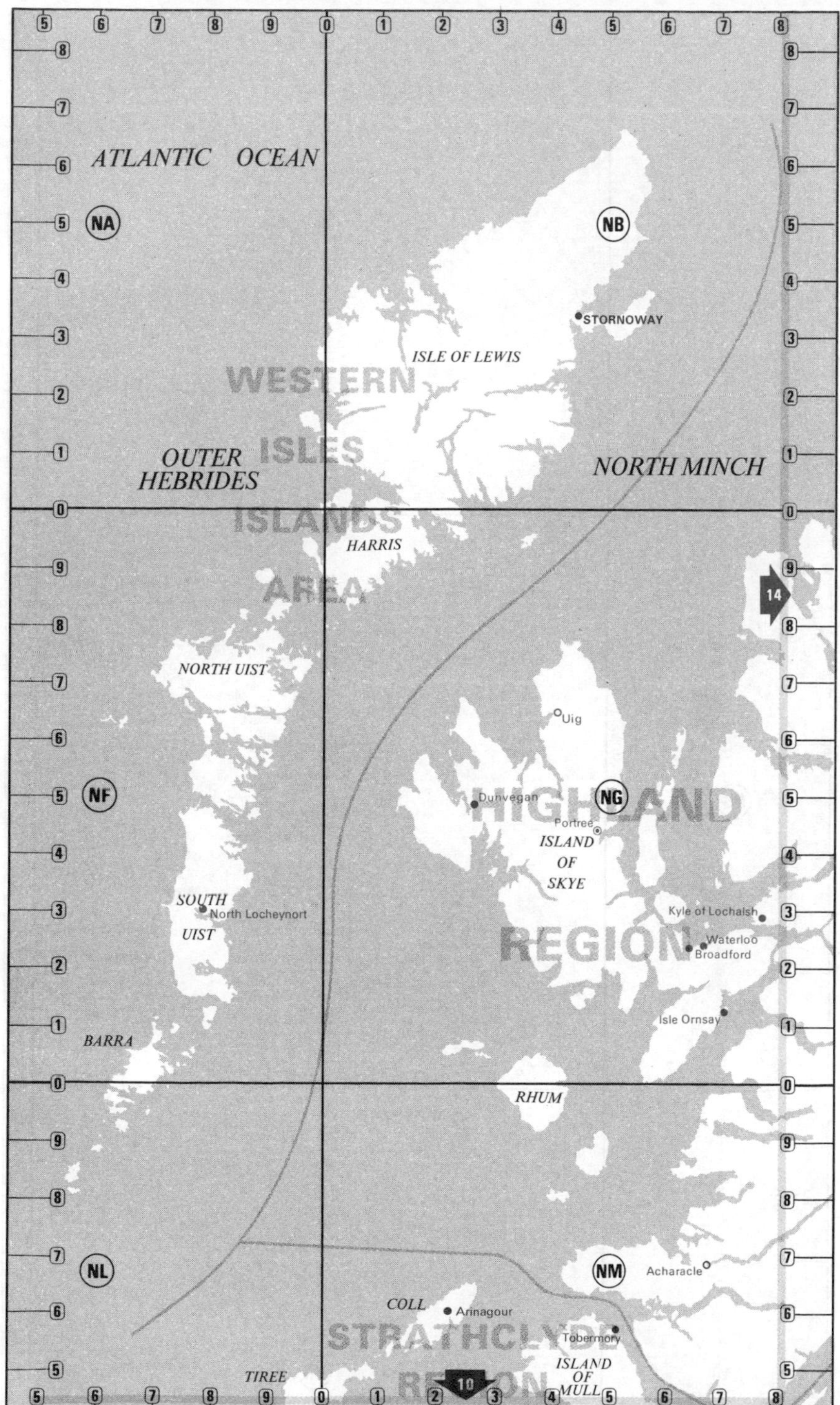
ATLANTIC OCEAN
NA
NB
STORNOWAY
ISLE OF LEWIS
WESTERN
ISLES
ISLANDS
AREA
OUTER
HEBRIDES
NORTH MINCH
HARRIS
14
NORTH UIST
Uig
NF
NG
Dunvegan
HIGHLAND
Portree
ISLAND
OF
SKYE
SOUTH
North Locheynort
UIST
Kyle of Lochalsh
REGION
Waterloo
Broadford
Isle Ornsay
BARRA
RHUM
NL
NM
Acharacle
COLL
Arinagour
STRATHCLYDE
Tobermory
ISLAND
OF
MULL
TIREE
REGION
10

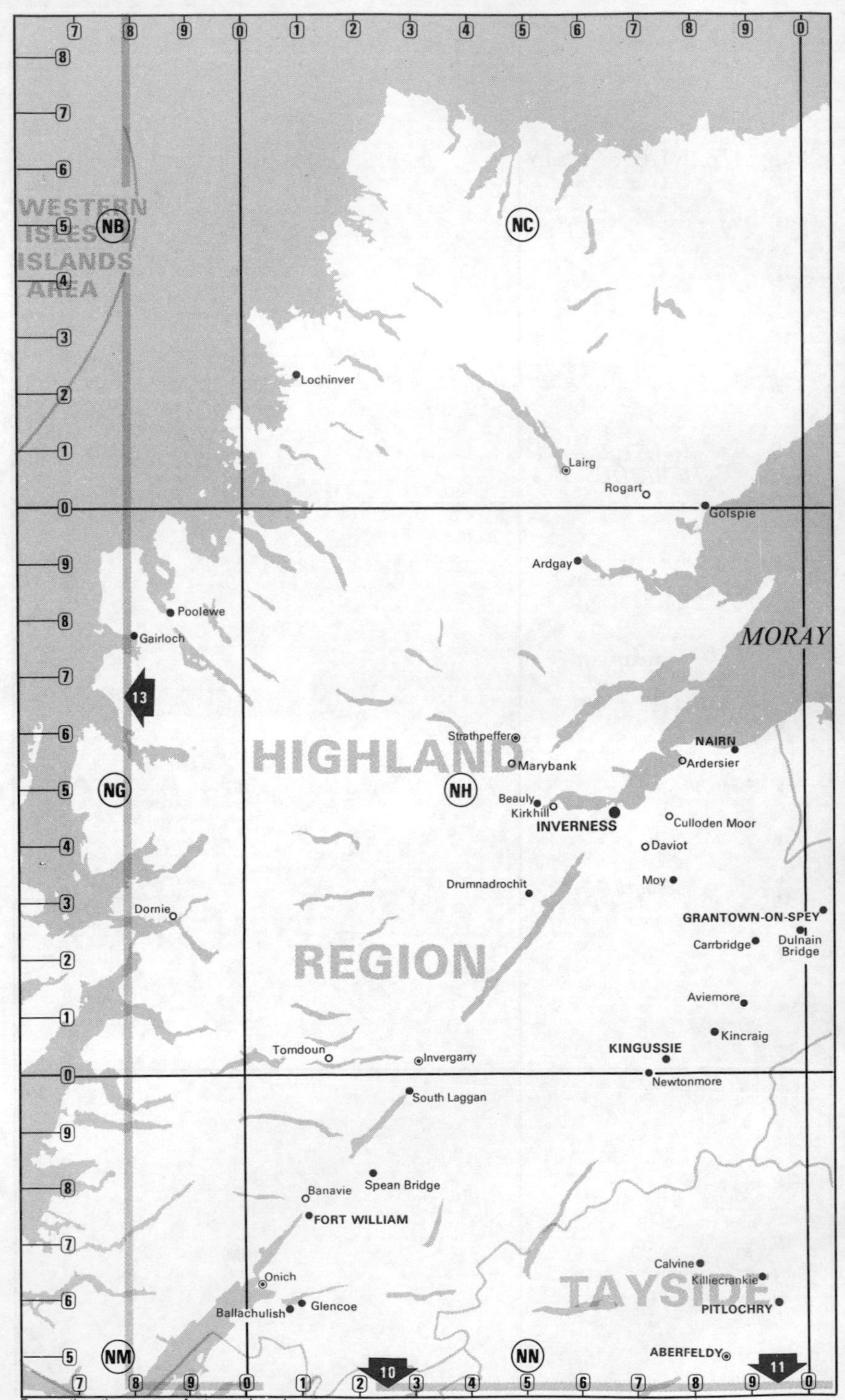

For continuation pages refer to numbered arrows

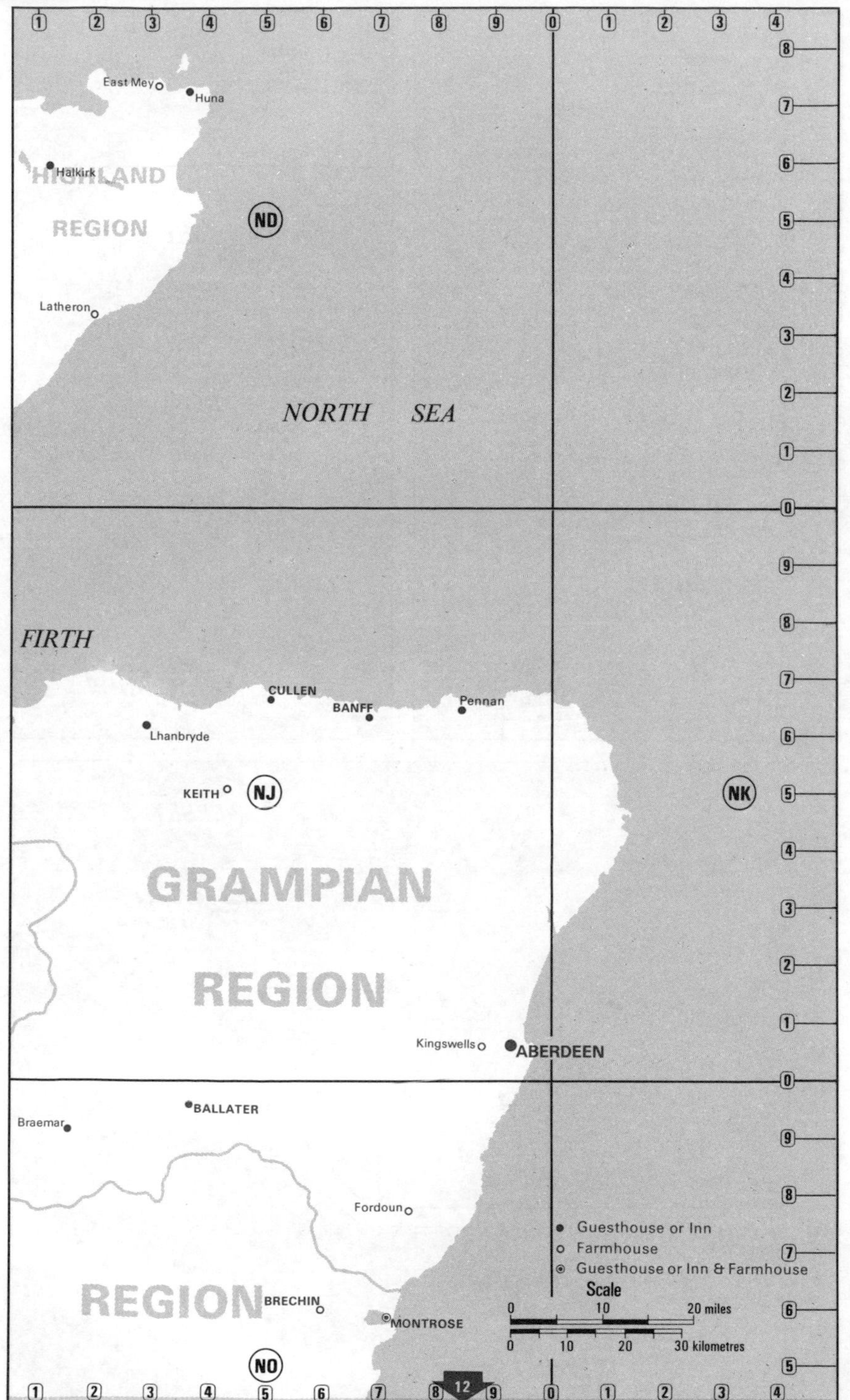
East Mey
Huna
Halkirk
HIGHLAND
REGION
ND
Latheron
NORTH SEA
FIRTH
CULLEN
BANFF
Pennan
Lhanbryde
KEITH
NJ
NK
GRAMPIAN
REGION
Kingswells
ABERDEEN
BALLATER
Braemar
Fordoun
REGION
BRECHIN
MONTROSE
NO
12
Guesthouse or Inn
Farmhouse
Guesthouse or Inn & Farmhouse
Scale
0 10 20 miles
0 10 20 30 kilometres

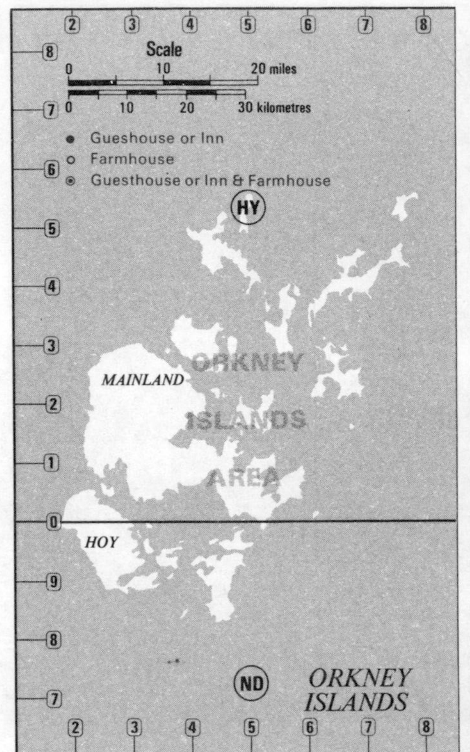

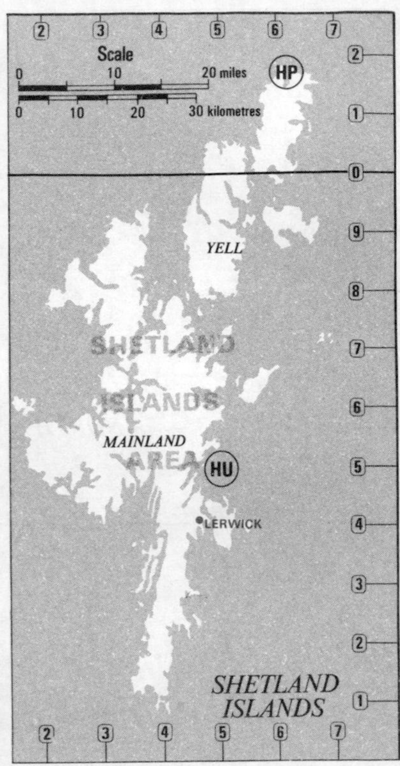

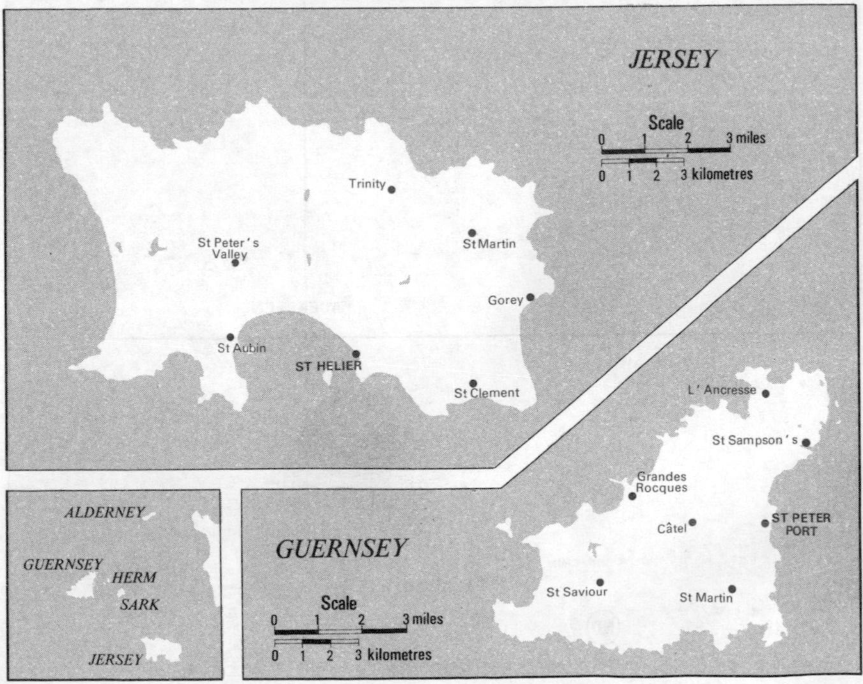

JERSEY

Scale
0 1 2 3 miles
0 1 2 3 kilometres

Trinity
St Peter's Valley
St Martin
Gorey
St Aubin
ST HELIER
St Clement

ALDERNEY
GUERNSEY
HERM
SARK
JERSEY

GUERNSEY

Scale
0 1 2 3 miles
0 1 2 3 kilometres

L' Ancresse
St Sampson's
Grandes Rocques
Câtel
ST PETER PORT
St Saviour
St Martin